Europe and the United States

COMMITTEE ON FOREIGN AFFAIRS

DANTE B. FASCELL, Florida, *Chairman*

LEE H. HAMILTON, Indiana
GUS YATRON, Pennsylvania
STEPHEN J. SOLARZ, New York
HOWARD WOLPE, Michigan
SAM GEJDENSON, Connecticut
MERVYN M. DYMALLY, California
TOM LANTOS, California
ROBERT G. TORRICELLI, New Jersey
HOWARD L. BERMAN, California
MEL LEVINE, California
EDWARD F. FEIGHAN, Ohio
TED WEISS, New York
GARY L. ACKERMAN, New York
WAYNE OWENS, Utah
HARRY JOHNSTON, Florida
ELIOT L. ENGEL, New York
ENI F.H. FALEOMAVAEGA, American Samoa
ANTONIO J. COLORADO, Puerto Rico
GERRY E. STUDDS, Massachusetts
AUSTIN J. MURPHY, Pennsylvania
PETER H. KOSTMAYER, Pennsylvania
THOMAS M. FOGLIETTA, Pennsylvania
FRANK McCLOSKEY, Indiana
THOMAS C. SAWYER, Ohio
DONALD M. PAYNE, New Jersey
BILL ORTON, Utah
(Vacancy)

WILLIAM S. BROOMFIELD, Michigan
BENJAMIN A. GILMAN, New York
ROBERT J. LAGOMARSINO, California
WILLIAM F. GOODLING, Pennsylvania
JIM LEACH, Iowa
TOBY ROTH, Wisconsin
OLYMPIA J. SNOWE, Maine
HENRY J. HYDE, Illinois
DOUG BEREUTER, Nebraska
CHRISTOPHER H. SMITH, New Jersey
DAN BURTON, Indiana
JAN MEYERS, Kansas
JOHN MILLER, Washington
BEN BLAZ, Guam
ELTON GALLEGLY, California
AMO HOUGHTON, New York
PORTER J. GOSS, Florida
ILEANA ROS-LEHTINEN, Florida

JOHN J. BRADY, JR., *Chief of Staff*
KRISTINE WILLIE, *Staff Assistant*
ANNE GREY, *Staff Assistant*

SUBCOMMITTEE ON INTERNATIONAL ECONOMIC POLICY AND TRADE

SAM GEJDENSON, Connecticut, *Chairman*

HOWARD WOLPE, Michigan
MEL LEVINE, California
EDWARD F. FEIGHAN, Ohio
HARRY JOHNSTON, Florida
ELIOT L. ENGEL, New York
AUSTIN J. MURPHY, Pennsylvania
BILL ORTON, Utah

TOBY ROTH, Wisconsin
JOHN MILLER, Washington
AMO HOUGHTON, New York
DOUG BEREUTER, Nebraska
BEN BLAZ, Guam

JOHN SCHEIBEL, *Subcommittee Staff Director*
EDMUND B. RICE, *Minority Staff Consultant*
KATHLEEN BERTELSEN, *Subcommittee Staff Consultant*
DONNA LA TORRE, *Subcommittee Staff Consultant*
PETER YEO, *Subcommittee Staff Consultant*

SUBCOMMITTEE ON EUROPE AND THE MIDDLE EAST

LEE H. HAMILTON, Indiana, *Chairman*

TOM LANTOS, California
MEL LEVINE, California
EDWARD F. FEIGHAN, Ohio
GARY L. ACKERMAN, New York
WAYNE OWENS, Utah
HARRY JOHNSTON, Florida
ELIOT L. ENGEL, New York

BENJAMIN A. GILMAN, New York
WILLIAM F. GOODLING, Pennsylvania
JAN MEYERS, Kansas
ELTON GALLEGLY, California
JIM LEACH, Iowa

MICHAEL H. VAN DUSEN, *Subcommittee Staff Director*
RUSSELL J. WILSON, *Minority Staff Consultant*
CHRISTOPHER KOJM, *Subcommittee Staff Consultant*
KATHERINE A. WILKENS, *Subcommittee Staff Consultant*
DAVID WEINER, *Subcommittee Staff Consultant*

Europe and the United States

Competition & Cooperation in the 1990s

Edited by Glennon J. Harrison

A STUDY SUBMITTED TO THE
SUBCOMMITTEE ON INTERNATIONAL ECONOMIC
POLICY AND TRADE
AND THE
SUBCOMMITTEE ON EUROPE AND THE MIDDLE EAST
OF THE
COMMITTEE ON FOREIGN AFFAIRS
U.S. HOUSE OF REPRESENTATIVES

M.E. Sharpe
Armonk, New York
London, England

Library of Congress Cataloging-in-Publication Data

Europe and the United States : competition and cooperation in the 1990s: a study submitted to the Subcommittee on International Economic Policy and Trade and the Subcommittee on Europe and the Middle East of the Committee on Foreign Affairs, U.S. House of Representatives / Glennon J. Harrison, editor.
p. cm.
Includes bibliographical references and index.
ISBN 1-56324-342-3 (cloth). ISBN 1-56324-343-1 (pbk.)
1. Europe—Economic integration.
2. Europe 1992.
3. European Economic Community countries—Foreign economic relations—United States
4. United States—Foreign economic relations—European Economic Community countries.
I. Harrison, Glennon J.
II. United States. Congress. House. Committee on Foreign Affairs. Subcommittee on International Economic Policy and Trade.
III. United States. Congress. House. Committee on Foreign Affairs. Subcommittee on Europe and the Middle East.
HC241.E78373 1993
337.4073—dc20
93-31505
CIP

Printed in the United States of America

The paper used in this publication meets the minimum requirements of American National Standard for Information Sciences—Permanence of Paper for Printed Library Materials, ANSI Z39.48–1984.

BM (c) 10 9 8 7 6 5 4 3 2 1
BM (p) 10 9 8 7 6 5 4 3 2 1

FOREWORD

I am pleased to receive the following report coordinated by the Congressional Research Service for the Subcommittee on Europe and the Middle East and the Subcommittee on International Economic Policy and Trade.

This study, which deals with European integration in the 1990's, is a follow-up to the 1989 CRS report on EC–92. The enhancement of European integration holds major implications for U.S. interests. It is important that we understand the likely impacts so as to be better prepared to respond and to manage our interests.

This study assists in analyzing and assessing those implications. It raises various questions and issues and begins to direct us in the proper policy direction.

The views and conclusions of the private experts contained in this volume are those of the authors and do not necessarily reflect those of their respective institutions, the Congressional Research Service, the Committee on Foreign Affairs or its members.

DANTE B. FASCELL,
Chairman, Committee on Foreign Affairs.

LETTER OF TRANSMITTAL

Hon. Dante B. Fascell,
Chairman,
Committee on Foreign Affairs,
House of Representatives,
Washington, D.C.

DEAR CHAIRMAN FASCELL: We are pleased to submit to you a study of European integration in the 1990's and its consequences for the United States. The study was prepared at the request of the Subcommittees on Europe and the Middle East and International Economic Policy. It is intended for use by the Committee on Foreign Affairs, the Congress and the interested public.

The study examines the emergence of a more united Europe as an economic and political power in the post-Cold War world, the implications of European integration for the United States, and options for U.S. policy toward Europe. The papers in this study consider, among other things, the Maastricht Treaty, EC enlargement, EC economic, social and agricultural policies, and the Single European Market. The study provides a starting point for examining long-standing U.S. policies with respect to Europe and considering the key question of where we go from here.

The successful conclusion of this project depended on the cooperation and contributions of many authors from the academic community, private research groups, and the Congressional Research Service of the Library of Congress. Glennon J. Harrison of the Economics Division of the Congressional Research Service planned, coordinated, and edited the study. Meredith Morris and Marietta Sharperson of CRS provided production assistance.

The views and conclusions of the private experts contained in this volume are those of the authors and do not necessarily reflect those of their respective institutions, the Congressional Research Service, the Committee on Foreign Affairs or its members.

Sincerely yours,

HON. LEE H. HAMILTON,
Chairman,
Subcommittee on Europe and the Middle East

HON. SAM GEJDENSON,
Chairman,
Subcommittee on International Economic Policy and Trade

CONTENTS

ABBREVIATIONS AND ACRONYMS

ACEA	Association of European Automobile Constructors
ACTPN	Advisory Committee on Trade Policy and Negotiations
AD	antidumping
AEA	American Electronics Association
ANSI	American National Standards Institute
APEC	Asia Pacific Economic Cooperation
ASEAN	Association of South East Asian Nations
BDA	Union of German Employers Associations
BEA	Bureau of Economic Analysis
BRITE	Basic Research in Industrial Technologies for Europe
CAFE	corporate average fuel economy
CAP	Common Agricultural Policy
CBI	Confederation of British Industry
CBO	Congressional Budget Office
CCMC	Committee of Common Market Motor Vehicle Constructors
CDE	Conference on Confidence and Security Building Measures and Disarmament in Europe
CEA	Commissariat L'Energie Atomique
CEC	Commission of the European Communities
CEFIC	European Chemical Industry Council
CEN	European Committee for Standardization
CENELEC	European Committee for Electrotechnical Standardization
CERN	European Center for Nuclear Research
CFE	Conventional Armed Forces in Europe Treaty
CFIUS	Committee on Foreign Investment in the United States
CFSP	common foreign and security policy
CIS	Commonwealth of Independent States
CMEA	Council of Mutual Economic Assistance

CNPF	Conseil National du Patronat Francais
Comitextil	Coordination Committee for the Textile Industries in the EEC
Confindustria	Confederazione Generale dell'Industria Italiana
COREPER	Committee of Permanent Representatives
CSCE	Commission on Security and Cooperation in Europe (Helsinki Commission)
CSFR	Czech and Slovak Federal Republic
DARPA	U.S. Defense Advanced Research Projects Agency
DASA	Deutsche Aerospace
DDR	see GDR
DESO	Defense Export Services Organization
DGA	General Armaments DelegationD
GATT	Defense General Agreement on Tariffs and Trade
DIHT	German Chambers of Commerce and Industry
EAEC	East Asian Economic Caucus
EBRD	European Bank for Reconstruction and Development
EC	European Community
ECB	European Central Bank
ECOFIN	Council of Economic and Finance Ministers
ECSC	European Coal and Steel Community
ECU	European Currency Unit
EC–92	Europe's 1992 program
EDC	European Defense Community
EDI	European defence identity
EEA	European Economic Area
EEC	European Economic Community
EFPIA	European Federation of Pharmaceutical Industries' Associations
EFTA	European Free Trade Association (Austria, Finland, Iceland, Liechtenstein, Norway, Sweden, and Switzerland)
EMS	European Monetary System
EMU	European Monetary Union or economic and monetary union
EOTC	European Organization for Testing and Certification
EP	European Parliament
EPC	European Political Cooperation

EPU	European Political Union
ERM	Exchange Rate Mechanism
ESA	European Space Agency
ESCB	European System of Central Banks
ESPRIT	European Strategic Program for Research and Development in Information Technology
ETSI	European Telecommunications Standardization Institute
EUCLID	European Cooperative Long-term Initiative For Defense
EURAM	European Research in Advanced Materials
EURATOM	European Atomic Community
EUREKA	European Research Cooperation Agency
Eurochambers	Association of European Chambers of Commerce and Industry
FDA	Food and Drug Administration
FDI	foreign direct investment
FRG	Federal Republic of Germany (west Germany)
FTA	free trade area
G–3	Group of 3 (the United States, the EC, and Japan)
G–4	Group of 4 (the United States, Japan, the EC, and Canada)
G–7	Group of 7 (the United States, the United Kingdom, Germany, Japan, Canada, France, and Italy)
GAO	General Accounting Office
GATT	General Agreement on Tariffs and Trade
GDP	gross domestic product
GDR	German Democratic Republic (East Germany)
GNP	gross national product
IEPG	Independent European Program Group
IGC	intergovernmental conference
ILO	International Labour Organisation
IMF	International Monetary Fund
ISDN	integrated-services digital network
ISO	International Organization for Standardization
ITC	International Trade Commission
JESSI	Joint European Submicron Silicon Project
JRC	Joint Research Center
LDDI	less developed defense industry

MBFR	Mutual and Balanced Force Reductions
MEPs	members of the European Parliament
MFA	Multifiber Arrangement
MNC	multinational corporation
MOSS	Market-Oriented Sector-Selective
MRA	mutual recognition agreement
NAFTA	North American Free Trade Agreement
NASA	National Aeronautics and Space Administration
NATO	North Atlantic Treaty Organization
NRC	National Research Council
OECD	Organisation for Economic Cooperation and Development
OTA	Office of Technology Assessment
PHARE	program of aid for central and eastern Europe
PROMETHEUS	Program for European Traffic with Highest Efficiency and Unprecedented Safety
QA	quality assurance
QMV	qualified majority voting
R&D	research and development
RAB	Registrar Accreditation Board
RACE	Research and Development in Advanced Communications Technologies in Europe
SEA	Single European Act
SII	Structural Impediments Initiative
TA	telecommunications authorities
UN	United Nations
UNCED	United Nations Conference on Environment and Development
VAT	value-added tax
VER	voluntary export restraint
VRA	voluntary trade agreement
WEU	Western European Union
WTO	World Trade Organization

OVERVIEW: THE CHANGING CALCULUS OF U.S. AND EUROPEAN INTERESTS

by Glennon J. Harrison *

Change in Europe, once gradual, is now occurring at a very rapid pace, and as the divisions between East and West give way to new concerns, questions have been raised about the types of adjustments the United States may find necessary to accommodate a more active, independent, and assertive Europe. At almost every level, Europe is redefining itself. This volume provides a framework for understanding the prospects for, as well as the causes and consequences of, change in Europe. Throughout, an attempt is made to explain change in terms of actual or potential effects on U.S. interests. Whether the issue is one of economics, politics, or institutional arrangements, a theme that recurs throughout this volume is that U.S.-European relations will be defined by competition and cooperation in the 1990s. For both the United States and Europe, a major concern is that relations need to be managed skillfully to ensure that competition remains healthy and that the challenges that confront the industrial countries are handled within a wider framework of cooperation.

The European Community (EC) is emerging as the core institution of post-Cold War Europe and as a superpower in a world where economic strength may increasingly be one of the most useful measures of power. EC integration has reached levels that many would have believed unlikely just a decade ago. But by the end of this century, a larger EC than the present community of twelve may achieve a single currency and closely coordinated economic, foreign, and defense policies. In the economic sphere, the EC is already showing signs of moving beyond narrow market unification toward economic integration, although numerous strains and stresses accompany this process. For many reasons, political union, with integrated defense policies, may prove more difficult to achieve. The significance of the European Community needs to be considered as the United States moves into the uncharted waters of a post-Cold War world.

During the 1990s, the challenge for the United States will be to develop policies that deepen political and economic ties with the EC, even as the EC sets its own agenda and on occasion goes its own way. The institutional framework through which the United States exercised political and military leadership during the Cold War period (mainly through the North Atlantic Treaty Organization—NATO) has been greatly diminished by events in Eastern

* Glennon J. Harrison is editor of this volume and a Specialist in International Trade and Finance, Economics Division, Congressional Research Service.

Europe and the former Soviet Union. Economics has taken on new significance, but no framework comparable to that provided by NATO is in place.

The declining utility of being the only military superpower in the post-Cold War world poses an obvious problem for the United States. Military might does not readily translate into economic strength, and in recent years many observers have come to believe that the relative international economic position of the United States has declined rapidly vis-a-vis the European Community, Japan, and other countries. The present inability of the United States to articulate a vision and muster the resources necessary to shape a new international economic environment characterized by multilateral cooperation and healthy competition is disturbing. Fortunately, leadership in this context does not depend exclusively on marshalling economic resources. It also depends on maintaining a high level of commitment to cooperation among the post-Cold War economic superpowers: the United States, the European Community, and Japan.

In most respects, the heightened importance of the European Community for the United States is directly related to dramatic changes that have occurred in Europe in recent years: the end of the Cold War and the strengthening of the EC as an economic and political actor. The collapse of the Soviet Union and the end of the Cold War mark a break with the past that may be comparable to the other significant break of the 20th century: the start of World War I in August 1914, which shattered the world of the 19th century and set in motion many of the political, economic, social, and cultural forces that effectively shaped the 20th century. A new configuration of forces has quelled fears of a global war, but uncertainty persists as to the significance of the Cold War's end.

During the post-World War II period, United States leadership was exercised directly and through a series of economic and political institutions [1] and programs [2] that were intended to promote the stability and strength of the West, on the one hand, and to contain Communism on the other. Economic, political, and military leadership of an alliance composed mainly of Western industrial countries came at a high cost to the United States. By the end of the 1980s the strengthening of Western Europe, Japan, and other industrial countries led many to question the vitality of U.S. economic leadership, as well as the competitiveness of the U.S. economy. A serious debate raged over Paul Kennedy's thesis about the decline of the United States as a "great power." Unexpectedly, the other "great power," the Soviet Union, collapsed in August 1991, following the demise in 1989 of its East European empire.

The end of the Soviet Union and the rising importance of economic "superpowers" represent changes of great magnitude and complexity. Policymakers in the United States, Japan, and in Europe face new challenges that will require constructive re-

---

[1] Examples of these include the United Nations, the International Monetary Fund, the World Bank, the General Agreement on Tariffs and Trade, the North Atlantic Treaty Organization, the Organization for Economic Cooperation and Development, and the Organization of American States.

[2] These would include, among others, the Marshall Plan, the Alliance for Progress, and the Peace Corps.

sponses, as well as leadership. To develop appropriate responses, they must understand more about the nature of the challenges that they face. The Western industrial countries no longer face a systemic challenge from a Communist bloc of countries. Capitalism, as a system, proved more durable than Soviet-style communism. But capitalism is not monolithic: the laws, regulations, and norms that govern markets and provide a structure in which property rights may be exercised differ widely from country to country. One consequence is that Japan's economic system differs markedly from European or American versions of capitalism, and Japan's obvious success is one reason the Japanese economic challenge has received considerable attention in the United States. [3] Within Europe, there are considerable differences between the German or continental system (with its collectivist or communitarian, "social market" model) and the Anglo-Saxon model (with its pronounced emphasis on individualism and competitive market solutions) that characterizes the British and American systems. Europe has traditionally not been regarded as a 'threat' in the way that Japan sometimes has. But it is now deeply involved in processes of economic, political, and social transformation that will most likely have major consequences for U.S. interests both at home and abroad.

Where common interests and common foes seemed to define the transatlantic relationship during the Cold War period, political and economic realignments within Europe may now provide a rationale to many Europeans for redefining the relationship on terms more favorable to Europe. As the transatlantic relationship comes to be defined by economics instead of security, Europeans might expect the United States to cooperate as an equal in the process of formulating international economic policy, and may expect to play a leadership, if not coequal, role on foreign and security policy decisionmaking. The United States made an initial move to foster closer cooperation in the post-Cold War period in the Transatlantic Declaration of December 1990. Semi-annual meetings are now held between the President of the United States and the Presidents of the EC Commission and the European Council. These meetings provide one forum for discussing the ever-widening range of issues that define U.S.-European relations. While the Transatlantic Declaration appears to be satisfactory at this time, European integration may one day reach a level that requires a more formal structure for coordinating policies.

Economic Policy and Decisionmaking

In recent years, the EC Commission has pointed to the Community's success with market integration (EC–92) as a factor responsible for improved economic performance, for new job creation, and for the renewed dynamism that the Community clearly experienced during the second half of the 1980s. Market integration provided a framework for formulating economic policies that are European in scope, but domestic economic policies, conditioned by domestic political considerations, may continue to be a significant determinant

[3] See U.S. Congress. Joint Economic Committee. *Japan's Economic Challenge.* Joint Committee Print. 101st Congress, 2nd Session. S. Prt. 101–121. Washington, D.C., U.S. Govt. Print. Off., 1990.

of overall macroeconomic performance. Section I provides an overview of economic performance, examines the institutions and processes involved in economic policymaking, and looks at relations between government and business in the Community.

Craig Elwell suggests that the growth spurt provided by EC–92 may now have run its course, and that the domestic economic policies required to achieve the convergence necessary for economic and monetary union (EMU) by the late 1990s may undermine the single market program and perpetuate slow growth in the future. Growth in the EC's real output (as measured by real GDP growth) during the 1980s advanced at an average annual rate of 2.5 percent, substantially below the 4.2 percent pace of Japan, and lower than the U.S. rate of 3.0 percent. Unemployment, which averaged 9.6 percent during the decade, was also significantly above U.S. and Japanese levels. In 1991, growth in real GDP in the EC advanced by only 1.3 percent, the lowest level since 1982, and unemployment rose for the first time since 1986 from 8.4 percent to 8.6 percent. The EC has projected that real output will advance by 2.2 percent and 2.5 percent in 1992 and 1993, respectively. Inflation, which moderated during the second half of the 1980s, should remain below 5.0 percent during 1992 and 1993.

Elwell finds that, if the European Community is to realize its *potential* for growth, significant constraints must be eliminated. Labor market rigidities, *dirigiste* economic and industrial policies, and protectionism represent the most serious obstacles. The growth prospects for the EC will be largely determined by the course of economic events in the four major countries, France, Germany, Italy, and the United Kingdom. The critical factors in these countries appear to be high interest rates (transmitted via the European Monetary System (EMS) from the German Bundesbank (the central bank) to the other member economies), reduced business activity, high unemployment, and slow growth. The overall weakness of the economies of the largest member states suggests a serious potential for political resistance to market opening if the benefits will likely accrue to foreign multinationals rather than domestic producers.

For the United States, the economic effects of market unification are thought to be relatively small, and positive effects, such as they are, will flow from the pursuit of aggressive market unification by the Community. Shifts away from unification toward protection of "coddled" sectors, such as agriculture, computers and electronics, automobiles, and airlines will reduce benefits for the United States. Such protection represents a far greater threat to the EC because of its dampening effect on economic growth. Finally, more rapid EC growth would be economically and politically beneficial to Eastern Europe and the former Soviet Union. Clearly, this would also represent a gain for the United States.

C. Randall Henning provides an overview of the complex interaction of institutions and processes affecting economic policymaking in Europe, and cautions that Community's ambitious agenda may well exceed the policymaking capacity of Community institutions. In the post-1992 period, that agenda includes completing the EC–92 program, economic and monetary union, and EC enlargement. The competencies of Community institutions in areas affecting economic policy will increase substantially as a result of these initiatives. At the same time, the role of European Community institutions in international economic affairs will grow as unification proceeds.

The evolution of Community institutions has been accompanied by debates over the degree and form of centralization, and the issue of democratic accountability. Some policy issues (competition, trade, and agriculture) are highly centralized, while others (taxation and budget policies) remain under the control of national governments. Macroeconomic policy is mainly influenced by decisions of national governments, but EC institutions will play an increasingly important role, especially if the momentum achieved at the December 1991 Maastricht Summit is sustained. At the Community level, the main policymaking bodies are the European Council, the Council of Ministers, the EC Commission, and the European Parliament.

Monetary policy in the European Community is largely set by national central banks, and is coordinated through the EMS. All of the countries of the EC participate in the Exchange Rate Mechanism of the EMS, except for Greece. Under the EMS, European currencies fluctuate within narrow bands and, consequently, national monetary policies tend not to diverge too greatly. The "nominal anchor" of the EMS is the German central bank, the Bundesbank. In practice, Germany's pursuit of a low-inflation monetary policy (at least until unification) has tended to be the dominant influence on monetary conditions within the EC. Monetary union, which was agreed in December 1991, will bring a number of important institutional changes, including a European System of Central Banks (ESCB) charged with maintaining price stability. This will mean that Europe will have a unified monetary policy among those countries qualifying for membership.

Fiscal policy is overwhelmingly a function of uncoordinated national policies (government spending and taxation). The EC budget plays a relatively smaller role in the overall determination of European fiscal policy. Nevertheless, the Community budget, which has been a significant irritant to the United States because of the Common Agricultural Policy (CAP), will probably grow in response to political demands for resource transfers from prosperous to depressed regions. National fiscal policies will be affected by the Treaty on European Union. The Treaty requires that national governments avoid excessive budget deficits and limit government debt, with a goal of fiscal convergence.

The extension of Community competence into new policy areas, according to Henning, means that the EC will become a more powerful and assertive bargaining partner for the United States. He finds it unfortunate that political and institutional reforms have not kept pace with economic and monetary union. As a result, the United States may discover that negotiating with the EC is as frustrating as ever. Changes in Europe may further restrict the scope of U.S. actions in the area of economic policymaking. For example, Henning argues that once national currencies are abolished and the common currency created later in this decade, Europe will be a larger, more cohesive monetary union, less vulnerable to fluctuations in its currency. He believes this will largely neutralize U.S. policymakers' ability to use the disruptive effects of rapid changes in the value of the dollar (the so-called "dollar weapon") to secure cooperation from European governments in the form of changes in their domestic demand policies. EC cooperation will most likely not come in response to pressure. Instead, it will probably be given in return for changes in American policies (e.g., reduction in the Federal budget deficit). Henning believes that the most likely and useful U.S. response to changing institutional and policymaking processes in Europe is cooperation and adaptation. Because the decisionmaking process in the Europe will remain decentralized, the United States will have to remain engaged with all of the decision centers in the EC.

Michael Calingaert provides a detailed view of how businesses in Europe engage the decision centers of the Community to promote policies and legislation that further their goals. He also examines (1) how government views and deals with business; (2) the intersection of government-business interests; (3) the roles that institutions and individuals on each side play; and (4) how interactions affect outcomes.

In Europe, individual firms and broader business organizations attempt to shape public policies and legislation. Business organizations may be Community-wide or national. At the EC level, there are umbrella (or non-sector-specific) groups; groupings of national umbrella organizations; and sectoral associations or federations. At the national level, umbrella groups, sector-specific organizations, and individual firms pursue business interests.

Business-government interaction takes place at both the Community and national levels, and interactions typically differ markedly from those in the United States. Calingaert identifies four main differences that distinguish government-business relations in the EC from those in the United States. First, decisionmaking in the EC is less transparent and more informal. Second, government-business interactions largely take place out of public view. Third, the tone of the relationship between government and business is more consensual and less confrontational. Finally, European parliamentary systems are very different from the U.S. system, in which power is divided among three strong branches.

Decisionmaking in the Community is decentralized: businesses must focus on European Community institutions as well as on national governments. The principal Community institutions are the EC Commission, the European Parliament, and the Council of Ministers. Dialogue between the EC Commission and business is important because of the Commission's power to initiate legislation. But the key decisionmaker is the Council of Ministers, which is composed of member state representatives, and business typically lobbies very hard at the national level to get its views aired, if not adopted, at Council.

Government-business relations at the national level vary from country to country. In France, relations are very close, and the government is quite attentive to French business interests. In Germany, relations are close, reflecting the social compact in which government, business, and labor strive for consensus. Italy is similar to France, but public administration is much weaker there than in France. Government-business relations are not as close in the

United Kingdom, reflecting a long-term practice of keeping business at arm's length.

Although the pattern of government-business relations in Europe differs markedly from that in the United States, U.S. firms are active participants in European representative organizations and as interlocutors of governments. To a considerable extent, those firms have been accepted on the same basis as European firms. Calingaert argues that there is little discrimination in terms of access and influence at the EC level for companies willing to invest in understanding the process of government-business interaction and adapting to it. Those U.S. companies with the least access to, or influence on, policy or legislation are those not "established" in the Community.

The Path to European Union

Many Americans do not fully appreciate the extent to which Europe is becoming integrated. European progress toward some greater union has always been quite abstract and shrouded in an institutional and linguistic fog that only initiates seem to understand. And even for close observers of Europe, interpretations of the significance of events and processes continue to vary widely. A partial explanation for this is that the Community is a work-in-progress: its shape, size, structure, and purpose continue to evolve. Stanley Hoffman, a Harvard professor, recently noted:

> The gradual formation of the Community, ever since its beginning in 1950, has necessarily been an exercise in ambiguity. The members could never agree on the ultimate shape of the Community (should it be a Federal state? a Europe of loosely associated states? something far tighter than a confederation yet far less so than a federation?). Each step forward has had to preserve this ambiguity, so that no one would drop out, and could only be taken after detailed bargaining on a narrow range of issues. [4]

For the United States and the member states of the Community, the nation-states of Europe have always mattered more than the Community, which, in its initial stages served several important purposes: it created durable bonds between former enemies; it served as a bulwark against new Cold War enemies; and it created a framework for sharing sovereignty to enhance the power and influence of European powers diminished by two world wars. During the postwar period, the most fundamental relationship between the United States and Europe has been symbolized by that other Brussels institution, NATO. The end of the Cold War signals the beginning of a new relationship between the major economic powers.

By any measure, Europe's progress during the past ten years—and especially since 1989—has been remarkable. The agreement to achieve a single market by 1992 is well underway, and the Community now has its sights set on a single currency, a central bank, political union, and possibly a substantial enlargement of Community membership. Although nation-states in Europe will continue to be

[4] Hoffman, Stanley. France Self-Destructs. *The New York Review of Books*, May 28, 1992. p. 28.

important, significant progress towards European union and the end of the Cold War strongly suggest that they will matter less than they formerly did. The nation-states acting in concert have invested the European Community with a portion of their sovereignty in economic matters and, at the December 1991 summit meeting in Maastricht, took momentous steps toward the formal creation of a European Union.

Yet Europe also faces many problems that may undermine the pace of integration and unification. Serious concerns continue to be expressed by citizens who fear that a "surrender" of sovereignty will amount to a loss of national identity. Next door, Eastern Europe and the numerous republics of the former Soviet Union appear to many West Europeans to threaten Western European stability and prosperity. Conflicts between Serbia and Croatia, Serbia and Bosnia-Herzegovina, and between Azerbaijan and Armenia over the enclave of Nagorno-Karabakh, raise the specter of nationalism and war in Europe. Even if other wars can be avoided, many wonder how the urgent task of reconstruction will be financed. Still others fear that failure to bring about material improvements in the east will cause waves of immigration to Western Europe. The plight of Eastern Europe and the former Soviet Union may have a significant impact on progress toward European union. If the pace of economic growth is sluggish during the 1990s, unemployment and immigration may pose the greatest risks to European union. The six studies in Section II provide a portrait of the European Community as it has evolved over the last 40 years. The studies also examine the issues that are likely to define the difficult path to European Union during the 1990s.

Desmond Dinan takes a wide-ranging look at the determinants of Community integration, and argues that an understanding of the Community's present course must be put within the context of its overall development. He suggests that there are a number of ways of looking at the evolution of the Community. Measures of progress toward integration include those events that stand out as constitutional landmarks, such as the 1951 Treaty of Paris, establishing the European Coal and Steel Community; the 1957 Treaty of Rome; the Single European Act of 1987; and the Treaty on European Union of 1992, which provides for economic and monetary union (EMU) and European political union (EPU).

These landmarks, however, mask the messy reality of *incremental* integration. And questions are once again being raised about Community momentum and about the political will of Europeans to confront fully the issues of enlargement, ratification of the treaty on monetary union and political union, and a host of other difficulties that now face Europeans. It is worth reflecting on the halting pace that has been so characteristic of Community development. Integration has been anything but a linear progression, and most observers would probably agree that progress usually consists of two steps forward and one step back. Rather that analyze EC development as a chronological progression, Dinan explores three sets of issues that will dominate the Community's future as they have its past: geo-political boundary setting; the evolving agenda; and the development of decision-making processes. He finds that a multitude of idiosyncratic and systemic factors account for the ways in which geo-political borders are set; political, security, and socioeconomic agendas are defined; and legislative decisions are made.

The geo-political boundaries of Europe and the Community are central issues in the debate over the new Europe. From a small core of six countries (France, Germany, Italy, Belgium, the Netherlands, and Luxembourg), the Community has grown to twelve as a result of three enlargements. Another enlargement is likely to take place during the 1990s as three or more western European nations join. But the end of the Cold War raises a number of questions about borders, especially where the borders of Europe are and whether the European Community will be "European" or, perhaps, be more limited in scope; and how will a Community of fifteen, or twenty, or twenty-five member states be managed? These questions are pressing as numerous potential applicants join a growing queue to join. The history of Europe and of the European Community provide a context in which answers might be developed.

For Dinan, the question of agenda, closely linked to enlargement, is also once again on the table. The original community of six had an agenda that was limited to sectoral economic integration (coal and steel). With each succeeding enlargement, some additional pooling of sovereignty has occurred and the agenda has grown. It now includes atomic energy, economic integration (the common market and the single market), agriculture, social policy, regional policies, research and development, monetary union, common foreign and security policies, and European Union. The Community's rapidly expanding agenda is shaped by a number factors including the external political and economic environment, a range of domestic internal issues, the changing dynamic of relations among member states, the day-to-day functioning of the Community's institutions, and bureaucratic behavior in Brussels.

The Community's decision-making process has also evolved into quite a complex system that involves intergovernmental negotiating and intra-bureaucratic bargaining. For many years, Community decision-making was hobbled by the requirement that all decisions be taken unanimously. Gradually, qualified-majority voting (QMV) has been extended to a range of increasingly important issues. While the straight-jacket of unanimity has been loosened, the institutions of the Community appear unlikely to assume the trappings of a supranational state in the near future. Instead, supporters of inter-governmentalism appear to have prevailed in the Treaty on European Union. As the Community grows in membership, the question of how best to structure decision-making will continue to be debated. Dinan's study provides a perspective on the large issues that are now at the top of the Community's agenda: EC–92, economic and monetary union, political union, and enlargement.

Anthony Wallace examines the source of Community momentum during the 1980s: the EC–92 program. The process of creating a single integrated market out of twelve distinct economies began long before the 1985 White Paper *Completing the Internal Market*, but progress toward such a market stalled during the 1970s. A combination of factors during the 1980s produced a favorable climate for renewed progress, including favorable economic conditions, strong demand by business leaders for reduced internal barriers, a series of legal decisions that broke down long-standing barriers around national markets, and an activist EC Commission that produced a plan and rigid timetable for creating a single market.

The EC–92 plan identified a series of obstacles to a single market: barriers to the free movement of people, goods, services, and capital; the use of standards, testing, and certification to impede competition; and closed markets for government procurement. It also identified a comprehensive set of changes (in the form of 282 EC Commission directives) necessary to eliminate those barriers. The EC Commission proved quite adept at pushing the EC–92 directives through the Community's legislative process. Success has, in part, depended on Commission flexibility, a willingness to compromise, and an ability to back down when necessary.

The attractiveness of the program to member states owes a great deal to the fact that it is not seen as a loss, but as a pooling, of sovereignty. Similarly, EC–92 eliminates layers of national regulations, and imposes new EC-wide rules that specify the 'essential requirements' that all member states must incorporate into their own laws and regulations. The program also has unleashed strong market forces that promote policy convergence in the areas of taxation, transportation, foreign investment, and environmental control. Perhaps most significantly, EC–92 provided a major impetus for monetary union. At the same time, many observers have noted that EC–92 can not be realized fully until a common monetary policy is adopted.

Monetary union has been on the EC's agenda since at least the early 1960s, and the first detailed plan for monetary union, the Werner Report, was adopted in 1971 but never implemented. In 1989, the Report on Economic and Monetary Union (called the Delors Report) was adopted by the European Council. Like the earlier Werner Report, it called for a three-stage plan for monetary union. In the 1990s, monetary union is once again on the Community's agenda.

Arlene Wilson provides a detailed analysis of the recently agreed provisions of the Treaty on European Union concerning economic and monetary union (EMU), and discusses the implications of the Treaty for the United States. EMU provides for a central bank, a common monetary policy, and a single currency. The Treaty specifies that the primary goal of EMU is price stability. The transition to EMU is to be achieved in three stages during which the EC countries will strengthen economic policy coordination and make the institutional changes necessary for an independent ESCB.

The Treaty provisions on economic union are not well defined, in marked contrast to those on monetary union. Economic union refers to those economic policies needed to complete EC–92 and monetary union. With the exception of monetary and exchange rate policies, responsibility for economic policies are to remain decentralized among national governments. Member states will coordinate their economic policies within the Council of Ministers, which will develop economic policy guidelines, monitor economic developments in each country, and determine exchange rate policy vis-a-vis non-EC currencies. Monetary union provides for centralized monetary and exchange rate policies. The ability of member states to determine their own money supply, interest rates, and exchange rates will pass to the ESCB. The transition to monetary union, which began in 1990, is to be complete by 1999. Monetary union, if completed, would probably stimulate growth because of better macroeconomic coordination and the efficiencies associated with the use of a single currency.

From the perspective of the United States, EMU is likely to deepen EC integration, and may contribute to increasing regionalism at the expense of multilateral approaches to trade. Regionalism is not an inevitable outcome of monetary union, however. EMU may also contribute to the decline in the dollar's role as an international currency and lead to dollar depreciation—although the extent of any dollar decline which may occur is difficult to estimate. EMU is likely to give the EC a significantly stronger voice in international economic policy coordination while U.S. influence in international policy coordination would decrease. While it may be easier for a Group of 3 (G–3: the United States, the EC, and Japan) to coordinate monetary policies, this will probably only be true in cases where policy prescriptions do not differ significantly. Coordination of fiscal policies is less clear, but assuming that the EC is successful at internal coordination among member countries, it is probable that a united EC position could reduce the U.S. leadership role. For Wilson, the magnitude of the effects is difficult to predict and unexpected developments could delay or lead to a postponement of the transition to EMU. She notes that, in addition to taking steps to maintain a healthy, low-inflation economy, the United States should monitor and analyze EMU developments carefully over the next few years.

Economic and monetary union represents a historic shifting of sovereignty from member states to the European Community. In a very real sense, EMU is more of a political act than an economic one. For the nations transferring their powers, EMU also represents a massive article of faith in Europe, and it inevitably furthers the cause of European political integration. The Treaty on European Union links economic and monetary union with political union. This linkage developed rapidly in the aftermath of the revolutions in Eastern Europe, and became pronounced with the reunification of Germany, and the decision to proceed simultaneously with two intergovernmental conferences at the Rome Summit in December 1990.

In his study of European Political Union, Roy Ginsberg focuses on the provisions of the Treaty on European Union that relate to the development of a Common Foreign and Security Policy (CFSP). Unlike the relatively straightforward provisions on EMU, political union is much more tentative and ill-defined. The Treaty also contains provisions on citizenship, internal security, social policy, and institutional reform. The Treaty widens the scope of foreign policy actions that the European Union may take to practically any action on which member countries can agree. The objectives of the CFSP include safeguarding the common values, fundamental interests, and independence of the Union; strengthening the security of the Union in all ways; preserving peace and strengthening international security; promoting international cooperation; and developing and consolidating democracy and the rule of law, and respect for human rights and fundamental freedoms.

With respect to security policy, the Treaty on European Union represents a dramatic departure from the Treaty of Rome and Single European Act: "the common foreign and security policy shall include all questions related to the security of the Union, including the eventual framing of a common defense policy, which might in time lead to a common defense." [5] The text of the Treaty refers to the Western European Union (WEU) as the defense component of the European Union and as a means to strengthen the Atlantic Alliance: "to this end, [the WEU] will formulate common European defense policy and carry forward its concrete implementation through the further development of its own institutional role." [6]

According to Ginsberg, the implications of a common European defense policy are quite significant for U.S. interests. Questions center on the U.S. presence in Europe, on burden-sharing, and, more generally, on the issue of security in the post-Cold War world. Ginsberg argues that both the open-endedness of the Treaty and the explicit linkage of the WEU to NATO will pose a major test for all of the members of the alliance as collective security arrangements are redefined. Finally, the CFSP may allow the European Union to speak with a single voice on many more issues than previously. Although this may benefit the United States when policies are complementary, a unified European voice might weaken the U.S. international leadership role when consensus cannot be reached.

Michael Smith, Helen Wallace, and Stephen Woolcock examine the implications of the Treaty on European Union for relations between the European Union and its international partners. Although it is too early to say how the Treaty will impinge on partners, those factors that will determine the future course of policy are discussed. These include Treaty provisions that affect the trade, monetary and exchange rate, foreign, security, and defense policies of the Union, as well as the perceptions that they engender. Smith, Wallace, and Woolcock expect the Union's role in the world to continue growing despite a preoccupation with developments within Europe. They believe that the balance between preoccupation and outward orientation depends on how the Union interacts with its partners (especially the United States and Japan) and on foreign perceptions of the European Union.

From the perspective of trade policy, the Treaty further extends the EC's more interventionist approach to the market economy and may have implications for the debate over competitiveness and 'fair' trade. The Treaty extends Community competence in the areas of industrial policy, research and development, and environmental policy. Eleven members, but not the United Kingdom, also signed a protocol and agreement on social policy that will further the development of the West European 'social market approach' to the market economy. As they have done with trade policy, the EC's partners will have to come to terms with the increasing power of the EC in monetary and exchange rate policy. A single European

---

[5] Council of the European Communities and Commission of the European Communities. *Treaty on European Union*. Brussels, 1992. p. 126.

[6] Ibid., p. 242.

currency will reduce the relative importance of the external component of the EC economy even as the external component of the U.S. economy continues to grow. The effect of EMU will be to strengthen the weight and importance of the EC in the international economy and thus in international economic cooperation.

For Smith, Wallace, and Woolcock, the common foreign and security policy offers the possibility of bringing greater coherence to the Union's external economic, monetary, and political actions. The success of the CFSP will depend on its implementation and on the substantive issues that emerge in the international agenda. The authors believe that the focus of the CFSP is likely to be on promoting economic and political stability in the rest of Europe rather than projecting EC power in other regions. The role of the Union in international security policy is less well defined because of differences among member states. The Treaty on European Union bridged these differences by recognizing the WEU as the defense element of the European Union and using it as the link between the Union and NATO. The defense policy element of the Treaty will be reviewed in 1996. By then, the accession of several new (neutral) members may have increased the heterogeneity of the Union and may have made a common defense policy less rather than more likely. Enlargement may also have a major impact on the ability of the Union to pursue coherent foreign and security policies. The authors conclude that the Treaty on European Union will not create a European 'super state,' and the Union is likely to focus more on regional issues and economic issues than on global or military concerns.

For the Community, enlargement is one of the most complex problems that it will face during the 1990s, and it is already a major topic of debate. Karen Donfried reviews the prospects for EC enlargement, analyzes the challenges enlargement poses for the EC, and considers the economic and political implications of enlargement for the United States. The growing list of aspirants to Community membership is likely to complicate the path to European Union. The number of potential new members is quite large, and rapid absorption could slow economic and political integration or possibly lead to an increased emphasis on one process over the other. Rapid enlargement might also alter the balance of power within the EC, and some are concerned that it will increase the power and influence of the unified Germany. A debate is also taking place within the EC over the economic, political, and geographical attributes necessary for membership in the Community.

Donfried suggests that, of three possible scenarios for enlargement, incremental enlargement is most likely. The other two options (accelerated enlargement or no enlargement) appear to be unlikely outcomes. Proponents of incremental enlargement believe that an unequivocal offer of future membership for non-EC countries will provide democratic stability and create a climate of confidence necessary for political and economic reforms. Second, incremental enlargement appears to presuppose major reform of Community institutions. Critics contend that EC membership is not a panacea for countries that will have difficulty, under the best of circumstances, meeting the minimum EC standards for membership. They also contend that enlargement will retard the integration process.

Incremental integration will most likely occur in three successive stages. The members of the European Free Trade Association (EFTA) are the most likely candidates for early entry into the Community. The conclusion of a treaty to create a European Economic Area (EEA), to take effect by January 1993, is a major step toward a 19-member European Community. Formal applications for membership have been made by several EFTA countries, including Austria, Sweden, Finland, and Switzerland. The other countries (Norway, Iceland, and Liechtenstein) are considering membership. The countries of Central and East Europe are a second group of potential EC members. Poland, Hungary, and the Czech and Slovak Federal Republic have stated that their ultimate goal is full EC membership. Although membership is a long-term goal, the conclusion of a series of "Europe Agreements" represents a step in that direction. Other countries in the second group include Bulgaria, Romania, and the republics of the former Soviet Union. A third group is made up of Southern European countries that have already applied for membership: Turkey, Cyprus, and Malta. Of the three, Turkey's application may prove to be the most contentious.

Enlargement has economic, political, and security implications for the United States. As with European integration generally, enlargement raises questions about the European commitment to the multilateral trading system. Will it remain open if the costs of enlargement are steep? Will trade diversion become an issue? What effect will the addition of traditionally neutral countries to the EC have on NATO? Will the transatlantic relationship be redefined? Will European unity pose a challenge to U.S. national interests or will a closer partnership emerge?

Given the number and complexity of issues, the path to European Union will clearly be difficult. Skeptics may well prove to be correct when they suggest that Europe is not up to the task it has set itself. The history of the Community demonstrates, however, that progress, when it occurs, happens slowly and fitfully. Moreover, progress to date has been critically dependent on strong European leadership. The 1980s and early 1990s marked one of the most vibrant periods of progress toward an integrated European Community. EC–92 and the Single European Act deepened the Community and set the stage for the Treaty on European Union. The collapse of the Soviet Union and East European communist regimes also contributed to the decision to place political union on the agenda. Whether the momentum towards union can be sustained is open to debate. But it should be remembered that European integration has, by and large, confounded the skeptics who seem to reappear at each new milestone to announce that Europe will never achieve the next stage or target. European integration has so far also confounded those critics who believe that a united Europe will pose a serious threat to U.S. national interests. Of course, there is no guarantee that, in the future, relations will not become severely strained as Europe changes or becomes frustrated by a lack of change. Consequently, the United States will increasingly be challenged to understand and respond appropriately to European integration.

Foreign Policymaking in the European Community

The European Community has pursued policies with a significant foreign policy dimension since its inception. Trade and development policies have historically been the most visible aspect of foreign policy, but the Community's domestic policies, which are transnational by definition, also clearly have implications far beyond the European Community. Additionally, the Community has gradually expanded its role as an international political actor in areas not covered by the Treaty of Rome. The foreign policy activities of the Community have been coordinated since the 1970s through the extra-treaty framework of European Political Cooperation (EPC). The provisions of the Treaty on European Union for a common foreign and security policy, which will not be incorporated into the Treaty of Rome, may represent a turning point for EC foreign policy.

Still, even as the EC achieves the status of economic superpower, it lacks political and organizational coherence in the formulation and implementation of foreign policy. Peter Ludlow, for instance, believes the problem resides in the "continuing addiction of the principal players in the member states to the prestige and privileges of parallel bilateral relationships" which characterized the bipolar era. [7] He concludes that "the EC has a long way to go before it plays the role in world affairs that it could and should." [8] The two studies in Section III examine how foreign policymaking may evolve in the EC during the 1990s and its implications for U.S.-EC relations.

Lily Gardner Feldman explores EC activism in the international arena and develops three scenarios for the EC's future as an international political actor and as an emerging world power: *Assertive Europe*, *Decisive Europe*, and *Diffident Europe*. Each scenario carries associated costs and benefits for the United States. Gardner Feldman notes significant impediments to EC external activities, including institutional obstacles to coherence and efficiency, and member state differences regarding goals and instruments. In spite of these difficulties, she believes that the EC is already an international political actor of significance and that its role will continue to evolve.

For the next decade, Gardner Feldman believes Assertive Europe to be the most likely scenario for the EC as an international political actor. Assertive Europe characterizes current reality, envisions the Maastricht Treaty as a milestone on an evolutionary path, and involves increased activity in the newer issues of international relations, including environmental concerns, human rights and development, and structural peace. In this scenario, the EC continues to develop as a "civilian power," emphasizes the political and economic aspects of security, and eschews traditional military notions of security that were held out as a long-term possibility in the Treaty on European Union. For the United States, this evolutionary path does not solve the problem of the variable identity of the EC inter-

[7] Ludlow, Peter. The Foreign Policy of the Union. In Ludlow, Peter, ed. *Setting European Community Priorities 1991–1992*. London, Brassey's, 1991. p. 138, 140.
[8] Ibid., p. 151.

locutor. The absence of a consistently unified position among policy sectors and member states means that the United States will not find an EC capable of responding as a single unit in a crisis. Instead, the EC will most likely pursue its growing agenda, with an emphasis on conflict resolution and peacemaking. This scenario has its advantages as well. It permits the United States a further flexibility to continue to deal with the EC both as a multilateral entity and as a collectivity of states with whom it has bilateral relations.

It is not inconceivable that the EC will transform itself from a civilian power to a world power, but this will probably not happen quickly. Decisive Europe assumes that agreement can be reached on a more federal structure for the EC and that foreign policy is formally integrated into the Treaty of Rome. The defeat of a "federal" EC at Maastricht probably delays the realization of Decisive Europe until at least 1996 when the next formal review of political union occurs. For the United States, Decisive Europe would provide a level of institutional and substantive coherence that would make Europe a more effective international actor, including in the military sphere. The United States would have the benefit of knowing with whom in the EC it must deal, but would no longer enjoy the close bilateral relations that it previously had with individual member states.

There is a third scenario, which Gardner Feldman believes less likely to occur, of a Diffident Europe characterized by hesitancy and lack of purpose. A Europe that fails to ratify the Maastricht Treaty or that experiences a resurgence of nationalism and even xenophobia, runs the obvious risk of losing momentum and falling back. While a united Europe poses certain foreign policy challenges in the international arena for the United States, a Europe of independent nation-states and renationalized foreign and security policies could pose new risks, including instability and anti-Americanism.

Stanley R. Sloan argues that U.S.-European relations have entered a period of fundamental change. The end of the Cold War has unmasked the differing interests that lay buried beneath the surface. These differences are challenging the cooperative instincts that defined the alliance. The competitive aspects of U.S.-West European relations are being raised to new levels, but it is unclear whether U.S. and European policymakers will choose to allow cooperation or competition to dominate the relationship during the balance of the 1990s.

Sloan focuses on the changing world around the Community-building process and the challenges that have been posed for the construction of a united Europe, with an emphasis on the political and security aspects of change. He considers a number of challenges that the Community has not yet resolved. Key issues include: Can the European Community be the vehicle for uniting all of Europe without sacrificing much of the organizational rigor and cohesion that exists among members? Can the momentum toward a united Europe be maintained without the motivation until recently provided by a threat from the Soviet Union? Does it make sense for the European Community to develop a common defense among its members without any apparent common military threat to their security? Can the United States develop a new concept of its role in the world consistent with a continuing partnership with its European allies and support for the process of European integration? Without a Soviet threat against Europe, will it increasingly appear to Americans that the main motivation for European integration is to be unified "against us" rather than "with us"?

After 1992: Trade Policy and the European Market

The European Community is one of the great success stories of international institution-building in the post-World War II period. Although primarily economic, the EC has provided an increasingly complex framework for making and implementing policies that transcend purely economic questions. As a framework, the Community has served as a confidence-building institution that has demonstrated that economic and political sovereignty can be shared for the benefit of member states. The EC framework has slowly evolved, often for domestic reasons or in response to external stimuli. That framework, however, has at times created serious frictions with its trading partners because the Community has demonstrated a willingness to move forward by shifting costs to third parties. The CAP and Airbus Industrie are examples of policies driven by domestic considerations that have significant externalities associated with them. EC–92, on the other hand, may be the outstanding example of a Community response to a perceived external challenge from Japan and the United States.

The CAP is a Community policy that serves a particular domestic interest group (farmers), although at an extremely high cost to European consumers and foreign agricultural interests. Similarly, Airbus Industrie is less of a response to U.S. preeminence in the commercial aircraft sector than a recognition that the aircraft sector is a strategic and critical industry that the Community can not afford to exit. On the other hand, the EC–92 program was clearly a response to the external challenge posed by Japan and the United States. American and Japanese competition in many manufactured goods, but especially in the area of high technology products, posed a significant challenge to European industry. Both as a long-term goal and as an immediate response to a serious foreign challenge, the Commission outlined a plan for strengthening European businesses by increasing competition within the European market. Section IV deals with bilateral and sectoral issues that are of concern to the United States. In the wake of the successful EC–92 program, a number of issues continue to be of concern, especially those related to market access, automobiles, aircraft, defense trade, and agriculture.

The EC–92 program is nearing completion, but, as Raymond J. Ahearn notes, U.S. business and government leaders continue to express concerns about specific aspects of the program that could affect American access to the EC market: the basic motivations behind the EC–92 program; "forced" investment; EC support for high-technology industries; and a potentially restrictive market access standard. In addition to the concerns that are raised by EC–92, Ahearn also reviews the opportunities that are created for U.S. exporters and investors.

The EC is a major market for the United States, and the EC–92 single market significantly expands opportunities for U.S. exporters and investors. For exporters, however, the benefits are not likely to be evenly distributed across industries or firms. Small- and medium-sized companies may face significant obstacles to taking advantage of the single market. Large firms may benefit in several ways, including EC–92-related growth in trade resulting from the removal of barriers to intra-European trade, increased competition, corporate restructurings, and new investment. For U.S. companies, the critical elements of the plan include harmonization of technical standards and more open government procurement policies, but other areas that are being reformed or deregulated are also important. These include border controls, transportation, taxation, antitrust policy, and intellectual property rights. U.S. investors in Europe will also gain from many of these same EC–92-related changes. The U.S. economy as a whole benefits from the linkage between foreign investment and exports. More than one-third ($34 billion) of all U.S. exports to the EC are shipped directly to the affiliates of U.S. firms.

EC–92 also raises a number of concerns for U.S. companies. At the most general level, concerns have been expressed about the basic motivations for EC–92. If EC–92 is viewed as a response to technological change and competition from Japan and the United States, it is also a response to the failure of national regulatory agencies to continue to provide benefits to the regulated. Deregulation at the national level is being accompanied by reregulation at the Community level. A number of forces representing very different interests at the EC and national levels have entered the fray, raising fears that EC–92 may have very uneven and unpredictable impacts on third countries.

Ahearn also examines the issue of "forced investment" in the EC. Although the single market is a natural magnet for foreign investment, the EC has used a variety of policy tools to encourage foreign firms to manufacture in the EC rather than export to it. These tools include new rules of origin and stringent local content guidelines, discriminatory public procurement policies, and aggressive anti-dumping actions. Research and development programs are also used to encourage foreign investment. The "forced investment" issue raises fears that high technology production, jobs, and exports are being stripped away from the U.S. economy.

Closely linked to the "forced investment" issue, EC support for high-technology industries may also become an obstacle to U.S. high technology exports. The EC promotes the competitiveness of firms in strategic industries such as telecommunications, computers, semiconductors, and automobiles through trade, procurement, and technology policies. Subsidy and antitrust policies are other areas of significant EC–92-related activity. Although the EC Commission has taken a strong position against national government subsidies to industry, the overall record is mixed. EC antitrust policy has raised questions about the extraterritorial reach of EC law, but the overall emphasis is on competitive factors and closely parallels U.S. standards. Concerns have been voiced that current EC competition policy may not survive beyond the tenure of the present EC Commissioner for competition policy, Sir Leon Brittan.

If his replacement takes a decidedly softer line towards mergers and subsidies, or if price-fixing or monopolization of markets were condoned, U.S. companies could suffer.

The fourth market access issue identified by Ahearn is reciprocity. In the Second Banking Directive of December 1989, the EC adopted a standard that combines "effective market access" and "competitive market opportunities." This goes beyond the U.S. standard of according "national treatment" to foreign companies. In addition to financial services, this restrictive reciprocity provision has been included in EC–92 directives affecting mergers and public procurement. The EC standard raises concerns that U.S. firms may be denied access to the EC market in cases where U.S. and EC regulatory standards diverge.

The EC–92 program presents U.S. policymakers with two basic policy challenges. First, the EC may use access to its market as leverage to effect changes in the U.S. legal and regulatory system. The EC–92 market will strengthen the EC's role in the international economy and will allow it to exert pressure on its partners to introduce reforms similar to those of the EC. Second, EC–92 may help make EC firms more competitive in global markets to the disadvantage of U.S. firms. This could put pressure on U.S. businesses and policymakers to emulate EC policies.

James P. Womack and Daniel T. Jones examine the European Community policies toward foreign trade and investment in the motor vehicle sector. Responsibility for public policy decisions have gradually shifted from national governments to the EC Commission in Brussels. The transition should be largely completed by 1999. Given the growing intensity of international competition in the automotive sector, concerns have been raised in the United States about how active the Community will be in developing policies to support and promote the European motor industry and whether such policies will be adverse to interests of the American motor vehicle industry.

European countries have a long history of providing substantial market protection to their motor vehicle industries. With the Treaty of Rome, the EC member states agreed to eliminate tariffs within Europe and to adopt a common auto and truck tariff with the rest of the world (currently at 10.5 percent). The Community continues to provide a very high level of effective protection for the European and American-owned automobile industry in Europe. Protection is provided through a number of EC and EC-sanctioned policies, including tariffs and quotas, investment aids, local content and rules of origin, energy pricing, vehicle distribution rules, technology policy, and restructuring policies.

Womack and Jones find that the European motor industry faces serious competitive problems with the Japanese motor vehicle industry and that, in conditions of completely open trade and investment, the European industry would be at significant risk. Within the European car industry, German and American-owned firms are in the strongest positions, while the French and Italian producers are the weakest. The European response to these problems has been to reach an agreement with Japan to restrict finished unit imports of Japanese vehicles to current levels (meaning the market share of imported cars from Japan will shrink as the European market grows). The agreement also includes understandings on the rate of increase of Japanese transplants and on the European content that is to be achieved by Japanese transplant factories. The European Community agreed to phase out existing national quotas for Japanese imports by January 1993 and to provide for a common European type certification for imported vehicles by that time.

Womack and Jones conclude that this agreement virtually assures that the Japanese share of the European market will steadily rise and the European share will steadily fall. Unit sales by European and American firms in Europe will stay practically constant, thus avoiding a crisis that might provoke a retrenchment or capacity reductions at least through 1999. Continued high levels of European protection, they suggest, mean that European policy toward imports from the United States is likely to be relatively open. The likelihood of significant trade frictions with the United States is, for the foreseeable future, relatively remote.

If friction between the United States and the EC is unlikely in the automobile sector, John W. Fischer argues that European policies in support of Airbus have been a continuing source of conflict. For the European Community, Airbus is a success story. For the United States, it is a product of unfair competition that has damaged the competitive position of both Boeing and McDonnell Douglas. In just two decades, with large subsidies Airbus has risen to become the number two producer of commercial jet aircraft (after Boeing). Airbus is a rare combination of successful industrial, technology, and trade policies. But Airbus has not proved to be an easily transferable model for policymakers, and many observers have noted that Airbus has yet to turn a profit and cannot be considered a commercial success. The Europeans have been less successful in applying a framework similar to Airbus to other sectors that are considered to be equally important, notably computers and electronics. According to Fischer, Airbus will not go away. In learning to live with Airbus, U.S. policymakers may have to face some hard questions about how best to bolster U.S. manufacturers in the face of subsidized competition.

Another frequent and longstanding source of friction between the United States and the EC is agriculture. Once again subsidies are a major irritant. Charles E. Hanrahan argues that reform of the CAP and the successful outcome of the Uruguay Round of the GATT would reduce trade distortions related to high levels of domestic support, import protection, and export subsidies. In 1990, European consumers subsidized European farmers to the tune of $50 billion and the CAP accounted for 60 percent of the total European Community budget. Additionally, Hanrahan notes that the CAP is responsible for high food prices, large stocks of surplus agricultural commodities, environmental deterioration related to the intensive farming practices that the CAP encourages, and unequal income distribution in rural areas.

Proposed CAP reforms would replace intervention buying with deficiency payments and land set-asides, but they would not dismantle the current systems of import protection or export subsidies. Variable levies and export restitution would remain centerpieces of EC agriculture policy. Thus EC producers and consumers will remain isolated from the world market. While CAP reform does not offer much of a prospect for eliminating the trade distortions of that system, a meaningful result in the Uruguay Round would presumably target the trade distorting effects of the EC's system of restitutions for elimination. If EC integration is going to progress much further, protection of agriculture will have to cease to be a central preoccupation of the Commission and member states.

As Theodor W. Galdi notes, no sector will be more affected by the end of the Cold War than defense, and decisions yet to be made in Europe will affect the fortunes of the U.S. defense industry. As governments and industry confront a shrinking defense market, excess defense production capabilities, and rising unemployment, questions have begun to arise about how to rationalize arms production and trade, while opening the sector to greater competition. The success or failure of Europe's defense industry to adapt to the changing international environment will have a direct impact on the level of U.S. arms exports to Europe and other areas of the world. Western Europe is the largest export market for the U.S. defense industry.

While the Treaty on European Union suggests the eventual creation of an integrated European defense policy, steps are already underway—through the Independent European Program Group (IEPG)—to create a European defense market. A major concern for the United States is that a closed market may be created that favors European producers. In an era of shrinking defense markets, the loss of an estimated $4 billion a year in defense trade could be a major blow to U.S. arms producers. Through its Ambassador to NATO, the United States put forward a proposal for a "Defense GATT" that addresses some of its major concerns. The proposal would foster efficiency and rationalization in the North Atlantic defense industry, maintain military strength at lower cost, and provide for NATO-wide open markets. Successful negotiations may stabilize a global industry that is clearly undergoing major changes.

Redefining the Rules of the Game

In the *Economics of 1992*, [9] the EC Commission noted that European integration promotes efficiency, competition, and greater economies of scale by reducing barriers across Europe. The study generally identified the various gains and benefits expected of the EC–92 program. Beyond the narrow calculation of benefits (and costs), the EC–92 program promotes measures that should improve the competitive position of firms and lead to improvements in living standards in Europe. These changes are to be achieved largely through a series of incremental reforms. Notions of national markets are abandoned, although local and national consumer preferences will obviously continue to play a significant role. And while local preferences may continue to matter, they will not provide either a basis for legal discrimination or a rationale for nontariff barriers.

---

[9] *European Economy.* No. 35. March 1988. The entire issue summarizes the findings of the European Commission-sponsored Cecchini Report, the 16-volume study entitled *Research on the "Cost of Non-Europe."* (Brussels, 1988).

The overall effect of the incremental reforms of the EC–92 program is a dramatic restructuring of the European marketplace. Layers of national regulation are being eliminated. Of course, deregulation is neither an end in itself nor is it the point of this particular exercise. Regulation and the activities of regulators are being refocused, and a common framework for competition is being established on the basis of a common European approach to regulation. Further, if a country wishes to impose heavy regulations on its own producers, it may do so. What that country cannot do is to block access to its market for producers that otherwise meet minimal EC requirements.

The benefits of EC–92 are well understood, or at least have received widespread attention in both the popular press and in specialized publications. What may be less understood are the overall implications of these changes for Europe's competitors. The European approach to development differs from those of the United States and Japan. Such a distinct approach will almost certainly create systemic frictions within the international economy. But given the size and importance of the European economy, competitors will be unable to ignore the European approach.

Although EC–92 and the other changes currently underway in Europe do not amount to a revolution or even a radical reformulation of market capitalism, the changes do effectively redefine many of the rules of the game. As with the development of the Community itself, however, it would be naive to assume that EC progress will be linear. Section V examines how the European framework of competition is being altered by the process of integration. Industrial policy, foreign direct investment, standards and conformity assessment procedures, research and development, and environmental policy provide case studies that are relevant to the United States. In each of these cases, changing rules in Europe have important ramifications for U.S. policy. Will changing rules affect U.S. competitiveness or access to markets? Can the United States learn from European experience? Have the Europeans chosen particular policies because of some set of conditions unique to Europe or as a response to change elsewhere? If a particular policy is being pursued, does it reflect a victory of special interests over common European interests? The studies in this section explore aspects of European integration that many believe will enhance competition in Europe. They also consider the prospects that the new European framework offers for international cooperation.

Robin Gaster explores the evolution of a new industrial policy in Europe that weaves together elements of traditional industrial policy, trade policy, and policy towards foreign investment. Gaster argues that the new policy establishes a framework in which the competing goals of equity and efficiency can be accommodated. A traditional goal for most of the nations of Europe during the postwar period has been the promotion of equity (or fairness) through the regulation of markets and the mitigation of market outcomes for a variety of economic and non-economic reasons. Emblematic of equity is the welfare state and social compact among business, unions, and government. Traditional industrial policy was used in conjunction with subsidies, trade barriers, restricted public procurement, and other means to achieve equity goals. The economic stagnation that overtook the European Community in the 1970s led many to conclude that traditional industrial policy instruments, including those designed to promote and protect national champions, had failed. Measures to promote equity had been transformed into a means of protecting existing jobs, existing firms, and the status quo.

The goal of efficiency, typically equated with a desire for unfettered markets, had come to be at odds with equity. EC–92 promised to create efficient markets by reducing internal barriers within Europe and creating a single European market. Underlying the entire program was the notion that a single market means a fair market, and a fair market is one in which national governments cannot favor domestic firms at the expense of the European competitors. EC–92 has severely eroded industrial policy tools at the national level, including subsidies, technical standards, public procurement, quotas and other trade-related barriers, and financial policies designed to funnel cheap capital to preferred firms. The results have been quite painful for national governments and for national champions faced with an urgent need to become efficient competitors at the European level.

Gaster argues that EC–92 has resulted in Europe-wide policies that recognize the principle of fairness (e.g., firms in one country cannot be granted favors at the expense of those in another) and are generally much more market-friendly than the policies of the past. Thus, European industrial policy by itself will probably not be sufficient to protect core European industries from competition. However, forces are arrayed on both sides of the industrial policy divide, and it appears that some of the goals of traditional industrial policy will continue to be pursued through the combination of protectionist external trade policies and the encouragement of foreign direct investment (FDI). For Gaster, FDI is the third and crucial element of Europe's new industrial policy. It bridges the gap between efficiency (by increasing competition, promoting free markets, and increasing consumer choice) and equity (by creating high-wage, manufacturing jobs and maintaining core industries). He suggests that the United States might benefit from examining how the EC is dealing with the economic challenges from Japan.

James K. Jackson further develops the topic of foreign direct investment in Europe by examining the patterns of flows and their implications for investment rules, competition (antitrust) policy, and the future of U.S.-EC economic relations. The creation of the single market has led to a dramatic acceleration of U.S. FDI in the European Community. Increased two-way flows of direct investment are forging closer ties between the United States and the European Community, but are also highlighting differences between the United States and the EC and its member states in fundamental beliefs over the nature of economic competition and market concentration, concepts of sovereignty, and the role of government in controlling or preserving competition in the marketplace.

For American and European firms, a number of investment-related issues, and their resolution, will determine whether the international investment climate is favorable or hostile. Changing systems of merger control in the EC and the United States have given rise to concern among businesses on both sides of the Atlantic. For

American business, concerns center on the merger control system adopted by the Community as part of the EC–92 process. This system differs considerably in approach from the U.S. system. European business is concerned with what it perceives to be a more vigorous enforcement of U.S. antitrust laws; potential effects caused by changes to the Exon-Florio provision of the Defense Production Act; and the possibility that Congress may enact new controls on foreign direct investment in the United States. Additionally, both the United States and the EC have recently initiated efforts to apply some provisions of their respective domestic laws to entities and events outside their territories. These differences in national legal standards and attitudes toward competition are potentially a major source of conflict and confusion for companies that are increasingly international in scope.

Standards are one of the building blocks of international trade and commerce. They assure product compatibility and maintain an agreed upon level of product quality and safety. However, incompatible standards and the way countries certify that a product complies with standards have also proved to be major stumbling blocks to trade. Testing and certification are perhaps the most prevalent means of using standards as a trade barrier. Lennard G. Kruger examines standards and conformity assessment activities in the EC and the potential impact these activities might have on U.S. firms. He also looks at the roles that might be played by government and the private sector to deal effectively with evolving EC standards and conformity assessment procedures.

As part of the EC–92 program, the European Community is harmonizing differing national standards and testing and certification procedures into a single EC-wide body of uniform standards and regulations. On balance, EC efforts to reform standardization procedures and conformity assessments are expected to be beneficial to American business. However, EC standards and conformity assessment procedures could, in some instances, constitute non-tariff barriers to trade, and some industrial sectors and individual companies (particularly small- and mid-sized companies) may be adversely affected by the EC approach. Some manufacturers worry that they will be compelled to subject their products to costly and duplicative conformity assessment procedures carried out by European authorities. Meanwhile, American standards and conformity assessment companies and organizations worry that they will lose business to their European competitors if they are not officially sanctioned and recognized by the EC to perform tests and issue certificates needed by regulated products to gain access to the EC market.

According to Kruger, the United States and the EC disagree on various options to allay the concerns of some U.S. exporters, standards organizations, and conformity assessment bodies. Issues under negotiation include mutual recognition agreements, subcontracting of quality registration functions to U.S. labs, and the extent to which the EC will allow manufacturer self-certification. A larger issue for Congress may be whether the U.S. standards and conformity assessment system will continue to meet the challenge of a changing and increasingly integrated international economy.

The process of European integration has produced significant changes in the way research and development (R&D) activities are structured in Europe. Glenn J. McLoughlin provides an assessment of the wide range of activities that the Europeans are engaged in, and asks what U.S. policymakers might learn from their experiences. The scope of European R&D activities is quite broad. Government-industry efforts range from basic research to commercial technology development, well beyond the "precompetitive" technology development threshold where joint U.S. Government-industry efforts end. European activities take place at three levels. Pan-European R&D (level 1) represents a wide range of efforts (particularly at the level of basic research) that involve the cooperation of nations, industries, and research facilities across Europe. R&D activities will also be affected by EC–92 directives (level 2), which are also likely to have a substantial and lasting impact on science and technology relations among the 12 member states, as well as with external partners. EC–92 will directly affect rules of origin, location of R&D facilities, standards, taxes, and flows of engineers, scientists, and technicians within the Community. Cooperative R&D activities are also supported by the Framework Programme (level 3). Government, industry, universities, and independent research facilities receive support in key science and technology fields directly from the European Community.

Questions have been raised about how well pan-European R&D fits in with the national scientific and technology priorities of each member state, and national support for pan-European R&D differs from country to country. EC R&D programs—as well as other pan-European programs—are not well funded in comparison with national programs, especially in areas where a technology is close to commercialization. A second issue raised by McLoughlin is whether pan-European R&D efforts add to European science and technology capabilities and knowledge, or merely subsidize R&D activity that would not have been undertaken in the absence of such an effort and that may be of questionable value. As European integration progresses, governments will also be challenged to find a balance between cooperation and competition in the fields of science and technology. Whether R&D activity should be restricted on the basis of regionalism (and possibly the rise of trading blocs) or links built to promote multiregional cooperation and sharing is a major issue that the United States, Japan, and the EC have yet to face fully.

In a paper on environmental policy in Europe, Mary Tiemann assesses how the Single European Act, the EC–92 process, and wider processes of integration are creating a new framework for more comprehensive policies of environmental protection. Although the pace and direction of European environmental policy is affected by a number of factors (including north-south regional disparities, differing national environmental priorities, German unification, and the vast needs of East European countries for environmental assistance), the Community is giving high priority to environmental matters. EC environmental policy is guided by three principles. First, pollution prevention is given priority over cleanup. Second, environmental degradation should be corrected at the source. And, third, the polluter pays. Community involvement in environmental matters will most likely be concentrated in the following areas: pollution prevention and control; improved natural resources management; international activities; and the development of means to promote environmental protection.

The development of comprehensive environmental regulations in the EC may be beneficial for U.S. business. Tiemann notes that, as EC environmental standards rise, environment-related business costs are likely to approach those in the United States, eliminating cost advantages that European firms may now enjoy. The degree to which U.S. business may gain may be mitigated by various EC policy instruments, including tax incentives, subsidies, grants, and EC-supported pollution-control research and development. U.S. firms that produce in Europe will also face rising costs associated with higher standards. The European market for environmental goods and services, which is expected to grow rapidly, should provide a boost to U.S. exports that meet EC standards and related technical requirements. A unified European Community voice on global environmental issues may influence U.S. positions, and Tiemann argues that the EC intends to challenge the United States for leadership on global issues. As European standards emerge, U.S. policymakers will have to decide whether U.S. standards should be set with a view toward greater harmonization with an increasingly powerful market.

The European Community in the International Economy

The United States has entered an uncertain period characterized by concerns over the reordering of the international system and the reemergence of domestic economic issues as top priorities for policymakers. The process of international reordering is the most obvious manifestation of a historical break that occurred with the collapse of the Soviet Union. The end of the USSR was accompanied by an almost immediate shift in attention to the European Community and to Japan as the major sources of competition and cooperation in the 1990s. As political and military confrontation with the USSR waned, the United States has begun to undergo a painful process of domestic economic readjustment as defense-related sectors decline and nondefense sectors seek to become more competitive. At the same time, the EC and Japan stand out as major competitors and, some believe, as threats to the international economic position of the United States. Increasingly, regionalism and the formation of trade and economic blocs appear to be attractive alternatives to the postwar multilateral economic system. The papers in Section VI examine many of the issues central to the emerging post-Cold War international economic order: the rise of economic superpowers, management of economic interdependence, the question of leadership, the challenge of Eastern Europe and the republics of the former Soviet Union, and the future of the multilateral trading system.

C. Michael Aho and Bruce Stokes contend that European economic unification is the third great economic shock to the world economy since the end of the Vietnam War, comparable to the oil embargoes of the 1970s and the Third World debt crisis of the 1980s. During the 1990s a new transatlantic relationship will be defined and tested, with the economy replacing security as the primary focus of bilateral relations. The European role in the international economic system will change in ways that are of fundamental importance to the United States. The authors note that, without the constraints of the Cold War, Washington can be expected to pursue aggressively its economic self-interest, but will consequently have less leverage with its allies. They also suggest that Europe will be more willing to assert its economic interests. The result will, they believe, will be ongoing confrontation.

The new transatlantic economic relationship will be defined by European economic unification, by macroeconomic coordination, by trade cooperation, and by a number of other factors, including developments in eastern Europe and the former Soviet Union, the emerging EC-Japan relationship, the changing nature of U.S.-European security arrangements, and political developments inside a united Europe. Aho and Stokes argue that it is now time for the United States to take the lead in launching an overarching dialogue with Europe on the future of the transatlantic relationship. They argue that a dialogue covering trade, investment, monetary and fiscal policy, defense, and global burdensharing would keep the United States engaged in and with Europe, while promoting an outward looking, global role for the European Community.

The economic triad of Europe, North America, and East Asia is the focus of a paper by Dick Nanto. The geo-economic centers of the triad comprise the leading industrial regions of the world and increasingly set international trade policy, generate consumer and industrial trends, and provide much of the capital and expertise for the rest of the globe. Within these regions, the United States, the European Community, and Japan take the leadership roles.

The triad is defined by a set of interactions consisting of three separate bilateral relationships that vary in intensity and balance. For Europe, increased competition threatens key industries and some perceive a U.S.-Japan axis in which Japanese and American companies act alone or in concert to threaten weaker European producers. The United States faces problems in resolving trade disputes with Japan, restoring macroeconomic health to its economy, and continuing to provide world leadership in economic matters. Domestic economic problems, rising protectionist sentiment, and the Federal budget deficit constrain international action by the United States. Japan is confronted with pressure from the United States and Europe to open its markets and internationalize its economy. At the same time, Japan must deal with the backlash directed against its aggressive export industries.

Nanto explores the evolving strategies of the EC, the United States, and Japan. These strategies are changing in response to changes in the nature of competition. Nations are no longer the exclusive beneficiaries of their own economic (or technology) policies, and the comparative advantage of nations is increasingly a function of the competitive advantage of firms within international industries. Successful national strategies may increasingly concentrate on ensuring that national industries are integrated into triadic consortia and networks. For Nanto, the changed international environment will lead to heightened competition among the triad economies and between the triad and the rest of the world.

George D. Holliday looks at the economic problems that confront Eastern Europe. The most difficult challenge to the overall process of European integration may well have been posed by the unexpected revolutions in Eastern Europe and in the republics of what was the Soviet Union. The dramatic reorientation of the region's economic, political, and security relations with the rest of the world would seemingly place those countries on a track moving toward eventual membership in the European Community. However, most of the countries of the region face formidable systemic and structural problems stemming from Stalinist central planning and decades of dictatorship. That legacy may prove to be a barrier to economic modernization, as well as an obstacle to closer economic relations among the countries of the region.

The United States and the EC share broad foreign policy interests in Eastern Europe and the former Soviet republics, including democratic transition and market-oriented economic reforms. The United States has supported closer cooperation between the EC and the countries in the East, and has encouraged the Community to take the lead role in coordinating foreign assistance to those countries. The United States also favors the elimination of barriers to trade between the EC and Eastern Europe through association agreements (the Europe Agreements). It is generally believed that this will stimulate economic growth in the East and create a favorable climate for foreign investment. Concerns have been raised over the possibility that closer trade ties with the East might serve as a pretext for higher third country trade barriers. U.S. officials are also concerned that the association agreements will be in violation of the GATT.

Since the mid-1980s, the nations of the European Community have contemporaneously pursued two important and seemingly complementary objectives: the creation of the single market and the Uruguay Round of multilateral trade negotiations. Jeffrey J. Schott examines the structure of EC trade and the factors likely to guide EC trade policy in the 1990s as the process of European economic integration grows wider and deeper. He then looks at how EC–92 has affected EC positions in the Uruguay Round, and how this could affect the prospective package of agreements. He concludes with an assessment of the reactions of non-EC countries to the expanding EC trading bloc.

Schott notes that the two initiatives juxtaposed and balanced the implicit inward-orientation of the EC–92 process, designed to remove obstacles to trade among the EC member states by the end of 1992, and the outward-orientation of the GATT round, designed to open markets to competition from third country suppliers. EC officials maintained that the two initiatives were mutually reinforcing, but others argued that while the Uruguay Round could provide substantial new opportunities for EC firms that would encourage the EC to lower its barriers to foreign suppliers, the EC–92 process might provide an excuse not to go forward in the GATT.

Schott posits success for the EC–92 process, but believes the GATT talks remain in doubt largely because of a dispute between the Community and most other GATT members on reform of farm support programs. The possibility that the talks may collapse or only achieve minimal results has revived concerns that the EC places greater priority on internal market reforms than on the GATT talks. EC policymakers also seem to be distracted by the unfolding events in Eastern Europe. A minimalist result, Schott argues, would likely place the GATT process in disrepute and lead countries to seek solutions though unilateral actions under national trade laws or through the negotiation of bilateral or regional trading arrangements. EC–92 and the Uruguay Round seem to be heading for a climax in 1992. Schott suggests that the outcome of the GATT talks will determine whether EC–92 leads the EC to open up to foreign competition or to curl up into an increasingly broadbased regional trading bloc.

I. ECONOMIC POLICY AND DECISIONMAKING

THE UNCERTAIN PROSPECT FOR ECONOMIC GROWTH IN THE EUROPEAN COMMUNITY

by Craig Elwell *

CONTENTS

INTRODUCTION

After accelerating in the late 1980s, economic growth in the European Community (EC) is ebbing and with it the prospects for realizing the large economic gain that could result from a successful implementation of the 1992 market unification (EC-92) efforts. Slow growth is a problem that has plagued the EC for most of the last two decades. In the 1980s real output advanced at an annual average pace of 4.2 percent in Japan, 3.0 percent in the United States, but only 2.5 percent in the EC. That the EC was growing below potential is evidenced by an unemployment rate that hovered above 10 percent for most of the last decade, well above unemployment rates in the United States and Japan (see table 1).

For many, the ambitious EC-92 plan outlined in the EC's 1985 White Paper, *Completing the Internal Market*, was the vehicle that would break down barriers to free trade and investment, and allow the EC to realize its potential for more rapid economic growth and a higher living standard. The size of the expected increase in national income is a matter of some disagreement. The Cecchini Report, sponsored by the EC, judged that over the medium term the move to the single market would boast EC GDP by a one-time gain of 4.3 to 6.4 percent, an acceleration that would generate a cu-

---

* Craig Elwell is a Specialist in Macroeconomics, Economics Division, Congressional Research Service.

mulative income gain to the EC of nearly $300 billion. [1] A Congressional Budget Office (CBO) study similarly concluded that the EC–92 program would raise EC GDP 6 percent above the level it would otherwise reach by the year 2000. The economist Richard Baldwin, however, has calculated that a full accounting of the potential supply-side improvements of EC–92 might add another 1 to 3 percentage points to the gains estimated by Cecchini and perhaps cause a permanent increase in the EC sustainable rate of economic growth. [2]

TABLE 1. Macroeconomic Trends in the EC, the United States and Japan

(annual percent change, unless otherwise noted)

	81	82	83	84	85	86	87	88	89	90	Average 1981–1990
Real GDP											
EC	0.2	0.7	1.6	2.4	2.4	2.7	2.7	4.0	3.5	2.9	2.5
U.S.	1.9	−25	3.6	6.8	3.4	2.7	3.4	4.5	2.5	2.5	3.0
Japan	3.4	3.4	2.8	4.3	5.2	2.6	4.3	6.2	4.7	5.6	4.2
Unemployment [a]											
EC	8.1	9.4	10.3	10.7	10.9	10.8	10.6	9.9	9.0	8.4	9.6
U.S.	7.5	9.5	9.5	7.4	7.1	6.9	6.1	5.4	5.2	5.4	7.2
Japan	2.2	2.4	2.6	2.7	2.6	2.8	2.8	2.5	2.3	2.1	2.5
Inflation											
EC	11.7	10.3	8.1	6.8	5.5	3.2	3.2	3.4	4.5	4.4	6.1
U.S.	9.2	5.7	4.1	3.8	3.3	2.4	4.6	3.9	4.5	5.0	4.6
Japan	4.5	2.7	2.0	2.5	2.2	0.4	0.2	−0.1	1.8	2.4	1.9

[a] % of labor force.
Source: OECD, Economic Outlook, December 1991.

The upshot of these estimates, whether the high or the low proves correct, is that the EC–92 program has the potential of making the citizens of the EC significantly richer. We may discover, however, that *who gains* and *who loses* as a result of these prospective initiatives may be more important in the implementation of the program than the size of the overall gains. The recent slowing of growth and the near-term prospect of only modest reacceleration could very likely undermine the resolve needed to implement the program fully. Poor economic times in the EC would make the necessary changes politically more difficult and perhaps impossible to achieve. By raising unemployment overall and particularly by increasing the burdens on Europe's weak industries, the current slowdown in growth cultivates a more fertile ground for the perpetuation and growth of mercantilism and protectionism. In this circumstance slow growth now may well breed slow growth in the future.

---

[1] Commission of the European Communities. *Research on the "Cost of NonEurope"*. 16 v. Brussels, 1988.

[2] Cecchini, Paolo. *The European Challenge 1992: The Benefits of a Single Market.* Aldershot, Gower, 1988; U.S. Congressional Budget Office. *How the Economic Transformation of Europe Will Affect the United States.* Washington, December, 1990; and, Baldwin, Richard. The Growth Effects of 1992. *Economic Policy*, October, 1989. p. 248–281.

What is at stake goes well beyond what the EC stands to lose or gain in terms of output and employment. The United States has substantial commercial interests in a more prosperous EC. Moreover, as Robert Samuelson of the Washington Post [3] recently observed, "It is Europe—much more than Japan —that will be decisive in shaping the new post cold-war international order." Slow growth in the EC would limit the flow of aid, whether direct transfers or export sales, to the emerging economies of Eastern Europe and the former Soviet Union, and reduce the prospects of a successful economic transformation in these nations.

Why Has Growth Slowed in the EC?

In 1991 economic growth in the European Community ebbed to its lowest point since 1982, with real output advancing only 1.3 percent, less than half the pace recorded in 1990. Among the big four countries, the UK remained in recession, while Germany, France, and Italy saw a sizable deceleration of economic growth. As would be expected in the very interdependent EC, economic growth in all of the smaller community members (except Greece) also slowed significantly and unemployment edged upward. For the EC as a whole, unemployment moved up for the first time since 1986, reaching 8.6 percent of the labor force in 1991. Inflation remained near 5.0 percent.

Protracted economic weakness in the UK has had a dampening effect on its EC neighbors, as has a generally weak world economy. Exports represent nearly 30 percent of final demand in the EC. Therefore, a slowdown in the world economy has strong negative reverberations on economic growth in the EC. In the last four years of the 1980s, world GDP (exclusive of the EC) expanded at about 3.8 percent a year, and world trade (minus EC imports) rose at an average 6.0 percent a year. In 1991, in contrast, the growth of world output was essentially zero, and the growth of trade fell to less than 2.0 percent.

The sizable deceleration in external demand was the result of normal cyclical factors, most likely exacerbated by the negative effects of the Gulf crisis, that generated recession in the United States, Canada, and the United Kingdom, and significantly slowed the economies of Japan and the Pacific rim. (In 1991 U.S. imports from the EC *shrank* by 8 percent.) As economic weakness in the world economy has proved more protracted than expected, the dampening effect on EC growth has also been more drawn out.

The world economy is expected to show a respectable recovery this year, with real output up about 2 percent, and to accelerate to about 3 percent real growth in 1993. It remains problematic whether overall EC growth will be buoyed as much as one might expect by this rise in external demand. The EC projects real GDP accelerating modestly to a 2.5 percent annual rate by 1993. That would not, however, be fast enough to prevent the unemployment rate from continuing to rise to over 9 percent in 1993. Slow growth leads to only a very modest reduction in inflation (see table 2).

---

[3] Samuelson, Robert J. Europe's Boom Has Come and Gone. *Washington Post*, February, 1992. p. A23.

TABLE 2. EC: Macroeconomic Trends and Forecasts

	1991	1992	1993
Real GNP (% change)	1.3	2.2	2.5
Unemployment 1(% of Labor Force)	8.6	9.0	9.2
Inflation (% change)	5.0	4.5	4.2
World Imports (excluding EC, % change)	1.8	5.1	6.1

Source: EC Commission, December 1991.

Perhaps of greater immediate effect on current and near term growth in the EC has been the recent steady increase in interest rates in Germany. Nominal long-term interest rates there averaged near 6 percent in 1988 but by 1990 had risen to nearly 9 percent and remained close to that level through 1991 despite significant slowing of the German economy. The German intent is to choke-off further acceleration of the inflation that has been prompted by the stresses of absorbing eastern Germany. Inflation which averaged less than 2.0 percent in the late 1980s has steadily accelerated to near a 5.0 percent annual pace in late 1991, high enough to prompt a countering action by the inflation-shy Bundesbank.

But the German anti-inflation program is dampening growth across the EC, not just in terms of the reduced stimulus of trade, but directly on each economy by forcing commensurate increases in interest rates across the Community. These rate increases occur because agreements under the European Monetary System (EMS) commit all EC members (except Greece) to maintain their current exchange rate alignment. If, for example, Italy did not raise its interest rates, capital would move from Italy into Germany, and in turn would depreciate the lira against the D-mark. Thus higher rates in Italy (and every other member country) are needed to hold the exchange rate steady.

The general economic implication of this arrangement is that, so long as Germany maintains its anti-inflation policy, the rest of the Community is constrained to slow growth. Of course, there is another course: EMS exchange rates could be allowed to rise. This would temporarily dampen inflation by cheapening imports, allow a respite for the tight monetary conditions, and allow a bit more growth. But to date, little serious consideration has been given this alternative.

The German anti-inflation program is of central importance in explaining the most recent EC growth slowdown, but there is probably a near-term anti-growth bias in the overall EC–92 program. Part of that program is the creation of a single European currency by the end of the decade. This is clearly important to the ultimate establishment of a true economic union. However, achieving that end has required the EC nations to work toward convergence of inflation and interest rates. These goals have and will continue to require sizable reductions in budget deficits and relatively tight monetary policies in most member nations. While certainly important to sustainable long-term growth, these policies work to dampen near-term growth.

Economic Conditions and Prospects

Nearly 80 percent of EC economic activity is accounted for by the four large members: Germany, United Kingdom, France, and Italy. Clearly economic events in these four economies will determine the growth prospects for the entire Community. Therefore this section will focus on the conditions and prospects in these key economics.

THE GERMAN LOCOMOTIVE SLOWS

Real GDP growth in Germany in 1991 rose at a seemingly impressive 3.3 percent, but this number belies the sharp deceleration of growth that occurred as that year progressed, and it is quite likely that in early 1992 real output is actually contracting (see table 3). The forecasts, however, do not envision western Germany tumbling into recession, as the economic state of consumers and investors remains sufficiently healthy to make the "cumulative decline" of a recessionary process unlikely.

TABLE 3. Western Germany: Macroeconomic Conditions and Forecasts

	1991				1991	1992	1993
	I	II	III	IV			
Real GDP (% change)	5.1	4.8	1.9	1.3	3.3	2.2	1.8
Unemployment (% of labor force)	3.3	5.5	5.5	5.4	4.6	5.0	5.6
Inflation (% change)	2.6	3.1	4.1	4.1	3.5	4.2	4.0

Source: DRI/McGraw-Hill and EC Commission.

The immediate cause of the recent slowdown was a weakening of consumer demand. German household budgets were hit by the 7.5 percent "solidarity surcharge" on their income tax (effective on July 1991), and at the same time by the effects of higher gasoline taxes. These, of course, are "one time" shocks to household budgets, so consumer spending can be expected to bounce back fairly quickly.

The push from external trade, exclusive of trade with eastern Germany, has not been very strong of late. Burdened by the strengthening of the German mark, as well as the general weakness in the world economy, export sales were up a very slim 0.9 percent in 1991. World demand can be expected to improve as the United States and Canadian economies move out of recession and the Japanese economy again accelerates. With buoyant world demand German exports will likely increase at a healthy pace.

Despite an improving world economy, the Bundesbank's program of monetary tightness and the associated high interest rates will likely keep the pace of economic growth moderate over the near-term. Short-term rates have risen sharply in recent months and long-term interest rates, although dropping moderately late in 1991, remain high. If they persist, such interest rate levels, will allow positive but moderate growth in Germany over the near-term (again, see table 3). But, as already discussed, continuation of high interest rates in Germany will also have a strong dampening effect on growth among the other members of the EMS.

The Bundesbank program of high interest rates and slow growth is the predictable response to recent strong inflationary pressure in Germany. In the last decade Germany moved aggressively to decelerate inflation and succeeded in the late 1980s at bringing inflation rates to below 2 percent. In the early 1990s however, in large measure due to the pressures and strains of absorbing eastern Germany, inflation again accelerated. In the late months of 1991 the GNP price deflator was rising at near 5.5 percent and is expected to go a bit higher in early 1992. The Bundesbank is likely to find this unacceptable and cannot be expected to ease its high interest rate program until far more moderate inflation prevails.

Sharply rising wages are the key factor behind the recent inflation surge. An average increase in wages of near 7 percent is likely for 1991, up from less than 6 percent in 1990 and well above the 3 percent average in the late 1980s. With productivity growth now weak, these wage increases have put sharp upward pressure on unit labor costs and prices. In fact, between January and October of 1991, unit labor costs rose 4.6 percent, more than the cumulative rise over the last four years. Because wage increases and the Bundesbank's reaction to them will likely be central to determining Germany's near-term growth prospects, the outcomes in the 1992 wage round is of obvious importance. If the 6 percent pay raise written into the new steel-workers contract and the 5.4 percent raise recently won by public sector unions are good predictors of settlements to come, the Bundesbank will not be much more willing to ease interest rates significantly this year.

Many observers judge that such inflationary tensions will persist well beyond 1992. As wage demands remain high and the Bundesbank stubbornly resists inflation with high interest rates, growth prospects will remain modest at best. Germany seems likely to be a slow moving "locomotive."

THE UNITED KINGDOM'S RECESSION CONTINUES

Britain is clearly stuck in a severe recession. Real GDP has steadily contracted since mid-1990 (see table 4). Some signs of recovery emerged in the third quarter of 1991, but conditions quickly deteriorated and the U.K. entered 1992 still in recession. The prospect is only for a modest boost in real output for the rest of 1992. The current British recession was bred in the exuberance of the economic expansion of the late 1980s. Rapid growth soon revealed Britain's two chronic economic weaknesses: overly large wage increases that quickly translate into accelerating inflation and a rapidly rising external deficit. By 1990, wages and prices were rising at nearly a 10 percent annual rate and the current account deficit had grown to nearly 4 percent of GDP.

To stem these pressures, monetary policy tightened in early 1990, pushing up interest rates and turning down real growth. External factors no doubt aggravated the process of decline: the Iraq-Kuwait war undermined business and consumer confidence, and the recession in North America reduced the pull of foreign demand.

TABLE 4. United Kingdom: Macroeconomic Conditions and Forecasts

	1991				1991	1992	1993
	I	II	III	IV			
Real GDP (% change)	−1.0	−3.7	−2.4	−1.4	−1.2	2.0	2.8
Unemployment (% of labor force)	7.0	7.9	8.5	8.9	8.4	9.8	10.0
Inflation (% change)	8.5	6.0	4.7	4.1	6.5	4.6	4.1

Source: DRI/McGraw-Hill and EC Commission.

But internal factors also played a role. Large increases in consumer and business indebtedness during the expansion presaged the need for eventual adjustment. In fact, the persistence of this recession is significantly rooted in the very large and successful adjustment that the private sector has made to bring their balance sheets to a more sustainable position. Another internal factor that added a heightened degree of uncertainty was the outcome of national elections in April 1992. The prospect that a Labor Party victory might bring major tax increases seems to have undermined consumer and business confidence. However, the Tory victory in April has allayed that fear.

The other major encumbrance to recovery and growth in Britain is high interest rates. Rates have certainly come down substantially from the heights reached in 1990. For example, long-term government bond rates have fallen from near 15 percent in mid-1990 to about 9.5 percent as 1992 began. Other instruments have seen similar large declines. Nevertheless, given the length and depth of recession, these lower interest rates are still high and remain a clear hindrance to more vigorous economic growth. Again, British interest rates are being held up by high German interest rates as a consequence of the EMS exchange parity system.

Despite these several encumbrances, most forecasts see the U.K. entering into a slow but steady economic recovery in 1992, and reaching real growth at near a 3 percent pace in 1993. Given the degree of slack in the economy and the prospect that wage demands will stay only moderately above productivity growth, inflation pressures should be tolerable and this growth pace sustainable. However, absent major improvements in the efficiency of British labor markets, more rapid growth is not probably sustainable. Over the longer term, with economic slack reduced, economic growth can be expected to slow to a more sustainable pace of about 2.5 percent. In this environment unemployment in the United

Kingdom will remain high at around 9 to 10 percent of the labor force for the next few years.

FRANCE NEEDS THE PULL OF A "LOCOMOTIVE"

Economic growth in France slowed markedly in 1991, falling to about a 1.3 percent annual rate of increase from nearly 4 percent growth in 1990. Activity continues to be sluggish in early 1992, but there is no widely held expectation of deterioration into recession. Rather the prospects are good for a moderate acceleration of growth in the coming year, if a sizable stimulus from external demand occurs. (See table 5.)

In many ways the French economy is in very good shape. Inflation ranging in the 2.5 percent to 3.0 percent range is the lowest among the big four European economies. Both the public deficit and the level of private indebtedness have been aggressively reduced to comparatively low levels. In addition, the French current account deficit remains modest and export competitiveness is good.

The principal constraint on the French economy is the gloomy prospect for domestic demand. The weakness of France's labor market has kept unemployment in recent years near 9 percent, even with relatively rapid economic growth. Unemployment is forecast as rising and will further undermine the purchasing power of French households. Add to that the dampening effect of now higher social security contributions (coming out of paychecks) and there is little prospect for much of a growth push coming from private consumption expenditures. Nor will public expenditures provide a boost to growth, as government officials are firmly committed to the process of tightening public finances. In the business sector low profitability limits investment prospects as does ongoing political instability. Of course, in both the business and household sector, the relatively high level of interest rates that now prevails due to the EMS linkage further dampens domestic demand.

TABLE 5. France: Macroeconomic Conditions and Forecasts

	1991				1991	1992	1993
	I	II	III	IV			
Real GNP (% change)	0.5	1.4	1.1	2.4	1.3	2.3	2.5
Unemployment (% of labor force)	9.3	9.9	9.8	10.0	9.5	10.1	10.2
Inflation (% change)	3.2	3.2	3.0	2.8	3.0	2.9	2.8

Source: DRI/McGraw Hill and EC Commission.

The upshot is that any sizable acceleration of economic growth in France will occur only with the pull of a foreign growth "locomotive." The German growth spurt of the late 1980s played this role, boosting France's net exports and overall growth rate. As Germany slowed it was hoped that the recovery of demand in North America and the UK would provide the external stimulus the French economy needs to achieve vigorous growth. But recovery in the United Kingdom and the United States have been delayed and, as a result, economic growth in France will most likely remain weak and unemployment high in 1992 and 1993.

ITALY SEEMS PERPETUALLY HOBBLED

After rising at a brisk 3.2 percent in 1989, Italian real GNP growth decelerated to 2.0 percent in 1990, and continued to slow to near 1.0 percent in 1991. While recession is not generally foreseen, the prospects are for below average economic growth and above average unemployment for the next several years. (See table 6.)

Since early 1990 Italy has pegged its currency to the EMS Exchange Rate Mechanism (ERM) and, to defend the lira, has steadily tightened monetary policy to raise interest rates in step with German rates. Monetary discipline has not been matched by fiscal discipline, however, as continued budget overruns have led to a high and growing stock of pubic indebtedness totaling over 100 percent of GDP in 1991. This inharmonious policy mix has steadily eroded financial market confidence, making the central bank's job harder, by pushing interest rates higher than they otherwise would be. High interest rates, as we have seen in France, Germany, and the UK, have dampened business activity in the Italian business sector and slowed economic growth. Although below its pace of the mid-1980s, inflation has risen to over 6.0 percent in recent quarters, even as the unemployment rate has risen to over 10 percent.

TABLE 6. Italy: Macroeconomic Conditions and Forecasts

	1991				1991	1992	1993
	I	II	III	IV			
Real GNP (% change)	0.7	1.4	1.0	1.3	1.2	2.0	2.5
Unemployment (% of labor force)	11.1	11.0	10.8	10.8	10.9	10.8	10.7
Inflation (% change)	7.0	6.6	6.4	6.3	6.4	5.2	5.2

Source: DRI/McGraw-Hill and EC Commission.

In contrast to France, a relatively healthy Italian household sector has given some buoyancy to Italian domestic demand, but this has not translated into a commensurate boost in economic growth, as consumers spend heavily on imports. Plagued by both competitiveness problems and now weak world demand, Italian exports have been weak, giving no offset to the sizable leakage of domestic demand abroad.

The Italian industrial sector remains weak as the problems of low profitability and eroding competitiveness add to the burdens of high interest rates. Further, the continuing instability in the Italian political arena does nothing to buoy investor confidence. Italy is quite unlikely to lead the EC to a high growth plateau, nor be led to one itself.

Slow Growth in the EC through 1993

If we extrapolate from the economic situation in the largest member economies to the whole EC, the near-term prospect of economic growth must be seen as modest at best. With little prospect of a strong near-term pull from the world economy and with the continued dampening effect of the German high interest rate policy persisting through the foreseeable future, it is likely that real GNP growth for the EC as a whole will average no more than 2.0 to 2.5 percent through 1993. That pace of real growth is not fast enough to prevent the EC-wide unemployment rate from rising to over 9.0 percent. This is not an economic environment that enhances the chances of implementing the set of measures necessary to realize the full economic benefits of the EC–92 unified market.

Even with much faster growth of world demand and some lowering of interest rates, it is doubtful that the EC can sustain the 3.5 to 4.0 percent rate of growth needed to reduce unemployment and to raise profitability sufficiently to create the economic environment needed to fully implement the unified market. Inflation in the EC will most likely rise quickly as growth accelerates, leading to a German braking of the expansion, and a general slowdown.

EC LABOR MARKETS ARE AN IMPEDIMENT TO ECONOMIC GROWTH

While it varies in degree from country to country, the rigid labor markets of the EC countries create an inflationary bias and are a major supply-side impediment to more rapid economic growth in the near term. When there is rising wage pressure, and the unemployment rate is above 9 percent, substantial structural problems undoubtedly exist. In their careful study of barriers to growth in European economies, Robert Lawrence and Charles Shultze concluded that past slow growth has been primarily the result of a hobbling interaction between growing structural rigidities in most European labor markets and insufficiently expansive aggregate demand policies of European governments. [4] Much has already been done to increase the flexibility of labor markets in many members countries, but significant rigidity obviously persists. As the Director Secretary General of the OECD recently observed; "Despite spending over 2 percent of their GDP on labor market policies, . . . the EC experienced a rising trend unemployment rate and a growing incidence of long-term unemployment. . . ." [5]

Indeed, greater change in the area of labor market flexibility may be a necessary precondition to successfully instituting the other important competitive initiatives of the EC–92 program. In its annual economic report the EC Commission outlines three areas of continued concern:

- Real wages do not adjust sufficiently to assure full-employment;
- Rigid wage structures, employment practices, and insufficient training preclude the entry of the unemployed into jobs; and

---

[4] Lawrence, Robert, and Charles Shultze. *Barriers to European Growth: A Trans-Atlantic View*. Washington, D.C., Brookings Institute, 1987.

[5] OECD. *Economic Outlook*, Paris, December, 1991. p. 41.

- An overemphasis on unemployment support rather than retraining limits needed adjustment and also keeps the unemployment rolls high. [6]

Further action on these fronts would greatly support a positive momentum for more rapid economic growth.

A Retreat from the Single Market?

A fundamental disagreement over economic ideology, exacerbated by recent poor economic performance, divides the EC and threatens to undermine the move to a single market. On one side France, Greece, Italy, and Spain push for a continued commitment to "dirigisme" (state-directed planning and industrial intervention). They believe that the single market can only work if the state continues to protect and support *key* enterprises. On the other side, Britain and Germany are ready to take the steps needed to move to a true free market and compete openly in the world market. They see this as the *vision* that, if fulfilled, will allow the EC to fully realize all of its seemingly elusive economic potential.

The large and growing presence of American and Japanese multinational corporations (MNCs) in Europe may also have served to raise the level of anxiety about the move to a single market. [7] The MNCs are hardened competitors in the world market, and many Europeans now see that they would surely become major participants and beneficiaries of an open European market. The MNCs would likely replace or greatly reduce the role of many now subsidized European enterprises, or in many cases, a European firm's survival would likely require significant cooperation with MNCs. Some nations see the MNCs as a threat. The benefits of the open market in their eyes should accrue to European enterprises not foreign transplants. France has been most hostile to Japanese MNCs locating there. Of course other nations see the MNCs as a boon that will raise the well-being of the whole EC economy even if certain established interests incur losses. In this spirit Britain is welcoming Japanese MNCs.

In any case, political resistance to full market opening is easier to sustain when slow growth keeps unemployment high and profitability low. Whether the EC will move further toward, or back away from, free trade internally will be clearer in the months ahead. *Fortune* magazine has observed that critical tests are forthcoming in what many see as Europe's big four "coddled" industries: agriculture, airlines, computers and telecommunications, and automobiles. [8]

European agriculture operates at small scale and high cost, and is sustained by an assortment of protective barriers that cost European consumers more than $100 billion a year. European intransigence in the GATT negotiations over these supports does not suggest that these walls are likely to fall substantially any time soon.

---

[6] Commission of the European Communities. *European Economy*. Brussels, December, 1991.

[7] For a fuller discussion of this theme see: Goldstein, Walter. EC: Euro-Stalling. *Foreign Policy*, November, 1985, Winter, 1991–1992. p. 129–146.

[8] Richman, Louis and Shawn Tally. The Real Danger in Europe's Slump. *Fortune*, July, 1991. p. 66–69.

Oversized European national flag airlines operate at a fraction of the efficiency of American carriers. Yet, moves to raise the level of competition seem half-hearted at best. While licensing may be liberalized it is not clear that more efficient new airlines can gain scarce landing slots from flag carriers.

The European computer and telecommunication industries have received significant subsidies and tariff protection, as well as the support of aggressive anti-dumping action, but still remain uncompetitive with U.S. and Japanese firms. There is now no evidence that this industrial support program will change.

In automobiles, the EC has clearly backtracked from its plan to eliminate all national auto quotas by 1993. Japan's market share will be allowed to rise slowly over the course of the decade, but this "quota" will include the production of Japanese "transplant" operations. This is good for Japanese profits but bad for the European consumer and the overall efficiency of European automobile production.

All in all, one cannot be sanguine that, in the current slow-growth, high-unemployment environment, the political will can be mustered to overcome the strong mercantilist forces within the EC. If this does indeed prove to be so, the EC will not realize its substantial long-run growth potential.

Implications for the United States

Potential economic effects on the United States of the EC–92 program could be transmitted via trade, foreign investment, and financial markets. The EC is the United States' biggest export market, purchasing 25 percent of American exports in 1990. Moreover, the EC is a particularly buoyant market for U.S. goods: rising income levels in the EC tend to draw in a more than proportionate increase in imports from the United States.

The standard framework used by economists to access the net impact of a preferential trading agreement such as the EC–92 initiative is whether on balance trade is "created" or "diverted." Trade creation leads to an increase in the demand for U.S. exports, while trade diversion is a measure of the amount of U.S. exports that would be replaced by output from within the EC.

The U.S. past experience with the formation and expansion of the EC over the last 32 years has been favorable, with trade creation out-weighing trade diversion by a comfortable margin. The effect of the EC–92 program is uncertain, but some analysts are cautiously optimistic that, if pursued fully, the program will favor "trade creation" over "trade diversion." [9] Prospects for a net gain to the United States from increased export earnings are positively related to the size of the boost given GDP in the EC by the "unified market" initiatives. Thus, from the standpoint of exports, the U.S. interest most likely lies on the side of a bold market unification program succeeding. Of course, if the program pursued by the EC is less far reaching, more protectionist, and generates less of a boost to the GDP of the EC, trade diversion could outweigh trade

---

[9] See Hufbauer, Gary C. *Europe 1992: An American Perspective.* Brookings Institution, Washington, D.C., 1990.

creation. The magnitude of gain or loss to U.S. exports is likely to be quite modest in size ($5 to $15 billion are plausible amounts) when compared to total U.S. exports of nearly $540 billion. [10]

Foreign investment is another dimension of U.S. economic interest in the EC. The countries of the Community have been major recipients of U.S. foreign direct investment, claiming 41 percent of the value of all U.S. direct investment abroad through 1990, and having a value well in excess of $200 billion. Sales of these U.S.-owned affiliates exceeded $700 billion in 1990, seven-fold larger than U.S. export sales to the EC.

American firms on the continent are well established and would likely continue to prosper even if EC–92 program devolved into the negative "Fortress Europe." One should also keep in mind that the EC's direct investments in the United States are also very large, and it is unlikely that the EC would risk the costly retaliation that could result from any diversion from strict national treatment for U.S. transplants, even as the EC moved to raise external barriers. But, it is equally clear that the large boost to EC growth that full market unification could bring would be very good for U.S. firms already established there and to firms which might enter. Clearly, in the areas of investment, U.S. economic interest is best served by a bold market unification program succeeding in the EC.

Finally, the EC–92 program could likely affect the United States through international capital markets. A sharp acceleration of growth in the EC has the potential to significantly raise the demand for capital and, perhaps, elevate interest rates in world financial markets. U.S. interest rates could rise, causing a dampening of interest rate-sensitive activities. The degree that interest rates will rise will also be contingent on what occurs on the supply side of the capital market in the EC and the United States. If the EC follows a fiscal policy that also increases the level of public savings, upward pressure on interest rates worldwide could be offset in whole or part. Recent budget consolidation in several EC member states suggests that this is quite possible. Of course, it would also be possible to mute the upward push on interest rates if the United States moved aggressively to reduce government deficits and raise its own national savings. Recent behavior gives no reason to be sanguine toward this prospect, however. If the EC–92 program transmits higher interest rates to the United States, the increase will be modest and unlikely to offset the temporary positive stimulus to U.S. GNP of growing U.S. export sales to the EC. [11]

The immediate overall economic effect on the United States, whether positive or negative, of the EC–92 program, whether a bold or timid manifestation, is likely to be relatively small. Positive effects on the United States are most likely to flow from an EC that continues to move aggressively toward market unification and free trade. If we also tally the wider economic and political benefits to the emerging economies of Eastern Europe and the former Soviet Union of the more rapid economic growth the single market would

---

[10] See Hufbauer, p. 22.

[11] See U.S. Congressional Budget Office. *How the Economic Transformation of Europe Will Affect the United States.* December, 1991.

bring to the EC, the gains to the United States of a more prosperous and stable world economy would be larger still.

MANAGEMENT OF ECONOMIC POLICY IN THE EUROPEAN COMMUNITY

by C. Randall Henning *

CONTENTS

SUMMARY

The process of integration is increasing the importance of the European Community in international economic affairs. The Single Market, Economic and Monetary Union, and the enlargement of country membership are creating a larger, more influential European partner for the United States and the rest of the world. The institutions of the Community, however, have been designed to advance economic integration and satisfy its political requirements. Those institutions have not been tailored primarily for expedient decisionmaking. Policymaking authority is widely dispersed within the Community, consensus is required on most important matters, and several actors can singlehandedly block Community action. The broad agenda before the Community might therefore exceed the policymaking capacity of its institutions, as presently constituted. Provided that the Community supports open multilateralism, European integration is in the general political and economic interest of the United States. But, between now and that indefinite point in the future when Community policymaking is streamlined, the United States must contend with a slow-acting and sometimes inward-looking partner and should therefore adapt its strategies of cooperation.

* C. Randall Henning, a political scientist, is a Research Associate at the Institute for International Economics in Washington, D.C., and is presently comparing economic policymaking in the United States, Europe and Japan.

INTRODUCTION

Western Europeans have conceived a peculiar political animal in the European Community. Created primarily to advance the process of integration, its decisionmaking organizations parallel neither international organizations nor national governmental structures. As the Community has evolved over the decades, its institutional architects have grappled with three enduring organizational questions.

The first is the question of *centralization*. Which matters should be collectivized and which matters should be left to national governments to determine independently? The issue areas considered in this volume lie at different points along a broad spectrum between centralized and decentralized decisionmaking. Competition, trade and agricultural policies are quite centralized in the Community structures. Despite efforts toward harmonization and convergence, national taxation and budget policies remain reserved primarily for national governments. [1]

The second major organizational question is that of *supranational* versus *intergovernmental* decisionmaking. To the extent that decisionmaking is centralized, should policy be set by Community institutions or the national governments negotiating among themselves?

The third organizational dilemma is the question of legitimacy and *democratic accountability* of European policies. Are Community officials sufficiently responsive to popular consensus, through the democratically elected national governments, or should they be made more directly accountable by answering, for example, to the European Parliament? The institutions of the Community, as presently structured, reflect the evolving answers to each of these questions.

The purpose of this chapter is to review the institutions and processes of the Community which affect economic policymaking in Europe. The chapter begins with a primer on the principal governing bodies of the Community. The following section discusses the institutions and processes associated with the management of the overall level of economic activity in the Community, monetary and fiscal policymaking. The final section discusses the ramifications of Community decisionmaking for transatlantic economic relations and U.S. policy.

PRINCIPAL GOVERNING BODIES OF THE COMMUNITY

The institutional structure of the Community defies simple comparison to the Federal governmental institutions of the United States or even European states. [2] Simply put, the Commission has

---

[1] Whether policymaking in any one issue area has devolved to the Community is a function of the strength of national governmental bureaucracies and the resistance of private sector constituencies. Goodman, John B. Do All Roads Lead to Brussels? Economic Policy Making in the European Community, in Ornstein, Norman and Mark Perlman, eds. *Political Power and Social Change: The United States Faces a United Europe*. Washington, D.C., American Enterprise Institute, 1991. p. 24–45.

[2] This section benefits greatly from several authoritative treatments of the community institutions: Nugent, Neill. *The Government and Politics of the European Community*. 2nd ed. Durham, Duke University Press, 1991; Keohane, Robert O. and Stanley Hoffmann, eds. *The New Europe-*

Continued

the right of initiative and proposal development, while the Council of Ministers has the right to pass judgment on these proposals and thereby establish Community law. The European Parliament is something of a proto-legislature: it is organizationally capable of acting as a true parliament but has not yet been granted the right to pass legislation. Instead, the Parliament renders an opinion on proposals made and passed by the Commission and Council. Though its role will be strengthened by the Maastricht treaty amendments, the Parliament strongly influences legislation only under exceptional circumstances. (The Court of Justice is the fourth important institution of the Community. While its decisions have advanced the process of integration, the Court is not central to policymaking *per se* and will not be reviewed here.)

EUROPEAN COUNCIL

The European Council is the name given to the summit meetings of the heads of state and government of the member states of the Community. An institutional innovation of the early 1970s, the body had no formal status in the European treaty until the Single European Act of 1986. Unlike the original institutions of the Community, it remains outside the jurisdiction of the European Court of Justice. The European Council has nonetheless evolved into the supreme political organ of the Community.

The European Council establishes the broad political framework for the work of the other Community institutions. Because these summit meetings bring together the most powerful political leaders in Europe, the matters of highest importance are subject to European Council review, and the development of the Community has proceeded at the pace and in the direction determined by the body. The crucial junctures on the road to the Single Market, Economic and Monetary Union, and Political Union, in particular, have been European Council meetings. The final bargain on EMU and Political Union, for example, was sealed at the European Council meeting at Maastricht in December 1991. Failure to take decisions in the European Council, on the other hand, can stall the Community machinery.

The European Council meets at least twice each year, once during each six-month Presidency of the group. (The chairmanship of the European Council coincides with the Presidency of the Council of Ministers, discussed below.) In addition, the Presidency might convene an extraordinary meeting to discuss particularly pressing problems, such as the Single European Act or Economic and Monetary Union. The European Council has no secretariat of its own; the President is principally reliant on his or her national ministries. Supporting the chairmanship of the European Council is an extraordinary burden, which the small-country governments find

---

an *Community: Decisionmaking and Institutional Change*. Boulder, Westview, 1991; Hurwitz, Leon and Christian Lequesne, eds. *The State of the European Community: Policies, Institutions and Debates in Transition Years*. Boulder, Colorado, Lynne Reiner for the European Community Studies Association, 1991; Peters, B. Guy. Bureaucratic Politics and the Institutions of the European Community, in Sbragia, Alberta M., ed. *Europolitics: Institutions and Policymaking in the "New" European Community*. Washington, D.C., Brookings Institution, 1992; and, Wallace, Helen, William Wallace, and Carole Webb, eds. *Policymaking in the European Community*. 2nd ed. Chichester, New York, John Wiley & Sons, 1983. This section is also indebted to suggestions made by Helen Wallace.

difficult to bear. But, in preparing summit meetings, the Presidency draws on the support of the secretariat to the Council of Ministers. Because the term of the Presidency is generally too short to complete initiatives, the outgoing, presiding and incoming chairmen—the "troika"—generally cooperate in setting the European Council's agenda.

COUNCIL OF MINISTERS

The power to establish Community law rests with the national governments in the Council of Ministers. [3] The Council meets in varying configurations depending upon the meeting's agenda. The most senior configuration is the General Council, the collection of foreign ministers of the member states. So-called Technical Councils in each substantive area also meet at ministerial level. They are assisted in their work by the Committee of Permanent Representatives (COREPER) of national governments, located in Brussels, and by working-level committees and groups created and configured for collective policymaking in the issue area concerned. A secretariat of roughly 2000 employees, also based in Brussels, supports the Council. Its Secretary General possesses substantial and growing influence within the Community. [4]

The Council system is chaired by the member country holding the Presidency. The President of the Council controls the number and timing of meetings, the agenda and whether a vote is to be taken on matters before the group. National governments like to show political leadership during their tenure in the Presidency by launching initiatives and concluding major agreements. The Presidency also represents the Council to other Community as well as non-Community institutions. It rotates on a six-month basis among the members. Portugal holds the Presidency until the end of June 1992 when it will pass to Britain. [5]

Once policy issues have percolated up through the working level and COREPER, they are addressed in the various Council meetings, the proceedings of which are confidential. There, the outcome depends greatly on whether decisions are subject to a vote by unanimity or a "qualified majority." [6] (The simple majority rule is applied generally to procedural matters only.) At the founding of the Community, it was envisaged that an increasing number of important decisions would be made by qualified majority voting (QMV). But QMV has been reserved until recently for only a relatively narrow range of decisions. The institutionalized practice within the

---

[3] Hereafter, the term "Council" refers to the Council of Ministers. The European Council, assembling the heads of state and government, is designated by its full name.

[4] Ludlow, Peter. A Major Step Forward. *International Economic Insights*, January-February 1992. p. 32–35.

[5] The order of rotation Belgium, Denmark, Germany, Greece, Spain, France, Ireland, Italy, Luxembourg, Netherlands, Portugal, United Kingdom is determined by the alphabetical sequence of the country name spelled in the national language.

[6] For a measure to pass under qualified majority voting it must receive 54 votes out of 76 allotted to countries roughly, but not proportionately, on the basis of size. Germany, France, Italy and Britain have 10 votes each; Spain, 8 votes; Belgium, Greece, Netherlands, Portugal, 5 votes each; Denmark and Ireland, 3 votes each; and Luxembourg 2 votes. This formula preserves some measure of balance of the interests of the large and small countries: the four large countries cannot enact measures without the support of at least three small countries; more than two large countries are needed to veto a measure generally favored. Abstentions weigh against adoption of decisions by qualified majority voting (but do not block unanimity decisionmaking).

Community has been to take major decisions—new policies, new policy frameworks, changing major existing policies, admitting new members to the Community—by unanimity. Since French President Charles de Gaulle balked at majority voting in 1965, national governments have retained the right to exercise a veto in areas that they themselves judge to affect vital national interests. If a matter of major importance does not command unanimity, no formal vote is taken in the Council. This pattern of practice is referred to as the "Luxembourg Compromise." It is a principal manifestation of intergovernmentalism in Community policymaking.

The Community has moved beyond the unanimity rule in an increasing number of areas, such as the implementation of the Single Market Program. A mixture of unanimity and QMV decisionmaking is well established. However, on the question of reform of the Common Agricultural Policy, for example, no formal vote has been taken in the Council (as of this writing) owing to the opposition at varying points of both France and Germany. A crucial institutional issue facing the Community, as well as the non-EC governments which negotiate with it, is whether national governments will surrender the veto option on agriculture and other important matters. The unanimity rule combined with further enlargement of the Community would be a recipe for policy paralysis. Movement toward greater qualified majority voting is widely expected among close observers of the Community, but it is by no means assured.

EUROPEAN COMMISSION

The Commission is charged with the responsibility of advancing the purposes of the 1957 Treaty of Rome, the founding document of the Common Market, and subsequent treaties. Its seventeen Commissioners are appointed to four-year terms. [7] Though Commissioners are not representatives of national governments, each government is effectively allocated one or two positions on the Commission, depending on country size. In principle individual Commissioners serve the Community as a whole and are appointed by "common accord" of the governments. Commissioners have in practice demonstrated varying degrees of independence from the governments that have nominated them. British Prime Minister Margaret Thatcher refused to renominate the independent-minded Lord Cockfield, for example, despite his successful stewardship of the Single Market Program (EC–92).

The Commissioners meet weekly as a group, the College of Commissioners, which takes collective responsibility for its actions. All important matters are brought to the group as a whole and decisions to propose, defer or reject initiatives are taken unanimously if possible, but by majority vote if necessary. The President, the first among equals, chairs these meetings, and gives more general direction and leadership to the Commission. National governments and the Council give his appointment particularly careful consideration.

---

[7] The number of Commissioners will be reviewed and probably reduced after the Maastricht amendments are ratified.

To assist it in its responsibilities, a bureaucracy has been placed at the Commission's disposal. With roughly 16,000 select, well-paid European civil servants, this bureaucracy is modest in size compared to its task: wide substantive responsibilities across twelve countries and nine languages. It is divided into 23 Directorates General, each responsible for different substantive areas. [8] Directorate General I (DG-I) covers External Relations; DG-II covers Economic and Financial Affairs; DG-III, the Internal Market; DG-IV, Competition (Antitrust); DG-VI, Agriculture; and so on. The Director General and staff of DG-I supports the Commissioner in charge of trade matters, for example, at negotiations at the GATT. DG-III supports the Commissioner responsible for overseeing the implementation of the Internal Market program. But in other cases, the division of responsibility among Directorates General might not match the distribution of substantive portfolios among the Commissioners. The relationship between Commissioner and Directorate General is not necessarily that between minister and ministry, and Commissioners do not have sole authority to appoint or remove officials in the Directorates General corresponding to their portfolios.

The Commission's main functions are three: (1) to propose initiatives, (2) to safeguard the European treaties, (3) to oversee implementation and execution of Community decisions. [9]

In its role as initiator, the Commission not only drafts legislation for consideration by the Council of Ministers and European Parliament but sets strategic goals, formulates policy, prepares the budget, mediates conflicts (among the member states and between the Council and Parliament), builds consensus and generally acts as a political entrepreneur for integration.

The Commission is charged with upholding Community law as embodied in the treaties and enforcing adherence on the part of private actors and national governments. The Commission's powers of enforcement are set by the Council and it takes member states charged with infringements to the European Court of Justice.

Among its Executive roles are the issuance of regulations which give force to legislation, management of Community finances and supervision of implementation of Community policy by national governments. In this sense the Commission is not a full-fledged executive branch: national governments are ultimately responsible for administering Community law and regulations, which to have effect must be incorporated by national parliaments into domestic legislation. The Commission has historically been better at policy initiation than management. [10] Conferring a greater executive role on Brussels would require an expansion of Commission resources.

The relationship between the Council and the Commission is complex. While law is enacted by the Council, the Commission retains the right to propose legislation. The phrase, "the Council may, on a recommendation of the Commission," permeates the European treaty and the proposed amendments. In practice, the Coun-

---

[8] The term "Commission" is often used to refer not only to the College of Commissioners but to the bureaucracy under their authority as well.

[9] Nugent, Neill. *The Government and Politics of the European Community*, Chapter 3; Ludlow, Peter. The European Commission, in Keohane and Hoffmann, eds. *The New European Community*. p. 85–132.

[10] Ludlow, Peter, *The European Commission*.

cil can prod the Commission to generate recommendations, and can undertake initiatives in new policy areas not specifically covered in the Treaties. [11] For its part, the Commission anticipates the lineup within the Council when formulating recommendations for its consideration. At the level of Ministers and Commissioners, and at the working level, the work of the Council and Commission is a mixture of cooperation and competition.

EUROPEAN PARLIAMENT

The European Parliament, originally quite weak, has been gradually strengthened over the lifetime of the Community. The one substantive economic area over which it has been given significant power is the Community budget. Since the first direct elections to the Parliament in 1979, the Parliament has consistently advocated even greater powers for itself to close the so-called "democratic deficit." The Single European Act gave the Parliament the power to approve all accession and association agreements, in addition to its modest legislative powers over the Single Market program.

The Parliament meets in Strasbourg, France, about twelve times each year for a period of about one week. Members of the European Parliament (MEPs) serve for five-year terms. The 518 seats within the Parliament are allocated among countries in proportions which enhance the influence of the smaller states. [12] The work of the Parliament is parceled out to eighteen permanent committees specializing in particular policy areas. These committees maintain connections to the Directorates of the Commission, national governments and private interest groups that also specialize in their policy area. [13] Because the influence of the Parliament in Community legislation in particular policy areas has not been strong, however, the Parliament has not been the point of access for private interest groups in the policymaking process. That could well change as the Parliament accumulates greater powers.

The Council of Ministers must take parliamentary views into consideration when adopting legislation. The Parliament reviews the "common position" of the Council and has the option of (1) approving (or declining to disapprove); (2) disapproving; or (3) proposing amendments. In the case of parliamentary rejection, the legislation fails unless the Council acts unanimously, with the approval of the Commission. If the Parliament offers amendments that are also supported by the Commission, the Council must vote by unanimity to overturn them. [14] The Maastricht treaty amendments strengthen the role of Parliament by providing it a "third reading" on legislation.

---

[11] Nugent, *The Government and Politics of the European Community*, Chapter 4.

[12] Germany, France, Italy and the United Kingdom, have 81 seats each; Spain, 60 seats; Netherlands, 25; Belgium, Greece and Portugal, 24 each; Denmark, 16; Ireland, 15; Luxembourg, 6. The number of voters per seat therefore varies greatly across the Community, from 747,000 in Germany to 64,000 in Luxembourg (as of 1989). Nor is the electoral process for the European Parliament uniform across the member countries, a situation which he Maastricht treaty amendment seeks to rectify. See Nugent, *The Government and Politics of the European Community*, Chapter 5.

[13] These are dubbed nascent "policy communities" by students of integration. See Peters, *Bureaucratic Politics and the Institutions of the European Community*, p. 91.

[14] Peters, *Bureaucratic Politics and Institutions of the European Community*, p. 91–92.

The Parliament is organized according to eleven political groupings, rather than national groupings as was the case in the early decades. The largest political grouping is the Socialists, with 180 MEPs in the current Parliament, followed by the grouping of the national Christian Democratic parties, called the European People's Party, with 122 MEPs. Both Groups contain considerable ideological diversity, ranging from left-wing socialists to moderate social democrats and from the Bavaria-based Christian Social Union to the Italian Christian Democrats. Few of these groupings are cohesive; none commands a majority of the Parliament.

Though the Strasbourg assembly possesses significant real authority, it is in many respects a Parliament in waiting. Its organizational capacity to participate in the policymaking process of the Community is fully constituted. But it awaits powers comparable to those of national legislatures: co-decisionmaking with the Council of Ministers, the right to initiate legislation, the authority to approve individual appointments such as the President of the Commission. As decisionmaking increasingly devolves to the Community from national governments, the Parliament will be increasingly needed to redress the democratic deficit. An intergovernmental conference scheduled for 1996 will be the Parliament's opportunity to assert its claim to greater powers. It has been suggested that the Parliament could withhold its approval of enlargement of the Community as a lever with which to wrest such powers from governments.

Community policies in specific sectors of the economy are developed among specialized subunits of the Commission, Council and Parliament, along with the relevant ministries of the national governments and private interest groups organized nationally and on a European basis. For each policy sector (agriculture, steel, autos, telecommunications, pharmaceuticals, financial services, etc.), there exists a Directorate General in the Commission, a specialized Council of the Council of Ministers, a Committee within the European Parliament. Thus, for the Common Agricultural Policy, the most important sectoral policy of the Community, DG-IV proposes measures to improve the efficiency of the CAP, which are considered by the Agriculture Council, supported by the Special Committee on Agriculture. In the area of external trade policy, DG-I drafts the terms of reference for EC negotiators (the chief among them being the Commissioner for trade), which are approved by the General Council, and closely overseen by the so-called "113 Committee," a special subcommittee appointed by the Council for the purpose of conveying guidance from the national governments. [15]

Managing Macroeconomic Policy

monetary policy

The Community does not yet have a collective monetary policy. Monetary conditions within Europe are determined at the national

[15] For a discussion of the making of trade policy in the Community, see Murphy, Anna. *The European Community and the International Trading System.* Volume 2: The European Community and the Uruguay Round, Chapter 7. Centre for European Policy Studies Paper No. 48. Brussels, 1990.

level by each country's central bank. Those national policies are coordinated, however, within the European Monetary System (EMS), which restricts the fluctuations of the European currencies against one another within narrow bands. As a logical consequence of exchange rate stabilization, the EMS requires that national monetary policies not diverge too greatly.

Because the regime of par-value exchange rates established at Bretton Woods dominated international monetary arrangements during the 1950s and 1960s, the Treaty of Rome was almost silent on monetary issues and did not explicitly require monetary cooperation among Community members. When the European countries decided to link their currencies—after the transition to floating exchange rates at the global level—their cooperation was outside the purview of the treaty. The founding document of the EMS, in fact, is a side-agreement to the treaty, concluded formally among the European central banks, sanctioned by the European Council. Not all of the members of the Community are members of the Exchange Rate Mechanism of the EMS. The United Kingdom, for example, did not join until Autumn 1990; Portugal not until April 1992. Greece is still not a member.

Three councils administer the EMS: the Committee of Central Bank Governors, the Monetary Committee, and ECOFIN. As its name implies, the former is strictly limited to the most senior central bankers. They meet in Basle, Switzerland, on the margin of the monthly meetings at the Bank for International Settlements. The Monetary Committee combines the senior deputies in the central banks with senior officials from the finance ministries and therefore bridges the two groups. The economic and finance ministers of the Community comprise the ECOFIN, the competent formation of the Council of Ministers. Both the Monetary Committee and ECOFIN meet monthly in Brussels. Members of the Commission attend these meetings. The Committee of Central Bank Governors and the Monetary Committee select chairmen from among their members for two- to three-year terms, a comparatively long tenure which contributes to the effectiveness of these bodies.

As long as there are no major disruptions within the EMS, the central banks can manage foreign exchange intervention and monetary coordination largely on their own. When central banks are unwilling to make the adjustments in monetary policy that would be necessary to stabilize exchange rates, however, they must appeal to ECOFIN, through the Monetary Committee, to approve a formal realignment of the central rates in the System. The prime ministers and presidents, as well as the cabinets, of each government are usually involved in realignment decisions. The ECOFIN ministers will each individually consult their governments when taking a decision to realign. European exchange rates have been quite stable since the last realignment in 1987.

This relatively efficient machinery does not constitute truly collective decisionmaking on monetary conditions within the Community countries, however. Monetary decisions revolve around the policies set independently by the German central bank, the Bundesbank. The Bundesbank took great pride in acting as the "nominal anchor" in the EMS. (Owing to unification, Germany no longer has the lowest rate of inflation in the Community.) Germany steadfastly pursued low-inflation monetary policy, while the other countries did their best to match it or, if necessary, devalued their currencies. Though it has not dictated, the Bundesbank has clearly dominated the setting of monetary conditions among the members of the EMS in practical terms. [16]

Substantial differences in national rates of inflation persist, nonetheless, and all Community members pledge in the Maastricht accord to reduce these discrepancies. During the transition to full monetary union, the Council of Ministers, on the basis of reports from the Commission, will conduct multilateral surveillance of members' economies. Inflation performance, long term interest rates, exchange rate stability and government deficits are the criteria on which their convergence will be judged. [17] As only one or two countries presently meet these criteria, many will have to tighten monetary and fiscal policies to meet these guidelines.

On the assumption that monetary union is achieved late in this decade—which is not a forgone conclusion despite the momentum of Maastricht—Europe will have a unified monetary policy among those countries qualifying for membership. The new European monetary policy will be governed by a new institution, the European System of Central Banks (ESCB), whose legal independence from political authorities is emphasized in the treaty amendments and whose primary objective will be price stability. [18] Without serious reform of the other Community institutions, the decentralization of political authority in the Community as a whole will ensure that governmental oversight of monetary policy will be weak.

FISCAL POLICY

Fiscal conditions within the Community are a function of the national fiscal stance of the member countries and the budget of the Community itself. The role of government spending, taxation and deficits in the Community-wide economy is overwhelmingly determined by national fiscal policies. The budget of the Community itself is small by comparison, amounting to about 1.2 percent of Community GDP and about 3.3 percent of the national budgets combined. But further integration will give rise to increasing political pressure to raise the size of the Community budget to transfer resources between prosperous and depressed regions. Community budget problems, moreover, bear heavily on sectoral issues complicating U.S.-EC relations, principally agriculture. Thus, the process and institutions of Community budget-making are also of interest.

---

[16] For the academic debate on whether empirical evidence supports this conclusion, see Gros, Daniel and Niels Thygesen. *The EMS: Achievements, Current Issues and Directions for the Future.* Centre for European Policy Studies Paper No. 35. Brussels, 1988; Giavazzi, Francesco, Stefano Micossi, and Marcus Miller. *The European Monetary System.* Cambridge, Cambridge University Press, 1988; and, de Grauwe, Paul and Lucas Papademos, eds. *The European Monetary System in the 1990s.* London/New York, Longman, 1990.

[17] Conference of the Representatives of the Governments of the Member States. *Treaty on European Union.* Article 109j and Protocol on the Convergence Criteria in Article 109j. Brussels, February 1, 1992. This document will be referred to as "Maastricht Treaty" hereafter.

[18] Maastricht Treaty, Articles 105–109 and Protocol on the Statute of the ESCB/ECB. For a discussion, see the contribution on EMU in this volume by Arlene Wilson.

Community Budget

The budget process is symptomatic of the non-hierarchical structure of decisionmaking in the Community. In the regular process, no actor is capable of imposing an overarching strategy or framework for the budget. The Council and the European Parliament are the dominant players, with the Commission formulating the draft budget but essentially on the sidelines thereafter. Until the late 1980s, budgets were merely adjusted incrementally, rather than substantively reworked with each budget cycle to reflect new priorities. When budget crises erupted, arrangements outside of the regular budget process—such as meetings of the European Council and a special Interinstitutional Agreement in 1988—were required to impose an overall framework.

The budget is relatively small, amounting to less that 49 billion Ecu in 1990. The largest component of the budget by far is the Common Agricultural Policy, claiming more than 55 percent, a proportion which is declining gradually in favor of the structural funds for depressed regions. These expenditures are funded mostly by a Community value-added tax (VAT) supplement (1.4 percent), plus customs duties, agriculture levies, and direct transfers from government budgets.

The financial flows through the Community are not intended to balance on a national basis. But the lack of balance has caused protracted political conflict over the budget. Britain, in particular, was aggrieved over its large net contribution during the 1970s and 1980s—a problem that was resolved, though not permanently, at the Brussels meeting of the European Council in 1988. The resolution of that budget crisis cleared the way for the far more important task of completing the Single Market and initiating EMU.

The Commission initiates the process by formulating the Preliminary Draft Budget during the spring prior to the commencement of the fiscal year (coinciding with the calendar year) to which it applies. The Commission submits it to the Budget Council (the competent body within the Council of Ministers) which amends the document before sending it to the European Parliament. The Budget Council takes its decision by qualified majority vote—the one important area where QMV has been used consistently over many years. The Committee on the Budget in Parliament considers, amends, and passes the draft to the floor. Amendments to the draft budget in the plenary session of the Parliament are admissible; the budget resolution is passed by a simple majority vote. The Budget Council accepts, rejects or amends these changes and resubmits them to the Parliament. During the Second Readings in the Council and Parliament, direct meetings among the key groups in the three institutions, the "tripartite dialogue," become the most intense. The President of the Budget Council, the Budget Commissioner and the Chairman of the Committee of the Budget might meet with the full Budget Committee, a special delegation of the Parliament or a special meeting of the Budget Council in an effort to reach a compromise.

After reconsideration in the Budget Committee, the Parliament votes in plenary session. If the budget is approved, the President of the Parliament declares it to be formally adopted. If the Parliament rejects the budget, program funding continues at the level of the monthly average for the previous year once the new budget year commences. The Parliament rejected the budget during the five years prior to the Brussels summit of 1988. In each case, though, the Parliament and Council have reached agreement eventually during the "current" year. Parliament has passed the budget during each of the last four years. The Maastricht treaty left budget procedures largely untouched.

National Fiscal Policies

The national fiscal policies of the member states of the Community are virtually entirely *uncoordinated*. Governments have jealously guarded their prerogative to set national budgets and raise revenue. The Community has impinged on these rights only indirectly, through prohibition on competition-distorting subsidies and an effort to make indirect taxes (principally VAT) more uniform to avoid distortions in the Single Market. The budget deficits of national governments, at present, are subject only to peer pressure and the uncertain discipline of financial markets which could balk at excessive deficits. These constraints have been manifestly insufficient to prevent wide disparities in the annual deficits and levels of accumulated national debt among the Community members.

As part of the Maastricht bargain, Germany secured assurance that other governments would restrain fiscal deficits during the transition to, and after the beginning of, the new monetary union. All Community members have agreed to avoid "excessive deficits," as one of the four convergence criteria mentioned above. The annual general government deficits are not to exceed 3 percent of GDP and the accumulated debt is not to exceed 60 percent of GDP. The force behind these rules is the possibility that a country will be excluded from monetary union. The European Council itself, on a recommendation from the Commission and with the advice of the Parliament, will decide by a qualified majority whether each country satisfies the conditions for entry. [19] Whether the European Council will exclude members that might not have met these criteria, such as Italy, will be a political not a technical decision.

After the establishment of monetary union, the Council of Ministers is empowered by the treaty amendment to levy sanctions including fines. Under this procedure, once the Commission and the Council have determined that a member state has an excessive deficit, the Council would act, on a recommendation from the Commission, by a two-thirds majority of the weighted votes, excluding those of the target country. [20] Under both the transitional and permanent arrangements to limit excessive deficits, therefore, the willingness of the Council to impose the ultimate sanctions remains unclear. The fiscal convergence strictures might nevertheless already be exercising a deflationary influence on budget deficits in the Community.

---

[19] Maastricht Treaty, Article 109j.

[20] Maastricht Treaty, Article 104c.

Ramifications for U.S. Policy

As Community competence extends to new policy areas and the Community membership grows, the EC will become a more powerful and assertive bargaining partner for the United States. Americans first encountered the Community as a negotiating partner during the Kennedy Round of negotiations in the GATT in the 1960s. Since then, U.S. negotiations with the EC have extended beyond the trade field to a broad spectrum of policy issues, ranging from trade, agriculture and sectoral regulation to foreign economic assistance and foreign policy. An increasing number of issues in U.S.-European economic relations, moreover, will be settled in bargaining with the Community in the future. [21] Community decision-making institutions and processes will therefore have increasing influence over the scope, frequency and content of transatlantic economic cooperation.

U.S. officials, however, have often been frustrated with the pattern of trade negotiations with the Community. Americans complain that the Community is slow to come to a consensus, and that, once arrived at, that position tends to be the "lowest common denominator" among the twelve (i.e., the stance of the least forthcoming national government). They further contend that the Community position is inflexible and leaves little room for give-and-take in international bargaining. The Community is typically reactive, responding to U.S. initiatives, rather than exercising trade policy leadership of its own, particularly in liberalizing market access. The Community can be inward-looking, and its policymaking lacks transparency.

Though Community machinery has at times worked efficiently, these American complaints are substantially valid. Community policy processes have indeed been cumbersome, slow and cautious as a general rule. (Europeans respond that the separation of powers and divided party control of the Executive and Congress have made the United States an equally difficult bargaining partner, and there is validity in that argument as well.) This stems not from deliberate foot-dragging on the part of the Community, necessarily, but from the need to reassure member states that their sovereignty would not be sacrificed for European integration. The unanimity rule on important decisions was required to provide that reassurance. As a result, the Community has a polycentric policymaking system in which no actor can impose solutions on others and a high degree of consensus is required.

Whether the American negotiating experience with the Community in trade policy will be replicated in the new policy areas is therefore a very important question. Unfortunately, the answer for the time being is that it probably will. Economic and monetary union has outpaced political union and institutional reform. This divergence runs the risk of overloading the policymaking capacities of the Community institutions. The prospective enlargement of the Community to the EFTA countries later this decade and perhaps the Central European countries thereafter will compound the already extraordinary demands on Community institutions and the

[21] Refer to the contributions in the section on international economic relations in this volume.

officials of national governments. Consider, for example, the future of U.S.-European monetary relations. [22] Once national currencies are abolished and the common currency created later in this decade, Europe will be a larger, more cohesive monetary union, less vulnerable to fluctuations in the external value of its currency. To secure cooperation from European governments in the form of changes in their domestic demand policies, U.S. policymakers in past decades often relied on the "dollar weapon," the substantially more disruptive effects of rapid changes in the value of the dollar on the European compared to the American economy. The Nixon administration, the early Carter administration and the two Reagan administrations employed this strategy with some success. The structural changes wrought by EMU, however, will render the dollar weapon impotent, as the effects of currency movements on the U.S. and European economies will become nearly symmetrical. European officials will be better able to resist U.S. pressure for policy adjustment, and if they choose to cooperate, they will be better able to insist on American policy changes, such as a reduction in the Federal budget deficit, as a *quid pro quo*.

These structural changes will be reinforced by institutional arrangements within the Community after monetary union. The European System of Central Banks will have independent control over European monetary policy. Because it will be primarily responsible for achieving internal price stability, it might well be unwilling to adjust domestic monetary policy to maintain a stable rate of exchange between the new European currency, the Ecu, and the U.S. dollar. The Council of Ministers will be empowered to ultimately decide whether to enter into formal exchange rate agreements with the United States and Japan and, in the absence of a formal agreement, to establish "general orientations" for exchange rate policy. But, on formal agreements, the Council must vote by unanimity and, on informal arrangements, must pursue a policy consistent with internal price stability in consultation with the ESCB. [23] These institutional arrangements are a recipe for flexible exchange rates rather than transatlantic coordination that would stabilize currencies.

Despite the difficulties that might arise in managing economic affairs with an integrating Europe, there is no realistic possibility that the United States could abandon this relationship. The high degree of interdependence between Europe and the United States compels cooperation. Moreover, to the extent that it has preserved economic and political stability in Western Europe and can contribute to stabilizing Eastern Europe and the successor republics to the Soviet Union, European integration is in the interest of the United States (provided of course that the Community becomes more open rather than closed).

The U.S. government will instead have to adapt to decentralized decisionmaking in Europe. When U.S. officials determine that

---

[22] See, Henning, C. Randall. Economic and Monetary Union and the United States., in Weber, Manfred, ed. *Europa auf dem Weg zur Whrungsunion*, Darmstadt, Germany, Wissenschaftliche Buchgesellschaft, 1991. p. 31740; Wake Up America, *The International Economy*, March-April 1991. p. 63-66; and, Pauly, Louis W. The Politics of Monetary Union: National Strategies, International Implications. *International Journal* 47, Winter, 1991-92. p. 93-111.

[23] Maastricht Treaty, Article 109.

American interests are engaged, they will have to mount a full-court press across all of the important decision centers in the Community. Second, the United States should firmly support international regimes and organizations that provide an open, multilateral, cooperative global context in which the new Europe will evolve. An hospitable global environment will favor those within the Community advocating open trade, investment, sectoral, regulatory and macroeconomic policies. Third, the United States should reexamine its own policymaking institutions with an eye to becoming more clearsighted and effective in pursuing its international economic goals. [24] The new global environment will be less forgiving of American vacillation on international economic policy.

The Community is committed to conducting a review of the need for larger-scale institutional reform than embodied in the Maastricht agreement on Political Union, and has agreed to convene an intergovernmental conference in 1996 to consider the question. Community experts recognize that unanimity should be increasingly abandoned as the Community expands to fifteen, eighteen and more member states. But, although Community decisionmaking might well be streamlined in the future, these reforms are a distant and uncertain prospect.

---

[24] For recommendations for changes in the process by which exchange rate policy is set, see Destler, I. M. and C. Randall Henning. *Dollar Politics: Exchange Rate Policymaking in the United States.* Washington, D.C., Institute for International Economics, 1989. For recommendations on changes in U.S. trade policy processes to deal with the Community on trade matters, see Greenwald, Joseph. Negotiating Strategy, in Hufbauer, Gary Clyde, ed. *Europe 1992: An American Perspective.* Washington, D.C., Brookings Institution, 1990. p. 345–88.

GOVERNMENT-BUSINESS RELATIONS

By Michael Calingaert *

CONTENTS

SUMMARY

Government and business interact in the European Community across a structure that consists of three EC institutions—the Commission of the European Communities (Commission), European Parliament (Parliament) and the Council of Ministers (Council)—and, on the business side, the entire range of companies and representative organizations. The latter, which play an important role in the interaction, include sector-specific bodies and bodies dealing with broader issues, in both cases present at the Community and national level.

The government-business relationship in Europe differs from the U.S. model in four significant ways. First, the process is less transparent and formal than in the United States. Second, much of the interaction takes place out of public sight. Third, the tone of the relationship is more consensual and less confrontational. And fourth, because of the European parliamentary system, there is no equivalent to the strong and direct role played by the U.S. Congress.

The interplay between the EC Commission and the private sector is crucial because of the Commission's power to initiate legislation. On the whole, the relationship is balanced in that each side needs the other. Although informal and rather personalized, there is intense interaction between business and the Commission in most areas. The Commission frequently uses the support of business, or

* Michael Calingaert is Director of European Operations, Pharmaceutical Manufacturers Association, and author of *The 1992 Challenge from Europe*. National Planning Association, 1988 and 1990. Previously a Foreign Service Officer, he served as Economic Minister at the American Embassies in London and Rome. The views expressed herein are his own.

a particular sector, to further its objectives, and business does the same.

At the level of the European Parliament the interaction to a great extent revolves around proposed amendments to draft legislation produced by the Commission. However, the mechanisms of Parliament are relatively undeveloped, thus the input of the private sector is far less extensive and structured than with the U.S. Congress.

The relationship between the Council and business is largely carried out at national level, since the Council consists of the member state representatives. The nature of the relationship varies considerably from one country to another, although in general it is quite close, with governments on the whole attentive to the concerns and demands of the private sector.

European business has closely followed the Uruguay Round trade negotiations, largely through contacts with national governments but also through the dialogue between the Commission and the European confederation of industry and employers federations.

U.S. business actively participates in this interaction between government and business in the EC. On the whole, it has been accepted as an equal in this process. At EC level, it enjoys good access and influence, directly and through the EC Committee of the American Chamber of Commerce and other bodies.

Introduction

As in the United States, governments and business interact in the European Community at all levels and in a multitude of ways. The web of interrelationships is vast and thus difficult to define and describe. In the case of the EC, analysis is rendered more difficult by the need to take account not only of what takes place at Community level—i.e., with the institutions of the EC—but also in the member states, whose collective actions and votes ultimately translate into decisions by the EC.

With that in mind, this study focuses on how government and business relate to each other in the development and execution of legislation and policy in the EC. In other words, how does government view and deal with business, and vice-versa? When and how do they intersect, what roles do the institutions and individuals on each side play, and how does that affect the outcome?

The Structural Context

The structure of the government-business relationship is relatively simple. On the *government* side, three Community institutions are directly involved in legislation and policy-making: [1]

- the Commission, the EC's bureaucracy, which has the exclusive power to originate legislative proposals and is the executor of EC policy;
- the Parliament, the directly elected representatives of the people of the Community, which scrutinizes draft legislation,

[1] The legal judgments of the European Court of Justice significantly affect Community legislation, similar to those of the U.S. Supreme Court, but by its nature the Court remains outside the scope of government-business relations.

expresses opinions and, under certain conditions, amends and votes on it; and

- the Council, the ultimate decision-making body, in which the member states debate, modify and ultimately adopt legislation and policies.

A fourth institution, the Economic and Social Committee, merits only passing mention. Divided into three groups—employers, workers and miscellaneous interests (e.g. consumers and the self-employed)—its opinion on draft legislation must be heard. However, its influence is marginal.

Business consists, of course, of individual firms and their representative organizations. Firms can be categorized by size, geographic location, and sector of the economy. Private sector activities are carried out directly by companies or through their representative organizations. The latter fall into the following categories:

- EC-wide umbrella or non-sector-specific groups (often with a membership extending beyond the 12 EC member states). Probably the most visible and representative of these organizations is UNICE (the Union of Industrial and Employers Confederations of Europe), consisting of 33 federations from 22 European countries, which was created in 1958 to represent and speak for European industry. UNICE primarily deals with issues that cut across sectors, notably environment and social policy. There are many other groupings of national umbrella organizations—Eurochambers (Association of European Chambers of Commerce and Industry) and the European Confederation for the Retail Trade, just to name two. Two other influential groups also fall into this category: the European Round Table of Industrialists, consisting of about 50 leading industrialists in Europe, maintains high-level contacts with the Commission and the member states, which it uses primarily to focus attention on key issues and problems in Europe, and the EC Committee of the American Chamber of Commerce in Belgium, which represents the subsidiaries of U.S. companies in Europe and lobbies the EC institutions on specific issues.
- European sectoral associations or federations. Such a group now exists for practically every industrial sector, but coverage is spotty in the services sector. Typically, the membership is made up of national associations, although in many cases individual companies are members as well. In banking, for example, the commercial banks are represented by the Banking Federation in the European Community, while parallel organizations exist for other categories of banks, including cooperative banks and savings banks. The Banking Federation consists of the national banking associations in the 12 EC member countries plus associate membership for the associations of six members of the European Free Trade Association. The European Federation of Pharmaceutical Industries' Associations (EFPIA) is structured along the same lines, with 16 national associations as members—11 from the member states plus five from non-member states. On the other hand, in what seems to be a trend, in the European Chemical Industry Council (CEFIC) the 15 national associations share membership with 44

major chemical companies headquartered in Europe on the basis of voting strength. It is inherent in these organizations that their strength and effectiveness is a function of the support and deference given them by their member associations, and, needless to say, that varies considerably from one to another.

The same pattern, then, obtains at the national level. On the whole, it is here that the preponderance of power of the private sector lies, because the member states hold the key to EC decisions and national representative bodies often find it difficult to arrive at a consensus among themselves and, in any case, often are reluctant to yield some of their prerogatives and freedom of action to an EC-wide body. On the other hand, they are not always quick to grasp EC issues or effective in dealing with them, hence the growth of EC federations and single issue groups in Brussels. The national organizations consist of:

- Umbrella groups. The structures of these groups vary among the member states. In some cases, notably Germany, separate employers and industry federations exist: the Union of German Employers Associations (Bundesvereinigung der Deutschen Arbeitgeberverbaende—BDA) and the Association of German Industry (Bundesverband der Deutschen Industrie—BDI). However, the general pattern is that the two are combined, as in the case of the Conseil National du Patronat Francais (CNPF) in France, Confederazione Generale dell'Industria Italiana (Confindustria) in Italy, and the Confederation of British Industry (CBI) in the United Kingdom. In some of these organizations the services sector is included, in others not; in some, publicly owned companies are included, in others not. Generally, the membership consists of national associations, but occasionally companies are included as well. In addition to these organizations, each country has its own national chamber of commerce (with compulsory membership except in the case of Ireland and the United Kingdom) plus a variety of other cross-sectoral organizations.
- Sectoral groups across the entire range of private sector activities.

The Nature of Interaction

Before describing and analyzing the relationship between government and business in the EC, it is necessary to underline four general considerations which characterize that relationship. While subject to the usual caveats of all generalizations, they represent important differences from the situation in the United States that should be recognized in understanding how interaction takes place at Community level.

First, the process is less transparent and formal. There is no equivalent to the publication in the *Federal Register* of proposed regulations on which public comment is solicited, only rare Parliamentary hearings on draft legislation, and virtually no structure of formal advisory bodies. That certainly does not mean that consultation, discussion and interchange do not take place. Quite the contrary. Such interaction takes place continually, but to a large extent it takes place informally.

As a corollary to that, much—though by no means all—of the interaction takes place out of public sight. Leading businessmen and business organizations are less likely than in the United States to take a public stance on an issue and to conduct their efforts of persuasion publicly. Chief executives of large European companies do not normally seek to influence governments through public pressure. Rather, they concentrate on private, informal means. One pan-European business group that had agreed on high-level approaches to governments, having heard nothing and seen no correspondence from its leading German industrialist member, inquired why no action had been taken and was told he had spoken to Chancellor Kohl, but nothing was done publicly or in writing.

Third, the tone of the relationship is more consensual and less confrontational. That does not mean that the European private sector does not fight for its interests. However, the interaction occurs largely within the context of an implicit understanding (a) on the limits of private sector opposition, both in substance and tone, to government proposals or action and (b) that an effort will be made to work toward a mutually satisfactory outcome. Thus, a European firm or association is less likely than its U.S. counterpart to attack government directly and publicly on a particular issue; rather, it is more likely to take what the government has proposed or done as the basis for discussion. This difference is in part a reflection of European culture and tradition; in part the reality that business is generally more dependent on government in Europe (where government involvement and regulation is more pervasive) and thus more reluctant to do battle with it; in part, insofar as the Community is concerned, the fact that the Commission has only a general obligation to hear business views, which limits the latter's willingness to make itself unpopular with its interlocutor.

However, it also reflects the difference between the parliamentary system in Europe and the balance of government powers in the United States. In the United States, the Congress is an independent and powerful participant in the governing process, and an individual or group may persuade members of Congress to apply political pressure rapidly and effectively on other members or on the executive branch. However, there is no equivalent in the EC member states. The leverage of one's elected representatives on the government and bureaucracy is considerably less because government and parliament are in effect synonymous and party discipline is strong. And, it should be added, financial support for parties and members of parliament is several orders of magnitude lower and less directly translatable into assistance for the providers of funds. Pressure can be applied, particularly through parliamentarians of the party or parties in power, but as a general rule its effects are less direct and more long-term—although on a specific issue, grass-roots support or opposition can force a government's hand, as it did, for example, in requiring the German Government to maintain protection for its trucking industry. The situation is mirrored at Community level, where the European Parliament's influence is limited and the upper hand is held by the Commission and the Council (in other words the member states) and where the link between local interests and parliamentarians is blurred by the system of voting for national or regional lists of candidates (except in Ireland and the UK) rather than one representative per district.

With these considerations in mind, let us turn to the government-business relationship involving each of the three main EC institutions.

Interaction with the Institutions

relations with the commission

Relations between business and the Commission revolve primarily around the Commission's power of initiation of legislative proposals and to a lesser extent the Commission's execution of policy. A central feature of the Commission-business relationship is that the formal consultative structures are far less extensive in Europe than in the United States. There is no equivalent in the EC to the range of committees consulted by various U.S. departments on sectors or issues, such as the 20-odd industry sectoral and functional advisory committees to the U.S. Trade Representative and the State Department's Advisory Committee on International Intellectual Property. The Commission has few formal consultative bodies to hear the views of business—as opposed to the vast number of consultative committees with the member states (on certain of which the private sector participates, but as experts rather than representatives of sectoral interests). For example, there are bodies in the fields of agriculture, the distributive trades, and banking (the Committee of Credit Organizations includes the various banking federations, consumer credit organizations and the public sector financial institutions, which meet semi-annually to be briefed by the Financial Services Directorate-General of the EC Commission and to give their views). However, their scope is quite limited relative to the range of EC legislation and policy. Nor is proposed legislation published for public comment before it has been officially approved by the Commission and submitted to the Parliament and Council.

Nonetheless, the Commission does have at least an implicit obligation to consult with interested groups on proposed legislation, and, indeed, it is required to notify the Parliament and Council that it has carried out such consultations. Usually, the appropriate groups are easily identified. Thus, in the case of pharmaceutical-specific legislation the Commission will consult with EFPIA, which is the representative of the European pharmaceutical industry. The only specific reference linking business to the Commission is the new provision of the Treaty of Rome, which stipulates that on social policy the Commission must take into account the views of the "social partners." Because UNICE represents the national associations of employers, it is clearly one body whose views must be heard. However, at times it is more difficult to identify the appropriate interlocutor, particularly when the proposed legislation is of a general nature. For example, on the proposed legislation to regulate gambling (as part of the harmonization of services), the determination of "interested parties" is far less apparent than in the case of regulating the use of food additives.

The most important stage in the development of legislative proposals is the drafting by the EC Commission. Once it has formally issued a proposal for consideration by the Parliament and Council, the broad outlines are unlikely to be changed substantially. Thus, the input of business during the initial stage is crucial. Such input takes place informally.

This is very much a two-way street. In most cases, the Commission lacks the expertise to draft effective and appropriate legislation, and it relies for a significant portion of its information, particularly in the preliminary stages, on the work of outside consultants and national experts. The staff of the Commission is small relative to that of almost any equivalent bureaucracy. While the responsible EC Commission official only occasionally starts with a "blank sheet," he or she almost invariably welcomes the views and experiences of the private sector—particularly in providing technical information and explanations—in aiding them to produce draft legislation that makes sense and will ultimately meet the approval of the Parliament and Council. In some instances, the Commission has actively sought out industry, as was the case before it began drafting legislation to harmonize medical devices regulations. And occasionally, for example in the rush to develop the EC–92 program, the Commission has preferred to get a draft on the table quickly and then use the consultative process to convert it into a viable version.

Thus, the interests of government and business converge, in that both want to undertake early discussions. Occasionally, the Commission will start the legislative process with a green paper (a "consultation document" outlining its thinking for public discussion) or a white paper (policy statement)—as it did in the cases, respectively, of the common market for telecommunications services and equipment in 1987 and the EC–92 program in 1985. Whereas these are public documents, the more usual procedure is that one or more memoranda are written, to be followed by drafts, none of which are officially published, but rather are made available informally to business, as well as member state experts and other interested groups, for their comments and input. The Commission and business are likely to remain in fairly close communication throughout the preparation of legislation. Thus, in fact the process is reasonably transparent: Commission officials are quite open and secrets are relatively few. Nonetheless, there is clearly room for improvement. [2] Access to, and the provision of, information is by no means uniformly open, and the situation is often the reflection of the personality or proclivities of one or more individuals. Indeed, in one key area, environment, private sector views are not well-received.

The key point is that virtually any business group with a serious message will be listened to. As a rule, the Commission does not discourage or prevent any interested group from expressing its views. What needs to be considered is who is "business" and to whom do they speak.

---

[2] This was also recognized at the Maastricht summit, one of whose declarations called for the EC Commission to submit a report "designed to improve public access to the information available to the institutions" no later than 1993.

On the whole, individual companies interact less with EC institutions than do their representative bodies (company activities generally are concentrated at national level other than for company-specific issues). However, there is no distinct pattern as between companies and associations, nor among the different types of associations. [3] On the whole, presentations made by representative organizations carry more weight because they represent a combined view. In addition, it is usually easier for the Commission to absorb a single, unified view, and it may be more responsive when compromises have already been worked out internally. Nonetheless, such consensus positions can represent too low a common denominator to be useful to the Commission, and, as is noted below, the Commission will occasionally have an interest in picking and choosing among conflicting private sector positions.

Dialogue with "the Commission" usually means the directorate-general with main responsibility for drafting a legislative proposal. However, in most cases other directorates-general will also have an input, and their views may differ from those of the main drafters. Thus, depending on the circumstances, these officials may seek business support and, conversely, business may seek to take advantage of internal splits in the Commission, although obviously such a tactic is best adopted cautiously.

Another locus of dialogue is the 17 EC commissioners and their cabinets, because decisions of the Commission are taken collegially. At this level political factors play a more important role. Although in a formal sense commissioners lose their national identity when they assume their duties, they are often the recipients of information and lobbying by compatriot business groups. This may enable business to gain allies among the other commissioners or at least increase the awareness of national perspectives that should be taken into account. In addition, at least some commissioners have formed private, informal groups to provide them with advice on a range of subjects.

To a considerable extent, the interaction described above takes place on the basis of a Commission proposal, followed by a reaction by business and other interested parties. However, that is by no means always the case. In many instances business takes the initiative and then develops support in the Commission. In a general sense this is how the EC–92 single market program was developed. The initial thrust, or at least much of it, came from business community sectors that were concerned about Europe's long-term ability to compete in an increasingly global market. Led by such firms as Philips, they developed a plan for removing the remaining obstacles to the free movement of goods, services, capital and people, an idea embraced by the new commission led by Jacques Delors, which entered office in 1985. Another example is the concern expressed by the European Round Table about infrastructure problems in Europe, which led to the development of a legislative program

---

[3] Whatever the pattern, the number of organizations, companies and other groups seeking to influence EC decisionmaking has jumped dramatically. Philip, Alan Butt, ed. *Directory of Pressure Groups in the European Community.* Harlow, Essex, U.K., Longman Group U.K. Ltd., 1991, lists over 800 pressure groups and other organizations, more than double the figure of ten years earlier. Another indicator is the membership of the EC Committee of the American Chamber of Commerce that has more than doubled in the past three years.

called Trans-European Networks (a Europe-wide program for energy, telecommunications and transportation). In another instance, EFPIA championed the need for an extension of patent protection for pharmaceutical products to recoup part of the time lost in testing and obtaining marketing approval, similar to legislation previously adopted in the United States and Japan. It presented its case and convinced the EC Commission, which drafted legislation and eventually succeeded in obtaining the necessary political agreement.

In some cases, business will seek a solution to a problem that it considers is not being appropriately addressed at national level by turning to the EC. That was the case with the banking community in the United Kingdom. The British Government refused to impose identical reserve requirements on public and private banks and the British private banks successfully pressed for passage of an EC directive.

On the other hand, the Commission often will enlist the support of business, or at least build on it, in order to overcome opposition to its proposals from member states unwilling to yield their prerogatives to the Commission and Parliament, which generally look for solutions at the Community level. In many cases business (or at least certain sectors) and the Commission are natural allies, in that both will desire a Community solution to a particular issue. For example, the Commission has benefited from the backing of the large industrial energy users in its battle against the state-owned electricity producers to liberalize the EC's electricity distribution. Another case in point is economic and monetary union, a goal strongly promoted by the Commission—not least by Jacques Delors—and supported by an important segment of the business community. An Association for the Monetary Union of Europe was established by Valery Giscard d'Estaing and Helmut Schmidt that consists of 250 leading companies plus 30 large banks. It works actively both at national level and with the Commission, providing the latter with various forms of technical expertise and assistance in gaining public support for monetary union and the common currency.

At times, the Commission will take one side of an issue that divides the business community. One example of this was the debate over the introduction of catalytic converters for automobiles, which French industry opposed but German manufacturers supported. Another is the different levels of liberalization of the postal monopoly sought by the small and regional couriers on the one hand and the large international firms on the other. In such cases, the Commission, in carrying out its campaign and developing its arguments, benefits from the assistance and expertise of one segment of the business community at the expense of the other.

RELATIONS WITH THE EUROPEAN PARLIAMENT

At the second stage of the legislative process—the one or two readings by the European Parliament—the relationship changes. For the most part, the process becomes more transparent. The status of a particular piece of legislation is clear, i.e., the text, which reading, the dates for discussion, the deadline for submitting amendments, etc. Although only slightly more than half of Parliament's committees are open to the public, most of those that deal with legislation affecting the private sector are open. (The Legal Affairs Committee, which usually has lead jurisdiction on financial services, is a notable exception).

Like the Commission, the Parliament has a small staff. On average, members of the European Parliament (MEPs) have one assistant (if that); such staff work as is carried out is done by the (again small) staff of the political group to which the MEP belongs and, non-politically, by the (small) Secretariat of the Parliament. To some extent this results in a receptivity to contacts with the business community. Many MEPs look to business to provide the knowledge and expertise they lack to assist them in arriving at their positions. However, that is by no means a unanimous view. A considerable number of MEPs believe that such contacts represent undue influence by interest groups, which gives them an unfair advantage vis-a-vis other groups that are likely to possess fewer resources. In fact, a debate is now going on in the Parliament as to whether regulations or controls should be instituted regarding the activities of lobbyists. [4] In any event, as Parliament gains in its ability to influence legislation, business groups are paying more attention to it and it is expected that interaction with the private sector will increase.

The focus of Parliament's activity is the drafting of amendments to legislative proposals of the Commission and, in cases where there are two readings by Parliament, to the first reading text agreed to by the Council (known as the "common position"). However, unlike the deliberations of the U.S. Congress, there is virtually no opportunity for business interests—or other outside groups—to communicate directly and officially with the Parliament or MEPs. In other words, there is rarely the equivalent of Congressional hearings, where private groups can present their views, orally and in writing, on legislation under consideration. As in Congress, the real work is conducted in committees. However, that work is carried out largely by the rapporteur, an MEP who is entrusted with drafting the sense of committee views on each piece of legislation and in so doing takes the lead in drafting amendments. Thus, the interaction between MEPs and business takes place outside the formal setting, and the degree of interaction is largely a function of the receptivity of the particular MEP to a dialogue with representatives of the private sector. The extent to which that relationship is fruitful, as measured by the ability of business to affect the legislation and by the degree to which the MEP considers that he or she has been aided by the input from business, varies in accordance with the particular circumstances and personalities involved. On one piece of major pharmaceutical legislation one committee rapporteur resolutely refused to meet with industry representatives, while rapporteurs on other legislation in the same sector were willing to devote considerable time to listening to interested parties.

---

[4] Taking its cue from the Parliament, the EC Commission noted in its 1992 work program that relations with interest groups must be more closely defined. Accordingly, it states that "[c]onsideration will . . . be given to the preparation of a code of conduct to govern relations with organizations set up for the specific purpose of handling relations with the EC Commission."

Despite a membership of 518 MEPs, the number of MEPs directly involved and directly interested in any specific issue is usually very small. That is a function of the system, under which each of the Parliament's ten political groups divides substantive responsibilities among its individual members. [5] Thus, for example, one member from each group is responsible for following pharmaceutical issues in the Environment Committee. That person will to a large extent determine the voting of the MEPs in his or her group because the other MEPs will not have the time or inclination to take an interest in the issue. Obviously, Parliamentary interest is a function of the degree of public interest and how technical an issue is. However, the net result usually is a relatively small target for a dialogue, and thus also limited scope for business to spread its views beyond a handful of MEPs.

RELATIONS WITH THE COUNCIL

Despite the changes brought about by the 1987 Single European Act and last year's Maastricht agreement, the Council of Ministers remains the key decisionmaker, and thus business' relationship with the Council is crucial. Because the Council consists of member state representatives, that relationship takes place essentially at the national, rather than the European, level.

The Council conducts its work at three levels. At the first level are working groups of experts consisting primarily of officials from the member state capitals. This level also includes the permanent Brussels-based representatives of member state governments (who represent various government ministries and form a sort of embassy to the EC). Working groups are expected to resolve technical issues so that the political aspects of the proposal can be addressed at the second level by the Committee of Permanent Representatives (COREPER), the Brussels representatives of the member states, before a decision is taken at the third, or ministerial, level, i.e. at Council. However, what distinguishes the work of the Council from that of the other EC institutions is that its deliberations, at all levels, are conducted in private. Information, including documents, are usually available only after the fact, but outsiders are not privy to the actual decision-making process.

There is minimal contact between the Council's General Secretariat and business. Some business organizations, such as UNICE and the American Chamber's EC Committee, send a position paper to the Secretariat on an issue being considered by the Council. The Secretariat's involvement is limited to circulating these papers to the Council members without comment. Interaction between government and business takes place with the national government during all three stages of the Council's work. Firms and organizations lobby their permanent missions. This is often a mutually beneficial activity because the information provided can improve the mission's understanding of an issue, and thus increase its effectiveness in promoting its government's position. of firms in promoting their government's position. However, the mission's initiative is largely limited to questions of strategy and tactics because posi-

[5] Naturally, some of the smaller groups do not actively participate in discussions on all issues.

tions are normally established in capitals. The degree of independence of the missions from capitals varies among the member states. As a general rule, those that are geographically closer to Brussels and/or have a strong bureaucracy are kept under tighter control.

The nature of the government-business relationship varies considerably from one country to another. Although it is difficult to ascribe relative shares of activity between Brussels and the national capitals, the balance of activity weighs heavily in favor of the capitals.

In *France*, the relationship between government and business is very close. In part, this reflects the tradition of *dirigisme* and the important role of government, both as a participant in the economy (the public sector accounts for about 25 percent of French GDP) and as a regulator. To a certain extent, business accepts "guidance" from government, and there is a considerable national consensus in favor of promoting French economic interests.

In many respects, this close relationship is cemented by the tight bond between the top echelons of government and business. That is a function of the education system, under which the brightest students attend one of the so-called "grandes écoles" as a path to both government and business careers, both of them enjoying high status. As a result, there is a considerable interchange of personnel between government and business and thus close personal ties exist irrespective of the political party in power.

On the whole, the French governmental system is quite opaque, and thus the government has considerable flexibility of action. Nonetheless, the government is very attentive to French business interests—this has been the case with the present Socialist government as well as with its predecessors. To a considerable extent, companies make their views known through the associations. France has what is called a unitary trade association system, at the apex of which is the Patronat. Made up of 80 federations of associations, the Patronat speaks for French industry, both officially and in regular informal consultations.

Germany has a long tradition of close government-business relations, although of a different nature than that in France. It forms part of a social compact, under which there is an implicit understanding that government, business and the unions will work together to reach decisions. Indeed, the pressures to arrive at a consensus are very strong, laying upon the private sector a measure of co-responsibility for decisions.

This relationship takes place very largely through representative organizations. Associations have the right to be asked for an opinion and the right to be heard. In fact, under German law they must be formally consulted—in hearings—first by government as it prepares legislation and then by Parliament as it considers this legislation. Officially, the government and Parliament deal only with the associations. At the top of the structure are the federations for industry, employers, the chambers of commerce, banking, insurance, and the retailers and wholesalers. In particular, the BDI and the German Chambers of Commerce and Industry (DIHT) play a leading role: the BDI, for example, represents 40,000 companies accounting for 85 percent of German industry and 40 percent of German GDP. In addition to formal consultations, these associations maintain an ongoing dialogue with government and Parliament.

The associations are strong and well-disciplined. The positions they reach set the parameters outside of which companies and individuals seldom venture. Individual firms' dealings with the government are largely restricted to company-specific issues. Similarly, individual businessmen are generally less involved with government than in some other countries. In part this is a function of business' somewhat negative view of government and the generally higher status that business enjoys. Nonetheless, Chancellor Kohl and government ministers seek out and listen to the advice of top businessmen, whose importance is also related to their role as sources of funds for political parties. Indeed, they are as likely to be visited by government ministers as vice-versa. On the whole, government and business sources agree, the German Government is quite responsive to business, an attitude which has prevailed under both Christian Democratic and Socialist governments.

In *Italy,* although the government-business relationship is less structured, in part reflecting the weakness of the public administration, relations are close. As in France, government plays an important role in the economy, particularly as a leading provider of assistance (the level of subsidies is the highest of the EC countries). Traditionally, relations between government and business have been relatively calm. However, there are indications of increasing friction, particularly as pressure increases on the Italian Government to bring its public debt and deficit closer into line with those of the other member states. The top business organization, Confindustria, carries out the main lobbying function. Business wields a strong influence over government, and on the whole the government, as one observer put it, is the standard-bearer of business.

Despite the long tenure of a Conservative government, the government-business relationship in the *United Kingdom* is less close than on the Continent. Although the Department of Trade and Industry has made a major effort to bring to the attention of British business the importance and opportunities of the single market, the government traditionally holds business somewhat at arm's length in its dealings. This is explained by a number of factors: the high level of expertise in the civil service; the close coordination and internal discipline among government ministries; and a desire by both bureaucrats and government leaders not to appear to give in to business pressures. Thus, government solicits the views of business, but it considers itself less bound by what it hears than certain other governments. As a result, government (at least until the recent election) has been subject to considerable criticism by the private sector. In the words of one leading businessmen, "government really does not like to listen, it likes to lecture."

Irrespective of the closeness of the relationship, business traditionally avoids public rows with the government, and seldom wins when it does engage in frontal attacks. The assertion some years ago by the director-general of the CBI that it was time for the Confederation to take its gloves off in its dealing with the government brought sharp criticism from his own membership and a marked cooling in its relations (and effectiveness) with the government.

INTERNATIONAL ISSUES

The foregoing pertains to internal policies of the EC. No less important are external policies of interest to the business community, foremost among those being the Uruguay Round trade negotiations. There is a widespread view in the U.S. business community that its EC counterparts have not taken a sufficiently active interest in the negotiations and thus have not wielded adequate influence over the positions of their governments, and, thereby, of the EC Commission's negotiators.

It is difficult to assess this criticism because it involves a subjective judgment. The European private sector has been deeply involved in the trade negotiations, although in a far less formal manner than in the United States. There is no counterpart of the Advisory Committee on Trade Policy and Negotiations (ACTPN) in the United States, with its elaborate structure and broad and direct involvement of the private sector. Rather, EC business has made its views known on the national level and with the Commission (which conducts negotiations on behalf of the EC), by all accounts with the preponderance of effort devoted to the national level. The mode and intensity of the government-business dialogue on the Uruguay Round varies among the member states. In the United Kingdom, for example, the government has consulted regularly with the CBI; the U.K. services organization, LOTIS; the Apparel and Textile Knitting Alliance; and a number of ad hoc groups for specific sectors or issues. Both government and business consider that adequate opportunity has been afforded business to make its views known.

At the EC level, the main business interlocutor has been UNICE, which has coordinated an extensive effort to follow and influence the negotiations. It has established a structure, headed by a leading French businessman, involving heavy input by the European sectoral federations. UNICE has worked closely and continuously with the EC Commission on its positions with, it believes, considerable success. At the same time, its national constituent associations have lobbied not only their national governments but often also the EC Commission. This pattern is not problem-free for the negotiators because UNICE does not represent the service sector, and in some areas the negotiators have faced conflicting voices from industry (e.g. from producers and consumers of semiconductors regarding tariffs). In addition to this effort, some sectors have lobbied directly at the national and the EC level, as, for example, in the case of the chemical industry through CEFIC, its Europe-wide federation.

One major difference between the United States and the EC is that chief executive officers have taken little direct interest in the Uruguay Round negotiating process. Among European companies, a comparable degree of interest, would, according to one participant, normally be shown only at the level of third-echelon company officials. Another difference is the almost total absence of ad hoc alliances of trade associations or companies on single issues. Finally, some observers note that the European private sector was slow to become involved in the negotiations and levels of intensity have been, on the whole, lower than in the United States. And, of course, active involvement does not necessarily translate into positions similar to those of U.S. business.

While the Uruguay Round is the centerpiece of trade negotiations, many other trade activities take place on a continuing basis. For example, bilateral textile agreements are negotiated under the framework of the Multi-Fiber Agreement. On the whole, the relationship between government and business is less tense than in the United States in this area, and EC Commission negotiators operate with less private sector (and member state) restraints. Although there is no formal pattern, regular contacts take place, in which the EC Commission works closely with European industry's representative body, the Coordination Committee for the Textile Industries in the EEC (Comitextil). The relationship is apparently based on mutual confidence, with the Commission relying on Comitextil to provide technical input, explain industry's problems and concerns, and identify bottom line positions.

Implications for the United States

The government-business relationship in the European Community is carried out in a setting sharply different from that in the United States. The differences relate to both substance and style. While the EC's separation of powers bears some resemblance to the U.S. federal system, EC institutions are significantly different in structure and in operation. Similarly, attitudes in both government and business are different. Personal relationships are more important in Europe than in the United States, and the way they are conducted can have a greater effect on the outcome, both positively and negatively. Overall, the government-business relationship takes place within more clearly defined parameters of expected conduct on both sides.

U.S. business can be—and is—an active participant in the European government-business relationship. U.S. firms established in the EC theoretically enjoy the same rights and privileges as any company, irrespective of the source of its capital or its headquarters, and thus can interact within the private sector and with government on an equal footing. In fact, however, the situation is more nuanced. The degree of acceptance of U.S. companies as equals in representative bodies and as interlocutors of governments, including the EC institutions, varies according to many factors on both sides of the equation. Nonetheless, to a considerable extent, the U.S. firms that have chosen to become involved have been accepted on the same basis as European companies. Such discrimination as exists—within the private sector and by governments—is seldom anti-American but more frequently aimed at protecting domestic interests against foreign companies.

Certainly, there is little discrimination in terms of access and influence at the level of EC institutions. The EC Committee of the American Chamber is a highly respected organization in Brussels. It closely follows developments in the EC and produces position papers that are widely read among EC decision-makers, who consider it a useful source of representative opinion. Its influence is probably enhanced by the parallel seen in the Community with experiences in the United States in developing its "single market."

Beyond the activities of the EC Committee, U.S. firms and other representative organizations are on the whole treated by the EC Commission and Parliament as recognized, valid players, whose views should be taken into account. The category of U.S. firms with less access and influence, of course, are those that are not established in the EC, and for them the route will generally be through other connections, either American or foreign.

The implications, then, for U.S. business of the EC government-business relationship are that it is possible to operate actively and effectively in what is a significantly different context from that in the United States. The degree of success in so doing will be largely a function of the effort devoted to understanding how the interaction works and adapting to it. The role of U.S. Government is secondary. It must continue to be supportive of business and to assist it in instances of discrimination.

II. THE PATH TO EUROPEAN UNION

THE DEVELOPMENT OF THE EUROPEAN COMMUNITY: BOUNDARIES, AGENDA AND DECISION-MAKING

By Desmond Dinan *

CONTENTS

Summary

The European Community is a unique international entity that combines elements of both intergovernmentalism and supranationalism. Its progress has not been linear. The course of European integration has ebbed and flowed with the tide of regional and global political, economic and ideological developments since the end of the Second World War. A number of notable events stand out in the Community's history: the Treaty of Rome in 1957, the Single European Act in 1987, and the Treaty on European Union, which provides for Economic and Monetary Union (EMU) and European Political Union (EPU), in 1992. But these constitutional landmarks mask the messy reality of incremental integration during the last forty years. A multitude of idiosyncratic and systemic factors account for the ways in which geo-political borders are set, political, security and socio-economic agendas are defined, and legislative decisions are made, in the contemporary European Community.

Introduction

In the last five years, the European Community has rarely been out of the news. Ratification of the Single European Act (SEA) in 1987 catapulted the Community to prominence. "1992," the target date set in the SEA for implementing the internal market program, became synonymous with the revitalization of Western Europe and the attainment of economic integration. Events in the

---

* Desmond Dinan is Director of George Mason University's Center for European Community Studies.

intervening period—from revolution in Eastern Europe to civil war in Yugoslavia—have pushed the Community to the forefront of international affairs. At a time of spectacular change on the Continent, with old ideas and institutions disappearing daily, the Community seems singularly stable and self-assured.

Clearly, the Community has entered a dramatic phase of its development. Completion of the single market program, leadership of the Eastern European aid effort, and involvement (however controversial) in the Croatian conflict emphasize the Community's newfound confidence and determination. By the same token, they exaggerate the discontinuity between the EC's present and past achievements. The Cold War may have ended abruptly and the Soviet Union collapsed unexpectedly, but underlying shifts in the international system stretch far back into the postwar period. Similarly, the single market program that grabbed public attention in the late 1980s could not have come about without the profound ideological, political and commercial changes of the previous decade. In short, the Gorbachev and Delors phenomena should not obscure deep-seated forces and influences that have shaped contemporary Europe.

Thus a proper understanding of the Community's current position is possible only by comprehending its overall development. Precisely because of historical continuity, that development is difficult to compartmentalize chronologically. Peter Ludlow divides the Community's history into two parts. [1] The first, from the early 1950s to the early 1970s, saw a "low-policy" Community thrive in the rigid Cold War climate of unquestioned U.S. hegemony, German diplomatic diffidence, relatively stable exchange rates, and unprecedented prosperity in the member states. The second, from that time onward, saw the Community gradually acquire a "high-policy" profile in the changing circumstances of fluctuating Superpower relations, marked American decline, growing German assertiveness, oscillating exchange rates, and widely uneven economic performance among the member states.

An alternative, but by no means contradictory division identifies four stages in the Community's development. The first, from the Monnet Plan (1946) to the Treaty of Rome (1957), covers the Community's emergence out of the postwar enthusiasm for European integration and concern about German revival. The second, from the Treaty of Rome to the Hague Summit (1969), involves President de Gaulle's "veto" of Britain's membership application, challenge to supranationalism and assertion of intergovernmentalism. The third, from the Hague Summit to the Fontainebleau European Council (1984), includes the Community's first and second enlargements, the relaunch of European integration, and the subsequent economic setbacks and disputes over budgetary contributions and resource allocation. And the fourth, from Fontainebleau to the Maastricht European Council (1991), charts the third enlargement, the SEA, the successful single market program and the Community's reaction to revolution in the East, culminating in the Treaty on European Union.

---

[1] Ludlow, Peter. *Beyond 1992: Europe and Its World Partners.* Brussels, CEPS, 1989.

Instead of adopting one or other of these chronological approaches, this short essay will analyze the EC's development by exploring a number of important topics and themes that dominate the Community's history. The first concerns the Community's geo-political boundaries, including previous and prospective enlargements. The second traces the impact on the Community's agenda of political, economic and systemic changes, in Europe and beyond, during the postwar period. The third deals with institutional issues and decision-making processes, as the Community adapted to incremental integration over the past forty years. These topics and themes are by no means exclusive or exhaustive. But their exploration helps to place the Community in a proper historical perspective.

Setting the Boundaries

At his famous press conference on May 9, 1950, in which he proposed pooling Franco-German coal and steel production, French Foreign Minister Robert Schuman declared that the new international authority would be "open to the participation of the other countries of Europe." [2] Schuman's statement suggests an inclusiveness that, in reality, his proposal plainly lacked. Although the ensuing organization had the word "European" in its title, membership of the Community was effectively confined to the West. Schuman and Jean Monnet, the brains behind the coal and steel proposal and the architect of European integration, never intended the countries of Eastern Europe to respond to their initiative. By 1950 the Cold War was at its height, and the Eastern European countries were firmly in the Soviet orbit. In his memoirs, Monnet claims to have advocated the European Community as a "third way," in part to try to break the bipolar mould. [3] In fact, Monnet expected the Community not only to operate within, but also to augment the existing international system. Monnet was too close to the American political establishment to have thought otherwise. For their part, American leaders would not have championed European integration had they suspected that the Community would some day challenge the postwar bipolar order, in which the United States, after all, was the Western hegemon.

Even within the West, the Community was effectively limited to "Little Europe" of the Six: France, Germany, Italy, Belgium, the Netherlands and Luxembourg. Monnet knew that the geographically peripheral countries to the north, south and west of "Little Europe" would remain outside the Community, but for radically different reasons. To the south, Spain was an international pariah; a legacy of its wartime sympathy and support for the Axis. To the north, the Scandinavian countries had demonstrated, during the negotiations that led to the launching of the Council of Europe in 1949, their reluctance to share national sovereignty. To the west, the United Kingdom, an economically and politically much more important country than its Scandinavian or Iberian counterparts, had displayed an even greater loathing of supranationalism. Moreover, in the run-up to the Treaty of Rome, Britain had attempted

---

[2] Monnet, Jean. *Memoirs*. Garden City, Doubleday, 1978. p. 46.

[3] Ibid., p. 92.

to abort the European Economic Community by proposing instead a broader, looser free trade area. When the Six went on to establish the Community anyway, Britain formed the rival European Free Trade Area (EFTA) with Austria, Denmark, Norway, Portugal, Switzerland, and Sweden.

No wonder that Monnet initially conceived of the "European" Community as a select group of countries centered on France and Germany. His government did not even inform London much in advance of the historic Schuman Declaration. Of course, the new Community did not preclude the possibility of enlargement. On the contrary, the little countries of Little Europe especially wanted Britain to join, if only to dilute Franco-German domination of the Community. But a consensus existed in the Community that new member states would have to subscribe to the fundamental principle of shared sovereignty, as a means of achieving the essential objectives of managing a resurgent Germany and promoting general prosperity. [4]

Although completely in sympathy with the Community's political and economic objectives, the United Kingdom never became fully reconciled to supranationalism. Yet Britain was the first country to ask for membership of the new Community. The reason for Britain's application was not only economic—a marked redirection of trade toward the Continent in the late 1950s and early 1960s—but also strategic—an awareness of the growing importance of the Community within the Western Cold War system. It was the latter point, and especially America's advocacy of it, that motivated de Gaulle to keep Britain out. De Gaulle's "veto" delayed the first enlargement of the Community until after his departure, when Britain and its economically dependent neighbors, Ireland and Denmark, finally joined in 1973. [5]

The second and third enlargements—Greece in 1981, and Spain and Portugal in 1986—amounted geo-politically to little more than tying up loose ends. Emerging from right-wing dictatorships in the mid-1970s, all three countries saw membership of the Community as the key to economic development and political stability. Greece applied first, playing the trump card of cultural affinity and democratic heritage. Disregarding an unfavorable Commission opinion, the Council of Ministers endorsed the Greek request. It is a decision which some in the Community now regret, not only because of the Greek government's political recalcitrance in the 1980s, but also because of Greece's persistent economic problems. Spain and Portugal, by contrast, acceded to the Treaty of Rome after difficult and protracted negotiations, and pride themselves today on being model Community countries, while tenaciously advocating their special interests. [6]

---

[4] For the early history of the European Community, see Gillingham, John. *Coal, Steel and the Rebirth of Europe, 1945–55.* Cambridge, Cambridge University Press, 1991; Hogan, Michael. *The Marshall Plan: America, Britain and the Reconstruction of Europe, 1947–1952.* Cambridge, Cambridge University Press, 1987; Lipgens, Walter. *History of European Integration,* v. I and II. London, Oxford University Press, 1981 and 1986; Milward, Alan. *The Reconstruction of Western Europe.* London, Methuen, 1983; and, Stirk, Peter, and David Willis, eds. *Shaping Postwar Europe: European Unity and Diversity, 1945–57.* New York, St. Martin's, 1991.

[5] See George, Stephen. *An Awkward Partner: Britain in the European Community.* Oxford, Clarendon, 1990.

[6] See Nicholson, Frances, and Roger East. *From the Six to the Twelve: The Enlargement of the European Communities.* Harlow, Longman, 1987.

By contrast, in the 1970s and early 1980s the remaining EFTA countries were content to remain outside the Community. All were democratically sound, economically prosperous and, with the exception of Norway (which had narrowly voted against EC membership in 1972) and Iceland, strategically neutral. After Britain and Denmark joined the Community, the remaining EFTA members negotiated individual trade agreements with Brussels. Given the relatively low level of economic integration attained by the Community in the 1970s, a level thought unlikely to be surpassed for some time, there was little incentive for the EFTA countries to seek another arrangement. [7]

Thus, by the early 1980s, the Community's boundaries seemed permanently set around the soon-to-be Twelve member states. Turkey was the only anomaly in an otherwise coherent Western system. Apart from Norway the sole European NATO member state outside the Community, but unlike Norway not only unwanted in the Community but also desperate to join, Turkey was the "odd man out." [8] After a troubled relationship with the Community, exacerbated by the invasion of Cyprus in 1974 as well as political and human rights violations at home in succeeding years, Turkey applied for membership in 1987. Turkey's performance in the Gulf crisis won American support for Ankara's application, and seemed to strengthen the country's case for membership. By that time, however, the end of the Cold War had eradicated the systemic imperative for Turkish participation. Paradoxically, the dramatic changes of the last three years have, on the one hand, made it less likely that the Community will admit Turkey as a member and, on the other hand, opened the Pandora's box of the Community's boundaries to the East.

Even before events in Eastern Europe began to speed up in the late 1980s, the Community's commercial and institutional revitalization in the immediately preceding years had reopened the enlargement question. Responding to both sets of circumstances, Austria reviewed its relationship with the Community and applied for membership in 1989. Sweden followed suit in 1991. In an effort to respond to the EFTA countries' concerns about exclusion from the single European market, and to ward off a rush of membership applications, the Community sought to establish a joint EC-EFTA "European Economic Area" (EEA). Negotiations almost faltered over three contested issues: fishing rights, Alpine trucking rights and a "cohesion" fund for the Community's poorer members to compensate for better EFTA access to EC markets. Agreement was eventually reached in October 1991, only to be rejected by the EC's Court of Justice two months later, on the grounds that the proposed EC-EFTA tribunal to adjudicate EEA-related disputes was incompatible with the Treaty of Rome. Apart from this legal obstacle to implementing the EEA, the earlier Austrian and Swedish applications suggest that an EC agreement with EFTA is unlikely in

---

[7] See Wallace, Helen. *The Wider Western Europe: Reshaping the European Community-EFTA Relationship.* London, RIIA, 1991.

[8] Burrows, Bernard. A Community of Thirteen? The Question of Turkish Membership of the European Community. *The Journal of Common Market Studies,* v. 17, no. 2, 1977. pp. 143–150.

any event to delay for long membership applications from that direction.[9]

By repeating the rhetoric of the architects of European integration, and citing the later examples of Greek, Spanish and Portuguese accession, the new democracies of Eastern Europe can make a compelling case for membership. When Vaclav Havel spoke about Czechoslovakia and Poland rejoining "Europe"[10] it would have been disingenuous for the Community to pretend that, to East European ears, Europe was no longer synonymous with the Community. But the prospect of numerous applications from the East greatly bothers Brussels, especially with the single market program not entirely implemented, and EMU and EPU still on shaky ground. Just as the Community has attempted to delay membership applications from the EFTA countries, so too has Brussels sought to discourage the Eastern European countries from attempting to join. The exception, of course, is East Germany, which entered the Community by default following German unification in October 1990. For the rest, Commission President Delors envisions a New Europe of "concentric circles."[11] Not surprisingly, the Twelve would form the inner circle, surrounded by the EFTA and Eastern European countries, with North Africa on the outer rim. A network of association and cooperation agreements would bind the circles together.

Czechoslovakia, Hungary and Poland, the three most economically developed countries in Eastern Europe, have the closest relationship with the Community. But strong protectionist impulses in the member states, especially in France, held up the Community's efforts to assist these countries economically. The Community finally signed separate "Europe Agreements" with Czechoslovakia, Hungary and Poland in December 1991,[12] as a means of promoting reform and putting off for as long as possible the inevitable accession applications. Brussels hopes eventually to conclude similar agreements with Bulgaria and Romania by the end of 1992. In the meantime, the Baltic States, Albania, the former Soviet Republics, Croatia and Slovenia all seek to cultivate closer contacts with the Community. None is apt to apply to join for some time, although most undoubtedly aspire to membership.

Thus the Community's boundaries are unlikely to stay set for long. As it is, the contemporary Community context bears little resemblance to the world in which Monnet operated, and the Community's size will soon be equally out of proportion to his original conception. By itself, the single market program acted as a catalyst for new applications, although from countries firmly within Western Europe and close to the Franco-German core. Unforeseen developments elsewhere in Europe and the erstwhile Soviet Union now raise the possibility of applications from prospective member states far to the East. With the Cold War over and a new international order emerging, future enlargements will raise fundamental questions not of the usual systemic sort, but of a more intractable

---

[9] Council of the European Communities General Secretariat. *Press Release 10323/91.*

[10] *The Guardian*, January 26, 1990.

[11] See Gauldesi, Marinella Neri. The European Community and Its Twelve Member States. *The International Spectator*, v. 25, no. 4, October-December, 1990. pp. 236–250.

[12] Council of the European Communities General Secretariat. *Press Release, 10324/91.*

kind. Specifically, where does Europe end? Which "Europe" is "Community Europe?" And how can a Community of fifteen, or twenty, or twenty-five member states be managed? [13]

Defining the Agenda

As the previous section suggests, the issues of enlargement and agenda are intrinsically linked. Despite the oft-declared, definitive objective of "European Union," for most of its history the Community had a relatively restricted agenda of sectoral economic integration. Yet the Community's first enlargement in the early 1970s led to a decision to broaden the agenda to include economic and monetary union and foreign policy coordination. The single market program in the mid-1980s acted like a magnet to attract new members from EFTA. Conversely, the collapse of communism in Eastern Europe, and the prospect of membership applications from the countries of the former Soviet bloc, compelled the Community to consolidate the single market initiative, revisit the question of economic and monetary union, and explore the feasibility of political union.

The external political and economic environment, a range of domestic internal issues, and the changing dynamic of relations between the member states help to set the Community's agenda. Less visible, more mundane factors are also important. Thus the day-to-day functioning of the Community's institutions, and bureaucratic behavior in Brussels, affect the agenda to an appreciable extent. A recent article cites the example of public health policy, for which the Community does not have legal competence, but in which it is nonetheless involved "through creative bureaucratic use of (non-political) powers." [14]

The Community confined itself initially to coal and steel because, for all their rhetoric about integration, the then member states could agree to share sovereignty only in a relatively restricted area. For Paris, the European Coal and Steel Community (ECSC) provided a means of harnessing Germany's industrial recovery and salvaging the postwar French modernization plan. For Bonn, the Community pointed the way to rapid economic recovery and international political rehabilitation. Germany was more than willing to widen the agenda of integration, but the French parliament's refusal to ratify the European Defense Community (EDC) in 1954 ensured that supranationalism would be confined to sectoral economic issues. [15]

A Dutch proposal during the EDC debate, to go beyond functional cooperation and establish a full a customs union, laid the basis for negotiations in the mid-1950s about rekindling the Community. Monnet thought the proposal too ambitious, and suggested instead an atomic energy organization, along the lines of the existing Coal and Steel Community. A reaction in France against the EDC deba-

---

[13] For some interesting answers to the first two of these questions, see Wallace, William. *The Transformation of Western Europe*. London, RIIA, 1990.

[14] Peters, Guy. Bureaucratic Politics and Institutions of the European Community. In Sbragia, Alberta, ed. *Europolitics: Institutions and Policy-Making in the "New" Europe*. Washington, D.C., Brookings, 1992. pp. 75–122.

[15] See the sources cited in footnote 5.

cle, and against the excessive nationalism exhibited in the 1956 Suez crisis, enhanced the political prospects for further economic integration. The ensuing Messina Conference eventually produced treaties for a European Economic Community (EEC) and a European Atomic Community (EURATOM). Both came into operation on January 1, 1958, with a membership identical to that of the ECSC.[16]

At French insistence, the new Community (the collective name by which all three Communities are known) encompassed agriculture in the proposed common market. Just as the last governments of the French Fourth Republic had insisted, against opposition from some of the other member states, that provision for a Common Agricultural Policy (CAP) be included in the Community, de Gaulle's government in the new Fifth Republic struggled equally tenaciously to bring the CAP into being. By linking progress on the CAP to implementing the industrial common market, which Germany especially sought, de Gaulle eventually prevailed. As a result, by the mid-1960s, a time of unprecedented economic progress, the Community was well on course.

Sustained economic setbacks would soon plunge the Community into rough seas. In the meantime, Britain's impending accession posed a challenge of a different sort. The Hague Summit responded with a call for "completion and deepening" to complement enlargement. Completion meant finalizing the common market and, especially, the CAP; deepening meant entering the "high-policy" areas of monetary and political union. Other external factors convinced President Pompidou, Chancellor Brandt and Prime Minister Heath to extend the Community's agenda. International financial instability, culminating in America's decision in August 1971 to float the dollar, and the corresponding erosion of American leadership within the Alliance, gave added impetus to new EC initiatives. Two Community reports, the Werner Report on monetary union and the Davignon Report on foreign policy coordination, pointed the way. At the Paris Summit of October 1972, the Community set 1980 as the target date for achieving economic and monetary union (EMU). Earlier, the member states had endorsed Davignon's findings and launched European Political Cooperation (EPC)[17]

The worsening international climate, especially in the aftermath of the 1973 oil embargo, almost submerged the Community. Not only was the new objective of EMU unattainable, but the common market itself seemed jeopardized. Huge divergences in member states' economic performances made monetary union impossible to achieve. More important, member states' separate, rather than collective, responses to the economic downturn undermined the political will for further integration. Coping with falling productivity, rising unemployment and soaring inflation, the member states reversed the achievements of the previous decade by championing national manufacturers and reinforcing non-tariff barriers. By the

---

[16] See Kuesters, Hanns-Juergen. The Treaties of Rome (1955–57). In Pryce, Roy, ed. *The Dynamics of European Integration*. London, Croom Helm, 1987. pp. 78–104.

[17] See Franck, Christian. New Ambitions: From The Hague to Paris Summits (1969–72). In Pryce, *Dynamics*, pp. 130–148.

end of the 1970s, especially in light of the second oil shock, "Eurosclerosis" had set in.

Given the seriousness of this situation, it seems remarkable that, less than a decade later, the Community had revitalized and recharged. The rise of "Europhoria" and the recasting of the EC agenda were due to a combination of interrelated economic, political and ideological developments, both inside and outside the Community. Together, they led to a conviction that, unless the eighties were to be as recessionary as the seventies, the Community would have to return to first principles. Simultaneously, the Community's southern enlargement diversified the EC's agenda by stressing the importance of regional policies, and highlighting the issue of resource redistribution.

Technological innovations in the 1970s and early 1980s provided a strong impetus for change in the Community. New technologies demonstrated the drawbacks of a fragmented European market, while growing competition from the United States and Japan forced European manufacturers to take the initiative. At the same time, an ideological shift toward deregulation and market forces, even in countries with surviving social democratic governments, led to a surge of political support for a "borderless Europe." Realizing that decisive action would have to be taken at the Community level, industrialists and entrepreneurs forged strategic links with Brussels. The Commission, or at least a few far-sighted Commissioners, reciprocated. Industry-Commission collaboration resulted in a number of diverse high-technology ventures: ESPRIT, BRITE, RACE, STAR, JESSIE and, to a different degree, EUREKA. [18]

Early experiences of private-public partnership, together with demands for unfettered competition and greater market access, created a climate in which the Delors Commission flourished. In 1985, Commission vice president Cockfield produced the celebrated "White Paper," a detailed description of the steps necessary to achieve a single market (EC–92). [19] Ironically, as far as the Community's agenda is concerned, the single market program represented a reversion to one of the Community's original objectives, rather than a bold assertion of a major new initiative. However, unrelated internal and external developments in the early 1980s had launched the Community on an unprecedented constitutional debate. Although the results of that debate proved disappointing, at least they provided a timetable and a decision-making framework in which the single market program could be implemented.

The first direct elections to the European Parliament, held in June 1979, were an important element in reopening the constitutional question. Altiero Spinelli, one of the newly elected members of the European Parliament (MEPs) and a veteran advocate of European integration, saw the directly elected parliament as a Constituent Assembly, charged with drafting a new treaty for the Community. His colorfully named "Crocodile Group" of like-minded MEPs eventually produced a "Draft Treaty for European Union."

---

[18] See Sharp, Margaret, and Claire Shearman. *European Technological Cooperation*. London, RIIA, 1987. For a discussion of high technology programs, see the study by Glenn McLoughlin, *European Research and Development*, in this volume.

[19] Commission of the European Communities. *Completing the Internal Market*. Luxembourg, Office of Official Publications, 1985.

The European Parliament's overwhelming approval of the Draft Treaty, in February 1984, challenged the member states to widen the Community agenda by encompassing security, defense, monetary and macroeconomic issues. Aware that the Draft Treaty might easily be dismissed as the work of irresponsible, over-exuberant MEPs, Spinelli purposefully presented a reasonable blueprint for a greater sharing of sovereignty. [20]

The member states would probably have ignored the Draft Treaty in any case, but for the their renewed interest in European integration. For one thing, the recent accession of Greece and the impending entry of Spain and Portugal gave the Community cogent reasons to consider constitutional reform. For another, rising U.S.-EC friction over how best to cope with the "Second Cold War," and EPC's limitations in the aftermath of the Soviet invasion of Afghanistan, added to the momentum. In November 1981, Hans-Dietrich Genscher and Emilio Colombo, the German and Italian Foreign Ministers, launched a joint initiative to revitalize the EC. Although it resulted only in a "Solemn Declaration on European Union", adopted by the Ten at the Stuttgart Summit in July 1983, the "Genscher-Colombo Proposal" nonetheless fuelled the impetus for a radical revision of the Treaty of Rome. [21]

Conflicting attitudes in the member states about how closely to cooperate, especially in sensitive areas like security and defense, contributed to the failure of the Genscher-Colombo proposal, and continue to inhibit European integration to this day. In the early 1980s, however, a number of unresolved disputes in the Community also impeded initiatives for a greater sharing of sovereignty. Most notable were the persistent and related problems of Britain's financial contribution, and the Common Agricultural Policy's bloated budget. The member states settled both issues at the Fontainebleau Summit in June 1984. Reform of the CAP and resolution of the British budgetary problem relieved the Community's pent-up frustration. Newly available energy soon found an outlet in the much larger question of the Community's future agenda.

Also at the Fontainebleau Summit, the member states decided to establish an "Ad Hoc Committee on Institutional Affairs" to consider the Community's response to internal and external change. Known by the name of its chairman, the "Dooge Committee" drew on the recent Genscher-Colombo and European Parliament initiatives, and "attempted to translate a wide range of existing views on the nature of European integration into politically acceptable reform." [22] The Committee's report, dealing with a variety of institutional issues and a plethora of policy options, from technology, to political cooperation, to the internal market, generated an intense discussion of European integration at the Milan Summit in June 1985. As a result, and based on a majority vote of the Heads of

[20] See Bieber, Roland, et al. *An Ever-Closer Union: A Critical Analysis of the Draft Treaty Establishing the European Union*. Brussels, European Perspectives, 1985; Capotorti, Francesco. *The European Union Treaty: Commentary on the Draft Adopted by the European Parliament on 14 February 1984*. Oxford, Clarendon Press, 1986; and, Lodge, Juliet, ed. *European Union: The Community in Search of a Future*. London, Macmillan, 1986.

[21] Bonvicini, Gianni. The Genscher-Colombo Plan and the "Solemn Declaration on European Union" (1981–83). In Pryce, *Dynamics*, pp. 174–187.

[22] Keatinge, Patrick, and Anna Murphy. The European Council's Ad Hoc Committee on Institutional Affairs (1984–85). In Pryce, *Dynamics*, pp. 217–237; p. 218.

State and Government, the Ten decided to convene an intergovernmental conference (IGC), similar to the one that recently ended in Maastricht, to propose Treaty amendments.

Despite the initial opposition and continued skepticism of Britain, Denmark and Greece, the IGC proceeded remarkably quickly. By February 1986 the Ten had approved the Single European Act, although full ratification was delayed until the following year. The SEA strengthened procedures for political cooperation, and brought EPC, the environment, research and development, and regional policy explicitly within the Treaty framework. Principally, however, the SEA endorsed the internal market program and set the target date of 1992 for its completion. [23] More hard negotiating followed, in 1987 and 1988, before the program was successfully launched. But the SEA's institutional provisions ensured at least that most of the single market program would be enacted in Brussels, whether or not enforced in the member states. With a secure legislative base, EC–92 soon took off. Confident that fiscal, physical and technical barriers would indeed be eradicated in the Community, business people behaved accordingly. Regardless of increasing productivity and employment, mergers and acquisitions certainly abounded.

But in terms of advancing the Community's agenda, the SEA was a disappointment. Earlier expectations of a radical Treaty revision proved unfounded. Yet the launch of the single market program, in which the SEA played a pivotal part, promoted three important areas of Community competence. First, neglect of workers' rights in the initial single market relaunch led to a debate in the Community about the so-called "Social Charter," [24] and ultimately to the controversial inclusion of a Social Chapter in the draft Maastricht Treaty on Political Union. Second, poorer member states' concerns about the program's lop-sided economic impact led, in 1988, to a renewed emphasis on regional policy, and a massive redeployment of resources from the "core" to the "periphery." Third, the success of EC–92 inevitably forced the Community to confront again the complementary question of a single currency and a coordinated macroeconomic policy.

Commission President Delors was more than happy to reopen discussion in the Community about Economic and Monetary Union. He eagerly set about exploring the issue and produced, in April 1989, the "Delors Plan," a three-stage proposal to promote economic convergence, establish a European central bank, and ultimately create a single currency. [25] The Spanish government, then in the six-month rotating EC Presidency, strongly supported Delors' initiative. At the Madrid Summit, in June 1989, the Twelve agreed that the Delors Plan provided a blueprint for EMU, and decided to

---

[23] See De Ruyt, Jean. *L'Acte Unique Europeen.* Brussels, Editions de l'Universite de Bruxelles, 1987; Moravcsik, Andrew. Negotiating the SEA: National Interests and Conventional Statecraft in the European Community. In *International Organization*, v. 45, no. 1, Winter 1991. p. 19–55; Sandholtz, Wayne, and John Zysman. 1992: Recasting the European Bargain. In *World Politics*, v. 42, no. 1, October 1989. p. 95–128; and, Cameron, David. The 1992 Initiative: Causes and Consequences. In Sbragia, *Europolitics*, p. 23–74.

[24] On the origins and politics of the Social Dimension, see Springer, Beverly. *The Social Dimension of 1992: Europe Faces a New EC.* Westport, Praeger, 1992.

[25] Commission of the European Communities. *Report on Economic and Monetary Union in the European Community.* Luxembourg, Office of Official Publications, 1989.

launch the first stage by July 1, 1991. Mindful of the Community's commitment in 1972 to achieve EMU by 1980, and aware of deep differences over how best to proceed beyond the first stage, the member states refrained at Madrid from setting a target date for a single currency.

Addressing the European Parliament on July 9, 1991, the Foreign Minister of the Netherlands declared that "the Dutch (EC) Presidency regards the internal market as its absolute priority.... [Without] it there would be no monetary union, and without monetary union there would be no political union." [26] This statement, and the momentum generated by the Delors Plan, suggest that the single market program was the sole reason for subsequent efforts to achieve European Union. Undoubtedly there is a causal connection between a single market and monetary integration; the point is made in the original Treaty of Rome. Yet even the enthusiasm surrounding the single market program was insufficient, by itself, to overcome the deep-rooted reluctance of some member states to go beyond the first tentative steps to establish EMU.

Moreover, the single market program might never have been launched but for an earlier initiative in the monetary sphere. Acting on the idea of Commission President Roy Jenkins, Chancellor Helmut Schmidt and President Valery Giscard d'Estaing proposed a European Monetary System in 1978. Concerned about persistent exchange rate fluctuations, and the supposed abnegation of American responsibility in that regard, Schmidt and Giscard sought a zone of monetary stability in Western Europe. [27] Begun in 1979, the EMS exceeded its authors' expectations by quickly acquiring the characteristics of a fixed exchange rate regime, with the German mark playing the part of a reference currency. The consequent fall in inflation and stabilization of prices among the participating states brought the Community back to where it had been in the 1960s, before the collapse of the Bretton Woods system. That, in turn, permitted the Community to turn its attention to the unfinished business of the single market. "In a sense, the creation of the EMS...represented a necessary precondition for the free flow of goods, services and capital within the Community. Thus it is understandable that the European Council would not consider (completing) an internal market until the EMS had been formed but that, once formed, attention would immediately turn" in that direction. [28]

Once off the ground, however, the single market program could not automatically ensure a further push toward EMU. Instead, it was the contemporaneous collapse of communism in Eastern Europe, and the revolutions there in 1989, that maintained the momentum of the Delors Plan, and clinched the imminent completion not only of EMU, but also of EPU. Delors rapidly realized that what he called the "acceleration of history" [29] in Eastern Europe,

---

[26] *The Financial Times*, July 10, 1991.

[27] See Ludlow, Peter. *The Making of the European Monetary System: A Case Study of the Politics of the European Community*. London, Butterworths Scientific, 1982.

[28] Cameron, 1992. In Sbragia, *Europolitics*, p. 47–48.

[29] *The Financial Times*, September 13, 1989.

culminating at the end of the year in the fall of the Berlin Wall and the rush for German unification, threatened not only to derail the single market program, but also to undermine the entire Community system. Events in the East forced the Community to revisit its political agenda, and to expedite EMU. The other member states' consent to German unification was the bargain upon which the Community's future hinged.

The deal was struck at the Strasbourg Summit in December 1989. An exuberant Chancellor Kohl sought to allay his partners' anxieties about German unification, and especially to overcome deep French suspicion. At the end of the historic meeting, the other member states acknowledged Germany's right to self-determination, but only in the context of European integration and unification. In concrete terms, that meant an end to German foot-dragging over EMU, and a commitment to proceed on EPU. Thus "by linking German unification to political union, and by making the latter conditional upon monetary union, (the Twelve) drew the lines along which the ensuing debate (on the Community's future) was to be conducted." [30]

The prospect of German unification nevertheless continued to cause strains within the Community, notably between Paris and Bonn. Only after the decisive East German elections of March 1990, when German unification appeared unstoppable, did France accept the inevitable and attempt to implement the agreement reached at Strasbourg. The famous Franco-German letter followed, endorsing European Union and calling for "fundamental reforms—economic and monetary union as well as political union—(to) come into force on January 1, 1993. [31] This proved the starting point for two years of frenetic discussions among the member states and the Commission about the nature, scope and competence of the proposed European Union.

EMU, at least, was easy to conceptualize. The Delors Plan already existed as an acceptable blueprint. At the Rome Summit in October 1990, Thatcher was isolated and outmaneuvered in her opposition to further monetary integration, contributing to her political downfall at home some weeks later. Thereafter the Twelve, including a more compliant United Kingdom, began to tackle the Plan's most pressing particulars, notably convergence criteria, composition of the European Central Bank (ECB), and the ECB's relationship to other EC institutions and the member state governments. Negotiations ebbed and flowed during the specially convened intergovernmental conference on EMU, that began in Rome in December 1990 and ended in Maastricht a year later. At Maastricht, the "member states in effect adopted the Delors Plan," [32] setting the definitive date of 1999 for a single currency in the Community.

By contrast, the parallel intergovernmental conference on EPU lacked focus and direction. Negotiations covered a wide range of

---

[30] Tsakaloyannis, Panos. The "Acceleration of History" and the Reopening of the Political Debate in the European Community. In *The Journal of European Integration*, v. 14, no. 2-3, 1991, p. 83–102; p. 88.

[31] *The Financial Times*, April 20, 1990.

[32] Wooley, John T. Policy Credibility and European Monetary Institutions. In Sbragia, *Europolitics*, p. 157–190; p. 157.

issues, including institutional reform, the Social Charter, and foreign and security policy. European Political Cooperation had always been an enigmatic issue in the Community. Defining a "security identity" and developing a Common Foreign and Security Policy proved especially arduous for the Twelve. The Gulf crisis highlighted once again the limitations of EPC, while demonstrating the difficulty of coordinating the member states' defense policies. On the one hand the United States cheerfully cited the Community's response to the Gulf crisis as proof of the EC's feebleness. On the other, discussions in the Community about acquiring a military capability provoked an intemperate American response, with warnings from Washington about the dangers of undermining NATO.

In the event, the Maastricht agreement gave the future European Union a defense dimension in addition to a common foreign policy, but within a framework that soothed Washington's sensitivities. The Western European Union (WEU) was the means chosen to satisfy both requirements. Formed in 1955 to bring Germany into NATO following the failure of the European Defense Community, the WEU will now be called upon to keep the EC's emerging defense identity compatible with the Atlantic Alliance. More likely, the WEU will be the midwife for a future EC army, conceived at the time of the Cold War's collapse but apt to endure a lengthy gestation, probably until the end of the 1990s.

The Maastricht Summit, the culmination of the intergovernmental conferences, addressed a wide range of issues encompassed by the contemporary Community. The Treaty on European Union brings a number of new items formally within the Community's confines. But Maastricht by no means represents the end of formal agenda setting in the EC. The dynamic of European integration, unlikely to diminish in the decade ahead, ensures that the Community's official agenda will continue to change.

Making the Decisions

Decisions in the Community are made at a number of levels. The most visible is that of the European Council, the biannual meetings, and occasional extraordinary sessions, of the Heads of State (in the case of France) and Government of the Twelve, together with the Commission President. The European Council ponders the Community's most controversial political and economic problems, and tackles issues incapable of resolution at lower decision-making levels. The Maastricht Summit is a striking example of the European Council in action. It took two days of hard bargaining to conclude the work of the intergovernmental conferences, and resolve the outstanding particulars of EMU and EPU. Only the Community's highest political leaders had the necessary authority to endorse a single currency by 1999, strike a deal on the Social Chapter (in the Treaty on European Union), and define a common foreign policy with a defense dimension.

The European Council is a relatively new institution. It emerged out of the occasional meetings of Heads of State and Government held during the Community's early years. In 1974, President Giscard d'Estaing proposed that such meetings take place regularly to conduct Community business. Giscard's initiative owed something to his predilection for intimate, high-level gatherings—he also proposed annual meetings of the industrialized world's top leaders (now the G–7)—and to his frustration with the Community's inertia in the mid-1970s. The European Council proved its worth four years later when Giscard and Schmidt used it as a forum to launch the European Monetary System (EMS). Subsequently, some meetings of the European Council have become synonymous with breakthroughs in the Community's agenda, although others have failed spectacularly. [33]

The EMS initiative, and the institutional environment in which it flourished, revealed Giscard's and Schmidt's suspicion of established Community organs and approaches. Both leaders disliked the Commission and distrusted the Brussels bureaucracy. They advocated intergovernmentalism as a means to get the Community going again. Although the European Council soon became an invaluable institution, however, its mere existence was not enough to end the decision-making deadlock that gripped the Community at the time.

The main problem, as Jacques Delors later declared, was "the ball and chain of unanimity that bedevils the whole Community system." [34] In 1965, General de Gaulle had exacerbated a bitter conflict in the Community over budgetary reform (the so-called "Empty Chair" crisis), by trying to prevent a provision of the Rome Treaty, on qualified-majority voting in the Council of Ministers, from coming into force. The others refused to renegotiate one of the Community's key supranational provisions. Faced with united opposition, and chastened by a surprisingly difficult victory over Mitterrand in the December 1965 Presidential election, de Gaulle sued for a settlement. The crisis ended with the "Luxembourg Compromise" of January 1966, an agreement to disagree over the question of qualified-majority voting. Although the Treaty's provision stood, the other member states noted France's consideration that "when very important issues are at stake, discussion must be continued until unanimous agreement is reached." [35]

The "Luxembourg Compromise" left a mixed legacy. On the one hand, it impeded effective decision-making in the Community for a long time to come. De Gaulle's insistence on unanimity heightened the member states' awareness of each others' special interests, and increased their reluctance to call a vote in the Council. For the next fifteen years or so, the Council made no decisions by majority vote on important issues (with the notable exception of the budget), even when national sensitivities were unruffled. But on the other hand, the intergovernmentalism that de Gaulle so bluntly asserted during the 1965 crisis laid one of the bases for the Community's survival in the 1970s and reinvigoration in the 1980s, as epitomized by the European Council.

---

[33] On the role of the European Council in launching the EMS, see Ludlow, XT3The Making of the European Monetary System; for an analysis of the evolution and impact of the European Council, see Bulmer, Simon, and Wolfgang Wessels. *The European Council: Decision-Making in European Politics*. London, Macmillan, 1986; and, Morgan, Annette. *From Summit to Council: Evolution in the EEC*. London, RIIA, 1976.

[34] Gazzo, Mariana, ed. *Towards European Union*, v. II. Brussels, Agence Europe, 1985. p. 26.

[35] The text of the "Luxembourg Compromise," and a good account of the crisis that preceded it, can be found in Lambert, John. The Constitutional Crisis of 1965–66. In *The Journal of Common Market Studies*, v. 6, no. 2, 1966. p. 195–228.

By the early 1980s, evidence emerged of the member states' willingness finally to question the norm of unanimity and, for the first time in fifteen years, to use majority voting. At the same time, enthusiasm for the single market initiative, and the need to revise decision-making procedures before an impending enlargement, convinced the member states to modify key provisions of the Treaty of Rome. The ensuing Single European Act extended majority voting to cover the bulk of the internal market program, while the political will to implement EC–92 ensured that, if necessary, decisions would be put to the vote.

The Commission's role in the decision-making process has fluctuated with the Community's fortunes. In 1965, the Commission provoked the "Empty Chair" crisis by proposing greater legislative power for itself and the European Parliament, in the full knowledge of de Gaulle's inevitable negative reaction. Robert Marjolin, a Commission vice-president, warned his colleagues not to persist with their proposal. Apart from its probable political repercussion, the proposal violated the Commission's "golden rule" of not taking any initiative "likely to encounter any outright veto (by a member state) that would have left no room for negotiation." [36] As Marjolin feared, the crisis resulted in a boost for intergovernmentalism, a setback for supranationalism, and a calamity for the Commission. Thereafter, the Commission refrained from asserting itself until the Jenkins' Presidency in the late 1970s.

The Commission has once again regained its confidence, not only because of the inspired leadership of Jacques Delors, but also because of the altered political and economic environment of the 1980s which gave rise to the single market program. The Commission is more likely once again to make bold proposals, although not if a single member state is apt to be isolated on an issue still subject to unanimity. The European Parliament, which also suffered a setback at de Gaulle's hands in 1966, has similarly reasserted itself. Subsequent budgetary agreements strengthened Parliament's hold over the Community's purse strings, while direct elections have bolstered the assembly's self-confidence. But the EP acquired little additional legislative power under the Single European Act, and did not fare much better in the European Union Treaty. The EP has undoubtedly become a key player in the Community's decision-making process, but its role cannot yet be compared to that of a legislature in a liberal-democratic state. [37]

At the level below the European Council, decision-making involves continuous interaction among government ministers, Commission officials, key MEPs on relevant Parliamentary Committees, member states' civil servants based either in the national capitals or in their country's Permanent Representations in Brussels, and officials of the Council Secretariat. As the Community's agenda increased over the years, the number of actors and the complexity of the decision-making process grew proportionately. More and more participants at the less politicized, and therefore less visible,

[36] Marjolin, Robert. *Architect of European Union: Memoirs, 1911–1986.* London, Weidenfeld and Nicholson, 1989. p. 314.

[37] See Jacobs, Francis, and Richard Corbett. *The European Parliament.* Boulder, Westview, 1990.

levels—below that of the Council of Ministers—make some of the most important decisions and push the parameters. Thus "progress toward supranationalism seems possible when manifestly political institutions are confined to the mere enregisterment of decisions made elsewhere. . . . The institutions of the European Community have not achieved that bureaucratized state perfectly, but they do permit substantial policymaking activity by bureaucracies before political officials ever see the prospective decisions." [38]

Decision-making in the EC, therefore, has evolved into a complex system of intergovernmental negotiating and intra-bureaucratic bargaining. Throughout, national and transnational interest groups play a vigorous part, lobbying government and Community officials at all levels, and lobbying elected representatives both in Brussels, where MEPs hold committee meetings, and in the national capitals, at critical points of the member states' political processes. Treaty revisions such as the Single European Act and the Maastricht agreement help to elucidate and streamline decision-making procedures, but have not unravelled the Community's intricate legislative system.

Conclusion

In his opening speech at the intergovernmental conference preceding the Single European Act, Jacques Delors remarked that "conferences like this one are not convened every five or ten years. There may not be another between now and the year 2000." [39] Little did Delors realize that not one, but *two* intergovernmental conferences, leading to far greater revisions of the Treaty of Rome, would begin in 1990. The latest IGCs took place so soon after the previous one because the success of the single market program, and revolution in Eastern Europe, had abruptly pushed the pace of integration. But milestones like accession treaties, new Commission investitures, or intergovernmental conferences should not obscure the reality of incremental integration in the European Community. Institutional evolution, economic undercurrents and long-term political trends have arguably been equally important in the Community's history as dramatic, news-worthy events. Thus the contemporary Community is a compound of constitutional construction, institutional design and accumulated operational experience. As for its policy-making persona, it is difficult to dispute Stanley Hoffmann's ironical observation that, today, the EC is "an improbable, yet not ineffectual, blend of de Gaulle and Monnet." [40]

---

[38] Peters, Bureaucratic Politics, in Sbragia, *Europolitics.*

[39] Gazzo, *European Union,* v. II, p. 23.

[40] Hoffmann, Stanley. Review of De Gaulle: The Rebel, 1890–1944. In *The New Republic,* December 17, 1990. p. 34.

THE 1992 SINGLE MARKET PROGRAM

by Anthony H. Wallace *

CONTENTS

Summary

As the European Community nears the end of its massive project to transform the economies of 12 countries into a single market of more than 340 million people, it is worthwhile to assess the progress to date and to measure the potential effects on the Community's trading partners. The process of reducing all barriers to the movement of goods, people, services and capital, delayed for 20 years by member state fears over loss of sovereignty, the oil shock and the recession, began again in the mid-eighties. Momentum was provided by pressure from European business, a few landmark court cases and the leadership of a remarkable group of commissioners in Brussels. These factors made possible the issuance of a plan (the White Paper and its 282 legal changes needed to get to

* Anthony H. Wallace is an international trade expert and adjunct professor in the International Institute of George Mason University.

the single market) and the amendment of the EC constitution to allow for majority voting on many of these legal proposals.

What has brought the Community to the present state in which almost all of the important proposals have been adopted has been a demonstration of resourcefulness and flexibility by Brussels and the strength of the market forces released in the process. As restrictive national rules in the areas of public procurement, transportation, financial services, telecommunications, environmental pollution and standards have been dismantled, the costs of doing business across borders in Europe look set to drop dramatically. This has convinced the member states of the value of "pooling" their sovereignty in order to increase the economic growth and competitiveness of Europe.

There are just a few sticking points to be resolved, including how to implement the goal of free movement of people, animals and plants across borders, and how to legislate the worker rights proposals in the Social Action Program. Of more concern is the fact that the rate of member state application of the already-adopted EC–92 directives has lagged and enforcement of some of those directives incorporated in member state law has been lax.

U.S. firms stand to gain from the progress achieved in moving toward EC-wide standards and liberalized public procurement and in opening up the telecommunications, financial services and transport sectors. The Community has, after expressions of concern from the United States and other trading partners, revised some EC–92 proposals, including those dealing with banking and standards-setting, testing and certification. The U.S. film industry has not been successful in getting the EC to remove local content provisions in the TV directive; credit card companies are concerned about proposed rules governing protection of personal data; and chip makers see a "forced investment" policy emerging from EC rules on origin, dumping, and procurement. Many U.S. firms have decided to establish production in Europe in order to avoid potential problems in implementation of EC product standards and public procurement programs.

Successful completion of the single market program will provide benefits to U.S. companies located in Europe and increase EC demand for U.S. exports, but it will also make EC firms more competitive in the global market. The framers of the EC–92 program did not set out to build a "fortress Europe." Vigilance will be required on the part of the United States, however, to assure that the Community and the member states do not stray from the game plan in important areas such as procurement, support for industry, and competition policy.

Introduction

Implementation of the 1985 blueprint to turn the European Community into a single market has progressed steadily in spite of a number of developments not foreseen by the framers. Two of these were the pressure for enlargement of the Community coming from some of the European Free Trade Association (EFTA) countries and former eastern bloc countries that desire closer association with the EC. Another unexpected development was the extent to which the EC has had to reexamine and revise the 1992 program in light of concerns expressed by the United States, Japan and other trading partners. In addition, the specter of recession and the imminent prospect of increased competition between enterprises within and without Europe has led to some foot dragging, characterized by requests for exceptions, delays in application and lax enforcement of EC–92 directives on the part of member states. On a more positive note, faster than expected progress in moving toward a single currency and monetary policy (economic and monetary union, or EMU) has served to encourage members to get their economic houses in order for the day when they will no longer be able to insulate themselves from their neighbors.

Because of these developments, the EC will probably not realize the growth and employment gains projected by the Cecchini Report [1] and other analyses as quickly as they had hoped. The United States and other trading partners will find they have to wait a bit longer than expected for totally free access to the single market in important areas such as standards, testing and certification, government procurement, and financial services. This does not mean that the single market project will fail, or that fears of "fortress Europe" will be realized. The EC states have come too far in the process of reducing barriers to go back. Although all 282 directives in the blueprint may not be enacted by the December 1992 deadline, EC–92 is a process which seems certain to accomplish its stated objective. The Europeans will find ways to get around most if not all of the sticking points they have encountered.

As far as the prospects for a fortress, the Commission of the EC is aware that it must work to keep the market as open as possible to reap maximum gains from international trade. What the EC's trading partners must watch for is the extent to which the Commission may, in the implementation process, find it necessary to pay for internal reform with compromises which have the effect of limiting foreign access to the EC market. Any movement away from the White Paper "vision" toward managed trade or interventionist industrial policy at EC level or member state level could result in a change in the generally favorable U.S. view of the single market project.

How the Process got Started

The idea of moving to a single market with freedom of movement of people, goods, capital and services was part of the vision of the founders of the European Community. The process of reduction of barriers to these four elements started well enough with the establishment of a customs union in 1968. With all internal tariffs and quotas gone, the Community then took another twenty years to begin the business of establishing a single market free of the more subtle barriers that limit trade.

Important catalysts which gave the 1992 project momentum included the following:

---

[1] Commission of the European Communities. *Research on the "Cost of Non-Europe"*. Brussels, 1988.

- Pressure from European business, concerned over the high cost of cross-border operations, and activist groups in the European Parliament forced Brussels to try again to enact market-opening laws that had languished for years.
- The development, through court cases, of the principle of mutual recognition made it possible to avoid the laborious process of harmonization of the legal systems of 12 nations.
- A break in the deadlock over the Community budget in 1988 resolved UK concerns about a fair return and promised increased regional aid to those less-developed members worried about problems of transition.
- The unique collection of personalities in the Commission who created an effective game plan (the 1985 White Paper) [2] and gave impetus to the movement to amend the Treaty of Rome, thus breaking the legislative log jam.

The action of these catalysts, on those who were concerned over the loss of sovereignty a single market might bring and those who feared they would be unable to compete, eased the acceptance of the White Paper and the passage of the Single European Act (SEA) of 1987. By introducing majority voting (instead of the old requirement for unanimity) for most single market measures, the SEA promised speedier implementation of the legal changes proposed in the White Paper. The act also blessed the White Paper and its deadline and managed to inject a bit more democracy into the decision-making process by allowing the Parliament to reject or amend single market proposals under certain conditions.

Progress toward 1992

In the process of evaluating what has been accomplished in the 1992 program and the impact of that progress on the United States, it is useful to note that the EC has proven to be very flexible in adapting to problems encountered on the way. Where something did not work, e.g. rigid harmonization of VAT and excise taxes, the Commission came up with an acceptable alternative. Where elements needed to be added to the program, e.g., energy, the environment, and social policy, the Commission moved to establish a "vision" in the form of a charter or green paper (outline of proposed legislation) and then drafted directives to implement the vision. Several proposed directives were considered unnecessary and were dropped.

As of early 1992, only about 50 of the 282 white paper measures had not been adopted by the Council of Ministers and therefore were not yet EC law. Many of these cover relatively technical areas such as animal and plant health controls and are not "deal breakers." Others, such as several pending controversial social policy directives dealing with working conditions, will, as a result of the December 1991 Maastricht Summit, be dealt with outside of the framework of the White Paper. Procedural delays and the EC's own special version of "log rolling" are holding up some of the initiatives, but the great bulk of single market legislation will be ap-

---

[2] Commission of the European Communities. *Completing the Internal Market.* White Paper from the Commission to the Council. Brussels, June 1985.

proved at Brussels level by the end of the year. A review of EC-92 accomplishments to date follows.

BARRIERS AGAINST PEOPLE

Progress is slow toward the goal of mutual recognition of education and qualifications of professionals and vocational school graduates. Those with lower level occupations can move freely, but the problem of pension and social benefits transfer has not been resolved. The Commission is using a ground-up approach, providing funding for exchange programs, placement, and cooperative development of training programs.

On the border security issues, eight nations (the Schengen Group) have agreed (effective January 1, 1992) to remove all checks (for drugs, guns, terrorism, art smuggling, espionage) on people as soon as the Schengen accord is ratified. The UK, Ireland, Denmark and Greece are not willing to end all checks on people. The Schengen eight hope to implement their policy through greater police and justice ministry coordination and information exchanges.

The success of this "two speed" approach to freedom of movement will depend on tighter control of illegal crossing of EC boundaries, a common visa policy, and agreement on procedures for dealing with requests for asylum. At the Maastricht Summit, the 12 agreed that Brussels competence would be limited to establishing a common visa policy. The remaining difficult immigration issues will be resolved through intergovernmental consultations. This may extend the process of fulfilling the White Paper goals considerably and may in the end limit the benefits of the Single Market.

BARRIERS AGAINST THINGS

As in the case of movement of people, the idea is to get rid of the checkers on EC internal borders. Convergence of VAT and excise taxes, abolition of CAP monetary compensation amounts, harmonization of plant and animal health standards are all on the agenda. Mundane things such as collection of trade statistics will be handled in the future by using the new VAT clearance system and other methods. Of considerable interest to the United States and Japan is the way in which the Commission has chosen to end the system of national quotas against non-EC products permitted under Article 115 of the Rome Treaty. The Commission has, under pressure from auto quota countries, had to compromise. In place of national quotas against Japanese cars, the EC will operate a restraint agreement until 1999.

Some observers are concerned that, as the remaining internal market barriers come down and competition becomes more intense, Brussels may be forced to make similar compromises in other sectors. This might, they contend, result in a perceptible bias against imports from non-members and a preference for foreign direct investment.

STANDARDS, TESTING, AND CERTIFICATION

Rather than attempting to harmonize the thousands of product standards in the 12 member states, Brussels has set out essential requirements in directives only for those items for which health and safety are important considerations (toys, some industrial machines, pacemakers, etc.) The European (19-country) standards bodies (CEN, CENELEC and ETSI) [3] are responsible for elaborating Europe-wide technical specifications for these products. For other non-sensitive products where differing national standards are not incompatible, members will be expected to recognize each others' standards. The Council has adopted all of the essential requirements directives outlined in the White Paper. Elaboration of the approximately 4000 EC-wide technical standards required by these directives will not, however, be completed by the end of 1992. This will delay full realization of the gains of the single market for EC members and pose problems for their foreign trading partners. [4]

U.S. firms have been concerned about limitations on their ability to participate in the standards-setting process of the EC. The U.S. Secretary of Commerce and EC Internal Market Commissioner Bangemann have met frequently since 1988 to assure that U.S. companies get early warning of proposed standards, and a right to comment on these drafts (directly if they are based in Europe and through the American National Standards Institute and the International Standards Organization if they are not). The EC has also promised to use existing international standards where feasible instead of devising a separate EC standard. The U.S. side is monitoring EC implementation of these commitments closely.

In the area of conformity assessment, the EC is establishing uniform procedures and criteria for its testing labs. U.S. labs seek to be accredited by the EC to test U.S. products that are to be exported to Europe. Without this recognition by the EC, U.S. firms would be forced to test a product twice—once in the United States and once in the EC. This duplication would increase costs for the U.S. supplier. The United States and the EC have agreed that the National Institute of Standards and Technology will be the central body responsible for assuring the competence of U.S. testing facilities. In the interim, U.S. labs hope to be approved as subcontractors to EC bodies for specific products.

GOVERNMENT PROCUREMENT

The EC government procurement market (not including defense) totals over $500 billion annually. Before the start of the EC–92 program, 95 percent of this total was supplied by national firms. The French government bought French goods and services, for example, even if they were not the best available in the world market in terms of quality or cost. The cost of this closed procurement market has been estimated at over $25 billion per year. [5] The single market program moved quickly to tighten up older directives on procurement of works and supplies and to open procurement in the formerly "excluded sectors" of energy, telecommunications,

---

[3] The European Committee for Standardization (CEN), the European Committee for Electrotechnical Standardization (CENELEC), and the European Telecommunications Standards Institute (ETSI) are the major standards-setting organizations in Europe.

[4] Until CEN/CENELEC elaborates an EC-wide standard for a particular product, U.S. exporters would still have to deal with an array of differing national standards for that product. This would continue to make it difficult for the U.S. exporter to sell the product throughout the EC.

[5] Commission of the European Communities. *Research on the "Cost of Non-Europe": Basic Findings. The "Cost of Non-Europe" in Public-Sector Procurement.* Volume 5, Parts A and B. Brussels, 1988.

transport and water. A directive dealing with procurement of services is also in the pipeline.

The excluded sectors directive accomplishes, at least for EC members, what the members of the GATT Government Procurement code have been trying to do since the end of the Tokyo Round. The EC, however, has taken the position that only those countries which offer reciprocal procurement opportunities can take advantage of this major opening of the EC market. The EC has asked the United States to put more procurement opportunities on the table (State and local government procurement and purchases by private utilities, transport, and communications entities) in order to demonstrate reciprocity. The GATT code covers Federal procurement only. The United States has informed the EC that the Federal government cannot force States and localities to remove Buy-America restrictions on procurement or require private companies such as the regional Bell Companies, electric utilities and private transport entities to open their procurement in a similar manner.

For U.S. firms bidding on EC contracts, the present situation is even less satisfactory than the former one. The EC reserves the right to reject bids with less than 50 percent EC content, even if they are price competitive and conform to specifications. There is also a three percent price preference for EC bids. Approximately 18 U.S. States interested in participating in the EC procurement market have expressed an interest in reexamining their restrictive procurement provisions. The next step in this process, which is being led by the U.S. Trade Representative, will be solicitation of specific commitments by States to abolish restrictive provisions. The USTR hopes to be able to put enough State, local and private procurement "on the table" to meet EC reciprocity requirements. The process has begun, but it raises important issues for the Congress and the States.

FINANCIAL SERVICES

The key to opening up the EC financial services market was the agreement to end controls on cross-border capital movements in mid-1990. Portugal and Greece are allowed more time for transition. In many ways,the EC–92 program seeks to emulate what the United States accomplished in its early attempts to create a single market. Trade between countries in Europe after 1992 will resemble the movement of goods among the States in the United States. In certain areas, however, the Europeans have made a conscious effort to do things differently.

In banking, for example, the EC has adopted a directive [6] which will entitle a bank established in one member state to establish branches without restriction in any other member state. That bank will be able to engage in the full range of activities permitted by the directive (the list includes traditional banking functions as well as sale of securities and portfolio management and advice). In addition, the bank will be governed by the laws of the home country. [7]

---

[6] See *Second Council Directive*. Dir. 89/646, *OJ*, no. L386, Dec. 30, 1989.

[7] Some local "conduct of business" rules will govern these branches, e.g., opening and closing hours.

This system is radically different from the U.S. system of restrictions on branch banking, prohibition of sale of securities, and host state control. In the early days of the second banking directive, the EC insisted on a "mirror image reciprocity" that would have forced the United States to give EC banks operating here more privileges than U.S. law allowed to American banks. The EC realized the intractability of this problem and modified the directive to call for "national treatment" reciprocity. This was one of the first single market areas in which the EC found it necessary to alter the EC–92 game plan in response to a problem with a trading partner.

With the exception of a few large institutions, U.S. banks have not responded to the opening of the EC banking market, especially at the retail level. The major beneficiaries of the "single passport" system will be the more efficient European commercial banks (including those in the EFTA countries such as Switzerland). In the coming banking shake-out in Europe, competition will be fierce and many banks will disappear. In anticipation of this, many European banks are merging.

The other areas of financial services are moving more slowly. In insurance, for example, cross-border sales of commercial fire, theft and auto insurance are permitted for large risks but not for individuals. Only national companies can insure individuals. [8] There are still significant restrictions on cross-border sales of life insurance. A directive granting a single passport for life insurance and commercial risk insurance sales is facing stiff opposition, mainly from Germany. U.S. firms see opportunities in Europe, especially in life insurance [9] but when the market is fully liberalized, U.S. insurers will almost certainly seek to establish a presence there.

The area of investment services (rules governing activities of securities firms and stock exchanges) is one of the few EC–92 initiatives which may fail. The directive is currently stalled over the issues of off-market trading [10] and capital adequacy rules for investment firms.

U.S. credit card issuers are concerned about proposed EC rules on protection of personal data. The proposed directive requires consent of all data subjects before data can be used and restricts transfer of personal data to third countries which cannot provide an "adequate level of protection." Member states are divided over the directive, with Germany pushing hard for strict rules. The data protection issue could be an important irritant this year.

The EC is concerned about reciprocity in the U.S. insurance market (some States discriminate against foreign companies in fiduciary requirements and taxation) and about language in the new U.S. banking reform legislation that, if not amended, may force European banks to convert their U.S. branches to subsidiaries at great expense.

---

[8] An earlier directive provided the right of establishment to service providers. Therefore, foreign subsidiaries may sell insurance.

[9] There would appear to be considerable scope for sales of life insurance in Europe. Per capita expenditures on life insurance premiums in Europe range from $13 in Portugal to $700 in the UK (EC average is $370 compared to $678 in the U.S.). Source: The Swiss Re Reinsurance Company.

[10] France and Italy support language banning off-market trading in stocks. The UK, Germany, the Netherlands and the Commission do not wish to abolish existing curb markets.

TELECOMMUNICATIONS EQUIPMENT AND SERVICES

The main purpose of the EC–92 telecommunications proposals is to open what has been a virtually closed market [11] enjoyed by the large public and private telecommunications authorities (TAs). The goal is to provide higher quality and greater variety of telecommunications services and equipment by liberalizing the market and providing a more consistent regulatory structure.

Voice communications (90 percent of the market) will remain the preserve of the TAs, at least for the moment. The EC has adopted a series of directives which open procurement of telecommunications terminal equipment, allow competition in non-voice communications (services such as e-mail, electronic data interchange and data communications), and set conditions for access by private service providers to the networks of the TAs. Two of these directives were enacted under the provisions of Article 90 of the Treaty of Rome which allows the Commission to take action against public monopolies that abuse their dominant position. [12]

U.S. companies will benefit from procurement liberalization, a move toward common standards, and the opening of the non-voice market. This segment should grow dramatically after deregulation in much the same way the U.S. market grew after the AT&T breakup. Several U.S. firms have moved to establish a presence in Europe to take advantage of the potential. Until the issue of reciprocity under the excluded sectors procurement directive is resolved, the extent of participation of U.S. exporters of equipment and services will be unclear.

TRANSPORT

By phasing out restrictive national rules governing road, rail, sea, and air transport, the Community hopes to reduce cross-border business costs and promote economic growth. In trucking, Brussels seeks to end cabotage restrictions; establish a freely-available EC license for cross-border haulage; harmonize truck taxes and excise duties on oil and gas; and standardize truck weights, dimensions, speed limits, driver qualifications and working conditions. Europe's stagnant rail sector will be revitalized by making the rail system more continent-oriented, upgrading lines for greatly increased use of high-speed trains, harmonizing of equipment and infrastructure and by rationalizing freight pricing. Member states will be required to open access to their rail lines to private carriers for a user fee.

Most of the directives in these areas have been passed, but because of member state reluctance, the Commission has had to include lengthy transition periods. U.S. transport firms established in the EC will be able to take advantage of these sweeping transport deregulation measures and U.S. firms in general will share in the benefits of a liberalized EC transport sector.

---

[11] In 1984, the UK privatized British Telecom and allowed a competitor, Mercury, to offer service. The UK later opened its market wider and Sprint is currently applying to supply full telephone services.

[12] France and others challenged the Commission's use of Article 90 in the terminal equipment directive in the European Court of Justice and lost. Another directive dealing with telecom services is also being challenged.

The EC's "open skies" program is an ambitious attempt to end the civil air cartels that have spelled high ticket prices and limited service in Europe for years. Directives that dismantle bilateral traffic-sharing agreements are gradually introducing competition and creating conditions for the entry of new airlines. The EC and its member states seek to rationalize Europe's inefficient and uncoordinated air traffic control system [13] and are developing plans to expand Europe's crowded airports. Resistance on the part of member states, particularly those concerned about the fate of their national airlines under "open skies," has been strong.

U.S. Government civil air negotiators will now have to deal with Brussels (which will be acting in the interests of 12 countries) rather than individual EC states. There will be considerable pressure from the EC to open new gateways in the United States and to allow for beyond rights and cabotage. U.S. airlines are better prepared to face the stiff competition which will come with "open skies." U.S. suppliers of air traffic control and communications equipment, terminal systems and computers should also do well, provided that the procurement market is open.

ENVIRONMENTAL POLICY

Under increasing pressure from Green movements all over Europe [14] the EC has increasingly focussed on environmental concerns and sustainable growth issues in pursuing the single market. The 1987 Single European Act gave Brussels competence in this area for the first time, but did not mandate establishment of an EPA-type body to enforce existing and new directives. [15]

The EC approach has been to develop rules governing the production of undesirable elements (air, noise and water pollution), the development of "safe" non-polluting products and packaging and the regulation of toxic waste treatment, shipment and disposal. Directives requiring procedures to deal with accident hazards and disposal and storage of toxic wastes are already in force. The EC has decided to adopt the U.S. principle of joint and several liability for accidents involving toxic wastes. Brussels has also adopted U.S.-level emission standards for small cars [16] and a tough requirement for large cars, buses and trucks which poses a major problem for the diesel engine industry. The Commission also seeks to set an EC-wide speed limit (there is strong German opposition to this). There are also directives dealing with landfill techniques, plastic and metal waste and treatment of non-toxic industrial and municipal waste.

U.S. companies, accustomed to tough EPA standards at home, will face few problems in adjusting to European rules. Firms in the toxic waste treatment and disposal business may find that EC con-

---

[13] Planes in the busy northeast air corridor in the U.S. can fly as close as five miles while flights in Europe must be separated by as much as 80 miles in dense corridors.

[14] As a result of the 1989 European Parliament election Green seats increased from 20 to 39. Green candidates received 15 percent of the total European vote in that election.

[15] Assuming the member states can agree on where to locate a European environmental agency, the body will, at least for the first several years, serve only as a collector of statistics.

[16] Passenger cars with a displacement of 1.4 liters or less make up 67 percent of the European fleet.

straints on cross-border shipments of hazardous materials limit opportunities in the Community.

Common Threads in the EC–92 Process

The Brussels bureaucracy has demonstrated considerable resourcefulness and flexibility in pushing through the single market program. Where rigid harmonization by means of directives proved unworkable, the Commission devised ingenious alternatives, as in the case of indirect taxes. Where member state fears arose that Brussels would attempt to micromanage social policy, the Commission has backed off. Irreconcilable conflicts have arisen in areas such as border checks on people and animals, voting procedures on sensitive social policy issues, and immigration policy. The Commission has tolerated "opt outs" or "two speed" formulas to deal with these issues. This approach, while allowing the 12 (and prospective members) to stay together, could result in a watering down of the original vision. Some of the elements which have contributed to the progress so far are discussed below.

POOLING OF SOVEREIGNTY

The Commission has been successful in allaying member concerns over loss of sovereignty as the single market process dismantles national regulations. This was accomplished in two ways. The Single European Act and the Maastricht Treaty on European Union now being prepared for ratification have helped to reduce the "democratic deficit," i.e., the perception that the people of Europe have no power in Brussels. Secondly, the inherent logic of the single market program has made a profound impression on even the most suspicious members. Lord Cockfield, the author of the White Paper has aptly described the process as a "pooling of sovereignty" rather than a loss of sovereignty.

DEREGULATION AT NATIONAL LEVEL AND REREGULATION BY BRUSSELS

EC–92 works because the dismantling of restrictive national laws that served as barriers to cross-border trade has unleashed powerful market forces. In general, Brussels has chosen carefully the areas to be governed by directive. The reregulation effort seeks to establish general principles only (e.g., the "essential requirements" that form the basis of CEN/CENELEC technical standards). Member states are free to devise their own laws and regulations provided they incorporate the essential requirements. This strategy has allowed Brussels to put its stamp on subjects which had been jealously guarded by the member states, including taxes, transport regulation, banking rules, and public procurement procedures.

CONVERGENCE

Perhaps the most powerful force contributing to the success to date of the single market effort is the pressure on member states, once market forces have been unleashed, to move toward harmonized direct and indirect taxes, and similar rules governing foreign investment, transport and environmental pollution. The urge to converge, for example will make it hard for one member to maintain substantially higher VAT, excise and company tax rates than other states. Shoppers will be attracted by lower indirect taxes and potential investors will move to the lowest-cost sites. Convergence will probably not work in some areas in which compromise is not feasible, such as ending all border checks on people and goods, or permitting off-market trading in stocks.

THINGS TO WATCH IN THE ENDGAME

The most important ongoing issue in the 1992 process will continue to be that of competency, i.e., who does what? The principle of subsidiarity [17] has served the Commission well, providing a guide to determining the extent of Brussels involvement in single market areas. The Maastricht Summit resolved serious differences of opinion concerning conduct of immigration and social policies. Another important sovereignty issue concerns voting in the Council of Ministers on single market directives. The Commission is seeking to maximize the use of qualified majority voting while some members insist on retaining unanimity for certain issues. The Maastricht Summit settled some of these problems. Proposed legislation in the areas of consumer protection, health, education, networks (transport, telecommunications, energy) and some environmental rules will be subject to qualified majority. Unanimity will be retained for culture and industrial policy proposals.

EFFECTS OF 1992—CHANGES IN THE LANDSCAPE

Even before the first single market directives were adopted, European companies began to anticipate reduced barriers to cross-border trade by engaging in a frenetic round of mergers and acquisitions. Mergers and acquisitions within individual member states rose from 100 in 1984 to 214 in 1988, mergers within the EC rose from 29 to 111 and international mergers in the same period rose form 29 to 58. A large percentage of the mergers within the EC during this early period were in the food business. Since 1988 there have been a growing number of alliances among small high-tech companies.

Foreign companies have moved rapidly in anticipation of the establishment of a single market. Japanese investment in the EC doubled between 1987 and 1990 and now totals over $60 billion (compared to $150 billion for the United States). Approximately 700 companies in Europe have Japanese ownership of ten percent or more. About 200 of these are in the UK where the climate for mergers and acquisitions is most favorable. Sweden and other EFTA countries are also aggressively buying into the EC in the belief that for purposes of standards conformity, rules of origin and public procurement it will be important to produce inside Community borders.

As the single market takes shape, the European consumer is also changing. The removal of barriers will stimulate increased travel and relocation for work. Tastes, fashions and trends will cross bor-

---

[17] This concept has its origin in the early history of the Christian church, when powerful bishops sought to share power with Rome. In the Treaty on European Union it means that Brussels will act only if the objectives of a proposed action cannot be achieved by the member states. Community actions are not allowed to go beyond what is necessary to achieve the objectives of the treaty.

ders more rapidly. In some market segments, pan-European life styles will emerge, allowing firms to take advantage of economies of scale in production, marketing, and advertising. EC–92 will not, however, result in the emergence of a lowest common denominator "European culture" with complete homogeneity of tastes.

How U.S. Firms are Dealing with the Single Market

U.S. firms interested in the European market have mastered the details of the 1992 program, determined which of their product/service areas will benefit most (or be threatened most) by single market directives, and are now implementing their strategies. Because of the way the market is developing, many companies see the need to establish a production, marketing, and research presence in Europe. For semiconductor companies, for example, the combination of EC provisions dealing with the chip rule of origin, [18] dumping and procurement make it difficult to compete in the EC market as an exporter. U.S. manufacturers of power generation equipment are seeking strategic alliances with EC manufacturers in order to avoid the restrictive content provisions in the excluded sectors procurement directive. Many U.S. firms see a need to produce locally in order to avoid difficulties posed for U.S. exports by expected delays in liberalizing the EC standards and testing and certification regimes.

For U.S. firms, the positive aspects of the move to an EC single market outweigh the negative prospects which stem from problems in certain directives and with the implementation process in general. U.S. companies will continue to monitor developments and will seek U.S. government assistance with major problems which may arise in the areas discussed below.

Fortress Europe or Not? Some Acid Tests

There are four areas to watch in the future. How they develop will determine to a great extent whether the open market the Europeans are building for themselves will be equally accessible for foreign goods and services. The 1992 directives, taken individually, are not meant to be protectionist and generally do not have that effect. In cases where the United States and other trading partners have found objectionable features in proposed EC legislation, the two sides have generally found an acceptable solution. An important exception is the TV Without Frontiers directive, which retains a local content provision which the U.S. film industry has found objectionable. In the case of semiconductors mentioned earlier, individual single market directives were not intended to affect U.S. exports adversely. However, when some of these directives are combined with changes in existing rules (e.g., dumping anticircumvention regulations and rules of origin) they have created the impression in the U.S. industry that a European presence would be necessary to compete in the EC market. This is why Intel chose to invest

[18] The EC rule of origin for integrated circuits considers a semiconductor chip to be European (and therefore not subject to the EC's 14 percent tariff) if the process of diffusion (etching the circuitry onto the silicon wafer) takes place in the EC.

in an EC production facility. An unknown number of other American businesses have felt the need to take similar steps.

IMPLEMENTATION OF 1992 DIRECTIVES

An EC directive does not have the force of law in a member state until it is incorporated into national law by the legislature of that state. Only about 50 of the 230 single market directives adopted by the Council have been incorporated into the laws of all 12 member states. Some of those incorporated have been accepted, but with derogations which reduce their effectiveness. Other incorporated directives have not been implemented, necessitating enforcement actions by Brussels. In those areas of great importance to EC trading partners, including government procurement and standards, foot-dragging by member states could greatly reduce the potential benefits of the single market for outsiders.

COMPETITION POLICY

The manner in which the EC implements the merger control regulations will affect the ability of foreign firms to make mergers and acquisitions in Europe. If the directive follows Treaty of Rome articles concerning abuse of dominant position (e.g., no blatant exceptions for national champions) and is not used in a way that discriminates against non-EC enterprises, U.S. firms will have nothing to complain about. The U.S. Justice Department and the Commission have recently concluded an antitrust cooperation agreement which provides for greater coordination in antitrust regulation. The agreement calls for increased contacts and exchange of information on investigations of business practices and proposed mergers. EC decisions on whether to block mergers will still be made independently by the Commission's task force on merger controls. Because of this, the agreement contains no dispute settlement mechanism for dealing with a situation in which a merger between two U.S. companies was approved by U.S. authorities but blocked by the Commission. [19]

AFTER NATIONAL QUOTAS, WHAT?

The way in which the EC has had to deal with national quotas against Japanese auto imports raises serious concerns for EC trading partners. The EC-wide arrangement which replaces those quotas is a grey area measure which may be very hard to displace in 1999 when it is supposed to end. Similar solutions may crop up in other important areas such as consumer electronics and office products which are now covered by national restraint measures. The auto arrangement has already raised the issue of how to treat imports of autos made in the United States by Japanese transplants.

---

[19] C&M International. *EC-US Business Report*, October 1, 1991. p. 3. The merger control regulation allows the EC to pass on mergers between two U.S.-headquartered firms if the combined turnover in the EC of these two firms is above a certain threshold (currently ECU 250 million, or $300 million).

INDUSTRIAL POLICY—AN END TO NATIONAL CHAMPIONS?

The most important area to watch is undoubtedly the continuing tug of war within the EC over implementation of the Commission's "new policy for industry." The two major elements of that policy of concern to U.S. companies are regional and structural aid and cooperative R&D policy. In the area of state aids, there appears to be a major difference between U.S. and EC views on what constitutes an unfair subsidy from the point of view of GATT rules. In R&D policy, U.S. firms will be watching closely to see the extent to which Brussels supports cooperative programs that operate relatively close to the market, i.e., fairly far down the continuum from the basic research programs common in the United States. In addition there is the problem of national industrial policies (such as those promoted by the government of Edith Cresson in France) that may not be consistent with the Commission's stated goal of ending support for white elephants. Concerns over the conduct of industrial policy surfaced at Maastricht, where Germany and the UK successfully turned back an attempt by France and Italy to shift decisions on EC R&D support to majority voting.

IMPLICATIONS FOR THE UNITED STATES

Successful completion of the single market program and non-protectionist implementation of that program will provide great benefits for the United States. A prosperous Europe will buy more from us. The efficiencies introduced by the reduction of barriers will lower costs for all firms operating in Europe and result in significant scale economies. European firms will become stronger and more competitive in the EC market as well as in our own backyard.

Major U.S. concerns in the areas of standards, testing and certification and procurement are moving toward resolution. Industrial policy, data protection, competition policy and implementation of the Community's social dimension will be among the important EC-U.S. issues of the 90s.

ECONOMIC AND MONETARY UNION

By Arlene E. Wilson *

CONTENTS

SUMMARY

The momentum towards monetary union is considerably greater now than in the first, unsuccessful attempt in the early 1970s. Growing convergence of inflation rates among the twelve European Community countries, the success of the European Monetary System in stabilizing exchange rates and the prospects of EC–92 all bode well for European monetary union. After being discussed for several years, monetary union is an important part, and, in fact, the raison d'etre, of the Treaty on European Union, agreed to in December 1991 at Maastricht, the Netherlands.

In economic and monetary union (EMU), as specified in the Treaty, the European Community (EC) countries would have an EC central bank, which would determine the EC's common monetary policy, and a single currency no later than 1999. Price stability is clearly specified as the primary goal of EMU. Although fiscal policies would remain the province of member countries, reduction of fiscal deficits is required before EMU goes into effect. The EC Council would determine exchange rate policy for the single currency vis-a-vis non-EC currencies. The transition to EMU would occur in three stages during which the EC countries would

* Arlene E. Wilson is a Specialist in International Trade and Finance, Economics Division, Congressional Research Service.

strengthen their coordination of economic policies, and begin institutional changes necessary for an EC central bank.

For the EC, monetary union would probably stimulate economic growth. After a single currency becomes effective, savings in transactions costs (by not having to convert one EC currency into another) would make the EC economy more efficient. Reflecting a common position, the EC would have a larger voice in international monetary policy coordination. The major cost is that individual EC countries could no longer use changes in monetary policy or exchange rates to adjust to country-specific economic shocks.

For the United States, the international role of the dollar and U.S. influence in international policy coordination would likely decline. But the magnitude of these effects are difficult to predict, and could range from marginal to potentially large. Those U.S. multinational firms operating in Europe would likely benefit from a stronger EC economy and from reduced transactions costs involved in a single EC currency, just as EC firms will. Although unforeseen events could deter EMU from becoming effective by 1999, at present the momentum towards EMU is strong, and it is much more likely than at any time in the past.

Introduction

At an historic meeting in December 1991 in Maastricht, the Netherlands, the 12 European Community countries agreed to a Treaty on European Union. The heads of state signed the Treaty on February 7, 1992, but it must be ratified by national parliaments by the end of 1992 to go into effect January 1, 1993. The Treaty amends the 1957 Treaty of Rome which established the EC.

The Treaty on European Union deepens the EC both politically and economically. Although the Treaty's main institutional changes refer to monetary union, the Treaty also includes steps towards political union. [1] Furthermore, the provisions on monetary union were, to some extent, politically inspired and have political implications. The radical changes in Eastern Europe, for example, probably hastened consideration of monetary union as a way to strengthen the EC. And monetary union is seen by many in Europe as an important step towards the ultimate goal of EC political union. For the most part, however, this paper focuses on the economic implications, especially for the United States, of monetary union.

The Treaty's provisions on monetary union are accompanied by provisions on economic union, which include requirements for limiting national budget deficits. Both economic and monetary union provisions are analyzed in this report.

Momentum Towards Monetary Union

Monetary union was not explicitly mentioned in the Treaty of Rome, which established the EC (originally called the European Economic Community) in 1957. The Bretton Woods system of fixed, but adjustable exchange rates among all major currencies was in

[1] The Treaty's provisions on political union are discussed in the next two papers in this volume by Roy Ginsburg and by Smith, Wallace and Woolcock.

effect at that time. Since the original six EC countries were part of the Bretton Woods System, stabilization of intra-EC exchanges rates was not a concern. More broadly, however, the EC was aimed at both political unification and market integration; consequently, monetary union was implicit in the long-term goal of the EC.

After problems in the Bretton Woods System became apparent in the late 1960s, the EC appointed a group of experts, headed by Pierre Werner, the Prime Minister of Luxembourg, to propose a plan for monetary union. The Werner Report, adopted in 1971, called for fixed exchange rates among EC countries within 10 years and a common monetary policy. Monetary union would be achieved in three stages. Coordination of monetary and fiscal policies was to be strengthened in the first two stages.

Initially, exchange rates were to be kept within designated margins of 2.25 percent against other EC countries in the Joint Float Arrangement (also called the Snake). [2] Although EC countries attempted to maintain these margins, fulfilling their commitments became increasingly difficult as a result of the oil crisis, the breakdown of the Bretton Woods System, and divergent policy responses of the EC countries. By the late 1970s, the system was no longer effective. The momentum towards monetary union faltered and the Werner Plan was never fully implemented.

The next attempt to stabilize exchange rates was the creation of the European Monetary System, which began operation in 1979. The primary goals of the European Monetary System were to reduce exchange rate fluctuations among EC member countries and to insulate EC countries from wide swings in the dollar's exchange rate.

A system of fixed, but adjustable, exchange rates was adopted. The exchange rate mechanism of the European Monetary System currently requires each participating country to limit its exchange rate fluctuations to 2.25 percent (6 percent for Portugal, Spain, and the United Kingdom) above and below its central rate, expressed in terms of the European Currency Unit (ecu), a weighted basket of EC currencies. All EC currencies except the Greek drachma currently participate in the exchange rate mechanism (Spain joined in 1989, the United Kingdom in 1990 and Portugal in 1992). Credit arrangements are provided for foreign exchange intervention by central banks and, if readjustment of exchange rates is necessary, both the deficit and surplus countries coordinate the realignment.

Considerable skepticism surrounded the establishment of the European Monetary System, given wide differences in inflation rates among EC countries in the late 1970s. And, in fact, exchange rate stability was somewhat elusive in the early years of the European Monetary System. Between 1979 and 1983, six realignments of currencies took place as countries attempted to maintain competitiveness while inflation rates continued to differ.

But the situation changed dramatically in the mid-1980s with a growing consensus among most EC countries that price stability was the most important economic goal. From 1983 to 1987, realign-

[2] In addition, from 1972 to 1973, each country agreed to keep its currency within a bilateral margin of 4.5 percent against the dollar (sometimes called the snake in the tunnel). This system ended in March 1973 when the EC currencies began to float freely against the dollar.

ments became less frequent as countries participating in the European Monetary System, especially France, attempted to reduce inflation levels towards that of Germany. [3] Countries other than Germany began pegging their currencies to the German mark, which became, in effect, the anchor for the system. The German Bundesbank (central bank) set the tone for monetary policy, which then had to be followed by other countries whose exchange rates were pegged to the German mark. Even though they lost monetary independence, the other countries found that price stability was politically easier to achieve in this way. Thus, exchange rates became more stable (no general realignments of currencies participating in the exchange rate mechanism occurred after 1987) and Italy reduced its margins from 6 percent to 2.25 percent in 1990. The success of the European Monetary System in stabilizing exchange rates and in encouraging greater economic policy coordination contributed directly to the current momentum toward monetary union.

FIGURE 1. Convergence of Inflation Rates

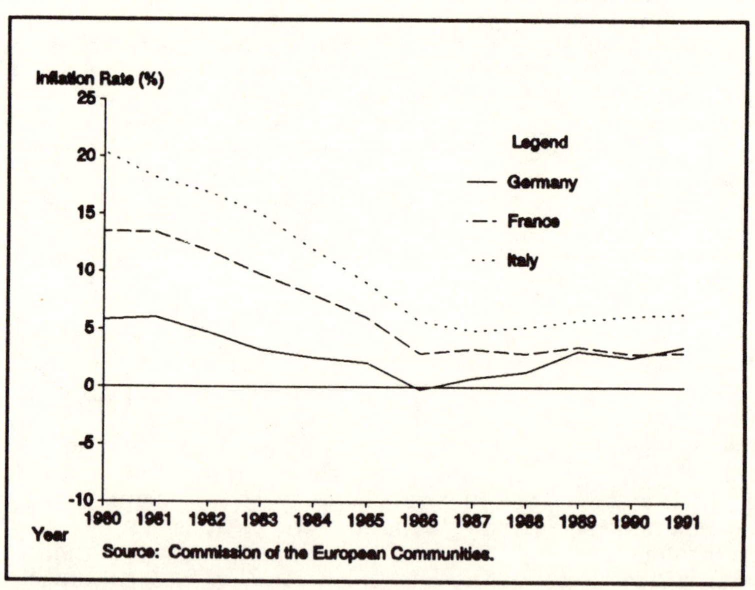

Another impetus for monetary union was the prospect of completion of EC–92. A monetary union is a natural complement to the

[3] Lambertini, Luisa, Marcus Miller and Alan Sutherland. *Inflation Convergence with Realignments in a Two-Speed Europe*. Discussion Paper Series No. 597. Center for Economic Policy Research. London, December 1991. p. 3.

EC-92 plan to integrate markets. With unrestricted movement of goods, services and people among EC countries, exchange rate fluctuations would be the only remaining trade barrier, especially since intra-EC trade is about 60 percent of all EC trade. Many analysts argue that the full benefits of a single market cannot be achieved unless potential exchange rate fluctuations are eliminated.

The scheduled removal of all restrictions on capital flows in EC countries by January 1, 1994 was also an important motivation for monetary union. It might be difficult for the fixed exchange rate system of the European Monetary System to maintain stable exchange rates if capital, especially speculative capital, was free to move in response to significant interest rate differentials among EC countries. The only way to eliminate interest rate differentials is by a common monetary policy, which requires an EC central bank. In other words, it is impossible for the EC to have full capital mobility, fixed exchange rates, and separate monetary policies at the same time.

In June 1988, the European Council approved the goal of economic and monetary union. The European Council appointed a Committee headed by Jacques Delors, President of the European Commission, and composed of 17 central bankers and other monetary experts, to study the concrete steps to achieve that goal.

The Committee released its Report on Economic and Monetary Union in the European Community (usually called the Delors Report) in April 1989. Like the earlier Werner Report, it outlines a plan for a common monetary policy, a common central bank and a single currency, to be achieved in three stages. Stage one focuses on strengthening monetary and economic policy coordination, while the transition mechanisms would be established in stage two. A common monetary policy and a single currency would be introduced in stage three.

The Delors Report provided no timetable for any of the stages, reflecting disagreement over the speed of monetary integration. West Germany, the United Kingdom and Luxembourg argued for a gradual approach (although the United Kingdom presented its own proposal), while France, Italy and Spain wanted to move more rapidly. The Delors Report emphasized, however, that the commitment to economic and monetary union should be made at the beginning of the process and the process should be considered irreversible.

In June 1989, at the Madrid summit, the European Council approved the concept of economic and monetary union as outlined in the Delors Report and decided that phase one would begin July 1, 1990. Since the proposed EC central bank is an institutional change that required changes to the Treaty of Rome, the Council authorized preparations for an Intergovernmental Conference (IGC), the forum for revising the Treaty of Rome, to be held from December 1990 to December 1991.

The Delors Report was the basis for discussion by the EC countries on monetary union. The main differences of opinion focused on the speed with which EMU was to be created, the steps creating a central bank, the procedures for coordinating budget policies, the possibility that some countries could elect not to join, and the responsibility for exchange rate policy against non-EC countries.

After much discussion and compromise, the Maastricht agreement was reached in December 1991 at the conclusion of the IGCs on EMU (and on political union). The central bank is be modelled on the German Bundesbank, with explicit priority to price stability, and is to be independent from national and Community authorities. Although France and Italy wanted a central bank established at the beginning of stage two (as did the Delors Report), the United Kingdom and Germany's position that it should be established at the beginning of stage three, when it would have full control of monetary policy, was adopted. France's argument for a single currency (and not fixed exchange rates) was accepted. Binding rules for budget deficits, supported by Germany and the Netherlands, are required. A date (1999 at the latest) was set for EMU so that it would be considered irreversible, as France and Italy proposed.

The United Kingdom was given an "opt-out" clause so that, although it signed the Treaty, it was not committed to a single currency. Denmark will be exempt from the third stage if a Danish referendum (which the Danish Constitution may require) does not support participation.

HIGHLIGHTS OF ECONOMIC AND MONETARY UNION

Considerable detail on the final shape, and the steps toward, monetary union are given in the Treaty on European Union.[4] By contrast, the economic part of EMU is not well defined. Generally, it refers to economic policies needed to complete EC-92 and monetary union. Responsibility for economic policies (other than monetary and exchange rate policies) remains decentralized among national governments, although coordination among countries, most notably limits on national budget deficits, is clearly specified. Monetary union, on the other hand, requires centralization of decisionmaking in the EC and the proposed European System of Central Banks.

ECONOMIC POLICY

A basic tenet is that economic policies would be based on the principle of an open market economy with free competition. Members would coordinate their economic policies within the Council, which will develop economic policy guidelines and monitor economic developments in each member country.

Several provisions are included to prevent fiscal imbalances from thwarting the goal of price stability. The EC would not be liable for the commitments of member states. National governments would not have overdraft facilities with the national central banks. Each member agrees to avoid excessive government deficits, defined generally as more than 3 percent of gross domestic product or government debt greater than 60 percent of gross domestic product. Budgetary developments would be monitored by the Commission, which would issue a recommendation, if necessary to the Council. The Council would decide if an excessive deficit exists, make recommen-

---

[4] The complete provisions on EMU can be found in Council of the European Communities and Commission of the European Communities. *Treaty on European Union*. Title VI. Luxembourg, 1992. p. 24-44; Ibid., *Protocols*, p. 148-195. An extensive summary of the provisions is Mapping the Road to Monetary Union. *Financial Times*, December 12, 1991. p. 5.

dations to the member country, and impose sanctions if the member does not rectify the excessive deficit. Such sanctions might include, among other things, requiring the member to publish additional information before issuing bonds or securities, or requiring the member to make a non-interest bearing deposit with the EC.

The Council may grant, under certain conditions, financial assistance to a member suffering severe difficulties caused by exceptional circumstances beyond its control.

EUROPEAN SYSTEM OF CENTRAL BANKS

In the final stage of EMU, the European System of Central Banks would go into effect. A federal structure similar to the German Bundesbank and the Federal Reserve System in the United States, the European System of Central Banks would be composed of the European Central Bank and the national central banks of the member states. [5]

Decisionmaking is centralized in the European Central Bank. The heads of state would appoint the six-member Executive Board, which implements monetary policy. The Governing Council of the European Central Bank, which makes broad monetary policy decisions, would be composed of the members of the Executive Board and the governors of the national central banks. In addition to participating in the formulation of monetary policy, the national central banks would assist in carrying out the functions of the European System of Central Banks.

Price stability is specified as the primary goal of the European System of Central Banks. After meeting this objective, the European System of Central Banks is required to support the general economic policies in the Community. The European Central Bank, the European System of Central Banks, and national central banks would be independent, and therefore may not take instructions from EC institutions or from any national government.

The tasks of the European System of Central Banks are to define and implement monetary policy for the Community, conduct foreign exchange operations, hold and manage official foreign reserves, and promote the smooth operation of the payment systems.

EXCHANGE RATE POLICY

At the beginning of the third stage, the EC would seek to speak with one voice on exchange rate policy towards non-EC countries. The EC's single exchange rate policy towards non-EC countries would be determined by the Council, acting on a recommendation from the European Central Banks or from the Commission, and after consultation with the European Central Bank. Such policy may consist of formal agreements on an exchange rate system or informal general exchange rate arrangements, such as the Louvre Accord, and may not compromise the goal of price stability.

[5] The European System of Central Banks gives more weight to regional representation, however, than does the Federal Reserve System. All national bank governors vote on major European Central Bank decisions, while only five of the twelve regional bank presidents vote on Federal Reserve decisions at any one time.

TRANSITION TO EMU

In stage 1, which began July 1, 1990, members agreed to remove restrictions on international capital flows and payments and to increase their efforts at economic convergence, particularly of inflation and public debt.

During the second stage, scheduled to begin January 1, 1994, the members would attempt to avoid excessive government debt and begin the process of making their central banks independent. The European Monetary Institute would be established to prepare for a single monetary policy. The European Monetary Institute would be managed by a Council consisting of a president (appointed by the heads of state), and the governors of the national central banks. The primary functions of the European Monetary Institute are to strengthen cooperation among national central banks and coordination of monetary policies among members, and monitor the operation of the European Monetary System. Monetary policy responsibility would remain with the national monetary authorities during the second stage.

Stage 3 could begin as early as January 1, 1997, if a majority of members have met the necessary economic convergence criteria, which are:

- Average inflation rate for one year no greater than 1.5 percent above that of the three EC members with the lowest inflation rate;
- Stable exchange rate (remaining within the normal fluctuations of the European Monetary System and not having devalued against any other EC currency) for two years;
- Budget deficit deemed to be not excessive using reference values set at 3 percent of gross domestic product and government debt at 60 percent of gross domestic product; and
- Average long-term interest rate no more than 2 percent above the three best EC performers for one year.

After reviewing reports from the European Monetary Institute and the Commission, the heads of state would decide, no later than December 31, 1996, whether or not a majority of members meet the criteria. If so, and if the heads of state decide that EMU is appropriate, they would set a date for the third stage to begin.

If no date has been set by the end of 1997, the third stage would automatically start on January 1, 1999. Before July 1, 1998, the heads of state would decide, based on reports of the Commission and the European Monetary Institute, which members have met the criteria. Those that meet the criteria would become part of EMU; others will have a "derogation" which will be reexamined at least every two years, or on request by a member.

When the third stage begins, the European Monetary Institute would be dissolved and the European System of Central Banks would go into effect. Those member states without a derogation shall, by unanimity, decide the conversion rates at which their currencies will be irrevocably fixed, and the rate at which the ecu will be substituted for the national currencies. The ecu would then become a currency in its own right.

How Likely is Monetary Union by 1999?

Achieving EMU by 1999 is not a certainty. EMU will be the result of a treaty among sovereign states which must be ratified and can always be amended, either before or after the third stage is reached. Given the strong momentum towards monetary union, though, it appears that only unexpected shocks, which by their nature are impossible to forecast, could make monetary union untenable.

Unanticipated shocks, domestic or external, that affect one or a few EC countries might make economic convergence difficult. For example, assume an East European country faces political or economic upheaval. Those EC countries bordering the East European country would likely be more affected than countries further away. Germany, in particular, due to its geographic, economic and cultural ties with Eastern Europe and the republics of the former Soviet Union, is more likely to be affected by shocks from Eastern Europe or the former Soviet Union than is the United Kingdom.

Another example is the strain imposed on economic convergence by German reunification. [6] West Germany's public debt rose to finance investment and consumption in East Germany, while the Bundesbank maintains high interest rates to restrain inflation. Even though Germany's increased demand for imports will ultimately stimulate other EC economies, in the short-run Germany's high interest rates are deflationary to other EC members, who must also maintain high interest rates to keep exchange rates fixed. Thus, desynchronized business cycles among EC countries, expected to be a short-term problem, are making coordination of economic policies difficult at present. Notably, though, the strain has not (as of late April 1992) caused a general realignment of exchange rates within the European Monetary System.

The Treaty recognizes the crucial importance of economic convergence in the success of EMU. The specific and clear convergence criteria which must be achieved before EMU becomes effective make it politically easier for countries to adopt policies which will meet these criteria. But Greece, Italy, Portugal, and Spain may have difficulty meeting the convergence criteria. Many analysts consider their participation in EMU quite unlikely by 1999. In 1991, the inflation rates of Greece (19.5 percent) and Portugal (11.4 percent) were especially high, although Italy, Spain and the United Kingdom, with inflation rates of 6.4 percent, 5.9 percent and 6.0 percent respectively, would also have not met the convergence criteria for EMU membership. (See figure 2). The government deficit as a percentage of gross domestic product in 1990 was 10.7 percent for Italy, and 20.2 percent for Greece, far above the convergence reference point of 3 percent. (See figure 3).

But there are many indications that EMU will go forward as planned. The political will among EC countries appears strong. In a Protocol to the Treaty, the members declare the irreversible character of the move to the third stage by signing the new Treaty. The relative shortness of the transition period reflects the willingness

[6] Ludlow, Peter, ed. *Setting European Community Priorities, 1991–92.* Center for European Policy Studies. London, Brassey's, 1991. p. 21.

FIGURE 2. 1991 Inflation Rates

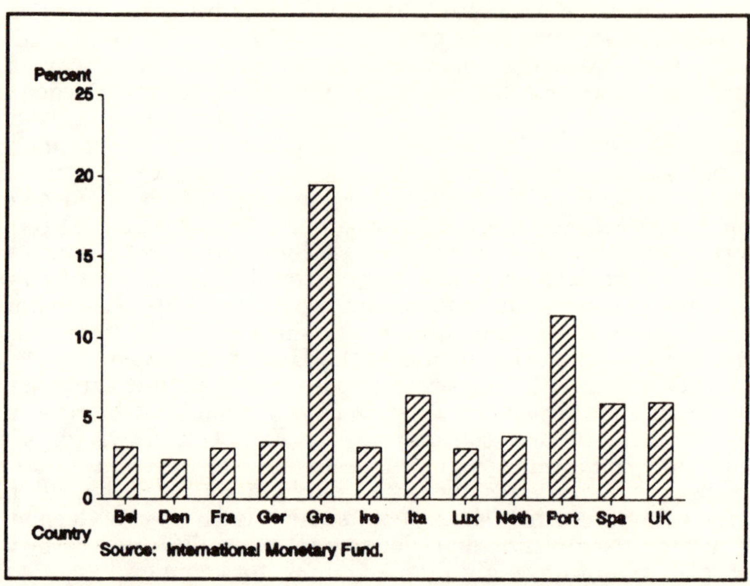

of EC members to pursue monetary union vigorously. Credibility of EMU is enhanced by the goal of a single currency, instead of fixed exchange rates, which are easier to abandon if the system is not functioning well.

The two-tier process in which some EC countries may join EMU in 1999, and others at some later point when they meet the convergence criteria, provides much-needed flexibility. Given the economic differences between Germany, the Netherlands, and France, on the one hand, and Spain, Portugal, Italy, and Greece on the other, such flexibility is realistic. (One remote possibility is that very few countries will meet the convergence criteria by 1999, and EMU, although officially in effect, will not be viable.)

Widening of the EC may also be facilitated by the two-tier process. Other countries could join the EC without having to participate in monetary union until they are ready. At the same time, some countries might be eager to join the EC because of the advantages of EMU. Austria, Switzerland, and the Scandinavian countries, in particular, may become EC members within a few years, and could likely participate in EMU when it becomes effective. Thus, the number of countries potentially eligible to join EMU at the beginning of the third stage could be greater than the current 12 members.

FIGURE 3. 1990 Government Deficit (or Surplus)

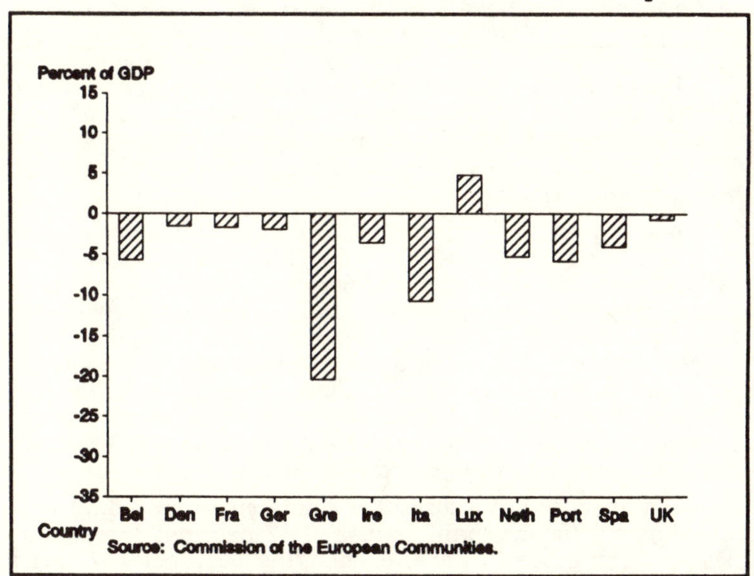

On balance, although EMU is not a certainty by 1999, the likelihood is far greater than at any time in the past. The conditions for monetary union appear more favorable now than in the era of the Werner Report. A great deal of economic convergence has already occurred, and the political will to support even more convergence appears strong at present. The major institutional changes, such as the amendments to the Treaty of Rome, and the decisions regarding the responsibilities of a central bank, are occurring faster than in the earlier attempt. The success of both EC–92 and the European Monetary System bode well for EMU.

Benefits and Costs for the European Community

When EMU becomes effective, each of the 12 member countries will relinquish sovereignty over monetary policy. Each country will no longer determine its own money supply, interest rates, or exchange rates, although each country's national bank governors will be represented in the European System of Central Banks. Monetary policy has a large influence on the economic health and social stability of individual countries. Giving up sovereignty in monetary policy has never been successfully accomplished by major countries with different histories and languages. In view of the importance of such a step, it is appropriate to ask what the major benefits and costs for Europe are expected to be.

The most important benefit is that EMU will likely stimulate EC economic growth. If EMU is successful, it will mean that coordination of economic policies has worked well, and economic convergence followed. Price stability will have been achieved, reasonable interest rates will have stimulated investment, and fiscal policies will have been responsible. These macroeconomic gains will likely provide the basis for renewed economic vigor by the private sector. According to an EC study,

> The larger part of the potential economic gains would not be the automatic results of the institutional changes. The full gains would require the concerted commitment of national governments, employers and employees as well as the Community itself to what amounts to a change of economic system. This is because systemic changes deliver only part of their economic benefits directly; in a larger measure the benefits would flow indirectly from policy changes induced by the new institutions and rules, and changed behavior in the private economy. [7]

Another gain is that the use of a single currency would be considerably more efficient than the use of 12 national currencies. As tourists have long been aware, exchanging currencies throughout Europe is generally costly and time consuming. Thus, transaction costs for consumers, and especially businesses, would be lowered by a single currency. Businesses would also save by not having to hedge against possible foreign exchange losses in their intra-EC trade and by simplified accounting requirements. For these reasons, businesses in the EC favor a common currency. [8] For the Community as a whole, the EC Commission estimates that savings from a single currency will total 0.3 percent to 0.4 percent of the EC's gross domestic product. [9] And elimination of the exchange rate risk within the Community would lower interest rates, stimulating economic growth.

EMU is expected to dramatically further the goal of EC political integration, since it reflects a new commitment to a European, not a national, future. Moreover, giving up monetary sovereignty is similar in some respects to transferring political power to the Community; consequently, the experience gained in establishing the European System of Central Banks may make political integration easier.

The EC would also benefit from a wider international use of the ecu when it becomes a common currency and from having a larger voice in international monetary coordination. [10]

The major cost of monetary union to individual EC countries comes from losing independence in monetary and exchange rate

---

[7] Commission of the European Communities. Directorate-General for Economic and Financial Affairs. One Market, One Money: An Evaluation of the Potential Benefits and Costs of Forming an Economic and Monetary Union. *European Economy*. October 1990, no. 44. p. 9, 11.

[8] Recently, however, some German business groups have expressed concern that the anti-inflationary policies of the European Central Bank may not be as strong as those of the German Bundesbank.

[9] Commission of the European Communities, One Market, One Money, p. 251.

[10] These benefits are discussed more fully in the section on implications for the United States.

policy. Individual countries will no longer be able to adjust to recessions or external shocks which affect EC members differently by increasing their money supply or allowing their currencies to depreciate. Instead, adjustment might have to occur through changes in nominal prices or wages, or in labor mobility, which is fairly low in the EC. Structural policies to encourage greater flexibility of prices, wages, and labor mobility are thus an important adjunct to monetary union. Fiscal transfers among EC countries may also be necessary if economic shocks differ among EC countries. In the United States, fiscal transfers are an important way of mitigating economic shocks that affect only one region of the country. Since the current EC budget is very low compared with that of the United States, however, fiscal transfers among EC countries may be more difficult.

It can be argued that the cost of losing independence in monetary and exchange rate policy may, in practice, be fairly low. To a considerable extent the EC countries have already given up monetary and exchange rate autonomy by following Germany's anti-inflationary policies, and through their participation in the European Monetary System. And some external shocks would affect all EC countries simultaneously, allowing Community monetary policy to deal effectively with them. Furthermore, the dollar-ecu exchange rate, which will remain free to fluctuate, may absorb some of the need for adjustment.

Another possible cost is that, during the transition phase, individual EC countries' attempts to achieve economic convergence by lowering inflation rates and budget deficits may be deflationary. But, with the relatively short transition period and the clearly specified timetable for EMU, the private sector may anticipate the future benefits of EMU when determining its business strategies. If so, its actions might mitigate the recessionary tendencies associated with convergence during the transition period. Indeed, this process is occurring as entrepreneurs anticipate the benefits of EC–92, stimulating the Community economy over the past few years.

EMU and the Multilateral Trading System

Over the postwar period, the United States has been a strong supporter of the multilateral trading system. Economically, the gains from multilateral free trade are greater than for regional free trade arrangements. Politically, multilateralism in trade tends to promote cooperation, while regionalism has the potential to be divisive, setting up competing, possibly even warring, blocs.

However, the United States has also strongly supported some regional initiatives. The United States encouraged EC integration since its inception as a way to inhibit future wars among European countries, and as a bulwark against a common enemy, the Soviet Union. And the United States supported the requests of Canada and Mexico for bilateral free trade negotiations, viewing them partly as a way station to multilateral liberalization.

EMU, by deepening the EC, may be the latest among several initiatives which might contribute to growing regionalism in world trade. Coming after the U.S.-Canada free trade agreement (in effect since 1989), current negotiations among the United States, Canada and Mexico (which may eventually be expanded to include the Western Hemisphere) and the difficulties in concluding the Uruguay Round, EMU may accelerate the trend towards regionalism. The EC may look inward as the size and depth of its own market increases. U.S. support for the EC may be tempered now by the loss of the Soviet Union as a common threat and the possibility that the EC may not keep its markets open. If so, U.S. and EC interests may diverge, weakening the U.S.-EC relationship.

On the other hand, it is not inevitable that regionalism replace multilateralism. Close links between the EC's financial markets and those of the rest of the world promote multilateralism. Since the activities of multinational firms are largely global, not regional, such firms are likely to support a multilateral approach to free trade. And U.S. exports are more geographically diversified than for most countries involved in regional integration. Europe, Asia and the Western Hemisphere took 30, 33 and 35 percent, respectively, of U.S. exports in 1990. By contrast, intra-EC trade is 60 percent of EC trade, while Canada and Mexico ship 70–80 percent of their exports to the United States. For the United States, at least, multilateralism appears to have more benefits than regionalism. Regional integration in the Far East may be hindered by the widespread concern of many Asian countries about potential economic and political domination by Japan. Finally, regionalism and multilateralism are not mutually exclusive; they can coexist with each other. And sometimes regionalism can stimulate multilateralism by breaking ground in difficult areas, such as investment and services.

Implications for the United States

International Role of the Dollar

At present, the dollar remains the most widely used currency in international trade and finance. Many internationally traded goods, such as oil, are priced, and paid for, in dollars. Bank loans and bonds often are denominated in dollars. The dollar is often an intermediary when selling one foreign currency and buying another, as, for example, when a bank first buys dollars with German marks and then sells dollars for French francs. Similarly, foreign central banks intervening in the foreign exchange market may use dollars for transactions from one foreign currency to another. Many central banks, corporations, banks and individuals hold dollar balances as reserves, due to their widespread acceptability in trade and finance.

The dollar's international role is based on the strength of the U.S. economy, the large size of U.S. international trade and investment flows, the breadth and depth of U.S. financial markets, the lack of exchange controls on international flows of funds, and the perception of the United States as a safe haven. Over much of the postwar period, price and exchange rate stability in the United States contributed substantially toward the U.S. dollar's international role.

The EC, combined with monetary union, will rival the United States in many aspects. With a 1990 population of 345 million and gross national product of $6 trillion, the EC countries combined exceeded the U.S. population of 250 million and gross national product of $5.5 trillion. EC 1990 exports of goods and services to non-EC countries were about $700 billion, also considerably greater than U.S. exports of goods and services of $535 billion. EC financial integration has progressed dramatically with EC–92, and capital controls in the EC are being removed. The goal of price stability is clearly specified in EMU. The perception of the United States as a safe haven might be the only way in which the EC will continue to lag behind the United States.

The extent to which the dollar's role might decline when the third stage of EMU begins is difficult to estimate. Although still predominant, the dollar's international role has been declining in recent years, while the German mark and, to a lesser extent the yen, have been growing in importance. Use of the ecu might speed up this trend, especially since it will be backed by strong anti-inflationary policies. And the international role of the ecu has been enhanced by the decisions of Norway, Sweden and Finland to link their currencies to the ecu in 1990 and 1991.

If EMU speeds up the decline of the dollar as an international currency, the process of selling dollars to buy ecus might result in dollar depreciation. Such dollar sales could be gradual, having a marginal effect on the dollar at any one time, and would perhaps be swamped by broader economic developments. One concern, though, is the "dollar overhang" (foreign exchange reserves currently held by individual EC central banks), estimated at about $300 billion, [11] of which perhaps $180 billion is in dollars. Fewer international reserves will be needed when EMU is implemented, since intra-EC exchange rate variability would no longer be an issue. Disposing of some of these dollars could lead to dollar depreciation, especially if private participants in the foreign exchange market sell in anticipation of central bank sales.

Another implication is that the United States would lose the seignorage gains (the ability to borrow money from foreigners at low or zero interest rates), which would then accrue to the EC. Such seignorage revenues to the United States are estimated to be relatively small now, [12] partly because most U.S. liabilities are interest-bearing.

Finally, even if the dollar becomes less of an international currency, it is unlikely to be a major problem for the United States. Until recently, the German mark and yen were not major international currencies, but this did not inhibit their international trade and finance, nor their economic growth.

INTERNATIONAL ECONOMIC POLICY COORDINATION

External relations with non-EC countries after EMU goes into effect are not covered in the Treaty. But since the Treaty provides that monetary and exchange rate policy will be decided by the Community as a whole (either by the European Central Bank or

---

[11] Computed by CRS based on data in International Monetary Fund. *International Financial Statistics.* March, 1991. p. 19 and 40.

[12] See Dornbush, Rudiger. *Europe's Money: Implications for the Dollar.* U.S. Congress. House. Committee on Banking, Finance and Urban Affairs. Subcommittee on Domestic Monetary Policy. Hearing, Implications of European Monetary Union. 102nd Congress, 1st Session. July 25, 1991. Serial No. 102–63. p. 52.

the EC Council), the EC will seek to speak with one, very likely stronger, voice in international negotiations. International negotiations will tend to become more tripolar between the United States, Japan, and the EC. Analysts differ regarding how much EMU could actually cause the U.S. leadership role to decline. To a considerable extent, this has already been occurring as the economies of Germany and Japan have grown, so some argue that EMU would have only a marginal effect on U.S. influence.

Currently, the major forum for coordinating monetary and fiscal policies is occasional meetings of the finance ministers and central bank governors of the Group of 7 (G–7) countries (United States, United Kingdom, Germany, France, Italy, Japan, and Canada). In practice, recent G–7 meetings focused mainly on exchange rate management, especially foreign exchange intervention. Relatively little coordination of monetary policies has been undertaken, and practically no fiscal policy coordination.

When EMU becomes effective, the four European central bank governors will be replaced by the governor of the EC central bank in these meetings. The United States, Japan, and the EC central bank governor (Group of 3) and possibly Canada (Group of 4) will coordinate monetary policy. EC countries who were formerly not part of the G–7 process would now be represented by the EC central bank governor.

With the G–3, it may be easier to reach agreement on monetary policies, since the EC countries will already have agreed on their position. On the other hand, an EC central bank governor will undoubtedly have a larger voice than the four national central bank governors did in the past. If the policy prescriptions of the EC and the United States differ substantially, coordination could become more difficult. Not only will the EC have a larger voice, but the process of negotiating with the EC, which might require substantial time to develop and reformulate its position, could become more complicated.

The effect of EMU on fiscal policy coordination with the United States is less clear. EMU leaves fiscal policies decentralized in each country, but requires close coordination among EC countries. EC institutional arrangements for fiscal policy coordination with non-EC countries are not yet decided. But if the EC is successful in coordinating fiscal policy among themselves, it is likely they would provide a united position, whatever the institutional arrangements, when negotiating with the United States, Japan and Canada. This again could reduce the U.S. leadership role.

EMU may mean that the EC is less interested in coordinating macroeconomic policies that affect the dollar-ecu exchange rate. At present, fluctuations in the dollar-German mark exchange rate can lead to wider spreads among EC currencies, creating tensions in the exchange rate mechanism of the European Monetary System. Such tensions could not occur with a single currency. Also, the EMU's emphasis on price stability may reduce the commitment of the EC to coordination and exchange rate stability. [13] And the EC

[13] Kenen, Peter. *EMU After Maastricht*. Group of Thirty, Washington, D.C., 1992. p. 106.

will become more self sufficient with EMU, and less interested in the dollar-ecu exchange rate. For the United States, however, the dollar-ecu exchange rate may fluctuate more than the dollar-German mark rate. As noted earlier, individual EC countries could no longer use exchange rate changes to adjust their domestic economies once a single currency is in effect. Some of the adjustment would then fall on the dollar-ecu rate. The United States might become more interested in coordinating policies that affect the exchange rate at the same time as the EC is losing interest.

EMU could also reduce U.S. freedom in determining its own fiscal and monetary policies. As has been occurring all along, international financial markets can, through capital flows, put pressure on other countries to adopt policies of the economically healthiest countries. If EMU is successful, it would reflect relatively low inflation rates and sound budget policies in the EC. If U.S. macroeconomic policies differed substantially from those of the EC, capital flows would quickly move toward the EC. All other things being equal, the dollar would then depreciate, worsening the U.S. inflation rate.

The transition to EMU could also be deflationary for the United States. Some argue that the attempts by Italy, Greece, Portugal and Spain to meet the convergence requirements before 1999 will require severe austerity measures, which might reduce economic activity in the EC, and ultimately in the United States. Others maintain that since the economies of these four countries are relatively small compared to France, Germany and the United Kingdom, economic retrenchment will have only a minimal effect on the United States.

U.S. influence in the International Monetary Fund would probably decline, but only marginally. If the EC members vote as a bloc, the EC would have a larger voice in International Monetary Fund decisions. But the United States would retain its ability to veto important International Monetary Fund decisions, which requires an 85 percent majority.

It is not clear whether the EC voting power in the International Monetary Fund would change. Voting power in the International Monetary Fund is determined by quotas, which reflect the size of each country's economy and international trade. Historically, membership in the International Monetary Fund has been open only to sovereign states. If this policy continues, each EC country would retain the same quota. If the policy changes, and the EC itself replaces the individual EC countries as a member, quotas would be recalculated to eliminate intra-EC trade, which would no longer be considered foreign trade. [14] Recalculating quotas is a complicated process heavily affected by political negotiations, so it is difficult to determine exactly how much the EC quota would decline. But, even if the quotas of the EC countries were adjusted to exclude 50 percent of all EC international trade, the EC quota would still be greater than 15 percent, [15] enough to veto major International Monetary Fund decisions.

---

[14] Quotas would also be recalculated if EC political union were achieved.

[15] Commission of the European Communities. *The Economics of EMU.* European Economy, Special Edition No. 1, 1991. p. 233.

U.S. BUSINESS FIRMS

A European Community enhanced by monetary union appears to offer more benefits than costs. A successful EMU will strengthen the EC economy which, in turn, will provide a healthier market for U.S. exports. The EC is already a large market for U.S. exports, taking 25 percent of all U.S. merchandise exports in 1990. It is likely that such U.S. exports will become even more important if EC economic growth is vigorous. It is important to note, however, that the United States will benefit only if the EC keeps its markets open.

U.S. multinational firms which pay bills or receive payments in national currencies of EC members will benefit by lower transaction costs associated with a single EC currency, just as European firms will. The need to hedge against intra-European exchange rate changes will disappear, also lowering costs for these U.S. firms. Companies such as IBM and General Motors likely will benefit from the single currency. At the same time, some U.S. financial firms, such as Citibank and American Express, will lose revenues currently associated with foreign exchange trading and hedging of EC currencies. [16]

CONCLUSION

Broadly, EMU will likely affect the United States in two major ways: the international role of the dollar will decline, and U.S. influence in international policy coordination will decrease. The magnitude of these effects, however, is difficult to predict and is quite speculative. EMU is still several years away, and although it appears likely now, unexpected developments could postpone the transition to stage three. Some analysts argue that EMU, when effective, will have only a marginal impact, at best, on the United States because it might only accelerate trends that have been underway for some time. Also, effects of EMU on the dollar or on the U.S. leadership position could be swamped by other global economic developments. Others maintain that the effects, even though not measurable, are potentially large.

Besides taking steps to support a healthy, low-inflation economy, there is very little the United States can do in anticipation of EMU. And, given the uncertainty about how much EMU will affect the United States, probably the only U.S. option is to monitor and analyze EMU developments carefully over the next few years.

---

[16] Putting Money on EC Currency; U.S. Firms See Both Sides of Coin in Unified Monetary System. *Washington Post*. December 26, 1991. p. D1–D2.

POLITICAL UNION

By Roy H. Ginsberg *

CONTENTS

INTRODUCTION

The Treaty on European Union, which establishes an economic and monetary union (EMU), also addresses political union. It introduces the idea of union citizenship and calls for a Common Foreign and Security Policy (CFSP). The new Treaty, which amends the 1957 Treaty of Rome, enables the European Community (EC) to act as a unit in most areas of international affairs provided that the members first agree on the principle of joint action and then on its implementation. The Treaty envisages a common defense policy that could lead to a common defense and would make the Western European Union (WEU) the EC's defense arm.

The foreign policy provisions of the new Treaty are evolutionary for the most part and do not suggest a quantum leap in EC institutional and policy development. The desire for a common foreign policy dates back to the early 1960s and gained momentum in the 1970s. This momentum has been sustained ever since. The EC has been an active foreign policy player throughout its history; between 1958 and 1990, it took 668 foreign policy actions that blended political and security objectives with its economic and diplomatic powers. [1] The Treaty could make the EC a more resolute foreign policy actor in areas in which the members agree to binding action, especially if the EC has a defense arm.

Unlike the foreign policy provisions of the Treaty, the security and defense provisions constitute a major development for EC integration. For the first time, EC members have laid out their defense objectives within the body's constitutional process. The idea of a defense community was broached, then aborted, in the 1950s. In 1987 the members agreed to formally consider joint action on political

* Roy H. Ginsberg is Associate Professor of Government at Skidmore College and Chairman of the European Community Studies Association of the United States.

[1] Ginsberg, Roy H. *Foreign Policy Actions of the European Community: The Politics of Scale.* Boulder, Lynne Rienner, 1989.

and economic aspects of security, although many previous EC foreign policy actions were implicitly security-oriented. The development of a common EC security policy, leading to a common defense, will, as in the case of foreign policy, ultimately depend on the extent to which the Europeans can agree on objectives. Despite its many fumbles and false starts in foreign policy, the EC is moving to complement and enhance the security of the common market with a common defense. The EC is the world's largest and richest group of states, yet it has not had the capability to defend its own interests outside the North Atlantic Treaty Organization (NATO) area. The Maastricht Treaty opens up the possibility for the EC to take foreign policy actions backed by military force. However, enlargement of the EC in the 1990s to include neutrals, such as Austria, Sweden, and Finland, could complicate the drive toward defense union.

Given the Treaty's relevance to the interests of the United States, the provisions for a common foreign and security policy (CFSP) will be analyzed. [2] Until very recently, many in the United States underestimated the EC's institutional and policy development. The United States began to adjust its policy toward the EC in the late 1980s by expanding consultations and areas of bilateral cooperation. The November 1990 Transatlantic Declaration not only reflected the heightened importance of the EC to the United States at the end of the Cold War, but it also laid out the objectives of U.S.-EC relations in advance of the EC's intergovernmental conference on political union. Neither able nor wishing to obstruct European integration, the United States may want to continue to engage the EC and its member states in the building of a post-Cold War international order. Such an approach may mean a greatly reduced role for NATO (and the United States) in the defense of Europe as the EC accepts a larger role for its own security.

A close EC-WEU relationship is likely to emerge in the next few years alongside NATO. However, a convergence of interests between NATO and the EC/WEU beyond the next five or six years cannot be assured. NATO and the EC/WEU will have a common interest in the defense of the traditional NATO area; yet the two memberships are not the same, and the thrust behind a merged EC/WEU will be the defense of European interests defined independently of NATO. Thus, future U.S. and European interests could diverge. As the EC-WEU link develops, the Conference on Security and Cooperation in Europe (CSCE) may prove a more lasting forum for retaining a U.S. voice in European security.

A much diminished U.S. role in Europe will have major implications for U.S.-EC relations. The key question before the United States and the EC is whether a new overall framework of bilateral relations can be built in the aftermath of the Cold War. Such a framework could enable the two to retain the mutual benefits of collective self-defense and economic interdependence, yet it would also allow them to maintain the flexibility necessary to cope with the emerging "new world order" and with their changing roles in that order. If a new relationship between NATO and the EC/WEU

---

[2] Much of this analysis is drawn from Featherstone, Kevin and Roy H. Ginsberg. *The United States and the European Community in the 1990s*. London, Macmillan, 1992.

can be constructed, perhaps in treaty form, and a more effective management of international trade and monetary affairs can also be achieved, then the U.S.-EC partnership of the 1950s may be revitalized to serve common interests in the 1990s.

EC Foreign and Security Policy: Background

The CFSP provisions of the Treaty on European Union should be interpreted within the context of the long-term institutional and policy developments of the EC because they spring from evolving processes and debates. The main foreign policy fora of the EC are as follows:

- The European Council—the biannual meetings of the EC Heads of Government/State.
- The European Council Presidency—the chair of the European Council. The chair rotates every six months.
- The Council of Ministers (also known as the Council)—the Foreign Ministers of the member states, aided by Political Directors.
- The EC Commission—the administrative/executive branch. It initiates/executes policy, represents EC interests abroad, and is advised by the Economic and Social Committee.
- The European Parliament—the only elected body of the EC. The Parliament has budgetary powers, participates in decision-making, and decides on enlargement and association agreements.

The following are milestones in the development of a Community foreign policy:

- The Treaty of Paris (1951) is the constitution of the European Coal and Steel Community (ECSC) and is the precursor of today's EC. It gave the Community a legal identity and provided it with limited powers to deal with foreign states on coal and steel trade;
- The Treaty of Rome (1957) is the constitution of the European Economic Community, now referred to as the European Community (or EC). This treaty gave the EC the right to act in international affairs on behalf of the member governments.
- European Political Cooperation (EPC; 1970). The EPC is an intergovernmental forum for foreign policy cooperation. EPC has been used to formulate and implement EC policies at the CSCE and at other international fora and to address such trouble-spots as the Middle East, Afghanistan, Cambodia, and Yugoslavia.
- The European Council (1974) consists of EC members' heads of government/state. It meets twice a year to resolve difficult questions. It allows the top political leaders to address foreign policy concerns.
- The Single European Act (SEA; 1987) was the first major amendment to the Treaty of Rome. The SEA brought EPC under the Treaty and set up a secretariat to coordinate EC foreign policy.

The Treaty of Rome spelled out the legal identity of the EC. Ten articles codify the powers of the EC to engage in diplomatic relations, international trade negotiations, association and cooperation agreements (with nonmembers), negotiations with states that are applicants for EC membership, and the work of international organizations in which the EC is a member or an observer. The key entree of the EC into the international system is the Treaty of Rome's provisions for a common external tariff. After joining the EC, members relinquished their powers to set external tariffs. The EC Commission handles all foreign trade matters, including the single external tariff of the common market.

The Treaty of Rome did not, however, expressly provide for EC foreign policy; yet by the late 1960s the EC was facing demands by nonmembers, as well as the pressures of international developments. It needed a mechanism that would allow it to act as a unified entity in an increasingly interdependent world. EPC was created for this purpose. It provided a forum for foreign policy cooperation among the EC members' foreign ministers and their political directors. Members made a commitment to consult before taking separate actions. Because no consensus existed at the time to bring such cooperation under the institutional umbrella of the EC, EPC remained a voluntary, intergovernmental grouping outside the Treaty. Its secretive and nonbinding procedures attracted member governments, which sought foreign policy cooperation but were not willing to give up sovereignty. EPC and the EC institutions eventually fused because of their identical memberships and overlapping interests.

With the passage of the Single European Act in 1987, EPC formally became a part of the EC decisionmaking process. The Single European Act, like the Treaty on European Union, codified past practices. Members committed themselves to work toward common foreign policies and to coordinate their positions more closely on the political and economic aspects of security. A permanent secretariat was established to provide EPC with both continuity, given the rotating Council Presidency, and an institutional base. The EC Commission became fully associated with EPC proceedings. The Single European Act allowed security issues to gradually be brought into EPC deliberations; enhanced the ability of the EC to take foreign policy actions; and ultimately paved the way for the Treaty on European Union's objective of a common defense policy.

EC foreign policymaking has not been uniform and, in many instances, EC unity has proved elusive. Yet when one compares the EC to other groups of states, the EC experiment with foreign policy coordination is unique and highly unorthodox. If anything, EC foreign policy cooperation is rooted in the experience and aftermath of World War II. Stripped of great power status, the European states eventually found that the only way they could reassert their influence in the world was through joint foreign policy action.

The Treaty on European Union

Following the agreement reached by the EC Heads of Government/State at the EC Council summit in Maastricht on December 9–10, 1991, member governments signed the Treaty on European Union on February 7, 1992. This paved the way for member state parliaments to consider ratification of the Treaty in 1992. [3] The Maastricht summit ended intergovernmental conferences on economic/monetary and political union that began in Rome in December 1990. Germany and France, with strong support from the EC Commission, broached the idea that the Treaty should incorporate provisions for political union to round out the EC's movement toward monetary and economic union.

The political provisions codify the rights of EC citizens; reform institutions and decisionmaking procedures; strengthen cooperation in environmental, police, and judicial affairs; and enable the EC to act in wider areas of international relations. Although the Europeans refer to these new areas of cooperation as "political union," a "United States of Europe" is not envisaged. The EC's legal mandate has been expanded into new areas, but member governments still retain many significant areas of sovereignty. Title V of the Treaty commits the EC to strengthen its security by establishing a CFSP. The gradual development of a common defense policy that may lead to a common defense is also provided for. The scope of EC action will be as large or as small as the member governments so choose. The wording of Title V is intentionally open-ended to give the member governments maximum room for independent maneuver.

FOREIGN POLICY

Most of the EC's foreign policy actions have a basis in specific articles of the Treaty of Rome, which established the European Economic Community, and are largely restricted to trade and commerce. These actions will continue to account for the majority of EC foreign policy actions because they relate to the day-to-day functioning of the common market and its effects on outsiders. However, the Treaty on European Union has expanded the traditional purview of EC foreign policy actions beyond the original design of the Treaty of Rome and has committed the members to binding joint action when they agree to act together.

Whereas the Treaty of Rome and the Single European Act restricted the areas in which EC members could take constitutionally-based joint foreign policy action, the Treaty on European Union opens the door to joint action in any area in which the member governments can agree. The extent to which the EC can branch out into new areas of foreign policy, such as arms control, will, again, depend on agreement. Based on over thirty-five years of foreign policy actions linked to the Treaty of Rome and later EPC, it would not be unreasonable to predict that the EC will continue to expand its foreign policy interests, not least because it is deeply and broadly connected to a wider interdependent world.

The European Council and the Council of Ministers will play a more decisive role in Community affairs. The European Council will decide which new foreign policy matters should be subject to joint action. If joint action is desired, the Council of Ministers will decide the scope, objectives, duration, and means for implementing the action. It is up to the Council of Ministers to decide whether

---

[3] Denmark and Ireland will also hold referenda on the Treaty's adoption.

voting will be by qualified (weighted) majority or by unanimity. If the European Council cannot agree on an area of joint action, or if the Council of Ministers cannot agree on the terms of implementation of a Council-approved action, the EC may be unable to act decisively. [4]

An individual member government can block consideration of a joint action or its implementation. During the treaty negotiations, the British pushed for unanimity on all foreign policy voting in order to protect the sovereign interests of individual member governments not wishing to act in unison. The EC Commission, Germany, and many of the smaller member governments were disappointed that qualified majority voting (QMV) was not adopted. They were concerned that without QMV, the EC would be unable to act with speed and resolution. The EC would certainly have had far wider latitude in making foreign policy had qualified majority voting prevailed. Instead, a dual system seems to have prevailed: QMV is used unless a member objects. The Treaty's foreign and security policy provisions are not a triumph of supranationalism, in which QMV is used, but of intergovernmentalism, in which unanimity can be used. In the supranational model, the European Council can decide an action by a qualified majority vote by which all member governments must abide. In the intergovernmental model, individual governments retain veto power and may either block a common response or the form that response may take.

The Treaty on European Union's decisionmaking purview and voting procedures are not a major break with past practice. Since the 1970s, the member governments, through EPC, the European Council, the Council Presidency, and the Council of Ministers, have decided which foreign policy matters outside the framework of the Treaty of Rome would be subject to common approaches. Veto power has not been regularly exercised because member governments do no want to appear divisive or obstructionist. Many Council Presidents have avoided unanimous voting by skillfully crafting decisions that could be adopted by QMV or by the consensus procedure. [5] By doing so, members are not forced to vote against a proposal.

At Maastricht, members agreed that deadlocks should be avoided to the extent possible. When decisions require unanimity, they agreed not to block the decision if a qualified majority emerges in favor of the action. Any member government or the EC Commission may submit foreign and security policy proposals to the Council of Ministers. In the event of an emergency, the Council Presi-

---

[4] Of all the EC institutions, the EC Commission and the EC Parliament are the most supranational, and they promulgate common policies more readily than the Council of Ministers. The new Treaty gives the Commission, the individual member governments, and the Council, but not Parliament, the power to initiate foreign and security policy actions beyond the traditional bounds of the Treaty of Rome. It also gives them the power to call emergency foreign policy sessions of the Council. Nonetheless, the Council Presidency, the European Council, and the Council of Ministers are likely to be the main initiators of foreign and security policy actions. The Commission and Council Presidency will keep the Parliament informed on foreign and security policy. The Council Presidency will consult the European Parliament on the mains aspects of policy to ensure that its views are taken into consideration. Members of the European Parliament may put questions to or make recommendations to the Council.

[5] Under the rule of consensus, a proposal is not brought up for a vote by the Council President until it is known that all parties concur with the wording.

dency may call a meeting of the European Council on its own or at the request of a member government or the EC Commission.

SECURITY POLICY

Title V of the Treaty on European Union commits the signatories "to strengthen the security of the Union and its member states in all ways." [6] It also states that CFSP "shall include all questions related to the security of the Union, including the eventual framing of a common defense policy, which might in time lead to a common defense." [7] Thus the scope of EC action will be as large or as small as the governments choose. The wording of Title V is intentionally open-ended to give member governments room for independent maneuver. Once member governments decide to take joint action and to implement it, they become bound to EC agreement. Until joint action and implementation are agreed to, the governments retain the freedom to act individually. The actual operation of a common defense policy will depend on many future developments that cannot now be predicted. The scope of EC action is potentially quite wide given the pressures on the EC to act as a single and cohesive state, and given the breadth of the EC's preexisting foreign policy experiences, interests, and actions.

The Treaty refers to the Western European Union as the defense arm of the EC. The WEU is the collective self-defense pact of nine current EC members that was established by the 1948 Brussels Pact. Of the EC members who are not in the WEU, Ireland is neutral, Greece has applied for membership, and Denmark may become an observer. The Council of Ministers and the WEU will determine the form that interinstitutional links will take. These new arrangements will be reviewed in 1996, the year the EC will most likely hold its next intergovernmental conference. Because the Brussels Pact expires in 1998, it is probably not a coincidence that the EC has chosen to consider its future defense before then. Article J.4 in Title V spells out the compatibility of the new EC/WEU link with NATO, and also provides for closer defense cooperation between two or more EC member states within the WEU and NATO frameworks.

In a declaration appended to the Treaty by the WEU members of the EC, the WEU agreed to a stronger role in the future defense of the EC. At the request of the EC, the WEU stated that it would implement actions of the EC that have defense implications. The WEU agreed to move its headquarters to Brussels, couple its meetings and venues with those of the EC, and establish close cooperation between its Secretariat and the EC Council Secretariat. The WEU committed itself to expand and strengthen military planning and cooperation in logistics, transport, training, and strategic surveillance.

Regardless of whether the objectives of the Treaty are fully realized, the EC will, for the first time in its history, have incorporated security into the European project. Even if the EC-WEU link does not result in the incorporation of the WEU by the EC before 1998,

---

[6] *Treaty on European Union,* Title V, Art. J.1.
[7] Ibid., Title V, Art. J.4.

a common defense is no longer taboo within the EC treaty context and European security will not necessarily be deferred to NATO as in the past. The Treaty's explicit linkage between the WEU and EC formalizes the longstanding ties between the WEU and EC—ties that include shared political leadership. This linkage issue has only come to the fore as NATO's monopoly over European security has been thrown into doubt by the Cold War's end.

The WEU will most likely be incorporated into the Rome Treaty later in the decade. Members of the WEU (except Ireland) are already committed to mutual defense through NATO and the principle of mutual military assistance in the event of war is longstanding. In addition, the WEU is not an integrated command; nor is there a European army, although the Treaty on European Union does not preclude such a development. The incorporation of the WEU into the EC would not require any additional new commitments on the part of most of the members but rather a reshuffling of institutional resources from the WEU to the EC. The incorporation of the WEU into the EC will enable the EC's NATO members to defend European interests outside the NATO area, thus giving the EC much wider latitude than NATO gives its members. [8]

Many EC-watchers are skeptical about the operational capability of the EC/WEU to launch a massive military action far away from Europe. The new EC/WEU link could be tested in the non-NATO European area, such as in Yugoslavia. Had the EC/WEU link been operational in January 1992, when Serbian forces downed a helicopter carrying EC peace monitors, the EC could conceivably have used the WEU if it had chosen to respond militarily. Similarly, had the new EC/WEU link been operational during the January 1991 Gulf War, the EC may have been able to play a more active military role in the allied operation. It also might have better coordinated its diplomatic and economic actions with the military actions of its member states.

Significance of the Treaty for the United States and U.S.-EC Relations

The new Treaty is an evolutionary document consistent with the EC's long-term development—a development long supported by the United States. If ratified, the Treaty would not appear to have any immediate adverse effects on the United States. The Treaty confirms the EC's already growing and active presence in the international system. Given the wide range of shared objectives between the United States and the European Community (e.g., peace in the Middle East, stability and growth in Eastern Europe and the new Commonwealth of Independent States, and promotion of international trade and development), a more coherent EC foreign policy presence should be welcomed by the United States. However, although a more independent and assertive EC will help spread the

---

[8] The Gulf War (1980–88) and the Iraqi invasion of Kuwait (1990) showed the Europeans how vulnerable they were to foreign security threats and how dependent they were on the United States to protect common Western interests. No doubt the EC's legal (and political) inability to act in the defense of Western interests during the crisis in Kuwait played a catalytic role in the decision to establish the WEU as the EC's defense arm. The EC's active attempt to mediate the conflict between the warring parties in Yugoslavia points to the strong desire to act responsibly in its own security interests in a non-NATO area.

burden of international management, the EC is likely to take actions from time to time that conflict with U.S. positions. The United States and the EC may, for example, differ over monetary policies, the speed and level of aid to the former Soviet Union, and the level to which agricultural subsidies should be reduced in the GATT negotiations. The United States must continue to adjust to the growing assertiveness of the EC in international affairs. Competition and cooperation in many areas of international relations will become part of the normal course of U.S.-EC relations in the 1990s.

The Treaty on European Union's provisions for a common defense policy, however tentative, are very significant for the interests of the United States. As the Europeans make progress toward a common defense, some in the United States and in Europe will question the utility of an American military presence in Europe, especially with the Cold War at end. Some Americans may question the need for and cost of leading NATO's integrated military command. Some Europeans may prefer to see the WEU, not NATO, become the major security framework for the EC.

The desire of Europeans to protect their own interests should not necessarily be viewed as either anti-NATO or anti-American. This desire should more properly be viewed as indigenously European and has strong links to European history and civilization. When viewed from this perspective, NATO and the EC represent two distinct dynamics. NATO was formed as a result of the Cold War, and has achieved its objective of deterring an attack on any of its members. The EC is a movement for European unity that transcends the Cold War. Its members view it as a means to enhance their power and influence in Europe and the world through joint actions.

In the Treaty on European Union, and especially in the WEU Declaration appended to the Treaty, the signatories took pains to link the WEU's development to the strengthening of the European pillar of NATO. [9] This position was championed by the British, the Italians, and the Low Countries. For the United States and many Europeans, the key question is whether the EC/WEU link with NATO is transitional or whether over time the two organizations will emerge as parts of a larger whole. Although both organizations are concerned with collective security, their compositions, histories, and functions are different. Maintaining links between NATO and EC/WEU in the face of changing security needs will test political will on both sides of the Atlantic. NATO and the EC/WEU could both serve as Western security organizations, but the growth of the EC/WEU security operation could cause some in the United States to question the U.S. commitment to European defense at a time when many believe Europeans could easily defend themselves.

For most EC members, NATO performs part of the task of providing for the security of the EC but cannot defend the interests of the EC outside the NATO area. The WEU is not regionally limited and could serve the members' security interests anywhere. The pri-

---

[9] The compatibility of the EC/WEU and NATO in operational terms poses many problems. For example, Spain and France are not members of NATO's integrated command structure but are members of the WEU. Therefore, one must question the extent to which the EC/WEU link can be properly viewed as a "European pillar" of NATO.

mary mission of the new EC/WEU link is to enhance the security of the EC; any complementarity of the WEU with NATO is likely to be a secondary objective of the WEU. Despite language in the new Treaty that connects the development of a EC/WEU defense policy with NATO, the main thrust is not to revitalize NATO but to create an independent European force that would defend EC interests in non-NATO Europe (at the least) and outside Europe (at the most). The EC/WEU link could potentially give the EC a much wider latitude of action than NATO provides.

In the 1980s and 1990s, the EC has started to fulfill the original vision of its architects, Jean Monnet and Robert Schuman, to become a full-blown economic and monetary union with substantially increased political powers. A strong movement now exists within the EC, supported by the Franco-German accord, to enhance overall economic security by developing a defense capability. Under the Treaty on European Union, closer military cooperation between two or more member states is permitted as long as such cooperation is conducted within the framework of the EC/WEU and NATO. But, the institutional compatibility of the proposed bilateral Franco-German unit, which would be tied to the WEU, with NATO is questionable because the basis of such cooperation would reflect only European interests. Although the United States might be associated in some way with such bilateral cooperation, the United States might prefer to see a strengthening of NATO capabilities.

An independent EC security capability would probably pose some problems for the United States, although such a capability could also be viewed as generally positive for U.S. interests. If the EC/WEU develops a rapid defense corps for use within the NATO area without U.S. participation, that force could take actions that affect U.S. interests without U.S. input. For example, the United States would probably be very concerned about a situation in which the EC/WEU became involved in a military conflict outside the NATO area and, as part of the conflict, an EC member of NATO came under foreign attack. In this scenario, the United States's NATO commitments could be activated by WEU/EC involvement.

The new EC/WEU link would not necessarily impede NATO or the fulfillment of its mission. NATO can continue to play a key role in the common defense of the alliance, while the EC/WEU takes on the primary responsibility for defending European security interests. However, if mishandled, there is a significant risk that NATO will collapse. If the WEU does formally merge with the EC by 1998, adjustments in NATO and in NATO-EC relations may have to be made to ensure the continued compatibility of the two organizations. Later in the decade, a U.S.-EC treaty may be necessary to adjust security ties to reflect developments within the EC. Such a treaty might build on the 1990 Transatlantic Declaration and might include provisions for better managing U.S.-EC commercial relations.

In sum, the CFSP provisions of the new Treaty are of moment to U.S. relations with the EC. The EC is attempting to adjust to the changing world order and to a new post-Cold War relationship with the United States by expanding the scope of its international operations. What does a more internationally active EC mean for the

United States? Many times in the past, the United States has sought—but not found—a common EC foreign policy position. In the post-Maastricht era, the EC is likely to increase the number of foreign policy areas in which it is able to act as a unit. Thus, when U.S. and EC policies are complementary, the United States will welcome a single EC voice. When policies clash, the United States will be challenged to reach agreement with the EC. Nonetheless, given the overall complementarity of many U.S. and EC interests in the wider world, the United States will most likely prefer to cooperate with a more unified and influential EC (even with differences), than a divided and ineffectual EC unable to influence external events.

THE IMPLICATIONS OF THE TREATY ON EUROPEAN UNION

Michael Smith, Helen Wallace and Stephen Woolcock *

CONTENTS

Introduction

This paper considers the implications of the intergovernmental conferences (IGCs) on economic and monetary union (EMU) and political union (EPU) for the relations between the European Union and its international partners. The IGCs were concluded in Maastricht with an agreement, the Treaty on European Union, reached in December 1991 and initialed in February 1992. The new Treaty, which when ratified during 1992, will create a European Union consisting of three columns, an extended and strengthened European Community (EC), common foreign and security policy (CFSP) and common internal security measures. [1]

In many areas it is too early to say exactly how the Treaty will impinge upon the Union's partners. This paper discusses the factors which will determine the future course of policy. It looks at how the Treaty will affect the trade, monetary and exchange rate, foreign, security and defence policies of the Union. It argues that, although there are indications that the Union may well be preoccupied with developments within Europe, it will still play a growing

* Michael Smith is Professor of International Relations at Coventry Polytechnic in Coventry, England. Dr. Helen Wallace is Director of the European Programme at the Royal Institute of International Affairs (RIIA) in London. Stephen Woolcock is Senior Research Fellow, European Programme, RIIA.

[1] For the text of the Treaty see Council of the European Communities and Commission of the European Communities. *Treaty on European Union*. Brussels, 1992.

role in the world. Given the high degree of interdependence that exists between the European Union and its partners, including in particular the United States, the balance between preoccupation and outward orientation of the Union will depend crucially on how it interacts with its partners and thus on foreign perceptions of the European Union.

Before addressing these questions it is important to emphasise the degree of interdependence that exists between the EC and its major partners. Whether in the field of trade, security, or defence, decisions taken in Europe and within the Union, will have an immediate impact on decision makers and public opinion in the United States or Japan, and vice versa. It is therefore not prudent to consider developments in European integration in isolation from decisions taken in Tokyo or Washington. Nor should the IGCs be seen in isolation from the other developments within the EC. For example, EC decisions on agricultural policy have immediate implications on the GATT trade negotiations and thus on transatlantic relations.

Although Vice President Quayle was no doubt misinterpreted by the European press when he was reported as suggesting that the absence of an EC concession on agriculture in the Uruguay round would affect the U.S. security commitment to Europe, such linkages have become more credible since the end of the Cold War. Certainly the proposals in the IGCs to create a European defence identity (EDI) had an immediate impact on the Washington security community. Likewise developments in other countries influenced the shape and pace of the IGC negotiations. The reform policies pursued by President Gorbachev in the Soviet Union and their consequences in terms of political change in eastern Europe and German unification also had profound implications for the course of the EC's negotiations.

Continuity and Change

The background to the Maastricht agreement on European Union was characterised by both continuity and dramatic change. Continuity was particularly marked in the field of economic and monetary union (EMU). There had, of course, been earlier plans for monetary union in the early 1970s, which were followed during the 1970s by the European "snake" and finally the European Monetary System (EMS) in 1979. The Maastricht agreement on EMU can be seen as the logical extension of the EMS, the internal market programme and the liberalisation of capital movements within the EC.

The current debate began at the Hanover European Council in July 1988, which asked the Delors Committee to produce proposals. At the Madrid European Council meeting in June 1989 the member states agreed that the resulting Delors Report provided a basis for preparing for an IGC on EMU and that the first of the three stage Delors process (participation by all member states in the exchange rate mechanism (ERM), full liberalisation of capital movements within the EC and surveillance procedures to encourage convergence and strengthen monetary cooperation) would begin in July 1990. The Delors Report set an agenda for the IGC which included an emphasis on independence for a European system of central banks and price stability. [2]

The element of change brought into the process was, of course, the reform and eventual collapse of the Soviet Union. This opened the way for reform and liberalisation in central and eastern Europe and German unification. The fall of the Berlin Wall and the end of the division of Europe created significant momentum for an acceleration of the EMU process and for the addition of a second IGC on political union. The rationale for intensifying integration in the EC included:

- the need to strengthen the EC as a source of stability in an otherwise rapidly changing Europe;
- the case for greater coherence in the external economic and political actions of the EC, in order to deal with the challenge posed by changes in the EC's external environment; and
- the exploitation of the "window of opportunity" offered by developments in 1989/90 to achieve the objective of German unification within European unification. [3]

The pressures emanating from political change in Europe were resisted at the time of the Strasbourg European Council in December 1989, at which Germany continued to resist an acceleration of the EMU process, although there was agreement to begin preparing for an IGC on EMU. [4] But by early 1990 the pressure for a political response from the EC was too great for those, such as the British, who sought to resist it. Agreement was reached to speed up the EMU IGC talks and to launch a second IGC on European political union.

The agenda for the EPU was set by a joint letter from Chancellor Kohl and President Mitterrand to the other heads of government a few weeks before the special Dublin European Council of April 1990. The Franco-German letter saw the objectives of the EPU as enhancing the democratic legitimacy of the Community, improving the efficiency of its institutions, achieving coherence in the actions of the union in economic, monetary and political spheres and defining of a common foreign and security policy. [5] This Franco-German initiative was aimed in part to ease strains caused by German unification (following Chancellor Kohl's failure to consult France on his 10 point plan for unification and prevarication in recognising the existing German-Polish border) and in part as a deal whereby France was to win a German commitment to bring the German mark (D-mark) into a single currency in return for a French commitment to greater political union. Had it not been for the political change in Europe the IGC on EMU would have followed a slower timetable and there might not have been a second IGC on political union at all. As it was the regular Dublin

---

[2] For a summary of the Delors Report see *Bulletin of the European Commission*, no. 6, June 1989.

[3] See for example the communique of the Dublin European Council meeting of April 28, 1990. "The point has now been reached where the continued development of the Community has become an imperative not only because it corresponds to the interests of the 12 member states but also because it has become a crucial element in the progress that is being made in establishing a reliable framework for peace and security in Europe."

[4] President Mitterrand had wished to see the IGC on EMU completed by mid 1991.

[5] For text of letter see *Le Monde*, April 12, 1990.

European Council meeting in June decided to convene both at the end of 1990.

Preparation for both IGCs was undertaken during 1990, but the EMU work started from the basis of considerable work already undertaken by experts. The IGC on political union was on a much tighter time scale and there was no consensus on what it should cover. When the IGCs were launched in Rome in October 1990 the EMU negotiations were already well advanced, even if the pace was too fast for Britain and for Mrs. Thatcher, the British Prime Minister, in particular. In contrast the EPU debate was only just beginning as regards, for example, the role of the EC in security and defence.

The Central Issues

A central issue in the whole negotiation touched the respective roles of the Council (read member states) and Commission and Parliament (read Community). This came to take the form of the "temple versus tree" debate. Advocates of the temple approach, such as the French authors and the British, argued that is was neither feasible nor desirable for the EC to absorb everything and that common foreign and security policy, defence and internal security issues, such as policing and immigration issues, should remain outside the formal Community structures. According to this view the "temple" of European Union should be supported by three columns: the EC, including economic and monetary union; a common foreign and security policy; and an internal security column. Of these only the EC would use Community procedures and be subject to European law and thus grant rights enforceable by the European Court of Justice. The other columns would be more intergovernmental.

The alternative view was that all of the policies of the EC should form branches attached to an EC trunk supported by common Community institutions and have their roots in European law. This seemed to be the majority view, in the sense that it was ostensibly supported by the European Commission and a majority of the member states. As the debate developed it became clear that even governments as *communautaire* as the Italian were less than convinced that such an extensive increase in Community competence was feasible.

At a crucial meeting of the member states in Dresden in May 1991 the French, supported strongly by the British, argued that the temple structure was the only realistic approach. As the alternative approach failed to convince, the minority view prevailed and was reflected in the draft Treaty texts produced by the Luxembourg Presidency for the June 1991 meeting of the European Council. After the Dutch took over the Presidency an attempt was made to reverse this decision, but the new draft Treaty text which aimed to do so was rejected in September 1991 by all member states except Belgium and the Dutch were obliged to go back to the Luxembourg draft. Only once this had happened could negotiations on the substance of each dossier of EPU begin in earnest. Thus the EPU negotiations started late and lost vital time during 1991. To make matters worse the Gulf crisis, which had begun in August

1990 with the Iraqi invasion of Kuwait, had the effect of raising serious doubts about the capacity of an EPU to develop an effective defence capability.

The Maastricht Agreement

ECONOMIC AND MONETARY UNION

The central issues of EMU were identified by the Delors Report. At German insistence the independence of the proposed central European bank and the constituent national central banks became a key question. Similarly as regards price stability the Germans, in particular the Bundesbank, argued that any European central bank would have to make this an absolute priority. The Germans and Dutch also stressed the need for economic convergence. The timetable for the whole process, and especially the move to stage three and irreversibly fixed exchanged rates, soon emerged as a crucial issue for, among others, the British. Indeed it was the commitment, made at the Rome launch of the IGCs, to move to stage two by the beginning of 1994 which precipitated Mrs. Thatcher's isolation and ultimately contributed to her removal from power. Although these were difficult issues during the negotiations, there was never any real doubt that agreement would be reached on EMU. This was true even though the British were still reserving their position and were later to seek a special agreement that would allow them to defer a full commitment to a single currency.

The Maastricht agreement on EMU built on the Delors Report's approach of three stages to a single currency [6] and the work of the Committee of Central Bank Governors among others. Stage 1 of the Delors process had in fact already been agreed at the Madrid European Council meeting in June 1989. With ratification of the new Treaty, stage 1 would also imply an irrevocable commitment to proceed to a single currency and a reinforced multilateral surveillance procedure.

As already decided in Rome in October 1990, stage 2 of EMU will begin on January 1, 1994. This will involve the liberalisation of capital movements with third countries, limitations on government access to privileged central bank finance, a commitment not to bail out countries facing mounting public debt and procedures to help bring debt of highly indebted countries onto the declining path needed to meet the convergence criteria of stage 3. These criteria were insisted upon by the Germans in order to ensure that only countries that had achieved convergence would be eligible to move to stage 3. The criteria are public deficits of no more than 3 percent of GDP, a total public debt of no more than 60 percent of GDP, inflation rates of no more than 1.5 percent and interest rates of no more than 2 percent above the EC best rate and finally, to have been within the narrow band of the EMS (2.5 percent band) for at least two years. If a majority of member states fulfil these requirements in 1997, they will move to stage 3, the irrevocable fixing of exchange rates. If not there will be two more years for member states to meet the criteria, but after 1998 the requirement

[6] In fact the Delors Report concluded that a single currency was not absolutely essential but was a firm commitment of intention.

for a majority meeting is dropped and those member states meeting the criteria will proceed.

A key question is how compliance with the convergence criteria will be determined and how much scope there is for interpretation of the quantitative criteria. The issue of who should decide was a controversial issue in the negotiations, but in the end the formula chosen was that the European Council, a political body, should decide, by qualified majority vote, whether a member state has done enough to meet the criteria, rather than the more technocratic Council of Finance Ministers, although finance ministers will clearly advise their heads of state and government. In the general debate on the convergence criteria there has been an assumption that the 60 percent debt-to-GDP figure is an absolute requirement, but in reality the wording of the Treaty allows for greater flexibility. What is required is to show that debt is on a declining path. Thus the fact that Belgium may not be able to reduce its current debt level to 60 percent by the end of 1996 does not necessarily mean that it will not be deemed to have met this criterion. In practice there is likely to be a strong desire to be inside and thus influencing European monetary policy rather outside but still having national monetary policy determined *de facto* by the European Central Bank (ECB) policy. This is one reason even a Conservative government in Britain is ultimately very likely to opt-in, and why the EMU Treaty with its deadline may provide a powerful incentive for economic convergence.

INCREASED POLICY POWERS FOR THE EC

The agreement on European Political Union (EPU) extends the competence of the EC into new fields. There is now new coverage of education, vocational training and youth, which is, however, primarily focused on promoting cross border contacts and exchanges. A policy on vocational training aimed at facilitating economic adjustment will be introduced. Culture, health and consumer affairs are also covered by provisions in the Maastricht text, although with only modest extension of Community competence in that, with the exception of measures that are already taken in these areas as part of the internal market programme under Article 100a, there is no provision for binding legislation based on qualified majority voting (QMV).

The areas in which Maastricht has changed things are those of the environment and research and development policy, where more QMV will apply once the Treaty is ratified. There was controversy over the chapter on industrial policy, sometimes called the "Cresson clause" after the French Prime Minister (see below). Efforts to extend QMV to social policy measures affecting working conditions, as opposed to health and safety provisions which have been subject to QMV since the ratification of the Single European Act (SEA), failed in the face of British opposition. The solution to this problem was found at the last minute with the other eleven deciding, as they had already done with the Social Charter in December 1989, to move ahead without the British. This meant that the "social chapter" became a curious agreement between the eleven outside the Treaty but following EC procedures, so that relevant legislation will not be applicable in Britain. At the same time the twelve agreed to a protocol which gave the eleven the right to use Community machinery to implement the social policy agreement among themselves.

The effort to increase the democratic legitimacy of the EC made less progress than some member governments, such as the German, and certainly the European Parliament (EP) itself, would have liked. Full co-decision, i.e. the requirement for EP assent to legislation, was the objective of the EP. In this it achieved only a partial success. In addition to the long established and rather weak *consultation* procedures (Article 189a) and the *cooperation* procedure established under the SEA (Article 189c), the new Treaty includes a (negative) right of co-decision (Article 189b). This means that the EP will in future be able to block EC legislation, if it wishes, but there will be pressure for the EP to compromise, since to throw out legislation could put back the cause of integration. Article 189b also introduces a Conciliation Committee based on parity between the Council and the EP in the event of a differences. The EP will also have the right to reject the slate of Commissioners proposed by the Council. This together with the procedural change to synchronise the term of office of the Commission and Parliament could well increase the political links between them and thus enhance the influence of the EP.

COMMON FOREIGN AND SECURITY POLICY

The second of the three pillars of the European Union comprises the common foreign and security policy (CFSP). This builds on nearly twenty years of experience with European political cooperation (EPC) and its first codification in the SEA. The CFSP as agreed at Maastricht is a significant advance on the EPC, because it puts the process onto a much more systematic and ambitious basis. Previously EPC rather depended on the voluntary engagement of the member states with the only sanction against non-implementation being peer pressure. But Maastricht leaves the member states in charge of foreign policy.

The European Council, the biannual meetings of heads of state and government, will set the broad guidelines for EC policy. The task of ensuring cohesion between the actions of the EC and CFSP falls primarily to the European Council. In pursuing these broad policy objectives, the Council of Ministers, acting unanimously, will determine in which areas joint action should be taken (Title V, Article J.8 of Treaty of European Union.) Proposals for areas of joint action can be made by any member state or by the Commission. This contrasts to the EC where the Commission retains an exclusive right of initiative, although under CFSP the Commission has won the right to be "fully involved with work carried out," having not been involved directly in EPC. In the agreed areas of joint interest the Council may now under certain conditions decide by qualified majority vote on the "specific objectives in carrying out" policy in areas of joint action, including "if necessary its duration, and the means, procedures and conditions for its implementation" (Article J.3). This will make it harder for individual member states to block decisions on foreign policy and is intended to lead to more effective and speedy decision making. The European Parliament plays no formal role in CFSP except that there will be an annual debate on progress towards implementing a CFSP and the Council Presidency must answer questions in the Parliament. The small secretariat of the EPC, established under the SEA, will also in the future have a more active role in supporting the CFSP.

The EC deliberations on defence and security were among the few areas in which the IGC on political union attracted the close attention of other countries, and in particular of the United States. Indeed within the EC there were difficult debates about how far a common security policy implied a common defence policy or common defence. This attracted U.S. attention because of its potential impact on NATO and in early 1991 the U.S. Administration became concerned about proposals to create a European defense identity (EDI). The Franco-German letter of April 1990 had referred to the need for a common policy on defence but it was not until proposals were made in late 1990 to strengthen the Western European Union (WEU) that the U.S., with the active encouragement of the British and Dutch, decided to enter the debate and seek to influence its outcome. The U.S. concern was that the EC would follow the French lead and produce fine rhetoric about European defence but that this would not be backed by any real resolve. An EC declaration that it was assuming responsibilities for defence would, it was argued, undermine NATO and domestic support within the United States for a continued U.S. commitment in Europe, with the result that NATO would be undermined without anything effective being put in its place.

In the field of defence the French effort to promote an independent EDI and the desire to integrate the WEU progressively into the EC clashed with the British and Dutch desire to avoid any action that might be seen as undermining NATO. The Maastricht text represents a compromise position and states that the CFSP "shall include all questions related to the security of the Union, including the eventual framing of a common defence policy, which might lead to a common defence" (Article J.4). On the WEU the text sees this as "an integral part of the development of the Union," but does not subsume the WEU to the guidelines of the European Council, as had been suggested at one stage. The compromise formula, with the WEU as a link between NATO and the EC, is used to diffuse the tensions caused by the possibility of an EDI undermining NATO.

In a separate declaration of the WEU its members agreed on the need to develop a "genuine European security and defence identity and a greater European responsibility in defence matters." It envisaged developing, in successive phases, the WEU as the defence component of the European Union, with the objective of strengthening NATO by creating a European pillar of the Alliance. The declaration refers to the WEU's preparedness "at the request of the European Union, to elaborate and implement decisions and actions of the Union which have defence implications." Specific concrete measures were agreed upon to help develop a close working relationship between the WEU and the EC including, for example, moving the secretariat from London to Brussels, a major concession from the French. In others words the WEU may be developed into the defence arm of the European Union but not at the expense of NATO. All the member states went to considerable lengths to stress the continued need for NATO.

INTERNAL SECURITY

The third pillar of the Union consists of provisions on justice and home affairs. This covers issues such as asylum, controls on external borders, i.e. the borders of the EC and common efforts to combat crime and drugs in particular. In contrast to the position in the EC the Commission has no right of initiative. This is shared with the national governments in most aspects of immigration and asylum policy. In the case of criminal matters the national governments have exclusive right of initiative. The Union can then adopt joint positions, take joint action and draw up conventions. The general rule on matters concerning justice and home affairs is that unanimity shall be required, although in certain circumstances decisions may be taken on the basis of a two thirds majority of the national governments. The fact that the provisions are outside the EC means that individuals have no automatic rights under European law and have no access to the European Court of Justice. Conventions may, however, stipulate that the European Court of Justice shall have jurisdiction to interpret their provisions and to rule on disputes regarding their application.

In other words this pillar of the Union remains outside the Community and retains a strong intergovernmental character. The agreement builds on the Schengen Agreement (named after a small town in Luxembourg at which it was reached) on the removal of frontier controls within the EC. The original signatóries were the Benelux countries, France, and Germany; Italy, Spain, and Portugal have now joined, but Britain does not participate. In general terms, however, the continental member states wish to see a removal of all frontier controls by the end of 1992, in line with Article 8(a) of the SEA. This is not accepted by the British who insist on retaining border controls as the most effective means of enforcing national immigration and asylum policies, and control of drugs.

The member states of the EC have also reached some pragmatic decisions on asylum policy. For example, the Dublin convention deals with the question of which national authority should deal with an asylum claim. The main purpose of the Dublin convention is to avoid possible abuse of the varied systems and multiple applications for asylum. There has also been some modest progress on common visa policies.

What Maastricht does is provide a strengthened, but primarily intergovernmental setting within which to conclude conventions or agreements in the fields of immigration and migration. All the member states have an interest in greater cooperation in this field, not least because large flows of migrants are seen to pose a difficult social and political dislocation in a number of EC member states. Large scale migration could also provide a conduit through which political instability in the Union's neighbouring countries could be channelled into countries such as France or Germany in the core of the EC.

On the other hand there are a series of difficult problems to be overcome before there can be much progress towards common policies. For example, asylum policies differ between countries. The rising number of asylum seekers is worrying all EC countries. Germany is facing a particular dilemma of what to do about the rapid increase in the numbers of people seeking asylum. Germany is attracting a high number of applicants because of its liberal asylum laws. But these laws are anchored in the German Basic Law (constitution). For historical reasons concerning the use made of asylum by Germans fleeing political prosecution during the Third Reich, any suggestion of change creates controversy. The German desire for a common European policy was in part related to a desire to bring about change in domestic policies through the introduction of a common EC policy. There was, however, also a genuine belief that common policies were needed for what is a growing issue of asylum and immigration in Europe.

Another example is in the field of visa policy where each member state's policies have been influenced by their established political relations with third countries, such as their ex-colonies. As a result it will be difficult to harmonise visa policy without there being implications for the general political relations between these countries.

RATIFICATION

The Treaty on European Union has to be ratified by all the member states and it is hoped that it will come into force on 1 January 1993. This poses one or two tricky problems in some of the leading member states. For once the difficulties are less likely to occur in Britain than some other member states. The pre-Maastricht debate in Britain was more intense than in any other member state. This combined with the "opt-in" for economic and monetary union and the "opt-out" of the social dimension seems to have largely succeeded in keeping the Europe issue out of the 1992 general election campaign and removed any difficulties a Conservative government might have had with its right wing voting against ratification. The only problem on this score was thought to be in the event of a very narrow conservative majority or a minority Conservative government which would provide an opportunity for the small minority of Conservative MPs opposed to "creeping integration" to reopen the question. The Labour Party, after a remarkable transformation in its position on the EC during the period 1987 to 1992, is likely to support ratification of the Maastricht Treaty.

In Germany most of the public debate about the IGCs has come after the event, because the Federal Government is judged by some to have failed to deliver on its promise of progress on political union in return for its commitment to take the D-mark into the single currency. In many respects this can be seen as a return to the *status quo ante* with regard to the caution of the Bundesbank and business community about a single currency. In the heat of German unification the Bundesbank lost some ground which it is now seeking to claw back. Committed federalists are also unhappy about the failure to make substantial progress towards redressing the democratic deficit by increasing the competence of the European Parliament. The federal states (Länder), whose support is also vital for agreement on the constitutional changes required to ratify Maastricht, are unhappy about their level of representation in under the new Treaty and threatening to make things difficult unless they get better representation. [7] Despite these difficulties Germany can be expected to ratify, because it looks as if the Länder will demand constitutional change in Germany rather than a change to the Maastricht text.

In France the Treaty provisions on European citizenship, and in particular those providing active and passive voting rights for non-French EC nationals in municipal elections will probably require a change in the constitution. This will not be easy at a time of considerable political uncertainty in France following the poor showing of the Socialist government in the March 1992 regional and local elections, the failure of the conservative opposition to make decisive gains and the rise of smaller parties such as the ecologists and the extreme right wing Front National (FN). If the Constitutional Court rules that a change of the constitution is required, a decision will have to be taken on whether to achieve this by parliamentary vote or by a referendum. The outcome of this is not certain but with all major political parties supporting it there should be enough support for ratification. Other countries, such as Denmark and Ireland may also have referenda to determine ratification. In both cases there are awkward elements in the internal debate. Despite these difficulties ratification should occur during the course of 1992.

The External Implications

THE EC AS A TRADING PARTNER

The focus of this paper is on what has changed as a result of the IGCs, but it is also worth noting that certain things have not changed. Trade and the operation of the EC's common commercial policy remain unchanged. This is important, given that trade policy has been the main external policy of the EC to date and one that has resulted in tensions with the Community's trading partners, including the United States. The core of EC trade policy is Article 113 (EEC) which provides for the Commission to make proposals to the Council on negotiations with trading partners and then to carry out the negotiations with a mandate from the Council. Decisions on the implementation of trade policy are already taken by qualified majority votes.

Likewise on investment policy. There is currently a split between national and Community competence on investment policy with a trend towards greater Community competence. For example, the Commission assumed the role of negotiator in the recent negotiations on "national treatment" within the OECD. Investment is, however, influenced by a wide range of policies and each time that the EC assumes competence for new areas its role in trade and investment increases.

---

[7] See *Financial Times*, March 14, 1992.

The IGCs also had an indirect impact on trade policy in the sense that one of the opportunity costs of the negotiating capital invested in them was that political leaders were distracted from other issues, such as the GATT round. This was *perceived* to be the case by the EC's trading partners, and in particular leading representatives of the U.S. Congress, in October 1990 when the European Council agreed to launch the two IGCs, but failed to agree on a negotiating position on agriculture for the Uruguay round ministerial meeting in Brussels in December 1990. The Brussels meeting had been intended to reach a political agreement on the Uruguay round. The failure to reach such an agreement has proved to be costly for the EC in a diplomatic sense. The EC has subsequently had to take much of the diplomatic flack for problems in the round and for the delays in the negotiations as a whole during 1990 and first half of 1991. The EC was perceived as being "inward-looking." Having missed the earlier timetable the negotiations subsequently ran into difficulties because of the preoccupations of the United States during the U.S. presidential elections.

TRADE POLICY BROADLY DEFINED

Trade policy is no longer mainly about tariffs. For some time EC efforts to promote competitiveness have been seen, especially by the United States, as "unfair" trade practices or policy. The end of the Cold War may mean that the market economy has won out, but there remain different types of market economy. Western Europe has traditionally been more interventionist than the United States, and the Treaty on European Union contains provisions which extend this approach within the EC. Seen from the EC's trading partners' point of view these have implications for the debate on what is "fair" trade.

The introduction of a formal provision in the Treaty on *industrial policy* was a major objective of the French. More liberal governments, such as those in Britain, Germany and the Netherlands resisted this attempt (as they have previous efforts over the past twenty years) to introduce broad discretionary powers to pursue EC industrial policy. A compromise was reached in which provision was made for an industrial policy (Title XIII) to "ensure that the conditions necessary for the competitiveness of European industry exist," but its implementation will require unanimity. [8] On the one hand, there has never been a unanimous view in twenty year-long debate about an EC industrial policy. This argues against the EC developing an interventionist policy. On the other hand, the economic liberals in the EC are concerned that, now that this provision is in the Treaty, there will be pressures to use it. The Treaty also increases Community competence in the field of *research and development* (Title XV) policy. [9]

As economic interdependence increases more and more domestic policy issues have an impact on commercial relations. In the internal market programme the EC has already extended its competence into many relevant areas. The Maastricht Treaty text also

---

[8] Council of the European Communities and Commission of the European Communities. *Treaty on European Union*. Brussels, 1992. p. 52.

[9] Ibid., p. 55.

extends the qualified majority voting provisions to *environmental policy.*[10] Environmental policy, along with competition policy in which the EC already has extensive supranational powers, is becoming a key issue in commercial policy. Maastricht thus confirms the trend towards Community competence in all important policy areas affecting commercial relations. The EC's trading partners will therefore have to come to terms with EC economic "muscle" in all important areas of commercial relations.

The *social policy agreement* reached among the Eleven, but without Britain, is also an expression of the West European "social market approach" to the market economy.[11] To be more accurate, it is about implementing a model of the social market economy already defined in International Labour Organisation (ILO) Conventions, in the Council of Europe's Social Charter drawn up in 1961 and the EC's Social Charter of 1989 (which was also adopted without the British). The SEA took a first step towards introducing the means to implement these principles through binding legislation by providing for qualified majority voting on health and safety at work (Article 118a). In the IGC on political union a majority of member states favoured extending QMV to working conditions and to sensitive issues such as the rights of workers to information and consultation in European works councils. Faced with a continued British veto of such efforts, the 11 decided to go ahead without Britain. In the past EC provisions have been a source of considerable tension with its trading partners. For example, U.S. companies with affiliates in Europe were bitterly opposed to the so called Vredeling proposals of the early 1980s to introduce provisions on consultation and information for workers, because they would have required U.S. parent companies to provide information to European employees and trade unions. The Social Action Programme, which aims to implement the Social Charter through EC legislation, includes a directive on information and consultation.

ECONOMIC AND MONETARY UNION

The Community's partners have had to come to terms with the increased economic power of the EC in the field of trade policy. The Maastricht agreement on EMU will mean that they will in the future also have to come to terms with a more powerful EC voice in the field of monetary and exchange rate policy. It is still too early to say exactly how significant the impact of EMU will be. In all probability its impact on the relative roles of the United States and EC in the international economic system will be gradual. This should make adjustment, both in real economic terms and in the perceptions of national policymakers, less painful. But the move to form EMU will confirm and consolidate the structural changes that have being occurring over a twenty year period, namely an increase in EC negotiating power and the decline in the U.S.'s ability to shape the rules of international economic relations. The gradualness of the change helps adjustment but it may mean that the underlying change does not attract the attention needed to avoid ten-

---

[10] Ibid., p. 59.
[11] Ibid., p. 196–201.

sions and false perceptions. Here the history of the "fortress Europe" debate is instructive.

When the EC adopted the SEA in 1987 it attracted little if any attention outside the EC. The consequences of it, including majority voting on internal market measures and the acceleration of the integration process led to the emergence, in 1988, of the "fortress Europe" debate. It was only then that the EC's trading partners realised the impact that EC–92 could have on market access in the Community. The absence of reaction in the EC's partners to the Maastricht agreement to form a single currency, with all the economic and political implications that this has for the member states, was even more surprising than their failure to note the significance of the SEA. The question is therefore whether this nonchalance is justified or merely short-sighted.

EMU will consolidate the existing trend away from the dollar as a reserve currency and could result in the ecu assuming a more important role. The degree to which assets will move from dollars into ecu is, however, difficult to assess. On the one hand, if the European Central Bank (ECB) follows the Bundesbank model, as many expect it will, the emphasis on price stability could mean that the ecu will take over from the dollar as the currency to which assets flow in times of uncertainty. On the other hand, some of the assets that are currently used to hedge against changes in European exchange rates could flow into the dollar; irrevocably locked exchange rates in the EC will remove the need for hedging between European currencies and increase the need for hedging between *the* European currency and the dollar or yen.

The creation of a single currency will tend to reduce the relative importance of the external component of the EC economy. Clearly adjustment problems will still be there, but will be internalised. In contrast the relative importance of the external component of the U.S. economy will continue to grow. This will reverse the position that existed in the 1970s, when the United States was able to take less account of the external component of economic policy when determining domestic priorities, than did the West European governments. This meant that the disruptive effects of rapid changes of exchange rates were greater in Europe than in the U.S. With a single European currency, to which non-EC member states could also tie their currencies, the effects of rapid changes in exchange rates may be more disruptive for the US. In the past this *dollar weapon* was used by the United States to secure cooperation from the Europeans in international economic policy coordination. [12]

In many respects it is the impact on the role of the EC in international economic coordination which will be most affected by EMU. Here a single currency will increase the weight of the EC in negotiations by virtue of the fact that there will be one monetary policy and one ecu exchange rate determined by the Council of Economic and Finance Ministers (ECOFIN). The EC's partners in, for example, the Group of Seven (G–7) could therefore face an agreed EC position which is likely to be less flexible than at present. For example, if one takes the situation in 1991, the United States was

[12] See also C. Randall Henning in this volume.

in a stubborn recession and the Administration wanted to stimulate the economy, not least because of the forthcoming election. It therefore tried to persuade the West Europeans to reflate. Now in 1991 this was hard enough, because the Bundesbank was concerned about inflation and more ready to raise rather than lower interest rates. With a single monetary policy in place the EC could be even less flexible. At the same time there will not be a single fiscal policy for the EC. The national ministers of finance will still be able to pursue reflationary fiscal policies subject to the criteria for budget deficits and debt as well as market pressures constraining profligate countries. The question is how will this discipline work in practice?

The picture that emerges from this assessment of the impact of EMU is that it will not have an immediate dramatic effect on the EC's partners, but that it will strengthen the existing trend towards a growth in the weight and importance of the EC in the international economy and thus in international economic cooperation. Once again perceptions of the impact of EMU may be as important as the reality of the impact. If U.S. domestic policy options, such as in running a large budget deficit are constrained by increased exposure of the U.S. economy to external factors, and if the EC fails to be sympathetic to U.S. requests for greater cooperation, there could be a political backlash in the United States against European preoccupations with their own interests. But this all remains hypothetical. The reality is that it is very difficult to be precise yet about what impact EMU will have.

U.S. policymakers have traditionally held a very sceptical view about the ability of the Europeans to "get their act together" on monetary policy. This view has persisted throughout the course of the IGC on EMU and may have been strengthened by the relatively easy access to Anglo-Saxon commentary on the feasibility of EMU. This has been both informed and sceptical. The continental European debate about EMU is also professional and informed, but has also a political dimension to it which tends to be underestimated or discounted by the Anglo-Saxons. But, as noted above, the political imperative has provided a momentum which has helped to overcome practical problems and thus contributed to the conclusion of a Treaty committing the eleven to the pursuit of a single currency, subject to the final decision in 1996 or 1999.

One final point concerns the important question of who determines the ecu exchange rate. The Treaty in Article 109 provides for ECOFIN, the Council of finance ministers, to determine participation in exchange rate systems. Once this broad political decision has been taken, it will be up to the ECB to deal with day-to-day management. But the text refers to "formal agreements" for exchange rates. At issue here is who decides on EC policy for meetings such as those of the G–7 where the Louvre or Plaza accords were reached? These agreements are not generally seen as "formal" agreements but understandings. This would suggest that the agreement reached in Maastricht was that any G–7 understandings of this type would be decided not by ECOFIN, the member states, but by the ECB. There are, however, some differences of view on how the Treaty is to be interpreted. If it is correct that the ECB will decide this would tend to strengthen the case of those who argue that after stage 3 the EC will be less flexible in multilateral negotiations on economic policy cooperation than the member states of the EC were.

COMMON FOREIGN AND SECURITY POLICY

The Maastricht agreement on CFSP is potentially of great significance. To date the EC has been an economic power and has not been able to articulate coherent foreign policy positions. If the objective of bringing greater coherence to the Union's external economic, monetary, and political actions is achieved, this would be a significant development. But Maastricht represents only a first step towards a CFSP; everything turns on how it is implemented and on the substantive issues that emerge in the international agenda.

The collapse of the USSR and the risk of economic and political instability on the European Union's eastern border are likely to be the first priorities for the Union's efforts to develop common policies. The fact that the instruments of foreign policy in this, as well as other regions, are increasingly becoming economic rather than political or military, also offers the EC a chance to play a more active role. Similar arguments apply to North Africa. In relations with the former Soviet Union, the EC (or some member states of the EC) are providing a large portion of economic aid. In relations with the central and east European countries it will be the new Europe agreements and the way they are developed that will play a crucial role in promoting or hindering economic and thus political stability in the region. The focus of the CFSP is thus more likely to be on promoting economic and political stability in the rest of Europe than projecting EC power in other regions. This could be seen as a preoccupation with Europe, but no one can be in any doubt that developments within the former Soviet Union and eastern and central Europe have global implications.

TOWARDS A EUROPEAN DEFENCE POLICY

The end of the Cold War has meant that security policy has begun to turn more on economics. This has opened the way to a greater role for the European Union in international security policy. But there remains the question of "hard" security issues, namely the projection of military power. In another initiative in advance of the Rome European Council meeting France and Germany argued that "political union must include a real common security policy leading over time to common defence." [13] A common defence policy is arguably still a key goal for the French who would like to see a greater independence for Europe from the US. For Germany the key was and remains the prevention of a renationalisation of defence policy. In order to prevent this and to keep the French on board Germany has been willing to seek joint action with France as a possible core of an EDI. France and Germany have continued to promote the idea of a common defence policy, as

---

[13] See *Le Monde*, December 9, 1990. The letter also suggested that the areas of joint action, in which policy is to be implemented by means of qualified majority voting, should be: relations with the (former) Soviet Union, central and eastern Europe, CSCE, disarmament negotiations and relations with countries bordering on the Mediterranean.

is illustrated by the second Franco-German proposal of October 1991. This was essentially a reiteration of the established Franco-German position, but also proposed a strengthened role for the existing Franco-German brigade.

In contrast Britain and the Netherlands have been at pains to avoid any action that might precipitate a reduction of the U.S. presence in Europe. All European members of the North Atlantic Alliance, including France, have continued to support NATO. Germany is also concerned to ensure a balance between its desire to maintain NATO and the compelling need to keep France involved in a defence policy at a European level. Hence the effort to present the development of an EDI as contributing to rather than undermining NATO.

In February 1991 the United States intervened in the internal debate by expressing concern about the impact that such an EDI would have on NATO. The concern was that the European rhetoric would result in a weakening of U.S. domestic support for NATO but would not produce any concrete results. Thus NATO would be "hollowed out," but nothing put in its place. Britain actively encouraged this U.S. intervention, in part because it wished to slow the process of integration down. The effect of the intervention was further to sour relations between the United States and France and thus to impede an effective dialogue about how to ensure a solid transatlantic security partnership in the post-Cold War era.

The Maastricht text strikes a balance between the desires of the French for an EDI and those of the Britain for placing priority on the transatlantic relationship. Institutionally the compromise has been reached by emphasising the WEU as the defence element of European Union, while seeking to ensure that it remains a bridge between NATO and the Union. This moves back from the immediate integration into the EC, as had been initially proposed by Italy in late 1990. Certain measures are taken to strengthen links between the European Union and the WEU and there are repeated references to the need to respect NATO and not to diminish its role in any way. It remains to be seen how the Maastricht agreement will work in practice, but the European Union is not about to develop a European defence policy which would enable it to project military power on anything like the scale of a superpower like the United States.

Once again the impact of EDI lies more in how it is perceived than in its substance. If it is perceived as making U.S. commitment to the defence of Europe less necessary this could well have an impact on the internal U.S. debate over how the U.S. commitment should develop. There is to be a review of the defence policy element of Maastricht in 1996, which will coincide with the WEU Treaty review. Before then the membership of the EC is likely to have been extended to include some EFTA countries. Austria, Sweden and Finland have already applied and neutrality is an issue in each case. It should be noted that the Swedes have not excluded the option of applying for membership of WEU and this is even being discussed in Finland. Enlargement will increase the heterogeneity of the European Union and make the likelihood of a common defence policy less rather than more likely.

ENLARGEMENT

Further enlargement of the EC is now inevitable and will affect the ability of the Union to pursue coherent foreign and security policies and will make the eventual development of a common defence policy for the whole of the Union much less likely. This could flow from an EFTA enlargement to include Austria, Sweden and Finland, which have already applied, with Norway and Switzerland possibly to follow, though of course Norway is a regular NATO member. The impact of EFTA enlargement is difficult to estimate in advance of negotiations, but the larger number of members, even if they are small, wealthy northern Europeans could make decisionmaking more cumbersome. The next intergovernmental conference scheduled for 1996 will have to address the institutional and political issues involved in making an enlarged Community effective.

The debate about enlargement tends to place the central Europeans, Poland, Hungary, and the Czech and Slovak Republic, in a second group of applicants. There is a danger that the interests of Germany and Britain in enlarging the Community to the east, albeit for different reasons, will create expectations that cannot easily be fulfilled. There is also an often unspoken assumption in the United States that it is the EC's duty to integrate the "central Europeans" and even perhaps some of the former Soviet republics. There is also a U.S. concern that the EC will neglect other NATO members that are not in the Community, for example, Turkey. The Turks have been seeking membership for some time but the majority of EC member states find this an unpalatable prospect, because of the size of the population, human rights problems and doubts as to whether it is a European country at all. To see the role of the EC as absorbing unstable countries into a stable and prosperous EC is, however, to underestimate the possible impact on either the process of integration or the EC's potential as an effective international entity.

The EC is probably most effective as a process of political and economic integration; and there is a case for arguing that this is what it will continue to be. [14] On the other hand there is a desire and probably a need within the EC to be able to articulate and prosecute its own foreign and security policies and thus act as a real partner for the United States. For Europe itself there is a case to be made that the EC should not deal with its relations with other European countries merely in terms of enlargement. The central and east Europeans will not be able to become members for some time. In the meantime there is a need to develop coherent policies which support foreign policy objectives, by promoting economic development and political stability in these countries through other Community policies such as the provision of access to EC markets. In order to achieve this the Union will have also to develop a more effective CFSP.

---

[14] Interdependence comes in here again, because if the Community approach to economic and political integration caught on beyond the EC itself, this would clearly influence the EC. In practice, however, the mutual recognition and supranational elements of the EC are unlikely to be accepted elsewhere.

Conclusions

Maastricht therefore represents an important step on the path towards an ever closer union in Europe. The success of the European Community has to date been mainly as a process of economic and political integration, but the political developments of 1989–91 have forced the EC to develop its ability to act on the international stage, to articulate and to implement common foreign and security policies. It is in the economic sphere, however, that the Union will continue to have the greatest impact on other countries.

In trade policy Maastricht confirms the trend towards an ever more comprehensive Community competence. Thus the EC's partners will face a common EC policy in new areas of trade policy such as the environment. The Maastricht agreement on economic and monetary union will mean that the member states will be working to establish a genuine monetary union. This could be *perceived* as another case of preoccupation on the part of the EC, especially if the ECB really follows the Bundesbank model and gives priority to price stability at the expense of what the rest of the world see as their interests.

The first step has been taken towards more common foreign and security policy. The possibility of recourse to qualified majority voting to implement policies in areas of joint action is an important development. Whether QMV will impart momentum to foreign policy as it did to the internal market process remains to be seen and will depend among other things on what substantive issues the EC will have to face in international relations. The focus of CFSP is likely to be on European issues and issues which are amenable to economic-type solutions. The European Union is not about to become a European "super state" and the prospects for a genuine common policy are even further in the future.

On balance therefore the Union is likely to be focused more on regional issues and economic issues rather than on global political or military concerns. In future the Union's policies and its relations with partners such as the United States will depend as much on how its actions are *perceived* and thus how its partners react.

EC ENLARGEMENT

By Karen E. Donfried *

CONTENTS

SUMMARY

Changes that have transformed Europe since 1989—the democratic revolutions in central and eastern Europe, the collapse of the Warsaw Pact, the radical arms reduction agreements, and the break-up of the Soviet Union—have presented the European Community (EC) with multiple opportunities and challenges. One of the most dramatic challenges has been the growing queue of potential applicants for membership in the EC. Formal applicants (Austria, Sweden, Finland, Switzerland, Turkey, Malta and Cyprus) have been joined by an increasingly eclectic group of aspirants. Norway, a colleague of Austria, Sweden, Switzerland and Finland in the European Free Trade Association (EFTA), is considering filing a membership application later this year. Poland, Hungary, and the Czech and Slovak Federal Republic have concluded unprecedented "Europe agreements" with the EC, and they have expressed their unequivocal desire to become full members. Bulgaria, Romania, Lithuania, Latvia, Estonia, and various members of the Commonwealth of Independent States may soon seek membership as well. This new pressure to "widen" EC membership comes as the EC is moving to "deepen" its own economic and political integration. The

* Karen E. Donfried is an Analyst in European Affairs, Foreign Affairs and National Defense Division, Congressional Research Service.

rapid transformation of the European continent is compelling the EC to take on both tasks simultaneously.

The questions surrounding the enlargement issue—whether the EC will expand its membership, and if so when and according to what organizing principle—remain open. Although the association accords with the three central European states have received considerable press attention, many believe the most likely new entrants to be the highly developed Austria, Sweden, Finland, and Switzerland. This paper reviews the prospects for EC enlargement, addresses the challenges enlargement would pose for the EC and, finally, considers the economic and political implications of enlargement for the United States.

The EC's Evolving Policy on Enlargement

Enlargement is not a new issue for the European Community. Since its inception in 1957, the EC has undergone three enlargements (Britain, Denmark and Ireland joined in 1973; Greece in 1981; Spain and Portugal in 1986), leading to a doubling of its original membership of six. What is new about the current situation is that a record number of states, some newly independent, are expressing interest in membership simultaneously. Seven states (Austria, Sweden, Finland, Switzerland, Turkey, Cyprus and Malta) have formally applied and at least four more (Norway, Poland, Hungary, and the Czech and Slovak Federal Republic) have indicated their interest in doing so. If the EC does open its doors to all potential applicants, the EC could grow to over 30 members.

Decisions Taken

The EC's Treaty on European Union states that any European state with a democratic system of government may apply for membership in the EC. Procedurally, an applicant's path to membership is straightforward. A country submits an application to the EC and, if that application is reviewed favorably by the Commission, the Commission undertakes negotiations with the applicant. Successful conclusion of these talks must be approved unanimously by the EC Council of Ministers and by a qualified majority of the European Parliament. The national parliaments of all twelve EC states and the parliament of the prospective member must then ratify the membership treaty. Applicants may also conduct national referenda to ensure domestic approval.

In contrast to these straightforward procedures stands the more byzantine reality of EC preferences regarding enlargement. To begin with, a state's application for membership does not activate an established procedural timetable. In fact, until recently, the EC had placed a moratorium on membership negotiations: no negotiations could begin until 1993, after the EC had put into place its 1992 single market program. This policy changed when the 12 member states met in Maastricht, the Netherlands in December 1991 to consider political, as well as economic and monetary union. The EC formally jettisoned its plan to delay membership talks until 1993 and issued a declaration stating that enlargement negotiations could begin in 1992. The start of those negotiations, however, is dependent upon the prior completion of a major overhaul of

EC finances. This condition makes it likely that talks will be delayed until the second half of 1992. [1] At the Maastricht summit, the Commission was charged with undertaking a study on enlargement to be submitted to EC leaders at their Lisbon summit in June 1992.

DECISIONS AHEAD

The Debate Defined

Three issues define the current debate within the European Community about enlargement. First, some EC members perceive a tension between "widening" the EC's membership and "deepening" its economic and political integration, and thus give priority to one process over the other. Second, some members are concerned that enlargement may affect the balance of power within the EC, in particular, by increasing the power and influence of the unified Germany. Third, no consensus exists as to what economic, political, and geographic attributes are necessary to become an EC member.

Deepening and Widening

The debate over enlargement is taking place against the backdrop of an ongoing process of deepening integration within the EC. The disparities, for instance, between the French and British positions on enlargement reflect divergent attitudes toward integration within the EC as much as they do sentiments toward new members. French officials worry that enlargement will slow EC integration. For the French, strengthening both economic and political integration in the EC has been a crucial counterweight to German unification, thus ensuring a Germany firmly imbedded in Europe. On the other hand, Britain has been the most enthusiastic about embracing Eastern Europe and expanding the EC. Prime Minister John Major said in January 1992, "I see no reason why we can't plan for a European Community which stretches from the UK right through to the Ural mountains in Russia." Major also said that a priority for Britain when it holds the EC presidency in the second half of 1992 will be widening the EC's membership. [2] Major's desire for enlargement may reflect, in part, the Conservative Party's lack of enthusiasm for deepening EC integration and hope that widening will thwart deepening.

The German Question

A second issue is whether enlargement would upset the fundamental balance of power within the EC. In the past, the partnership between France and Germany has been critical to the EC's success and ability to move forward. German unification automatically extended the EC eastward. While Germany appears committed to deeper integration and willing to cede more of its sovereign-

---

[1] The budget is a difficult issue for the Community. The EC has committed itself to substantial increases in fiscal transfers to its four poorest member states and intends to continue aiding eastern Europe and the successor states of the former Soviet Union. A draft budget broadly agreed on by the European Commission in mid-January 1992 did not include reforms of the common agricultural policy, which absorbs almost three-fifths of the EC budget. See Gardner, David. Brussels Targets Poorest States. *Financial Times*, January 20, 1992. p. 3.

[2] Timmins, Nicholas. EC Should Plan to Let in Russia, Major Says. *The Independent*, January 2, 1992. p. 1.

ty to the EC, some of Germany's EC partners worry that the united Germany will extend its own sphere of influence through eastern enlargement and come to dominate the EC. Germany already is the largest source of investment and aid for eastern Europe. One Spanish official lamented in September 1991: "We think the Bonn-Paris axis has been replaced by the Bonn-Berlin axis." [3] Those who share this belief cite as evidence Germany's campaign, in late 1991, for EC recognition of Slovenia and Croatia. Other observers argue that an enlarged EC would serve to contain German ambitions because Germany is less likely to exert undue influence over its eastern neighbors if those states become EC members. Furthermore, these observers doubt a Germanic voting bloc (consisting of Germany, Austria, central Europe) would coalesce in an enlarged EC because the central European states, in particular, harbor suspicions about German intentions based on their historical experiences.

Necessary Membership Attributes

Different attitudes toward enlargement reflect, in part, different conceptions of necessary membership attributes. What makes a given state "European"? Should all member states share certain economic, political, geographic, or ethnic attributes—and if so, what should those attributes be?

When contemplating whether to admit a given applicant, officials from the EC and member states accord the same factors different weight. For example, some believe that economic symmetry should form the bedrock of the EC and thus a certain level of economic development should be the fundamental prerequisite for membership. For the existing community of highly industrialized states, eastward enlargement raises the specter of a development community. For the rich states, enlargement may conjure up economic nightmares of having to subsidize new, poorer members, thereby lowering the standard of living for the EC as a whole. The EC's southern members share this skepticism toward eastern enlargement, but for a different reason: they fear competition for regional development funds. Another concern is that enlargement, when coupled with the free movement of people (a fundamental principle of the 1992 single market), could lead to a mass migration of Poles, Hungarians, Czechs and Slovaks (not to mention Turks, Bulgarians, or Russians) to the higher wage states of western and northern Europe. If priority is given to the economic measuring stick, only the EFTA states would seem likely entrants; central European states and Turkey would probably be ineligible to join the EC during the 1990s.

Another view, based on the EC's Treaty, is that a democratic political system is the only prerequisite for entry. If this were the standard, the list of likely newcomers would grow markedly longer. According to this yardstick, the most important factors are the existence of a multi-party democracy and respect for human rights. Those who give precedence to the level of political development believe that the primary goal of EC expansion should be to help anchor democracy and political stability in the newly independent

---

[3] United versus Rovers. *The Economist*, September 14, 1991. p. 60.

states of Eastern Europe and the former Soviet Union, as well as in Turkey. The driving force behind this political conception of enlargement is the hope that broad integration would make it inconceivable for European states ever to take up arms against one another again.

A final factor in the enlargement equation is geography, i.e., the definition of European as those states lying within the geographic boundaries of the continent. This factor favors the EFTA states, central and eastern Europe, and the European states of the former Soviet Union. Turkey, the great bulk of which lies in Asia, and the Asian members of the Commonwealth of Independent States—all states with large Muslim populations—would stand to lose if geography were to become an important qualification. This concern with geography reflects an equally fundamental concern with ethnicity.

Certainly, any definition of who belongs in the European Community would consist of some combination of economic, political, geographic and ethnic factors. Certain applicants receive high marks in every category. Austria or Sweden boast highly industrialized economies, advanced democratic cultures and are unquestionably "European." Turkey's prospects for entry vary, however, depending on which factor is stressed. The political goal of enhancing regional stability weighs in favor of Turkish entry, whereas economic indicators, cultural differences and geography weigh against it. Prospects for EC admission for the central and east European states lie somewhere in between these two extremes.

The Scenario of Incremental Enlargement

In light of this ongoing enlargement debate within the European Community, there are three theoretical scenarios for EC action on the enlargement issue: accelerated enlargement, incremental enlargement, and no enlargement. Accelerated enlargement (taking in all applicant countries at an expedited pace) and no enlargement represent the parameters of the EC's enlargement debate. Neither path is likely to be followed. Consensus does exist among EC members that Austria, Sweden and Finland should be granted membership, perhaps by mid-decade; the EC has no substantive objections to their applications. Opposition to enlargement centers primarily on expansion to the east rather than inclusion of the EFTA states. The balance of opinion within the EC seems to favor incremental enlargement.

Incremental enlargement, as the term implies, would entail increasing the membership of the European Community gradually, neither embracing all membership aspirants simultaneously nor categorically excluding them. The first phase of this enlargement scenario would likely involve welcoming the EFTA states as full members, while establishing loose economic and political associations with other membership aspirants, such as the central and east Europeans. Eventual membership in the EC for non-EFTA aspirants would be pegged not to any firm timetable, but rather would depend on the fulfillment of clearly defined economic, political and social requirements. Under this scenario, the EC could grant the central European states full political membership together with long economic transition periods, in keeping with the membership model of Greece, Spain and Portugal. This would result in a multi-tiered European Community with members and aspirants at different levels of participation.

The rationale for incremental enlargement is two-fold. First, proponents believe EC membership is critical for anchoring democratic stability throughout the central and eastern part of the European continent. According to this view, while the economic and political development of those states is not sufficient to welcome them into the EC fold immediately, the EC should extend an unequivocal offer of future membership. In support of this position, proponents cite the positive impact of EC membership on Spain and Portugal, where EC membership helped create a climate of confidence crucial for attracting foreign and domestic investment and proved to be a source of pressure on the governments to undertake necessary political and economic reforms. [4]

Second, supporters argue that incremental enlargement would force the EC to undertake radical and beneficial institutional reform. They see no tension between deepening and widening. From their perspective, widening makes further deepening inevitable. The larger the number of members, the greater would be the need both for a further extension of majority voting within the European Council (if not a renunciation of unanimity) and for increased democratic control through a more powerful European Parliament that would resemble a genuine legislative assembly. Jacques Delors, President of the European Commission, believes a EC of 20 or more members would need a strengthened government. He proposes that the heads of state meet at regular intervals each year and charge someone with forming the EC's government. That individual would represent Europe in all areas of EC competence. In the absence of such institutional reforms, Delors believes the European Community would degenerate into a simple free trade zone, forfeiting the economic and political gains of 30 years of integration. [5]

Critics of enlargement do not believe EC membership is a panacea for the problems facing the fledgling democracies in the east. They see a fundamental incompatibility between continuing the integrative process begun by the Single European Act and enlarging the EC eastward. From their perspective, the central and east European states, even if exempted from certain EC economic policies and granted aid for an extended period of time, would be hard-pressed to reach minimal EC standards unless the EC froze its integration process and allowed these new, less developed members to catch up. Joining the EC after 1992 will entail a much deeper commitment to political and economic integration than joining before

---

[4] Blum, Patrick. A Moment in the Sun for the South. *Financial Times*, December 27, 1991. p. 11.

[5] Buchan, David. Delors Signals More Powers for Brussels. *Financial Times*, April 8, 1992. p. 2; Buchan, David. Maastricht Deal Will Open Way to Enlarged EC. *Financial Times*, November 25, 1991. p. 1; Ash, Timothy Garton, Michael Mertes, and Dominique Moisi. Let the East Europeans In! *New York Review of Books*, October 24, 1991. p. 19; Foreign Broadcast Information Service. EC Commission President Delors Grants Interview. *Daily Report, Western Europe*, January 6, 1992. p. 8–11. For possible reforms of the EC presidency, see Big is Beautiful. *The Economist*, January 11, 1992. p. 48.

1992 did.[6] Furthermore, the cost of aid could be prohibitive. Critics point out that Germany, the paymaster of the EC, is already feeling financially strapped, particularly given the enormous cost of its own unification.

On a more general level, critics are pessimistic about the EC's ability to reform its institutions to allow for effective policy-making in a considerably larger EC. They point out that some enlargement enthusiasts (such as Britain's John Major) express reservations about strengthening EC institutions and relinquishing more sovereignty to the EC. Rather than revitalizing the EC and making substantive reforms inevitable, enlargement, opponents fear, would sound the death knell for European integration.

The Line of Aspirants

What is most striking about the states pursuing EC membership is their diversity. Yet three distinct groupings are discernible: the European Free Trade Association (EFTA) states, the Central Europeans, and the Southern Europeans. Admitting a handful of EFTA states first—the likeliest scenario—would set a precedent of organizing applicants into groups and admitting them in successive stages, perhaps over the next two decades.

The EFTA States

EFTA members, a mixture of neutral states (Austria, Finland, Liechtenstein, Sweden and Switzerland) and NATO allies (Iceland and Norway), are the most likely candidates for early entry into the EC. A first step toward this goal was taken on October 22, 1991, when the EC and EFTA agreed to establish a European Economic Area (EEA) in 1993 that will enable goods, services, capital, and people to move without restriction. The 19 countries will coordinate social, educational, environmental, and other policies. Special arrangements will cover energy, coal, steel, fish, and food. EFTA countries will also maintain their domestic farm policies. The EC conducts 60 percent of its trade with EFTA, thus making EFTA the EC's largest trading partner. With 380 million consumers, the EEA will be the world's largest free trade area.

EEA enthusiasts, particularly among EFTA's neutral states, extol the virtues of gaining the economic benefits of a single European market without having to participate in EC political and security undertakings. EEA critics argue that the circumscribed rights of political participation awarded EFTA states under the EEA accord force EFTA members to adopt EC legislation that they have no voice in creating. From the perspective of these critics, simply retaining foreign policy autonomy is too high a price to pay. This imbalance between economic benefits and rights of political participation may lead all EFTA states eventually to seek full membership in the EC.[7]

---

[6] De la Serre, Francoise. The Integration Dilemma: Enlarging and/or deepening the Community. *Futures*, September, 1991. p. 741; Sbragia, Alberta M., ed. *Euro-Politics: Institutions and Policymaking in the "New" European Community*. Washington, Brookings Institution, 1992. p. 14–15.

[7] Rodger, Ian. Austria: Big Step Towards Full EC Membership. *Financial Times*, October 9, 1991. sec. III, p. II; Dempsey, Judy. European Community: A Mood of Optimism Prevails in Vienna. *Financial Times*, June 25, 1990. p. 12; Barnard, Bruce. The European Economic Area. *The Journal of Commerce*, December, 1991. p. 19.

At the time the EEA was established, two EFTA states already had filed membership applications with the EC. Austria applied for membership in July 1989; Sweden followed in July 1991. Both states are concerned that they will become marginalized, politically and economically, if they remain outside the EC. Finland and Switzerland followed their example and formally applied for membership in March and May of 1992, respectively. Norway's Prime Minister, Gro Harlem Brundtland, has indicated her desire to apply for EC membership and negotiate alongside her EFTA colleagues.

The issue of "neutrality," once an insurmountable obstacle to EC entrance for the majority of EFTA members, has changed fundamentally. Pursuing an independent foreign policy seems much less inviolable a principle in light of the changes that have transformed Europe since 1989. Swedish Prime Minister Carl Bildt no longer objects to cooperating with other Europeans on foreign policy matters, although he maintains clear limits in the area of security policy: "what remains, what usually is the hard core of our security policy, is the fact that we are outside the military alliance systems. We have our own responsibility for the defense of the land, the sea, and the airspace. This will certainly not change." [8] Similarly, Finland's Prime Minister Aho has made clear that Finland could not join the EC if supranational decisions on defense policy were required. At present, the EC has neither a common foreign nor security policy. The scheduling in 1996 of an EC review conference on economic and monetary union, as well as political union, has created an incentive for EFTA states to join by mid-decade in order to influence the outcome. In the interim, many officials in EFTA governments are counting on continued EC hesitation to impose the binding rule of the majority or of a qualified majority in the areas of foreign and security policy. If that expectation withstands the test of time, each state would retain a certain degree of autonomy over those issues within the framework of the EC. Thus, at this juncture, the path to EC membership for interested EFTA states appears unobstructed.

The Central and East Europeans

Poland, Hungary, and the Czech and Slovak Federal Republic (CSFR) are on a much more circuitous path to EC membership—one that is littered with stumbling blocks. These three states passed a crucial junction on December 16, 1991, when they signed association agreements with the European Community. These unprecedented accords provide for regular top-level political consultations and the establishment of a free trade zone through a phasing out of trade barriers. Acquiring better access to EC markets was a key goal of these three states, particularly given the collapse of their largest existing market, the Soviet Union. During the negotiations, Poland, Hungary and the CSFR encountered stiff EC commercial protectionism, particularly in the sectors of steel, textiles and agriculture. Nonetheless, the agreements will lead to free trade over a ten-year period, with the EC lowering its barriers to

---

[8] Oschwald, Hanspeter. Carl Bildt: Swedes Feel Mature Enough for Europe. *Die Welt*, December 23, 1991. p. 7, as quoted in Foreign Broadcast Information Service. *Daily Report, Western Europe*, December 24, 1991. p. 18–20.

industrial imports more quickly (within five to six years) than the central Europeans will be required to do. Some restrictions in the area of agriculture will remain in place at the end of the ten-year period.

The so-called "Europe agreements" will involve the central European states in a much closer political dialogue with the EC, thus assuring central Europeans some degree of inclusion in the ongoing process of European integration. Unlike the EFTA states, Poland, Hungary and the CSFR desired a political as much as an economic association with the twelve states of the EC. Political ties to the EC should help alleviate central European concerns over the security vacuum in which they find themselves and over possible regional instability due to the breakup of the Soviet Union. [9]

Representatives of the three central European states stress that their ultimate goal is full membership in the EC. The preamble of the agreements acknowledges this aim, but does not commit the EC to achieving it. In the words of Pablo Benavides, the European Commission's chief negotiator for the accords: "This is not an entrance ticket. It's a kind of trial run [to see] if they would like to become members later on." [10] Rather than guaranteeing future membership, the Europe agreements serve two primary purposes from the EC's perspective: to foster the transition from command to market economies, and to encourage the establishment of stable, pluralistic democracies.

Beyond their immediate economic and political value to the three central European states, these agreements will serve as useful precedents for planned association accords with Bulgaria and Romania. The EC will also negotiate more modest trade and cooperation agreements with the newly independent states of the former Soviet Union. On January 9, 1992, Frans Andriessen, a senior EC official, said that few of the former Soviet republics could be considered candidates for more extensive "Europe agreements." He further warned that even the most European and economically advanced among them could not expect quick integration into the EC: "We should not overload the boat of relations with the EC." [11]

The Southern Europeans

Malta and Cyprus have applied for EC membership, but, among the southern European applicants, it is Turkey's bid for admission that has received the most attention. Turkey has been an associate member of the EC since 1963; in April 1987, it applied for full membership. In December 1989, the EC Commission responded to the Turkish bid by stating that Turkey's membership could not be considered until 1993, after implementation of the EC's 1992 single market plan. The Turkish government focused on the positive as-

---

[9] Buchan, David. Central Europeans Sign EC Accords. *Financial Times*, December 17, 1991. p. 2; Barnard, Bruce. EC Signs Pacts With Poland, Czechoslovakia and Hungary. *Journal of Commerce*, November 25, 1991. p. 3A; Buchan, David. Aim is a Circle of 22 Nations. *Financial Times*, December 18, 1991. sec. III, p. III.

[10] Hill, Andrew and Christopher Bobinski. EC Paves Way for Free Trade with E. Europe. *Financial Times*, November 24, 1991. p. 2.

[11] Foreign Broadcast Information Service. EC Prepares Accords with Former Soviet Republics. *Daily Report, Western Europe*, January 10, 1992. p. 3.

pects of the Commission's report: first, the report reaffirmed Turkey's qualification to become a full member at some point; second, it underscored the importance of creating a customs union between Turkey and the EC by 1995. [12]

Several concrete obstacles lie in Turkey's path to EC membership. First, Greece is likely to continue to oppose Turkish membership until disputes over Aegean sea and air rights and over the status of Cyprus are resolved in a mutually agreeable manner. [13] Second, the EC harbors doubts about Turkey's commitment to democracy and its respect for human rights. Third, some observers argue that Turkey's comparatively low level of economic development disqualifies Turkey from membership. According to World Bank figures, Turkey's per capita GNP in 1989 was one third that of the EC's poorest member, Portugal. Beyond these factors, some analysts sense a more fundamental bias against Turkey based on the perception that Turkey is too Muslim and not truly "European." [14]

The EC committed itself to the "possibility" of full membership for Turkey in the association agreement of 1963. Despite its long wait, Turkey in 1992 is not at the head of the enlargement line. Turkish officials argue that the economic potential and strategic importance of Turkey is great, that Turkey's inclusion in the EC could help stabilize the Balkans and Caucasus regions, and that Turkey could serve as Europe's bridge to the Arab world. Although many believe Turkey has no meaningful alternative to Western orientation and integration in the EC, the current geopolitical map of Europe is allowing Turkey to expand its ties to the Commonwealth of Independent States (CIS). Turkey and Iran appear to be vying for influence in the Muslim republics of the former Soviet Union. In February 1992, Turkey initialed a Black Sea economic cooperation accord to foster economic ties with Russia, Ukraine, Georgia, Armenia, Azerbaijan, Moldova, Romania and Bulgaria. [15] Turkey views its increased attention on Central Asia as a foreign policy course complementary to its desire for admission to the EC. While some observers believe these ties to other Muslim states could corrode the secular character of the Turkish state, other observers point out that the appeal of Turkey to Central Asia is precisely its Western orientation, both politically and economically. The balance of opinion in the EC does not favor Turkish member-

---

[12] Kuniholm, Bruce. Turkey and the West. *Foreign Affairs*, Spring, 1991. p. 41; Brown, John Murray. Turkey, EC in New Push for Customs Union. *Financial Times*, December 6, 1991. p. 3.

[13] In 1974, the island of Cyprus was divided when the Cypriot National Guard, led by Greek officers, seized control of the government. In response, Turkey invaded and the Turkish-Cypriots gained control of northern Cyprus. Turkey alone recognizes this self-proclaimed Turkish-Cypriot state which is protected by Turkish troops. Until Turkey and Greece resolve their dispute over Cyprus, it will remain an obstacle to Turkey's membership in the EC. For more on this subject, see U.S. Library of Congress. Congressional Research Service. *Cyprus: Status of U.N. Negotiations.* Issue Brief 89140, by Carol Migdalovitz. Turkish officials were angered when the EC received the Republic of Cyprus' application for admission. Turkey insisted that the Greek Cypriots had no right to request EC membership on behalf of the divided island (see Cohen, Sam. Turks Weigh Prospects after European Rebuff. *Christian Science Monitor*, July 24, 1990. p. 4).

[14] Kramer, Heinz. Turkey and EC's Southern Enlargement. *Aussenpolitik*, v. 35, no. 1, 1984; Haberman, Clyde. Turkey Remains Confident It Will Join European Community. *New York Times*, March 17, 1990. p. 7; Cowell, Alan. Turkey's Westward Yearnings. *New York Times*, July 12, 1987. sec. 4, p. 2.

[15] Cohen, Sam. Expected Strong Shifts in Turkey's Foreign Policy Fail to Materialize. *Christian Science Monitor*, December 17, 1991. p. 3; Ozal, Turgut. Turkish Model in a Triangle of Turmoil. *Washington Times*, January 20, 1992. p. E4.

ship during the 1990s, a reality which may encourage the further development of a distinct Turkish-CIS economic area with links to the EC.

EC Enlargement and the United States

The members of the European Community are essential economic and political partners of the United States. As a bloc, the EC is the United States' largest trading partner: total U.S.-EC trade in 1990 was $190 billion. In 1990, EC products comprised 19 percent of total U.S. imports, and the EC received 25 percent of all U.S. exports. Thus, changes within the EC are highly significant for U.S. interests.

The enlargement of the EC carries both economic and political implications for the United States. Economically, enlargement could affect the level of protectionism within the EC, the growth of regional trade blocs, and the speed with which a single European currency is introduced. A major political issue for the United States is how enlargement would affect progress toward a single EC foreign policy. In terms of U.S. security interests, questions arise as to whether the inclusion of formerly neutral states and former members of the Warsaw Pact would enhance the stability of the European continent, or instead would lead to an EC security policy unresponsive to U.S. interests.

Economic Effects

Those who fear that enlargement could lead to greater protectionism are particularly concerned about the entry of central and east European states. Since industries in those states are not yet competitive in world markets, they may require some degree of protection for many years to come. On the other hand, inclusion of the EFTA states could help Brussels resist protectionist pressures because those states have more liberal external trade regimes and generally give more modest subsidies than the EC.

Some observers express concern that a larger European Community might trigger disintegration of the present world trading system, leading to protectionist regional trading blocs, with the EC, the United States, and Japan heading rival groupings. Certainly, the importance of Europe as a trading region is growing. For instance, the European Economic Area negotiated with the EFTA states will establish a market of 380 million consumers when formed in 1993, accounting for over 40 percent of world trade. It is also fair to say that Europe, in trade terms, is relatively introverted. EC member states now conduct 59 percent of their trade with other countries in the EC, up from 53 percent in 1989. That trend is expected to continue.

Whether a stronger European bloc would necessarily be more protectionist, however, is uncertain. Some analysts do not see the emergence of regional trading blocs as undermining the existing global trading regime, the General Agreement on Tariffs and Trade. Harvard economist Robert Lawrence argues that emerging regional trade blocs "are more likely to represent the building blocks of an integrated world economy than stumbling blocks which prevent its emergence." [16]

Finally, enlargement could affect the speed with which a single European currency is introduced. The EC's adoption of a single currency could pose a serious challenge to the dollar's role as the world's premier reserve currency. The existence of a strong alternative to the dollar could impose, in turn, constraints on U.S. financial policy. The EC has not chosen an exact date on which a single currency will be adopted. At the EC's Maastricht summit in December 1991, the EC decided to create a single currency and a regional central bank by 1999 at the latest, as the culmination of a three-stage process of monetary union. The single currency could be introduced as early as 1997 if seven EC states meet strict economic criteria on inflation, budget deficits and interest rates. Based on these convergence criteria, Austria and Sweden appear better prepared to join the EC's economic and monetary union (EMU) than do many current EC members. If Austria and Sweden were offered full EC membership by mid-decade, the EC could adopt a single currency in 1997. The two newcomers could join Germany, France, Denmark, and the Benelux countries in forming a core group. Excluding the EC's southern "periphery" would reinforce claims that a two-tier Europe is developing, but Germany, in particular, would prefer EMU without those economically more troubled states. France would also be satisfied with this scenario because it would like to achieve EMU as soon as possible. [17]

POLITICAL IMPLICATIONS

Enlargement carries implications for the United States in both the foreign policy and security areas. The EC did make limited progress on improving European cooperation on foreign policy matters at its Maastricht summit, but most decisions in that area still require unanimity. In all likelihood, increasing the EC's membership would impede further integration on foreign policy matters. For instance, the Scandinavian and central European states have foreign policy traditions and geopolitical realities different from those of current EC members. Some U.S. officials fear that the inclusion of formerly neutral countries and former members of the Warsaw Pact in the EC could shift the European policy debate and result in an EC foreign policy less compatible with U.S. priorities.

Some American officials believe increased EC foreign policy coordination would benefit U.S. interests, because political integration would increase European unity and virtually rule out a repetition of the internal rivalries that led to two world wars. From this perspective, enlargement serves U.S. interests as long as it does not jeopardize the process of deepening integration. Other officials worry that one unified European voice in foreign policy decision-making could pose a grave challenge to U.S. interests and U.S. leadership in global affairs. From their vantage point, an EC delegation in Washington for negotiations would be wedded to a posi-

[16] As quoted in Dodwell, David. Anxiety and Europhoria. *Financial Times*, December 18, 1991. sec. III, p. III.

[17] Balls, Edward. Why Widening the EC Makes Deepening Less Risky. *Financial Times*, December 16, 1991. p. 4.

tion agreed upon in Brussels and thus could not engage in compromises with its American counterparts. Furthermore, these observers argue that the United States has benefited from its "special" relationships with the United Kingdom and Germany and would have to forfeit those bilateral ties. These critics favor enlargement because they hope it will forestall further foreign policy integration.

Were the EC to speak with one voice, certainly that voice would command more attention than a welter of 12 or, after enlargement, perhaps 20 or more, national voices. Potentially, this new-found strength could lead to greater EC foreign policy activism, particularly in Africa and other areas of the world where EC member states have special historical ties and continue to both wield political influence and provide considerable economic assistance. To the degree that a deeper and wider EC could promote stability, democracy and growth in these areas, the United States would benefit. On the other hand, if enlargement and the resulting transfer of resources to the east depleted EC coffers, one might see a decline in the amount of assistance the EC provided to developing countries. In that case, the United States might be faced with appeals from those countries for increased foreign assistance.

On the security side, American advocates of enlargement contend that widening EC membership to include the central and east European states would enhance stability on the European continent. The more inclusive the EC, the greater would be the sense of political and economic certainty in the new eastern democracies and the smaller the risk of inter- and intra-state violence. Less optimistic observers disagree, reasoning that if the EC prematurely admitted states to its east without having sufficient financial resources to hasten economic development in those states, membership would not ease political, social or economic tensions. These skeptics warn that EC membership should not be viewed as a panacea for the multiple ills facing central and eastern Europe.

At Maastricht, the EC agreed on a defense role for itself. The Western European Union (WEU) will be the EC's defense arm and it will maintain close links to NATO. Since the WEU included only nine of the EC 12, membership offers were extended to Ireland, Denmark and Greece. The WEU will also "involve" European NATO members (i.e., Turkey, Norway) in its activities without full membership. Establishing a vigorous security role for the EC would be even more complicated following enlargement than it is at present. EFTA neutrals have expressed their intent to remain outside of military alliances. Should those states join the EC, they would likely oppose developing a military dimension to the EC. EFTA states would be more likely to support a looser policy of security coordination, particularly if the EC were to act in conjunction with the Conference on Security and Cooperation in Europe. If current EC members were concerned that EFTA neutrals might block progress on the security front, the EC could allow newcomers to "opt out" of a common security policy.

The central and east European states, in contrast to EFTA neutrals, want to join traditionally west European security arrangements and would likely endorse an EC defense role. These states also favor a continued U.S. military presence in Europe. Uncertainty over the future of the Commonwealth of Independent States (CIS), among other concerns, has led the central and east Europeans to conclude that the United States is the best guarantor of their security at present. The former Warsaw Pact "allies" of the Soviet Union could join NATO before joining the EC. Even Russia has requested membership in NATO. At its November 1991 summit, NATO decided to form a cooperation council with the Soviet Union, Poland, the Czech and Slovak Federal Republic, Hungary, Romania, Bulgaria, Estonia, Latvia, and Lithuania. In February 1992, NATO extended an offer of membership in the council to all CIS members, except Georgia. The aim of this pan-European relationship is to encourage security cooperation in post-Cold War Europe by creating a forum in which to discuss regional security issues and promote confidence-building measures. The cooperation council essentially grants these states political membership in NATO. Thus, further European integration on security matters could take place within the NATO framework without involving the European Community.

In the security area, an enlarged NATO could feature a greater clarity of purpose and unity of action than an enlarged EC. Ambivalence on the part of EFTA neutrals toward common security action in an enlarged EC would greatly complicate joint undertakings. For this reason, widening the EC could enhance NATO's importance as a European security organization.

The economic, political and security implications of EC enlargement for the United States are not clear. Ultimately, it is not enlargement per se that will determine the compatibility of transatlantic policies, but rather the political will exercised on both sides of the Atlantic.

III. FOREIGN POLICYMAKING IN THE EUROPEAN COMMUNITY

THE EC IN THE INTERNATIONAL ARENA: A NEW ACTIVISM?

by Lily Gardner Feldman *

CONTENTS

SUMMARY

The Maastricht Treaty is a milestone in the evolution of the EC as an international political actor. In its external activities, the EC will continue to be plagued by institutional obstacles to coherence and efficiency and member state differences regarding goals and instruments. Nonetheless, the EC is already an international political actor of significance and will build on its past record through the further institutionalization of ties to a variety of international actors in an ever-expanding range of issues.

Three scenarios of EC international activism are possible, "assertive Europe," "decisive Europe," and "diffident Europe." "Assertive Europe" characterizes current reality and will frame developments in the next decade; it involves increased activity in the

---

* Lily Gardner Feldman is Research Director of the American Institute for Contemporary German Studies.

newer issues of international relations: environmental concerns, human rights and development, and structural peace. The other two scenarios could emerge by the end of the decade as a function of political will both within the EC and its member states and impulses from the international arena. One scenario implies further integration, the other disintegration in Europe.

There are costs and benefits of each scenario for the United States. It should support "assertive Europe," promote "decisive Europe," and work actively to avoid "diffident Europe." The United States must play an active role in devising an international and bilateral agenda with the EC as a political actor.

INTRODUCTION

The role of the European Community (EC) as a formidable international economic actor is undisputed by the United States, as both cooperative (Central and Eastern Europe) and contentious (the GATT) U.S.-EC relations demonstrate. Less clear, from the U.S. perspective, has been the power and purpose of the EC as an international political actor.

Yet, the Maastricht Treaty reveals international activism as fundamental to political union. The Community's overall intentions are now transparent: the Treaty's Common Provisions define explicitly as one of five main objectives "to assert [the EC's] identity on the international scene, in particular through the implementation of common foreign and security policy." [1] Maastricht failed to absorb common foreign and security policy (CFSP) into the Treaties of Rome, but did codify and elevate its goals and structures on the EC's agenda. Whether and how the EC can translate renewed political will into expanded political action externally is the focus of this chapter.

"Common foreign and security policy" clearly does not embrace all of the EC's international relations. Significant external activity has been conducted on the basis of the Treaties of Rome, largely in the economic realm (for example, according to articles 110, 111, 113, 131, 228, 229, 230, 231, 237, 238, some of which have been repealed or revised by Maastricht). [2] The diversity and potency of the EC's international economic activity are dealt with elsewhere in this study. Here, then, the weight of analysis rests largely on the political and security spheres broadly in the extra-treaty framework of European Political Cooperation (EPC); treaty-based activity will be examined to the extent that it reveals the EC as a political actor.

The chapter develops three scenarios for the EC's future as an international political actor, distinguished by the type of activism involved. [3] The strength and effectiveness of activism are deter-

---

[1] Council of Ministers. *Treaty on European Union*. Brussels, Council of Ministers. CONF-UP-UEM 2002/1/92, REV 1, Title I, Common Provisions, Article B. February 12, 1992. p. 2; hereafter called "Maastricht Treaty."

[2] For a comprehensive treatment of foreign policy and external relations, including the legal basis for activity, see: Ginsberg, Roy. *Foreign Policy Actions of the European Community: The Politics of Scale*. Boulder, Lynne Rienner Publishers, 1989.

[3] These three visions are similar to Christopher Hill's pre-Maastricht formulations of the EC as "power bloc," "civilian model," and "flop." See his chapter in Rummel, Reinhardt, ed. *The Evolution of an International Actor. Western Europe's New Assertiveness*. Boulder, San Francisco, and Oxford, Westview Press, 1990.

mined by the volume of activity, its nature, and, ultimately, its coherence and consistency. Coherence and consistency, in turn, are a function of both the EC's pro-active, self-definition as an international entity and the EC's internal structures for converting vision into reality. *Assertive Europe* envisions Maastricht as a milestone on an evolutionary path. It involves incremental growth of activity, building on past experiences and structures that are now firmly institutionalized in intergovernmental form. *Decisive Europe* goes further than Maastricht by assuming a more federal structure for the EC, and integration of foreign policy into the Treaties of Rome. It projects greater institutional rationalization, resulting in a more purposeful and efficacious international presence. *Diffident Europe* is a hesitant international actor, stymied by lack of purpose. It implies a retreat from Maastricht's intentions, and renationalization of foreign and security policies among the twelve.

The three scenarios differ according to definitions of power, goals, institutional base, and instruments. Each entails different implications for the United States, both positively and negatively. For the next decade, the first scenario, which describes and explains current reality, will dominate. Nonetheless, the other two cannot be ignored as possible models for the first decade of the twenty-first century.

ASSERTIVE EUROPE

The robustness of European foreign policy assertiveness is rooted in four factors: (1) entrenchment of CFSP's development; (2) density of global activity; (3) diversity of international activity; and (4) institutionalization of foreign ties. The limits of assertiveness have been forged in the crucible of international crises.

THE EVOLUTION OF CFSP

Since the 1969 Hague Summit, at which the EC took stock of achievements, identified deficiencies and outlined priorities, a regular and gradual accretion of foreign policy consultation and coordination has occurred: the 1970 Luxembourg Report, the 1972 Paris Summit; the 1973 Copenhagen Report; the 1974 Paris Summit; the 1976 Tindemans Report; the 1981 Genscher-Colombo Initiative; the 1981 London Report; the 1983 Stuttgart Solemn Declaration; and the 1986 Single European Act. [4] The Luxembourg Report began the process by seeking "continuous collaboration among the foreign ministries and foreign services of the member states" through regular exchange and the establishment of working groups, and a Political Committee (comprising foreign ministries' political department heads), as well as a liaison in each member state. The 1970s delivered real achievements both politically (commitment to a distinct profile in international relations, consultation and joint activity) and organizationally (the creation of the European Council to

---

[4] On the genesis of common foreign policy, see: Ginsberg, *Foreign Policy Actions of the European Community,* p. 47–51; de Ruyt, Jean. *European Political Cooperation: Toward A Unified European Foreign Policy.* Washington, DC, The Atlantic Council of the United States, 1989. p. 11-15; and, Ifestos, Panayiotis. *European Political Cooperation. Towards a Framework of Supranational Diplomacy.* Aldershot, Hants, Avebury, 1987. For the texts of the main documents, see: Press and Information Office of the Federal Government of Germany. *European Political Cooperation.* Bonn, Press and Information Office, 1988.

preside over EPC and a telex network to link foreign ministries). The early 1980s efforts already set the specific common foreign policy goals that would be realized in the Single European Act (SEA).

The Single European Act was the harbinger for the Maastricht Treaty, suggesting that current EC common foreign policy intentions are hardly the product of recently-gained international recognition, but more the outgrowth of long-term thinking. A comparison of the Single European Act and the Maastricht Treaty confirms their intimate connection and details the nature of European Political Cooperation.

From the Single European Act to the Maastricht Treaty

The goals of common foreign policy enunciated in the SEA and reiterated at Maastricht are at once pragmatic and idealistic. The EC attaches primordial importance to the protection of "common" and "fundamental interests," particularly the "security" and "independence" of the Union, yet emphasizes broader values of international cooperation and international peace, democracy and the rule of law, human rights and fundamental freedoms. The tentativeness of the SEA to "endeavor jointly to formulate and implement a European foreign policy" has been replaced by the firmness of Maastricht to "define and implement a common foreign and security policy . . . covering all areas."[5]

Both the SEA and Maastricht have recognized that the preliminary stages for "joint action" and "common positions" are consultation, coordination and convergence and have developed structures accordingly. The European Council provides the basic guidelines for deliberations by the Ministers for Foreign Affairs either in the Council of the EC or in their regular meetings (at least four times a year) on EPC with a member of the Commission. The Political Committee plays a maintenance and continuity role. Under the Political Committee's direction, the European Correspondents' Group (junior foreign ministry officials) monitors the implementation of EPC. Regional and thematic working groups aid focussed attention and preparation. The Presidency of the Council is ultimately responsible for implementation and for representing the twelve on CFSP to EC institutions, in third countries and in international fora; it is assisted by a five-person secretariat that rotates with the Presidency.

While the preponderance of the Presidency's authority reinforces the intergovernmental character of EPC, the Commission and the Parliament are integrated into the EPC system. Through the Maastricht Treaty, the Presidency's obligation under the SEA to "inform" the Parliament has been augmented to "consult." In addition, the Parliament now possesses the formal role of asking questions, making recommendations and holding debates on CFSP. By Maastricht's assignment of the right to submit questions and proposals a similar agenda-setting role accrues to the Commission which already under the SEA was mandated to be "fully associat-

[5] See Preamble and Title III of the SEA in: Commission of the European Communities. Single European Act. *Bulletin of the European Communities*. Supplement 2/86; and, Title V of the Maastricht Treaty.

ed" with EPC and to maintain consistency between external relations and EPC. [6]

The potential for diluting national interests, for example through the shaping activities of the more supranational Commission and Parliament, also has been increased by Maastricht's provision for qualified majority voting in CFSP. Yet, just as in the final analysis CFSP elevates the Council over the Commission and the Parliament, unanimity dominates majority voting: "The Council shall decide ... that a matter should be the subject of joint action. ... The Council shall, when adopting the joint action and at any stage during its development, define those matters on which decisions are to be taken by a qualified majority." [7]

CFSP's intergovernmental nature does not imply, however, that the EC is merely a reactive entity with an ad hoc, lowest common-denominator agenda. The provisions of the SEA and Maastricht as well as the reality of the EC's existing foreign policy behavior suggest otherwise. To capture the full scope of the EC as an international political actor, we must look at both EPC and treaty-based external relations in quantitative and qualitative terms.

THE DENSITY OF GLOBAL ACTIVITY

The fact alone of EC international activity does not reveal its effectiveness, but aggregation of foreign policy actions according to type and cause does demonstrate an evolutionary, substantial and durable pattern of foreign policy behavior. On the basis of a systematic study of the nature, motivation and volume of EC foreign policy in the period 1958–85, Roy Ginsberg has shown the salience and sustainability of the EC as an international actor.

From the creation of the Community until the negotiation of the SEA, there were 480 EC foreign policy actions (both treaty-based and EPC). [8] In the five-year period since 1985, a further 189 actions were taken, revealing significant growth. [9] In all periods, most of the activities have been multilateral (dealings with international organizations, fora and issues) and bilateral (dealings with non-member states or groups of states), but there has been an increase in security-related actions and in relations with other regions.

The majority of activity is engendered by the effects of the EC's internal integration which causes other international actors to look to the EC for mitigation or compensation. However, increasingly EC activity must be explained also by the reality of international economic interdependence and by the EC's own efforts to shape the international agenda.

---

[6] For the institutional structure of EPC, see: Commission of the European Communities. *Single European Act.* Title III, points 3,4,5 and 10. p. 18–19; Maastricht Treaty, Title V, Articles J.3, J.5, J.7, J.8, and J.9, p. 173–78.

[7] Maastricht Treaty, Title V, point J.3, p. 173.

[8] Ginsberg, *Foreign Policy Actions of the European Community*, p. 90–116.

[9] . See Ginsberg's updated data in *The European Community as an International Actor in the 1980s and into 1990s.* Paper presented to the Conference on Franco-German Partnership and the European Project, Northwestern University, May 4-5, 1991.

CIVILIAN POWER IN PRINCIPLE AND PRACTICE: THE DIVERSITY OF EC ASSERTIVENESS

Both the SEA and Maastricht envision a "contribution to the preservation of international peace and security" in line with the United Nations Charter and the principles of the CSCE's Helsinki Final Act and Charter of Paris. This vision is based on the EC as a "civilian power." It means continuation of the SEA's emphasis on the broad "political and economic aspects of security" and eschews traditional military notions of security held out as a long-term possibility in Maastricht's reference to the "eventual framing of a defence policy."

First developed in the early 1970s by François Duchêne and Andrew Schonfield, the concept of "civilian power" has reemerged in the 1990s, particularly in the work of Christopher Hill and Hanns Maull. Cooperation, reciprocal dependence and supranationalism are identified as key structural qualities. Non-military, especially economic instruments, take precedence over military power which becomes a "residual" tool. Negotiation and open diplomacy are the preferred methods, international solidarity (particularly with the Third World) and responsibility (especially regarding the environment) the chosen values. "Persuasion," or "soft" power, dominates "coercion," or "hard" power.[10]

In the strictly EPC framework, the EC has been active internationally in five main ways: *declarations* on international events on every part of the globe; *consultations* with countries on every continent; *ministerial missions* to areas of tension, including the Middle East and Yugoslavia; *participation* in international fora, including traditional organizations like the United Nations and newer organizations like the CSCE; and *diplomatic sanctions,* against, for example, Argentina, China, cold-war Poland and the Soviet Union, Iraq.[11]

The Council's role in external affairs is not restricted to EPC. It provides the directives on which the Commission negotiates with third parties (in consultation with Council-appointed special committees) and then finalizes the process through decision and signing. The areas of treaty-based activity are numerous: *international agreements* across the globe, stepping up in complexity from trade through trade and cooperation agreements to association agreements, and to the newer forms of European Agreements (with Central and Eastern Europe) and the European Economic Area (with EFTA); *aid,* whether financial and technical assistance to a variety of areas (aid to Central and Eastern Europe under the PHARE program is one of the most visible recent examples; less well-known is the assistance to countries like Syria and Israel, as well as to the

---

[10] For the genesis of the term, see: Hill, European Foreign Policy, p. 41–5; and, Bull, Hedley. Civilian Power Europe: A Contradiction in Terms? In Tsoukalis, Loukas, ed. *The European Community: Past, Present, and Future.* Oxford, Basil Blackwell, 1983. p. 149–51. See also: Maull, Hanns W. Germany and Japan, "The New Civilian Powers". *Foreign Affairs,* Winter, 1990/91.

[11] For an inventory of EC international activity, both in the Treaty of Rome nd EPC frameworks, from 1958 until 1985, see: Ginsberg, *Foreign Policy Actions of the European Community,* p. 90–106. For a comprehensive review of recent activity, see: Burghardt, Günther. Political Objectives, Potential and Instruments of a Common Foreign Policy. In Weidenfeld, Werner and Josef Janning, eds. *Global Responsibilities: Europe in Tomorrow's World.* Gütersloh, Bertelsmann, 1991. p. 85–95. For details of international activity, see the section on EPC in the Commission's monthly publication *Bulletin of the European Communities.*

occupied territories); or emergency, humanitarian and food aid (for example, to the Soviet Union and Central and Eastern Europe, but also assistance for the Kurds, the repatriation of Vietnamese exiles or help to Lebanon); *economic sanctions* (such as those against China, Iraq, Israel and South Africa); *representation* in international organizations of all kinds. [12]

Consistent with the notion of the EC as a civilian power, there are three issues on which the EC's external activity has increasingly concentrated: the environment, human rights, and conflict resolution.

The SEA formally introduced environmental concerns into the EC's internal affairs and put them on the agenda of international activity. Given its status "as a main producer and recipient of pollution" and as, for example, "the largest importer of tropical woods," [13] Europe cannot ignore ecological issues. Maastricht has gone beyond the SEA by setting as a goal of EC environmental policy "promoting measures at international level to deal with regional or worldwide environmental problems." [14] The environment has also featured in EC relations with specific countries/regions, for example in development of Mediterranean policy, in the Cooperation Agreement with Chile, in the PHARE Program for Central and Eastern Europe, and in the Joint Declaration on the Baltic States.

Human rights have been highlighted by the SEA and Maastricht and have been integrated into practice, both in public declarations (approximately 120 in 1991) and confidential d'marches (approximately 150 in the same period), as well as in international fora (particularly at the UN and CSCE). [15] Both the Commission and the Council have connected human rights observance with economic relations and development cooperation, both in Central and Eastern Europe and the Third World, elaborating graduated responses to violations, including the suspension of cooperation. [16] In articulating its views on development cooperation as a separate title of the Maastricht Treaty, the EC recognizes that development aid should help consolidate democracy, the rule of law and human rights. For the EC, these are fundamental issues: "Human rights are on the international agenda to stay and require the same sort

---

[12] For detailed summaries of external activity, see the section entitled Role of the Community in the World. In the Commission's *Bulletin of the European Communities.*

[13] Janning, Josef. A New Transatlantic Deal: European–American Relations in the 1990s. In Clesse, Armand, and Raymond Vernon, eds. *The European Community after 1992: A New Role in World Politics*? Baden-Baden, Nomos Verlagsgesellschaft, 1991. p. 218–219.

[14] See Title VII in Commission of the European Communities, Single European Act, p. 16; and, Title XVI of the Maastricht Treaty, p. 76–7. See also the Commission's documents for the United Nations Conference on Environment and Development, including *A Common Platform: Guidelines for the Community for UNCED 1992.* SEC(91) 1693 final. Brussels, Commission of the European Communities, October 30, 1991; and, *Report from the Commission of the European Communities to the United Nations Conference on the Environment and Development.* SEC(91) 2448 final. Brussels, Commission of the European Communities, March 20, 1992.

[15] For a review of EC human rights activity in 1991, see: European Communities. *European Political Cooperation.* Press Release. Brussels, December 10, 1991.

[16] See, for example, the Commission's proposal for a Council Regulation on financial and technical assistance, and economic cooperation with the developing countries in Asia and Latin America in: Commission of the European Communities. *Bulletin of the European Communities*, March, 1991. p. 52–3; and, the Council's November 28, 1991 Resolution on Human Rights, Democracy and Development in Commission of the European Communities. *Bulletin of the European Communities*, November, 1991. p. 120–123.

of responsible handling accorded to other items of international cooperation."[17]

The growing magnitude of EC-related development aid confirms its potential in the pursuit of human rights: in the period 1989–91, the EC increased development aid as a proportion of its budget from 2.7 percent to 4.2 percent. Combining EC and member states contributions, 0.51 percent of GNP goes to development aid (compared to 0.15 percent in the United States and 0.32 percent in Japan).[18]

On both the environment and human rights, the European Parliament has been an important voice, frequently placing the issues on the agenda and monitoring them through resolutions and questions, for example with reference to Central and Latin America, the Gulf, the Kurds, and Central and Eastern Europe.[19] The Parliament has also played an active role in promoting conflict resolution in a variety of regional settings. The belief in a particular EC contribution to peace-making is common to all EC institutions and derives from the EC's achievement of one of its basic goals: the curtailment of centuries of conflict among European powers, especially between France and Germany.

At least since the mid-1980s, the EC has explicitly viewed itself as a model for regional integration and conflict resolution. This vision has been particularly prominent in German leaders' references to the "peace initiatives," "peace community" and "role model" of the EC.[20] It is obvious for the twelve in the Community's declarations on regional conflicts in areas as diverse as Central and Eastern Europe, the Middle East, Central America, and Africa. For example, the Commission has recently noted that "the European Community is now seen as the main focus for peace, democracy and growth by all of Europe and the neighbouring countries to the South and East," and President Delors has referred to the Community as "a focus of attraction in Europe and throughout the world, a model of regional integration serving the interests of peace."[21] In the EC's Mediterranean policy, the Commission has promoted the "process of integration in the region," as has the Parliament.[22] The EC has been particularly vocal regarding conflict in the Middle East, for example in its Venice Declaration of 1980. Although the United States has clearly been responsible for bringing the parties to the negotiating table, as chair of the Middle East peace conference's working party on the region's economic development the EC will influence the quality of peace among Israel, the

---

[17] See Title XVII of the Maastricht Treaty, Article 130u, p. 80; and European Communities. *European Political Cooperation*, December 10, 1991. p. 3.

[18] Burghardt, Political Objectives, Potential and Instruments of a Common Foreign and Security Policy, p. 91.

[19] The European Parliament's resolutions are recorded in the Commission's publication *Bulletin of the European Communities*.

[20] See: Press and Information Office of the Federal Government of Germany. *European Political Cooperation*. p. 343–344, 349; and, Ungerer, Werner. EC Progress under the German Presidency. *Aussenpolitik*, v. 39, no. 4, 1988.

[21] Commission of the European Communities. *From the Single Act to Maastricht and Beyond. The Means To Match Our Ambitions*. COM(92)2000. Brussels, Commission of the European Communities. p. 15; and, Commission of the European Communities. 1992: A Pivotal Year. Address by Jacques Delors, President of the Commission, to the European Parliament, February 12, 1992. *Bulletin of the European Communities*. Supplement 1/92. p. 44.

[22] Commission of the European Communities. *Bulletin of the European Communities*, January/February, 1991. p. 78; and, July/August, 1991. p. 86.

Palestinians and the Arab world. The EC has vigorously supported regional integration in Central America, particularly through various economic arrangements and the creation of a Central American parliament, and has sought consistently to invigorate the regional Contadora peace process. [23]

Part of the EC's peace strategy is institutionalization of its relations with regions of conflict to facilitate transparency and consistency, and to allow the EC to link economic incentives to political behavior. Institutionalization and regionalization extend beyond ties to areas of conflict; they define also the EC's approach to international relations in general, as suggested already in the SEA, [24] and in the EC's constructive role in the evolution of the CSCE, the embodiment of a broad conception of peace and security. The EC has become, then, both a model and a magnet with large implications for the twelve as an international actor: "The political consequence of this position is the Community's global political responsibility." [25]

THE INSTITUTIONALIZATION OF FOREIGN TIES

Most extensive of all is the EC's multi-faceted relationship with sixty-eight African, Caribbean and Pacific states. The latest, ten-year, agreement between the two sides, the December 1989 Lomé IV Convention, has been referred to as "the updated version of a genuine international cooperation charter with a view to economic and social development of the APC states." In addition to cooperation in areas such as agriculture, mining, energy and the environment, and adherence to fundamental human rights, the heart of EC-APC ties lies in trade and financial cooperation. Trade cooperation involves access to the EC market, trade promotion, and stabilization of APC export earnings. [26]

The Middle East has long represented a consistent focus of the EC, and links have been deepened through the EC's Mediterranean policy, its trade and financial agreements with individual Maghreb and Mashreq countries, regular consultations with the Organization of Arab Petroleum Exporting Countries, and the creation of both the Euro-Arab Dialogue and the Gulf Cooperation Council.

Ties have been institutionalized with Central America and Panama (and Mexico, Colombia and Venezuela as "cooperating countries") largely through an annual Ministerial Conference, and associated agreements, on political and economic dialogue that

---

[23] See, for example, the joint political declaration from the Managua Ministerial Conference in: European Communities. *European Political Cooperation.* Press Release. Brussels, March 19, 1991.

[24] Commission of the European Communities. *Single European Act,* Title III, Point 8. p. 19.

[25] Weidenfeld, Werner and Josef Janning. After 1989: The Emergence of a New Europe. In Weidenfeld and Janning, *Global Responsibilities: Europe in Tomorrow's World,* p. 20. For a discussion of the EC as an international actor, both as model and magnet, see: Gardner Feldman, Lily. 1992 and the Federal Republic's European Identity: Implications for Relations with the United States. In Cooney, James A., Wolfgang-Uwe Friedrich, and Gerald R. Kleinfeld, eds. *German-American Relations.* Yearbook 1. Frankfurt/New York, Campus Verlag, 1989; and, The Architecture of a European Peace Order: Concepts, Actors, Institutions. In Lee, J.J. and Walter Korter, eds. *Europe in Transition: Political, Economic and Security Prospects for the 1990s.* Austin, Lyndon B. Johnson School of Public Affairs, 1990.

[26] Flaesch-Mougin, Catherine, and Jean, Raux. From Lomé III to Lomé IV: EC-APC Relations. In Hurwitz, Leon and Christian Lequesne, eds. *The State of the European Community: Policies, Institutions and Debates in the Transition Years.* Boulder, Lynne Rienner, 1991. p. 343.

began in 1984. A similar dialogue exists with Latin America through ties to the Rio Group.

The dialogue with the Association of South East Asian Nations (ASEAN) originated in 1978. It has been less comprehensive than with other regions, but does involve a cooperation agreement and an annual Ministerial Conference focussing on political and economic issues.

The largest and most complex regional challenge for the EC is now Central and Eastern Europe. One of the main reasons for the EC's ability to develop so rapidly a panoply of instruments for confronting and channelling change in Central and Eastern Europe after fall 1989 was its regional perspective prior to the upheavals. Consistent with its other regional foci, the EC was already structuring its relationship to Central and Eastern Europe in the mid-1980s, culminating in the June 1988 joint declaration to normalize relations with the Council for Mutual Economic Assistance.

The EC's major involvement in helping to shape the future of Central and Eastern Europe has demonstrated its strength as an international actor. The Community's efforts in South Eastern Europe have both reinforced its contributions and revealed its limits, just as the Gulf War did earlier.

THE TEST OF ASSERTIVENESS: THE GULF AND YUGOSLAV CRISES

Five standard criticisms concerning both goals and means have been levelled against the EC as an international political actor, leading to the charge that EC "foreign policy is a resounding flop."[27] The broadest and most frequent indictment argues that the intergovernmental character of EC foreign policy guarantees the preponderance of national interest in times of crisis, precluding fulfillment of the SEA's goal to "speak ever increasingly with one voice" and confirming declarations as the single expression of agreement.

Intergovernmentalism brings with it institutional constraints that affect the instruments at the EC's disposal. The need for consensus through the pre-Maastricht exclusive use of unanimity voting ensures sluggishness when crises situations demand speed of response. The constant rotation of the presidency every six months is hardly a recipe for consistency and coherence. Consistency and coherence are further impaired, according to the critics of EC foreign policy, by the institutional cleavage between EPC and external relations, between the Council and the Commission, resulting in political and economic instruments running at best parallel, instead of in concert. Even if there is linkage between political and economic tools, the key instrument for crises, according to detractors, is military power which is non-existent in the Community's foreign policy arsenal.

In both the Gulf and Yugoslav crises, many of these weaknesses were present, but there were also countervailing factors suggesting

---

[27] Hill, European Foreign Policy, p. 48. In addition to Hill, for analyses of EC foreign policy deficiencies, see: Dinan, Desmond. European Political Cooperation. In Hurwitz and Lequesne, *The State of the European Community*; and, Ifestos, European Political Cooperation. Towards A Framework of Supranational Diplomacy.

the EC is an international political actor of note.[28] This view accepts fundamental features of the EC's general development and applies them to foreign policy: integration is a process that is both evolutionary and non-linear, such that the "community method" invariably involves two steps forward and one step back.

Clearly, national interests abounded during the Gulf War and the Yugoslav crisis. Britain, France, Italy, Belgium and the Netherlands eventually crafted individual policies to contribute to the U.S.-led military effort in the Gulf, but four of the five at least also attempted a common approach. In the Yugoslav civil war, Germany, Italy and Greece have played dominant roles on the question of recognizing Croatia, Slovenia, and Macedonia. Yet, for all its threats of unilateral action, Germany was able to convert its intentions into EC policy.

It is true that declarations have been a regular feature of the EC's response to both crises, but the twelve have gone beyond mere exhortation to action, even if its construction has been difficult. In the Gulf War, the EC responded with a range of activity: economic sanctions (oil import embargo, freezing of Iraqi assets, cessation of arms sales, postponement of cooperation); relief aid to Jordan; a new energy policy; a revived Mediterranean policy; and diplomatic missions.

On Yugoslavia, declarations have been accompanied by a similarly diverse set of responses: arms and military equipment embargo; suspension of financial protocols; suspension of trade and cooperation agreement and of various trade and aid benefits to Yugoslavia; trade concessions for Bosnia-Herzogovina, Croatia, Macedonia and Slovenia; convening of peace conference; facilitation of cease-fires; dispatch of cease-fire monitors; diplomatic missions; and creation of both guidelines for recognition of new states and arbitration commission for their implementation.

While there was considerable wrangling among the member states, it is by no means clear that this delayed EC reactions dramatically. In the Gulf case, the EC decided on an oil embargo immediately after the Iraqi seizure of Kuwait and prior to the UN's response, and the twelve provided relief aid to Jordan before anyone else. Already at the end of August 1991, the EC foreign ministers took the initiative to convene a peace conference which opened in September, a remarkably speedy undertaking compared to the decades-long delays in comparably intractable conflicts such as the Middle East and Northern Ireland. Similarly, the differences in member states' positions concerning recognition were essentially overcome in one, albeit marathon, negotiating session on December 16/17, 1991.

The rotation of the presidency in both crises did mean a difference in style and priorities (from Italy to Luxembourg during the Gulf War; from the Netherlands to Portugal during the Yugoslav

---

[28] For details of what the EC did and did not do during the two crises, see: Salmon, Trevor. Testing Times for European Political Cooperation: The Gulf nd Yugoslavia, 1990–1992. *International Affairs*, v. 68, no. 2, April, 1992; and, Steinberg, James B. *The Role of European Institutions in Balkan Security: Some Lessons from Yugoslavia.* RAND N-3445-FF, forthcoming. The texts of EC statements and policy decisions during both crises can be found in the monthly Commission *Bulletin of the European Communities* for August, 1990 through February 1991 and for March 1991 through December, 1991.

civil war), but the ongoing, comprehensive role of the Commission helped mitigate the effects of formal leadership change.

For example, when the 'troika' (past, present and future presidents of the Council) visited Jordan, Saudi Arabia and Egypt at the beginning of the Gulf crisis, it was accompanied by Commissioner Matutes, to facilitate coordination between EPC and treaty-based action. Similarly, Mr. Matutes participated in the troika's meetings with Slovene and Croatian representatives, and with federal Yugoslav authorities; he and Commission President Delors took part in the July 30 Brussels meeting between the twelve's foreign ministers and Yugoslav representatives. The Commission also was included in the group of EC observers dispatched to monitor the Brioni cease-fire agreement. More generally, the EC's interactions with international organizations during both cases (the UN and the CSCE) meant both the Council and the Commission were involved in parallel and connected ways.

Following a long tradition in the Middle East (for example, the postponement of trade and financial arrangements with Israel after the 1982 invasion of Lebanon and during the *intifadah* to try to change Israel's political behavior), the EC linked political and economic aspects of policy during the Gulf War. While using the economic "stick" of sanctions, the twelve offered the "carrot" of a "global approach to the region," including the support of an international peace conference on the Middle East. In the Yugoslav case, the EC again withdrew economic benefits from the federal state in an attempt to alter political behavior, but in November 1991 also explicitly offered incentives to individual republics: "Positive compensatory measures will be applied to parties which cooperate in a peaceful way towards a comprehensive political solution, on the basis of EC proposals." [29]

Critics of EC positions during the Gulf maintain the EC was ineffectual because it lacked the technical capacity and political will to use military force. The EC clearly had no competence to engage as a unit in military activity, but was stimulated into serious discussion about a defence identity, via the West European Union (WEU), by the Gulf War. While the Gulf War uncovered the limits of EC influence, it also revealed the limits of using force; Saddam Hussein is, after all, still in power.

The subsequent EC debate about common defense was not yet concluded when the Community became actively involved in the Yugoslav crisis, once more leaving the twelve without legal competence for military action (the cease-fire observers did include retired military personnel and active military officials in civilian clothing). Although the situation of civil war does not appear susceptible to outside military influence, it nonetheless has further stimulated the debate, at Maastricht, over CFSP and the specific role of WEU as the EC's security arm.

Commission President Delors had already concluded after the Gulf War that "the Community must assume its share of political and military responsibility if it is to meet the challenges of the

---

[29] For the linkage on both occasions, see: European Communities. *European Political Cooperation.* Press Release. January 14, 1991; and, Commission of the European Communities. *Bulletin of the European Communities*, November, 1991. p. 92.

1990s," and is convinced of this necessity as the Yugoslav crisis worsens.[30] This image projects the EC as a world power and entails a more resolute Community. The expansion from civilian power to world power will not occur quickly, but some of the elements are already in place while others are being developed with an eye to the next formal review on political union in 1996. If the Community expands its external activity, and possesses the capacity for consistency, coherence, and flexibility of action, then by the end of the decade, decisive Europe could emerge.

Decisive Europe

The EC's potential for decisiveness in the international arena will depend on two sets of conditions: (1) the nature and agenda of the international system; and (2) the commitment and attendant institutional change within the Community.

EUROPE IN THE NEW INTERNATIONAL SYSTEM: AN EMERGING WORLD POWER

According to the German Research Group on European Affairs, leading and influential analysts of the EC, the new concept of world power contains six elements: exceptional economic strength (accessibility to raw materials, size and productivity of domestic market, world trade position, innovation, and potential for capital formation); large population (high education level, tight infrastructure, and industrial and societal capacities for creativity and absorption); sophisticated military efficiency (relative invulnerability, capacity for both deterrence and power projection); dynamic political system (ability to mobilize resources and international partners); political consensus for world order (inclination toward multilateralism); and experience with order-making and leadership activities (management of regional environment).[31] The group concludes that the EC is a nascent world power according to the first three criteria, but that it has yet to fully achieve the last three. Nonetheless, after the United States, the EC approximates these characteristics more than other actors in the international system. There are both external and internal reasons for the possibility of genuine political union by the beginning of the twenty-first century.

THE PROSPECT OF POLITICAL UNION

External crisis has frequently been one of the main stimuli for EC integration; disintegration of the former Soviet bloc, the Gulf War and the Yugoslav civil war are no exception, as the path to Maastricht demonstrated. Pressure in each of these regions, whether political, economic or social, and the related potential for large-scale migration, will probably intensify rather than diminish. Re-

---

[30] Commission of the European Communities. *Europe After 1992: Signposts to Where.* Address by Jacques Delors to the Council on Foreign Relations, New York, April 24, 1991. p. 5.; and, Commission of the European Communities, *From the Single Act to Maastricht and Beyond,* p. 3.

[31] For a detailed analysis of Europe's future by the Research Group on European Affairs at the University of Mainz, see: *The Future of Europe: Alternatives—Strategies—Options.* Document presented to the International Bertelsmann Forum, Guest House of the Federal Government of Germany, Petersberg, April 3-5, 1992.

gardless of its own inclinations, as one of the few factors of stability in the international system, the EC will be beckoned by other actors to increase its international role.

Widening of the Community, whether to sixteen, twenty, twenty-three or twenty-seven members, inevitably will cause both a recalibration of power and purpose and a rationalization of institutions and procedures within the Community. With the threshold of twenty-three members, two blocs are envisioned: "the South Western European part of the Romance states and the North Eastern European part." In this scenario, the Franco-German dyad will continue its role of motor and innovator for the EC, but add responsibility for stability and cohesion. [32]

Franco-German initiatives have been central for movement toward political union, for example in the run-ups to the SEA and to Maastricht. As in the past, agreement is hardly automatic between France and Germany, but the density and institutionalization of the relationship still promise resolution of differences, particularly in the context of a united Germany. To prove its Europeanness, the new Germany will reaffirm its commitment to political union, including the common foreign and security policy aspects. That commitment has been consistent and consensual, spanning the German political landscape. Indeed, from the beginning of EPC in the early 1970s, Germany has been a vital force at critical junctures of substantive and institutional development. [33] France and the rest of the Community will likely move forward on CFSP to guard against German unilateralism or German dominance. [34]

A further internal stimulus toward political union will be progress in other areas of EC integration. Consistent with Jean Monnet's vision of the EC's evolution, Community officials predict that completion of the internal market and progress toward economic and monetary union will either require or provoke a "political counterpart." [35]

INSTITUTIONAL CHANGE

The characterization of the EC as "federal" was defeated at Maastricht, but only after vigorous and serious debate. The goal, form and process of federation-building will continue to be disputed among member-states and scholars. [36] However, if there is to be real institutional change (as opposed to incremental tinkering with the Maastricht structure), it will likely occur in the direction of the Commission's preferred "federal-type organization" in two main re-

---

[32] Research Group on European Affairs, *The Future of Europe: Alternatives—Strategies—Options*, p. 16.

[33] The most recent examples of German commitment to political union have come in Chancellor Kohl's speech to the Bertelsmann-Forum in: Press and Information Office of the Federal Government. *Bulletin*, no. 38, Bonn, April 8, 1992; and, in Foreign Minister Genscher's April 27 resignation speech to his party's presidium.

[34] On the Community's response to German unification, including progress toward political union, see: Gardner Feldman, Lily. The EC and German Unification. In Hurwitz and Lequesne, ed., *The State of the European Community*.

[35] Burghardt, Political Objectives, Potential and Instruments of a Common Foreign and Security Policy, p. 93. This is a common perspective among Commission officials.

[36] See, for example, Sbragia, Alberta M. Thinking about the European Future: The Uses of Comparison. In Sbragia, Alberta M., ed. *Europolitics. Institutions and Policymaking in the "New" European Community*. Washington, The Brookings Institution, 1992; and, Weiler, Joseph H. H. The Transformation of Europe. *The Yale Law Journal*, v. 100, no. 8, June 1991.

spects: it will be a "single Community" whose competence covers all areas of policy; and it will entail a division of power and labor among the Community and its constituent parts. To improve management, efficiency, and legitimacy the powers of the Commission and the Parliament would be increased, but, as Peter Ludlow has pointed out, not to the detriment of the Council. [37]

In the foreign and security policy area, the views of both the Commission and the Parliament expressed, but not fulfilled, in the Maastricht process indicate the next stage in 1996. The Commission advocates a "flexible and pragmatic approach" to meet the "historic challenge" of "unity and coherence in the Community's international action." [38] Mindful of the historic and geopolitical diversity of the member states, unity connotes for the Commission "common" as opposed to "single" policies. However, the necessity of a "single Community" to close the gap between internal and external policies and between EPC and external relations mandates a "single institutional structure."

The Commission addresses four elements of the policy-making process: initiation of decisions; decision-making; implementation; and accountability. The right of initiative would be shared among the Council Presidency, the member states and the Commission. A strengthened political secretariat joined with Commission representatives in an institution attached to the Secretariat-General of the Council would prepare decisions. The European Council would define the areas of common policy, with the Foreign Ministers thereafter making decisions by a qualified majority for foreign policy issues and by unanimity for security questions. The Commission would play a central role in implementation, helping the Council to ensure "one voice." Consultation with the European Parliament would be regularized. Apart from this last provision, where the European Parliament has called for "scrutiny" of the EC's foreign policy, the Parliament has largely concurred with the Commission on CFSP. [39]

By 1997 the Commission promises expansion of external activity both substantively (in areas such as human rights, development and the environment) and financially (the "external action" component of the budget would increase by 81 percent between 1992 and 1997 whereas finances for the common agricultural policy and for structural operations will grow by only 12 percent and 58 percent respectively). [40] At the same time, the Commission recognizes that enlargement will require institutions to be "radically reformed" to avert a regression into "loose arrangements for foreign policy consultation." [41]

---

[37] Ludlow, Peter. Europe's Institutions: Europe's Politics. In Treverton, Gregory F. *The Shape of the New Europe*. New York, Council on Foreign Relations, 1992. p. 64.

[38] Commission of the European Communities. *Commission Opinion of 21 October 1990 on the Proposal for Amendment of the Treaty Establishing the European Economic Community With a View to Political Union*. COM(90)600. Brussels, Commission of the European Communities, October 23, 1990. p. 4. See also Delors' April 24, 1991 speech to the Council on Foreign Relations.

[39] European Parliament. *Second Interim Report Drawn Up on Behalf of the Committee on Institutional Affairs on the Intergovernmental Conference in the Context of Parliament's Strategy for European Union*. Document A 3-166/90. June 25, 1990. p. 7–8.

[40] See Commission of the European Communities, *From the Single Act to Maastricht and Beyond*, p. 39; and, Delors, 1992: A Pivotal Year, p. 44.

[41] Commission of the European Communities, Commission Opinion, p. 4.

For the post-1996, second stage of decisive Europe's development one prediction is the transformation of the Commission into the government or executive branch of the Community, including a cabinet (the European Council would become the collective head of state and the Council of Ministers would constitute a second chamber). The Commission would be elected by Parliament which, through uniform election laws, would represent the citizens of Europe. Both the Commission and the Parliament would, then, take over competences and responsibilities from the member states.[42]

Meeting the criteria for a world power through internal political rationalization, does not necessarily imply an abandonment of a civilian power's definition of international priorities and instruments in favor of traditional "strength and power," as some fear.[43] The EC's growing experience with peace-making combined with the problem of neutrality for both members (Ireland) and potential members (Austria, Switzerland, Sweden and Finland) probably relegates military intervention to a tool of last resort and then only in a larger multilateral context (UN or CSCE). Germany's commitment to eschewing traditional conceptions of power will frame the EC debate.

An institutionally redrawn European Community, particularly one based on the subsidiarity principle enshrined at Maastricht, would also need to account for the growth of regions, both within and across member states. The practical and conceptual attention to sub-national levels of government in EC internal policy-making has not extended to the foreign policy area, yet, as both the Canadian provinces and U.S. states demonstrate, this may be one of the toughest challenges for federalism.[44] Sub-national governments can be benign complements or useful conduits for federal governments, but they can also be open competitors. It is precisely at this level of government that one finds apparent opposition to Maastricht.

Diffident Europe

Before the Maastricht Treaty can go into effect it must be ratified by the member states of the EC. The European Parliament has voted for the Treaty, thereby clearing the way for the Italian and Belgian parliaments which have linked their ratification to the European Parliament's assent. However, ratification will not be automatic elsewhere, particularly in Germany where dissatisfaction with the treaty has been vociferous.

Ratification hurdles exist in both of the Federal Republic's parliamentary chambers. The prime ministers of Germany's sixteen federal states who come together to vote in the second chamber,

---

[42] See: Weidenfeld and Janning, *Global Responsibilities: Europe in Tomorrow's World,* p. 30; and, Research Group on European Affairs, *The Future of Europe: Alternatives—Strategies—Options,* p. 17.

[43] Weiler, *The Transformation of Europe,* p. 248283.

[44] On the general issue of federalism and foreign policy, see: Michelmann, Hans J. and Panayotis Soldatos, eds. *Federalism and International Relations: The Role of Subnational Units.* Oxford, Oxford University Press, 1990; and, Duchacek, Ivo D. *The Territorial Dimension of Politics Within, Among, and Across Nations.* Boulder, Westview Press, 1986. For comparative examples, see: Feldman, Elliot J., and Lily Gardner Feldman. Canada. and, Fry, Earl H. The United States of America. In Michelmann and Soldatos, *Federalism and International Relations.*

the *Bundesrat*, have attached three stipulations to their acceptance of the treaty: amendment of the German Basic Law to require the states' consent for any future transfer of sovereignty to multinational organizations; receipt of a report by 1996 on member states' fulfillment of the political preconditions (reduction of the democratic deficit through strengthening the European Parliament) and economic criteria (convergence) for moving to the third stage of economic and monetary union; and clarification of the financial consequences for the states of the EC's five-year budget plans.[45]

Similar concerns have been expressed among parliamentarians across the political spectrum in the *Bundestag*, with some voicing conditional acceptance and others promising formal opposition.[46] While vigorously defending the Maastricht Treaty, reflecting parliament's mood the German government has balked at the Commission's new budget proposals.

Parliamentary qualms are accompanied by popular fears about the loss of political sovereignty and choice and economic stability and control. State elections in Baden-Württemberg and Schleswig Holstein seem to confirm these sentiments with losses for the major parties and increases for the right-wing "Republican" party (a 9.9 percent jump in Baden-Württemberg) and German People's Union (a 5.7 percent growth in Schleswig-Holstein). If this development is reinforced in the 1994 national election against a background of economic malaise and growing public disenchantment with the cost of German unification, then the third scenario of a diffident Europe could occur.

Instead of internationalism and supranationalism, nationalism would be the order of the day. In place of interdependence and integration, independence would be the foreign policy goal. CFSP would be a target of attack rather than a target of opportunity.

Even though this scenario of a weak EC is possible, for several reasons it is the least likely of the three this chapter has outlined. The view of the federal states, unlike that of the right-wing, nationalist parties is not one of opposition in principle to the EC, but rather disaffection with the German federal government (the same is true for the Italian Northern League). If subsidiarity does develop in practice, then regional governments and parties could find an ally in the EC. Secondly, the increase in nationalist sentiment in the state elections was offset by a counter trend, for in Germany (as in France, and to a lesser extent Italy) the Greens also did well. Increasingly, environmental groups are looking to the EC to define both the agenda and the solution to European environmental problems.

On one of the key subjects attracting voters to the political right—immigration and asylum—the German government, like others, has looked to Brussels to Europeanize the issue. The threat of xenophobia and nationalism will likely be an incentive to institutionalize the EC's overall achievements now through ratification and later by moving forward in 1996.

---

[45] See *Financial Times*, March 13, 1992; and, *Süddeutsche Zeitung*, March 13, 1992.

[46] See *Süddeutsche Zeitung*, February 15, March 6, March 10, April 9, 1992; and, *Frankfurter Allgemeine Zeitung*, March 6, 1992.

Implications for the United States

Since 1989, the United States has become sensitized to the EC as an international political actor, reflected in statements by President Bush and Secretary of State Baker, in the expansion of EC-U.S. consultations, and in the November 1990 signing of the Transatlantic Declaration.[47] As both partners continue to define their foreign policy identities in the post-Cold War world, the EC-U.S. relationship inevitably will change. Each of the three scenarios described here holds different policy implications for U.S. reactions to the EC in the international system and for EC-U.S. relations.

ASSERTIVE EUROPE

Maastricht's continued institutional separation of external affairs and EPC together with the intergovernmental character of CFSP reinforce an old American complaint regarding the variable identity of the EC interlocutor. The absence of a consistently unified position among policy sectors and among member states means the United States cannot expect what it hoped for in the Gulf War, namely rapid military action in a crisis situation beyond Europe. What the United States should anticipate is a renewed EC commitment to conflict resolution in the Third World, an arena where the United States historically has seen little room for EC involvement. Both in Europe and elsewhere, the EC will pursue its peace-making approach in the context of multilateral institutions, particularly the CSCE and the UN, actively seeking definition of the growing agenda and participation in attempted solutions. The EC will present, then, challenges of inaction and of action.

Yet, the United States will derive certain advantages from this scenario. It will permit a further flexibility of approach, where the United States can still deal with the EC both as a multilateral entity and as a collectivity of states with whom it has bilateral relations. The current inability to mount a common military stance adds to the likelihood of further EC priority to development aid and the environment, areas where the United States lends rhetorical support but lacks the financial means for initiatives. The EC may have a head start over the United States in according importance to the UN and the CSCE, but the United States is still a key member of both institutions.

The United States should pursue three responses to assertive Europe. It should finally acknowledge that the EC is a political actor, not just in Europe, but in the international system as a whole. Whether the United States chooses then to see the EC as a competitor or as a complement, it should recognize that the EC's international strength lies in its institutionalized regional relationships. The EC's extensive ties with other parts of the world make foolhardy any plans to act on the Pentagon's prescription of a one-superpower world.

---

[47] See, for example, President Bush's speech of May 31, 1989, at the Rheingoldhalle, Mainz. Washington, D.C., Office of the Press Secretary, White House; and, Secretary of State Baker's December 12, 1989 speech in Berlin. Washington, D.C., U.S. Department of State. Bureau of Public Affairs. The text of the Transatlantic Declaration is in *European Community News.* Washington, D.C., EC Office of Press and Public Affairs, November 27, 1990. Current consultation arrangements are detailed in the Declaration.

Again, whether for cooperative or competitive purposes, the United States must be active in the same fora as the EC, and, therefore, should expand its efforts to shape the institutions and priorities of the CSCE and the UN.

Until the EC has clarified further its institutional future, the framework of the Transatlantic Declaration is probably adequate for airing differences and planning cooperation. However, the United States should use the arrangements fully and imaginatively. It would be unfortunate if the United States paid lip service to the Declaration just when the July 1991 Joint EC-Japan Declaration is going into effect. And, even if the EC cannot yet speak with one voice, in the context of the Transatlantic Declaration machinery the United States should try to by improving bureaucratic coordination of policy toward Europe.

DECISIVE EUROPE

The institutional and substantive coherence of decisive Europe will render the EC more effective internationally, including in the military sphere if it so chooses. The United States will have the benefit of knowing with whom in the EC it must deal, but no longer will enjoy the possibility of playing bilateral favorites with Germany and the UK.

A decisive EC will expand its involvement in conflict resolution, not only in terms of regions of the world, but as in Yugoslavia, with respect to stages of the process. The firm linkage of political and economic tools, backed up by the potential for military action, may make it impossible for the United States to resist the EC as a co-organizer in regional peace-making.

The United States should prepare now for the eventuality of Europe as a world power. It should determine specific areas for burden-sharing, not only in Central and Eastern Europe and the CIS, but in other regions of the world, particularly those where Europe has comparative political and economic advantage. It should anticipate that a larger gap in interests will emerge, requiring more regular and more powerful consultation mechanisms. As the EC establishes synergy between its economic and political dimensions, so should EC-U.S. consultations through a treaty.

The process of concluding a treaty would force both sides to confront the competitive and cooperative elements of their interactions, would elevate the relationship for both parties and for third countries, and would facilitate management of an increasingly complex partnership. In the past few years, a variety of specific models has been floated in American policy circles, including a revival of the 1967 resolution of the Committee of Action for the United States of Europe (the "Monnet Committee"); and a transformation of the individual Friendship, Commerce and Navigation treaties (made obsolete by the completion of the internal market) that exist with most EC members into a bilateral treaty.

DIFFIDENT EUROPE

A Europe of independent nation-states might be easier for the United States to deal with, and certainly would not pose the same kind of challenge in the international arena as united Europe.

However, renationalization of foreign and security policies might not bring with it renewal of traditional bilateral ties for the United States, but rather anti-Americanism. Moreover, the reassertion of nationalism probably would occur in the context of profound economic problems and political confusion. The ensuing effective disintegration of Europe would be highly destabilizing. After all, the United States has come to rely on the EC as the force of stability in Central and Eastern Europe and in the Commonwealth of Independent States.

The United States can promote policies to help forestall the unravelling of Western Europe. It can welcome ratification of the Maastricht Treaty and recognize openly the virtues of further institutionalization of integration. It can support other European institutions, particularly those in which the EC is active, thereby increasing the density of transnational networks and making their undoing harder. The United States can also embed the EC as a partner in international organizations.

In the transatlantic relationship, the United States can acknowledge in principle and in practice the greater symmetry of the EC to avoid the perception on the political right of the EC as an object of U.S. domination.

For the next decade, the United States can anticipate an assertive EC in the international arena, but it must plan now for a more decisive Europe at the beginning of the next century and be prepared for the least desirable situation of disintegration.

U.S.-WEST EUROPEAN RELATIONS AND EUROPE'S FUTURE

By Stanley R. Sloan *

CONTENTS

SUMMARY

The Cold War has ended in victory for the West; a victory for the power and productivity of Western political and economic systems, and a victory for the principles that underlie those systems. That victory, however, has raised questions about the future of the West and of the institutions that were instrumental in fashioning the successful outcome. Without a Soviet/communist threat as a cohesive force holding the North American-West European alliance together, differing interests have been exposed, challenging the cooperative instincts that defined the alliance.

The democratic revolutions in Eastern and Central Europe, the unification of Germany and the disintegration of the Soviet Union have fundamentally altered the European political landscape. The fledgling democracies aspire to membership in the successful institutions of the Western system. To guarantee their future security, most aspire to some form of association with NATO and its integral security link to the United States. To confirm their entry into the Western system and to guarantee a higher standard of living in the future, they aspire to membership in the European Community. For the EC, this poses a number of basic questions. Can the EC stick to an ambitious program of economic, political and military integration while at the same time responding to the political and

* Stanley R. Sloan is a Senior Specialist in International Security Policy, Office of Senior Specialists, Congressional Research Service.

economic needs of the new democracies? Can the momentum of the integration process be maintained without the impetus previously provided by the Soviet/communist threat? What are the dangers that U.S. and West European policies will increasingly emphasize the competitive areas of transatlantic relations to the detriment of cooperation in those relationships?

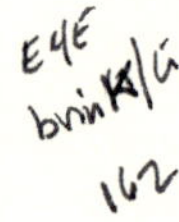

Meanwhile, the entire nature of the U.S.-EC relationship may be up for grabs in the growing debate in the United States over its future role in the world. The United States has supported the process of European integration for over four decades on the assumption that the process benefited rather than undermined U.S. interests. Much of the U.S. self-interest in the integration process related to the imperatives of the Cold War confrontation with the Soviet Union. Without the Cold War justifying framework, some in the United States question the wisdom of supporting a uniting Europe that is in economic and political competition with the United States. Whether or not the United States and Europe can sustain a relationship in which the cooperative aspects outweigh the competitive aspects could be the next major test for the stability of the international system.

The Roots of U.S. Support for European Integration

For nearly four decades, the goal of creating a European Union among the members of the European Community has been an ambitious plan. The community-building process has never moved rapidly, and at times has been required to take a step backwards before managing a few steps forward. The construction of Europe has been likened to that of a cathedral—section by section, generation after generation of architects and stonemasons, the structure rises; the shape and size of each section depends on the imagination and resources available at the time; and the final contours remain unknown, and perhaps unknowable, as the cathedral is built.

Throughout the construction of the European "cathedral," each EC member has pursued its own national agenda and preferences within the EC decisionmaking framework, ensuring that consensus-building would require laborious negotiations and difficult compromises. The still-strong force of nationalism has limited the use of majority voting to carefully proscribed areas outside of what any member would consider "vital interests." And yet, in the long view of history, the process has moved ahead with a certain persistence in spite of its sometimes-glacial pace.

Once again, at Maastricht in the Netherlands in December 1991, the EC leaders met to give new impetus to the process. This time, the leaders agreed to complete a monetary union and to adopt a common currency during the next decade. The EC leaders also decided to expand the process of European Political Cooperation (EPC) into the area of defense. They agreed that the Western European Union (WEU) would become the EC's defense arm, within the overall framework of the transatlantic alliance. They decided to move the WEU's headquarters from London to Brussels, to be near the other EC institutions. But the leaders did not resolve a number of critical issues about how to coordinate force commitments and command and control between NATO and WEU missions.

U.S. foreign policy for the last forty years has supported the process of West European integration. This process was seen initially as a way of facilitating recovery from World War II, avoiding post World War I mistakes by establishing a constructive and yet constraining framework for Germany, and blocking the advance of Soviet power and communist ideology.

The United States was prepared to pay a price for European integration in the earlier years, but much less so once Western Europe was once again flourishing economically, relatively stable internally, and apparently resistant to Soviet encroachment. The main "prices" that have occasionally raised questions about U.S. support for the EC have been the economic/trade consequences of the Common Agricultural Policy and the danger, posed mainly by French attitudes toward integration, that the political definition of "Europe" would have the effect of attenuating ties to the United States.

Contemporary U.S. policy has been marked by an inherent schizophrenia regarding the European integration process. Pressured by Members of Congress, U.S. administrations have for many years encouraged the European allies to lessen U.S. defense burdens by taking on more responsibility for their own defense. Now that Europe is becoming much less reliant on U.S. military power for its security, some in the United States are troubled by the consequences of greater European self-reliance and a diminished U.S. leadership role.

U.S. officials still say that they favor a European "pillar" in the Western alliance, but not a European bloc. The distinction between the two images presumably is based on the judgment that a pillar is supportive of the transatlantic community while a bloc just gets in the way. It is nonetheless difficult to imagine how the EC can constitute a pillar without having at least some of the attributes of a bloc. In any case, U.S. support for the European Community in today's context is much more qualified than in the past.

European Integration in a Changing Europe

In 1991, the Community faced perhaps the biggest challenge in its history. The internal dynamics of the integration process suggested that the EC had reached a point where the member governments would have to push political cooperation ahead once again or perhaps stagnate, perhaps irretrievably. At the same time, the neighborhood around the EC cathedral experienced a more-or-less peaceful revolution that produced many potential new members for the congregation, new supplicants to draw on the parish's coffers, and pressure to fortify as well as enlarge the edifice to accommodate the new demands.

This essay focuses on the changing world around the community-building process and the challenges that have been posed for the construction of a united Europe. It concentrates mainly on the political and security aspects of change. It then assesses some of the implications for U.S.-EC relations of the evolving structure of European and international relations. Some of the key issues that have not yet been resolved that will come into play in future decisionmaking include:

- Can the European Community be the vehicle for uniting all of Europe without sacrificing much of the organizational rigor and cohesion that exists among current members?
- Can the momentum toward a united Europe be maintained without the motivation until recently provided by a threat from the Soviet Union?
- Does it make sense for the European Community to develop a common defense among its members without any apparent common military threat to their security?
- Can the United States develop a new concept of its role in the world consistent with a continuing partnership with its European allies and support for the process of European integration?
- Or, without a Soviet threat against Europe, will it increasingly appear to Americans that the main motivation for European integration is to be unified "against us" rather than "with us."

The Key Changes in the European Neighborhood

The European Community was forged in the Cold War crucible, as were most of the post-World War II European and transatlantic institutions. A major part of the Community's rationale was to fortify the members sufficiently to be able to resist Communist subversion and economically strong enough to be able to help balance Soviet military power. NATO is usually seen, justifiably, as the main bulwark against communist ideology and Soviet power. But the community-building process in Western Europe was as important a part of the West's Cold War arsenal economically as NATO was militarily. Both institutions also were designed to help create circumstances in which the participating nations would have no future incentive to war against one another.

Given these historical roots, the end of the Cold War and of the Soviet threat creates different circumstances for the EC, just as it does for NATO. The difference may be that, while NATO is searching for a new definition of its mission, the European Community has long since developed roles and capabilities that extend beyond its post-World War Two origins.

THE DEMOCRATIC REVOLUTIONS IN EASTERN EUROPE

Most of the key changes in the European neighborhood grew out of decisions made in Moscow. The failure of communism to serve as an effective political and economic system for the Warsaw Pact members had been obvious for many years, but the Soviet Union used its overwhelming military superiority to keep those systems afloat. Historians may debate the cause and course of the fall of the Soviet empire for many years. But for contemporary political analysts it may be sufficient to note that it was Mikhail Gorbachev who acknowledged the system's shortcomings and, most importantly, signaled that the Soviet Union would no longer be willing to spend additional political capital to keep failed systems intact in other countries.

Gorbachev's promotion of *glasnost* and *perestroika* in the Soviet system implied that greater openness and reform would be appropriate for Moscow's allies as well. Granted, Gorbachev had no idea that the process of change that he promoted would lead to the end of the Warsaw Pact, dissolution of the Soviet Union, and his own downfall, but he indeed let the genie out of the bottle. Once it became clear that the Soviet Union would no longer enforce any strict ideological or systemic line on its allies, the old regimes fell in rapid succession, first to a mixture of reform-minded communists and opportunists from within the old system and then, in most cases, to those seeking a more complete break with the past.

The main consequence for the European Community of these revolutions was that virtually overnight an entirely new set of potential applicants, aid recipients and investment opportunities stood knocking at the door. None of the new regimes promised to be ready for membership in the near future, but Poland, the Czech and Slovak Republic and Hungary laid claim to future membership and some form of associate status as soon as possible. Bulgaria, Romania, and even Albania moved in similar directions, albeit from the position of substantially lower levels of economic development and with a mixture of questions about the potential for democracy to take root.

GERMAN UNIFICATION

The most significant collapse in Eastern Europe was that of the regime in the German Democratic Republic (GDR). Once Gorbachev removed the Soviet prop for Erich Honnecker's East German regime, its future was in doubt. The fact that reform governments had begun to surround the GDR intensified pressure on the regime, and in 1989–90 led to a rapid sequence of events symbolized by the breaching of the Berlin Wall in November 1989, transformation of the East German regime, and, in 1990, a decision by the East German people to join their West German cousins in recreating a united Germany.

This stunning development fundamentally altered political realities within the European Community and in Europe as a whole. No longer would West Germany be politically handicapped by its unfulfilled goal of reunification. Germany could complete the process, underway for several years, of becoming a "normal" state in the international system, even if several self-imposed inhibitions still characterized German policy (such as strong domestic opposition to a German military role outside Europe).

Importantly, the dramatic change unsettled some of Germany's European neighbors, particularly those who believed that Germany's division was for the best, sharing French novelist Francois Mauriac's sentiment, "I love Germany so much that I am happy there are two of them." Even though united Germany will be preoccupied with the trials and tribulations of the unification process for several years, once these costs have been absorbed, a united Germany could be the economic and political powerhouse of Europe. Even if such a strong Germany would likely abstain from a strong military role, France and some other countries have looked nervously toward a prospective future of German hegemony in Europe.

In part to ensure that future German power remains contained within an acceptable European framework, France has become increasingly prepared to make more substantial sacrifices of national sovereignty than previously in order to strengthen the European Community framework. In addition, some observers have speculated that the strong French push toward political and military cooperation on the European level was intended to play on France's strength (her status as a nuclear weapons state) to maintain balance in her relationship with a larger and economically stronger Germany. Not unaware of French motivations and the concerns of other neighbors, the German government has judged that a strong push toward European union was in its interest. German unification, according to this perspective, therefore has provided new incentives for the process of European community-building.

DISBANDING THE WARSAW PACT

As the communist dominoes fell throughout Eastern and Central Europe, some Western observers believed for a brief time that it might be convenient if the Warsaw Pact were somehow maintained to ensure that NATO would have a negotiating partner in the East to continue the process of arms control and disarmament. This, however, was not the preference of the new regimes in the Warsaw Pact countries. Each new government in the East saw the Warsaw Pact as a symbol of previous Soviet domination and as a source of support for the communist regimes that they had just cast aside. NATO would have to do without an Eastern negotiating partner, because no reform government in Eastern Europe had any interest in keeping the Warsaw Pact alive.

The end of the Warsaw Pact, which came on July 1, 1991, left an institutional vacuum in Central Europe. All the former Warsaw Pact governments participated in the Conference on Security and Cooperation in Europe (CSCE), but none of them saw the CSCE as a sufficient framework for their inclusion in the European system as free, democratic nations. Poland, the Czech and Slovak Republic and Hungary wanted to be associated as quickly as possible with Western institutions, particularly NATO and the European Community. NATO was attractive because it symbolized a link to the United States. The new democracies wanted to intensify that link sufficiently to deter any future Soviet attempt to reimpose control and, perhaps more imminently, to block any counter-revolution by supporters of the old regimes.

NATO countries were wary of taking on any defense commitments in Eastern and Central Europe, and throughout 1990 and most of 1991, were wary of doing anything that might provoke the Soviet regime and stimulate a turn away from reform there. Nevertheless, once the disintegration of the Soviet Union accelerated after the failed coup attempt in Moscow, the NATO members agreed (at their November 1991 summit meeting in Rome) to create a North Atlantic Cooperation Council as a vehicle for consultations with representatives of all former Warsaw Pact governments and, subsequently, new states emerging from the dissolved Soviet

Union. As a result, all these governments became participants in the transatlantic alliance even though they are not "members" of NATO.

At the same time, the East European reformist regimes aspired to membership in the European Community as the symbol of acceptance in the Western economic system, the route to more open markets in Western Europe, and the main source of investment in their nascent free market systems.

One problem for the Community is that none of the former Warsaw Pact countries is yet sufficiently developed to participate in the highly competitive EC market without some level of protection for their fledgling free market economies, and a commitment to membership for the new states implies a willingness to help them advance economically to a point where they could stand up to the rigors of the market. Yet another set of challenges is presented by the fact that eventual membership for former Warsaw Pact countries threatens to make even more cumbersome both the EC decisionmaking process and to swell further the EC bureaucracy, as countries claim their share of EC policymaking positions.

DISINTEGRATION OF THE SOVIET UNION

Coming hard on the heels of the abolition of the Warsaw Pact, the disintegration of the Soviet Union has posed additional challenges to the European Community. The initial challenge has been the threat of instability. It was clear that the Cold War victory over communism, in which the success of the European Community played a major part, could not be consolidated if the successor regimes were not insulated against a backlash inspired by political and economic chaos. The prospect of winning the (cold) war and then losing the peace emerged as a very real threat. And Europeans could not rely on U.S. leadership and resources to meet this new threat to the degree that they had relied on U.S. military power and strategic leadership throughout the Cold War.

From a coldly calculated perspective, the situation in Europe following the abolition of the Warsaw Pact and the dissolution of the Soviet Union was more directly threatening to the interests of the West European states than to those of the United States. Recognition of this fact is reflected in the fact that of the $80 billion in assistance pledged to the former Soviet Union since September 1990, over 75 percent of the total has been pledged by EC countries, 57 percent by Germany alone. The United States share represented only 6.5 percent. [1]

The disappearance of the Soviet military threat, and its replacement by the potential for political and economic chaos, accompanied by mass migrations out of the former Soviet Union and East European states, reversed fundamentally the U.S.-European dependency relationship. The relationship shifted from one in which West European nations depended heavily on U.S. military power for their security to one in which military power was, in the near term, much less relevant, and the main threat required economic

[1] Friedman, Thomas L. Bush to Press Congress to Approve $645 Million for Ex-Soviet Lands. *New York Times*, January 23, 1992. p. 1, 8.

and political assets that the Europeans are deploying more effectively and generously than the United States.

The disintegration of the Soviet Union therefore largely liberated Western Europe from its previous reliance on U.S. military power. At the same time, however, the disappearance of the Soviet threat also removed one of the original motivations for West European integration, and raised questions about what would motivate the process in the future as it became more and more demanding and difficult with most of the rest of Europe wanting to join in a Europe united from the Atlantic to the Urals. The East European countries that aspire to EC membership will surely be joined in line by those former Soviet republics that get on track toward democracy and free market economies. Latvia, Lithuania and Estonia, the former Soviet Baltic republics might be the first to apply, but the potential for Russia and Ukraine someday to ask the EC to open its gates suggests a much more challenging scenario.

COOPERATIVE EUROPEAN SECURITY FRAMEWORK

Even before the Warsaw Pact started to unravel, the initial stages of a new European security framework appeared to be emerging. This new system was also primarily the consequence of Gorbachev's decision that the Soviet Union no longer needed, and could no longer afford, the defensive glacis that it had thrown up around its periphery. This implied not only that Warsaw Pact nations could be allowed to evolve their own reformed socialist systems of government and economy, but also that past Soviet and Pact defense efforts could be reduced substantially without putting the security of the Soviet Union at risk. This was the essential message delivered by Gorbachev to the United Nations in December 1988. [2]

Gorbachev's 1988 initiative opened the way for consideration of an entirely new approach to security in Europe, one that depended increasingly on cooperative structures and relationships and less on confrontation and military balance. Progress toward this more cooperative system developed in two parallel frameworks. One, the Conference on Confidence and Security Building Measures and Disarmament in Europe (CDE), concentrated on building up a structure of information exchanges, constraints and inspections that had begun in the adoption of voluntary confidence building measures included in the 1975 Helsinki "Final Act" of the conference on Security and Cooperation in Europe (CSCE). The second, the negotiations on Conventional Armed Forces in Europe (CFE), succeeded the long-running negotiations on Mutual and Balanced Force Reductions (MBFR) in 1989 as the framework for negotiating reductions in military forces from the Atlantic Ocean to the Ural Mountains.

A new set of confidence and security building measures negotiated in the CDE was approved at the Paris summit meeting of the CSCE in November 1990. A treaty reducing conventional armaments in Europe was signed at the same meeting. Implementation

---

[2] Statement by Mikhail S. Gorbachev, President of the Presidium of the Supreme Soviet of the USSR, General Secretary of the Central Committee of the Communist Party of the Soviet Union, at a Plenary Meeting of the United Nations General Assembly, December 7, 1988.

of the treaty has been complicated and delayed by the dissolution of the Soviet Union. But as the measures from the two negotiations take effect, the rudimentary structure of a cooperative security system will be in place. In addition, NATO's North Atlantic Cooperation Council now constitutes another part of the framework for cooperative management of European security relationships.

These nascent cooperative security mechanisms are helping translate the political changes in Eastern Europe and the Soviet Union into a new set of institutional relationships. This emerging cooperative security system is an important part of the EC's European neighborhood. To the extent that it helps ensure peaceful relationships on the continent and promotes reductions in armaments, it will complement the EC's efforts to overcome Europe's division. But the complex set of old and new consultative frameworks will require that the EC coordinate its own discussions of foreign and defense issues both in substance and timing with the discussions going on in the other fora.

THE PERSIAN GULF AND YUGOSLAV CONFLICTS

In the year before the EC reached agreement at Maastricht to begin shaping common foreign and defense policies, the Community members were challenged to try to deal cohesively with the Iraqi invasion of Kuwait and, closer to home, the internecine conflict in Yugoslavia. The Gulf crisis demonstrated how unprepared Europe was to translate the European Community's impressive economic strength into concerted political and military action. The failure of the EC to mediate a peaceful settlement in Yugoslavia suggested that the crisis was beyond the current limits on EC security cooperation, whatever its future potential might be.

The European Community countries eventually made important contributions to allied military forces in the Gulf as well as providing important financial contributions to underwrite U.S. military efforts there. Many Americans were disappointed, however, at Europe's inability to act more cohesively. European Community naval contributions to the Gulf War effort were coordinated through the Western European Union, strengthening the case for recognizing the WEU as the "military arm" of the European Community, as was done at the Maastricht summit. Because the Gulf war tended to emphasize the fact that Europe did not have adequate means to behave as an influential actor in the international system, it gave new impetus to the effort to shape a European defense identity. But it also made clear that the members of the Community are many years away from a sufficient political consensus to make the sacrifices of national sovereignty necessary to subordinate their national military efforts to any common European military structure.

Two factors led the European Community to its involvement in its Yugoslav mediating efforts. First, prior to the attempted coup in the Soviet Union in August 1991, the Soviet government opposed outside intervention in Yugoslavia that might set precedents that could be used to justify international intervention in its own growing internal crisis. Moscow could have blocked any UN role with its veto in the Security Council. The Soviets also opposed any CSCE-based intervention for the same reason.

Second, the United States was not inclined to take the lead in dealing with the Yugoslav crisis. At the time, the Bush Administration was still preoccupied with the Gulf crisis and presumably had the additional incentive of wanting to avoid a Soviet-U.S. confrontation over the Yugoslav case. Perhaps an additional factor was domestic criticism of the Bush Administration for being preoccupied with foreign affairs and insufficiently attentive to domestic problems. As a result, the Administration encouraged the Europeans to take the lead.

The EC's numerous failed attempts to broker a successful ceasefire was interpreted by some observers as revealing the fact that the Community did not yet have much clout in the foreign and defense policy arena. To be fair, however, it might be suggested that as long as the Yugoslav factions preferred fighting to a peaceful settlement, no international peace efforts would have had much luck. Ultimately, with Soviet objections removed, the United Nations was able to assume greater responsibility for attempting to deal with the crisis. History may nonetheless record, whether fairly or not, that the European Community failed in its first serious attempt to exercise its international influence in crisis conditions.

Perhaps the most interesting historical footnote to the Yugoslav crisis, however, will be the fact that it produced a watershed development in German diplomacy. Germany's desire to recognize the breakaway Yugoslav republics of Slovenia and Croatia and its ability to force EC-wide recognition of these states early in 1992 may be recorded as Germany's first post-Cold War attempt to use its increased international clout to achieve a national foreign policy objective. Whether this signals the beginning of a new era of more assertive German diplomacy or is merely a case of Germany seeking in somewhat difficult circumstances to define its role in the post-Cold War world could have a major influence on future political dynamics within the European Community and between the EC and the rest of the world.

U.S. Perspectives on European Integration

This combination of changes and challenges in Europe has coincided with growing irritations in U.S. relations with the European Community, particularly with two of its leading members. Early in 1992, the press reported what were portrayed as tensions between U.S. and French officials on a wide variety of issues ranging from trade to leadership of the Western military alliance. [3] Other stories suggested some official U.S. concern about a growing unilateralist tendency in German policy. Unnamed officials told reporters that Germany had not taken the interests of its allies into account in a variety of political and economic decision taken in recent months. [4] President Bush, while still supporting the process of European integration, nevertheless raised questions about the depth of American support when he accused the European Community of hiding behind an "iron curtain" of protectionism. Trade differences be-

[3] For example, see Drozdiak, William. Tensions Between France and U.S. aid to Turn Allies into Rivals. *Washington Post*, January 22, 1992. p. A25.

[4] See Fisher, Marc. U.S. Dismisses Unease over Germany's Role. *Washington Post*, January 23, 1992. p. A17.

tween the United States and its allies are not new. But harsh words for trading partners appear no longer tempered by a core of security interdependence as they were in the past.

A "YES, BUT" PERSPECTIVE ON THE EC

There has always been a variety of tendencies in the U.S. attitude toward the EC. Public opinion is still very favorable toward Europe and, in particular, toward the EC members, reflecting deep European roots in American society, perceptions of shared values, and alliance relationships, among other factors.

Only within the policy elite is there much specific focus on the EC and the integration process. With some experts and officials, there still is a tendency to support European integration because of the belief that it generally reaffirms American values and benefits U.S. interests. This might be called the "traditionalist" school, located in the center of the U.S. political spectrum, which envisions a stronger EC as part of a continuing transatlantic community of shared interests and cooperation. The traditionalists largely applaud the results of Maastricht as having given the process of European integration an important push forward. Some among them might be disappointed that a more "federal" outcome was not possible, but on balance they will be pleased.

Another tendency sees the EC as part of the answer to the need for the United States to respond more effectively to its internal agenda. This perspective, which has deep roots in the defense burdensharing debate of recent years, supports the goal of the EC taking full responsibility for its own security and assuming progressively larger burdens and international leadership roles in relief of the United States. Such observers might be mildly disappointed that the Maastricht outcome did not promise any near-term burden relief for the United States. Nonetheless, those with this perspective have been inclined to seize on the summit's outcome as further evidence that the United States can move more rapidly toward the exits from the European theater to return more rapidly to the home front where so many domestic problems call out for money and political attention.

A third tendency, skeptical of the benefits of European integration for the United States, focuses more on particular U.S. economic and political interests. This tendency suggests that the United States must actively defend its interests in the European integration process and should, if necessary, disrupt community consensus if such consensus might operate against U.S. self interests. Particularly in the absence of an active Soviet threat against Europe, the process of European integration may have mainly negative consequences for U.S. interests, according to this approach.

Current U.S. policy reflects the influence of all these perspectives. The traditional approach still dominates the rhetoric of U.S. policy, but the desire to escape from overseas burdens has become a much more important factor in American politics, and the tendency to look more skeptically on U.S. support for European integration has become more influential in the absence of the strong geopolitical requirement to support European union during the Cold

War. In a "yes, but" policy environment, the "but" therefore has more emphasis.

CONTEMPORARY U.S. POLITICS AND U.S.-EC RELATIONS

The immediate future of U.S.-EC relations will be directly affected by the campaign leading up to the November 1992 elections. The political climate in the United States is not at the moment particularly conducive to the United States playing a leading international political role. In this election year, most American politicians will try to demonstrate that their priorities put the United States first, and all other concerns second, even if they do not espouse an "America first" political outlook. The overwhelming political weight of the domestic agenda may make it impossible for leading politicians in 1992 to contribute to a consensual redefinition of a pro-active U.S. foreign and international security policy. The principal justification—and source of domestic political support—for the leading U.S. role in the world over the past forty years has been the *fear* of communism and its embodiment in the policies of a powerful, expansionist Soviet Union. Now that the Soviet threat no longer serves as an effective rationalizing and mobilizing force for the U.S. role in the world, the search has begun for a new approach, but it may take several years for a new consensus to emerge.

As a consequence, the next few years may provide an opportunity for the EC nations to assume new leadership responsibilities in global political and economic affairs. U.S. preoccupation with domestic issues could create a "leadership gap" internationally. At a time of economic malaise, public pessimism about the future, mounting social ills and structural weaknesses, the United States is not well-positioned to be a confident promoter of "the American way." Under these circumstances, perhaps the United States, for better or worse, will continue to drift in its international role until it gets a better handle on its internal agenda and develops sufficient renewed self-confidence to play once again a strong, effective international leadership role.

The challenge for the European Community at this stage of development of American policy formulation is to avoid becoming part of a newly perceived external threat to U.S. interests while taking on a greater degree of international responsibility and making it clear that it does so in partnership with the United States rather than as a critic of a seemingly floundering U.S. foreign policy. Had the Maastricht summit outcome created the impression that Europe was uniting "against us instead of with us," a groundswell of criticism might have arisen.

Meanwhile, the "deepening" of European integration that was decided in Maastricht should be sufficient to ensure that the Community becomes even more of a global economic and political force in the years ahead. The most difficult test for the EC, however, may be the one posed by the great variety of candidates standing at or near its door asking for admission. From an American point of view, the most important contribution to international peace and stability that the EC could make in the 1990s would be to develop supportive political and economic ties to Europe's new democracies. Whether the EC can successfully meet this challenge while continuing the long march toward closer union remains to be seen.

A Longer Term Perspective on U.S.-European Relations

Over the longer term, the Europe that the United States has grown used to is gone, never to return. Given the rapid process of political change, it is difficult to anticipate all the possible elements of future European developments. Current trends, however, suggest some general directions.

NATO will likely continue in some form. The North Atlantic Treaty expresses a community of political, economic, and security interests among the signatories that transcends the former "Soviet threat." The creation of the North Atlantic Cooperation Council in NATO has brought all former Warsaw Pact countries and the governments that have succeeded the Soviet government into the NATO consultative process. In the coming years, several former Warsaw Pact states, including even Russia, might be invited to join the alliance, fundamentally altering its nature. Under these circumstances, NATO could become the main military security component of a cooperative security system from "Vancouver to Vladivostock."

For several years into the future, many practical areas of cooperation in defense may be coordinated through existing NATO channels. NATO's defense planning mechanisms could play an important role in ensuring that the inevitable reductions in Western military efforts and defense spending are accomplished efficiently and without creating destabilizing military weaknesses. Further down the road, the European Community and the Western European Union might assume many of these functions, particularly if the U.S. military presence on the ground in Europe is reduced to token levels. NATO's main function at such a time might be to provide a consultative forum linking the United States with European democracies. It will also likely remain the principal framework for U.S.-European military cooperation as long as such cooperation is deemed mutually beneficial.

The European Community could become the most vital and important European institution of the future if the EC members can find a formula that both permits the core membership to deepen their economic, political, and even perhaps military cooperation while linking themselves politically and economically to the new East European democracies, other West European countries, and the post-Soviet successor states. Nevertheless, the process of European integration will likely remain an evolutionary one. Wider European participation in the EC will tend to slow down the process of integration. Barriers to rapid political and military integration probably would not be overcome even if stimulated by a total withdrawal of U.S. forces from Europe.

The Conference on Security and Cooperation in Europe will arguably serve as the vehicle for all CSCE signatories, including the United States, Canada, and the successor regimes to the former Soviet Union, to participate in the shaping of a new Europe. The process of conventional arms control within the CSCE framework will be restructured to encourage stable and peaceful military relations among all participants, viewed on a bilateral and regional basis, and not just on the East-West level as originally intended.

IMPLICATIONS FOR U.S. POLICY

These potential developments raise a series of important issues for U.S. foreign and defense policy. A fundamental question is what role the United States wants to play in the new European architecture. The process of change in Europe and in the former Soviet Union appears to have unleashed a new Great Debate in the United States about the allocation of resources between U.S. international involvement, particularly defense spending, and domestic problems. Already, the desire to provide economic assistance to emerging democracies in Eastern Europe has come into conflict with competing domestic program requirements, previous foreign aid priorities, and the desire to reduce the U.S. budget deficit.

President Bush has stated his resolve to see that the United States remains an active participant in Europe, politically, economically, and militarily. However, a Europe in which military alliances are less important will make dealing with our allies more complex. The United States is currently exploring questions about what the full range of its means of influence are, beyond its military strength within NATO; which of these is likely to be most important in the years ahead; and which may require additional resources or new impetus. Such changes may also create subtle or overt alterations in ongoing U.S. bilateral relations.

West European economic and political cooperation has progressed to the point where these countries can achieve consensus on a wide range of issues and can act in a coordinated way in many circumstances. There are still, however, many issues on which the major European powers disagree. This is particularly true when it comes to the "big" issues such as future monetary cooperation, Third World issues, and defense organization, to name a few. Recent events have raised questions about whether the United States still has a useful role in shaping Europe's future. Such splits as exist among our allies, however, suggest that the United States probably still has a potentially constructive "leadership" role to play at least in shaping approaches to and compromises on future pan-European issues.

Perhaps the key argument for the United States remaining actively involved in European security arrangements is the fact that twice in this century the United States has had to send soldiers into combat in Europe. Officials on both sides of the Atlantic are reluctant to remove completely what has been a major component of a peaceful European system since World War II. In addition, NATO still provides the one established forum in which U.S. military forces can develop habits of cooperation with allied military forces. The infrastructure for cooperation could in the future support U.S.-allied military operations outside Europe, for example as part of United Nations-authorized peacekeeping or even peacemaking efforts or for other projects, such as disaster relief and humanitarian assistance.

It appears certain now that the United States will be able to reduce its military forces in Europe substantially below current levels. Those cuts will reduce dramatically that portion of U.S. defense expenditures that are "NATO-related." The Bush Administration has projected a reduction in U.S. force levels in Europe over the next several years down to 150,000 military personnel. Increasingly, however, Washington observers expect U.S. force levels in Europe to drop to below 100,000 by the mid-1990s.

Whether or not even such a reduced presence can be sustained in the United States is debatable. In recent years, many Americans have questioned why the United States should still be defending "fat cat" Europeans. The logic of such a question suggests the desirability of pulling out all U.S. forces from Europe, irrespective of any positive political role the U.S. presence might play. From another perspective, however, continuing U.S. military cooperation in NATO could be seen as actually facilitating reductions in overall U.S. military efforts. As the U.S. reduces its overall forces levels and defense spending, it will become increasingly dependent on cooperation with other nations to deal with future security threats. NATO is currently the only forum with a track record of promoting such cooperation on a continuing basis.

In any case, as the prominence of the U.S. military role in Europe recedes, it is possible that U.S. political influence will recede as well. As the importance of military instruments of power diminishes in relations among European countries, influence may depend much more on political and economic instruments of power. Under such circumstances, future U.S. influence in Europe may depend increasingly on the political and economic roles that it plays than on the extent of its military presence.

As long as the European countries believe, as virtually all European governments currently do, that the involvement of the United States in European security affairs is in their interest, they will provide both a measure of political and financial support for a continued U.S. military presence, albeit limited, in Europe. Because for the Europeans that military presence will have largely political significance in the absence of an imminent threat, however, they will not likely respond favorably to attempts by the United States to gain concessions in trade negotiations or in other aspects of the relationship that run counter to their own domestic interests. In other words, the United States will retain a degree of influence in European affairs due to the fact that the Europeans want us there, but the United States risks jeopardizing this degree of influence if it overplays its hand.

We have entered a period of fundamental change in U.S.-European relations. Former enemies have become new potential allies. A diminished sense of military threat has raised the competitive aspects of U.S.-West European relations to new levels. Whether the cooperative or competitive aspects will dominate the relationship in the next period of history remains for policymakers on both sides of the Atlantic to decide. From an objective perspective, there would appear to be no single conflict or even set of conflicting issues that would warrant a break in the tradition of cooperation between the United States and European democracies. But without a Soviet threat to enforce an alliance, the United States and its allies—new and old—will perhaps have to make even greater efforts to realize the full potential benefits of their cooperation and to minimize the potential costs of the competitive aspects of the relationship.

IV. AFTER 1992: TRADE POLICY AND THE EUROPEAN MARKET

U.S. ACCESS TO THE EC-92 MARKET: OPPORTUNITIES, CONCERNS AND POLICY CHALLENGES

By Raymond J. Ahearn *

CONTENTS

SUMMARY

Europe's 1992 program (EC-92) is intended to create a larger and more unified market for the movement of goods, services, capital, and labor. Although this is intended primarily to benefit Europeans, the movement towards a single, integrated market substantially free of internal barriers to trade also has the potential for creating new export and investment opportunities for U.S. business. For most U.S. businesses, particularly large multinational corporations, EC-92 will provide tangible benefits. Some U.S. businesses, mostly small and medium-sized exporters, however, may not realize any gains.

Although fears have eased that the drive by the European Community for a barrier-free market by the end of 1992 would discriminate against foreign exporters and investors, U.S. business and gov-

---

* Raymond J. Ahearn is a Specialist in Trade Relations, Foreign Affairs and National Defense Division, Congressional Research Service.

ernment leaders still are concerned about specific aspects of the program that could affect access to the EC market. Four issues—the basic motivations behind the EC–92 program, EC actions that are seen by some as "forcing" foreign firms to invest in the Community, EC support for high-tech industries, and a potentially restrictive market access standard—continue to be a source of concern to U.S. firms.

Aspects of the EC–92 process are also challenging longstanding U.S. policies. In some areas, particularly financial services and government procurement, the Community may be moving towards a deeper and more comprehensive standard of market liberalization than exists in the United States. If the EC does achieve a more open market in certain sectors, it could make access to its own market contingent upon changes in U.S. laws and regulations. Moreover, the EC–92 program is a major element in the creation of larger European firms that may be positioned to challenge U.S. companies for market leadership in the years ahead. If Europe prospers under a system of greater state intervention, support in the United States for emulating aspects of the EC model could also develop.

Introduction

Given the importance of the EC market to U.S. economic interests, the consequences of the EC–92 market for U.S. exports, investments, and competitiveness are critical. This chapter summarizes existing research findings on the market access opportunities, concerns, and policy challenges posed by EC–92. A qualification to bear in mind is that many of the research findings summarized in this chapter were completed between 1988 and 1991, a period of optimism about the prospects of EC integration. Consequently, potential benefits may be overstated.

As the deadline for the completion of the single market program approaches in 1992, the widespread European confidence about EC–92 that characterized an earlier period seems to be eroding. A more somber mood appears to be permeating Europe during 1992 as a result of slower growth, the reappearance of structural problems, the emergence of escalating immigration problems, and rising demands for enlarging the Community. Whether these changes in the economic and social landscape of Europe translate into political pressures for slowing the pace of liberalization to the outside world remains a critical unknown.

The European Community is a major market for U.S. exporters and investors. In 1991, the United States exported over $100 billion of goods to the Community, a sum that accounted for nearly twenty-five percent of total U.S. exports. Over one-third of U.S. exports to the EC are high value-added capital goods such as computers, power generating machinery, telecommunication equipment, aircraft, and industrial machinery. [1]

Demand for American goods varies with changes in economic growth and exchange rates. When economic growth in the member

[1] Cooney, Stephen. Europe 1992: The Opportunity and The Challenge For U.S. Economic Interests. *SAIS Review*, v. 10, win/spr 1990. p. 81.

countries of the Community accelerates and the dollar remains priced at a competitive level, demand for American goods picks up substantially. Recent strong EC imports have helped the United States reduce its global trade deficit. [2]

In 1986, the U.S. ran a $27 billion trade deficit with the EC and a $170 billion trade deficit with the world. By 1991 the United States was experiencing a $16 billion trade surplus with the EC and a $66 billion trade deficit with the world. Over this five year period, the $43 billion turnaround in the trade balance between the U.S. and EC accounted for over 40 percent of the reduction of the U.S. global trade deficit. [3]

The EC is also the most important destination for U.S. foreign direct investment, accounting for over 50 percent of the total value of all U.S. companies' manufacturing investment abroad. With an asset base totaling over $170 billion, European affiliates of U.S. companies had sales totaling over $700 billion in 1991, an amount seven times greater than the value of U.S. exports to the EC. [4]

Opportunities

EC–92 provides significant new opportunities for both U.S. exporters and investors. While overall U.S. exports to the EC should expand as a result of faster economic growth in Europe and more deregulated markets, the benefits are not likely to be evenly distributed across industries and firms. Some U.S. exporters, particularly small and medium sized companies, may face considerable obstacles in taking advantage of the single market. On balance, the opportunities are more clear-cut and tangible for U.S. investors than for U.S. exporters. From an investment perspective, EC–92 is highly attractive to American firms, particularly those that have a longstanding presence in Europe.

POTENTIAL EXPORT GAINS

Most studies have found that EC–92 offers U.S. exporters potential major gains. The potential benefits are based on the growth-promoting effect of economic integration and on opportunities created by more specific reduction of trade barriers within the EC. [5]

EC–92 is expected to promote economic growth in Europe in a variety of ways. The most important mechanisms are through the removal of intra-EC trade barriers, increased competition, corporate restructurings, and additional investment. If EC–92 does substantially increase the growth of the Community's GNP, as many believe, the demand of European consumers and companies for American goods should increase. While the internal trade liberalization will also increase trade among EC countries at the expense of more efficient producers in the United States, most research predicts that the trade creation effects will outweigh the trade diversion effects. One estimate is that if EC–92 generates its promised growth,

---

[2] Ibid., p. 80.

[3] Department of Commerce trade data, Foreign Trade series 990, various editions.

[4] U.S. Department of Commerce. *Survey of Current Business*. various editions.

[5] See *Annual Report of the Council of Economic Advisers*. February 1992. p. 224.

trade creation will exceed trade diversion for the United States by over $4 billion. [6]

The removal of a variety of intra-European trade barriers, particularly in the areas of standards and government procurement, could also make it easier for U.S. firms to sell and distribute their products throughout the EC. In addition to harmonized standards and more open procurement policies, deregulation and single market reforms of such areas as customs controls, transportation, taxation, antitrust policy, and intellectual property rights should in principle help generate increased trade and growth. [7]

Unified Standards

A central element of EC–92 is the creation of an unified standards and conformity assessment system in Europe which is the subject of more than half of the 282 Commission directives. Uniform standards would allow products that comply with EC standards to freely circulate within the $5 trillion EC market. Producers based in Europe would be able to allocate production and marketing facilities across EC borders more efficiently and reduce costs. U.S. exporters could obtain comparable benefits because they now could be assured that complying with whatever product standard is adopted will provide access to the entire EC market instead of having to make costly changes to meet as many as 12 different national standards.

Different principles apply to unregulated and regulated products. For unregulated products (those not covered by EC-wide directives, such as paper and furniture), the EC will apply the principle of mutual recognition of national standards for non-safety aspects of a product. A U.S. exporter of an unregulated product can certify that U.S. standards are met and, if these standards are accepted in at least one EC country, they will be accepted in the EC. Most U.S. exports will benefit from mutual recognition. [8]

The EC is developing harmonized European standards for products requiring minimum safety and health levels (so-called regulated products). Estimates are that close to 50 percent of $50 billion of U.S. exports to the EC are subject to harmonization requirements. Three European regional standards bodies are developing harmonized and "voluntary" European standards. U.S. exporters have the option to use other standards in certifying compliance with EC legal requirements, but this option will likely require the involvement of a third party. Thus, if a manufacturer is interested in self-certifying a product, he must apply European standards. [9]

Despite the widespread perceived benefits to be derived from harmonized standards, U.S. companies are concerned that potential gains will be constrained by regulations on content, standards de-

---

[6] See Hufbauer, Gary Clyde. *Europe 1992: An American Perspective.* Brookings Institution, 1990. p. 23.

[7] The U.S. International Trade Commission has completed detailed analyses of the anticipated changes in EC markets and the potential effects on the United States. See U.S. International Trade Commission. *The Effects of Greater Economic Integration within the European Community on the United States.* USITC Publication 2204, July 1989; USITC Publication 2268, March 1990; and USITC Publication 2368, March 1991.

[8] Hagigh, Sara E. Hundreds of New Product Standards Will Apply to Sales in EC After 1992. *Business America*, January 13, 1992. p. 16.

[9] Ibid., p. 16.

velopment, and certification. On content, U.S. firms have found that the technical drafting committees tend to base standards on European equipment and specifications. While pride in existing products and greater familiarity with one's own equipment may explain this tendency—not some secret agenda to keep out foreign products—the content of new standards will affect costs and the relative attractiveness of the EC market for many U.S. exporters. [10]

The EC's delays in adopting and implementing new standards will also constrain the realization of new business gains. Although the number of new standards developed has accelerated over the past years, the current pace will not be sufficient to meet the January 1, 1993 deadline. In the view of the U.S. Chamber of Commerce, the delays mean that in the near term, U.S. business will not be able to take advantage of one of the most touted benefits of the single market. [11]

A third potential obstacle relates to where and how products will be tested and certified for export to the European market. U.S. firms will most benefit if their products can be tested in their home territory. U.S. industries are pushing the EC to license U.S. test laboratories as certified bodies, or allow EC certified bodies to subcontract testing to U.S. labs. But little progress in negotiating access for U.S.-based testing and certification laboratories has been made. Guidelines for subcontracting testing laboratories outside the EC and establishing mutual recognition agreements between testing and certification bodies in the U.S. and EC have yet to be negotiated. [12]

More Open Government Procurement Policies

The value of government procurement in the EC is huge—an estimated $1 trillion, but this market has been heavily protected in the past. National champions traditionally are awarded contracts based on tailor-made and pre-negotiated tenders. On average only two percent of the public supply contracts and two percent of public construction contracts have been awarded to firms from other EC member states. The long-range EC goal is to open about 80 percent of public purchasing to EC-wide competition. [13]

A single and more open EC procurement market could provide greater opportunities for U.S. business. New procurement procedures that will require greater openness, less discrimination, and broader coverage could break the hold that many national champions now enjoy as favored suppliers. To become a reality, this will require tough national implementation. However, a recent EC survey revealed that nearly one-third of 2,000 public procurement transactions involved instances where member countries continued to protect their own national champions. [14]

---

[10] Burgess, John. Competing in a Diverse Market. *Washington Post*, December 2, 1991. p. A6.

[11] U.S. Chamber of Commerce. *Europe 1992, A Practical Guide for American Business*. 1991. p. 30.

[12] Ibid., p. 31.

[13] U.S. Library of Congress. Congressional Research Service. *European Community: 1992 Plan for Economic Integration.* CRS Issue Brief 89043, by Glennon Harrison. p. 5–6.

[14] U.S. Chamber of Commerce, p. 50.

Potential benefits also will be limited by the September 1990 Excluded Sectors Directive. The four excluded sectors—water, energy, transport, and telecommunication—account for at least one-quarter of all public procurement in the EC and for substantial U.S. exports of telecommunications equipment. The directive requires that all goods or services supplied to these sectors contain at least half European content by value. Companies that cannot confidently claim 50 percent EC content may even be deterred from bidding. Even if a foreign company can meet a 50 percent content threshold, the member governments are required to give a three percent price advantage to goods and services of EC origin. [15]

POTENTIAL GAINS FOR U.S. INVESTORS

EC–92 should provide expanded business opportunities for U.S. companies already established in Europe. For these companies, the primary issues are local content restrictions and rules of origin. To the extent that these companies are "European" by the Community's definition, the implications of EC–92 are no different for these non-European companies than for a native EC company. [16] Therefore, they are particularly likely to gain from uniform standards and a reduction of intra-EC trade barriers. [17]

In some respects U.S. multinationals that have longstanding ties to Europe may even have advantages over Europeans firms because they tend to have more diversified operations and are less dependent on a single, national market. Ford and IBM, for example, already are accustomed to serving a pan-European market with plants in several countries and widespread sales and service networks. In addition, they may have more flexibility in shifting production facilities among different countries in Europe. German or French companies, by contrast, may have to weigh more heavily the reactions of home-country labor unions concerning possible production relocation decisions than non-national firms. [18]

Financial Services Opportunities

EC–92 offers many new opportunities and benefits for U.S. financial institutions—banks, investment banks, and insurance companies—currently operating in the EC. U.S. banks are active in every Community country, holding over $200 billion, or 5 percent, of total Community bank assets. U.S. securities houses rank among the world's largest in their Euromarket activities. And some U.S. insurance companies are increasing their presence in the EC in anticipation of new opportunities. [19]

The EC–92 program to deregulate financial markets should enable institutions to consolidate operations and offer more products. Central to the liberalization of financial services under EC–92 is the concept of a "single passport." Once a financial firm is estab-

---

[15] U.S. Office of Technology Assessment. *Competing Economies: America, Europe and the Pacific Rim.* 1991. p. 199.

[16] Devinney, Thomas M. and William C. Hightower. *European Markets After 1992.* Lexington Books, 1991. p. 188.

[17] *Annual Report of the Council of Economic Advisers*, 1992, p. 225.

[18] Devinney and Hightower, p. 13.

[19] U.S. General Accounting Office. *U.S. Financial Services' Competitiveness Under the Single Market Program.* NSIAD–90–99. p. 3.

lished and licensed in one member state, its home country, that firm can use a single passport to offer financial services anywhere in the Community, either directly across borders or through branches. Firms offering investment services should also benefit from increased corporate financial activity, such as expansions, restructurings, and mergers and acquisitions. [20]

To date the EC has passed most of the legislation required to establish a single European banking market by the end of 1992. Legislation on investment services and insurance lags far behind, thus preventing U.S. investment and insurance firms from being able to take advantage of the benefits of a single market for the time being. [21]

While insurers and investment firms wait for their single passports, bankers beginning in January 1993 will be able to compete across borders as mandated by the Second Banking Directive. Banks based in countries with universal banking regimes will be particularly advantaged since they will be allowed to provide investment services and insurance throughout the EC with a single license, based on home country control. [22]

Concerns

Despite the potential opportunities EC–92 provides U.S. exporters and investors, there are numerous ongoing concerns that could undermine the realization of tangible gains. Four major concerns—the motivations behind EC–92, "forced" investment, government support for sensitive industries, and reciprocity—tend to predominate. Specific sectoral concerns affecting agriculture and transportation are discussed elsewhere in this volume.

CONCERNS INHERENT IN THE BASIC MOTIVATIONS FOR EC–92

EC–92 has often been billed as the building of a "Europe for Europeans", implying that the winners will be Europeans. While this does not necessarily mean that foreign companies will not also benefit, it is clear the overriding objective is to strengthen European industries against international competition. Due to changes in information technology and to the rise of Japanese and American economic competition, EC–92 can be viewed as a process driven in part by the inability of member state regulatory agencies to continue to provide benefits to the regulated. [23]

The deregulation that is occurring under the banner of EC–92 is a battle among many different interests. The main actors are the EC member states, pan-European business interests who stand to benefit from a single market and less national regulation, national economic interests who stand to lose from deregulation, and the European Commission in Brussels. The interests of these main actors often conflict so that deal-making, coalition building, and bargaining are common. French agreement to allow the British to ship Japanese-built cars into the Community, for example, may re-

[20] Ibid., p. 14.
[21] U.S. Chamber of Commerce, p. 52.
[22] Ibid., p. 54.
[23] Devinney and Hightower, p. 171 and p. 188.

quire the British to return the favor on something the French want, such as minimum requirements for EC TV programming. [24]

Given this process, EC-92 may have very uneven and unpredictable impacts on third countries. Stark black and white monikers such as "Fortress Europe" or "Opportunity Europe" can be misleading. EC-92 is not driven primarily by concerns for consumer interests or free trade ideology. Where necessary, and where the political coalitions allow it, the deregulation process will open some markets to the outside world. Where the costs of more competitive markets outweigh the gains to specific political coalitions, deregulation could serve to restrict market access. While most of the impacts are likely to be favorable to U.S. economic interests because the process of deregulation has an inherent free trade dimension, the longer term effects on U.S. interests may vary greatly. [25]

FORCED INVESTMENT

The EC movement toward a single, integrated market has served as a natural magnet for increased foreign investment. The reasons seem clear. A larger and more dynamic market, an improved business climate, and close proximity to emerging market economies in Eastern Europe and the Commonwealth of Independent States provide strong incentives for foreign companies to produce locally to better serve a growing regional market.

There are concerns, however, that the attraction of economic opportunity is not the sole reason why firms locate in the EC. Although there is little evidence to suggest that the EC is pursuing a coherent and unambiguous policy of forcing foreign firms directly or indirectly to invest in the EC, it appears to be the practical effect particularly in high-technology industries.

Many EC leaders are strongly and explicitly committed to encouraging inward investment in forms that promise to create well-paid knowledge-intensive jobs and that transfer valuable technology to local firms. That commitment is backed by a variety of tools the EC has at its disposal to compel investment and by some very specific actions taken by the EC in recent years. [26]

A combination of new rules of origin combined with stringent local content guidelines, discriminatory public procurement policies and aggressive antidumping actions have been used by the EC in recent years to push foreign firms to manufacture in Europe rather than export. In addition, the EC has used its research and development programs as an encouragement to foreign investment.

- U.S. semiconductor exports have been affected by a 1989 EC rules of origin decision. The EC adopted a general rule of origin that requires the country of origin to be defined not by testing and assembly of chips, as had been the case, but by the location of wafer fabrication (where the diffusion process occurs). Semiconductors that no longer qualify as EC made (i.e. are not fabricated in Europe) face a relatively high 14 percent tariff. This rule allegedly forced one U.S. semiconductor manu-

---

[24] Ibid., p. 79.
[25] Ibid., p. 125.
[26] U.S. Office of Technology Assessment, p. 205.

facturer to build a plant in Ireland to serve the EC market in lieu of exporting from the United States. [27]

- The 50 percent content requirement provided for in the Excluded Sectors procurement directive is based on both goods and services in the contract, including R&D. This could pressure U.S. companies to increase foreign R&D in order to meet such a content requirement. Liberalization in the excluded sectors is of particular interest to U.S. telecommunications and heavy electrical equipment suppliers.
- Another EC trade policy action that affects U.S. exports, especially in electronics, is the EC's recent aggressive pursuit of antidumping (AD) actions. From 1985 to 1990, the EC initiated over 200 AD cases, directed mainly against Japanese and East Asian exports. These actions and penalties have most likely encouraged Japanese and other foreign firms to locate and manufacture in Europe. A fear is that the increased local production by Asian producers in Europe could displace traditional markets for U.S. exports. [28]
- Foreign company access to EC research and development programs is predicated on a company having an "integrated European presence." Many large American companies such as IBM that have manufacturing plants and research and development labs in Europe have participated in EC research consortia. For U.S. companies that just export to the EC, meeting the condition of an "integrated European presence" is not possible.

U.S. anxieties about EC investment pressures are fueled by the view that exporting from the United States, particularly in the case of high-technology products, contributes more to the vitality of U.S. economy than foreign investment. While increasing sales by U.S. firms operating in Europe may enrich the U.S. economy when profits earned overseas are returned to enrich stockholders or to be plowed back into domestic investment, U.S. exports are said to strengthen the U.S. economy more directly by creating jobs and additional production in the United States. Some fear that foreign investment could undermine the vitality of the United States as a geographical base for exports that provide high wage jobs and strong linkages to national security.

A contrary view is that foreign direct investment in Europe serves as an important beachhead for U.S. exports. According to the latest Department of Commerce data, 34 percent of all U.S. exports to the EC, or $34 billion, go directly to the affiliates of U.S. companies with direct investments there. Based on the Commerce Department estimate that 20,000 U.S. jobs are associated with every $1 billion in U.S. exports, U.S. investments in the EC account for about 680,000 jobs in the United States. Without those investments, it can be argued, U.S. exports and U.S. employment would be lower.

---

[27] Ibid., p. 198.
[28] Ibid., p. 200.

SUPPORT FOR HIGH-TECHNOLOGY INDUSTRIES

The "forced investment" concerns are closely related to EC support for high-technology industries and companies. A number of European industries such as computers, semiconductors, and telecommunications equipment are struggling to compete against stronger Japanese and American companies. In an effort to help European firms compete more vigorously in these areas, the EC has employed trade, procurement, and technology policies to bolster their competitiveness. Given that high-tech exports are the most important and largest category of U.S. exports to the EC, there is considerable concern that EC support for strategic industries could at some point become an obstacle to U.S. exports. [29]

To date the EC has actively used rules of origin and local content requirements and antidumping and anti-circumvention measures to protect its computer, semiconductor and automobile industries; it has negotiated an understanding with Japan that will control the number of Japanese automobile sales in Europe; it has instituted restrictive procurement provisions limiting non-EC access to key public procurement markets of transportation, telecommunications, energy and water; and has provided huge subsidies to its aerospace industry. The future direction of these and other policies affecting competition and subsidization of industry remain key concerns.

One of the more blatant industrial policy efforts by the EC involved the photocopying industry. To bolster four European companies against their Japanese rivals, the EC in the mid-1980s applied antidumping duties averaging 20 percent to limit Japanese imports. To avoid the antidumping duties, Japanese companies then invested in European plants to get around or circumvent the antidumping duties. Even with European plants, the EC later agreed to lift the antidumping penalties only if Japanese goods produced in Europe contained at least 40-percent non-Japanese content. In July 1989 the EC extended new rules of origin to copiers that based the country of origin determination on where the most technically sophisticated components were manufactured. Although the EC did not explicitly state that the sophisticated components would have to be made in the EC in order for Japanese photocopiers to escape antidumping penalties, that could be the practical effect. [30]

State Subsidies

In contrast to the trade, procurement and technology instruments used by the EC to foster high-tech industries, the current EC Commission has adopted an aggressive position against the use of government subsidies by member state governments to bolster national industries. The Commission's Directorate for Competition has blocked dozens of government fund transfers to ailing companies in recent years. In addition, the Commission has established a state subsidy reporting system that requires large nationalized EC manufacturing companies to file annual financial statements. This requirement, which will apply to approximately 100 to 150 companies that are majority-owned by EC governments, should make it

---

[29] Ibid., p. 196–7.
[30] Ibid., p. 200.

easier to identify public subsidization of EC industries. [31] But state aids to private companies, which the Commission estimates are five to ten times larger, go largely unreported. [32]

The most controversial and difficult Commission actions on state aid have involved the politically sensitive automobile, computer, and electronics sectors. In these sectors, the Commission's rulings have been mixed.

In 1990, the Commission forced Renault, the French automaker, to repay half of a $2.4 billion loan for failing to meet prescribed targets for scaling down production. In the same year, the Commission also ruled that the British government provided over $80 million in illegal subsidies in the sale of carmaker Rover Group to the British Aerospace consortium. But the Commission allowed in 1991 a $370 million French government capital infusion to Air France. [33] It is expected to approve a $721 million French government subsidy to the struggling French computer manufacturer later this year. [34]

An aggressive stance by the EC Commission against state aid to industry is in the interest of U.S. business. A number of governments, however, particularly France and Italy, are strongly opposed to the Commission's aggressive policy on state subsidies. These countries, which have large public sectors, complain that the Commission is favoring the private sector over state industry, despite EC laws forbidding such discrimination. Tough budgetary conditions agreed to at the signing of the European Monetary Union in December 1991, however, compel greater fiscal discipline on member governments and may make the state aid question less important over time. [35]

Competition Policy

Under the leadership of Sir Leon Brittan, the EC Commissioner for competition policy and financial institutions, the EC has also pursued a tough policy against monopolies in recent years. Since September 1990, an EC task force under Sir Leon's direction has been policing the competitive implications of all large mergers, acquisitions, and joint ventures that could affect the European market. This review has included mergers and takeovers involving companies that are located outside the EC. For example, the acquisition of NCR by AT&T, the takeover of MCA by Matsushita, and the sale of assets by PanAm to Delta have all been reviewed by the EC task force, prompting concern on the part of U.S. business about the potential extraterritorial reach of EC law. [36]

---

[31] U.S. Chamber of Commerce, p. 15.

[32] Barnard, Bruce. Fighting Dirigism in the EC. *Journal of Commerce*, December 16, 1991. p. 7A.

[33] Rockwell, Keith M. Trustbusters Play Influential Role in the EC. *Journal of Commerce*, January 6, 1992. p. 3a.

[34] While the Treaty of Rome is silent on the question of private versus public ownership of companies, EC statute requires that the fairness of government transfers to individual companies be judged by whether a private party would make such an investment under normal market conditions. A recent decision by IBM to invest $100 million in Groupe Bull could make the French government support acceptable to the Commission. See Rockwell, Keith M. EC Expected to OK French Aid To Groupe Bull. *Journal of Commerce*, March 5, 1992. p. 3A.

[35] Rockwell, Trustbusters Play Influential Role in EC, p. 3A.

[36] U.S. Chamber of Commerce, p. 21.

As provided by EC regulations, a merger proposal must be reviewed for market impact if each company in a proposed merger has annual sales within the Community of more than $315 million. The key standard in assessing a proposed merger is whether such an action would lead to abuse of a dominant position in the marketplace. By EC definition, a company holds a dominant position if it has power over industrial behavior without regard to competitors. [37] This EC emphasis on competitive factors closely tracks U.S. antitrust standards. [38]

Since it was established in 1990, the EC task force has examined 50 mergers or acquisitions, conducted five full investigations, and blocked one deal. That one deal involved the proposed takeover of de Havilland, a Canadian-based but American-owned producer of commuter aircraft by a joint venture between Aerospatiale of France and Alenia of Italy. The decision to block the merger was based on the grounds that the merged entity would have over half the global market and nearly three-quarters of the EC market in the production of some commuter aircraft. [39]

French and Italian government officials reacted angrily to the decision. A number argued that the decision undermined the aircraft producer's attempts to lower costs and expand into new markets. Others called for a major reduction of Sir Leon's powers.

Whether the vigorous pro-competitive policies by the EC will last beyond Sir Leon's tenure remains to be seen. There are fears that when his term as competition commissioner expires at the end of this year, France and Italy will push hard for a replacement who takes a decidedly softer line towards mergers and subsidies. If price-fixing and monopolization of markets were condoned by the EC, U.S. companies that compete in those markets could be adversely affected. [40]

RECIPROCITY

A fourth U.S. concern is that the EC has put in place a potentially restrictive market access standard that could adversely affect U.S. exporters and investors. Under the Second Banking Directive issued on December 15, 1989, the EC set forth a standard that called for a combination of "effective market access" and "competitive market opportunities." The intent apparently is to condition access for U.S. financial institutions to the EC market on U.S. treatment of EC firms in the U.S. market. Under the directive, if the U.S. does not offer EC financial institutions "reciprocal treatment" in the U.S. market, then the EC would seek negotiations to change the status quo. [41]

This EC standard of reciprocity goes beyond the traditional concept of "national treatment" (according the same regulatory treatment to foreign companies that is accorded domestic companies). The concepts of "effective market access" and "competitive market opportunities" imply that national treatment alone is not necessar-

---

[37] Rockwell, Trustbusters Play Influential Role in EC, p. 3A.
[38] U.S. Chamber of Commerce, p. 21.
[39] Ibid., p. 21.
[40] Ibid., p. 22.
[41] U.S. General Accounting Office. *U.S. Financial Services' Competitiveness under the Single Market Program*. p. 15–16.

ily sufficient to provide reciprocity in trade relations when regulatory structures vary cross-nationally. That is to say that national treatment in a restrictive and highly regulated environment would not provide the same degree of effective market access as in a less restrictive and less regulated environment. The EC concern seems to be that its financial market, as a result of EC–92, is becoming more open and less regulated than the U.S. financial market, and consequently, EC banks would not be receiving "reciprocal" treatment in the U.S. market.

The Second Banking Directive's reciprocity provision may foreshadow an even more powerful challenge to U.S. access to the EC market. Given a divergence in regulatory structures in a range of other markets, there is a possibility of similar kinds of reciprocity provisions being included in other directives. To date reciprocity provisions have also been included in directives affecting mergers and public procurement.

In the area of mergers, the EC has left itself the option of blocking a non-EC merger, pending bilateral discussion, if another government attempts to block an EC merger or acquisition in that country on national security grounds. This provision apparently was motivated by the U.S. Exon-Florio provision in the 1988 Trade Act which authorizes review of merger activity involving U.S. companies on national security grounds. [42]

Two proposed public procurement services directives concern U.S. business because both contain a clause which allows the Commission to suspend or restrict the award of contracts to non-EC companies if that country does not award national treatment to EC firms in its market. This is based on a similar clause in the Second Banking Directive. The U.S. concern is that the complex system of local, State, and Federal "buy America" legislation may be in some respects more restrictive than the EC procurement procedures, thereby allowing the EC the pretext to restrict American access to its lucrative services procurement market. [43]

Policy Challenges

EC–92 presents two basic policy challenges to U.S. policymakers. The first is that the EC could attempt to use access to its market as leverage to effect changes in the U.S. legal and regulatory systems. The second is that EC–92 could help strengthen the competitiveness of European firms to the disadvantage of American firms and serve as a more liberalizing and attractive approach to economic integration than the U.S. approach.

INCREASED LEVERAGE IN THE U.S. MARKET

The establishment of a powerful European trading bloc may well give the EC greater clout to exert pressure for reform of various aspects of the U.S. legal and regulatory structures. The movement towards a single EC banking market provides the EC with considerable leverage to seek changes in the more restrictive U.S. financial services market. Similar developments could occur in other

[42] U.S. Chamber of Commerce, p. 2.
[43] Ibid., p. 49.

areas, including public procurement and standards. At issue is whether the United States will consider changing its regulatory system in such sectors as banking and public procurement to stay in tune with global market developments.[44]

Due in part to EC–92 financial reforms, many big U.S. banks have been advocating changes in U.S. regulations that they now perceive as undermining their ability to compete both in the U.S. and foreign markets. In the U.S. market they are particularly concerned that interstate banking regulations and limits on the mixing of banking and securities activities undermine their competitiveness and growth by keeping the U.S. market segmented. Overseas they are concerned that U.S. regulatory limits restricting the absolute and relative size of various nonbank activities, such as securities dealing and underwriting, puts them at a competitive disadvantage compared to EC banks that can offer both kinds of services under the EC's universal banking model.[45]

During 1991, the Bush Administration backed a plan to bring the U.S. banking system more in line with the universal EC banking model by removing restrictions on interstate banking. Strong congressional opposition to the plan indicates that far-reaching reform is not imminent.[46]

U.S. policymakers face similar challenges in the government procurement area. EC coverage of entities (federal, state, local, and regulated private firms) in government procurement directives is much more comprehensive than the solely Federal U.S. procurement coverage. For this reason, the EC has been in a position to push the United States to include State and local procurement programs under the GATT Procurement Code. The discriminatory provisions of the Excluded Sectors directive were intended, in part, as leverage to get the U.S. to expand its public procurement coverage to cover State and local procurement rules.[47] The EC also wants to require coverage of U.S. private sector entities such as AT&T, regional Bell operating companies that are regulated by State or Federal entities, in the GATT Code. Official U.S. policy has opposed broader coverage for legal and constitutional reasons. In lieu of State and local coverage, the U.S. has proposed a separate monitoring process, which would involve official U.S. commitment to use its best efforts to ensure open and non-discriminatory procurement procedures in the State, local, and private sectors.[48]

COMPETITIVENESS OF U.S. COMPANIES

The ability of U.S. companies to remain competitive in the world marketplace will be influenced by European developments both directly and indirectly. If EC–92 bolsters the competitiveness of European firms, U.S. firms could face increased competition in the world marketplace. Such a development, in turn, could create pressures in the United States to adopt or emulate aspects of the EC–92

---

[44] For extended analysis of this issue, see Woolcock, Stephen. *Market Access Issues in EC-US Relations.* Royal Institute of International Affairs, London, 1991.

[45] U.S. General Accounting Office. *U.S. Financial Services' Competitiveness Under the Single Market Program*, p. 4.

[46] U.S. Chamber of Commerce, p. 54.

[47] Woolcock, *Market Access Issues in EC-US Relations*, p. 78–79.

[48] National Association of Manufacturers. *Update on EC–1992.* October 1991. p. 32.

economic integration model to foster the competitiveness of U.S. firms.

EC–92 has led to an outpouring of mergers, acquisitions, and joint ventures among European firms. Large European industrial and banking conglomerates can be expected to account for a larger share of total sales in European markets in the years ahead. Combined with the existence of huge Japanese conglomerates, the emergence of new European giant corporations might serve to push U.S. industrial and financial firms further down the ranks of the world's largest corporations. [49]

Size alone, of course, is no guarantee of profitability and increased competitiveness in world markets. Some analysts believe that large firms are at a competitive disadvantage in reacting quickly to changing market developments and in cutting excessive costs. Yet huge conglomerates do have advantages in having deep pockets to support research and development on cutting-edge technologies, in absorbing short-term losses in the hopes of long-term profits, and in initiating high risk undertakings. [50]

While the evidence concerning the relationship between the size of firms and competitiveness is not clear-cut, it is apparent that many aspects of the EC–92 are more in tune with the pressures of the global marketplace than selected U.S. policies. In liberalizing the areas of government procurement and financial services, the EC has relied on concepts that limit the ability of national policymakers to insulate their states from the international economy. In contrast, liberalization of these areas in the United States is constrained by Federal-State constitutional divisions. The rights of States such as New York and California to pursue "Buy American" programs and to restrict interstate banking makes the U.S. less able to adapt to the demands of global international economic integration. [51]

Whether the EC achieves a higher level of liberalization in all sectors compared to the United States remains to be seen. The EC, for example, has made very little progress in liberalizing its transportation, telecommunications, and energy sectors. But it is clear that the EC has a large regulatory sphere of influence as the EFTA countries (Sweden, Norway, Finland, Austria, and Switzerland) and East European countries adopt regulations and standards set in Brussels. The net effect of the EC's internal dynamism could be increased influence in international economic fora. [52]

An equally broad policy challenge may follow if EC–92 succeeds in helping European industries and firms regain their international competitiveness. The philosophic underpinnings of the European experiment entail a strong and interventionist government role across a range of economic policies such as support for high-tech industries, more formalized labor-management relations, substantial regional development aids, and a large public sector. If Europe prospers under a system of greater state intervention, pressures for

---

[49] Hufbauer, *Europe 1992: An American Perspective*, p. 45.
[50] Hufbauer, p. 45.
[51] Woolcock, *Market Access Issues in EC-US Relations*, p. 113.
[52] Ibid., p. 117.

emulating aspects of the EC model to increase competitiveness may grow in the United States.[53]

[53] Ibid., p. 49.

EUROPEAN AUTOMOTIVE POLICY: PAST, PRESENT, AND FUTURE

By James P. Womack and Daniel T. Jones *

CONTENTS

Summary

The European Community has been transferring public policy decisions regarding the motor industry from national governments to Brussels since 1957. This process will be largely completed by about 1999 when the Community has a uniform set of rules in place governing vehicle standards, state aids to industry, intra-European trade of vehicles manufactured in Japanese "transplant" factories in Europe, and trade between the Community and the rest of the world.

The Community's policy toward foreign trade and investment is the special concern of this chapter. In particular, the chapter examines the likely implications of EC auto policy for the American-based motor vehicle industry. The findings are as follows:

- The European industry faces serious competitive problems with the Japanese motor vehicle industry. In conditions of completely open trade and investment, the European industry would be at significant risk.
- Within Europe, the German and American-owned producers are in the strongest positions while the French and Italian producers are the weakest.
- The recent trade and investment negotiations between the European Community and Japan have produced an understand-

* James P. Womack is Principal Research Scientist, Center for International Studies, Massachusetts Institute of Technology. Daniel T. Jones is Professor, Cardiff Business School, University of Wales in Cardiff, Wales.

ing that finished unit imports of Japanese vehicles will not increase from the current level (meaning their market share will decline as the European market grows). In addition, it is understood that Japanese transplant factories will achieve roughly 80 percent European content in their vehicles within a few years of the start of production. Finally, it is understood that the rate of increase of Japanese transplant production in Europe will be roughly synchronized with the growth of the overall vehicle market. The Japanese firms will be allowed to capture practically all of the growth in the European market in the 1990s, but the existing European and American-owned firms producing in Europe will not have to reduce their overall production volume and will avoid the "downsizing" agony currently experienced in Detroit.

- Given this very high level of effective protection for the European and American-owned auto industry in Europe, it seems highly unlikely that there will be trade friction in the 1990s between the United States and the EC over vehicle shipments across the Atlantic from the United States to Europe, even if these vehicles do not have a high level of American content.

Introduction

The European Community has been concerned about its motor vehicle industry since the signing of the Treaty of Rome in 1957. However, it has taken many years to transfer the most important aspects of public policy relevant to the motor vehicle sector from national governments to Brussels, a process which will not be complete until at least the end of the 1990s.

Recently, plans to "complete" the market within Europe by the beginning of 1993 have greatly accelerated the shift of policy from national governments to the Community. Given the growing intensity of international competition in the motor vehicle sector, these steps have raised understandable concerns in the United States that the Community plans an active program of industrial promotion which, under certain circumstances, could be adverse to the interests of the American motor vehicle industry.

This chapter assesses this situation. We begin by reviewing the general competitive stance of the European motor industry. We then examine each of the areas of public policy in which the Community may seek to support and promote its motor industry. Finally, we offer an assessment of Community policy in the 1990s and the consequences for the American motor vehicle industry.

The Competitive Position of the European Motor Industry

Until recently, policy makers in Europe considered their motor vehicle industry to be internationally competitive. A steady decline in small car exports had meant a steadily shrinking trade surplus in whole-vehicle units (as shown in table 1). At the same time, growing exports of high-value luxury cars and heavy truck components had kept Europe's historic trade surplus in motor vehicles, as measured in value, from declining significantly (as shown in table 2). (Table 3 breaks out 1989 motor vehicle trade, measured in value, into separate categories for cars, trucks, and parts.)

TABLE 1. European Community Unit Trade in Motor Vehicles, 1979, 1986, and 1989

(thousands of units)

	1979	1986	1989
Western European Exports			
to EFTA	560	625	602
to North America	552	576	302
to Japan	39	58	142
to ROW	979	533	523
Western European Imports			
from EFTA	83	82	71
from North America	144	13	37
from Japan	780	1104	1238
from ROW	n.a.	n.a.	n.a.
Total			
Exports	2130	1792	1569
Imports [a]	1007	1199	1346
Balance [a]	1123	593	223

Note: EFTA is the European Free Trade Area (Austria, Finland, Iceland, Liechtenstein, Norway, Sweden, and Switzerland). ROW is the rest of the world.

[a] Data on imports from ROW are not available for Europe as a whole. We estimate that these have been stable since 1979 at about 200,000 units per year (from Korea, Malaysia, and Eastern Europe/Russia.) Thus the European Community import figures are slightly larger and the trade surplus is slightly smaller than shown.

Source: Directorate for the Internal Market (DG-III), Commission of the European Communities.

TABLE 2. European Community Trade in Motor Vehicles and Parts By Value, 1979, 1986, and 1989

(billions of constant dollars at 1989 prices and exchange rates)

	1979	1986	1989
Western European exports			
to EFTA	7.2	10.4	11.0
to North America	6.8	14.4	9.8
to Japan	.5	1.1	3.3
to ROW	11.9	10.2	11.5
Western European imports			
from EFTA	2.2	4.1	4.2
from North America	1.5	1.4	1.5
from Japan	2.7	6.6	9.9
from ROW	1.0	2.0	2.3
Balance			
exports	26.4	36.1	35.6
imports	7.4	14.1	17.9
balance	19.0	22.0	17.7

Source: Directorate for the Internal Market (DG-III), Commission of the European Communities.

TABLE 3. Constituent Elements of European Community Trade in Motor Vehicles and Parts by Value, 1989

(in billions of dollars)

	EFTA	North America	Japan	ROW	Total
Cars					
Exports	7.3	7.4	3.1	6.2	24.0
Imports	1.1	.8	7.8	1.3	11.0
Balance	6.2	6.6	−4.7	4.9	13.0
Trucks					
Exports	1.7	.3	.0	1.9	3.9
Imports	1.0	.1	.7	.4	2.2
Balance	.7	.2	−.7	1.5	1.7
Parts					
Exports	2.0	2.1	.2	3.4	7.7
Imports	2.1	.6	1.4	.6	4.7
Balance	−.1	1.5	−1.2	2.8	3.0
Total					
Exports	11.0	9.8	3.3	11.5	35.6
Imports	4.2	1.5	9.9	2.3	17.9
Balance	6.8	8.3	−6.6	9.2	17.7

Source: Directorate for the Internal Market (DG-III), Commission of the European Communities.

In addition, for a remarkable eight year period from 1984 through 1991 the European motor vehicle market was extraordinarily robust, sustaining production and sales at a far higher level (as shown in tables 4 and 5) than any analysts had predicted at the beginning of the 1980s. This bull market emerged just at the end of a long period of rationalization and consolidation, driven by stagnant sales in the decade 1974–1983, in which the number of European car companies shrank and the number of workers in the industry was reduced dramatically, as shown in table 6. Thus, every surviving company was able to operate at a high level of capacity utilization and to show profits in the late 1980s.

Within the past two years, however, the view of policy makers in Brussels has begun to change. The first independent global survey of company performance in plants, research and development operations, and supply chain management, [1] indicates that European companies—both the mass producers (Volkswagen, Fiat, Renault, and PSA) and the specialists (Mercedes, BMW, Volvo, Saab, Jaguar, and Rover)—lag Japanese and even American performance significantly in terms of fundamental productivity, product quality, [2] and responsiveness to changing market demand.

---

[1] Womack, James P., Daniel T. Jones, and Daniel Roos. *The Machine That Changed The World.* New York, Rawson Associates/Macmillan, 1990. The findings of this report on the competitive stance of the European industry will not be summarized here. Rather, the reader is directed to this source.

[2] Defined as the number of manufacturing defects in cars reaching customers, not as durability or "luxury".

TABLE 4. Motor Vehicle Production in the EC, 1973–1990

(thousands of units)

	Germany	U.K.	Spain	Italy	France	Belgium	Netherlands	Total
1973	3,949	2,164	822	1,958	3,569	299	107	12,868
1978	4,186	1,607	1,144	1,656	3,508	303	85	12,489
1981	3,897	1,184	987	1,434	3,019	237	101	10,859
1982	4,062	1,156	1,070	1,453	3,149	278	109	11,277
1983	4,154	1,289	1,288	1,575	3,336	285	122	12,049
1984	4,045	1,134	1,309	1,601	3,062	249	129	11,529
1985	4,445	1,311	1,418	1,573	3,016	267	128	12,158
1986	4,578	1,203	1,307	1,913	3,195	295	142	12,633
1987	4,634	1,389	1,704	1,913	3,493	352	152	13,637
1988	4,625	1,545	1,866	2,111	3,678	398	149	14,372
1989	4,852	1,626	2,046	2,221	3,920	389	149 [a]	15,203
1990	4,661	1,295	1,679	1,875	3,295	313	140 [a]	13,258

[a] Estimated.

Note: Spanish production is included although Spain was not a member of the EC until 1985. Japanese transplant production in the U.K. and Spain is included.

Source: For all countries except the Netherlands: *Automotive News Market Data Book*. 1991 edition. p. 3. For the Netherlands: Motor Vehicle Manufacturers Association of the United States. *World Motor Vehicle Data*. various years.

TABLE 5. Passenger Car Sales in Western Europe, 1973–1990

(thousands of units)

	Total New Registrations	Japanese Share
1973	8,787	3.9
1978	9,479	6.7
1981	9,330	10.0
1982	9,493	10.0
1983	9,928	10.6
1984	9,655	10.7
1985	10,525	10.7
1986	11,547	11.7
1987	12,393	11.4
1988	13,004	11.3
1989	13,461	10.9
1990	13,249	11.6
1991	13,530	12.3

Note: These registration data are for passenger cars only. The data in table 3 are for all motor vehicles.

Source: 1973–1988: Motor Vehicle Manufacturers Association of the United States. *World Motor Vehicle Data*, 1990 edition. p. 114, 1989–90. *Financial Times*, January 21, 1991. 1991: *Financial Times*, January 21, 1992.

This information was accompanied by the dramatic revaluation of the dollar. Those firms with heaviest dependence on the American market (Jaguar, Saab and Volvo) had to seek buyers (Ford for Jaguar) or joint venture partners (GM for Saab and Renault for Volvo) in order to survive. At the same time, the failure of Rover to reestablish itself in the U.S.-Canada market meant that its fate came to be controlled by Honda.

TABLE 6. Employment in the European Motor Industry [a]

(thousands of workers)

	1973	1975	1978	1980
A. 1973–1980				
West Germany	625	566	650	784
France	529	507	534	524
U.K.	510	457	471	424
Italy	290	253	282	285

B. 1980–1986

	1980	1986
West Germany	726	772
France	485	370
U.K.	437	265
Italy	295	209
Spain	160	122

Note: Data for years more recent than 1986 are not available. The general view of industry executives is that automotive employment has increased slightly since 1986.

[a] We have had great difficulty in obtaining consistent time series employment data for the European industry. The material presented above should not be taken to be completely accurate with regard to absolute numbers of workers, due to differing definitions of the industry from country to country and over time. We believe it does accurately reflect the general trend in which employment has fallen substantially in every national auto industry in Europe since 1973 except Germany.

Source: 1973–1980: Altshuler et al. *The Future of the Automobile*. Cambridge, MIT Press, 1979. p. 201. 1980–1986: *Twenty-Second Report from the European Communities Committee*. p. 20.

The realization that the European industry has a serious disadvantage in fundamental productivity and quality and that many of its vaunted "specialists" have failed as independent European-owned companies, has emerged just as the Japanese have launched a major attack on the European industry. In 1991, the recently introduced range of Japanese luxury cars outsold European luxury cars in the United States for the first time [3] and the gap is likely to widen rapidly as the number of Japanese products on offer continues to increase. Equally ominous, the Japanese have made a major commitment to direct investment in new production capacity for small- and medium-sized cars within Europe (as shown in table 7).

At the same time, the European market has run out of steam, with sales falling in all markets but Germany by the beginning of 1991. (The extraordinary burst of sales in Germany after unification boosted the automobile sales total for Europe as a whole for 1991 but this masks the underlying reality of a severe recession in most markets offset by a one-time burst of sales in one market.) Thus it has begun to occur to European policymakers that the European motor industry may face in the 1990s what the Americans

[3] A First: Japanese Makes Far Outsell Europeans in 1991 U.S. Luxury Sales. *Ward's Automotive Reports*, January 27, 1992. p. 1.

TABLE 7. Japanese Production Capacity in Western Europe [a]

(thousands of units)

	Actual for 1990	Announced for 1994
Vehicle Assembly		
Toyota:		
Burnaston, U.K.	0	200
Lisbon, Portugal	0	15
Honda:		
Swindon, U.K.	0	200
Nissan:		
Washington, U.K.	200	300
Barcelona, Spain	0	74
Mitsubishi:		
Boorn, Netherlands	0	100
Suzuki:		
Linares, Spain	50	50
Esztergom, Hungary	0	50
IBC (Isuzu-GM):		
Luton, U.K.	45	45
Total	295	1,034
Engines		
Honda:		
Swindon, U.K.	0	120
Nissan:		
Washington, U.K.	0	300
Toyota:		
Deeside, U.K.	0	200
Total	0	620

[a] The capacity figures given are for incremental capacity beyond that currently existing. The Barcelona, Linares, Boorn, and Luton plants are facilities already being operated on a smaller scale by European or American companies. They will continue to produce European designs exclusively for their European or American joint-venture partners while adding the capacity shown in the table to produce Japanese designs to be sold by both partners.

Source: Company announcements and *Financial Times*, January 17, 1992. p. 13.

faced in the 1980s: a catastrophic loss of global and European market share at the hands of the Japanese.

In fact, this prospect is greatly exaggerated, as we will endeavor to show in the final section of this chapter. However, the European motor industry does face serious competitive challenges in the 1990s which will probably generate significant policy responses. In the final section of this chapter we will examine what these might be and what they may mean for the American motor vehicle industry. As background for that analysis, we will review the range of policy instruments utilized by European governments and the Community over time to shape the fate of the European motor industry.

Community Policies Toward the Motor Industry

TARIFFS AND QUOTAS

Since the 1920s almost every European country with a motor industry has maintained a substantial degree of market protection. When the Treaty of Rome was signed in 1957, the six members of the Community agreed to eliminate tariffs within Europe and to adopt a common auto and truck tariff with the rest of the world, a process completed by the initial members of the Community in 1967 when internal tariffs were finally eliminated and a common external tariff of 17.6 percent was imposed. (This has gradually fallen with succeeding GATT rounds to the current level of 10.5 percent.)

However, the later entry of Britain, Ireland, and Denmark (in 1973) meant that these countries did not complete their tariff transition until 1978 and the entry of Spain, Portugal, and Greece (in 1985) means that a completely common external tariff for the twelve-member Community will not exist until the end of their transition period in 1992. Even then, the process will not be complete. It seems certain that many of the European Free Trade Area (EFTA) (Austria, Finland, Iceland, Liechtenstein, Norway, Sweden, and Switzerland) countries will join the Community by the end of the century and highly likely that some of the Eastern European countries will be added early in the new millennium.

While the trend in European tariffs has been steadily downward, it is important to remember that the current 10.5 percent tariff is somewhat higher than the U.S. tariffs of 2.3 percent on cars and parts and 25 percent on light trucks (meaning a rough average of about 7.5 percent tariff protection on all vehicles), and a significant trade barrier compared with the 0 percent Japanese tariff on cars, trucks and parts, effective since 1978.

In the period since 1975, when Britain and Japan reached an informal agreement limiting Japanese imports to 11 percent of the British domestic market, quotas have supplanted tariffs as the predominant means of protecting European-based auto and truck production from Japanese competition. What's more, even as tariff policy was being harmonized across the Community, quotas and "voluntary restraints" were being adopted country-by-country at different levels.

France imposed a 3 percent market share limitation in 1977. The Italian government chose to retain a limit of about 2500 imported Japanese automobiles annually, which was agreed with the Japanese government in the 1950s prior to the Treaty of Rome. (This limit does not apply to Japanese four-wheel drive vehicles or to vehicles imported new by Italian citizens from other European countries. The consequence has been that the Japanese have captured slightly more than 1 percent of the Italian domestic market in recent years.)

The situation in Germany is both the most important, because of German dominance of the European auto industry, and the most confusing. There is no formal or informal agreement on market share limitations by the Japanese in Germany. However, it is widely reported that at the time the American voluntary trade agreement (VRA) was announced in 1981, the Japanese government addressed fears of diversion of Japanese products from the United States to the more open European markets (such as Germany) by informing the German government that its companies would not increase their sales in the German market by more than 10 percent a year (or about one percentage point of market share).[4]

Since 1984 the European and German domestic markets have grown so strongly that German auto production has increased steadily, as shown above in table 4. Thus, despite a steadily increasing Japanese share of the German domestic market, as shown in table 8, the German firms have mainly been concerned with finding additional production capacity to meet growing demand rather than fending off Japanese competition. Obviously, this lack of interest in restraint on the Japanese could change quickly if German sales fell dramatically, a possibility we will return to in the final section of this report.

TABLE 8. Company Shares of German Auto Market

(thousands of new car sales)

	1982		1989	
	Sales	Share	Sales	Share
German Companies	1,396	64.8	1,693	59.8
German Companies Plus Ford	1,639	76.0	1,978	69.9
French Companies	170	7.9	199	7.0
Italian Companies	107	4.9	137	4.8
Japanese Companies	211	9.8	429	15.1
Total	2,156		2,832	

German companies: Volkswagen-Audi (but not including Seat), Mercedes, BMW, and Porsche.

French companies: Renault, PSA.

Italian companies: Fiat (including Lancia and Alfa Romeo).

Note: These are sales by companies in the German domestic market wherever the vehicles may have been produced. Opel has been counted as "German" despite its American parent because Opel's top-to-bottom European manufacturing system is predominantly located in Germany. Ford has been treated both as German and non-German because its substantial activities in Germany are balanced by large production complexes in Britain and Spain.

Source: 1989: Calculated by the authors from *Automotive News Market Data Book*, 1990 edition. p. 25. 1982: Calculated by the authors from *Automotive Market Data Book*, 1983 edition. p. 36.

Elsewhere in Europe, governments with no domestically owned motor vehicle industry have generally avoided quotas and other market impediments on the Japanese,[5] with the result that Japanese market shares in Europe fall into two bands—less than 15 percent in the five countries with major domestically owned motor

[4] The Swedish, Dutch and Belgian governments are commonly thought to have received similar assurances at the same time.

[5] The Dutch and Belgian governments did reach understandings with the Japanese government to moderate car imports during the recession year of 1981. However, these agreements have not been renewed.

industries, and 20–40 percent in those countries with no domestically owned motor industry, as shown in table 9.

TABLE 9. Japanese Share of European Car Market, 1989

Country	Share
Finland	39.6
Ireland	39.4
Norway	37.8
Denmark	31.8
Austria	30.3
Greece	29.9
Switzerland	29.4
Netherlands	25.9
Sweden	24.7
Belgium and Luxembourg	19.2
West Germany	14.8
U.K.	11.3
Portugal	6.1
France	2.9
Italy	1.6
Spain	1.1

Note: Sweden is an exception in having a large domestically owned motor industry and a high level of Japanese imports. However, the Japanese imports are almost entirely in the smaller size classes where no Swedish products are offered.
Source: *Financial Times*, February 5, 1990.

INVESTMENT RULES

One of the most contentious objectives of the Commission in Brussels has been to transfer the authority for investment aids from the member states to the Community. Historically, most of these aids were justified as part of regional development schemes—for example, the Chrysler plant at Lynwood in Scotland and the Fiat plants in the south of Italy—often with disastrous consequences for the companies agreeing to them. [6]

The Commission's determination has been strengthened by the evident desire of some member states to preserve their domestically owned auto industries during the recent wave of sell-offs and restructurings. The Commission has claimed that some companies have been sold at below-market values, specifically the British government's sale of Rover to British Aerospace and the IRI (Italian state-owned industrial combine) sale of Alfa-Romeo to Fiat. It has also claimed that the French government has inappropriately written down debts in converting Renault from a state enterprise able to borrow directly from the French treasury to a publicly owned enterprise run on market principles. In each case the Commission succeeded in forcing at least some repayment.

Recently an additional weapon used by the Commission in gaining control over these tendencies is the widely shared perception that without Community-wide rules the Japanese companies now investing are likely to receive large public windfalls in the form of investment aids which serve to undermine the established, Europe-

[6] The initial savings from government aid for obtaining the site and constructing the plant were soon offset by high transport costs, poor coordination with distant suppliers, and low skill levels of the local work force.

an-owned firms. This perception arose initially when Nissan received 125 million pounds in British government aid for its 610 million pound investment in its Washington complex. The Commission allowed this but required that in the future any state aid for a new automotive investment exceeding 12 million Ecu (about $15 million) be cleared in advance with Brussels.

Thus Toyota in 1990 received no British state aid for its 850 million pound investment in its Derby complex and the local aid it initially received from the Derby County Council to buy the site has been largely been paid back as the result of an investigation by the Commission. Honda located its plant in Swindon, a full employment area not eligible for state aids. [7]

The state aids controversy is tied directly to a second one. This is the permissible level of local content needed to create a "European" product which can be sold into other European countries without counting against the quotas in effect on Japanese finished units.

Currently, there is no Commission regulation on local content. The matter has only been dealt with formally in the EC-EFTA trade treaty which states that a product is "European" if the last major transformation in manufacture occurred in Europe. (This would mean that vehicles assembled in Europe with as little as 25 percent of their value-added in Europe could be counted as European rather than imports.)

However, as the British government negotiated with Japanese companies in the early 1980s about manufacturing investments in Britain, it was able to demand much higher levels of European content, both to qualify for state aids and in order not to count the transplant vehicles against the 11 percent British quota on Japanese finished units. [8] The result is that a strong precedent has been set [9] in which the three largest Japanese automotive investments in Europe (Nissan at Washington, Toyota at Derby, and Honda at Swindon, all in the U.K.) are committed to higher levels of local content (60 percent) in their initial production runs than most of the Japanese transplants have reached in North America after some years of production.

What's more, these facilities are committed to 80 percent European content by two to three years after start up, a level not current-

[7] This approach is consistent with Honda's policy throughout the world. It neither requested nor received government aid for its Marysville, Ohio; Alliston, Ontario; and Guadalajara, Mexico facilities. The company maintains that speed in getting started, freedom to pick the best location, and lack of future political entanglements more than compensate for state aids.

[8] It is commonly thought that the British government's primary aim was to save its domestic components sector, although the official explanation given for the high content demand was that other European states with Japanese quotas, notably Italy and France, would count British assembled Japanese vehicles against Japanese import quotas in those countries unless the vehicles had very high levels of European content. The French and Italian governments supported this strategy at several points in the late 1980s by claiming that the initial British-built Nissan vehicles were not actually meeting the agreed European-content levels and threatening to subtract them, if imported, from their quotas on Japanese vehicles.

[9] This precedent has no formal force of law but all European governments seek Japanese investments with very high levels of local content. Brussels has damped direct investment aids but car companies still need considerable help of many types from a host government in making a success of a new investment and it seems unlikely that any government would think it a good bargain to provide assistance when the investment plan calls for low levels of European content.

ly contemplated by any North American transplant. [10] (This level of content requires that the body, most major mechanical components, and either the engine or the transmission be fully manufactured in Europe.)

The lower levels of state aids recently available to the Japanese in Europe and the significantly higher levels of local content required seem to have had two major effects. First, they have slowed the rate of Japanese assembly plant investment in Europe because these operations could be established more rapidly in the United States with a considerably higher level of government aid. This does not mean the Japanese are not coming to Europe or that their long-term objective in establishing a major production presence is different from their intentions in North America, only that the number of finished units from their European transplants (each with a high level of European content) has grown more slowly, giving the European assembler firms more time to improve their performance (or withdraw).

Second, European investment policies have spurred Japanese use of existing, European-owned suppliers in order to meet the high content requirements as rapidly as possible. By contrast, the complete lack of American content requirements has permitted the Japanese transplants to utilize only as much content from domestic suppliers as seems commercially advantageous. In consequence, the Japanese assemblers are forcing improvements in the performance of European supplier firms who also supply the European-owned assemblers, while in many cases they are ignoring the American suppliers servicing the Big Three. This should provide a clear benefit for the European industry as a whole in the 1990s. [11]

ENERGY PRICING

While hardly adopted as a conscious industrial strategy, the fact that European energy pricing at the pump has been nearly identical to Japanese pricing has meant that the product mix demanded in Europe has been similar, on balance, to Japan (obviously with some variation from the north of Europe to the south). This meant that the major product development efforts of the European producers were in smaller cars and that the industry was not vulnerable to a dramatic shift in demand after 1973. By contrast, the Americans had no products in the smaller segments at all and were forced to spend much of the 1970s and 1980s gaining experience in making smaller vehicles.

More relevant to this chapter, in the 1990s as concern seems to be shifting from fuel shortages to the greenhouse problem, the European industry will again be in a better position to respond because its product portfolio still favors smaller vehicles which consume less fuel per unit of travel. In the United States by contrast,

---

[10] Indeed, under the current Corporate Average Fuel Economy (CAFE) regulations which specify 75 percent U.S.-Canada value-added as the break point between "import" and "domestic" vehicles, Japanese companies will be reluctant to go far beyond 75 percent domestic content in any vehicle which they may need to shift from the "domestic" to the "import" column to meet the separate fuel economy averages each company must maintain.

[11] It is important to note that the Japanese assessment of European suppliers was much more favorable to begin with than their assessment of American suppliers, many of whom they regard as unredeemable. Some of their reasoning is given in Chapter 6 of *The Machine That Changed The World*.

the Big Three critique of the Bryant bill for a 40 mile per gallon corporate average fuel economy (CAFE) quite correctly argues that a rapid move to shift the mix to smaller cars (where the Big Three make no profits) could drive the American industry to the wall.

DISTRIBUTION RULES

Few analysts of the motor vehicle industry have noted the critical connection between distribution rules and the competitive position of national/regional industries. However, the United States has been quite different from the rest of the world in the way it has set rules for selling motor vehicles.

The United States has always been a large market without internal barriers where a vehicle of given description sold for the same price in every region. [12] In addition, since the late 1940s, assembler firms in the United States have not been able to require their dealers to sell only one brand from a single site. By contrast the European Community has permitted assemblers to enforce "selective distribution" and "exclusive selling" rules which limit the freedom of the customer and the dealer, to the distinct advantage of the established assemblers.

Selective distribution has flourished in the absence of a European-wide type certificate and, in the case of the U.K. and Ireland, due to the difference between left and right hand drive. The assemblers have simply refused to provide dealers vehicles with the steering arrangement and national type certificate for any other than the local market. (For example, German assemblers have refused to ship right-hand drive vehicles to Belgium, from whence they could be re-shipped to Britain—a market with much higher prices for most German models.)

What this has meant in practice is that assemblers are able to sell the same car for vastly different amounts in different countries in Europe and to dramatically increase the cost to a newcomer of establishing a sales network. The predominant approach has been to price very low in the assembler's home market to establish a volume base and keep others out (including Japanese imports), and to sell at much higher prices in other markets (in much the same way European luxury cars have for many years been sold at much higher prices in the United States and Japan than in Europe).

At the same time, the European (and American) assemblers in Europe have forbidden their dealers from "dualing", which is to say taking on Japanese brands at established dealerships. Aggressive use of "duals" was precisely the technique which permitted first the Europeans (in the late 1950s) and then the Japanese (in the early 1970s) to rapidly build nationwide dealing networks in the United States with a relatively modest investment.

TECHNOLOGY POLICY

There were apparently few explicit attempts by governments to aid the development of automotive technologies in Europe until the

---

[12] There were, of course, minor variations in prices (e.g., convertibles fetched a higher price in California than in Michigan), but the ease with which middlemen could move vehicles around the country by means of a well developed auction system for new cars meant that significant differentials in prices never endured.

first energy crisis in 1973. At that time environmental and safety demands on the motor vehicle began to grow rapidly as well. Therefore, it was hardly surprising that the French and German governments undertook modest programs in the late 1970s to enhance motor vehicle technology in ways which would deal with environmental, safety, and energy concerns. The main German effort was Auto 2000, funded by the Ministry of Research and Technology between 1978 and 1982. This program shared the cost of developing prototypes at Mercedes, BMW, Porsche, and Volkswagen, which incorporated as many new technologies as possible. The French government responded in 1979 by funding a series of technology demonstration vehicles (Eve and Eco 2000 at Renault and Vera and Vesta at Peugeot-Citroen) through the mid-1980s.

Given their modest size and funding level (for example, the total government contribution to Eve and Vera together was only about $10 million), it is also hardly surprising that these programs had little effect. Indeed, in a report prepared by the authors in 1982, [13] we found that these programs had given a modest boost to future-oriented thinking in some of the German companies (particularly VW) and had effectively subsidized existing research and development activities in the French companies, but had not yielded any technology which would not have been developed otherwise. Indeed, by contrast, the U.S. Government's funding of research on alternative power sources for motor vehicles was truly massive. [14] Unfortunately, it yielded the same results: none.

The Commission has not been deterred, however, by lack of past success in developing commercially attractive automotive technologies. In the late 1980s it embarked on an ambitious set of programs under the names Prometheus and Drive, sub-components of the Eureka program designed to boost the technological position of all European industries in global competition. [15]

Prometheus (Program for European Traffic with Highest Efficiency and Unprecedented Safety) is designed to develop new vehicle/highway electronics which will simultaneously permit more efficient and safer use of European highways while aiding European automotive and electronics firms in gaining a larger share of the global automotive electronics market. The idea is to develop communication and navigation capabilities for motor vehicles which permit them to avoid congestion and accidents and to move in the direction of automatic operation.

Prometheus was initially promoted by the German auto and electronics firms but now includes practically all of the European-owned companies in these sectors. The Americans and Japanese were initially excluded although Ford has gained access through its purchase of Jaguar and GM has been given associate status after

---

[13] Womack, James P. and Daniel T. Jones. *Government Policy and Automotive Technology*. Report prepared by the U.S. Department of Transportation, Transportation Systems Center, March 1982.

[14] The Advanced Automotive Power Systems Program received nearly $1 billion in Federal funding between its origination in 1969 and its demise in the mid-1980s. For a critical review of this program and its results see Womack, James P. *Public Policy for a Mature Industrial Sector: The Auto Case*. PhD dissertation, Massachusetts Institute of Technology, September 1982. p. 150–165.

[15] This section is based on Graves, Andrew. *Prometheus: A New Departure in Automobile R&D?* International Motor Vehicle Program Working Paper, MIT, May 1989.

protests from the company and the American Government. In addition, over 100 automotive and electronics supplier firms and 70 research institutes and universities are participating. The program is to run from 1989 through 1995 at a total cost of about $800 million. About two thirds of this sum is to come from industry.

Prometheus concerns in-vehicle technologies. It is coupled to a second program, Drive, which will develop technologies for roadway management which permit vehicles to communicate with traffic managers and with each other by means of information networks incorporated in the roadway.

In our IMVP work we were only able to look a the initial phase of Prometheus and Drive, specifically the selection of technology targets and the designation of research teams. The structure of the Programs is enormously complex and there is no guarantee that the technologies developed, even if successful, will convey competitive advantage to the European industry. It is taken as a given that auto producers from other regions would be allowed to license any technology so their vehicles could use the European roadway system. Thus the competitive advantage may lie in the amount of licensing fees and their method of collection.

RESTRUCTURING POLICIES

At a number of points during the past twenty years the European Community and its member states have faced the problem of what to do with failing producers. Similar challenges are likely to arise in the 1990s because a number of European car industries, led by the French, are in a very weak competitive position. It seems logical, particularly from an American perspective, that European governments unable to revitalize failing firms will resort to protectionism as their primary response.

In the 1970s, a number of European governments did undertake far reaching "restructuring" of their national industries. However, in the end government assistance proved to be little more than a subsidy to keep "national champions" alive. Very little restructuring occurred. And, not coincidentally, the companies being "restructured" improved very little. Gradually, most of the countries, as well as Brussels, grew disillusioned with the notion that simple financial backstopping could turn around firms which were otherwise not competitive.

Thus the British government after 1979 stopped underwriting losses at British Leyland/Rover and made massive cuts in operations instead. The Spanish government reached a similar conclusion in the mid-1980s and gave up on efforts to make Seat into an independent Spanish "champion". The company was sold to Volkswagen with the understanding that employment would be cut despite a large program of new investment designed to raise Seat's product quality and productivity dramatically. The Italian government took a more active course in 1979 by agreeing to accept about 40,000 workers from Fiat into a state-run retraining and job-bank program. However, the result was the same: a dramatic decline in automotive sector employment.

Indeed, a brief glance at table 10 (which restates data from table 6), suggests that contrary to the common perception in the United

States, European governments have been willing to accept very large declines in automotive employment and do not invariably seek to protect uncompetitive firms. Overall the European auto industry shed about 265,000 jobs between 1978 and 1986, a level of "restructuring" nearly twice as great as that occurring in the United States during this period. Only the dominant German industry was spared the need to downsize payrolls, an important point we will return to in the next section.

TABLE 10. Shrinking Automotive Employment: Europe vs. United States

(thousands of workers)

	1978	1986	Percent Change
Germany	602	772	+28
France	494	370	−25
U.K.	485	265	−45
Italy	292	209	−28
Spain	160	122	−24
U.S.	1005	843	−16

Note: We have used 1978 and 1986 as the relevant years to compare because both were very strong years for automotive demand. Employment in all countries was probably considerably lower during the depths of the world recession of 1981–83.

Source: European data derived from table 6. We have assumed that Spanish employment was the same in 1978 and 1980. We have adjusted the 1978 employment totals for all countries on the presumption that the 1980 data supplied by the European Commission is more accurate than the 1980 data we obtained independently from national sources. For example, the Commission's data show 726,000 employees in the German industry in 1980, compared with an estimate of 784,000 obtained from national sources. We have therefore decreased the 1978 national source estimate by a proportional amount. U.S. data: 1978 from U.S. Department of Labor, Bureau of Labor Statistics. *Employment, Hours, and Earnings, United States, 1909–1984*, Volume 1. p. 313–314. 1986 from U.S. Department of Labor, Bureau of Labor Statistics, *Employment and Earnings*, March 1987.

European Policy in the 1990s: Consequences for the American Motor Industry

Thus far we have reviewed the competitive situation of the European motor vehicle industry at the beginning of the 1990s and examined the policy instruments used by national governments and the Community to shape the development path of the motor vehicle industry in the past. Now we need to ask what the prospects are for the European industry in the 1990s, what the government response (particularly the Commission's) is likely to be in the case of poor performance, and what this may mean for the American-based motor vehicle industry.

We may begin with the policy framework likely to be worked out for the "completion" of the market in 1993. When the debate on this matter commenced in 1988 it appeared that the Commission was likely to back a very liberal position with no limits on imported Japanese units and Japanese direct investment after 1999. 1988, after all, was the midst of a great market boom in Europe and the Commission was mainly concerned that European car prices seemed to be quite high in relation to prices for similar products in the United States. Perhaps more competition was the answer. The discovery that the European industry was inefficient in comparison with both the Japanese and the American industries gave ammunition to the liberals. [16]

Gradually, however, the dawning awareness that the European industry has severe competitive problems and that the bull market of the late 1980s could not continue forever influenced thinking in Brussels. The critical event was the decision by Volkswagen chairman Carl Hahn to join Raymond Levy, the Renault chairman, and Umberto Agnelli, deputy chairman of Fiat, in a submission sent to the Commission in December of 1990. This submission argued that a continuing Europe-wide share limit on Japanese imports would be needed along with a transition period for dropping the country-by-country restrictions on the Japanese within Europe. It clearly represented a move by the Germans from the free-trade to the protectionist camp.

When an agreement was finally reached in July 1991, it was quite restrictive with regard to finished unit imports through 1999 and open to wide interpretation with regard to restrictions on Japanese direct investment. [17] The agreement, the full details of which have never been made public, limits Japanese finished units to 1.23 million per year through 1999, roughly the level of 1991. After that time it states that there will no be no barriers on finished unit imports into Europe, an assertion which quite literally no one in either Japan or Europe believes. Rather, it is universally assumed that as 2000 approaches there will be a new negotiation.

The agreement further states that there will be no limit on Japanese direct investments in European motor vehicle production but that the Commission "expects" that Japanese transplant production will not exceed 1.2 million units by 1999. The meaning of this "expectation" has been interpreted variously. The French and Italian governments have stated that this is a firm upper limit, while the Japanese and British governments maintain that it is nothing more than the Commission's estimate of the likely trend in production. The British government has offered its own "expectation," notably that Japanese transplant production in Europe, overwhelmingly in the U.K., will total 2 million units in 1999.

The agreement provides for the phasing out of individual national quotas on Japanese finished-unit imports as of January 1, 1993, and provides for a common European type certification for imported vehicles from that point in time. However, the Agreement also "forecasts" that Japanese sales in individual European markets which currently have quotas on Japanese finished-unit imports will only increase gradually to the following levels by 1999:

Finally, the agreement places no restrictions on the import of cars and parts from Japanese transplant factories in North America into Europe. [18]

---

[16] The European Commission was a sponsor of the International Motor Vehicle Program. The authors provided several briefings to the Commission staff, beginning in 1988, on the relative competitive standing of the European industry.

[17] Tokyo Holds Out Over EC Car Sales Deal. *Financial Times*, July 28, 1991. p. 2.

[18] This openness will presumably hold as long as Japanese imports from North American transplants are modest in number, contain a substantial amount of North American content (which they will), and the overall European trade balance with North America in motor vehicles continues to be positive.

TABLE 11. Individual National "Forecasts" of Sales of Japanese Imported Automobiles and Market Shares, 1999

Country	Sales	Market Share [a]
France	150,000	5.26
Italy	138,000	5.3
Spain	79,000	5.3
Portugal	23,000	8.36
U.K.	190,000	7.03 [b]

[a] The share estimates are based on an EC Commission forecast that the total European auto market in 1999 will be 15.1 million units.

[b] This represents a decline in Japanese import market share in the U.K. based on the presumption that the great bulk of Japanese transplant production will occur in the U.K. and be sold there. Thus imports are likely to decline but not due to the agreement.

Source: EC Vehicle Sales Accord with Japan to Include Light Trucks. *Financial Times*, August 5, 1991.

What do all of these forecasts and "expectations" really mean? From discussions with the EC Commission staff in Brussels we believe that the unspoken objective of the Agreement is as follows: At least through 1999, and very probably for an indefinite period beyond, the Japanese producers will be allowed to capture the growth in the European market. Taking the realistic British forecast of transplant production and extrapolating the DRI projections for the size of the automobile market in Europe (as shown in table 12) to the 15.1 units estimated by the EC Commission in 1999, we find that the combination of freezing imports of finished units at 1.23 million and allowing 2.0 million units of transplant production to be sold in Europe results in the Japanese producers capturing the entire 1.9 million units of market growth expected between 1991 and 1999.

TABLE 12. Forecast Auto Production and Sales in Europe [a]

(thousands of units)

	1989 [b]	1991	1992	1993	1994
Production	13,749	13,467	13,670	13,957	14,454
Sales	13,424	13,250	13,452	13,649	14,140

[a] Actual for 1989, estimated for future years.

[b] Europe = EC + EFTA, does not include Eastern Europe.

Source: *DRI World Automotive Forecast*, September 1990.

Thus the Japanese share of the European market rises steadily and the European share steadily falls. However, the number of units sold by the European and American firms in Europe stays practically constant. Thus there is no need for retrenchment or reductions in production capacity at least through 1999.

For the Americans these rules have straightforward and important consequences: They mean that Europe will so thoroughly protect itself against serious losses of sales by its American and European producers that no "crisis" is likely to emerge soon. This means in turn that European policy toward the U.S. imports is likely to be relatively open. We will elaborate on this logic in a moment.

This is particularly true because of the likely pattern of trade across the Atlantic. Many American observers have noted the potential of the Japanese transplants in the United States to supply vehicles for European markets and Honda recently announced plans to export about 6,000 Accord station wagons from Ohio to Europe in 1991.[19] Because these plans are being announced at the same time that European imports to the United States are falling substantially, some analysts have predicted a reversal in the European trade balance in motor vehicles with North America and growing pressure in Europe to restrict imports from the United States and Canada, particularly those of the transplants.

The most likely path of events is quite different. First, the weakest European specialists have all been taken over recently by much stronger partners (e.g., Jaguar by Ford and Saab by GM) who have the resources to develop the new models these marques urgently need. In addition, the stronger European specialists such as Mercedes and BMW now understand that the Japanese threat is very real and are taking steps to shorten product lives and push harder on new technologies to remain competitive. Finally, much of the effect of the Japanese luxury cars has been to expand the market in the United States for these classes of vehicles. Thus the flow of European vehicles to the United States is likely to fall somewhat further in the next few years but then to stabilize.

At the same time, the Japanese transplants in Europe are likely to illustrate the very different thinking these firms bring to international strategy. We expect that the limited flow of transplant vehicles from the United States to Europe over the next few years[20] will be balanced later in the decade by a flow of Japanese transplant vehicles from Europe to the United States and Canada. These vehicles will be produced at only one site in each producer's global production system, in Europe or North America, for high volume sales within the region of production and for export in much lower volumes to fill market niches in the other region. The same process will be occurring between Europe and Japan and between North America and Japan, as shown in table 13, which summarizes export plans already announced.

(Candidate vehicles for shipment from Europe to the United States are the Honda Synchro, to be launched at Swindon, U.K. in 1992, the Nissan Primera from Washington, U.K. (which may show up in the Infiniti product range), and the Toyota Carina from Burnaston, U.K.)

Summing these trends (as shown in table 14), we expect a modest additional decline in European vehicle imports to the United States and a modest increase in American and Canadian exports to

---

[19] U.S. Honda to Ship Wagons to Japan. *New York Times*, January 8, 1991. p. D4.

[20] Probably never exceeding 50,000 units. The major problem facing the transplants most likely to export—notably those of Toyota, Nissan, and Honda—is not a lack of domestic markets in the U.S. which might tempt them to "dump" vehicles in Europe, but instead the inability to produce enough vehicles to supply the U.S. market from North America as pressures to continually reduce imports from Japan continue.

TABLE 13. Cross-Regional Export Plans by Japanese Transplants

Company	Production Site	Product	Exported To	Volume	Date
Toyota	Georgetown, KY	Camry	Japan	40,000	1992
	Georgetown, KY	Camry	Taiwan	7,200	1991
	NUMMI (CA)	Corolla	Taiwan	10,000	1991
Nissan	Cuernavaca, Mexico	Pickup	Japan	35,000	1992
	Smyrna, TN	2-door Sentra	Japan	13,000?	1992
	Washington, U.K.	5-door Primera	Japan/Taiwan	10,000	1992
	Australia	Bluebird Stationwagon	Japan	13,000?	1992
Honda	Marysville, OH	Accord Coupe/ Stationwagon	Japan/Taiwan	50,000	1992
	Marysville, OH	Accord Stationwagon	Europe	6,000	1991
Total				184,000	

Source: Based on company press releases as reported in the media.

Europe over the next few years. However, the eastward flow of vehicles will hardly be a flood and will not precipitate a trade crisis between the United States and Europe.

TABLE 14. Pattern of Trans-Atlantic Motor Vehicle Trade

(thousands of units)

	1986	1989	1990	1995 [a]
European Exports to U.S.	657	448	357	300
U.S. Exports to Europe	20	40	70	100
Balance [b]				

Source: U.S. International Trade Commission for 1986, 1989, and 1990; 1995 estimated by authors.

A final point concerning the relation of the American auto industry to Europe is important. For eighty years, since Ford established an assembly plant in the U.K. in 1911, the American companies have been treated as outsiders in Europe. At times they have been welcomed, often in Britain, less frequently in other countries. At times they have found a very hostile reception—for example when Ford was repeatedly denied permission to invest in France and Italy in the interwar years.

However, the arrival of the Japanese transplants has had a curious effect. The organization formed in the 1970s to promote the interests of the European-owned motor vehicle firms in Brussels, the Committee of Common Market Motor Vehicle Constructors (CCMC), resisted all efforts by the Americans to join, becoming essentially a club of the chairmen of the European-owned companies.

In the debate about the approach to take with Brussels on the Japanese in the context of 1992, the tensions within the CCMC became so great that eleven of the twelve members resigned at the end of December 1990, to protest the intransigence of Jaques Calvet, the PSA chairman. (Calvet was insisting that Japanese transplant vehicles must count directly against import quotas no matter what their level of local content and that the overall quota on Japanese vehicles must be reduced to a point where the Japanese were allowed two vehicle imports into Europe for each European import into Japan. This would mean more than halving Japanese imports.) A new organization, ACEA (Association of European Automobile Constructors), has been formed which includes the European and the Americans but, of course, exclude the Japanese (and Calvet)!

Thus the course of events has strengthened the perception that the two American firms (Ford and General Motors), with their top-to-bottom production systems spread across the continent, are now "European" after eighty years on probation. The likelihood of the Commission turning on these firms' American parents in the next few years by threatening to bar imports or to increase investment barriers must be judged very remote. This is true even if the European market proves to be much less ebullient than the current forecasts suggest.

A Final Thought: The Very Long Term

At some point in the longer term, perhaps in the downturn after the current downturn—say 1997/99—the steady growth of the Japanese transplants may began to place severe pressures on the weaker European-owned firms. The European industry might then at last begin to exhibit the stress shown by the American industry in the 1980s.

We would judge that the key question, if this begins to happen, is the relationship between the Japanese and the Germans. The German industry has not to date faced a need to restructure. What's more, its employment commitments to its workforce present a very difficult problem in restructuring. Thus it seems obvious that the smart Japanese strategy is to focus their marketing efforts on the weaker non-German companies and, if necessary, to enter into joint ventures or wholly-owned German investments which could help deal with the need to remove excess workers from the German companies.

However, this is so far away and so many things may happen—for example, an upheaval in the entire world motor industry driven by regulatory demands to meet the challenge of greenhouse gases or, more positively, a significant improvement in the competitive performance of the European firms—that it seems pointless to speculate. In this chapter we have simply argued that for the next five years or so, the European-owned motor vehicle industry—despite lower productivity and quality than the American-owned industry in North America—is likely to escape the need for traumatic restructuring and that, therefore, the likelihood of significant trade friction with the United States is very remote.

AIRBUS INDUSTRIE AND SUBSIDY IN THE EUROPEAN CONTEXT

by John W. Fischer *

CONTENTS

Airbus Industrie, from the European view, is a major success story. From a company that produced a single product only two decades ago, Airbus has become the number two firm in the small universe of producers of commercial jet aircraft. Only Boeing is larger. Airbus is essentially a "chosen instrument" of a European policy that calls for participation in the high visibility, technology leading sectors that constitute commercial jet aircraft manufacturing. Airbus employs large numbers of skilled professionals and technicians and keeps related industries at the forefront of advancing technology. In the process it has also shattered what Europe saw as a virtual American monopoly of an industry to which it feels it has equal or better historical claims.

The fact that Airbus has devoured large quantities of governmentally provided subsidy, while never providing a significant return on investment, is not an important issue in the European view. Market participation in this industry apparently is seen as more important than profit. Subsidy is an important part of European industrial policy. Even in the soon to be established single market, activities like Airbus, with a European rather than a national focus, will continue to be eligible for significant governmental assistance.

The United States has long objected to the continued subsidy of Airbus. While U.S. manufacturers continue to dominate this indus-

* This report is largely taken from U.S. Library of Congress. Congressional Research Service. *Airbus Industrie: An Economic and Trade Perspective*. CRS Report no. 92-166 E, by John W. Fischer (coordinator), David J. Cantor, Glennon J. Harrison, and Lenore M. Sek. February 20, 1992.

try, their combined market share of production over time has declined. The United States view is that direct subsidy is unfair and trade distorting, and that in this specific instance it has damaged the competitive position of the two U.S. market participants, Boeing and McDonnell Douglas (Douglas). As a result the United States and the European Community have been involved in a long running dispute over the efficacy and legality of continued subsidy. [1] This dispute may have been settled, at least temporarily, as a result of a tentative agreement announced by the parties on April 1, 1992.

The creation of Airbus could be viewed as the beginning of a trend toward internationalization of the aircraft manufacturing market. As additional nations demand a role in the production of the strategically and technologically valuable commercial aerospace market, political will is becoming more of a determinant of market participation than are economic forces. Ironically, new politically motivated production within Europe itself may damage the long term prospects not only of U.S. producers, but of Airbus itself.

This report examines the importance of aircraft manufacturing to the U.S. economy and then looks at a number of aspects of the Airbus controversy. First, the role of Airbus in the international marketplace for commercial jet aircraft is analyzed. Second, the report looks at subsidy as an element of European policy generally and as part of the aircraft manufacturing industry specifically. Third, the dispute between the United States and the EC over subsidy policy is reviewed. Finally, U.S. policy options are considered.

Aircraft Production and the U.S. Economy

Aircraft production in the United States to some degree affects nearly 80 percent of the economy. Directly or indirectly, about 340 sectors of the economy—out of about 429 defined sectors—produce goods and services as a result of the output of aircraft. Of these 340 sectors, 150 supply outputs directly to the aircraft industry.

Increasing shipments of domestic aircraft by $1 billion in 1991 is estimated to generate an increase in total output in the economy of about $2.31 billion. Of this amount, $1 billion accounts for the additional output shipped to the marketplace. [2] The remainder represents the output of all sectors of the economy required for these additional shipments. As a result of this total increase in output, an estimated 34,840 jobs are created throughout the economy. Just as an increase in demand and output to satisfy that change could stimulate economic activity by the estimated magnitudes, a decrease in demand could have a similar, but negative effect on output and employment.

Every additional dollar of shipments of aircraft to the market generates about $1.31 of output from all other sectors of the econo-

[1] There is a considerable body of literature on the subsidy issue. This report accepts as a basic premise that Airbus receives direct governmental subsidy as detailed in U.S. Department of Commerce sponsored research (also referred to in this report as the Gellman Study). Although the EC disputes parts of this claim and has sponsored separate research to show that U.S. industry has received large indirect subsidies it has not provided a full accounting of its financial practices. See Arnold and Porter. *U.S. Government Support of the U.S. Commercial Aircraft Industry*. Prepared for the Commission of European Communities. November, 1991.

[2] All value figures in this section of the report are expressed in constant 1977 dollars.

my. Shipments of $1 billion more of new aircraft to the market create about 11,500 new jobs in the aircraft industry itself, and about 23,335 new jobs elsewhere in the economy. For every new job in the aircraft sector, about 2.03 jobs are created in other sectors.

Excluding the aircraft sector, about $1.31 billion of additional output is generated elsewhere in the economy as a result of an increase in demand for aircraft of $1 billion. Twenty-eight sectors account for about $972 million of the additional $1.3 billion produced by all other sectors in the economy as direct or indirect inputs to aircraft production; their share of the increase in total output of all other sectors is estimated to be about 74.3 percent. With respect to direct inputs to the aircraft sector, 28 sectors produce about $630.1 million, or about 86.5 percent of all direct inputs supplied to the aircraft industry. Finally, these 28 sectors account for about 75.0 percent of the total increase in employment other than in the aircraft industry; about 17,500 new jobs would be created in the 28 sectors out of about 23,235 jobs elsewhere in the economy other than in the aircraft sector.

The Market for Commercial Aircraft

At the end of 1990 over 55 percent of all the commercial jet aircraft ever produced had been produced by Boeing. The next largest producer in the market, Douglas, had done less than half as well with close to 25 percent of the market. Airbus, a consortium of French, German, British and Spanish firms, is a relative newcomer to the market having made its first deliveries in 1974. The 6 percent share of the historical market that it has garnered since that date is therefore reasonably impressive. [3]

Much of Airbus' success occurred in the later half of the 1980s. During this period it aggressively expanded its presence in the market by launching new products and rapidly expanding its airline customer base.

It is unlikely that the management of Boeing and Douglas would be happy with the appearance of a strong new competitor in any event. Airbus, however, is not any ordinary competitor. Its efforts have benefited significantly from direct governmental assistance in the launch of its aircraft products. According to the Gellman Study, launch aid and other supports made available to Airbus to date exceed $13.5 billion. No comparable direct support has been provided to U.S. manufacturers by the United States Government.

The growing Airbus presence can be seen in figures 1 and 2. Boeing has continued to dominate the new aircraft market. In terms of new aircraft orders, and the dollar value of orders, Airbus took a lead over Douglas in the boom year of 1989, a lead that it has not relinquished. In 1991 Airbus' lead in orders over Douglas has expanded even in the existing recessionary new aircraft market.

---

[3] Boeing Commercial Airplane Group. *World Jet Airplane Inventory: Year End 1990.* March, 1991. p. 13.

FIGURE 1. New Jet Aircraft Orders
1985-1991 (aircraft)

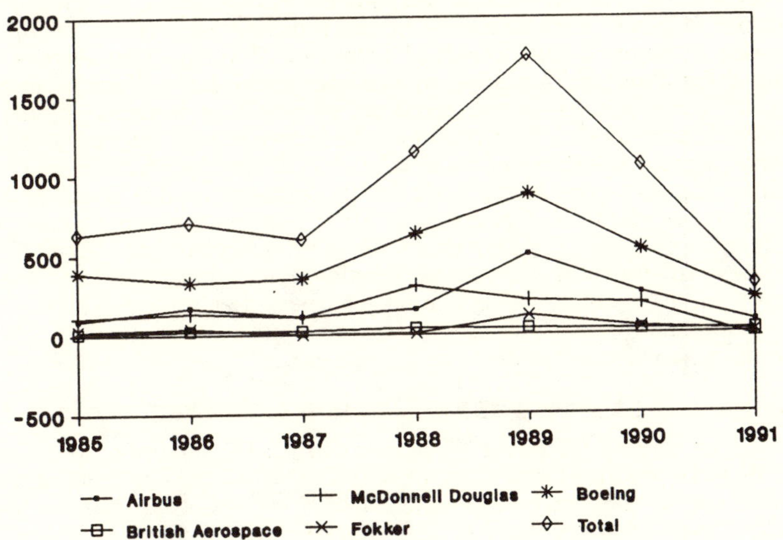

Source: Compiled by CRS

INTERNATIONALIZATION

The production of commercial aircraft today is an international undertaking. This represents a fundamental change in the market from conditions that predominated as little as a decade ago. By way of example, Airbus says that on average 30 percent of the dollar value of its aircraft comes from the United States. Similarly 30 percent of the Boeing B767 has it origins outside the United States. The list of firms supplying major components (subcontractors) for the B747–400 includes such well known non-U.S. aerospace firms as, British Aerospace (an Airbus partner), Aeronica, Fuji, Kawasaki, Mitsubishi, Hawker de Havilland (Australia), Rolls Royce, and Short Brothers.

Today no aircraft is put into production, "launched" in industry parlance, without careful attention to choosing suppliers. While all of these relationships are ultimately commercial, some are also political.

The international commercial aircraft industry is most often thought of in terms of a single firm or product. This is not necessarily a good frame of reference. Airbus is, itself, an example of internationalization. Although Europe has a long and significant aerospace history, European cooperation in the production of commercial aircraft is actually of recent origin. The technologically

FIGURE 2. New Jet Aircraft Deliveries
1985-1991 (aircraft)

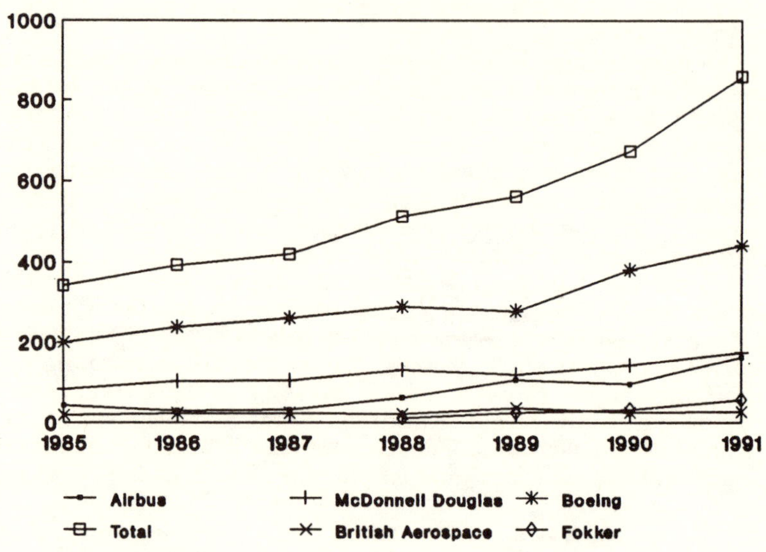

Source: Compiled by CRS

successful and economically disappointing Concorde was the first real evidence of a European ability to cooperate in commercial aircraft manufacturing. Airbus, now in its third decade, has not been without its problems and disputes. At various times the British either did not participate or threatened to withdraw from the consortium. National politics continues to be a primary force in the consortium's business decisions. Most recently Germany demanded, and got, a role in aircraft final assembly with the establishment of the A321 line in Hamburg.

OVERCAPACITY AND FINANCE

A question raised continuously since Airbus was founded is the issue of whether the world aircraft market really needs additional competition. It could be argued that sufficient capacity to meet all of the needs of all of the world's airlines already existed at the time Airbus production began in the mid-1970s and that at least some overcapacity existed.

Airbus generally views the overcapacity issue as irrelevant to its founding. Airbus has frequently stated that its goals were to break up what it saw as an American monopoly in the manufacture of commercial jet aircraft and to give Europe an opportunity to participate in what it views as an important technological sector.

The Gellman Study supports the contention that Airbus has never had to base its decisions to launch new aircraft types solely on market factors. The firm's access to direct government subsidy with the consequent elimination and/or lessening of financial risk has greatly reduced its need for an economic rationale to enter new product markets.

The same research and Airbus' own statements indicate that it has never returned a profit over the long term. It can be further argued that Airbus has yet to have a profitable product. Airbus has stated that it has made an operating profit in each of the last two years, but there are questions as to how the firm defines profit. Douglas has also acknowledged that over the long run it has lost money on its commercial operations. In fact, Boeing has been the only consistently profitable player in this market.

Against this backdrop a case could be made that the decision to pursue much of the new investment in the production of aircraft is not market based. As figure 3 shows, this industry is likely to operate in a constant state of overcapacity for the foreseeable future. The figure shows the 1991 stated capacity of the five current producers of aircraft with 100 seats or more in relation to forecasted demand for new aircraft. For the purposes of this figure, stated capacity is the announced production rate of each of the manufacturers.

FIGURE 3. 1991 Stated Production Capacity vs. Delivery Forecasts

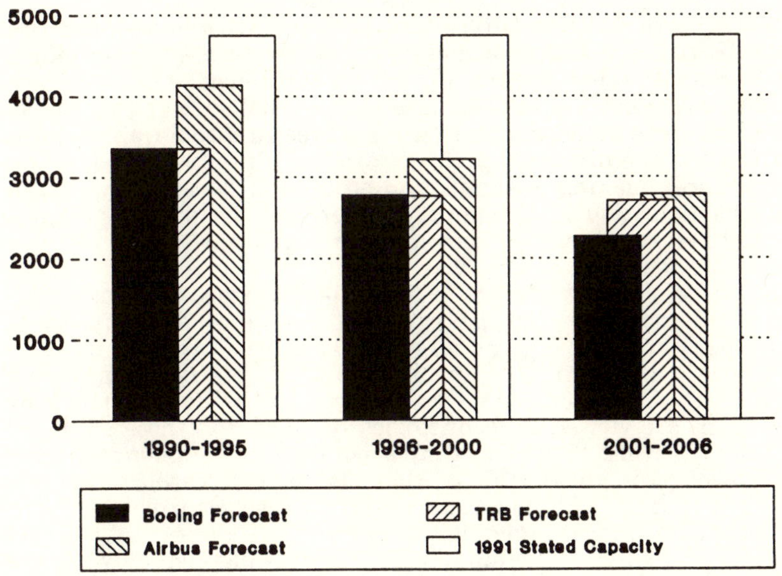

Source: compiled by CRS

FRAGMENTATION AND PROLIFERATION

In 1991, a number of new players were indicating an interest in joining the commercial jet aircraft manufacturing club. Perhaps the most interesting development in this regard is taking place in Airbus' own backyard. Deutsche Aerospace (DASA), the parent company of Deutsche Airbus (Germany), along with Aerospatiale (France), also a firm in the Airbus consortium, and Alenia (Italy) are proposing to build a family of small 80–130 seat aircraft. They propose to do this with significant governmental assistance. They also propose to do this in spite of the fact that Airbus has suggested producing a product for the same market, a smaller version of the A320, tentatively named the A319. It could be said, therefore, that these firms are proposing to compete with Airbus for subsidy, even though two of the firms have ties to the Airbus consortium. The most striking difference between Airbus and the new consortium appears to be the leadership position. In the new consortium the lead partner would be DASA, and assembly would take place in Germany.

As the DASA-led consortium moved toward a launch decision at the end of 1991, two other European producers already in the 100-seat market, British Aerospace (an Airbus partner) and Fokker (a parts supplier to certain Airbus aircraft) found themselves faced with the prospect of subsidized competition from within the European Community (EC). It is believed that either of these firms could seek the intervention of the EC Commission to block the formation of the DASA-led firm. The outcome of such a move, however, is unpredictable.

All of these products will compete, at the high end of the seating spectrum, with existing aircraft such as the B737 and MD80/90 series. In perhaps a countermove Douglas is proposing to build a new low-cost 100-seat aircraft, the MD95, in China.

All of this activity is taking place in a market segment that most analysts believe could support two or three profitable products at best. If all of the discussed products are built, the likelihood of any one producer making a significant profit will be severely diminished. Participation in this market, therefore, is likely to require not good market incentives, but a either a guaranteed market or a dependable source of subsidy.

Another group of producers in the former Eastern bloc could also enter the market over the next decade. The aerospace industry of the former Soviet Union, and its not so long ago Warsaw Pact partners, have a demonstrated capability to produce aircraft in a wide range of configurations. At this writing the products offered by these firms are viewed as technologically inferior to those produced by Western firms. Providing that a political and economic framework develops in these regions, there is no real reason to assume that these nations will choose to absent themselves from the international market for commercial jet aircraft.

Interest in aircraft manufacturing is growing not only at the completed product level, but at the supplier level as well. Interest in subcontracting is increasing worldwide, most often with strong governmental support. Manufacturers have increasingly sought alliances outside their original supplier base for any number of reasons, such as market access. The expansion of manufacturing activity worldwide is acknowledged as a potential threat to certain parts of the U.S. aerospace production base. What is often overlooked in many discussions is that the production base of the Airbus Consortium, and its supplier base is equally threatened by these trends.

Most of the information in this section would point toward a future with more internationalization of the aircraft manufacturing sector. Airbus can be viewed as a regional, managed trade model, of how to run an aircraft manufacturing firm. Airbus is primarily European in its focus, with its products having a significant North American content. Airbus policy is heavily influenced by the industrial policies of its member firms' parent governments. These firms in turn are dependent on government as a guarantor of the firms continued existence. Aerospatiale's January 1992 request for specific French Government financial assistance demonstrates the continued closeness of the relationship.

SUBSIDIES IN THE EUROPEAN COMMUNITY

Subsidies have long been an important component of the industrial policies of many European Community countries. The plan for completing the single market by 1992 (EC–92) has undercut many of those industrial policies that permitted individual member states to champion national industries. In recent years, the Commission of the European Communities (CEC) has been particularly aggressive in taking action against state subsidies that create unfair advantages for national producers. Nationally focused industrial policies, including the use of subsidies, are inconsistent with EC–92. Nevertheless, many member countries continue to use industrial policy and subsidies to promote national economic objectives.

The CEC, while committed to eliminating discriminatory policies that hinder the development of an integrated European market, is not opposed to subsidies that have a European basis rather than a national one. The European venture into aircraft production, via the Airbus consortium, is an example of subsidies that have been determined to be compatible with the creation of a greater European market and that fit the profile of economic activities that are encouraged.

EC MEMBER STATES AND SUBSIDIES

Subsidies have been widely used by the European Community and its member states for a number of specific purposes, including support for new industries, support for declining industries, support for small and medium-sized enterprises, support for research and development, support for regional development, and export promotion and trade-related assistance. [4] Recent studies of subsidies in the European Community and several EC member states, demonstrate that subsidy levels are considerably higher in the EC than in either the United States or Japan. [5]

---

[4] "State aids" is the term commonly used for subsidies in the European Community.

[5] Ford, Robert and Wim Suyker. Industrial Subsidies in the OECD Economies. *OECD Economic Studies*, no. 15, Autumn, 1990. p. 37–81; Commission of the European Communities, *First Survey on State Aids in the European Community*, 1989, and *Second Survey on State Aids in the European Community*, 1990.

For EC member states, total aid to industry amounted to 4.0 percent of industrial output (sectoral GDP) for the 1986 to 1988 period, while such aid in the United States (in 1986) and Japan (in 1985) amounted to 0.5 percent and 1.0 percent of sectoral GDP, respectively. For all EC countries, total aid to all sectors amounted to 2.8 percent of GDP in the 1981–86 period and 2.2 percent in the 1986–88 period. The data contained in this part of the report are largely drawn from EC sources, especially the first and second *Survey on State Aids in the European Community.* [6]

Of the EC member states, the largest providers of subsidies (on an average annual basis) were Germany ($26 billion), Italy ($23 billion), France ($17 billion), and the United Kingdom ($7 billion) during the 1986–88 period. Total subsidies by national governments amounted to $91 billion and exceeded subsidies provided by the European Community, which amounted to $27 billion, by a ratio of more than 3 to 1 during the same period.

THE EC COMMISSION AND SUBSIDIES

The CEC has expressed concern about the volume and proliferation of subsidies among the EC member states. The CEC has stated that subsidies have a negative impact on "the unity of the common market, competition, and therefore the successful completion of the internal market." [7]

The objective of the CEC's subsidy policy is not to eliminate subsidies but to restrict them to recognized Community objectives. Article 92 of the Treaty of Rome forbids any subsidy that "distorts or threatens to distort competition by favoring certain undertakings or the production of certain goods." Such a subsidy is incompatible with the common market insofar as it affects trade between member states. [8] However, not all subsidies are regarded as incompatible with the common market.

Although the CEC has, in recent years, tended to take an increasingly narrow view of subsidies that it would be willing to permit, individual countries continue to rely on industrial and other subsidies. The CEC has concluded that reductions in industrial subsidies have not been significant, despite efforts to bring such subsidies under firm control.

The French electronics sector is a case in point of support for state-owned industry through fresh infusions of equity capital. In April 1991, the French government announced that it would provide $320 million in capital to Thomson, a French consumer and defense electronics company, and $640 million to Groupe Bull, a state-owned computer company. In June 1991, the French government announced that it would suspend this support while it undertook a study of the entire electronics sector. At the same time, it continued to maintain the government's right to provide fresh cap-

---

[6] Considerable variation exists as to the type and level of subsidies among EC member states. For information on subsidies, see Ford, Robert and Wim Suyker. Industrial Subsidies in the OECD Economies. *OECD Economic Studies*, no. 15, Autumn, 1990. p. 37–81; Commission of the European Communities, *First Survey on State Aids in the European Community*, 1989, and *Second Survey on State Aids in the European Community*, 1990.

[7] *Second Survey on State Aids*, p. 50.

[8] For a basic statement of EC policy with respect to subsidies and a summary of the relevant articles of the Treaty of Rome, see: Commission of the European Communities. *EEC Competition Policy in the Single Market.* Second edition, 1989.

ital for public sector companies. [9] In December 1991, the French Government announced that it planned to merge two loss-leading state enterprises with two of France's most profitable state-owned industries. Thomson would be merged with the Commissariat à L'Energie Atomique (CEA), the country's state-owned civil nuclear power industry. Bull would be merged with France Télécom, the state-owned telecommunications monopoly. Various news reports also suggested that France's aerospace industry will be merged into another money-making state-owned entity that could provide a ready source of cash for that industry while avoiding accusations of subsidy. [10]

In November 1991, the CEC approved a $350 million recapitalization of Air France, a state-owned carrier, against the advice of Leon Brittan, the CEC vice president with responsibility for competition policy, who considered the payment to be an "unfair state aid." [11] The CEC also recently authorized a $465 million capital injection by Crédit Lyonnais, a state-owned bank, into the money-losing steelmaker Usinor Sacilor. According to William Dawkins, a *Financial Times* reporter, "the French Government could well take this to mean that it is free under EC regulations to cross-subsidize between different parts of the public sector—just as a private conglomerate might channel profits from one subsidiary to another." [12]

The continuing reliance on subsidies by EC members undermines the single market by reducing the overall competitiveness of industry by preventing or delaying necessary industrial restructuring and by distorting trade and causing harm to unsubsidized foreign competitors. As the European Community comes closer to realizing an EC-wide market without internal barriers, some national governments are likely to push for greater use of subsidies to support failing businesses and national champions, and to promote social or other economic objectives. Greater competition in the European Community in sectors such as air transport and electronics is already resulting in new subsidy strategies (via the old capital-injection route) on the part of member countries. There are concerns that the CEC will not be successful in the battle to limit the use of subsidies as long as member states can—and do—prevail in their efforts to provide additional new subsidies through capital injections.

---

[9] *Financial Times*. Brittan to Challenge French Subsidies Plan. June 13, 1991. p. 3; Hill, Andrew and George Graham. France to Suspend Thomson Support. *Financial Times*. June 20, 1991. p. 1.

[10] Dawkins, William. France May Set Up Public Sector High-Tech Concern. *Financial Times*, December 16, 1991. p. 1; Dawkins, William. France Forms Electronics To Nuclear Energy Giant. *Financial Times*, December 19, 1991. p. 1; *The Economist*. Edith's Edifice. December 21, 1991–January 3, 1992. p. 83. *The Economist* makes the point that, at a time when Siemens is having difficulty digesting another computer maker (Nixdorf) and IBM is restructuring itself into smaller, more agile operating units, the French attempt to create a new group of national champions appears to be another foray into industrial policy, as well as an attempt to get around EC controls on unauthorized state aids.

[11] *Reuters*. EC Clears Large State Cash Injection for Air France. November 20, 1990; *Reuters*. Air France Rivals Criticize EC's Approval of State Aid. November 21, 1991.

[12] Dawkins, William. Cresson's Champions. *Financial Times*, December 19, 1991. p. 16.

EC SUBSIDIES POLICY AND AIRBUS

Subsidies to Airbus are a major source of conflict in U.S.-EC bilateral relations. The notion that state subsidies are acceptable if they promote sectors of economic and technological importance is not widely accepted in the United States—although proponents of strategic trade policy and industrial policy often assert that the Government should use specific, highly targeted subsidies and other measures as a means of promoting U.S. industry and U.S. competitiveness. [13]

Estimates of government subsidies to Airbus are difficult to determine because Airbus Industrie does not publish financial statements. The Gellman study notes that "only incomplete information is available on government support for Airbus." [14] Although government support for the Airbus consortium is understated, Gellman concludes that France, West Germany, and the United Kingdom committed a total of about $13.5 billion in support of Airbus programs through 1989. Types of support fall into several categories, including launch aid and other supports such as equity infusions, non-program specific operating loans, research and development funding, and production subsidies. Using an alternative method for determining the true economic value of public support for Airbus-related activities, Gellman conservatively estimated that the value of committed net government support by 1989 had reached almost $26 billion. [15]

THE AIRBUS DISPUTE IN THE GENERAL AGREEMENT ON TARIFFS AND TRADE

The General Agreement on Tariffs and Trade (GATT) administers an aircraft agreement, but that agreement does not clearly provide strong rules pertaining to some practices, especially aircraft subsidies. Multilateral negotiation of an aircraft code occurred in the latter part of the Tokyo Round of multilateral trade negotiations (1976–1979). The U.S. industry had the major share of world trade in aircraft, but it viewed the newly formed Airbus consortium, with solid government financing, as a potential major threat to that U.S. dominance. The aircraft code included many provisions to liberalize aircraft trade; for example, it eliminated tariffs, prohibited licensing requirements, and banned discriminatory procurement. However, it did not include clear rules covering aircraft subsidies and said only that the multilateral subsidies code, which was negotiated at the same time, would apply to aircraft.

Through the first half of the 1980s, the U.S. aircraft industry was increasingly concerned about market loss to Airbus and government support for that consortium. In 1986, high-level U.S. negotia-

[13] See U.S. Congress. Office of Technology Assessment. *Competing Economies: America, Europe, and the Pacific Rim.* OTA-ITE-498. October, 1991. See especially chapters 1 and 2.

[14] Gellman Research Associates, Inc. *An Economic and Financial Review of Airbus Industrie.* A study prepared for the International Trade Administration, U.S. Department of Commerce. September 4, 1990. p. 2-1. The Gellman study provides detailed summaries of subsidies provided by the French, German, and British governments, as well as an economic analysis of the Airbus program.

[15] Ibid., p. 2-3.; U.S. Department of Commerce. International Trade Administration. *Airbus Models/Programs: Historical Summary Information.* May 3, 1991.

tors travelled to the EC to hold discussions on the subsidy of Airbus. At that time, negotiators were trying to resolve the issue bilaterally rather than pursue a formal procedure through the GATT. [16]

Bilateral discussions continued for a few years, but eventually the United States brought a dispute to the GATT in response to a German government program. The German government wanted to free itself of losses to Deutsche Airbus, which was a subsidiary of Messerschmitt-Boelkow-Blohm (MBB). [17] It approved acquisition of MBB by Daimler Benz AG and promised that it would cover exchange rate losses if the dollar went below a given rate. In March 1989, the United States formally requested consultation under the GATT Subsidies Committee, charging that the exchange rate guarantee was clearly prohibited by the Subsidies Code. The Subsidies Code does not prohibit all subsidies; it bans export subsidies, but says that "subsidies other than export subsidies are widely used as important instruments for the promotion of social and economic objectives . . ." The EC argued that the proper forum for the dispute was the Civil Aircraft Committee.

Bilateral negotiations on Airbus continued and the two sides made some progress on a ceiling for development subsidies. The United States moved from a position of no government subsidies for development to a limit of 25 percent. EC representatives moved from a 75 percent limit to the 40–45 percent range. The United States threatened to request a GATT dispute panel if the EC did not agree to a lower ceiling.

In February 1991, the EC proposed again the 45 percent limit and two days later the United States filed for dispute resolution of the exchange rate complaint. The dispute panel reached its final decision in January 1992 and found in favor of the United States. The panel decision, however, does not necessarily mean that Germany will drop its exchange rate guarantee. Almost every dispute that has reached the panel report stage in the Subsidies Committee has been blocked by the party that lost the case and thus has not been adopted.

In May 1991, the United States formally requested consultations with the EC on a second Airbus issue: government subsidies. This complaint also was filed in the Subsidies Committee. After unsuccessful consultation the United States formally asked for conciliation in August 1991. Early in October, the EC presented a proposal that set a cap on development subsidies in the 30–39 percent range. The United States could have requested a dispute panel, but after conferring with industry representatives U.S. officials said that they would pursue further negotiation with the EC. [18]

---

[16] The Bureau of National Affairs. U.S., European Negotiators Trade Charges as Talks on Subsidized Airbus Funding Convene. *International Trade Reporter*. March 26, 1986: 412-413.

[17] A German official was quoted as saying in November 1988, "The German government's desire was to get out of the Airbus business. We were far behind other world producers, there were too many other competitors, and the government had no way to carry the losses. The only company that had the economic muscle to [take over our share] was Daimler, and they were not prepared to take it without some coverage for the risks." The Bureau of National Affairs. Yeutter Criticizes German Decision to Provide Risk Support or Daimler Benz Airbus Venture. *International Trade Reporter*, November 16, 1988. p. 1498.

[18] Administration Decides to Explore Further Flexibility on Airbus Negotiations. *Inside U.S. Trade*, October 25, 1991. p. 1.

On April 1, 1992 negotiators for the United States and the EC announced a tentative settlement of the Airbus dispute. The settlement, subject to governmental approval, would cap development and indirect subsidy, and provide for increased transparency of financial information. The stated goal of the negotiators is to expand this agreement to include other aircraft producing countries and other related products, such as aircraft engines. The tentative agreement provides for review of its implementation after one year. There have been statements of concern about the agreement from congressional and additional sources, but other U.S. officials are reported to find the agreement acceptable. It is far too early to predict whether this tentative agreement will conclude the Airbus dispute, or whether the debate will continue.

Without the GATT committees and dispute process, the United States and the EC might not have had an adequate alternative forum and the dispute might have ended in a destructive trade war. Further, the stages for dispute resolution (consultation, conciliation, dispute panel) allow the parties several opportunities to come to an agreement. A problem in using the GATT, however, is the slow pace in resolving the dispute. A stronger GATT dispute process with tighter deadlines might have led to resolution sooner and not allowed the talks to continue for over five years without a successful conclusion.

Developments resulting from the GATT Uruguay Round could make the GATT a more practical forum for the commercial aircraft sector. A proposed draft by GATT Director General Arthur Dunkel in December 1991 appears to contain much stronger dispute resolution procedures. Specifically a single nation could no longer block a decision by a GATT panel or implementation of the decision. The effect of these new dispute procedures, while possibly helping the U.S. aircraft sector, might be damaging to other U.S. industries.

Policy Options

Some have expressed considerable concern over the years that U.S. policy toward Airbus has been somewhat "waffling." At times the United States has demanded in the GATT that the Airbus subsidies be reduced, a short time later the United States was stating that it was open for further discussion, and so on. Some of this is attributed to changes in overall U.S. trade policy, of which aircraft manufacturing is only a single part, and some to the reluctance of the U.S. aircraft manufacturing industry to get involved in a trade dispute that might cause them to lose access to European markets.

The requirement is for an accommodation (possibly reached on April 1, 1992). For a number of years representatives of the U.S. industry have been stating that what they really want is the so called "level playing field." Given the internationalization of the market and strong national policies toward continued participation found in some parts of the world, the level playing field is probably unattainable. Something closer to this ideal might be reachable, however, if a clear U.S. policy advancing it existed.

In 1992, the U.S. commercial aircraft manufacturing sector is troubled. Orders for new aircraft have fallen to a level not experienced since the early 1980s. The recession is obviously a major factor, but there are others, and the existence of Airbus, with its enhanced product line, is one of them.

In the early 1980s, Airbus' product line was limited and its impact in world markets was relatively small. Now Airbus is a competitor in almost all market segments and it is threatening to get into the small and jumbo markets as well. Where the limited business of the recessionary periods of the early 1980s was split among two large U.S. firms and a small Airbus, it is now Douglas that is the small player, apparently having captured less than 10 percent of 1991 new aircraft orders.

The position of the two U.S. aircraft manufacturers could be further eroded in the years ahead by reductions in defense spending. McDonnell Douglas is still the Nation's largest defense contractor and its profits in recent years, when it had some, came largely from the military side. Boeing is less dependent on defense spending, but certain military products have contributed significantly to the firm's bottom line.

Although it is not always noted, the status quo might not necessarily work to Airbus' advantage. The Airbus partners' military business is also subject to decline in the years ahead. Problems that result from this standdown at any one of the partner firms could affect the whole consortium. Aerospatiale, as mentioned earlier, is now having financial problems. There is also a reluctance by partner Governments to subsidize new projects at this time, putting both the small aircraft and jumbo aircraft projects in jeopardy. [19] In addition, DASA seems intent on having a larger role in the consortium, and seems determined to become an aircraft producer in its own right. The likelihood of independent DASA action would seem to be setting the stage for considerable friction with its French partner. The outcome of this potential instability on Airbus' long term business plan remains to be seen, but for the moment the consortium may be undergoing something of a retrenchment. None of these forces, however, should be viewed as life threatening to Airbus. A subsidized Airbus has consistently shown itself to be a long-term player.

Airbus' success has been financed primarily with massive government subsidies. These subsidies are frequently called loans, although the pay back periods and interest charged (if any) bear little resemblance to a loan obtained in the open market. In addition, as Department of Commerce studies have shown, the computation of expected paybacks appears to forgive most historical losses. It should be kept in mind that these subsidies have been provided over what is now a 20 year period, and the actual annual cost to the government of any particular Airbus partner is no more than a few hundred million dollars. [20]

Obviously the provision of the same level of subsidy to two U.S. firms would cost the U.S. Government considerably more. The reality, however, is that a comparable level of subsidy would not

---

[19] Betts, Paul. Finance Problems Threaten New Airbus. *Financial Times*. January 10, 1992. p. 2.

[20] Golaszewski, Richard. *Foreign Targeting of U.S. Industry: Can the U.S. Respond?* Presentation at NASA Alumni League. September 11, 1990. p. 6.

likely be needed to maintain the competitiveness of U.S. firms in this marketplace, if it were needed at all. As has been discussed, Boeing has managed to stay profitable even in the face of subsidized competition. Douglas has not done as well, but has not lost anything near to the huge sums parted with by the governments of Airbus' partners.

Airbus will not go away. EC actions to date, make it clear that subsidies will remain available to firms with a clear European industrial policy goal. Many believe the goal of U.S. policy, therefore, must concentrate on bolstering U.S. manufacturers in the face of subsidized competition and enabling them to introduce new products, while at the same time maintaining access to world markets.

EUROPEAN INTEGRATION: IMPLICATIONS FOR U.S. FOOD AND AGRICULTURE

by Charles E. Hanrahan *

CONTENTS

Introduction

European integration has important implications for U.S. food and agricultural sectors. Completion of the single European market (EC-92) is one among several potent forces for change in future U.S. and European Community production, processing, and trade of food products and agricultural commodities. Others include German unification and its effects on EC food and agriculture, political and economic reforms in Eastern and Central Europe, and possibly, wider European economic and political union. The success of envisaged reforms of the EC's Common Agricultural Policy (CAP) and the outcome of agricultural negotiations in the Uruguay Round of multilateral trade negotiations will bear importantly on how U.S. food and agriculture are affected by continuing European integration.

EC-92: Its Implications for Agricultural and Food Trade

EC-92 is not an effort to reform EC agricultural policy nor is it directed at the EC's foreign agricultural trade. Nevertheless, the creation of a single market will have important effects—both direct and indirect—on agricultural policy and on trade in food and agricultural products. EC-92 has direct implications for U.S. processed food trade, while its effects on trade in agricultural commodities will be more indirect and less certain. [1]

---

* Charles E. Hanrahan is a Senior Specialist in Agricultural Policy, Congressional Research Service.

[1] See various articles in U.S. Department of Agriculture. Economic Research Service. *EC 1992: Implications for World Food and Agricultural Trade*. David R. Kelch, ed. Staff Report AGES 9133. Washington, D.C., October, 1991.

More than one third of the 282 directives for implementing EC–92 will affect trade barriers for intra-EC food and beverage trade. [2] EC member states' laws concerning production, consumption and trade of food and agricultural products must conform to these EC-wide laws. This EC-wide harmonization of sanitary and phytosanitary standards for plant, animal, and human health should facilitate entry into the EC market from countries with similar standards. Countries with lower or different standards, however, may face new difficulties in gaining access to the EC food market. Additional EC–92 directives for transportation, financial services, and the harmonization of value-added taxes and excise taxes will also affect production and trade of processed foods and agricultural products.

U.S. and European analysts have identified other effects of the 1992 integration process on agriculture, not related to the food and agricultural directives. These include

- reduced prices for agricultural commodities due to reform of the monetary system [3];
- increased food consumption attributable to such macroeconomic effects as increased employment, income growth, and income redistribution;
- a possible weakening of the EC farm lobby and consequent loss of support for the CAP;
- a restructuring of markets for agricultural inputs, agricultural raw materials, and processed foods; and
- the establishment of EC-wide institutions that may regulate EC agriculture, such as an EC-wide environmental agency.

On balance, these developments would tend to lower prices for agricultural products in the Community, reduce EC food and agricultural production, and lower net agricultural exports. These effects would be welcomed by U.S. producers and exporters of agricultural commodities.

The U.S. processed foods and agricultural sectors will be likely to benefit from lower EC agricultural production and macroeconomic changes that lead to higher food consumption. These production and consumption effects of EC–92 together with other forces for change should lead to reductions in the EC's exports of agricultural products. Under EC–92, U.S. processed food companies already operating in the EC should benefit from opportunities to expand intra-Community trade. U.S. exporters of processed products should benefit from both reductions in the number of import restrictions from EC member states and their harmonization.

U.S. food processors, however, could face stronger competition from EC companies in world markets for processed foods. EC food processors will be able to take advantage of economies of scale made possible by a larger European market. Some EC–92 food directives have already created problems for U.S. exporters. The EC's bans on meat from animals treated with hormones and on pork

---

[2] *EuroFood.* London, AgraEurope, Ltd. Various issues.

[3] See Josling, Timothy E. and Walter H. Gardiner. Dismantling the EC's Agrimonetary System: Effects on European Agriculture. *EC 1992: Implications for World Food and Agricultural Trade.* Kelch, David R., ed., cited in footnote 1.

slaughtered in U.S. facilities that do not meet internal EC standards have created significant problems for U.S. meat exporters. A Uruguay Round agreement on harmonizing the use of such food health and safety measures would contribute to resolving difficulties created by different international standards and practices. If exports from third countries that do not meet new Community-wide standards are diverted from the EC market, they may seek access to U.S. markets, resulting in stiffer competition for some U.S. producers of processed foods.

The effects of EC-92 on trade in agricultural commodities is more difficult to gauge. Many analysts think that EC-92 will result in expanded U.S. agricultural trade to third country markets, but not to the EC market itself. The magnitude of the trade effects, which depends on changes in the net export position of the EC, is likely to be small, according to most analysts. As a result of changes in the agrimonetary system (a direct result of EC-92) and price cuts envisaged in CAP reforms (see below), EC prices for wheat, corn, dairy, and beef should fall, leading to reduced growth in production. Macroeconomic effects of EC-92 (increased employment, income growth, and income redistribution) should contribute to increased food consumption in the Community. Thus net exports should fall. The United States could expect to capture some portion, but probably not all, of this change in EC net agricultural trade. Other major agricultural exporting countries such as Argentina, Australia, and Canada would take some portion of the change in world trade. An expansion of U.S. exports could mean U.S. prices and farm income would increase and reduced budget outlays for price and income support. [4]

Some U.S. agricultural exports to the Community may be adversely affected by the move to a single market. If EC grain prices fall as a result of both EC-92 and proposed CAP reforms, U.S. exports of nongrain feeds such as corn gluten could decline as livestock producers increase their use of domestically produced grains as feedstuffs.

German Unification

Another important factor is the integration of east German agriculture into the EC. German unification has already had important implications for EC production and trade of agricultural products and is adding to the budgetary impetus for policy change. German unification has contributed to increased production of commodities already in surplus in the EC-12 and added to the cost of the CAP. [5] In their first year under the CAP (the 1990-1991 marketing year), east German farmers achieved high levels of self-sufficiency in milk, meat and rapeseed production and increased their self-sufficiency for wheat and feed grains. East German additions to supplies of grain and beef, already in surplus in the Community, severely depressed commodity prices in Germany. These depressed

---

[4] See McDowell, Harold. Implications of EC 1992 for U.S. Agricultural Commodity Trade. *EC 1992: Implications for World Food and Agricultural Trade.* David R. Kelch, ed., cited in footnote 1.

[5] U.S. Department of Agriculture. Economic Research Service. *Western Europe: Agriculture and Trade Report.* RS-91-4, October, 1991.

prices spilled over into other EC countries necessitating large intervention buying of grains and meat. German unification increased CAP spending in 1991 by about one billion dollars.

East German farm structure, dominated by very large collective farms, is in the process of adjusting. While farms sizes are expected to drop, east German agriculture will not likely face the problems confronted by the very small farms in west Germany. The German government has instituted adjustment programs aimed at facilitating the restructuring of east German agriculture. The government has also introduced land set-aside programs to remove marginal land from production. Despite efforts to take land out of cultivation in the east, yields there are expected to increase rapidly as farmers intensify production on better lands remaining in production and shift from rye and potatoes to wheat, barley, and rapeseed. Already farmers are reported to be applying improved inputs from West Germany such as fertilizers, pesticides, and high-yielding seeds. The pace and effectiveness of this adjustment process will determine how efficient these farms can become.

Analysts of German agriculture predict that, in the medium and long term, east Germany will become a net exporter of agricultural commodities, adding to the EC's net export position, especially for grains. [6]

Reforms in Eastern and Central Europe

Political and economic reforms in Eastern and Central Europe also have important implications for European and U.S. trade in food and agricultural products. As in the case of Germany, those reforms are likely to increase the production of temperate zone products already in surplus in the EC. Most of these countries have expressed a desire to join the EC, to increase agricultural exports to the EC, and to share in generous EC price supports and export subsidies.

Some Eastern and Central European countries appear to be moving toward the adoption of agricultural policies modeled on the CAP. Czechoslovakia's announcement of its intention to adopt CAP-like agricultural policies reflects its hopes for eventual union with the EC. The proposed policy includes intervention buying systems, price guarantees, import controls, and export subsidies. The Czechoslovak plan appears intended as a transition to a free market in agricultural products, but Czechoslovakia would adopt the CAP if it became a member of the EC.

The EC has been willing to extend expanded market access to Eastern and Central European countries for many products, but has been reluctant to open its borders in the near term for agricultural products. Differences between the EC and Hungary, Poland, and Czechoslovakia over the extent of market opening for agricultural products almost torpedoed association agreements in negotiations between those countries. Final association agreements provided for several years of limited access to the EC market for Eastern

---

[6] U.S. Department of Agriculture. Economic Research Service. *EC 1992: Implications for World Food and Agricultural Trade.* October, 1991. See especially the paper by Henrichsmeyer, Wilhelm. The Effects of Integration of East Germany on the CAP; First Calculations and Indications.

Europe's agricultural products. Most observers expect that Eastern and Central European countries will eventually seek membership in the EC.

The European Economic Area

Agriculture is likely to play a relatively subordinate role in the European Economic Area (EEA), a free trade zone, which includes the twelve member states of the EC and the seven member states of the European Free Trade Association (EFTA)—Austria, Finland, Iceland, Liechtenstein, Norway, Sweden, and Switzerland. Agriculture was left out of the EEA because it was judged by negotiators to be too "sensitive" for inclusion. EFTA countries, with smaller agricultural sectors than their EC partners, maintain highly protectionist agricultural policies.

Sweden, however, which had been operating an agricultural policy much like the EC's CAP, has adopted a sweeping reform program. Its previous agricultural policy, which dated from the 1930's, included high, administered prices reinforced by import levies, export subsidies, and a high degree of market intervention. Sweden's revised agricultural policy abolishes the agricultural price support system and export subsidies. Border protection measures, however, will remain in force pending the outcome of the Uruguay Round negotiations on agriculture. Direct income support will be provided to grain farmers whose prices will be reduced and who take land out of production in order to reduce surpluses. Dairy farmers will get incentives to take early retirement. Payments will be made to dairy farmers who cull their dairy herds.

Most EFTA countries may become full-fledged members of the EC. The EC Commission has indicated that it will not consider new membership applications until after January 1, 1993, the date when the single market is to be fully established. Sweden has officially applied for EC membership and the changes it has made in its agricultural policy mirror the reforms proposed for the CAP (see below). Austria has also applied for EC membership as have Finland and Switzerland. Iceland and Norway are debating future membership in the EC. Unlike Sweden, however, these countries have not undertaken reforms of their highly protectionist agricultural policies.

THE IMPORTANCE OF CAP REFORM AND THE URUGUAY ROUND

How continuing European integration affects U.S. food and agriculture will depend in large measure on (1) the success of envisaged reforms of the EC's Common Agricultural Policy (CAP) and (2) the outcome of agricultural negotiations in the Uruguay Round of multilateral trade negotiations. The United States is pushing the EC to make significant reforms in its agricultural policy in the current GATT round. At the same time, the Community is debating far reaching internal reforms in the CAP.

THE ROLE OF CAP REFORM

Prior to ratification of the Single European Act in 1987, agriculture had been central to European integration. The 1957 Treaty of Rome included significant agricultural objectives:

- increasing agricultural productivity
- maintaining a fair standard of living for the rural population
- stabilizing markets
- assuring regular food supplies, and
- maintaining reasonable consumer prices.

Agriculture was central in the drive for European economic integration for several reasons. [7] For EC member states with vivid memories of widespread malnutrition and hunger during and after World War II, food security was a prime concern. Food price inflation was widespread, thus stabilizing food prices was important to stabilizing wages and incomes in Europe. Food expenditures as a percent of disposable income in 1957 varied widely, but reached as high as 60 percent in some member states. Finally, many Europeans thought it would be easy to integrate existing highly interventionist country agricultural policies.

The Common Agricultural Policy took its present form in 1967, ten years after the signing of the Treaty of Rome by the original six member states of the EC. The basic goals of the CAP as set forth in 1967 are to :

- guarantee food supplies at stable and reasonable prices;
- improve productivity through technical progress and a more rational production; and
- ensure a fair standard of living for farmers.

The CAP relies on three principal policy instruments to accomplish these goals. The *variable levy* (a kind of sliding tariff) applied to most agricultural imports; a Community-wide and largely open-ended system of *intervention buying* for major agricultural commodities; and *export restitutions* or subsidies for the disposal of surplus production. There are three "pillars" of the CAP: (1) common financing (primarily from value-added taxes (VAT) and the variable import levies; (2) common prices (which have been difficult to maintain because of monetary differences in member states); and (3) community preference.

These policies, especially high internal prices for agricultural commodities, have encouraged domestic production, which has increasingly met domestic demand, and displaced imports from the United States and other sources. As a result of the CAP, the EC has moved from being a large net importer of many crop and livestock products to that of a large net exporter. For example, in 1970, the EC imported 6.5 million metric tons of wheat and wheat flour, but in 1991, exported 23 million metric tons. In 1986, the EC temporarily surpassed the United States as the world's largest agricultural exporter. Despite the production increases stimulated by the CAP, the EC remains the world's largest importer of agricultural products, importing $63.5 billion of food and agricultural products in 1990. The United States traditionally maintains an agricultural

[7] U.S. Department of Agriculture. Economic Research Service. *The Role of Agriculture in European Unification, in EC 1992: Implications for World Food and Agricultural Trade.* David R. Kelch, ed. Washington, D.C., October, 1991.

trade surplus with the EC. At $2.4 billion in 1990, however, it is only 27 percent of the 1980 surplus. [8]

Many of the goals of the Treaty of Rome as implemented in the CAP have been realized. Farm incomes in the Community have been enhanced. The EC enjoys high rates of self-sufficiency (more than 100 percent for most basic staple commodities) and there is a stable food supply. However, food prices are relatively high and budget outlays for agricultural support and protection are enormous. The EC's export restitutions for major traded commodities have outraged other major exporters such as the United States, Argentina, Australia, and Canada who say that such subsidies distort world trade in agricultural commodities. Intensive farming practices, including applications of chemical fertilizers far in excess of crop nutrient requirements, encouraged by high internal prices, have had adverse environmental consequences.

While reaching many of its goals, the CAP has proved an incredibly costly undertaking. Not counting the outlays of individual member states, budget costs of the CAP amounted to more than $50 billion in 1990, according to OECD. [9] By way of comparison, the United States spent about $55 billion over the five-year life of the 1985 farm bill. Member states pay out an additional $10 billion for national agricultural programs. The CAP accounts for about 60 percent of the total EC-wide budget.

Huge budget outlays and other factors such as large stocks of surplus agricultural commodities, environmental deterioration, and unequal income distributions in rural areas have led to a far reaching effort by the EC Commission to reform the CAP. [10] The major features of the Commission's reform proposal to be phased in over three years are:

- a steep reduction in prices paid to cereal producers and lesser cuts for producers of milk, butter, and livestock products
- the introduction of set-aside programs for cereals, oilseeds, and protein crops (modeled on U.S. acreage reduction programs)
- deficiency payments to compensate farmers for price cuts and for taking land out of production (also modeled on U.S. income support programs),
- programs to encourage less intensive crop production or grazing and to limit environmental damage, and promote early retirement of farmers.

These reforms would radically alter the CAP. Deficiency payments would replace intervention buying as the main policy instrument for supporting farm income. Land set-asides would be introduced into the CAP for the first time ever. As noted, both these features of CAP reform have been modeled after U.S. agricultural policy measures. The reforms do not, however, dismantle EC sys-

---

[8] For information on U.S.-EC agricultural trade see U.S. Department of Agriculture. *Foreign Agricultural Trade of the United States*, various issues; Commission of the European Communities. *The Agricultural Situation in the Community*, various issues; and, U.S. Department of Agriculture. *Western Europe: Agriculture and Trade Report*, various issues.

[9] *Agricultural Policies, Markets and Trade: Monitoring and Outlook 1991.*

[10] Commission of the European Communities. *Commission Communication to the Council and the European Parliament: The Development and Future of the Common Agricultural Policy, Follow-up to the Reflections Paper* (COM(91) 100 of 1 February 1991)—Proposals of the Commission COM(91) 2568. Brussels, July 22, 1991.

tems for import protection or export subsidization. The variable import levies and the export restitution would remain as integral components of EC agricultural policy and continue to restrict market access and have the effect of isolating EC producers and consumers from world markets.

CAP reform would affect both internal and external EC food and agricultural trade. Jacques Delors, President of the EC Commission, has suggested, that if the reforms are adopted, the EC will "produce less, export less, and import more" agricultural products. EC consumers could benefit from lower prices due to price cuts for the major commodities. USDA analysts expect agricultural production in the EC to stabilize somewhat below current levels, if the proposed reforms are enacted. Reduced EC grain prices could render EC grains more competitive with imported feedstuffs, notably oilseeds and nongrain feeds such as corn gluten. U.S. exports of such feedstuffs to the Community could be adversely affected, although by how much is difficult to determine. Stocks and exports should decline as EC production declined and domestic consumption increased. The EC would still be an exporter but at a reduced level. U.S. exporters of grains, especially wheat to third country markets might benefit in the long run from reduced EC wheat exports. [11]

The effect of CAP reforms on the EC budget are another matter. Reducing budget outlays for agriculture is a prime reason for CAP reform, yet the effect of the reforms on the budget would be to increase outlays in the near term. The EC Commission estimates CAP spending, if the reforms were implemented, at 38.84 billion ECU ($44.67 billion) in 1997, compared with 32.5 billion ECU ($37.38 billion) for 1991. According to the Commission, this represents a savings of 5.4 billion ECU ($6.21 billion in 1991 dollars) over 1997 outlays in the absence of CAP reform. [12] The Commission expects that budget outlays would decline thereafter as a proportion of EC spending. Some analysts speculate, however, that outlays could be higher because of additional administrative costs and enhanced possibilities of fraud.

AGRICULTURE IN THE URUGUAY ROUND

The CAP is also under considerable international pressure, especially in the Uruguay Round of multilateral trade negotiations where the United States and other major exporting countries are demanding substantial changes in the EC's system of agricultural support and protection. The trade-distorting effects of the EC's system of export restitutions has been singled out particularly as a target for change and reduction. [13]

The Uruguay Round is a way to deal with the EC's border measures (that would not otherwise be affected by the current proposals for CAP reform) by converting variable levies and other nontariff trade barriers to tariffs (tariffication) and by placing strict limits

---

[11] U.S. Department of Agriculture. Economic Research Service. *Western Europe: Agriculture and Trade Report.* RS-91-4. October, 1991. p. 48-49.

[12] See footnote 4.

[13] U.S. Library of Congress. Congressional Research Service. *Agriculture in the GATT.* Issue Brief no. IB89027. Updated regularly.

on budget outlays and quantities of commodities that could be subsidized. A proposed Uruguay Round agreement [14] would also impose discipline on domestic policies that distort trade by imposing cuts in programs that stimulated surplus production of agricultural commodities.

A major obstacle to reaching an agreement on agriculture in the Uruguay Round concerns the way in which to deal with trade distorting effects of the compensatory income payments envisaged under the CAP reform proposals. The "Dunkel text" now lists these payments in the category designated for cuts. The EC is holding to its reform proposal, although some compromises, for example, classifying compensatory payments as "transitional" measures during the implementation phase of the Uruguay Round agreement on agriculture, have been taken up by U.S. and EC trade negotiators. Reaching agreement on how to treat direct income supports is not the only obstacle to reaching a Uruguay Round agreement on agriculture. The EC is evidently resisting the efforts of other GATT members to limit the quantities of commodities, particularly wheat, that may be exported with the aid of subsidies. In addition, some members of the EC (especially France) are holding out for some form of "rebalancing" of protection. Under rebalancing (which the United States has resisted), levels of protection on some commodities, such as nongrain feeds (corn gluten, citrus pulp, cassava chips, and the like) would be raised, as protection is lowered on grains and other commodities.

A Uruguay Round agreement with meaningful agricultural provisions is potentially significant for CAP reform and for U.S. food and agricultural trade. Financial and quantity limits on subsidized exports would enhance the prospects for U.S. grain exports, particularly wheat and wheat flour, which the EC now subsidizes heavily. Conversion of nontariff barriers to tariffs and provisions for minimum import access would lay a basis for enhancing market access over the long term. The greatest impact on U.S. agricultural trade from a Uruguay Round agreement would likely be not in terms of expanded exports to the EC itself, but in expanded exports to third country markets heretofore the recipients of large quantities of subsidized EC exports of grains, meat, and other products.

Conclusion

The effects of European integration on trade in food and agricultural products could be magnified if combined with accelerated CAP reform and a Uruguay Round agreement on agriculture that significantly reduced trade distorting domestic support and export subsidies, not only in the EC, but across Europe. Some suggest that there is a critical link between CAP reform, a Uruguay Round agreement on agriculture, and wider European integration. The desire to forge a single Community-wide market reflects in part a desire to shift Community resources away from agriculture toward other ends. CAP reform offers at least a longterm promise of facilitating such a shift, although in the near term, it may make agri-

[14] General Agreement on Tariffs and Trade. Trade Negotiations Committee. *Draft Final Act Embodying the Results of the Uruguay Round of Multilateral Trade Negotiations*. December 20, 1991. This document is commonly referred to as the "Dunkel text."

cultural policy more rather than less expensive. EC–92 and further progress toward wider integration may enable the EC to move beyond agriculture as the central focus of European integration, allowing greater scope for dealing with broader economic, monetary, and political issues.

THE EUROPEAN DEFENSE INDUSTRY: RESPONSES TO GLOBAL CHANGE AND EUROPEAN INTEGRATION

By Theodor W. Galdi *

CONTENTS

Overview

Accelerated movement toward economic, political and social integration of the European Community (EC) and the practical disappearance of a major Soviet and Warsaw Pact threat have taken place in an environment of worldwide excess defense production capability. Notwithstanding the eventual overall success of the EC in achieving higher rates of economic growth, one sector—defense—faces a clearly shrinking market. How the European defense industry adapts to this rapidly changing, uncertain environment could have far-reaching consequences for both Europe and the United States. For individual European countries, the fate of their arms producers will affect employment and export levels, perceptions of international competitiveness, and the ability to be self-sufficient in the production of major weapons systems. The success or failure of Europe's defense industry in adapting to the changing international environment will also have a direct impact on the level of U.S. arms exports to Europe and other areas of the world. Western Europe is the largest export market for the U.S. defense industry; in the period 1983–1987, about 78 percent of the defense imports of NATO-Europe came from the United States.

* Theodor W. Galdi is a Specialist in International Political Economy, Foreign Affairs and National Defense Division, Congressional Research Service.

Because of the close linkage between arms production and sovereignty, problems in the defense area that in other sectors might be resolved primarily on economic grounds have been—and remain—heavily politicized. In addition, there exists a long tradition in Europe of direct state intervention in many economic matters, not just defense. Thus, recent proposals by the EC Commission, by the Independent European Program Group (IEPG), and by the United States through the North Atlantic Treaty Organization to rationalize arms production and trade and to open up the sector to greater competition have faced significant obstacles.

In keeping with the very general language agreed to at the December 1991 Maastricht EC summit concerning the "eventual" creation of a common European defense policy, it appears that for now the EC Commission will concentrate on harmonizing the treatment by member states of dual-use commodities. While even this step is controversial, it is more likely to be accepted than earlier proposals to extend EC-wide tariffs to all defense imports or to abolish completely the special status accorded the defense industry and trade under article 223 of the Treaty of Rome.

The steps by the IEPG to create a European defense market are—in addition to opening up trade opportunities among European suppliers—leading to the rationalization and concentration of the European defense industry. From a U.S. perspective, the main danger is that these policies may lead to the creation of a closed market favoring European producers. The loss of the European defense trade—estimated at more than $4 billion a year—would strongly affect U.S. arms producers in this period of shrinking defense markets worldwide.

The proposals to create a "defense GATT," first made in March 1990 by U.S. Ambassador to NATO, William Taft, led to the creation of a special group of experts which issued an interim report on limitations to the defense trade among NATO countries. The special group is currently examining more detailed steps needed to create an open, market-based, trading system among NATO allies. Among the issues under discussion are the wisdom and content of a "Code of Conduct" for defense trade. Because of the resistance of some Europeans, particularly the French, to unregulated defense trade, the final outcome of the discussions in NATO is uncertain.

Current Structure and Near Term Outlook for West European Defense Producers [1]

The tendency for European arms production to become more concentrated is not a new phenomenon. Since the late 1950s, the size of both aircraft and shipbuilding industries in some European countries have shrunken from several firms in each country to at

---

[1] There have been a number of recent studies by U.S. government agencies concerning the evolution of the European defense market. Among these are: U.S. Library of Congress. Congressional Research Service. *EC 1992: Potential Implications for Arms Trade and Cooperation.* Report No. 89-643 F, by Margaret Berry Edwards. Washington, 1989; U.S. Congress. Office of Technology Assessment. *Arming Our Allies.* OTA-ISC-449, May 1990. Washington, U.S. Govt. Print, Off., 1990; U.S. Congress. Office of Technology Assessment. *Global Arms Trade.* OTA-ISC-460, June 1991. Washington, U.S. Govt. Print. Off., 1991; and. U.S. General Accounting Office. *European Initiatives: Implications for U.S. Defense Trade and Cooperation.* GAO/NSIAD-91-167, April 1991. Washington, 1991.

most one or two. In the last few years this process has accelerated. Concentration took place first on a national basis, and more recently, on an international basis. The cross-border mergers and acquisitions that formerly characterized the civilian sector have recently taken place in the military sector. In 1989–1990 alone, there were 22 major international takeovers. The same period saw eight international mergers and new companies formed. [2] One outcome of the mergers and acquisitions has been the creation of "national champions" in specific weapons areas.

TABLE 1. Principal European Defense Firms, 1990

Country	Aircraft	Tanks	Missiles	Electronics
France	Dassault Aérospatiale	GIAT	Matra Aérospatiale	Thomson-CSF
U.K.	British Aerospace	Vickers	British Aerospace	General Electric (U.K.)
Germany	Daimler Benz/MBB	Krauss-Maffei	Daimler Benz/MBB	Siemens

Source: U.S. Congress. Office of Technology Assessment. *Global Arms Trade*. OTA-ISC-460, June 1991. Washington, U.S. Govt. Print. Off., 1991. p. 74.

The demise of the Soviet Union and Warsaw Pact is likely to affect the European defense industry in several ways. First, demand for military equipment by the producer's host government for use in NATO will fall significantly. This decline will remove the major source of financing for base levels of production for weapons systems. In the past, these base levels have helped finance the research and development phases of new weapons which require by far the largest initial capital outlays. Without these base level expenditures, the unit costs of existing weapons systems will increase greatly, making them less competitive, and the costs of future weapons systems may become uneconomic to finance. The phrase "constructive disarmament" has been used to describe the long-term results of this situation. Second, the recent rationalizations in the European defense industry paradoxically may well work against future production. One of the main characteristics of these rationalizations is the separate establishment inside corporations—or even as separate entities—of the defense portions of the firm's overall business. Although there is some disagreement on this point, these rationalizations will likely make it much more difficult, if not impossible, for civilian-related activities to cross-subsidize defense-related activities in the near future. As a result of the mergers and rationalizations, and the expected declines in demand due to the changed situation in Eastern Europe and the former Soviet Union, employment in West European defense industries could decline from 1.5 million in 1987 to as low as 910,000 by 1995. [3]

Future European defense exports to other NATO or Third World countries are likely to be lower than in the past. For potential exports to NATO countries, limits under the Conventional Forces in Europe (CFE) Treaty combined with the disappearance of Soviet

[2] Anthony, Ian, Agnes Courades Allebeck, and Herbert Wulf. *West European Arms Production*. Stockholm International Peace Research Institute (SIPRI), October 1990. p. 13–14.

[3] Ibid., p. 60–61.

and Warsaw Pact threats have removed major justifications for arms purchases. The level of European arms exports to Third World countries will depend on several factors. First, how quickly will Third World countries pay off the costs of large-scale exports received in the 1980s and incorporate the new equipment into their operational inventories? Second, to what extent will the potentially large quantities of advanced equipment become available at cut rate prices from the former Soviet Union and Eastern European countries? In late February 1992, Russian President Yeltsin indicated that conventional arms production and exports would, of necessity, continue to be a major source of employment in his country. [4] Third, since the number of significant buyers of first-line European equipment (aircraft, missiles, naval combatants, electronic equipment) is fairly limited, what economic and strategic circumstances do they face? All of the likely major Middle East arms-buying countries—including OPEC members like Saudi Arabia, Kuwait and the United Arab Emirates—are currently facing strong budgetary constraints. These will limit the size of their arms purchases. There might be some potential growth in South and East Asian markets, and in certain specialized markets for specific technology, such as non-nuclear submarines. Fourth, how will Europeans respond to the superior performance of U.S. equipment during Operation Desert Storm, an outcome that apparently provided a boost to the competitiveness of U.S. firms in export markets? European competitors in the area of high-end weapons systems will likely experience the most direct effects of this factor. Fifth, how strong will competition be in the market for less-advanced armaments? Sales by countries such as Israel, Brazil, South Korea, or Singapore may displace lower-technology sales from European firms. Like the effect of the loss of sales to host country governments, any loss of sales of lower-level technology armaments will reduce the total turnover of European firms. This, in turn, will make the amounts devoted to high-technology products a larger portion of the total. Essentially, because of lower turnover, the "commodity sectors" of the European defense firms will be less able to finance the "leading edge" sectors. A judicious assessment of all of these factors indicates that the market will be much smaller—and more highly competitive—than in the past.

Major West European Arms Exporters [5]

France, the United Kingdom, and Germany are by far the largest West European arms producers and exporters. Between 1986 and 1990, the three together accounted for 90 percent of West European arms exports and, during the same period were the third, fifth and six largest exporters of conventional weapons systems worldwide. Because of this market position, and the potential for increased competition with U.S. arms producers, most attention fo-

---

[4] Russia Boosts Weapons Sales to Aid Economy. *Washington Post*, February 23, 1992. p. A1.

[5] This section is drawn from four documents published by the Stockholm International Peace Research Institute (SIPRI): Anthony, Ian, Agnes Courades llebeck, and Herbert Wulf. *West European Arms Production*. October 1990. 71 p; Ian Anthony, ed. *Arms Export Regulations*. Oxford University Press, 1991; and, SIPRI. *World Armaments and Disarmament*. Yearbooks for 1990 and 1991. Oxford University Press.

cuses on the arms exports of France, the United Kingdom, and Germany.

FRANCE

The French government is very heavily involved in the French arms industry. In terms of output, 60 percent of the industry is majority state-owned, and another 28 percent is wholly state-owned. Only 12 percent of the output of the French arms industry is generated by private firms. According to a report to the French Parliament, exports accounted for 31 percent of the total turnover of the arms industry in 1989. [6] The French tradition of government intervention in the economy is reinforced by the need to maintain exports—and employment—from arms production.

In France, all armaments production, whether private, state-owned, or state-operated, is regulated by the Ministry of Defense through the General Armaments Delegation (DGA). [7] The DGA directs all aspects of the arms production process and makes the overall decisions on military exports as well as what is to be purchased for use by French military forces. In the DGA, the Directorate for International Affairs controls arms exports and French military technical assistance. The Directorate for International Affairs has played a major role in marketing French weapons and in the past has prompted the DGA to develop specific products for export. The Directorate for International Affairs has more than 10 sales departments dealing with specialized armaments areas, such as the Office Général de L'Air, which concentrates on the sales of French aircraft overseas. The DGA maintains a global network of sales personnel.

Each proposed export sale is referred by the Directorate for International Affairs to the Interministerial Committee for the Study of Arms Exports. This committee includes representatives from the Ministries of Defense, Foreign Affairs, Economy, and Finance, and the military services and military intelligence. The decisions of the Interministerial Committee must be unanimous before an export license will be granted.

France was the third largest—after the United States and Soviet Union—exporter of conventional weapons systems in the period 1981–1990. One source places the value of deliveries of major French weapons systems during this period at over $33 billion. [8]

An examination of the destinations and amounts of exports of major French weapons over the last decade indicates a very wide

---

[6] Cited in SIPRI, *Arms Export Regulations*, p. 64–65.

[7] U.S. Executive Office of the President. Office of Management and Budget. *Financing Defense Exports*. November 1990. Report to Congress as required by Section 825 of the National Defense Authorization Act for Fiscal Years 1990–1991; and, SIPRI, *Arms Export Regulations*, p. 64–71.

[8] SIPRI, *Arms Export Regulations*, p. 64. These data should be used with caution. Since there are often significant differences between SIPRI and U.S. Arms Control and Disarmament Agency (ACDA) figures, some explanation of the methodology used by SIPRI to derive the arms export data is necessary. First, the arms export data are given in constant 1985 prices. Second, the figures do not include total arms exports, but rather only exports of *major* equipment. Third, the SIPRI figures are trend indicators of the deliveries of major conventional weapons systems and not figures on what was paid for the weapons. While not precise, the figures provide an indication of the comparative magnitude of the actual exports of major arms from Western Europe. The last point is very important because of the very common occurrences of modifications or cancellations of arms deals after they have been announced. For a fuller discussion of the SIPRI methodology, see Anthony et. al., *West European Arms Production*, p. 61.

range of political regimes and levels of development, with the Middle East as the most common destination. Over 40 countries imported more than $100 million in French arms in the period 1981–1990. Of this group, only 15 percent of the importers were developed countries, most notably the United Kingdom, Spain, and Greece.

TABLE 2. French Major Arms Exports

(millions of 1985 U.S. dollars)

Recipient	1981	1982	1983	1984	1985	1986	1987	1988	1989	1990	Total
Iraq	951	189	778	865	722	757	234	271	79	42	4,888
Saudi Arabia	297	264	58	184	1069	1221	424	374	403	306	4,600
India	36	72	40	48	613	761	555	178	143	138	2,584
U.K.	190	220	311	265	188	208	88	80	62	58	1,670
Egypt	76	121	363	127	151	163	484	6	0	16	1,507
United Arab Emirates	166	91	41	37	0	0	13	8	617	508	1,481
Spain	304	252	89	15	22	147	125	175	142	153	1,425
Qatar	69	139	281	258	130	42	73	131	50	29	1,200
Argentina	231	256	275	240	138	22	0	0	38	0	1,199
Greece	182	0	0	0	0	0	0	395	444	81	1,103
Peru	315	71	78	32	11	133	243	0	0	0	884
Jordan	0	387	343	0	0	0	30	61	3	0	824
Brazil	94	30	30	47	60	82	178	90	94	61	765
Libya	20	510	140	70	0	0	0	0	17	0	758
Nigeria	122	248	0	120	119	0	6	17	15	30	677
Kuwait	0	0	40	182	310	30	23	0	0	0	586
Morocco	219	126	111	61	14	8	14	13	0	0	566

Source: Anthony, Ian, Agnes Courades Allebeck, and Herbert Wulf. *Arms Export Regulations.* SIRI, October 1990. p. 70.

During the 1980s, Iraq was the largest importer of French arms, followed closely by Saudi Arabia, and more distantly by India. The consistently high level of French weapons deliveries to Iraq tapered off quickly in 1989 after the end of the eight-year war between Iran and Iraq, while deliveries to Saudi Arabia and India grew substantially after 1984. In 1988 and 1989, the United Arab Emirates received more than $1.1 billion in French weapons, mainly aircraft.

Recent levels of arms exports by France have fallen from those of the early 1980s. Exports are likely to remain lower than in the past, but future arms export possibilities do exist. Even though Iraq will most likely not be in the market for French arms in the near future—because of the U.N. embargo and also the very high levels of indebtedness from past arms purchases—four other former buyers in the Middle East: Saudi Arabia, the United Arab Emirates, Qatar, and Kuwait might be. Recent press accounts indicated that South Korea ordered $180 million worth of Mistral anti-aircraft missiles from the French firm Matra. With the cutoff of U.S. sales to Pakistan, it is possible that Pakistan will turn to France for weapons. News reports indicate that Pakistan might purchase older Mirage 2000 aircraft in addition to three mine-hunters sold by France. India also might be interested in purchasing weapons if financing were available.

It is unlikely that French arms sales to Latin America will return to the scale reached in the early and mid-1980s because of the general decline of tensions in the region and the high levels of indebtedness. In addition, the expense of parts and maintenance for recent Latin American purchases of French weapons decreases the amount of funding available for new purchases. Military air transport equipment in the region, however, is notably obsolescent and country modernization programs could provide sales for France.

UNITED KINGDOM

Although the British government continues to consider arms exports as a major economic and foreign policy tool, one of the more significant changes made by the Thatcher government during the 1980s was the effort to shift all arms production out of government hands and into the private sector. These privatization efforts and the recent decline in defense procurement have been the most important elements in restructuring the U.K. arms industry.

While the arms industry is now almost entirely in private hands, the United Kingdom possesses a well organized government arms sales promotion system supported by the highest levels of government. British companies receive the full cooperation of the Ministry of Defence and the Foreign and Commonwealth Office in the Foreign Ministry.

TABLE 3. U.K. Major Arms Exports

(millions of 1985 U.S. dollars)

Recipient	1981	1982	1983	1984	1985	1986	1987	1988	1989	1990	Total
Saudi Arabia	0	0	8	29	51	174	442	452	930	814	2,898
India	361	529	145	137	140	196	460	343	122	45	2,478
Oman	7	60	168	105	78	5	120	180	100	28	851
Chile	0	266	6	224	0	19	323	6	0	0	844
Indonesia	45	0	38	23	170	230	194	102	0	0	801
Switzerland	0	0	107	214	244	107	0	0	8	113	794
U.S.A.	58	0	109	86	151	0	39	12	188	78	720
Denmark	5	0	50	50	60	60	11	0	240	0	476
Nigeria	7	22	44	154	160	30	0	0	0	0	418
Jordan	77	74	108	69	69	0	9	6	0	0	412
Egypt	130	218	2	3	3	3	3	6	6	6	381
Turkey	0	0	0	129	114	115	0	0	8	0	366
Pakistan	0	207	0	0	0	0	0	125	0	0	332
Argentina	324	0	0	0	0	0	0	0	0	0	324
Finland	38	38	38	53	83	0	0	0	40	15	304

Source: SIPRI. Anthony, Ian, ed. *Arms Export Regulations.* Oxford University Press, 1991. p. 181.

Established in 1966, the Defense Export Services Organization (DESO) in the Ministry of Defense is responsible for marketing, promoting, and selling British military equipment overseas. The DESO coordinates interdepartmental reviews of arms sales. According to one source, the DESO relies on U.K.-based teams with specific regional knowledge to provide market expertise. Rather than having a separate field organization, like the French, the DESO teams draw upon information provided by trade and military attachés in British embassies around the world. [9] There are three Di-

[9] SIPRI, *Arms Export Regulations*, p. 179.

rectorates in the DESO: Defence Sales, Marketing, and Sales Supply and Defence Secretariat. Of the three, the Marketing Directorate promotes overseas sales and sponsors displays of British military equipment abroad.

The United Kingdom has consistently been the fourth largest arms exporter in the world. SIPRI data indicate that Britain exported over $15 billion in major weapons systems during the period 1981–1990—half the amount exported by France. Compared with France, a much greater proportion of British arms sales went to industrialized countries.

For Britain, Saudi Arabia was the largest purchaser of weapons during the 1980s. The bulk of British sales to the Saudis came after the conclusion of the so called Al Yamamah arms deal in 1985 which resulted in over $2.7 billion in arms deliveries—mostly aircraft—from 1986–1990. The level of British arms exports to its second largest buyer—India—remained relatively stable throughout the 1980s but was higher in the early years and in 1987 and 1988. During the 1980s, India took delivery of over $5 billion in arms from Britain and France, and *another $18 billion* worth from the Soviet Union. Other major recipients of U.K. arms exports in the 1980s were Oman, Chile, Indonesia, the United States, and Switzerland.

Several possibilities exist for future U.K. arms sales. If the Al Yamamah II Agreement is concluded as expected, Saudi Arabia will continue to make substantial follow-on purchases from British Aerospace. News reports in early February 1992 indicated that Kuwait was expected to sign a memorandum of understanding leading to several hundred million pounds sterling in military sales. [10] Although there has been some discussion that India, in the wake of the Soviet collapse, may refocus its arms relationship to the United States, India's former colonial ties, and price and availability would appear to give Britain an advantage if India can obtain financing. In addition, Oman and the United Arab Emirates also might be potential buyers of British arms. The bottom nine countries listed in table 3, however, are unlikely to be in the market in the near future. The possibility of other major sales to Third World countries on the same scale as the Al Yamamah agreements appears low.

FEDERAL REPUBLIC OF GERMANY

Unlike France and the United Kingdom, Germany has no state agency to promote the sale of German defense equipment. However, the German government must approve all transfers of military equipment. While there has been a great deal of controversy over the export by German firms of dual-use commodities and industrial processes to Libya, Iraq, and other Third World countries, controls over weapons exports are strict and German laws prohibit the export of arms to "conflict areas," including much of the Middle East. A company wishing to export weapons is required to formally request a permit from the Ministry of Economics. In routine cases, officials at the Ministry approve the request. In other cases, the

[10] Kuwait to Sign U.K. Pact. *Defense News*, February 3, 1992. p. 26.

Foreign Ministry and Defense Ministry are consulted. If a disagreement arises or it becomes evident that the export would be politically sensitive, the case is referred to the Federal Security Council, consisting of the Chancellor and the Ministers of Defense, Economics, Foreign Affairs, Finance and Interior for final decision on the export license. Except for ships, German exports of military equipment to Third World countries have been small.

TABLE 4. German Major Arms Exports

(millions of 1985 U.S. dollars)

Recipient	1981	1982	1983	1984	1985	1986	1987	1988	1989	1990	Total
Argentina	54	115	695	764	185	271	125	0	0	248	2,456
Turkey	112	186	180	247	173	130	240	574	208	102	2,152
Netherlands	14	299	299	299	299	303	0	0	0	0	1,513
Greece	187	106	109	150	42	0	0	146	67	4	810
Nigeria	473	72	10	20	88	69	0	0	3	0	735
Switzerland	0	0	0	0	0	0	123	147	147	147	564
Colombia	0	0	266	269	2	0	0	0	0	0	537
Malaysia	0	34	67	320	0	10	0	0	0	0	431
India	0	0	0	0	0	200	18	9	126	30	383
Bahrain	10	10	44	44	0	44	44	158	0	0	354
United Arab Emirate	181	0	0	0	0	0	0	0	0	158	339
Indonesia	144	5	5	30	17	44	43	1	10	14	312
Kuwait	0	0	13	189	88	0	0	0	0	0	289
Norway	0	0	0	0	0	0	0	0	88	176	264
Chile	0	0	0	180	0	2	0	0	9	3	194

Source: SIPRI. Anthony, Ian, ed. *Arms Export Regulations*. Oxford University Press, 1991. p. 85.

According to SIPRI, Germany was the sixth largest exporter of weapons during the period 1981–1990. The value of German exports of major weapons systems was estimated to be $12.4 billion in that period.

Argentina was the largest importer of German weapons during the period 1981–1990, receiving an estimated $2.4 billion. These exports consisted almost entirely of ships and submarines for the Argentine navy. Imports from other West European arms producers were used to outfit the ships. NATO ally Turkey, the second largest importer of German arms, received a wide range of equipment during the 1980s including secondhand F-104G fighters and Leopard tanks. Other German arms to Turkey included Koeln class frigates and substantial numbers of anti-tank missiles. Exports to the third and sixth largest importers of German weapons—the Netherlands and Switzerland—consisted almost entirely of Leopard-2 tanks.

It is difficult to predict what future markets for German arms will be. Even if Germany finally decides to participate in the production of the European Fighter Aircraft, exports are unlikely because of very high unit costs and strong competition. Some reports had indicated that the South Koreans were interested in buying Tornado strike aircraft from the Germans. There has been no recent follow-up to the reports. The weapons Germany has exported to NATO countries, especially tanks, are clearly in surplus worldwide. However, the expertise gained in producing and exporting high-quality, relatively inexpensive non-nuclear submarines and smaller surface combatants may allow Germany to continue to be a major player in this particular arms market in the future.

Activities of International Organizations Dealing with European Defense Production and Trade Issues

At the present time, there are three major international actors in matters dealing directly with European defense production and trade: the Independent European Program Group (IEPG), North Atlantic Treaty Organization (NATO), and the European Community (EC).[11]

INDEPENDENT EUROPEAN PROGRAM GROUP (IEPG)

The IEPG was established in its present form in 1976 as an informal group to promote an integrated European armaments market and to foster European cooperation in research, development, and the production of defense equipment. The original impetus for the formation of IEPG was to bring France into the deliberations of the NATO-related Eurogroup. A major goal of IEPG is to develop and maintain a strong European defense industrial base. The membership of IEPG includes all EC members of NATO plus Norway and Turkey. Originally an organization of national armaments purchasing directors, the IEPG was reconstituted in 1984 to the Minister of Defense level, thereby assuming greater importance. In December 1988, the IEPG was given formal status with the establishment of a permanent secretariat and headquarters in Lisbon.

In 1986, the IEPG issued a report, *Towards a Stronger Europe*—also known as the Vredeling Report—advocating a much greater degree of European collaboration in weapons production. With the Vredeling Report as a policy foundation, in November 1988, European Defense ministers endorsed a European Armaments Market Action Plan. The Action Plan listed five major goals: 1) establishing an open European market for defense procurement, 2) assuring "juste retour," or an amount of return from joint or cooperative defense production commensurate with the extent of investment and production of each participating country, 3) creating technology transfer policies that promoted the dissemination of government-sponsored defense research and development to all IEPG members, 4) providing assistance to less developed defense industry (LDDI) members of the IEPG, and 5) creating a common fund for defense research and development to be allocated by the IEPG. While the proposals to assist the LDDI members were perhaps necessary to obtain some sort of consensus, the shrinking arms market worldwide will make it very difficult for the IEPG to assist some members to grow—and perhaps export—while others are cutting back and losing export markets. Also, institutionalizing a mechanism for

[11] The Eurogroup (all European NATO countries except France) and the Western European Union (Belgium, France, Germany, Italy, Luxembourg, the Netherlands, Portugal, Spain, and the United Kingdom) have also undertaken defense cooperation initiatives in the past. At the moment, however, the major focus of European defense procurement policy is IEPG. The Western European Union appears destined to play a much greater defense role in the future based on its coordination of European responses to the Iraqi invasion of Kuwait and on the recognition of its increased competence by the Maastricht EC summit and the North Atlantic Council.

insuring *juste retour* will be very difficult short of creating an IEPG trade manager.

The IEPG has had partial success in meeting some of the goals of the Action Plan, especially those making the armaments bidding process more transparent and creating, in June 1989, a European defense research program called EUCLID (European Cooperative Long-term Initiative For Defense) under French direction. EUCLID's 1991 budget was $96 million, a level increased to $124 million for 1992. The goal for 1994 is a budget of $164 million. The "Coherent Policy Document" endorsed by the IEPG Ministers in November 1990 was intended to incorporate the principles of the Action Plan into an agreed working document to assure competition on a European scale.

The true long-run goals of the IEPG dealing with the United States—independence and cooperation—are somewhat contradictory. As an Office of Technology Assessment report observed:

> In Europe it is widely understood that the impetus behind the Vredeling Report and the Action Plan was the fear of domination of the European market by U.S. producers. However, in explaining the IEPG for U.S. consumption, the emphasis is on how the creation of a "European Pillar" in defense will make the Europeans stronger and better NATO allies. [12]

One of the best statements of the position of the IEPG was made by the Belgian Defense Minister in an article discussing the IEPG program and proposals for a more open NATO-wide defense market:

> The IEPG ministers have therefore agreed to conduct in parallel an intensification of the IEPG's efforts in Europe, and an initial listing of the obstacles which stand in the way of a transatlantic defense equipment market. The aim is to advance towards the elimination of these obstacles with a view to an opening up of markets when the IEPG countries as a whole have become sufficiently strong economically, industrially, technologically and politically, thereby constructing a true European pillar of the Atlantic alliance. [13] (emphasis added)

NATO AND THE "DEFENSE GATT" PROPOSAL

In March 1990, U.S. Ambassador to NATO William Taft made a proposal which appeared to address directly some of the major concerns the United States had about the evolution of the European defense trade. In a speech to the German Strategic Forum in Bonn, Taft suggested a four point plan to foster efficiency and rationalization in the North Atlantic defense industry and to maintain military strength at lower cost. The four points were: 1) to use the NATO Conventional Armaments Planning System to insure that

---

[12] U.S. Congress. Office of Technology Assessment. *Arming Our Allies: Cooperation and Competition in Defense Technology.* OTA-ISC-449, Washington, U.S. Govt. Print. Off., May 1990. p. 56.

[13] Coeme, Guy. *NATO Review*, v. 39, no. 4, August 1991. p. 20. Belgium holds the presidency of IEPG for 1991 and 1992.

cooperative programs truly had alliance support, 2) to examine restrictions on intra-alliance technology transfer, 3) to expand the definition of the Alliance's industrial base and establish formal links between the U.S. Defense Advanced Research Projects Agency (DARPA) and the EUCLID Program of the IEPG to coordinate and conduct joint research, and 4) to establish the equivalent of a Defense General Agreement on Tariffs and Trade (DGATT) for NATO. In his initial proposal, Taft suggested that the "defense GATT" should also include Japan, Korea, and Australia and have an agreed code of conduct limiting protectionist practices, eliminating tariffs on defense goods and establishing dispute settlement mechanisms. [14]

In October 1990, a special Task Group was established by the NATO Conference of National Armaments Directors [15] to examine the issues raised by the "defense GATT" proposal. The Task Group's initial report, published in March 1991, reflected the divergent visions of the members of NATO on the respective roles of governments and the market place in determining defense production and trade. For each reference to the economic advantages of obtaining arms from the most efficient source there was a reference to the need to prevent unacceptable trade imbalances, insure continuity, and achieve *juste retour*. References to ending restrictions to acquisition and trade were followed by references to the need for long transition periods.

The report identified the key constraint: the limited amount of defense trade among NATO allies. It discussed the need for reform, the many obstacles to the defense trade, and lessons learned from a number of existing institutions—including the GATT, the IEPG, the EC and the U.S.-Canada Free Trade Area. Among issues requiring decisions were: membership in a "defense GATT"; problems with technology transfer and foreign ownership; the impact on existing cooperative arrangements; *juste retour* on a NATO-wide basis; third country sales; and how to deal with the LDDI nations. The report concluded with four possible options: a code of conduct, a NATO treaty on defense trade, a NATO purchasing agency, and extending bilateral cross purchasing agreements NATO-wide.

In July 1991, the North Atlantic Council established a formal group on defense trade to continue studying the issue, and also to develop a code of conduct for defense trade. One of the key areas of concern was the lack of good statistics on the arms trade. Except for the United States, most other NATO countries were very secretive about the size and destinations of their arms exports for both commercial and foreign policy reasons. Throughout the fall of 1991, the task group met to develop a draft code of conduct and also to try to gather statistics on the defense trade.

As of January 1992, the proposed draft code of conduct appeared essentially to restate the IEPG Action Plan provisions relating to market opening, technology transfer, and less developed defense industries—except it would now be on a non-discriminatory NATO-

---

[14] *Atlantic News*, no. 2203, March 16, 1990. p. 3.

[15] Established in 1966 to coordinate defense procurement throughout NATO, the Conference of National Armaments Directors (CNAD) is the highest body dealing with acquisition. All members of NATO are part of the CNAD.

wide basis. The information sharing and transparency provisions were very close to those of the IEPG. If adopted, these provisions would essentially divert the focus from Europe to NATO. The current negotiating draft still contains a transition period of unstated duration as well as a provision resembling *juste retour*. While U.S. State Department officials were moderately satisfied with the progress toward the code of conduct, the U.S. position apparently has been that a satisfactory code was only the first step toward opening markets and that all parties would have to take additional market-opening steps during the phase to be negotiated next.

THE EUROPEAN COMMUNITY (EC)

The legal basis for current EC policy toward the defense industry and trade lies in two provisions: Article 223 of the 1957 Treaty of Rome and Article 30 of the Single European Act of 1987. In the Single European Act members of the European Community established the goal of creating a single European market without barriers to the movement of goods, services, capital and people by the end of 1992.

The most pertinent part of Article 223 states that any member state may take such measures as it considers necessary for the protection of the essential interests of its security which are connected with the production of or trade in arms, ammunition and war material. However, the second part of article 223 states that the measures should not prejudice the conditions of competition in the common market for products not intended specifically for military purposes. A list of military equipment covered by the provision was drafted by the Commission of the European Community.

Article 30 of the Single European Act of 1987 deals with treaty provisions on European cooperation in the sphere of foreign policy. Section 6(a) of Article 30 states that the parties consider that closer cooperation on questions of European security would contribute to the development of a European identity in external policy matters. They were, according to the text, ready to coordinate their positions more closely on the political and economic aspects of European security. Section 6(b) states that the parties were determined to maintain the technological and industrial conditions for their security. To this end, they were to work at both the national level and within the framework of competent Community institutions and bodies.

An active state of tension exists between parts of Article 223 and the goals of the European Community. Article 223 allows the member states to exclude defense production and trade from the Common Market requirements limiting physical, technical, and fiscal barriers to internal trade. After passage of the Single European Act in 1986, the Commission made proposals to harmonize the external tariff regimes of member states. Commission proposals made in September 1988 appeared to cover all trade except for the military equipment specifically listed by the EC as being covered by article 223. Prior to this time, each EC member had determined for itself which articles it considered to be strategic military items, and thus not subject to tariffs. The result was a wide divergence of treatment among member states, ranging from a very restrictive interpretation of the coverage of Article 223 to a very loose definition of military usefulness. The United Kingdom justified its tariff-free defense imports on the grounds of economic efficiency, limiting the spread of knowledge of certain classified imports, and meeting overriding alliance responsibilities. On the other hand, the Commission asserted that Article 223 was not intended to justify any unilateral tariff waivers. The EC Commission's September 1988 proposals made it clear that the intention was to afford better protection for European defense firms, since the tariff waivers deprived member country firms of the benefits of Community preference. The Commission also argued that the divergent treatment by member states involved the loss of customs duties reaching $250 million a year. For the United States, the existing arrangement allowed relatively tariff-free access for defense exports to European NATO members based on a series of separate bilateral procurement agreements.

Following the strong negative reaction of the United States and several EC members to the idea of harmonizing the tariff treatment of defense items and several attempts by the Commission itself to modify the proposal, in April 1990 Commission President Delors announced that the issue was "dormant." More recent Commission proposals have concentrated on covering so-called dual-use items and creating a Community-wide export control regime.

In the period prior to the Maastricht Summit, several proposals were made concerning Article 223. Among these, in February 1991, the Commission asserted that implementation of a common foreign policy implied the revocation of Article 223. Also, in March 1991, the Netherlands submitted a proposal to amend Article 223 to abolish by the end of 1997 the list of products exempted. At that time, the existing EC treaty would apply to all aspects of arms production and trade. Other proposals made during this period would have indirectly affected the operation of Article 223.

Results of the Maastricht Summit

Although proposals were made prior to the Maastricht Summit to abolish or modify Article 223, there were no revisions made at the summit. Instead, the summit issued "Provisions on a Common Foreign and Security Policy" as a separate part of the Treaty on European Union. Article A of these provisions stated that the political union and its member states would define and implement a common foreign and security policy (CFSP) covering all areas of foreign and security policy. Article D of the provisions stated that the common foreign and security policy should include all questions related to the security of the European Union, including the eventual framing of a common defense policy, "which might in time lead to a common defense." However, other parts of Article D exempted issues with defense implications from the majority voting requirements in the provision, and stated that the new policy of the political union would not prejudice the specific character of the security and defense policy of member states and would respect the obligations of member states under the North Atlantic Treaty. Another part of Article D stated that the existence of the Article was not to prevent the development of closer cooperation between two or more members on a bilateral level, in the framework of the

Western European Union (WEU) or in NATO, as long as such cooperation did not run counter to or impede the cooperation envisaged by the new provisions on common foreign or security policy. The results of the summit appear to continue the existing state of tension between the intentions of the Commission to harmonize EC policy and the desire of some members to continue to have the flexibility in defense procurement allowed by Article 223.

For the future, there appear to be at least three potential options. Under one option, the members would allow the EC Commission to do little more than it has up to now—discuss the creation of a common external tariff on dual use items. Under a second option, the EC Commission would develop a very restricted list of goods that Article 223 would continue to cover. Everything else would be open to EC-wide bidding and be subject to EC competition policy. Under the third option, Article 223 would be abolished and EC policy would apply to defense like any other sector. Which of these outcomes is most likely is unclear at present since there are very strong, and at times contradictory, pressures at work.

Other EC Policies Affecting the Defense Industry

Although the focus of this section has been on the current status and future of Article 223, there are other EC activities and policies which directly influence defense industries and trade. The four major ones are EC-financed or coordinated research and development, EC competition policy, subsidy policy, and industrial adjustment policy.[16]

It is absolutely necessary to conduct research and develop advanced technologies and materials to remain active in the defense field today. While EUCLID was designed as an IEPG program to focus on military research, a number of EC research programs will also affect the ability of European arms producers to be competitive. ESPRIT (European Strategic Program for Research and Development in Information Technology), for example, is a program focusing on microelectronics, software development and computer integrated manufacturing, and advanced information processing. Expenditures for ESPRIT will total more than $3 billion over a decade. The BRITE program, estimated to cost more than $475 million during the period 1987-1991, involves the application of new technologies to manufacturing. Finally, EURAM, dealing with advanced materials technology, was budgeted for more than $250 million for the period 1987-1991.[17]

The mergers or acquisitions which created the "national champions" in defense discussed above were approved—or modified—by national antitrust authorities. However, beginning in September 1990, the Commission was given jurisdiction over mergers or acquisitions of firms whose combined turnover exceeded $6 billion. Using this authority, in October 1991, the Commission voted to reject the acquisition of de Havilland Aircraft of Canada by a European consortium consisting of Alenia of Italy and Aérospatiale of

---

[16] For an excellent discussion of the current state of EC competition and antitrust policy, see Survey: Business in Europe. *The Economist*, June 8, 1991. 26 p.

[17] Budget figures from Commission of the European Communities. *Research and Technological Development Policy*. European Documentation Series. February 1988. p. 26.

France on European antitrust grounds. Whether this authority will be used to limit further consolidation in industries clearly covered by Article 223 is unclear. However, because of the firms' large civilian and dual-use production, future Commission action is likely.

Some of the EC efforts to limit state aid to manufacturing have affected the defense industries. Among other steps, the EC Competition Commissioner has launched investigations into France's decision to award almost 6 billion francs to Groupe Bull and Thomson, a state-owned defense and electronics group, and the 44 million pound subsidy British Aerospace allegedly received from the state as part of its purchase of Rover Group, the nationalized automobile manufacturer. In both cases, repayment of the subsidies was requested. Since Italy, Germany and France provide the largest subsidies to manufacturing, these countries would be most heavily affected by a successful anti-subsidy policy.

Finally, EC policy on industrial adjustment could affect the defense industry. Some members of the European Parliament have advocated "transitional" subsidies for defense industries to cushion the expected declines in employment. These "transitional" subsidies—if spent—will directly increase the competitiveness of European defense firms.

U.S. Policy Responses and Issues for Congress

There is little disagreement that, at the present time, the U.S. defense industrial base is deeper, stronger, and technologically more advanced in the production and integration of major weapons systems than its competitors. What is not clear is how this group of companies will function in the near future as defense markets shrink worldwide. The Department of Defense, in its November 1991 report to Congress on the defense industrial base, saw a shrinking DoD aircraft and helicopter market offset to some unspecified extent by increased commercial and export sales. According to the report, other segments of the defense industrial base were expected to adapt to the smaller—or non-existent—market, but to be prepared to expand again if needed. Reliance on market mechanisms was to be the watchword. [18]

The NATO "defense GATT" proposals of Ambassador Taft, the IEPG Action Plan, and proposals by the EC Commission all envisage opening up the European defense market to greater competition. However, the IEPG proposal is Eurocentric and only speaks of true open competition at some future date. The ultimate impact on the defense industry of EC proposals to foster inter-European competition in non-defense areas is not yet clear. Earlier EC defense tariff proposals were designed specifically to provide greater protection to European arms producers. The rejection by the EC Commission of the de Havilland acquisition by Alenia and Aérospatiale suggests that the EC will actively pursue market-oriented solutions in areas relating to commercial and dual-use activities. However, future EC anti-trust efforts may depend heavily upon the views of the EC commissioner for competition. If Sir Leon Brittan, the EC

[18] U.S. Department of Defense. *Report to Congress on the Defense Industrial Base.* November 1991. 47 p. plus appendices.

Vice-President for Competition Policy, is replaced by a less active commissioner, non-competitive activities by EC defense firms may not receive the same degree of opposition. Finally, while language apparently postponing true competition until some future date appeared in the first draft of the NATO "defense GATT" study, more recent drafts of a proposed code of conduct appear to be moving to establish the requirements for a NATO-wide market and reciprocal access to all NATO members. In code drafts in early 1992, problems remain with the proposed transition phase and attempts to keep some form of the principle of *juste retour*.

There appear to be a number of ways in which Congress could influence the trends of European defense trade. If Congress determines that access to European markets is very important, it then would become necessary to consider which U.S. restrictions on defense trade and investment may have to be modified to obtain access to European markets. Buy American provisions, the Exon-Florio Amendment, and a number of specific limitations on U.S. purchasing decisions may need to be examined in this light. Second, in dealing with the reauthorization of the Export Administration Act, Congress may decide to reconsider the provisions which require permission for the reexport of U.S. systems or subsystems to third countries. Some argue that European firms will refuse to use U.S. systems or subsystems if they are unable to export the completed object without first obtaining permission from the United States. Third, Congress may wish to exercise its oversight authority concerning existing bilateral memoranda of understanding on defense cooperation and trade with our NATO allies. Several questions may arise: Are they useful any longer? What are their disadvantages and advantages in opening up the European market? Assuming they should be retained, should changes be made in them? Fourth, congressional actions to reduce arms transfers to the Middle East or other areas could have a significant impact on U.S. and European arms producers. Finally, Congress will, directly or indirectly, determine the extent of U.S. influence in NATO—and by extension U.S. influence over the defense trade—by the degree to which it supports an active U.S. role in the alliance. The U.S. voice will much more likely be heeded if it remains a major actor in the alliance.

V. REDEFINING THE RULES OF THE GAME

EUROPEAN INDUSTRIAL POLICY

By Robin Gaster *

CONTENTS

SUMMARY

The Europe Community appears to be reaching a critical turning point in industrial policy and trade policy. The context within which those policies are formulated has been revolutionized by the Single Market program (EC–92), and, with the signing of Treaty of European Union, further economic integration has been agreed. The impact is likely to be immediate as countries struggle to align monetary and fiscal policies. Monetary union and a single currency may come sooner rather than later, and geographic expansion will likely occur in the next few years as consideration is given to membership applications by Austria, Sweden, and Finland.

The New Europe is therefore emerging, but as change takes on a more permanent cast, new problems are emerging. Since World War II, Europe has struggled between opposing visions of economic and social life. On one side lies the demand for efficiency, which has come to mean a relatively unfettered, and, in Europe's case, integrated market. On the other side lies equity, and the belief that markets must be regulated, and market outcomes mitigated for a variety of economic and non-economic reasons. Europe's struggle has been to accommodate efficiency and equity at the same time.

For nearly 30 years after World War II, the balance tilted heavily toward equity. Government policies sharply limited competition,

* Robin Gaster is president of North Atlantic Research Inc., a Washington research and communications firm.

encouraging instead the creation of "national champion" firms which dominated their home markets. In the context of the long post-War boom, this did not appear to be such a great problem, because the rising economy lifted all ships, including those that remained tethered to the shore. By the end of that golden age (around 1970), the Europeans discovered that growth was not automatic. They had to confront harder choices between equity and efficiency, as economies slowed and inflation and unemployment rose.

Traditional solutions were tried first. Industrial policy had worked in the past, albeit better in some sectors than others. Because industrial failure has consequences that go far beyond the firm, one major European response to slowing growth was to prop up failing industries to help ensure a graceful transition. However, the internal contradictions of this logic were quickly exposed as favored firms simply failed to adjust fast enough to meet the competition. Protectionism was another option. Yet as global competition increased, a retreat into national markets too small to support modern industries was simply not a viable option.

The solution to the impasse came in the mid-1980s with the drive to establish a single market in the EC. The EC–92 program is fundamentally about market liberalization and the opening of tightly controlled national markets. In consequence, the balance of policy has been tilted away from equity within national markets toward an efficient European market. This has been accomplished partly by preventing European governments from using the industrial policy tools they have long favored to help domestic firms survive and compete.

EC–92 has been a roaring success. But as a direct result, it is now becoming its own victim. Europe faces an imminent future of radical—and in some cases catastrophic—change, as market forces threaten to demolish some of the well-established national champions. In France alone, Renault, Thomson, Bull, Usinor, and even Matra are only some of the chosen firms now in deep trouble. The national champions of other countries face similar problems. Firms, workers, and governments are unlikely to accept sweeping changes of this magnitude, even though they may continue to favor the overarching strategy behind EC–92. The equity tradition will not be easily discarded.

As a consequence, Europe is now going through another policy revolution. Out of the conflicting pressures to save old industries and yet create competitive firms, an entirely new industrial policy seems to be developing as a middle way between equity and efficiency. This new European industrial policy weaves together elements of traditional industrial policy, trade policy, and, most importantly, a policy toward foreign direct investment. Gradually, and without any action that even approximates a conscious policy choice or coherent decision on the part of the Community, foreign direct investment is coming to play a pivotal role in the New Europe.

Foreign direct investment is adding a massive dose of efficiency by challenging domestic producers on their home turf. Comfortable national champions are comfortable no longer as invaders from Asia, the United States, and indeed other European countries attack long-dormant markets. Yet at the same time, the Europeans are taking a more activist approach to foreign investment, with a focus on attracting it and then managing it in such a way that it makes a positive contribution to European development. The result is that foreign investment is beginning to produce European jobs with a high level of European content and value-added. It is also contributing the skills and technology that will help to cushion needed transitions. In effect, the Europeans are trying to make foreign direct investment into an engine for promoting both efficiency and equity.

THE OLD REGIME IN EUROPE: THE TRIUMPH OF EQUITY

Between 1945 and the 1970s, European governments largely managed to avoid tensions between equity and economic efficiency. For most of that period, a comfortable agreement between business, unions, and the government in most European countries led to rapid growth, as countries caught up from the devastation of World War II and the legacy of the Great Depression. To the extent that choices were in the end required, they were very largely made in favor of equity. Fairness mattered a great deal, after the bitterness and divisions of the Depression and then the War, so the social compact and welfare state became powerful political icons. As growth seemed to come anyway, this presented few problems.

During the 1970s, this golden age came to a gradual close. Growth rates slowed, unemployment rose, world market shares stagnated, and inflation began a steady secular increase. Countries like France and Italy, which had achieved remarkable progress—even economic miracles—during the 1950s and 1960s, saw their progress slow or halt. Worse still, the very vehicles of past success looked increasingly like the source of the new problems. In most countries, core growth areas had been in manufacturing, often by means of national champion firms. These firms—such as Renault or Thomson in France, SGS is Italy, Siemens in Germany, British Steel and Rover in the U.K.—were deliberately encouraged to become dominant in their respective national markets.

The idea in Europe was that giant U.S. firms could not be matched without an equivalent structure, so big was beautiful. Equally, big losers could not simply be abandoned. They had to be helped to cope. Governments use a range of policies to pursue both objectives:

- *Subsidies* in many cases reached enormous proportions. As recently as 1989, each coal-mining job attracted support of around $60,000 in France; in Germany, that figure was $40,000. Italy still spends more than 6 percent of GDP on direct government handouts.
- *Trade barriers* were crucial. National markets were defended to make sure that national champions had a secure domestic base, where they could earn the profits needed to take on competitors elsewhere. Quotas, tariffs, intricately-designed technical standards—all had an important role.
- *Government procurement* was directed at supporting national champions. The EC estimated in 1985 that less than 2 percent

of all government purchases in Europe went to firms headquartered outside the purchasing country.

- Even the *financial system* was geared to support these champions. Savings attracted only low interest rates, but savers were still forced to use national banking institutions. In some countries, that allowed the banks—directed by the government—to offer concessional loans to chosen firms.

The overall results of these policies were mixed. They did indeed produce national champions, as they were designed to, but at the same time they largely failed to produce firms which could compete effectively in world markets. The net result was that the search for efficiency had turned into the protection of equity—which had come to mean protecting existing jobs, existing firms, and the status quo.

By the end of the 1970s, the bankruptcy of the national champion and lame duck strategy was apparent. Governments started to cast around for ways out of what had become a very expensive and tenacious trap. Ironically, the solution lay in a set of visionary commitments whose import was probably not widely understood when they were adopted in 1985. Had they truly foreseen the impact and extraordinary power of the changes they were about to let loose, many European leaders might well have rejected the single market program altogether. Fortunately for Europe, such accurate vision was not available in the mid-1980s.

The Single Market: Efficiency in the Driver's Seat

In 1985, the EC countries committed themselves to creating a single market within the EC by the end of 1992. Two institutional changes made this more than the pipedream it had been for almost 30 years. First, the program was laid out in the form of 300 specific and concrete reforms which would have to be implemented in order to create the single market. Second, the national governments agreed that these reforms would all be implemented on the basis of modified majority voting. No single country would be able to block progress. This latter change was accomplished through the Single European Act (1987).

The results have been remarkable. The single market is now already a reality in the minds of those making economic decisions. While the recent forward movement at Maastricht takes that process to a new level for governments, companies long ago concluded that unless they adapted to the notion of a single market, they would die. U.S. and Japanese companies have responded by repositioning themselves in Europe to take advantage of the single market. European companies are much further along: cross-border mergers and acquisitions have now overtaken domestic mergers within all the European countries combined, by value. More widely, transnational arrangements are the order of the day, ranging from R&D to production to marketing to service agreements. At the corporate level, the single market is now completely irreversible.

Although the program has been a success and Europe has taken the leap forward that many had hoped for, EC planners did not understand or predict the devastating effect of EC–92 on European countries' industrial policies, especially those that supported national champions.

In fact, the single market carries with it a simple philosophy of remarkable power and depth: the notion that a single market means a fair market, and a fair market is one in which *domestic governments cannot favor domestic firms at the expense of their European competitors.* [1]

The single market has therefore introduced what might best be understood as the European equivalent of the commerce clause of the U.S. Constitution. Just as Federal law prohibits the states from actions that interfere with interstate commerce, so Europe is adopting rules and regulations that block national governments there from doing the same thing. And because European governments have been in the aid business for so long, the impact is powerful—even devastating in some cases. The result is that each of the crucial tools of industrial policy is being systematically disarmed and removed from the control of national governments:

- *Subsidies* are being slashed, and the EC Commission must now approve all significant subsidies on the basis of specific and limiting criteria. The Community has been taking a tough and effective line against industrial subsidies.
- *Technical standards* have been a key barrier, but that is now being dismantled. In general, products acceptable in one EC country are now acceptable in all others.
- *Public procurement* polices are being made equitable and transparent. Tenders must be published in the *Official Journal of the European Communities*, and accepted procedures used to selected winning bids.
- *Trade policy,* long ago taken from national governments and given to Brussels, is being further transformed by the removal of border barriers. National quotas and other trade-related barriers used by national governments will be very hard to maintain even in the medium term without border controls.
- *Financial policies*, which channeled national savings into the coffers of selected firms or industries, are being systematically undermined by the new freedom of capital movement. Savers can now vote with their feet, so government-controlled pools of low-cost savings are becoming a thing of the past.

The efficiency-based reforms of EC–92 have brought some painful results, which present Europe with new challenges. The great national champions are being dismantled: British Steel, now the most efficient producer in Europe, shed two-thirds of its labor force in three years; Philips, still the largest employer in Holland, fired 30,000 workers last year with more to come; and the chairman of Renault warns with conviction, if not convincingly, that without massive aid from the EC the European auto industry will collapse. The market is working, but it is not necessarily working well for

[1] Thus Groupe Bull (the giant French computer company), for example, survived for years on government aid and slanted government procurement. But as borders have come down, Bull can be supported no longer. While the idea behind the single market was to create a huge market in which Bull (or any other EC company) could grow to giant size, Bull's own market was the stake that had to be put on the table to play. And many consider that Bull has turned out to be a loser.

the European champions and their supporters. With EC–92, rapid transitions are the order of the day. Vast numbers of workers face a future with lower and more uncertain wages, a reduced standard of living, and collapsed communities around them. But unlike the United States, Europe has a tradition of government industrial policy activism, a tradition which is very widely accepted. So European governments have tried hard to head off the impending disaster that some believe will occur without a coordinated European response to the demise of national industrial policies.

Toward a European Industrial Policy

INDUSTRIAL POLICIES FOR A POST–1992 EUROPE

Quite naturally, the Europeans began their response by trying to recreate the mechanisms that served them so well in the past. The first attempt has been to rebuild traditional industrial policies, but this time at the European level. Each of the policies adopted at this new level does have two new aspects in common. First, the fairness principle has been accepted. None of these Europe-wide policies favor firms in one country at the expense of those in another. [2] Second, these policies are in general much more market-friendly than the policies they replace. They indicate a much greater understanding and acceptance of the need for efficiency.

The Commission has dramatically increased its powers over industrial policy, and the recent agreement at Maastricht specifically provided the Commission with greater competency over industrial policy issues. Thus even though it is may be somewhat misleading to call the policies discussed below a coherent *European industrial policy*, it should be recognized that these policies have wide support within the Community and do nonetheless offer at least the skeleton of a coordinated, if not especially coherent, approach.

EUROPEAN CHAMPIONS

Much of the original impetus behind EC–92 came from those who believed that what Europe needed above all was larger companies to compete with the American and Japanese giants, and who argued that larger companies could only come from a larger home market. That belief was certainly reflected in the massive wave of cross-border mergers that occurred in the late 1980s and early 1990s. [3] Yet despite the high level of merger activity, the Eurochampion solution faces serious legal obstacles. The European Commission now has sweeping antitrust powers in cases crossing national jurisdictions, and it appears to be taking its new authority seriously. [4] The new powers of the Commission suggest that a strat-

[2] The very limited exception to this rule is aid granted to lagging or declining regions (regional aid policy).

[3] Even though the initial wave is over, there can be no doubt that more shakeouts are on the way. The next set of candidates probably include the airline and chemical industries, while in the medium term there will almost certainly be another massive restructuring in the auto industry which is unlikely to support all the existing manufacturers into the next century.

[4] The key case so far has been de Havilland, where the Commission used its new powers to block the takeover by Aerospatiale and Alenia, despite fierce lobbying from the French and Italian governments, and strong support for the takeover within some parts of the Brussels bureaucracy itself.

egy of translating national champions to a European level is highly unlikely to be permitted, especially if such champions might dominate the market.

Nor is the "big is better" theory very compelling. The current radical downsizing at Philips suggests that, in some industries, smaller and more agile firms may have a distinct advantage, as IBM's corporate chief for example now also admits. Of course, synergies and savings can be achieved by merging companies, especially when the aim is to rationalize fragmented production or to create distribution networks that respond to the needs of companies operating in a borderless Europe. Still, many European firms have come to see that size alone is not a sufficient condition for success, and in some cases it may be a serious handicap.

TECHNOLOGY POLICY

The Community's massive technology effort amounts to the most important Europe-wide industrial policy so far. Backed by the Commission as well as all the big high-tech players in Europe, such as Philips, Siemens, and Thomson, these research and development (R&D) programs have received approximately $3 billion annually in government funding alone. This has been matched more or less equally by the private sector. Unfortunately, the programs are not solving Europe's competitiveness problems for two main reasons. First, though big, they are still only a drop in the R&D bucket. At 3 percent of total R&D spending in Europe, they may simply not be big enough to make a real difference, despite the Commission's optimistic talk about the "catalytic effects" of such programs. More important still, the European programs have been directed at *precompetitive* R&D. That avoids antitrust problems, and the possibility that these programs might interfere with market efficiency. Yet European firms are falling behind Japan not in basic research, not in precompetitive R&D, but in the application of technology to manufacturing itself. These programs have only marginal impact at that level.

TRANSNATIONAL EURO-PROJECTS

Transnational Euro-projects lie much nearer the market than precompetitive R&D, and range from Airbus to JESSI to projects still on the drawing board. Well-favored by the EC Commission and the national governments which largely pay for them, their transnational character means that they do not breach the fairness principle. The best example is Airbus, for though it has yet to show a bankable profit, Europeans still see it as a winner. Billions in subsidies have been spent to produce a viable world-class competitor that is steadily gaining market share in one of the world's great knowledge-intensive industries. However, Airbus may well be a unique case in a unique industry, and the JESSI consortium in microelectronics may be more typical. It is the last European hope in commodity semiconductors. However, conflicting commercial and national interests seem to have made JESSI too cumbersome to operate effectively. In short, while there is only one Airbus, there will probably be many JESSI's.

ECONOMIC TRANSITIONS

Support for winners is one thing, but Europe has a sorry record of pouring massive and continuing support into losers. This is a problem that the Commission wrestles with constantly on a case-by-case basis. However, there are signs that change is taking place. The Commission has insisted, with considerable success, that such aid be dedicated specifically and exclusively to economic transitions (exit from a market or restructuring). Indefinite subsidies are now just about dead. In some very important cases, transition aids have in fact turned out to be the crucial element that allowed an industry the breathing space to recover, as the steel industry has done with very considerable success. For the EC, the trick is to ensure that the aid really does create a transition. There is also a very clear intention on the part of the Commission to reduce such aids or phase them out altogether in the near future. Thus, for example, the current EC plan for the shipbuilding sector is to phase out all aids by the end of 1993. Given the politics involved, this is a remarkable display of Commission power and initiative.

Industrial policy, by itself, is unlikely to shield the core European industries from market forces, and the institutional measures and market reforms that accompanied EC–92 no longer allow a return to the old ways. Indeed, industry has already restructured sufficiently to make that impossible. Nevertheless, Europeans are determined not to "lose" key industries. They fully understand that large segments of the workforce do not have the training or aptitude to move from blue-collar jobs to high-end service jobs. And for those forced from manufacturing into the service sector, few believe that the pay will be equal or better. Some European governments (France and Italy in particular) also accept the argument that some industrial sectors are "strategic". These sectors include autos, electronics, aerospace, computers, semiconductors, machine tools, and advanced materials, at a minimum. A number of European countries also have big defense industries that are considered strategic assets worthy of protection.

TRADE POLICY: THE NEW EUROPEAN PROTECTIONISM

European industrial policy might be regarded a failure, except for a collateral emphasis on trade policy and other mechanisms that have contributed to stronger European borders, which provide considerable protection to firms operating within them. While there is room for discussion about the finer points of EC trade policy, there is little doubt that many foreign corporations believe that the EC has not become less protectionist in recent years. If anything, they argue that the EC has erected more barriers to entry, including tariffs, quotas, voluntary restraint agreements, antidumping policy, anti-circumvention policy, rules of origin, and government procurement policies.

Given these beliefs, and the siren song of the huge European markets, it is easy to see why many businesses in both Japan and the United States are worried about future EC trade policy. In fact, according to a Peat Marwick survey, many executives erroneously believe that unless they make a move into Europe soon, they will be blocked from doing so in the future. The reality is that they should really be worrying about problems in exporting to the EC and the development of new EC investment policies.

The EC still maintains significant *tariffs* on key imports (especially autos and electronics). Some, like the 14 percent tariff on semiconductors, offer a crucial advantage for EC-based manufacturers. Partly as a result, EC semiconductor producers hold more than 30 percent of the European market, far above their shares in the rest of the world.

Quotas have been used widely by EC countries to restrict imports ranging from sewing machines to autos. EC–92 has eroded national quotas, so EC-level agreements have become increasingly important. The recent auto deal between the EC and Japan is one example of the move from national- to EC-level trade restrictions.

Antidumping policy has been the EC's most controversial trade weapon. The EC's antidumping procedures are rather opaque, allowing very wide administrative discretion. Asian electronics companies believe, with some justification, that they are the primary targets. And following upon antidumping rulings, the EC has used anti-circumvention policy to ensure that firms do not circumvent dumping rulings by building an assembly (or "screwdriver") plant in the EC. Japanese and Korean manufacturers have again been singled out as targets. A GATT panel found these anti-circumvention policies to be GATT-illegal, but the finding has not had much of an impact on EC policy.

Rules of origin determine exactly where a product was made. This can be important for complex products like autos or VCRs, and the EC has made some controversial rulings with protectionist overtones. In one key case, it ruled that semiconductors originate where they are diffused (cut from the raw silicon), not where they are assembled into subcomponents. After the ruling, U.S. and Japanese semiconductor imports faced a 14 percent tariff, and at least one U.S. firm, Intel, reportedly decided that it had to establish a European production facility to remain competitive in the European market.

Even in *public procurement,* where EC–92 has important liberalizing effects, public authorities can still reject any bid where at least half of the value of the bid was created outside the EC (a GATT deal on the Uruguay Round may change this, however). Where foreign bids are considered, they face a mandatory 3 percent price penalty (which is similar to the 10 percent preference granted under "Buy American" laws).

The EC's version of protectionism is relatively porous: in only a few cases are imports blocked altogether. This makes good economic sense. The EC has simply placed hurdles in the way of importers in key industries, making sure that only imports with a considerable cost advantage over domestic producers are likely to be imported. The U.S. firm Intel has referred to EC protectionism as "the death of a thousand cuts."

Still, for proponents of protection, trade barriers have not necessarily produced the expected results. A flood of foreign direct investment has occurred since 1986. The inward flow of Japan investment grew from around $1 billion in 1980 to more than $14 billion by 1988. In the first quarter of 1991, Japanese investment in the

U.K. grew at an annual rate of $12 billion, although Japanese firms have since retrenched.

EFFICIENCY MEETS EQUITY: MANAGING FOREIGN DIRECT INVESTMENT

The new European industrial policy depends on the translation of narrowly conceived industrial policies and trade policies from the national to the European level. As discussed above, the fairness principle dictates that policies that protect national markets and national firms from competitive forces within the larger Europe be eliminated. This has been the primary thrust of EC–92. Painful adjustments naturally accompany such a process, so it is not entirely surprising that the European Community has struggled over the extent to which national trade policies and national industrial policies should become European policies.

Many of the fears of "Fortress Europe" that initially greeted EC–92 were directly related to a fear that Europe would seek to externalize many of the costs associated with EC–92. The EC Commission sought to allay such fears with a publicity campaign entitled "Europe: World Trade Partner." By and large, the campaign had a soothing effect. Nevertheless, many of the costs of EC–92 have been externalized through the "Europeanization" of national industrial and trade policies (as described above).

Europe's success in achieving the single market can largely be ascribed to its handling of foreign direct investment (FDI). Foreign direct investment, the third major element of Europe's emerging industrial policy, bridges the gap between the efficiency of the EC–92 market and the equity principle. Efficiency demands competition and relatively free markets and free choices for consumers. Equity insists that industrialized countries cannot afford to relinquish certain core manufacturing industries and the jobs associated with them. If managed properly, foreign direct investment addresses both concerns successfully by boosting efficiency and enhancing equity.

FDI clearly promotes efficiency, and there are some very good reasons to believe that FDI is an effective mechanism for spurring competition in domestic markets. Thus, encouraging, or even forcing, foreign firms to locate production in or close to markets can be beneficial to consumers, business (including direct competitors), and labor. Nevertheless, if forced, FDI still amounts to another form of protectionism, especially if investors find this is the only way to gain access to a market. This particular variant, however, sidesteps the classic complaint against protectionism, i.e., that it reduces competition and allows domestic firms to avoid adjustment. Pre-EC–92 policies produced such a result in the EC. Under the single market program, this is extremely unlikely, even if the EC externalizes most of the costs of the program to non-European competitors.

That leaves equity considerations. Here the crucial issue is the behavior of foreign firms, and it is here that the European and American experiences differ most. For equity to be addressed effectively, foreign competitors must in some—but not all—respects replicate the attributes of their domestic competition. This is difficult, because part of what makes these foreign firms so successful is precisely their different approach. Still, the Europeans are clearly drawing a delicate line in the sand on this aspect of foreign direct investment.

Europeans begin with jobs, especially those crucial, high-wage manufacturing jobs that require few formal pre-employment skills. But they want much more. They have pushed hard to make sure that Japanese plants in the EC do not just assemble expensive components made elsewhere. European demands are quite comprehensive. They want high levels of local content, with the associated high value-added production. They want training for their workers, to make them more productive. They want hiring and training of their managers, to make them understand the foreign way of doing things that seems so successful. They want a chance to do the most interesting work and to retain key capacities in high technology areas. They want design and then R&D transferred to local facilities. They want not just the big operations, but the supplier base too: foreign firms should use local (i.e., domestic) suppliers in a given industry, training them to international standards, if necessary. And where foreign suppliers are used, they want these firms to shift production into the EC too, and to follow the same ground rules as their big brothers.

Less specifically, Europeans want foreigners to respect their way of doing business, and to adjust to them as much as they expect to adjust to foreigners. In many cases that means operating within a unionized shop, as Nissan does in Britain but not in Tennessee, or even taking on board the whole panoply of elaborate European labor relations—worker directors, works councils, codetermination, local working hours, local holidays, etc. Beyond the factory gate there are also expectations: becoming part of the community, helping to maintain and build facilities from libraries to sports fields.

The ultimate shopping list is a long one; Europeans don't expect to get everything. The evidence so far, though, is that they are going to get much of what they want. And the remarkable thing is that they will do so despite having few formal tools at either the national or EC levels with which to lever concessions out of investors. True, bucking the French administration is always going to be a poor way to get a tricky project off the ground. Yet foreign investors have given in on many of these points to a remarkable extent.

Honda, Toyota, and other Japanese firms recently announced firm commitments in Europe to "Europeanize" their facilities. While Toyota has formally agreed to reach 60 percent local content at its British plant by August 1993 and 80 percent two years later, it now apparently plans to reach 90 percent by 1995. This would imply the construction of a transmission plant as well as the planned engine plant. Honda has also announced sourcing plans for its new British plant, now under construction. UK suppliers alone are expected to provide 50 percent of component inputs. Honda has released a long list of agreed suppliers, which indicates that, in this case at least, it is European-owned components manufacturers like Valeo, Bosch, Lucas, and GKN who stand to benefit most from Honda's new European transplant.

When compared with American results, the comparisons are quite dramatic. The American Electronics Association (AEA) estimates that the local content of color TVs made by Japanese firms in the United States is 28 percent, while for sets made by Japanese firms in Europe, local content is 79 percent. The same firms appear to have taken quite different sourcing decisions on the two continents: for example, Alpine's car audio plant in Greenwood, Indiana, imports 98.6 percent of its component purchases; its plant in Soisson, France, imports only 60 percent. Overall, Japanese electronics companies in Europe sourced 56.7 percent of their components in Japan in 1989; the figures for the U.S. was 74.3 percent. These differences persist even though these Japanese electronics companies have four times the amount of sales in America that they have in Europe.

The contrast can be biting. The AEA reports that, while one American chipmaker uses its European production to supply Japanese TV makers in Europe, the same TV makers will not accept chips made by the same firm in the United States. The limited evidence on issues other than local content points in the same direction. Workforces in Japanese firms are often unionized in Europe, but not in the United States. Design and R&D work has shifted into the United States, but the pace is picking up in Europe: NSK (a big bearings manufacturer), for instance, recently announced a new design center in England, explicitly in response to calls for "deeper" integration of manufacturing into the host economy.

On training, the interests of Japanese firms and foreign governments can run side by side. Lean (or Japanese-style) production can only work if workers are fully involved in the production process, and that requires much more engagement and knowledge than is allowed by the Taylorized assembly lines common in the United States and EC. Nissan recently announced that it planned to devote 14 percent of its total salary bill in England to training, including 8 days "off the job" and 12 days "on the job" for each employee. In sharp contrast, British employers howled at a recent proposal from the Labour Party for a 0.5 percent training levy, even though it would be paid only by those employers not spending an equivalent amount on training.

The Europeanization of Japanese firms is still in its infancy. Many Japanese firms in Europe continue to employ working practices that non-Japanese find difficult. Consensus-oriented decision-making is one thing, but the wide open office plans, the largely Japanese senior managements, and the assignment of Japanese "shadows" to even senior executives are less easy to take. Nor are all Japanese firms alike. Working patterns, and attitudes toward foreign investment and even foreigners, vary widely even within the same industry. Thus Honda is the most internationally oriented of the auto companies, perennially rumored to be moving its head office to Los Angeles; Toyota is the most Japanese, venturing abroad most reluctantly; while Nissan has in one expert's phrase "gone native," as its U.S. operations have become the most American of all, especially in terms of management.

There is certainly a difficult contradiction to be reconciled here. On the one hand, the single largest benefit of Japanese foreign investment is the influx that it brings of Japanese management skills: the new lean production techniques. On the other, a primary purpose of any FDI policy is to indicate the kinds of foreign behavior that are desirable and those that are not. Japanese behavior in

Europe is definitely changing, under pressure from the Europeans. Key circles in Japan openly recognize that, in the European case, globalization means adopting a European cast. The influential Industrial Bank of Japan acknowledged that point on the cover of its 1990 overview of EC–92. It noted that Japanese investors in Europe would have to increase levels of local content, shift design and R&D to Europe, and use local suppliers and local managers where possible.

In similar vein, MITI has produced a diagram which shows the shifting European pressures on Japanese firms. First came a requirement to assemble in Europe. This was followed by further requirements to locate complete manufacturing facilities in Europe with high levels of European value-added and sourcing. Finally, design and R&D activities must be located in Europe.

How much of this been a result of government pressure? The EC has explicitly called for local content, though it has been very reluctant to enshrine it in EC regulations. Even the best-known case, the 1991 EC-Japan auto agreement, contains no explicit language on local content. What is more, it is simply an agreement, not EC legislation. Yet surveys by JETRO indicates that about 65 percent of Japanese manufacturing establishments have been asked for specific performance guarantees by host governments. Most requests target employment, but there are also pressures for technology transfer and the development of exports. In addition, many European leaders have been explicit about what is expected of companies investing in Europe.

Thus while one can argue—and the Commission, wearing its free trade hat, certainly would argue—that the EC has no explicit policy on foreign investment and that these perceptions are misplaced, exaggerated, or even hallucinated, they have nonetheless clearly had a tremendous impact on executives making decisions about the level and form of their involvement in Europe. Perhaps the most important point of all is that, in the end, the approach adopted in Europe seems very familiar to Japanese investors. There have been very few public complaints. Just as Japanese firms accepted guidance from MITI or the Japanese Ministry of Finance in the past, they are now willing to accept it from host governments elsewhere.

The European approach is predicated on a core assumption: with sufficient incentives or pressure, Japanese and other foreign investors will adapt to local demands because the market is attractive enough to make it worthwhile. In Europe, this assumption has so far been proved correct. The United States might benefit from a closer look at some of the industrial policies being developed in Europe today. Given the increasingly market-friendly orientation of these places and the broad concern that the benefits of foreign direct investment be shared by the host country as well as the source country, these new policies may fit better with the needs and traditions of the United States and, at the same time, avoid any further slide toward old-fashioned protectionism and isolation. As the United States moves forward with some trepidation into a world newly-populated with potentially dangerous commercial rivals, it is worth bearing in mind that the strategies adopted by other major players matter. And there are good reasons to look closely at the experiences of Europe, the region that offers the most useful and applicable lessons.

AMERICAN DIRECT INVESTMENT IN THE EUROPEAN COMMUNITY

by James K. Jackson *

CONTENTS

SUMMARY

American direct investment in the twelve member states of the European Community has increased sharply since 1985, when the Community embarked on its plan to develop a single European market. These investments arise from the largest and most well-known American multinational companies and from small operations that are investing abroad for the first time and run the spectrum of countries and industries in Europe. As a result of these investments, American direct investment in Europe was a larger share of total U.S. direct investment abroad in 1991 than it was in 1985.

The increased flows of investment between Europe and the United States are challenging some of the basic economic and legal philosophies and principles of both the EC and the United States. Acquisitions of firms on both sides of the Atlantic are causing members of the EC and the United States to confront differences between them in fundamental beliefs over the nature of economic competition and the role of government in controlling or preserving competition in the marketplace. In addition, the investments are challenging some of the basic assumptions many in the United States hold concerning the role of U.S. antitrust laws in controlling the accumulation of market power. Moreover, at the same time

* James K. Jackson is a Specialist in International Trade and Finance, Economics Division, Congressional Research Service.

that the Federal government is considering using U.S. antitrust laws to challenge foreign economic practices, U.S. businesses are arguing that U.S. antitrust laws are impairing their ability to compete with foreign firms in domestic and foreign markets. Recent decisions by both the EC and the United States to extend further their legal reaches outside their territories, raise prospects of significant conflicts between the EC and the United States over economic issues.

Direct investment across the Atlantic in both directions is also challenging philosophical and political differences in the United States and the EC over the role of government in aiding industries and in protecting firms from foreign acquisition for "national security" reasons. The U.S. Congress is reviewing a number of proposals that would interject more of an economic content into the Nation's view of national security. Objections raised in Congress to the proposed sale of the bankrupt LTV firm to a French company may be a harbinger of increased conflicts between the United States and the EC as the United States attempts to characterize the role of economics in defining the nature of national security. For American multinational firms, these conflicts could compound an already confusing clash of laws and national attitudes over the role of multinational firms in national markets.

American Direct Investment Abroad

American businesses have increased their interest and direct investment [1] in Europe since 1985, when the Commission of the European Community published its White Paper plan to develop a single European market by 1992. [2] As a result of this interest, U.S. direct investment in Europe in the later half of the 1980s eclipsed U.S. foreign direct investment to all other regions of the world. As figure 1 shows, U.S. direct investment in the EC grew at a faster rate than U.S. direct investment elsewhere. (See appendix A.) Data on U.S. direct investment in the EC also show that acquiring existing EC firms, rather than greenfield, or new investments, was the most prevalent form of investment.

In the first half of the 1980s, U.S. direct investment abroad was stagnant. In some cases, U.S. multinational companies actually reduced their investments overseas as U.S. economic growth outpaced that in Europe. According to the U.S. Department of Commerce, this reversal in U.S. investment abroad was keyed to much stronger economic growth and higher interest rates in the United States than abroad. The attractive U.S. investment climate, combined with increased merger and acquisitions activity, spurred U.S. parent companies to increase their demands for funds to finance their domestic operations. In turn, U.S. parent companies turned to

---

[1] U.S. direct investment abroad is defined as the ownership or control, directly or indirectly, by a single person (individual, branch, partnership, associated group, association, estate, trust, corporation and any government) of 10 percent or more of the voting securities of an incorporated foreign business enterprise or the equivalent interest in an unincorporated foreign business enterprise. 15 CFR § 806.15(a)(1).

[2] For a discussion of the plan, see: U.S. Library of Congress. Congressional Research Service. *The European Community's 1992 Plan: An Overview of the Proposed "Single Market"*. Report no. 88-623 E, by Glennon J. Harrison. Washington, 1988. 33 p. The 12 member countries comprising the European Community include: Belgium, Denmark, France, Germany, Greece, Ireland, Italy, Luxembourg, the Netherlands, Portugal, Spain, and the United Kingdom.

their foreign subsidiaries as a source of funds: a sizeable portion of the resulting capital inflows was channeled to U.S. parent companies through their foreign affiliates, thereby reducing the U.S. direct investment position abroad. [3]

FIGURE 1. U.S. Direct Investment Outflows By Year For Selected Geographic Regions (in billions of dollars)

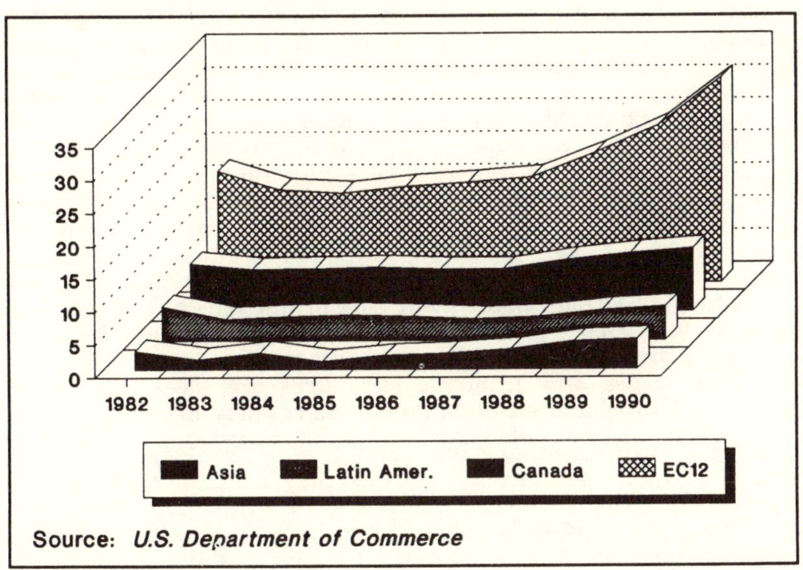

Between 1984 and 1990, however, U.S. direct investment abroad doubled, rising from $211 billion to $421 billion. [4] American direct investment in the European Community more than doubled in the 1984–1990 period, rising from $72 billion to $173 billion. As a result, U.S. direct investment in the EC increased as a share of total U.S. direct investment abroad (from 34 percent in 1984 to 41 percent in 1990). Some of the increase in U.S. direct investment in Europe reflects exchange rate changes that are related to the depreciation of the dollar since 1985. The depreciation of the dollar

---

[3] U.S. Department of Commerce. Bureau of Economic Research. *Survey of Current Business*, June 1985. The International Investment Position of the United States in 1984, by Russell B. Scholl. p. 30. For an empirical assessment of the interactions between a multinational's domestic and foreign investment, see: Stevens, Guy V.G., and Robert E. Lipsey. Interactions Between Domestic and Foreign Investment. *Journal of International Money and Finance*, February, 1992. p. 41–62.

[4] Some analysts argue that the direct investment position data understate the value of U.S. assets abroad because they measure the investments at their acquisition prices instead of at their market values. In 1991, the Department of Commerce published two alternative estimates for the historical cost data on direct investment: current cost and market value estimates. (See: U.S. Department of Commerce. Bureau of Economic Analysis. *Survey of Current Business*, May 1991. Valuation of the U.S. Net International Investment Position, by J. Steven Landefeld and Ann M. Lawson.) Since current cost and market value estimates are not published for individual countries or for industries, historical cost data are used in this report. Also see: U.S. Library of Congress. Congressional Research Service. *Foreign Investments: How Much Are They Worth?.* CRS Report no. 91-865 E, by James K. Jackson. Washington, December 9, 1991.

affects the foreign direct investment position of the United States, because large capital gains accrue for the foreign affiliates when their earnings are converted from the appreciating foreign currencies into dollars. These gains are included in the foreign affiliates' earnings statements and, therefore, become part of the foreign affiliates' reinvested earnings. In most years, reinvested earnings comprise the major component of foreign direct investment flows, enhancing the U.S. foreign direct investment position.

In other regions of the world, U.S. direct investment has grown at a much slower pace. U.S. direct investment in Africa declined over the 1982–1990 period, while direct investment in the Middle East grew by about one-third. By contrast, U.S. direct investment in Asia increased slightly faster than the overall rate of growth in U.S. foreign direct investment. U.S. direct investment in Latin America also increased at a faster pace than did U.S. direct investment as a whole, but much of this growth arises from investments in the Bahamas and the Netherlands Antilles, which are often used as tax havens.

Overall, American direct investment abroad challenges conventional notions of foreign investment as a primary means of shifting production to low-cost producers in developing countries. Instead, U.S. foreign direct investment is concentrated in developed countries where wages and economic structures are most similar to those of the United States. Such developed country investments account for three-fourths of total U.S. direct investment abroad, a share which remained virtually unchanged during the 1980s, despite the doubling in the value of U.S. direct investment abroad.

U.S. Direct Investments in Europe

American direct investment in Europe surged during the 1980s; such investment in Europe by American firms, however, is not a recent development. Samuel Colt was among the first Americans to invest in Europe when he built a factory in London in 1852 to manufacture repeating firearms. [5] By one account, the first American multinational business to invest in Europe was Singer Co., founded by I.M. Singer. In 1867, Singer established sales offices in Glasgow, Scotland and in London, England and soon built manufacturing facilities to gain some economies of scale in production and warehousing and to gain from lower wage costs in England. [6] Conversely, European investment in the United States was one important factor in the early development of the American industrial infrastructure. During the nineteenth century, for instance, European investment helped to accommodate sharp bursts in U.S. economic growth and in the domestic expansions of canal and railroad facilities. [7]

---

[5] This factory never was profitable and Colt sold it in 1857. Wilkins, Mira. *The Emergence of Multinational Enterprise: American Business Abroad From the Colonial Era to 1914*. Cambridge, Harvard University Press, 1970. p. 29–30.

[6] Ibid., p. 37–41. Singer Co. was acquired in 1988 by Bilzerian Partners LP. *Mergers & Acquisitions*, September/October, 1988. p. 97.

[7] For a discussion of the role of foreign investment in the U.S. economy see: U.S. Library of Congress. Congressional Research Service. *Foreign Ownership of U.S. Assets: Past, Present, and Prospects*. Report no. 89–458 E, by James K. Jackson and William D. Jackson. Washington, July 1, 1988. 29 p; and, *Foreign Direct Investment in the U.S.: A Decade of Growth*. Report no. 91–349 E, by James K. Jackson. Washington, April 12, 1991. 46 p.

U.S. direct investment in the United Kingdom reached $65 billion in 1990, or 38 percent of U.S. direct investment in the EC. Investments in Germany, the Netherlands, and France account for the next largest shares of U.S. direct investment in the EC, representing 16 percent, 13 percent, and 10 percent, respectively of U.S. direct investment in the EC. While the flow of American direct investment into the EC member states varies from year to year, the shares of U.S. direct investment in the individual EC states in 1990 closely resembles the makeup of those investments that existed in 1981. Five of the twelve EC members gained during the 1980s as a share of total U.S. direct investment in the EC (Ireland, Italy, the Netherlands, Spain, and the United Kingdom), but these increases were small.

American direct investment within the EC is concentrated in the manufacturing and finance industries, as indicated in table 1. These two sectors account for over 60 percent of American direct investment in the EC and one-third of total American direct investment abroad. Investments in the petroleum industry in the EC account for 80 percent of all American foreign direct investment in that industry. Also, direct investment in EC manufacturing industries accounts for nearly half of American investments there, a share that is higher than the worldwide average of 40 percent.

RECENT INVESTMENTS AND ACQUISITIONS

A European market without internal barriers to trade and investment offers American and other firms attractive business opportunities. The names of American firms that have established or have expanded their presence in Europe reads like a directory of the largest American multinational companies: General Motors, Ford Motor, E.I. du Pont de Nemours, and Procter & Gamble, to cite a few. Many of these large U.S. multinational companies already have sizeable operations in the EC countries and may be investing primarily to round out their European operations.

Other U.S. multinationals, however, have moved aggressively to shore up their positions since 1985. These investments likely are spurred by a combination of high promise and concern over the prospects of a single European market free from internal barriers. American investors apparently reason that even if all the EC's directives are not carried out, a more liberalized internal market could enhance overall business opportunities in Europe. At the same time, some American businesses are concerned that Europe may become more protectionist following the removal of internal barriers. Data compiled on publicly announced investment transactions indicate that the majority of American transactions in the EC are acquisitions of existing European companies. [8] Appendix B lists the largest American acquisitions in Europe over the 1985–1991 period where the value of the acquisition, if stated publicly, is over $50 million.

---

[8] Data on transactions are taken from *Mergers & Acquisitions*, which collects information from publicly announced mergers and acquisitions transactions. While this coverage is as comprehensive as possible, these data are not as complete as those compiled by the U.S. Department of Commerce, which collects data for its reports on U.S. direct investment abroad and foreign direct investment in the United States.

TABLE 1. U.S. Direct Investment Position, Historical Cost Basis, 1990

(in billions of U.S. dollars)

	All industries	Petroleum	Manufacturing	Wholesale trade	Banking	Finance (except banking), insurance, and real estate	Services	Other industries
All countries	421.5	59.7	168.2	41.4	21.4	98.9	10.8	21.0
Europe	204.2	24.4	84.0	24.5	8.7	52.2	6.5	3.9
EC (12)	172.9	18.8	81.3	15.4	7.5	40.7	5.5	3.8
Belgium	9.5	0.3	4.3	2.2	(D)	2.1	0.4	(D)
Denmark	1.6	(D)	0.3	0.6	(D)	0.3	0.1	(*)
France	17.1	(D)	11.1	3.0	0.2	1.0	0.4	(D)
Germany	27.7	3.1	17.5	1.5	1.7	2.9	(*)	1.1
Greece	0.3	(*)	0.1	0.1	0.1	(D)	(D)	(D)
Ireland	6.8	(*)	4.9	(D)	(*)	1.5	0.4	(D)
Italy	13.0	0.6	8.5	1.7	0.4	1.0	0.3	0.5
Luxembourg	1.1	(*)	0.5	(D)	0.3	0.2	(*)	(D)
Netherlands	22.8	1.6	8.1	2.5	0.2	8.6	1.4	0.3
Portugal	0.6	(D)	0.3	0.1	(D)	(D)	(D)	(D)
Spain	7.5	0.1	5.0	1.0	0.9	(*)	0.3	0.2
United Kingdom.	65.0	11.3	20.6	2.7	3.6	23.1	2.2	1.4
Other Europe	31.3	5.6	2.7	9.1	1.2	11.5	1.0	0.2
Austria	0.8	(D)	0.1	0.3	(*)	(D)	(*)	(*)
Finland	0.5	(D)	0.1	0.4	(D)	(*)	(*)	(*)
Norway	3.6	3.0	0.1	0.4	(*)	(D)	(*)	(D)
Sweden	1.5	(*)	1.1	0.3	(D)	(*)	(*)	(D)
Switzerland	23.7	(D)	1.2	7.4	1.0	11.1	(D)	0.1
Turkey	0.5	0.2	0.1	0.1	0.1	(*)	(D)	(D)
Other	0.6	(*)	0.1	0.1	(*)	0.3	(D)	(D)

Note: An asterisk (*) represents values less than $500 million (+/−). A (D) indicates that data have been suppressed by the Department of Commerce to avoid the disclosure of data of individual companies.

Source: U.S. Department of Commerce. Bureau of Economic Analysis. *Survey of Current Business*, August 1991. U.S. Direct Investment Abroad: Detail for Historical-Cost Position and Balance of Payments Flows, 1990.

The largest changes in American direct investment abroad and in the EC are in the petroleum and finance industries. American direct investment in the petroleum industry in Europe was marked by a number of major purchases, including Atlantic Richfield's purchase of shares in Britoil PLC for $700 million in 1987, Tricentrol PLC in 1988, and E.I. du Pont de Nemours' acquisition of Tenneco Oil Norway and Triton Europe PLC. These investments pushed American direct investment abroad in the petroleum industry to $18.8 billion in 1990, but they run counter to the general trend in U.S. direct investment in the petroleum industry: American direct investment abroad in the petroleum industry was generally flat during the 1985–1990 period. As a result, U.S. investment in the petroleum industry fell by nearly half as a share of total U.S. direct investment abroad during the 1985–1990 period.

American direct investment in foreign, especially European, financial concerns rose by more than four times during the 1985–1990 period, reaching $99 billion. As a result of these investments, American direct investment in foreign financial businesses alone accounts for 40 percent of the increase in U.S. worldwide direct investment since 1985. Within the EC, American direct investment in the financial industry stands at $41 billion and represents an array of American investments in European credit, securities, insurance, and investment companies. General Electric, with $7 billion, or about 13 percent, of its revenues generated abroad,[9] acquired a number of credit firms in the United Kingdom, including Burton Group Financial Service for $330 million in 1990. American Express, which generates 20 percent of its total revenues from its foreign operations, acquired Signet Ltd., a British credit firm in 1991 for $235 million. Such American firms as Citicorp, McGraw-Hill Inc., Bankers Trust, Aetna Life & Casualty Co., and Gulf & Western Inc. also have invested in financial businesses in a number of EC countries. Most of this investment, however, has been in the United Kingdom: half of the $17 billion in new American direct investment in the United Kingdom in the 1985–1990 period is from investments in British financial businesses.

American direct investments in the wholesale trade, services, and manufacturing industries in the European Community have also grown rapidly. Within manufacturing, American direct investment has grown most rapidly in the chemicals, transportation, and metals industries. Procter & Gamble, which is rated among the largest U.S. multinationals with 40 percent of its revenue generated from its foreign operations, acquired the West German company, Blendax-Group, in 1987 for $400 million. E.I du Pont de Nemours & Co., which ranks among the top ten American multinational companies, acquired shares in firms in Italy and Denmark. The Sara Lee Corp. made one of the largest investments in the EC chemicals industry when it acquired AKZO NV, the food and consumer products unit of Royal Dutch Shell NV for $600 million in 1987.

In the transportation sector, the three major U.S. auto manufacturers acquired EC companies. General Motors, which already derives $34 billion in revenues, or one-fourth of its total revenues, from its foreign operations, acquired the British sports car manufacturer, Group Lotus, in 1986. In 1987, Chrysler Corporation acquired the Italian firm, Nuova Automobili L. Lamborghini; Ford Motor Company had the largest investment with its acquisition of the British firm, Jaguar PLC, for $2.6 billion in 1990. In addition, United Parcel Service has acquired nearly a dozen transportation firms since 1989 in the United Kingdom, Spain, France, Switzerland, Belgium, and Denmark. These purchases should help move the company more into the ranks of the larger American multinational companies.

Other American companies have also been active in investing in Europe. For instance, Borden Inc., one of the smaller American multinational companies with $1.8 billion in foreign revenues, acquired more than a dozen European companies in industries ranging from food and produce to chemicals and rubber in the United Kingdom, West Germany, Italy, and the Netherlands. Campbell Soup Company, which has also been active in investing in the food and produce industry, acquired half a dozen firms across Europe, including locations in Italy, Belgium, France, West Germany, and the United Kingdom. Whirlpool Corp., which bought out Philips

---

[9] Data on the foreign revenues of American multinational corporations are taken from: U.S. Firms With the Biggest Foreign Revenues. *Forbes*, July 23, 1990. p. 362–365.

Electronics' $611 million stake in a joint venture between the two firms, Whirlpool International, has been successful in conducting a pan-European advertising and marketing campaign that has increased its market shares in Germany, France, and Britain. [10] Whirlpool International markets and services major home appliances in Europe, the Middle East, the Far East, Africa, and South America.

CAPITAL EXPENDITURES

Another way of measuring U.S. direct investment in Europe is by evaluating the capital expenditures by majority-owned affiliates of U.S. companies. This measure includes funds raised in foreign markets that are not recorded as part of the balance of payments flows and, therefore, provide another estimate of the capital expenditures of the American affiliates in Europe. As table 2 indicates, capital expenditures in the EC by the foreign affiliates of U.S. firms fell from $17.3 billion in 1981 to $13.7 billion in 1984. Since 1984, capital spending increased annually through 1991, when it reached $34.5 billion. Between 1987 and 1990, capital expenditures increased by more than 20 percent a year; the latest estimates indicate that spending rose by 10 percent between 1990 and 1991. Since 1985, U.S. firms have devoted an increasingly larger share of their capital expenditures to investments in EC countries. As a result, capital expenditures in the EC rose from 42 percent of total U.S. capital expenditures abroad in 1981 to 51 percent in 1991. [11]

The Department of Commerce's Bureau of Economic Analysis (BEA) surveys the foreign affiliates of U.S. companies every June and December on their capital expenditure plans. From these surveys, it is possible to track the investment spending plans of firms as far ahead as 18 months of the year end data. [12] Comparing the revisions in investment plans over the various surveys with the actual investments for the year provides one indication of how the firms have altered their investment plans over the tracking period. As figure 2 shows, between 1980 and 1987, the actual investment outlays of U.S. foreign affiliates were consistently below their earlier, planned levels. This trend suggests that the affiliates curtailed their capital expenditures during the course of the 18-month planning cycle surveyed by the BEA from the levels the affiliates had originally planned. Both the planned and the actual capital expenditures of the affiliates declined through the first half of the 1980s as U.S. multinational companies withdrew capital from their

---

[10] Nelson, Mark M. Whirlpool Gives Pan-European Approach a Spin. *The Wall Street Journal*, April 23, 1992. p. B1.

[11] U.S. Department of Commerce. Bureau of Economic Analysis. *Survey of Current Business*, September 1991. Capital Expenditures by Majority-Owned Foreign Affiliates of U.S. Companies, Revised Estimates for 1991, by Mahnaz Fahim-Nader. p. 32–38.

[12] The Bureau of Economic Analysis is changing the timing of its surveys on the capital spending plans of U.S. foreign affiliates. A study by BEA indicates that June is too early in the affiliates' budget cycle for most firms to obtain reliable capital spending plans for the year ahead. Part of the difference between the initial spending plans, which are based on the June survey, and the actual spending outlays may arise from partial information the affiliates were using to complete the survey. U.S. Department of Commerce. Bureau of Economic Analysis. *Survey of Current Business*, September 1991. Capital Expenditures by Majority-Owned Foreign Affiliates of U.S. Companies, Revised Estimates for 1991, by Mahnaz Fahim-Nader. p. 34.

foreign subsidiaries to fund their investment programs in the United States.[13]

TABLE 2. Capital Expenditures By Majority-Owned Foreign Affiliates of U.S. Companies

(in billions of U.S. dollars)

	1981	1982	1983	1984	1985	1986	1987	1988	1989	1990	1991*
Total	43.7	43.8	36.0	34.7	34.9	34.3	34.4	42.6	51.5	61.2	67.3
Developed	31.3	30.0	25.3	25.3	25.5	26.0	27.3	33.9	40.4	47.9	52.8
Canada	8.1	7.4	6.5	6.6	6.8	6.5	6.5	7.9	8.9	9.6	9.6
Europe	20.1	19.5	16.5	16.4	16.2	16.8	17.7	21.5	26.1	33.7	37.6
EC12	17.3	17.1	14.2	13.7	14.7	15.3	16.1	19.8	24.0	31.2	34.5
Japan	0.8	0.9	0.6	0.8	1.0	1.0	1.2	1.8	2.0	2.1	2.3
Developing	11.1	12.5	10.1	9.1	8.9	7.9	6.7	8.0	10.2	12.4	13.8
Latin Am.	5.7	5.2	3.3	3.7	3.9	3.7	3.3	3.6	4.6	5.1	5.6
Africa	1.6	2.5	1.9	1.5	1.5	1.1	0.7	0.9	0.9	1.4	1.4
Mid. East	0.5	0.7	0.8	0.7	0.5	0.4	0.5	0.4	0.5	0.8	0.8

* Indicates that the data are estimated expenditures based on a survey of the foreign-owned affiliates of U.S. firms in June 1991.

Source: U.S. Department of Commerce. Bureau of Economic Analysis. *Survey of Current Business*, various issues. Capital Expenditures by Majority-Owned Foreign Affiliates of U.S. Companies.

Figure 2 shows that actual investment spending by the EC affiliates of U.S. firms has exceeded the affiliates' original spending plans since 1987, reflecting a shift in the flow of capital between the EC affiliates and their U.S. parent companies. Actual investment outlays by U.S. foreign affiliates in EC countries in 1987 increased by 5.2 percent from the initial survey taken 18 months prior to year end 1987. In 1988, investment outlays increased 34 percent from the $14.8 billion indicated in the June 1987 survey to $19.8 billion by year end. Similar increases were experienced in 1989 and 1990 and may be seen again in 1991. While the affiliates' motivation for increasing their actual capital expenditures over their planned levels is not apparent in the data, the increase in expenditures above the planned levels suggest that American firms have grown more positive about investing in Europe. These expenditures may also reflect the global view of U.S. multinational corporations that leaving profits in the hands of the affiliates for investing in Europe is a better use of the funds than repatriating them to the United States.

Motives for Investing Abroad

One question raised by the EC single market proposal is the influence the proposal itself is having on the observed increase in U.S. direct investment in the EC. Part of the increase in investment spending could arise from concerns that U.S. firms share with other non-EC firms that a unified European market might eventually be a more protectionist market.[14] Also, U.S. firms could have increased their investments to take advantage of opportunities that may arise from an expanding and integrating market, such as economies of scale in production and advertising. Econo-

---

[13] Stevens and Lipsey, Interactions Between Domestic and Foreign Investment, p. 40–62.

[14] U.S. Library of Congress. Congressional Research Service. *U.S. Trade Restraints: Effects on Foreign Investment*. CRS Report no. 89–447 E, by James K. Jackson. Washington, August 4, 1989.

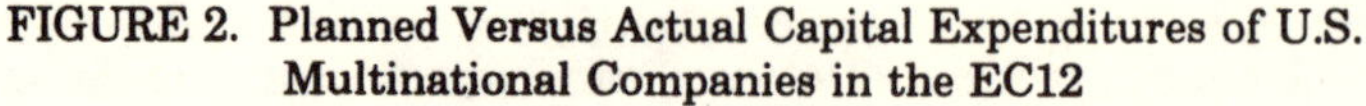

FIGURE 2. Planned Versus Actual Capital Expenditures of U.S. Multinational Companies in the EC12

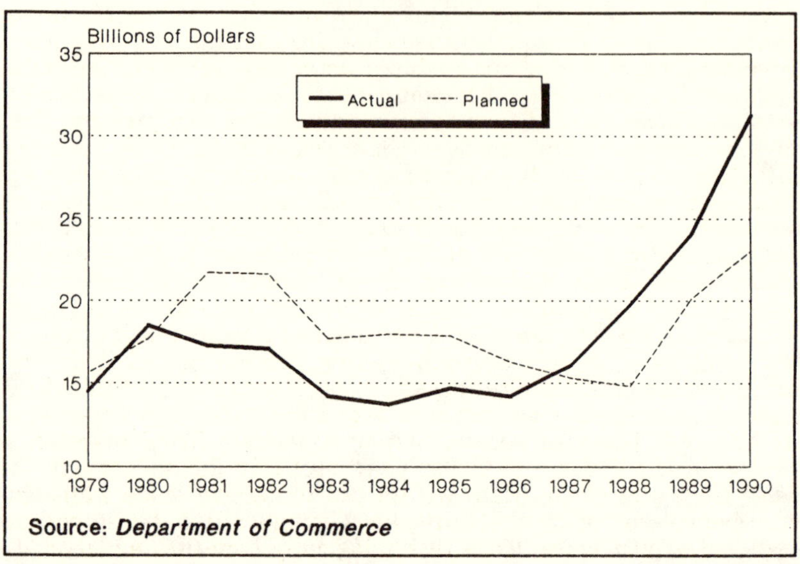

mists argue that such factors as relative growth rates among national economies, exchange rate movements, relative changes in productivity, and monetary and fiscal policies in the United States and elsewhere are the most important factors influencing foreign investment.[15] Furthermore, some economists argue that foreign direct investment is keyed to gaining proximity to the European market and to the size and growth of the market: to the extent that the single market enhances European growth, they contend, it likely will attract more investments.[16]

The pull on investments might be strong for American firms even if they discount the ability of the EC to accomplish the full slate of goals it has set for itself. This appeal seems to be based on an appraisal that the effects of the EC–92 plan will be felt among all the EC countries and is most apparent in the spread of American direct investment across a broad range of EC countries. American firms may well believe that national markets and national borders will continue to remain strong business considerations in the EC, despite whatever unifying effects may arise from the EC–92

[15] U.S. Department of Commerce. Bureau of Economic Analysis. *Survey of Current Business*, October 1978. Manufacturing Affiliates' Capital Expenditures and Host Country Output, Prices, and Exchange Rates. p. 50–53; Lipsey, Robert E. and Merle Yahr Weiss. Foreign Production and Exports in Manufacturing Industries. *The Review of Economics and Statistics*, November, 1981. p. 488; and, Ray, Edward John. *The Determinants of Foreign Direct Investment in the United States: 1979–1985*. Cambridge, Mass., National Bureau of Economic Research, 1988. p. 2.

[16] Nicolaides, Phedon and Stephen Thomsen. The Impact of 1992 on Direct Investment in Europe. *European Business Journal*, v. 3, no. 2. p. 8–9.

plan. As some economists argue, "the removal of the barriers to trade within the EC will not necessarily make national markets homogeneous, either in terms of consumer tastes or available tangible or intangible assets." [17]

American multinational firms may also increase their investment spending in Europe because they are continuing a progressive movement abroad of their business activities. As such, American firms are investing abroad to compensate for market imperfections or to take advantage of firm-specific advantages that give the firms some economic advantage over their competitors. [18] Some economists argue that such macroeconomic factors as monetary and fiscal policies are the prime determinants of U.S. trade performance and investment behavior through their influence on exchange rates, prices, and wage and productivity behavior. [19] Firms are also influenced in their decision to invest abroad by relative growth rates among national economies, exchange rate movements, productivity, trade restraints, and the desire to acquire technology. [20] The complexity of this decision-making process makes it difficult for economists and others to assess the relative importance firms place on such specific activities as acquiring technology or avoiding protectionist trade measures. When American firms invested in Europe in the 1950s and 1960s, they probably did so not only because they wanted to locate within the protective trade walls that were being erected by the European Community, but also because they had grown large, were technologically superior, and had significant amounts of trade with Europe that encouraged them to invest there.

RELATIVE GROWTH RATES

Differences in the rates of growth between the U.S. and European economies appear to be especially important factors at times influencing U.S. direct investment in Europe and elsewhere. For instance, reinvested earnings of the European affiliates of U.S. companies fell sharply during the early 1980s as foreign affiliates returned capital to their U.S. parent companies while U.S. economic growth outpaced that in Europe. Real capital expenditures (adjusted for the effects of inflation) by U.S. foreign affiliates in the EC (*RCEM*) barely increased from 1984 to 1987, after falling steadily since 1980 as indicated by figure 3. Figure 3 also shows recent trends in three measures of real economic growth that are prob-

---

[17] Ibid., p. 16; and, Shapiro, Alan C. Europe 1992: Competitive Threats and Opportunities Facing Multinational Corporations. *European Business Journal*, v. 3, no. 3. p. 8–18.

[18] Horst, Thomas. Firm and Industry Determinants of the Decision to Invest Abroad: An Empirical Study. *The Review of Economics and Statistics*, August, 1972. p. 258–2266; Caves, Richard E. Causes of Direct Investment: Foreign Firm's Shares in Canadian and United Kingdom Manufacturing Industries. *The Review of Economics and Statistics*, August, 1974. p. 279–293; Grubaugh, Stephen G. Determinants of Direct Foreign Investment. *The Review of Economics and Statistics*, February, 1987. p. 149–152;Ethier, Wilfred J. The Multinational Firm. *The Quarterly Journal of Economics*, November, 1986. p. 837–841; and, Benvignati, Anita M. Industry Determinants and "Differences" in U.S. Intrafirm and Arms-Length Exports. *The Review of Economics and Statistics*, August, 1990. p. 481 488.

[19] Lipsey, Robert E. and Irving B. Kravis. *The Competitive Position of U.S. Manufacturing Firms*. Cambridge, Mass., National Bureau of Economic Research, 1985. (Working Paper No. 1557.) p. 2; and, Albier, Robert Z. A Theory of Direct Foreign Investment. In Kindleberger, Charles P. *The International Corporation*. Cambridge, Mass., The M.I.T. Press, 1970.

[20] Lipsey and Kravis, The Competitive Position of U.S. Manufacturing Firms, p. 2; and, Ray, The Determinants of Foreign Direct Investment in the United States: 1979–1985, p. 2.

ably major determinants of U.S. investment in the EC: real gross fixed capital formation among the EC countries (*ECGFCF*), real gross domestic product of the EC (*ECRGDP*), and U.S. real gross national product (*USRGNP*).

While comparisons such as these admittedly are imprecise measures, they provide an indication of some of the factors which drive U.S. investments in the EC countries. In particular, figure 3 shows that the capital expenditures of U.S. affiliates roughly follow the same pattern as European firms, represented by EC real gross fixed capital formation. The investment plans of U.S. firms also are affected by the differential between U.S.-EC growth rates: as U.S. real economic growth outpaced economic growth in the EC between 1982 and 1984, the American affiliates scaled back their investments in order to supply capital to their parent companies.

FIGURE 3. Real Capital Expenditures of U.S. Multinational Companies in the EC12

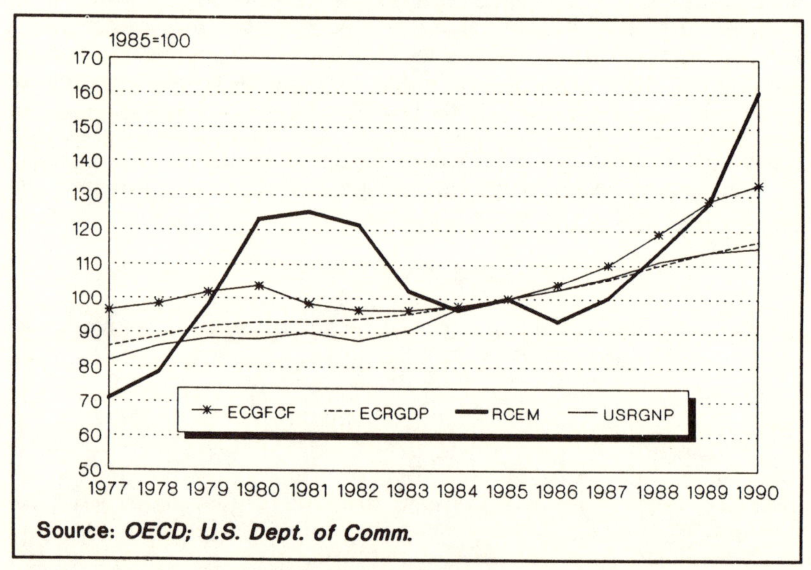

Source: *OECD; U.S. Dept. of Comm.*

REMAINING CONCERNS

Some U.S. firms are looking to invest and to expand their operations in the EC as a result of increased economic activity that is expected to arise from the single market. Others, however, hold a number of concerns about the single market plan. [21] These concerns can be grouped into four general areas: national treatment, reciprocity, rules of origin, and social policy. [22] National treatment

[21] Mossberg, Walter S. Obstacle Course: As EC Markets Unite, U.S. Exporters Face New Trade Barriers. *The Wall Street Journal*, January 19, 1989. p. A1.

[22] Calingaert, Michael. *The 1992 Challenge From Europe: Development of the European Community's Internal Market*. Washington, The National Planning Association, 1988. p. 85–91.

is the concept that U.S. firms will be treated no less favorably than are EC firms. Reciprocity, on the other hand, refers to a feeling within the EC that nonmember firms should not be allowed to enjoy the benefits of the integrated EC market unless EC firms are allowed to enjoy similar treatment in the nonmember's country. [23] Rules of origin relate to the factors the EC will use to determine if goods produced in the EC by a subsidiary of a foreign company qualify for designation as an EC product: such rules ensure that goods accorded EC status are produced substantially from EC-originated parts rather than merely goods assembled from parts imported from outside the EC. Social policy is a broad rubric that includes such issues as workers' rights and safety standards.

For the most part, developments in the four areas likely will not affect American subsidiaries in the EC as much as they will affect other, non-EC (especially Japanese) firms. Many U.S. subsidiaries have carried out conscientious policies of attempting to integrate into the local scene and to gain acceptance as local firms. Some analysts argue that U.S. firms did this by maintaining minimal non-national staff, participating in local cultural and charitable activities, and playing down their U.S. origin. [24] American businesses have focused their attention on rules of origin and local content requirements because they believe the EC countries have sought and gained protection from foreign competition. Japanese firms, in particular, concluded that they must invest in the EC now, because they believe the EC will become more protectionist in the future, locking them out of the EC market. [25]

ANTI-MERGER MOVEMENT

American and European firms have grown cautious over the way their ability to trade and invest abroad may be affected by changes in U.S. and EC laws that govern certain types of investments, primarily mergers and acquisitions. These concerns arise in the United States because of the merger control system adopted by the European Community's Council of Ministers on December 21, 1989, which took effect September 1990. For their part, Europeans are concerned over: a perceived move toward a more aggressive enforcement of U.S. antitrust laws; potential effects from changes in the Exon-Florio provision of the Defense Production Act; and the possibility that Congress may enact new controls on foreign direct investment in the Untied States. In addition, both the United States and the EC are beginning to apply their respective domestic laws to entities and events outside their territories, i.e., extraterritoriality. As more American firms expand their operations abroad, differences in national legal standards regarding competition raise

[23] For a discussion on reciprocity see: U.S. Library of Congress. Congressional Research Service. *The European Community: 1992 and Reciprocity.* Report no. 89-227 E, by Glennon J. Harrison. Washington, 1989. 8 p.

[24] Calingaert, The 1992 Challenge From Europe: Development of the European Community's Internal Market, p. 87.

[25] Garnett, Nick, and Ian Rodger. Part of the Scenery But Not Yet art of the Culture. *Financial Times,* August 27, 1986. p. 1; Dullforce, William. Japan Protests to GATT at EC 'Screwdriver' Measures. *Financial Times,* May 10, 1988. p. 7; Rodger, Ian. Japanese Strive to Become Good Europeans. *Financial Times,* June 20, 1988. p. 6; and, de Jonquieres, Guy. Toyota Pondering European Strategy. *Financial Times,* October 28, 1988. p. 5.

the prospect of conflicts and confusion between nations over acceptable corporate actions. One observer concludes:

> One of the greatest challenges facing the field of antitrust is the harmonization of American and European laws governing competition. Conflicting competition laws are a consistent source of discord in international relations. The United States and the multi-national European Community (EC) constitute the world's largest economic powers and in an increasingly interdependent global economy, the conflicts and contradictions of United States and EC laws regarding antitrust often hinder trade across the Atlantic. This makes it increasingly difficult for transnational firms to successfully operate in both markets. [26]

American and EC competition policies share a common goal—to increase and protect consumer welfare, but U.S. and EC policies approach this goal in very different ways. For example, there are some fundamental differences between the U.S. antitrust policy toward mergers and acquisitions and the EC's merger control system, the two systems having been developed at different times, at different paces, and from different perspectives. [27] Although attempts to make generalizations about the two are subject to gross oversimplification, many commentators believe that the most fundamental difference between them is their approach to market power. United States antitrust law generally prohibits the active creation or acquisition of monopoly power in the marketplace, [28] while EC competition policy is generally neutral toward the acquisition of a dominant market position: U.S. antitrust policy is directed at preventing the *potential* for abuse of a dominant market position; EC competition policy, on the other hand, is concerned with the *actual* abuse of such a position.

EC competition policy allows regulators to permit mergers, joint ventures, and other transactions that would normally be illegal because they would have a negative effect on competition between European businesses if there are procompetitive effects in global markets; or if there are other advantages such as increasing a corporation's ability to compete with American, Canadian, and Japa-

---

[26] Overton, Todd R. Substantive Distinctions Between United States Antitrust Law and the Competition Policy of the European Community: Comparative Analysis of Divergent Policies. *Houston Journal of International Law*, Spring, 1991. p. 315. (Hereafter cited as: Substantive Distinctions)

[27] U.S. antitrust laws have evolved through a series of statutes dating from 1890 and 1914 on up to the present, and have reflected continuing congressional concerns over the growth of large business trusts and monopolies. EC antitrust laws, however, had no foundation until 1958, when the European Economic Community was created in the Treaty of Rome, which included articles 85 and 86, directed at the establishment of a uniform competition policy for the Community. This original Treaty "policy" was not so much a competition policy as it was primarily a means of integrating the laws and economies of the EC member countries. By contrast, the new EC regulations on competition, which date from 1990, confer jurisdiction on the EC Commission to determine whether proposed mergers (1) with a "Community dimension" (those in which the aggregate worldwide sales of all the parties concerned total more than 5,000 million ECU *and* the aggregate Community-wide turnover (sales) of each of at least two of the parties concerned must be more than 250 million ECU) or (2) over a certain size are compatible with the common market. (Compatible mergers are those which do not create or strengthen a dominant market position that impedes effective competition. Stewart, Terrence P. and Delphine A Abellard. Merger Control in the European Community: The EC Regulations "On the Control of Concentrations Between Undertaking" and Implementing Guidelines. *Northwestern Journal of International Law and Business*, Fall, 1990. p. 334)

[28] "Monopoly," however, is not subject to precise definition.

nese competitors. [29] Mergers may violate U.S. statutes if they are deemed to be monopolies under section 2 of the Sherman Act (15 U.S.C. § 2); if their effect "may be substantially to lessen competition, or tend to create a monopoly" in any section of the country (section 7 of the Clayton Act, 15 U.S.C. § 18); or could be considered "unfair methods of competition" under section 5 of the Federal Trade Commission Act (15 U.S.C. § 45).

American and some European firms are concerned that after a period of somewhat lenient enforcement of the antitrust laws, antitrust enforcement in the United States has become more aggressive. [30] For example, James F. Rill, then Assistant Attorney General, Antitrust Division, U.S. Department of Justice, stated on the 100th anniversary of the Sherman Antitrust Act that criminal and merger enforcement had become the Department's top priorities and that it would be placing "renewed emphasis on our role as competition advocates." [31] In April 1992, the Department of Justice and the Federal Trade Commission, which share responsibility for antitrust enforcement, issued revised Horizontal Merger Guidelines; it was the first time that the agencies had issued joint guidelines, and thus, underscores the importance with which both view merger enforcement. [32]

In addition, some legal observers believe that American courts have become more aggressive in prosecuting violations of U.S. antitrust laws. At the same time, other legal observers point out that the courts have altered their view of mergers as nearly *per se* violations of the antitrust laws, and have become more willing to consider arguments to the effect that efficiencies may justify an otherwise anticompetitive merger [33]—in other words, to ask whether the merger may be acceptable, even though it technically violates the antitrust statutes, because it has a net-positive effect on competition. Nevertheless, American courts appear to have rejected the argument that an increased ability to compete internationally justifies anticompetitive effects in the U.S. marketplace that may arise from a merger or acquisition.

EXTRA-TERRITORIAL ISSUES

Both the EC and the United States have moved toward applying their laws to anticompetitive practices conducted outside their territory. Under a policy announced by the U.S. Justice Department in April 1992, the United States will challenge such anticompetitive practices as boycotts and other exclusionary activities carried

---

[29] Overton, Substantive Distinctions, p. 334–335.

[30] Pitofsky, Robert. The Renaissance of Antitrust. *The Record of the Association of the Bar of the City of New York*, November, 1990. p. 851–861.

[31] *Congressional Record*. Daily Edition, v. 136, July 20, 1990. p. S10139.

[32] ". . . one of the most important aspects of the joint Guidelines is the fact that both of the Federal antitrust agencies have now formally subscribed to the same statement of merger enforcement policy. This benefits all those who come into contact with the system of dual merger enforcement at the federal level, including the courts, the business community and the bar. The joint guidelines are an important milestone in cooperation at the federal level. . . ." Janet Steiger, Chairman, Federal Trade Commission, Speech Before the Section of Antitrust Law of the American Bar Association, Washington, DC., April 3, 1992.

[33] *Per se* violations are those for which there can be no justification, i.e., automatic violations. Mergers are not, in reality, ever considered as *per se* violations. Violations which are not considered as *per se* violations are analyzed under the Rule of Reason, which employs a balancing approach i.e., do the procompetitive consequences of a practice outweigh the anticompetitive aspects?

out abroad, that hinder U.S. exports to foreign markets. [34] Under this initiative, foreign companies that operate subsidiaries in the United States will be liable for actions they commit abroad, even if those actions are legal where they occur, if the actions would be illegal under U.S. antitrust laws had the actions occurred in the United States. [35] The EC Commission has also ruled that it can investigate and rule on transactions even between two non-EC firms, if the firms are over a specified size and each realizes sales over a specified value within the EC. [36]

NATIONAL SECURITY

The EC has expressed concerns about the Exon-Florio provision [37] of the Defense Production Act. This provision grants the President the authority to take what action he considers to be "appropriate" to suspend or prohibit foreign acquisitions, mergers, or takeovers of U.S. businesses which threaten to impair the national security. Neither the legislation, nor the implementing regulations define the term, "national security." The Committee on Foreign Investment in the United States (CFIUS), chaired by the U.S. Treasury Department, was given the responsibility to investigate cases under the Exon-Florio provision. A statement issued by the European Community expresses concerns that:

> . . . the uncertainties created by the wide and undefined scope of this legislation have the potential to damage business confidence. Already these uncertainties have left investors with little choice but to voluntarily notify proposed acquisitions for screening by the Committee on Foreign Investment in the U.S. Moreover, if in the future the concept of national security were to be abused, by applying it to one or another key industrial sector for essentially protectionist reasons, the damage could be very serious indeed. That would be a major setback to global economic recovery and to the economic relationship between the Community and the United States. [38]

The EC has had first hand experience with the Exon-Florio provision. It was the proposed sale by Schlumberger Ltd. of France of one of its subsidiaries, Fairchild Semiconductor Co., to the Japanese company Fujitsu in 1987 that sparked the development and eventual passage of the Exon-Florio provision. [39] Through mid-

[34] For a more complete treatment of this issue, see: U.S. Library of Congress. Congressional Research Service. *Extraterritorial Application of U.S. Antitrust Laws: Some History And Implications.* Report no. 92-367 A, by Janice E. Rubin. Washington, April 13, 1992.

[35] *The Proposed Application of the U.S. Antitrust Laws to Foreign Markets.* Report of the Commercial and Federal Litigation Section of the New York State Bar Association; and, Davison, Joe. U.S. Decides to Enforce Antitrust Laws Against Collusion by Foreign Concerns. *The Wall Street Journal*, April 6, 1992. p. A10.

[36] Overton, Substantive Distinctions, p. 335.

[37] Public Law 100-418, Title V, Subtitle A, Part II, 50 U.S.C. App. § 2170. For additional information, see: U.S. Library of Congress. Congressional Research Service. *Foreign Investment: The Exon-Florio National Security Test.* CRS Report no. 90-463 E, by James K. Jackson. September 26, 1990.

[38] EC Statement on U.S. Policy on Foreign Direct Investment. *European Community News*, February 18, 1992.

[39] Auerbach, Stuart. Cabinet to Weigh Sale of Chip Firm. *The Washington Post*, March 12, 1987. p. E1.

March 1992, nearly half of the cases investigated by CFIUS involved firms located within the EC.[40] While the potential for discord between the United States and the EC is always present, a new conflict erupted when the French company, Thomsen-CSF, outbid a consortium of the Martin Marietta Corp. and Lockheed Corp. to acquire the missile division of the bankrupt LTV Corp.[41] CFIUS is conducting an interagency review of the proposed acquisition: this is the first step in a process that could lead to a more in-depth CFIUS investigation. The U.S. Defense Department, which also participates in the CFIUS investigation, told U.S. Senators that the acquisition should only be allowed if Thomsen-CSF would separate itself from day-to-day control of the company.[42] Even if CFIUS recommends that President Bush disallow the acquisition, the President is not required to follow CFIUS' recommendation.

By a conservative count, at least 36 legislative proposals were introduced through March 1992 in the 102nd Congress that relate to foreign direct investment in the United States. These proposals reflect frustration over the CFIUS process among some Members of Congress and concern that foreign investors may be adversely affecting the technological prowess of the United States. Representative Cardiss Collins introduced legislation (H.R. 2624) that would explicitly require CFIUS to consider the economic effects of proposed mergers and acquisition in its deliberations. Similarly, Representative Levine is sponsoring legislation (H.R. 2386) that would add certain criteria for CFIUS to consider in judging the effects of a proposed merger or acquisition on the economic or national security of the United States. In particular, this proposal would require CFIUS to assess the concentration of foreign direct investment in the industry in question and the impact of additional investments on the industry and the presence of "critical technologies." Another proposal sponsored by Representative Sharp (H.R. 2631) would have CFIUS review all proposed mergers and acquisitions above a certain size based on assets or sales for possible anticompetitive effects.[43]

Conclusions

The European Community's plan to develop a single European market by 1992 is confronting the United States with as many challenges as it is offering American firms attractive business opportunities. Large, American multinational firms and small firms venturing abroad for their first time have increased their investments in Europe since 1985. While there are any number of explanations for this surge in investment, the draw of a potentially more

---

[40] These cases include: the acquisition of Monsanto Electric Materials Co. by the German company, Huels AG; a joint venture between Westinghouse Electric Corp. and the Swiss-based Asea Brown Boveri; the acquisition of three divisions of Fairchild Industries by Matra Aerospace Inc., a subsidiary of the French-owned Matra SA; the acquisition of Norton by the French Compagnie de Saint-Gobain-Pont-a-Mousson.

[41] Pearlstein, Steven. Undoing a Done Deal: How a Few Key Days Broke Marietta's Grip on LTV Aerospace. *The Washington Post*, April 19, 1992. p. H1.

[42] Pearlstein, Steven. Pentagon Cites Security Issue In Sale of LTV to Thomsen. *The Washington Post*, March 1, 1992. p. B1.

[43] For additional information, see: U.S. Library of Congress. Congressional Research Service. *Foreign Direct Investment: The Economics of National Security Issues*. Issue Brief no. IB90143, by James K. Jackson, March 20, 1992 (continually updated).

unified European market likely is a tantalizing incentive for these firms.

The growing ties between the United States and Europe forged by the increased flows of direct investment across the Atlantic in both directions are challenging traditional concepts of sovereignty, market concentration, and the role of the government in the market. As more American and European firms operate globally, the United States will face increasingly difficult policy choices over the role of economics in defining the Nation's security and the appropriate focus of U.S. antitrust laws. In addition, the United States and Europe will be confronted with the differences between their respective laws governing the role of multinational firms in national markets and the role of government in monitoring and enforcing competition in markets that defy categorization.

Congress is facing a number of legislative proposals that may require making some tough choices. Congressional efforts to strengthen U.S. laws to limit foreign direct investment in the United States likely will find little support among U.S. multinational companies that would fear a foreign backlash against their own sizeable foreign investments. At the same time, these firms likely would support a loosening of U.S. antitrust laws because they believe it would enhance their ability compete against foreign firms. On the other hand, these same firms likely would support U.S. efforts to extend the reach of U.S. antitrust laws abroad to attack anticompetitive actions of foreign firms.

With the passing of the Cold War, pressure is likely to increase on Congress to adopt some form of national economic security policy. Such a policy might shift the emphasis in a number of fields from defense, or military, to economic, including the international competitiveness and success of U.S. multinational corporations. If such a policy provoked a strong foreign response, especially in the European Community, the United States and U.S. multinational firms could face a more difficult and potentially more hostile international investment environment.

APPENDIX A. U.S. Direct Investment Position in Europe, Historical Cost Basis

(in billions of U.S. dollars)

	1982	1983	1984	1985	1986	1987	1988	1989	1990
Total	207.8	207.2	211.5	230.3	259.6	314.3	335.9	370.1	421.5
Europe	92.4	92.0	92.0	105.2	120.7	150.4	157.0	175.2	204.2
EC (12)	74.3	72.6	72.0	83.8	98.6	124.0	131.1	149.5	172.9
Belgium	5.5	4.4	4.6	5.0	5.0	7.3	7.5	7.9	9.5
Denmark	1.2	1.1	1.1	1.3	1.1	1.1	1.2	1.2	1.6
France	7.4	6.6	6.2	7.6	9.0	11.9	13.0	14.1	17.1
Germany	15.5	15.3	14.8	16.8	20.9	24.4	21.8	24.6	27.7
Greece	0.4	0.3	0.3	0.2	0.1	0.1	0.2	0.3	0.3
Ireland	2.0	2.5	2.8	3.7	4.3	5.4	5.9	5.5	6.8
Italy	4.3	4.5	4.6	5.9	7.4	9.3	9.5	10.3	13.0
Luxembourg	1.1	1.2	0.4	0.7	0.8	0.7	0.8	1.1	1.1
Netherlands	6.8	6.6	6.2	7.1	11.6	14.8	16.1	18.1	22.8
Portugal	0.3	0.2	0.2	0.2	0.3	0.5	0.5	0.5	0.6
Spain	2.3	2.3	2.2	2.3	2.7	4.1	5.0	6.1	7.5
United Kingdom	27.5	27.6	28.6	33.0	35.4	44.5	49.5	59.8	65.0
Other Europe	18.1	19.4	20.0	21.4	22.1	26.4	26.0	25.7	31.3
Austria	0.6	0.5	0.5	0.5	0.7	0.7	0.7	0.6	0.8
Finland	0.2	0.2	0.2	0.3	0.3	0.4	0.4	0.5	0.5
Norway	2.7	3.1	2.8	3.2	3.2	3.8	4.4	3.5	3.6
Sweden	1.1	0.9	0.9	1.0	1.0	1.1	1.1	1.1	1.5
Switzerland	12.9	14.1	14.9	15.8	16.4	19.7	18.7	19.2	23.7
Turkey	0.1	0.1	0.2	0.2	0.2	0.2	0.2	0.3	0.5
Other	0.5	0.5	0.5	0.4	0.3	0.5	0.5	0.4	0.6
Latin America	28.2	24.1	24.6	28.3	36.9	47.6	51.0	62.7	72.5
Africa	6.5	6.1	5.9	5.9	5.5	5.9	5.5	4.8	4.7
Middle East	3.6	4.5	5.0	4.6	4.9	4.1	3.8	4.2	4.8
Asia and Pacific	28.2	30.3	32.3	34.0	36.7	44.8	50.4	54.1	63.3

Source: U.S. Department of Commerce. Bureau of Economic Analysis. *Survey of Current Business*, various issues. U.S. Direct Investment Abroad: Country and Industry Detail for Position and Balance of Payments Flows.

APPENDIX B. Selected U.S. Direct Investments in Europe

(in millions of U.S. dollars)

US Firm Name	Foreign Acquisition	Loc	City	Amount	Type	Year
Philip Morris Co. Inc.	Jacobs Suchard Ltd.	SZ	Zurich	$3,800.00	AQ	1990
Ford Motor Co.	Jaguar PLC	UK	Allesley, Coventry	$2,640.00	AQ	1990
PepsiCo Inc.	BSN SA	FR	Paris	$1,350.00	AQ	1989
Newgateway PLC	Gateway Corp. PLC	UK	Milton Keynes	$1,100.00	EI	1989
Atlantic Richfield Co.	Britoil PLC	UK	Glasgow, Lanarkshir	$696.80	EP	1987
Whirlpool Corp.	Whirlpool International BV	NE	Eindhoven	$610.56	AQ	1991
Sara Lee Corp.	AKZO NV	NE	Arnhem	$600.00	AQ	1987
Sun Co. Inc.	Atlantic Petroleum Maatschappi	NE		$513.00	AQ	1988
Emerson Electric Co.	Leroy-Somer	FR	Angouleme	$460.00	AQ	1990
Goldman, Sachs & Co.	Wolters Kluwer NV	NE	Amsterdam	$444.20	EP	1990
E.I. du Pont de Nemours & Co.	Vickers PLC	UK	London	$400.00	AQ	1989
Procter & Gamble Co.	Blendax-Group	WG	Mainz	$400.00	AQ	1987
Du Pont & Fujifilm Electronic	Crosfield Electronics Ltd.	UK	Hempstead	$377.00	AQ	1989
General Electric Co.	Burton Group Financial Service	UK	London	$329.00	AQ	1990
Coca-Cola Co.	Societe Parisienne de Boissons	FR	Paris	$312.40	AQ	1989
International Paper Co.	Aussedat-Rey SA	FR	Yvelines	$297.40	AQ	1989
American Brands Inc.	Whyte & Mackay Distillers Ltd	SC	Glasgow	$273.76	AQ	1990
James River Corp. of Virginia	Kaysersberg SA	FR	Paris	$263.00	EP	1987
PepsiCo Inc.	Seven-Up International	SZ	Lausanne	$246.00	AQ	1986
Ecolab Inc.	Henkel KGaA	WG	Dusseldorf	$240.22	AQ	1991
American Express Co.	Signet Ltd.	UK	Basildon	$235.00	AQ	1991
Southeastern Asset Management	Saatchi & Saatchi PLC	UK	London	$226.90	EP	1989
Cannon Group Inc.	Screen Entertainment Ltd.	UK		$226.00	AQ	1986
International Paper Co.	Cookson Graphic Arts	UK		$215.00	AQ	1990
ICN Pharmaceuticals Inc.	F. Hoffman-LaRoche & Co. AG	SZ	Basel	$211.00	EP	1987
Private investor(s)	F. Hoffman-LaRoche & Co. Ltd.	SZ	Basel	$209.00	EP	1988
Arvin Industries Inc.	TI Silencers	UK	Lancaster	$204.00	AQ	1988
Arrow Electronics Inc.	Lex Service PLC	UK	London	$198.25	AQ	1991
Sara Lee Corp	Van Nelle Holding NV	NE	Rotterdam	$185.40	AQ	1989
Old Bond Street Corp.	SmithKline Beecham PLC	UK	Brentford	$182.00	AQ	1990
Ralston Purina Co.	COFINEA	FR		$169.00	AQ	1989
Nalco Chemical Co.	Imperial Chemical Industries	UK	London	$168.00	AQ	1991
Newmont Mining Corp.	Aminoil (Netherlands) Petroleum	NE		$165.00	AQ	1985

Boise Cascade Corp.	Hanson Trust PLC	UK	London	$150.00	AQ	1986
Rockwell International Corp.	Baker Perkins	UK	Peterborough	$143.90	AQ	1989
Scott Paper Co.	Feldmuehle AG	WG	Fritz-Vomfielde-Plat	$130.00	EP	1990
American Brands Inc.	NSS Newsagents PLC	UK	Woking	$120.00	AQ	1986
Tandy Corp.	Datatronic AB	SW	Stockholm	$119.40	AQ	1989
E.I. du Pont de Nemours & Co.	Tenneco Oil Norway A/S	NO	Sandnes	$115.00	AQ	1988
Owens-Corning Fiberglass Corp.	Pilkington Brothers PLC	UK	St. Helens	$114.00	AQ	1986
Investco	Waterford Wedgewood PLC	IR	Kilbarry, Waterford	$112.50	EP	1990
John Head & Partners LP	Anglo American Insurance Co.	UK	London	$110.00	AQ	1990
NYNEX Corp.	Business Intelligence Services	UK	London	$109.00	AQ	1987
State Farm Mutual Auto. Ins.	Blue Arrow PLC	UK	London	$104.06	EP	1990
Multiple acquirers	American Multi-Cinema Inc.	UK		$98.00	AQ	1988
Bausch & Lomb Inc.	Dr. Gerhard Mann chem-pharm	WG		$97.00	AQ	1986
Banner Industries Inc.	Avdel PLC	UK	Welny Garden City	$95.50	AQ	1989
Schlumberger Ltd.	Thorn EMI PLC	UK	London	$94.80	AQ	1989
Maralou Netherlands Partnership	CLAM Petroleum Co.	NE		$90.00	EP	1985
Delta Air Lines Inc.	Swiss Air Transport Co. Ltd.	SZ	Zurich	$90.00	EP	1989
Management Co. Entertainment	Virgin Vision Ltd.	UK	London	$85.00	AQ	1989
Philip Morris Co. Inc.	Pietro Negroni SpA	IT	Cremona	$80.52	EI	1990
James River Corp.	Celtona BV	NE	Katwyk Nb	$77.00	AQ	1989
Metropolitan Life Insurance Co	Albany Life Assurance Co.	UK	London	$75.00	AQ	1985
Chicago Pacific Corp.	Rowenta-Werke GmbH	WG	Offenbach	$75.00	AQ	1986
Private investor(s)	Storehouse PLC	UK	London	$74.00	EP	1988
IVAX Corp.	Harris Pharmaceuticals Ltd.	UK	Edmonton	$73.43	AQ	1990
Allied-Signal Inc.	Valeo SA	FR	Paris	$71.96	AQ	1990
UNUM Corp.	National Employers Life Assur.	UK	Docking, Surrey	$70.80	AQ	1990
Harris Associates LP	Blue Arrow PLC	UK	London	$70.40	EP	1989
Newport Corp.	Micro-Controle SA	FR	Evry	$70.00	AQ	1991
Cooper Industries Inc.	Dubilier International PLC	UK	Abingdon	$69.40	AQ	1988
Kaneb Services Inc.	Furmanite PLC	UK	Kendal	$66.00	AQ	1991
Aetna Life & Casualty Co.	Montagu Investment Management	UK		$64.00	AQ	1985
Borden Inc.	Sooner Snacks Ltd.	UK	Scunthorpe	$64.00	AQ	1988
Viacom Inc.	MTV Europe	UK	London	$62.27	AQ	1991
ICN Pharmaceuticals Inc.	Galenika RO	YU	Belgrade	$62.00	AQ	1991
E.I. du Pont de Nemours & Co.	Triton Europe PLC	UK	London	$61.00	AQ	1990
C.R. Bard Inc.	Radi Medical Systems AB	SW	Uppsala	$60.00	AQ	1989
ITT Corp.	BICC PLC	UK	London	$60.00	AQ	1988
Scott Paper Co.	Bowater-Scott Corp. Ltd.	UK	East Grinstead	$60.00	EI	1986
Sara Lee Corp.	Compack Trading & Packing Co.	HU	Budapest	$60.00	EP	1991
Federal Paper Board Co.	Thomas Tait & Sons Ltd.	SC	Inverurie	$60.00	AQ	1989

APPENDIX B. Selected U.S. Direct Investments in Europe—Continued

(in millions of U.S. dollars)

US Firm Name	Foreign Acquisition	Loc	City	Amount	Type	Year
General Electric Co.	Thorn EMI PLC	UK	London	$57.00	EP	1991
Baroid Corp.	Diamant Boart Stratabit SA	BE	Bruxelles	$56.00	AQ	1991
Borden Inc.	Borges GmbH	WG	Osnabruck	$55.00	AQ	1987
Teleflex Inc.	Willy Rusch AG	WG	Stuttgart	$54.00	AQ	1989
Corporate Partners LP	Albert Fisher Group PLC	UK	Windsor, Berkshire	$52.44	EP	1990
Sara Lee Corp.	DIM SA	FR	Paris	$51.00	EP	1987
American International Group	Kleinwort Benson Lonsdale PLC	UK	London	$50.90	EP	1988
Thermo Electron Corp.	E. & M. Lamort SA	FR	Vitry	$50.60	AQ	1990

Note: Data represent publicly announced transactions where the values of the transactions were indicated. For transaction type, AQ indicates acquisition; EI represents equity increase; EP represents equity participation.

Source: Data compiled by CRS from *Mergers & Acquisitions*, various issues.

EC-92: STANDARDS AND CONFORMITY ASSESSMENT

By Lennard G. Kruger *

CONTENTS

SUMMARY

Standards serve to facilitate international trade and commerce by assuring product compatibility and maintaining an agreed upon level of product quality and safety. However, incompatible standards and the way a country certifies that a product complies with a standard can often create barriers to international trade. Testing and certification are perhaps the most prevalent means of using standards as a trade barrier. In recent years, the great majority of standards-related comments received by the United States Government from American exporters have concerned the nonacceptance by foreign governments of test data generated in the United States and the burdensome and time-consuming approval and certification procedures that are required for product acceptance in foreign markets. [1]

The European Community (EC) is composed of twelve member nations, each with its own set of laws, regulations, standards, and conformity assessment procedures which govern the trade of goods and services. In preparation for economic integration, the EC is accelerating and streamlining its ongoing effort to harmonize differing national standards, as well as testing and certification procedures, into a single EC-wide body of uniform standards and regulations. Products that are not regulated by EC member governments

* Lennard G. Kruger is a Specialist in Science and Technology, Science Policy Research Division, Congressional Research Service.

[1] U.S. Departments of Agriculture, State, and Commerce and the U.S. Trade Representative. *Second Triennial Report to the U.S. Congress on the Agreement on Technical Barriers to Trade.* Washington, U.S. Govt. Print. Off., 1986. p. 16.

for health, safety, or environmental reasons will be granted legal access to the entire EC market. Standards-related trade problems will be a matter for the private sector to resolve.

For products that are regulated by European governments, the EC has embarked on a three step process to counteract standards-related trade barriers. First, the EC has issued product directives that lay out essential health and safety requirements which each regulated product sold in EC markets must meet. Second, the EC has charged European voluntary standards organizations with the task of developing standards that manufacturers can use to meet those essential requirements. And third, EC product directives will specify a set of testing and certification procedures that manufacturers can follow in order to certify that their products conform to the EC's essential requirements.

While many analysts view a unified European marketplace as largely beneficial to U.S. exporters, concerns have been raised that standards and conformity assessment procedures formulated by the EC could, in some instances, constitute non-tariff barriers to trade. Some U.S. manufacturers worry that they will be compelled to subject their products to costly and duplicative conformity assessment procedures carried out by European authorities. Similarly, American conformity assessment bodies (such as testing laboratories and quality assessors) are concerned that U.S. exporters will bypass their services for their European competitors. Controversy has focused on whether U.S. conformity assessment bodies will be officially sanctioned and recognized by the EC to perform tests and issue certificates needed by regulated products to gain access to the EC market.

The United States and the EC disagree on various options for allaying the concerns of some U.S. exporters, standards organizations, and conformity assessment bodies. Subcontracting, mutual recognition agreements, and the extent to which the EC will allow manufacturer self-certification are a few of the options that continue to be debated by Congress, the Administration, and the private sector.

This paper will focus on standards and conformity assessment activities in the EC, the potential impacts these activities might have on U.S. firms, and what roles might be played by government and the private sector in order to deal effectively with evolving EC standards and conformity assessment procedures.

DEFINITIONS—STANDARDS AND CONFORMITY ASSESSMENT

There is no commonly accepted definition of a *standard.* In the broadest possible sense, standards can be seen as "a category of documents whose function is to control some aspect of human endeavor." [2] More specifically, the American National Standards Institute (ANSI) defines standards as "formal agreements that define the contractual, functional, and technical requirements necessary to ensure that a product, service, process, or system does what it is supposed to do." [3]

---

[2] Sullivan, Charles D. *Standards and Standardization.* New York, Marcel Dekker, 1983. p. 2.

[3] Global Connections: The Quest for Worldwide Standardization. *Fortune,* November 4, 1991. p. 186.

Technical standards, whether adopted voluntarily by industry or mandated by government regulation, are used to specify the characteristics of a wide variety of industrial and agricultural goods and services, ranging from paints to pressure vessels, vegetable oils to electrical outlets. Standardization offers many acknowledged benefits, including: an assurance that different parts and components will be compatible within a "system," a uniform level of product quality and safety, a means for implementing new technology, and many others.

Conformity assessment is the process whereby a government or private sector authority determines if a product meets a prescribed standard. The goal in this process is certification, which is defined as "the act of issuing a warranty, certificate, or mark or other appropriate evidence that attests that a product or service conforms to specific standards or specifications." [4] It is up to the authority granting the certification to prescribe what procedures should be used for a given product or service to receive a certification mark. According to the General Accounting Office (GAO), the EC and the United States "use two types of certification—self-certification, whereby the manufacturer uses his mark, symbol, or statement to tell the consumer that the product meets a specific standard, and third-party certification, which is normally performed by an outside organization that owns and controls a certification mark." [5]

Depending on the product, there are a variety of procedures and combinations of procedures that might be followed in order for a product to receive a certification mark. For example, manufacturers may be allowed to perform product testing in-house, or they may be required to have products tested by an outside laboratory that is accredited by an approved laboratory accreditation organization. If the manufacturer is permitted to self-certify, it may also be required that the manufacturer have a quality assurance program in place. Furthermore it may be necessary that a company's quality assurance program be registered and inspected by an accredited independent third party organization known as quality system registration body. The array of procedures which might be used to receive a certification mark can be grouped under the general term *conformity assessment,* which can be defined as any procedure used, directly or indirectly, to determine that relevant requirements in technical regulations or standards are fulfilled. Conformity assessment procedures can include sampling, testing and inspection; evaluation, verification and assurance of conformity; and registration, accreditation and approval, as well as their combinations. The combinations which may be required depend on the product being certified—generally the more the product relates to health, safety, or environmental considerations, the more stringent the requirements that must be met in order to receive certification.

---

[4] Unpublished document. American National Standards Institute.

[5] U.S. General Accounting Office. *European Single Market: Issues of Concern to U.S. Exporters.* Report to the Chairman, Subcommittee on International Trade, Committee on Finance, U.S. Senate. GAO/NSIAD-90-60. Washington, February 13, 1990. p. 15.

The New Approach: Standards and EC–92

Incompatible product standards among European nations has made trade needlessly difficult. For example, in the EC alone, there are 29 different types of electrical outlets, 10 kinds of plugs, 12 kinds of cords, 3 kinds of television sets, and 15 types of cake mixers. [6] Thus, companies seeking to sell their products in the European market must often make costly modifications to products in order to meet country-specific requirements, and there can be lengthy delays in sales due to the need to get products repeatedly tested and certified.

For 25 years, the EC Commission recognized this problem and attempted to "harmonize" the different national standards into a unanimously agreed upon set of European-wide norms. Because progress was extremely slow, the EC has opted for a new approach. In 1985, the EC Commission published a White Paper entitled *Completing the Internal Market* that set out a plan to unify the European marketplace by 1992. One of the major goals of the White Paper is the removal of barriers to trade caused by incompatible or differing product standards and testing and certification procedures among EC nations. A cornerstone of this new approach is *mutual recognition* which holds that any product legally manufactured and marketed in one member state must, in principle, be admitted to the markets of all other members.

Standardization activities initiated by the EC will involve not only the European Community, but also the nations of the European Free Trade Association (EFTA), which include Austria, Finland, Iceland, Norway, Sweden, Switzerland, and Liechtenstein. Additionally three Eastern European countries (Hungary, Czechoslovakia, and Poland) plan to form a coalition (affiliated with the EC) for the purpose of achieving economic cooperation, including free trade of industrial products. As a result, there will be a total of 22 countries—12 EC countries, seven EFTA countries and three Eastern European countries—in which products will be sold under a common standardization regime.

Products which are *not* regulated by EC member governments for health, safety or environmental reasons will be granted legal access to the entire EC market. However, for products that are regulated by each member state for health, safety, or environmental reasons, the EC Commission has issued a series of directives which lay out essential requirements that must be met by regulated products. EC member governments are expected to adopt these directives, and their accompanying essential requirements, into their own national legislation. Meanwhile, private sector European standardization groups, such as the European Committee for Standardization (CEN) and the European Committee for Electrotechnical Standardization (CENELEC), are developing standards which manufacturers *can elect* to use in order to manufacture their product to the essential requirements. According to EC officials, international standards, where they exist, will be adopted as the

[6] Uncommon Market: Philips Finds Obstacles to Intra-Europe Trade are Costly, Inefficient. *Wall Street Journal*, August 7, 1985. Cited in: Chambord, Antoine B. European Standardization. *ASTM Standardization News*, December 1986. p. 44.

standard of first choice. In areas where international standards do not exist, existing European standards will be harmonized, or new standards will be written. A special effort is being made to quickly develop a body of technical European standards for high-technology goods such as advanced composite materials and telecommunications equipment.

Standards developed by CEN and CENELEC will be voluntary. The EC Green Paper on European standardization explains that: "Community legislation must be limited to laying down essential requirements for safety, health, and so on. It is up to producers to choose by what means they wish to comply with these requirements." [7] However, while the use of European standards is not mandatory (meeting the essential requirements is mandatory), EC officials have indicated that a product meeting EC standards will probably be approved on a "fast track," thereby gaining quicker and/or easier access to the EC market.

Since 1985, CEN and CENELEC have developed about 1100 standards. However, it has been estimated that 1000 or more additional standards are needed, and the EC Commission is concerned that a large number of standards will not be ready by 1993. [8] Slow progress in standards development creates uncertainty and confusion for manufacturers, who need to know what standards their products may meet in order to most easily satisfy the EC's essential requirements.

Over 200 EC directives have already been issued which seek to harmonize differing national standards among member nations. However, the implementation of a directive does not necessarily mean that it will be enforced right away. For some product directives there will be a transition period between the date of implementation and the date of total enforcement. For example the directive on electromagnetic compatibility, while formally implemented on January 1, 1992, will not be enforced until December 31, 1995 because the legislatures of the individual member nations have been slow in adopting the directive, and because the necessary standards are not yet developed. Table 1 lists implementation and transition dates of the major EC regulated product safety directives.

EC Procedures for Conformity Assessment

The European Community is currently in the process of developing a testing and certification system that is intended to remove trade barriers within the planned internal market of 1992. The philosophical guidelines for this new system are set forth in the "Global Approach," a proposal submitted to the Council of Ministers by the EC Commission. The Global Approach relies on two key principles: *mutual recognition*, which means that countries will recognize each other's ability to test and certify that a product meets a standard; and *reciprocity*, which means that countries have equivalent access to each other's testing and certification systems.

---

[7] Commission of the European Communities. *Commission Green Paper on the Development of European Standardization: Action for Faster Technological Integration in Europe*. Brussels, October 8, 1990. p. 2.

[8] A Survey of Business in Europe. *The Economist*, June 8, 1991. p. 54.

TABLE 1. EC Product Safety Directives—Dates of Implementation and Transition

Product	Implementation Date	Transition
toys	1/1/90	—
simple pressure vessels	7/1/90	7/1/92
construction products	7/27/91	INDEFINITE
electromagnetic compatibility	1/1/92	12/31/95
machinery	12/31/92	12/31/94 (nonmobile) 12/31/96 (mobile)
personal protective equipment	7/1/92	—
gas appliances	1/1/92	12/31/95
weighing machines	1/1/93	TEN YEARS
medical devices	7/1/94	6/30/97
active implantable medical devices	1/1/93	12/31/94
telecommunications terminal equipment (mandatory standards).	1/1/93	—
low voltage (no uniform mark)	8/19/74	—
furniture flammability	DRAFT	
measuring and testing instruments	DRAFT	
used machinery	12/31/92	12/31/95
recreational craft	DRAFT	
cable ways	12/31/93	—
lifting appliances	12/31/93	12/31/96
equipment for use in explosive atmospheres	DRAFT	
amusement park and playground equipment	DRAFT	

Source: U.S. Department of Commerce

In order for a regulated product (e.g. toys, medical devices, telecommunications equipment) to gain legal access to the European market, it must bear a "CE" mark of certification. [9] A CE mark signifies that the product meets the essential health, safety or environmental requirements set forth in the EC directives that apply to that product. According to the Global Approach, there are a variety of ways, depending on the product, that conformance to essential requirements can be demonstrated in order to receive the CE mark. [10] For some products (like toys, for example), a manufacturer can "self-certify" meaning that the manufacturer can attach a document of conformity to the product and affix the CE mark itself. In other directives (such as medical devices) the manufacturer must submit products to a testing laboratory officially recognized by the EC (a "notified body") for proof of conformity.

For many of the products regulated by the EC, it will be necessary for producers to implement a quality assurance (QA) system [11] in their manufacturing operation. In many cases, QA systems must

---

[9] For unregulated products, the EC has established the European Organization for Testing and Certification (EOTC) which will provide a framework to help the private sector harmonize conformity assessment procedures used for products and services not addressed by EC legislative requirements. The majority of products traded in the EC are unregulated.

[10] Procedures for conformity assessment are spelled out in eight "modules" which describe various options a manufacturer might use to obtain a CE mark on its product. Available modules for a given product will be cited in the harmonization directive for that product.

[11] QA systems in Europe will be required to meet the ISO 9000 standard. Published in 1987, ISO 9000 is a set of quality system standards and guidelines that manufacturers can follow to ensure uniformity and a consistent level of quality in manufacturing operations. See: Gosch, John. The Key to Europe '92. *Electronics*, May 1991. p. 43–47.

be audited, approved, and registered with an EC-recognized notified body. Table 2 shows the certification options available for each product directive.

According to the Global Approach, products originating outside the EC (such as the United States) will be granted access to certification systems on an equal basis with products originating within the EC. For products requiring certification conferred by a third party, the EC has stated that only laboratories and assessment bodies located in the EC will be *initially* designated as "notified bodies." However, the EC has stated that conformity assessment bodies outside the EC may eventually be granted notified body status for a given product sector pending mutual recognition agreements (MRAs) in that sector. The view of the EC is that an MRA between the EC and a non-EC entity should guarantee that both parties obtain "broadly equivalent opportunities to participate in each other's certification systems for the products concerned and thus similar opportunities for improved access to each other's markets." [12]

Notified bodies, though presently limited to EC member nations, are permitted to subcontract certain conformity assessment functions to bodies outside the EC. The scope of subcontracting remains undefined. The EC Council of Ministers will allow subcontracting for strictly technical activities such as laboratory testing. However, the more evaluative activities, such as granting certifications or auditing quality systems, as yet, must be performed by notified bodies within the EC.

TABLE 2. EC Regulated Products: Certification Options

Product Type	Certification Options
toys	manufacturer self-declaration
construction products	at a minimum, manufacturer registration of production quality assurance system
simple pressure vessels	EC type examination
large pressure vessels	EC type examination and quality assurance
electromagnetic compatibility	manufacturer self-declaration
machinery	manufacturer self-declaration
personal protective equipment	EC type examination, with quality control system registration for higher risk equipment
gas appliances	EC type examination and either quality assurance system registration or on-site checks
non-automatic weighing instruments	EC type examination and quality assurance registration or EC verification
medical devices	various options depending on risk level, ranging up to full quality assurance or EC type examination and product quality assurance
telecommunications terminal equipment	EC type examination or declaration of conformity with full quality assurance

Source: Department of Commerce.

[12] Ludolph, Charles. *The European Community Program for Conformity Assessment.* Presentation given January 31, 1991 at the ASME/NIST Workshop on Pressure Vessels. In: U.S. Department of Commerce. National Institute of Standards and Technology. *Conformity Assessment Workshop on Pressure Vessels.* NISTIR 4542. April 1991. p. 44.

IMPACT OF EC STANDARDIZATION ON THE U.S.

It is difficult, if not impossible, to generalize on the possible impacts of EC standards activities on U.S. companies. There are hundreds of different types of products traded internationally and each product and industrial sector has a unique set of variables affecting its performance. On balance, however, many analysts believe that EC standardization will be beneficial for U.S. businesses. In its report, *European Single Market: Issues of Concern to U.S. Exporters*, GAO concludes:

> Under EC 1992, a U.S. exporter will have to meet only one standard and have its product tested in one EC member state to sell throughout the EC. Therefore, U.S. exporters will probably not be any worse off than they are under the current system and could be much better off. [13]

In a similar vein, the International Trade Commission (ITC) reports that "the adoption of common standards by the EC is widely seen by U.S. industry as a major benefit." [14] According to the ITC, the EC–92 program will enable some exporters to "reduce design, engineering, marketing, transportation, and compliance costs currently incurred in producing for export to the various EC national markets. Completing one conformity assessment procedure will also guarantee their products free access to the entire EC market." [15]

Concerns have been raised, however, that for some exporters, the EC standards program may increase costs of exporting, thereby making it more difficult for these companies to compete in the European market. Specifically, concerns have centered on 1) standards development activities by CEN and CENELEC; and 2) conformity assessment rules and procedures being developed by the EC Commission.

STANDARDS DEVELOPMENT

As new standards are written and adopted by CEN and CENELEC, many worry that incompatible European product specifications will force U.S. exporters to make costly modifications to their products. In general, it is in the interest of American companies for European standards to conform as closely as possible to American standards. The issue has arisen—how much influence will U.S. manufacturers be able to exert within the CEN/CENELEC standards writing committees? When CEN/CENELEC began its EC–92 standards development activities in 1985, committee meetings were strictly limited to EC members, and U.S. companies without European subsidiaries or affiliates were allowed very limited access to the standards development process. Due partly to intensive lobbying by U.S. industry and the U.S. Government, the EC has allowed greater access to its standards development process. CEN/CENE-

---

[13] U.S. General Accounting Office. *European Single Market: Issues of Concern to U.S. Exporters*. p. 27.

[14] U.S. International Trade Commission. *The Effects of Greater Economic Integration Within the European Community on the United States: First Followup Report*. Investigation No. 332–267. USITC Publication 2268. March 1990. p. 6–44.

[15] Ibid., p. 6–45.

LEC committees now allow participation by representatives from international standards organizations. Additionally, mechanisms have been set up whereby U.S. parties receive early notification of new EC standards work, and may submit written comments to European standards writing committees. A Federal advisory committee on the EC common approach to standards, testing and certification has found that:

> These efforts have improved the means for U.S. input into the content of new EC standards, and a number of U.S. industries have already succeeded in achieving meaningful results in terms of having EC standards be consistent with their products. Not all U.S. industries have, however, been equally successful in achieving this desired goal. [16]

CONFORMITY ASSESSMENT

Because the EC's Global Approach for conformity assessment is still an evolving concept and not yet a practice, its effect on U.S. exporters is unclear. For some, the effect of the Global Approach could vary depending on what kinds of products they export. For nonregulated products, testing and certification will be a matter between the buyer and the seller. For regulated products which require only the manufacturer's self-certification (such as toys), U.S. exporters who self-certify that their products meet EC standards will not be subject to third party approval and will enjoy the same access to European markets as their EC competitors. [17] The United States (both the private sector and the Federal government) continues to urge the EC to accept manufacturer's self declaration of conformity whenever possible.

For products which do require submission to an EC notified body, U.S. exporters may be required to get their products tested in European laboratories. Some European countries already require testing in their own labs. Thus, the Global Approach would be a relative advantage to exporters doing business in these countries, because certification via a notified laboratory in any EC member country guarantees access to the entire EC. On the other hand, for exporters dealing with EC nations which may currently require no certification for a given product, or which may currently recognize U.S. certification via bilateral agreements, the Global Approach could be a relative disadvantage.

While an American exporter should be able to obtain a CE Mark for its product by following the procedures available to European manufacturers, these procedures, though equally applied, may be less costly for EC-based manufacturers to follow than their American counterparts. Concerns have been raised that some U.S. exporters may be at a disadvantage if the EC does not confer notified body status to U.S.-based conformity assessment bodies (i.e. testing, certification, quality assessment, and accreditation organizations).

---

[16] *Report to the Secretary of Commerce of the Federal Advisory Committee on the EC Common Approach to Standards, Testing and Certification in 1992.* G. Lee Thompson, Chairman. May 1991. p. 2.

[17] However, if the product is not manufactured to meet EC standards, the product will be subject to testing by an EC notified body to determine whether it meets the essential requirements necessary to receive the CE mark.

The ITC, in its series of reports, *The Effects of Greater Economic Integration Within the European Community on the United States*, has cited private sector concerns over the EC's Global Approach. For example, the ITC noted that medium- and small-sized firms that produce heavy machinery worry about the effect third-party inspections required by the EC's machinery safety directive might have on their export costs, arguing that "it would be excessively costly and physically impossible to ship large, heavy equipment (machine tools or industrial forklift trucks) to designated testing and certification laboratories in the EC unless these facilities were equipped with special hoists and heavy duty foundations on which to place this equipment. To alleviate these potential problems, all U.S. exporters of machinery indicated that in order to maintain current U.S. export levels it would be necessary for the EC to allow U.S. laboratories to certify their products." [18] The ITC found similar concerns echoed in other industries, such as medical devices, pulp and paper, and forest products. [19]

Testing laboratories in the United States, particularly the smaller independent laboratories, have also expressed concern over the potential negative effects the EC's global approach could have on their business. They worry that U.S. exporters will be inclined to bypass domestic testing services and instead have their products tested in EC-approved European laboratories. While the EC has stated that it will eventually recognize notified bodies outside the EC (after negotiation to assure that these bodies meet EC criteria), representatives of the U.S. small laboratory industry worry that by the time they get recognition as notified bodies, domestic manufacturers will have already initiated business relationships with European laboratories.

Subcontracting is another possible way in which U.S. laboratories may be able to test regulated products bound for European markets. However, the ITC notes that:

> Smaller U.S. testing labs [have] charged that subcontracting arrangements were not likely to be widespread and were thus no substitute for the formal designation of U.S.-based labs as notified bodies. In particular, since European-owned labs were generally free to become accredited by U.S. regulatory agencies and since a number of prospective notified bodies have set up affiliated labs in the United States, there was little incentive for such bodies to extend subcontracting relationships to nonaffiliated U.S. based labs. [20]

Quality assurance systems and the means by which manufacturers must register or obtain approval for their QA systems could also have an impact on exporters. For many regulated products, one of the principal routes to obtaining the CE mark is for a manu-

---

[18] U.S. International Trade Commission. *The Effects of Greater Economic Integration Within the European Community on the United States: Second Followup Report.* Investigation No. 332-267. USITC Publication 2318. September 1990. p. 4-65.

[19] U.S. International Trade Commission. *The Effects of Greater Economic Integration Within the European Community on the United States: First Followup Report.* p. 6-64, 6-83, 6-103.

[20] U.S. International Trade Commission. *The Effects of Greater Economic Integration Within the European Community on the United States: Second Followup Report.* p. 4-23.

facturer to register its quality system to the ISO 9000 standard. According to machinery exporters interviewed by the ITC, if ISO 9000 is implemented it "may require third-party assessment of each firm's quality control procedures. Conformity to this distinctive standard will require that a team of assessors visit a production facility to verify production processes and product design and to ensure that an updated quality control manual be maintained at each individual production facility." [21]

A key issue for U.S. exporters as well as conformity assessment bodies is: who will be authorized by the EC to register QA systems of U.S. manufacturers? Currently, the EC has stated that only European bodies, officially notified by the EC, would be able to perform this function. In the future, however, it is conceivable that U.S. bodies could register QA systems, (at manufacturing plants producing regulated products bound for EC markets) if they receive notified body status through a mutual recognition agreement (MRA) between the United States and the EC, or if quality registration functions are eventually subcontracted to a U.S. entity or entities. Both of these possibilities are a continuing subject of speculation and negotiation.

MUTUAL RECOGNITION AGREEMENTS

A mutual recognition agreement would ensure that both parties accept and recognize each other's conformity assessment work. In theory, the principle of mutual recognition seems simple: the EC recognizes U.S. certification marks, while the United States recognizes EC certifications. In practice, however, MRA's are enormously complicated and controversial. Several major issues have been raised in association with MRAs.

First, the United States and the EC disagree on the conditions under which an MRA might be agreed upon. The EC insists upon "reciprocity," meaning that it should be as easy for an EC manufacturer to access the U.S. market as it is for a U.S. manufacturer to access the EC market. The United States, on the other hand, argues for "national treatment" which means that EC manufacturers would have the same access to U.S. markets as U.S. manufacturers. In other words, EC manufacturers would be required to meet the same Federal, State, or local criteria as U.S. manufacturers must meet to gain access to a U.S. market. This fundamental difference in approach (reciprocity vs. national treatment) reflects key differences in the regulatory structures of the United States and the EC. In the EC, a centralized entity (the EC Commission) is creating a system whereby regulated products will be certified and approved. In the United States, on the other hand, the Federal government, States, localities, and the private sector authorize their own certification and approval criteria. In order to reach MRA's based on the principle of reciprocity, it would be necessary, for example, for the Federal government to guarantee EC access to a State or municipal certification system. This is seen by many as untenable.

---

[21] Ibid., p. 4–66.

Second, the EC has insisted that other countries seeking MRAs must be able to guarantee that their conformity assessment bodies will maintain their ability to perform adequately. In the EC, the EC Commission, a governmental body, would act as guarantor. With respect to the United States, the EC asks: who would serve as the guarantor or accreditor of U.S. conformity assessment bodies?

Again, fundamental differences in the testing and certification systems between the EC and the United States can cause difficulties. In the EC, conformity assessment for regulated products is overseen by the EC Commission, and conformity assessment for unregulated products will be coordinated by the newly formed European Organization for Testing and Certification (EOTC). In the United States, no one organization or entity exists which oversees or accredits the hundreds of private and public conformity assessment programs nationwide.

If MRAs are pursued, they will be negotiated on a sector by sector basis. In regulated product sectors, where clear Federal authority exists, Federal agencies should be able to negotiate MRA's with the EC. For example, the Food and Drug Administration (FDA) currently has an agreement with the British Department of Health and Social Security for the mutual recognition of inspections of manufacturers of medical devices. FDA officials believe that similar agreements with the EC are a possibility, although much work remains before such an agreement could be negotiated. [22] However, for products which are regulated in the EC and not regulated in the United States (such as pressure vessels and construction products), negotiations between the EC and the United States could be more problematic. According to a Department of Commerce official:

> The U.S. Government has some serious concerns in the area of proposed mutual recognition agreements (MRA's) which would confer notified body status to parties in the U.S. Our concerns include such issues as who would be the responsible body in the U.S. to enter into MRA's (government or private sector bodies), whether or not the U.S. Government would be responsible for guaranteeing the performance of notified bodies, and ultimately whether MRA's are in the best interest of the U.S. [23]

The Federal Advisory Committee to the Department of Commerce also cautioned that mutual recognition agreements with the EC could bear costs and risks that may not ultimately be desirable. The committee stated that:

> ... it is premature to seek U.S.-EC mutual recognition agreements as a general policy at this juncture when the implications for product development, financial responsibilities and costs, and reciprocal obligations are unknown. ... In seeking mutual recognition agreements, U.S. policy

---

[22] Ibid., p. 4-64.

[23] Ludolph, Charles M. International Trade Administration. *The European Community Program for Conformity Assessment.* In: U.S. Department of Commerce. National Institute of Standards and Technology. *Conformity Assessment Workshop on Pressure Vessels.* NISTIR 4542. April 1991. p. 45.

> must be mindful of the need to prevent entry into the U.S. market of EC-certified products meeting substantially lower standards than those prevalent in the United States.[24]

Regardless of whether or not MRAs are in the best interest of the United States, no negotiations between the United States and the EC on MRAs can take place until the EC Council of Ministers approves formal negotiating mandates necessary to conclude agreements with third countries on the mutual recognition of test results. These EC negotiating mandates are expected sometime in 1992. In the meantime, as the Federal Advisory Committee notes:

> Until the EC notified body system is established, the initial preferred general response is to seek subcontractor status for U.S. testing and certification entities. The EC should be encouraged to establish a flexible policy for subcontracting and to rely on private sector agreements between test houses. The responsibilities and rights of U.S. subcontracting bodies should be as broad as possible, in keeping with the objective of minimizing product testing and certification costs by avoiding duplication in multiple locations.[25]

Public and Private Sector Activities

Both the Federal government and the private sector have sent a series of delegations to meet European officials in an effort to ensure that U.S. exporters will not be hurt by the evolving EC–92 standards and conformity assessment procedures. While the transparency of the EC standards-setting process remains a concern in some product sectors, most attention now centers on the conformity assessment area. The EC has expressed a preference for dealing with some sort of national testing, certification and accreditation system in the United States (whether public or private) that can guarantee that U.S. conformity assessment bodies meet EC criteria. While many feel that the United States should not mirror the highly centralized EC system, most parties in the United States recognize a need for a more coherent, less fragmented system for providing accreditation of conformity assessment bodies.

ACCREDITATION OF CONFORMITY ASSESSMENT BODIES

In the private sector, the American National Standards Institute (ANSI) has established an expanded program to accredit third party certification programs. ANSI has also established, in conjunction with the Registrar Accreditation Board (RAB),[26] an American National Accreditation Program for Registrars of Quality Systems. This program will accredit bodies that audit organizations for compliance with quality standards, particularly the ISO 9000 series of quality standards. The purpose of these programs is to ensure that

---

[24] *Report to the Secretary of Commerce of the Federal Advisory Committee on the EC Common Approach to Standards, Testing and Certification in 1992.* G. Lee Thompson, Chairman. May 1991. p. 18–19.

[25] Ibid., p. 18.

[26] RAB is an affiliate of the American Society of Quality Control (ASQC).

a domestic certification of a U.S. manufacturer's product or manufacturing process is ultimately recognized as sufficient in the EC market.

The Federal government is also considering steps to help U.S. conformity assessment bodies achieve recognition and legitimacy in the EC. On June 21, 1991, Secretary of Commerce Mosbacher and EC Commission Vice President Bangemann agreed to: (1) develop confidence-building systems in the field of conformity assessment, in particular accreditation, based on international standards and documents; and (2) consider the steps proposed by the Secretary of Commerce to strengthen the coherence of the U.S. system to provide an assurance that U.S. conformity assessment programs satisfy international guidelines. Currently, the National Institute of Standards and Technology is contemplating a program which could provide interested industrial sectors with an accreditation which would demonstrate the competence of their conformity assessment programs. Whether or not public and private initiatives in this area are complimentary, duplicative, or at cross-purposes is as yet unclear. Recent efforts to accredit conformity assessment bodies, both governmental and private sector, are either new, extremely small in scope, or not yet implemented. Their ultimate success is by no means assured, and Congress may wish to monitor their progress.

CONGRESSIONAL ACTIVITIES

In the area of EC–92 standardization, Congress continues to monitor potential impacts on U.S. exporters and on domestic standards, testing and certification organizations. The House Committees on Foreign Affairs, on Small Business, and on Science, Space and Technology have all held hearings specifically on the possible effects of EC–92 standards and conformity assessment programs. Legislative options in this area have been limited, largely because the EC–92 process is still evolving; because a wide diversity of industrial sectors are involved, each with different sets of concerns and needs; and because the respective governmental and private sector roles in dealing with these issues are not clearly defined.

However, a few legislative initiatives have been advanced. In the 101st Congress, a series of bills introduced by Rep. Gejdenson (H.R. 4471, H.R. 4472, H.R. 4463, H.R. 4474, and H.R. 4476) would have denied the current and ongoing certification of EC companies by five Federal agencies [27] unless the Secretary of Commerce certified that the EC "is setting product standards and requirements in an open and fair manner and has established equitable rules for testing and certifying products for compliance with product standards and requirements." None of these bills were enacted into law.

The 1990 Farm Bill (P.L. 101–624) expresses congressional displeasure with the EC standards process. In Title XV, Section 1555 of P.L. 101–624, Congress finds that the EC has "refused to guarantee that such United States exporters will be able to show compliance with European Community product standards and require-

[27] The five agencies were: the Federal Communications Commission, the Environmental Protection Agency, the Food and Drug Administration, the Department of Energy, and the Department of Labor.

ments by using United States laboratories or through self-certification." Congress also "denounces the European Community's nontransparent process of setting standards and requirements for agricultural commodities and products thereof, and the Congress further denounces the refusal by the European Community to guarantee that United States exporters of such commodities and products will be able to show compliance with European Community standards and requirements by using United States laboratories or through self-certification." The legislation "urges the President to use all available means to bring about significant and far-reaching changes in the standards and testing policies of the European Community in order to protect and maintain United States access to the European Community market for agricultural commodities and products thereof."

In the 102nd Congress, a provision exists in the American Technology Preeminence Act of 1991 (P.L. 102–245) that directs the Secretary of Commerce to contract the National Research Council (NRC) to conduct "a thorough review of international product testing and certification issues." The following issues will be addressed in the NRC study: (1) the impact on United States manufacturers, testing and certification laboratories, certification organizations, and other affected bodies of the European Community's plans for testing and certification of regulated and nonregulated products of non-European origin; (2) ways for United States manufacturers to gain acceptance of their products in the European Community and in other foreign countries and regions; (3) the feasibility and consequences of having mutual recognition agreements between testing and certification organizations in the United States and those of major trading partners on the accreditation of testing and certification laboratories and on quality control requirements; (4) information coordination regarding product acceptance and conformity assessment mechanisms between the United States and foreign governments; and (5) the appropriate Federal, State, and private roles in coordination and oversight of testing, certification, accreditation, and quality control to support national and international trade.

The study is due eighteen months after the Department of Commerce signs a contract with the NRC. Another study, requested by the House Committee on Science, Space and Technology and conducted by the Office of Technology Assessment (OTA), is examining the effectiveness of the U.S. standards system in helping U.S. business compete in foreign markets. The OTA study was released in March 1992.

GATT STANDARDS CODE NEGOTIATIONS

As part of the Uruguay round of multilateral trade negotiations, the U.S. government is participating in negotiations on possible revisions of the 1979 GATT standards code, which addresses technical barriers to trade. EC representatives are advocating the adoption of a "Code of Good Practice for Standardizing Bodies," which would obligate governments to monitor the performance of their national standards organizations. Industry groups in the United States strongly oppose the Code of Good Practice provision, stating that it would lead to government regulation of the existing U.S. voluntary standards system. ANSI is advocating the adoption of a voluntary code of good practice developed and administered by a non-governmental body—the International Organization for Standardization (ISO). Another issue in the GATT standards code negotiations is whether countries should be required to recognize conformity assessment procedures performed by other parties. The provisional text of the GATT standards code encourages, but does not require, this recognition.

CONCLUSIONS

On balance, it appears that efforts by the EC to reform its procedures for standardization and conformity assessment will be beneficial to American companies seeking to do business in the EC. However some industrial sectors and individual companies (particularly small- and mid-sized companies) are concerned that their ability to compete in EC markets may be adversely impacted in the future. Similarly, some standards and conformity assessment companies and organizations in the United States worry that they too may lose business to their European competitors. The nature of MRAs, the scope of subcontracting, the extent of manufacturer self-certification allowed, and the transparency of the EC standards development process are all issues under negotiation which could affect the impact of EC standardization and conformity assessment on the United States.

Congress continues to monitor standards and conformity assessment in the EC, and its possible effect on United States-EC trade. The question of how and whether Congress might address this issue is unclear, largely because the EC–92 process is still evolving; and because a wide diversity of companies and industrial sectors are involved, each with different sets of concerns and needs. While direct congressional influence over EC activities is limited, Congress can influence how the U.S. government responds to EC initiatives, while also scrutinizing the extent to which government and the private sector are effectively working together to ensure that U.S. businesses will flourish in an integrated European market. A more fundamental question which Congress may ultimately address is whether the long standing standards and conformity assessment system in the United States can continue to function adequately in a changing world.

EUROPEAN RESEARCH AND DEVELOPMENT

By Glenn J. McLoughlin *

CONTENTS

Summary

The EC–92 harmonization process brings into sharp focus how European integration is changing research and development (R&D) performed in Europe. It also has heightened interest in a wide range of European R&D efforts, some now several decades old. How do these programs function, what issues do they address, and what do they tell U.S. policymakers about our own R&D priorities and policies?

The first thing that strikes the interested observer of European R&D policies and programs is the wide range of programs across Europe (often called "pan-European") and particularly in the EC. In the United States we have some R&D programs which join Government and non-government interests, ranging from basic research to "pre-competitive" technology development. However, except for defense, the U.S. Government's role and interests usually end when it comes to applications of technology with a specific commercial purpose. In Europe, there are a greater number of Government-industry efforts, from basic research to commercial technology development, and increased interest in transnational levels of support.

Therefore, many of the current pan-European efforts to support R&D are worthy of attention. These efforts can be categorized on three levels: Pan-European R&D, actions arising from the 1992 harmonization process, and the Framework R&D Programmes. The

* Specialist in Science and Technology Policy, Science Policy Research Division, Congressional Research Service.

pan-European R&D programs represent a wide range of R&D efforts, many of which were in existence before the SEA. These pan-European R&D efforts set a precedent for cooperation of nations, industries and research facilities across Europe, particularly in basic research. Second, the EC–92 process itself, in an attempt to harmonize internal and external policies, will have a significant impact on "rules of origin" and the location of R&D facilities, potential non-tariff barriers such as mechanical and electrical standards, and the "flow" of scientists, engineers and technicians across European borders. Third, the EC Framework Programmes—arising out of the SEA mandate for the EC to establish a "framework" for science and technology R&D—has continued the process by which governments, industries, universities and independent research facilities are supported throughout the EC in key science and technology fields.

It is important to remember that most European R&D is still performed at the national and industry level. In 1987, the EC's total budget for R&D was approximately 1.5 percent of the total the twelve EC nations spent on R&D. But Europeans supporting these EC efforts also recognize that transnational R&D creates ties and linkages which go beyond funding figures. The pan-European, EC–92, and Framework Programmes are all attempts to leverage scientific, technical, human and other resources in areas where national and industrial R&D efforts have not, or cannot, support R&D.

Still, these collective European efforts raise many questions. Can the national R&D priorities of the member states fit into the broader European, and especially EC, goals and objectives? At what point do these programs truly support R&D, at what point are they government subsidies for technology development which might not ordinarily be supported, and in either instance, how do issues of measuring "success" help us evaluate their progress? Finally, what do transnational R&D programs tell Europeans, Americans and others about cooperation and competition in R&D?

European Science and Technology

Since the end of World War II, many European nations have formally recognized science and technology as part of larger national priorities for economic growth and development. At the same time, some programs were begun to support transnational research and development across western Europe. [1] These programs and projects range from those which support basic scientific research to commercial technology development. [2] In a variety of fields—now numbering over thirty—the European response has been for national governments, industries, universities and national laboratories to

---

[1] While science and technology and research and development are used frequently in this chapter, science and technology policies may include a wide range of other policies as well, including tax, regulatory, and infrastructure policies. R&D policies and actions are the outcome of science and technology policies, and encompass either a specific activity or a wide range of activities from basic research to technology commercialization.

[2] The difference between a "program" and a "project" is not always clear, but most often an R&D program is a large-scale science or technology field receiving support (e.g., information or energy technology); a project is a targeted science and technology area within a program which addresses specific goals and objectives (e.g., the EC's European Strategic Programme for Research and Development in Information Technologies, or ESPRIT, described later).

combine resources and jointly to support R&D. [3] While intense interest has focused on the EC–92 harmonization process, it is important to note that European R&D policies as a whole—those predating the Single European Act and those which are part of the EC Framework Programme—must be considered as part of a dynamic and continuous process changing modern Europe.

U.S. interest in how the European Community—and Europe in general—supports R&D is based on several issues. The first is that pan-European support for transnational R&D may provide some lessons for the United States. Pan-European R&D efforts may suggest to U.S. policymakers and industry leaders of how best to leverage R&D efforts during a time of static or declining economic resources. Some policymakers and industry leaders are beginning to question whether the United States can fund or otherwise support a wide range of science and technology policies and programs by itself. [4] They ask: do current programs in Europe demonstrate that partnerships to share costs and benefits in R&D provide for greater options? Or will these programs demonstrate to Americans that transnational R&D efforts cannot supplant national and industrial R&D priorities in a competitive global economy?

A second and related issue is regionalization. U.S. interests and concerns in the EC have often been reduced to their broadest terms as either "Opportunity Europe" or "Fortress Europe." However, it may be appropriate to ask whether European R&D programs demonstrate that regional R&D priorities can coexist efficiently and smoothly with national science and technology policies. The North American Free Trade Agreement (NAFTA) under negotiation between the United States, Canada and Mexico has raised some expectations for formal R&D ties in the western hemisphere. If the industrial world is moving towards three regional blocs—Europe, North America and Asia—how would transnational R&D programs such as those supported in Europe fit into this archetype?

Finally, the European R&D programs and the EC–92 harmonization process, when taken together, raise a series of pertinent R&D issues. At what point, or should, government policies and actions go beyond support of "pre-competitive" technology? Is there a Federal interest in the types of programs which the Europeans are currently supporting? What are the criteria for "success" of Government-industry partnerships; can such a set of criteria be quantified and measured when examining pan-European programs? Should existing U.S. government-industry efforts be expanded to include European participation?

Pan-European Programs

Pan-European R&D efforts both pre-date the 1992 harmonization process and are ongoing. The EC has several roles in a variety of programs in pan-European R&D, including primary and supporting

---

[3] The number and scope of these programs does not allow for all of them to be listed in this chapter, although many will be described. For a more comprehensive examination of these efforts, see: Kaplan, Gadi. Europower. *IEEE Spectrum*, June 1990. p. 20–38, 43–62.

[4] Cozzens, Susan E., Peter Healey, Arie Rip and John Ziman. *The Research System in Transition*. NATO/ASI Series D: Behavioral and Social Sciences, v. 57. Dordrecht, Kluwer Academic Publishers, 1990. 407 p.

roles. To some outside of Europe, they represent a puzzling array of programs and projects and an alphabet soup of acronyms. Programs include efforts like CERN (basic nuclear research) and ESA (basic research to applications in space science and technology); recent pan-European R&D efforts include EUREKA (seed money for technology development) and JESSI (microelectronics R&D); and EC-sponsored R&D includes the JRC (basic research and applications).

PRE-SINGLE EUROPEAN ACT

In basic research, the European Laboratory for Particle Physics, or CERN, was established in 1954. CERN serves as a research facility where scientists and researchers from all over Europe can collaborate on "nuclear research of a pure and fundamental character." [5] CERN enjoys a reputation as one of the premiere physics laboratories in the world. Its particle accelerator is currently the most powerful in the world, and has spurred global efforts in advanced particle physics in the United States and Japan. [6]

The European Space Agency (ESA) was established in 1975 by the merger of the European Scientific Research Organization and the European Launcher Development Organization. [7] ESA receives its funding directly from the European nations which support it. ESA has three main activities: basic scientific research and technological development; a development program that includes space launch vehicles, space station modules, other space facilities, and spacecraft to study the solar system and universe; and ground facilities and launch installations. [8] Therefore, ESA supports activities ranging from basic research to the technology development for space launches.

PAN-EUROPEAN

The EUREKA program is a pan-European program begun in 1985. The stated objective is to provide a "technological renaissance of Europe," specifically for commercial technology development. [9] While EC members also support this program, EUREKA goes beyond the EC both in membership and scope. Its purpose is to provide "seed" money to undercapitalized small and medium sized European firms seeking to bring technologies to the marketplace. Since its inception in 1986, there is evidence that it has enhanced the sharing of risk, complemented existing scientific and technological capabilities, and increased the sales and market shares of firms participating in its funding. [10]

[5] Martin, Ben R. and John Irvine. CERN: Past Performance and Future Prospects. *Research Policy*, Part I, v. 13, August 1984. p. 183.

[6] Peterson, Thane. A Big Bang for European High Tech. *Business Week*, September 4, 1989. p. 102.

[7] U.S. Library of Congress. Congressional Research Service. *Space Activities of the United States, Soviet Union and Other Launching Countries/Organizations: 1957-1990*. CRS Rept. No. 91-621 SPR, by Marcia S. Smith. July 31, 1991. p. 113.

[8] European Space Agency. *European Space Agency; 1989 Annual Report*. Paris, European Space Agency, 1989. p. 8-9.

[9] Bradshaw, Richard. *European Community Science and Technology Programs of Particular Relevance to NSF*. Paper presented at the Europe 1992 Conference, George Mason University, Reston, VA, May 1988.

[10] Richardson, Jacques J. Eureka Gets High Marks from French Participants. *Research and Technology Management*, July-August 1990. p. 3.

One of the larger projects started in part with seed money from EUREKA in 1989 is the Joint European Sub-Micron and Silicon Initiative, or JESSI. Often described as the European answer to the U.S. semiconductor consortium SEMATECH (Semiconductor Manufacturing Technology), JESSI began as a trans-national government and industry effort to advance the knowledge and technology of European companies for manufacturing semiconductor chips. While JESSI was created with great hopes and expectations, it has since narrowed its objectives and it is uncertain it will be continued beyond 1997, when its first eight year funding cycle concludes.

EC-SPONSORED

The primary EC-sponsored R&D program is the Framework Programme, described in the next section. Before the Framework Programme, however, the EC had supported some R&D efforts, primarily in basic research. The Joint Research Center (JRC) was created in 1960 to conduct joint research on nuclear energy. However, in 1973, it broadened its mission into other basic and target-oriented research areas, although its main clients are still scientific, regulatory, and administrative bodies of the EC Commission. [11] JRC research areas include measurements and standards, exploratory research in mass spectronomy and image processing, specific technical support for the EC in energy, agriculture and other areas, and work for third parties in industrial technology. [12]

What interests observers in these various European programs, projects and efforts is the breadth of these activities. [13] While some similar U.S. efforts in space (NASA) and advanced electronics (SEMATECH) exist, there is really nothing to compare with other efforts like EUREKA. [14] Some argue for broader and deeper support of American R&D along lines of the European efforts. However, it is unclear how successful these pan-European efforts are, or how much they will add to future R&D efforts across Europe.

EC–92 Harmonization

The Single European Act, intended to eliminate most technical, physical, and financial barriers among the twelve EC nations, did not address science and technology explicitly, except for a broad reference to a science and technology "framework." However, many of the EC directives outlining the harmonization process do address areas which will have a substantial and lasting impact on

---

[11] Foreign Broadcast Information Service. Science and Technology: Foreign Data Bases. *EC 1992: EUROSCOPE Report on R&D Programs*, June 24, 1991. p. 9.

[12] Commission of the European Communities. *Joint Research Center; 1989 Annual Report*. Brussels, Commission of the European Communities, 1989. 124 p.

[13] For a more comprehensive description of these and other European science and technology programs, see: U.S. Congress. House of Representatives. Committee on Energy and Commerce. *Transfer of Technology from Publicly Funded Research Institutions to the Private Sector [A Report Prepared by the Congressional Research Service]*. Committee Print 102-G, July 1991. p. 51–68.

[14] Some early supporters of EUREKA, including French President Francois Mitterand, compared EUREKA to U.S. efforts in the Strategic Defense Initiative (SDI), contending that the European effort would have the same desired effect as SDI on respective defense technology bases. However, EUREKA is not defense-oriented, nor is there any indication that a European SDI will emerge from EUREKA. Marum, John M. The Technology Gap: Europe at a Crossroads. *Issues in Science and Technology*, September 1986. p. 3–5.

the scientific and technology exchanges between the twelve member nations, as well as with non-EC stakeholders.

This impact can be seen in many different areas. For example, EC "rules of origin," particularly as they are applied to microelectronics products, have had the effect of shifting some R&D and manufacturing facilities of American, Japanese, Korean and other non-EC semiconductor firms to the EC. Some U.S. high technology industries, most notably the microelectronics industry, contend that this will add significant expense to how American firms do business in Europe. [15] Yet it may also have the long-term effect of providing greater EC market access to firms which do relocate R&D facilities. Non-tariff barriers, particularly in standards, may also have a significant impact on the nature, location and funding of R&D beyond 1992. For example, a single EC electronics standard for computers may permit U.S. and Japanese computer manufacturers greater economies of scale in meeting that standard for all of their products. A distinctly EC computer standard different from other non-EC nations, however, may create a substantial cost and technical barrier to computer firms as well. EC–92 also will open the flow of people across national borders, which in turn will have an impact on the movement of scientists, engineers, technicians and other types of researchers from the public and private sectors, from EC and non-EC organizations, and from many R&D fields. [16]

Science and technology policy considerations may include tax, fiscal, regulatory, education, training and other issues beyond just R&D activities. Therefore, the EC–92 harmonization process provides an insight into how a wide range of transnational policies may have an impact on a still-evolving EC-wide science and technology policies. It is the outcome of this evolving process which leaves observers uncertain about the final status of R&D in Europe. After 1992, it is likely that in some areas there will be greater opportunities for non-EC firms to utilize EC resources with EC-based R&D, including the possibility for transnational R&D efforts, from basic research to technology development. There is, however, concern in the United States that only the larger multinational firms will be able to take advantage of the EC harmonization process, and that small and medium-sized firms will not be able to shift R&D functions and facilities to the new Europe. Some directives and regulatory measures may further impede free flows of personnel and technology outside of Europe, changing the nature of how R&D is performed both inside and outside the EC alike.

Framework Programmes

Background

In addition to the specific directives coming from the Single European Act, the members of the EC also recognized the importance of further encouraging R&D among EC members. The idea of cooperative R&D efforts among the EC nations was broadly addressed

---

[15] Fine, Frank L. A United Europe, The Effects of 1992 on Suppliers of Semiconductor Equipment and Materials. *Channel.* Mountain View, CA, Semiconductor Equipment Materials International, January 1992. p. 35.

[16] Ibid., p. 4–5.

in the SEA and subsequently the EC Commission formed the Framework Programme for Community R&D—known simply as the Framework Programme—in 1987. [17]

The Framework Programme is designed to pool national resources among the EC members in critical science and technology areas, and as such has two broad objectives. The first is to promote coordination among the twelve EC nations without duplicating existing national science and technology development programs. In this respect the Framework Programme is intended to be *subsidiary* to these national programs, to supplement not supplant national R&D priorities. But whether it is truly achieving this goal is still being debated within the EC. The second objective is the encouragement of pre-competitive technology development. While the exact nature of pre-competitive development is open to interpretation, it lies beyond basic research and involves increasing the broad understanding of science and product technology development for specific goods and services. Often the cost and risk needed to nurture pre-competitive technology makes it unattractive for any one company or even an entire industry to undertake it by itself. The intent of the Framework Programme is to help nurture scientific research to a point of being commercially viable to the research sponsors. [18]

There have been three Framework Programmes: Framework I (1987–1991), Framework II (1988–1992) and Framework III (1990–1994). The twelve EC nations support the total funding for each Framework Programme, although Germany, Great Britain and France provide almost 75 percent of the total Framework budget. [19] The Framework R&D priorities have evolved as the EC has moved from Framework I through Framework III (figure 1). For example, energy R&D, a high priority in Framework I, has received a small level of funding support in Framework II and Framework III. The funding for Framework is provided over four-year bands. The EC contends that this allows for a carry-over of R&D programs without interruption and provides continuity from Framework I through III.

While the Framework Programmes support many different scientific and technological projects, four fields have received a considerable amount of attention not only in Europe but also in the United States. These are information technology (ESPRIT); communications (RACE); advanced materials (EURAM); and industrial technology (BRITE) (see table 1). Each of these areas has very broad technology objectives, and ideally, industrial participants will use the "pre-competitive" technologies developed under ESPRIT, RACE

---

[17] The 1957 Treaty of Rome provided for a "framework" to cover coordination of national policies and research projects in science and technology. Under the Single European Act, Title VI, articles 130 F through 130 P amended the EC charter to include a broad "framework" to encourage greater research, technology and development (RTD) cooperation among the twelve nations, while not interfering or usurping national RTD policies. Commission of the European Communities. Single European Act. *Bulletin of the European Communities.* Supplement 2/86. p. 14–15.

[18] Interview with Gilbert Fayl, Counselor for Science and Technology, Delegation of the Commission of the European Communities, Washington, DC, September 28, 1990.

[19] U.S. National Science Foundation. *Science and Technology Integration in Europe and Influence on U.S.-European Cooperation [A Report of the National Science Board Committee on Europe in 1992].* Washington, DC, 1990. p. 4.

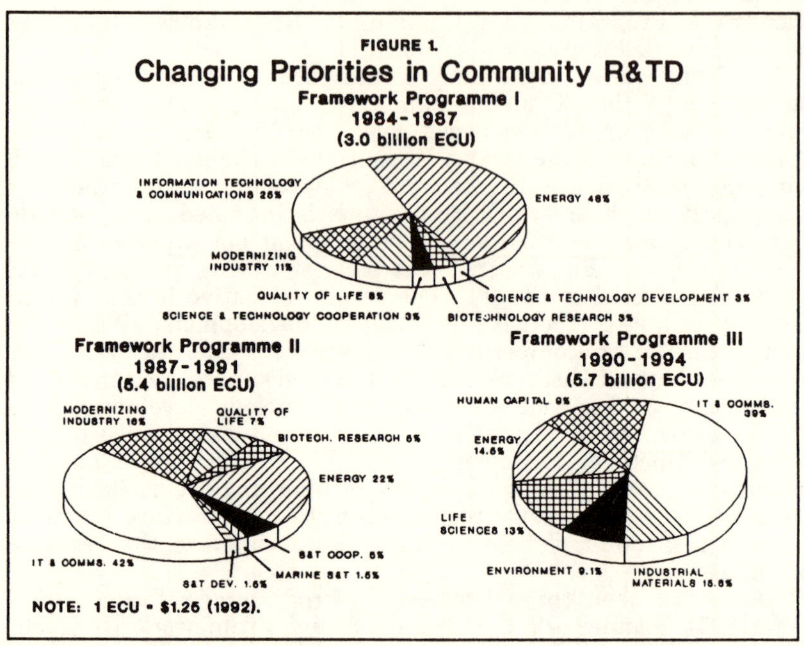

and EURAM/BRITE to bring to market specific products and services for EC and global use.

While the EC administers funding for the Framework Programme, the national laboratories, private research and development groups and firms actually perform the research. When a broad program has been outlined by the EC Commission and approved by the member states, the EC publishes a call for research proposals. Respondents—called "investigator teams"—may be any "natural or legal person or public or private body" registered in an EC nation.[20] Preference is given to projects in which partners from several EC nations will work together.[21] Proposals for projects are assessed through a peer review process which considers such criteria as compatibility of the proposal to the Framework Programme, scientific and technical merit, feasibility of the proposal, and other characteristics to determine the merit of each application.

Yet other considerations, often political, come into play as well. The R&D priorities of member states as they fit into the Framework Programme, are clearly considered, as are the goals of European industrial firms, universities and other research institutions. Thus, Framework projects which might conflict or compete with

---

[20] Foreign Broadcast Information Service. Science and Technology: Foreign Data Bases. *EC 1992: EUROSCOPE Report on R&D Programs*, op. cit. p. 10.
[21] Ibid., p. 10.

TABLE 1. Major Framework Projects of the European Community

Name	Goals	Duration of Current Phase	EC contribution, in millions of ECUs[a] ($U.S.)
The European Strategic Programme for Research and Development in Information Technologies, second phase (Esprit-II)	Provide the European information technology industry with the basic technologies it needs for meeting the competitive requirements of the 1990s; promote European industrial cooperation.	1988-92	600 ($480)
R&D in Advanced Communications Technologies in Europe (RACE)	Contribute to the introduction of broadband communications, in line with the evolving integrated-services digital network (ISDN); prepare for international standards.	1987-92	550 ($384)
European Research in Advanced Materials (EURAM)	Support of programs in advanced materials, particularly in ceramics and composites.	1987-92	500[b] ($400)
Basic Research in Industrial Technology for Europe (BRITE)	Improve European competitiveness in industrial manufacturing and advanced materials technology	1989-92	500[b] ($400)

[a] ECU = European currency unit, worth about $1.25 as of January 1992.

[b] In 1988 both BRITE and EURAM were combined and listed under "Enabling Technologies." However, most EC documents continue to refer to BRITE and EURAM as major programs, assisting specific aspects of European industry. The total budget for these two programs is 500 million ECUs, of which BRITE received approximately 60 percent.

Source: Commission of the European Communities, EC Research Funding, Jan. 1990; and IEEE Spectrum, June 1990, p. 38.

the objectives of European industry are thoroughly reviewed. But it is increasingly clear that European corporations will not participate in Framework projects that may crowd out support which they might otherwise receive from their Government for development of commercial technologies. These issues are discussed more explicitly in the next section.

Issues

RECONCILING R&D POLICIES

A significant issue arising out of these many pan-European R&D efforts (including those supported by the EC) is how well they fit in with the national science and technology priorities of each member state. How are differing regional and national R&D objectives reconciled; and does consensus building reduce the impact and effectiveness of pan-European efforts?

For pan-European programs in general, many R&D programs are given broad national support, although this varies from program to program. The JRC and CERN are widely considered the "crown jewels" of European R&D, and their basic research and applications missions are scientific. The EC Commission claims that it makes a strong effort to ensure that for basic research institutions like CERN and the JRC, complete dissemination of research is permitted through published papers, travel to conferences and exchanges between the facilities and the national and university laboratories. [22] However, in other areas, particularly where efforts are being made to develop technology close to commercialization, national support varies. EUREKA also has wide national and industry support, because it is seen as an important adjunct to national and industrial technology development. [23] On the other hand, some in European government and industry have criticized JESSI for not fully representing the member states and the goals and objectives of their industries. [24]

As a part of the 1992 process, the member states must implement directives passed by the EC. This has created problems when EC objectives have not matched national priorities. [25] To date, it appears that serious conflicts between member states and the EC regarding R&D priorities, have been minimized. A 1990 report on the EC Framework Programme stated that " . . . Close intra-EC cooperation in S&T [science and technology] matters is rapidly unfolding as an integral component of the larger scheme of integration." [26] Generally, the EC Commission has skillfully balanced R&D priorities with those of the member states, so that EC priorities not only run parallel to the national goals and objectives of member states, but also avoid conflicting with their R&D priorities as well.

Still, there are several areas where national and transnational priorities may produce areas of potential conflict. [27] The reunifica-

---

[22] Ibid., p. 10.

[23] Fels, Xavier. Eureka, A Model for the Future. *Science and Public Policy*, December 1988. p. 373–375.

[24] Peterson, Thane and Gail Schares. Europe's High Tech Titans Put Their hips on JESSI. *Business Week*, November 14, 1988. p. 82.

[25] Policing Europe's Single Market; Laws Unto Themselves. *The Economist*, June 22, 1991. p. 76.

[26] U.S. National Science Foundation. *Science and Technology Integration in Europe and Influences on U.S.-European Cooperation*, op. cit. p. 10.

[27] Ibid., p. 10–11.

tion of Germany may create short-term national disruptions that will divert the will and energy of that nation away from larger EC-wide priorities in science and technology. A second issue is the "deepening vs. broadening" issue: should EC ties among nations be deeper and more complex or should the integration movement seek to broaden its scope? This question directly reflects a similar debate concerning the Framework Programme, as supporters and critics discuss whether the Framework III Programme should be deepened or broadened and how either outcome would affect individual national priorities. Finally, member state leaders and other observers caution that pan-European programs, and particularly EC R&D efforts, need to be kept in perspective. In 1987, the most recent year member state and EC R&D funding figures are available, total EC R&D programs were only 1.5 percent of the over ECU 54 billion (or about $70 billion) spent by member states on their own R&D programs. [28] While the EC R&D programs—and other pan-European R&D programs—receive a great deal of attention, it may not be commensurate with the amount of funding EC nations are committing to their national programs.

These issues are important to U.S. policymakers on two levels. First, the United States and the EC Commission have discussed coordinating bilateral and multilateral science and technology agreements into one overarching EC-U.S. policy. [29] While these talks have progressed towards establishing a single science and technology policy, it is clear that a single EC-U.S. policy will not supplant current nation-to-nation agreements. Therefore, there is the potential of bifurcation of policies, one U.S.-EC and the other U.S.-member state, with separate policies and objectives. Second, if national European priorities conflict with EC science and technology policies, U.S. firms may also face difficulties. Several of the larger U.S. firms are positioning themselves in the post-1992 Europe, as well as actively soliciting to participate in many pan-European R&D efforts. Federal policymakers may find themselves formulating both bilateral and multilateral policies to accommodate industry competition or cooperation with the many European transnational R&D programs. [30]

SUPPORT OF R&D

A second major consideration is whether the pan-European R&D efforts truly add to European science and technology capabilities and knowledge, or do they subsidize R&D which would not be undertaken in the absence of these programs and may be of questionable value? Whether programs support needed R&D or are attempts by some interested stakeholder—the EC, the industry in question, or member states—to subsidize marginal R&D, calls into

[28] The total R&D budget of the twelve Member States in 1987 was approximately ECU 56 billion; one fourth of the Framework III Programme (19871991) was ECU 1.35 billion. Member States R&D budgets derived from: National Science Foundation. *International Science and Technology Data Update: 1991.* NSF 91-309. Washington, National Science Foundation, 1991. p. 115.

[29] Pandolfi, Filippo Maria. *Science and Technology and European Market Integration.* Washington, National Academy of Sciences Forum. March 5, 1990. 22 p.

[30] U.S. Department of Commerce. European Community '92 Update. *Business America.* Washington, DC. February 25, 1991. 36 p.

question the very reason why these R&D efforts began and if they should continue.

The subsidy or support question has been raised several times recently within the EC. In 1990, several anonymous senior EC officials were quoted as raising serious doubts about both the ESPRIT project—a part of the Framework Programme—and JESSI—which is not an EC program but receives some financial support from the EC Commission. [31] Complaining that these projects were simply subsidized collaborative efforts that contributed little to European competitiveness, they called for a complete rethinking of these and other pan-European R&D programs. [32] In May of 1991, this issue was raised again when the EC Council published a report on the Framework Programme. [33] This report, the result of an internal audit, critiqued the Framework Programme for having a limited impact on how its research results are utilized. The report states that the EC Commission needs to review the Framework Programme in areas of research publications, dissemination of information, patents, and other methods of promoting EC R&D and improve efforts in these areas so that Framework research is better utilized. [34]

Central to this issue for European policymakers, researchers, industry leaders and others is defining "success"—what is expected of an R&D program, and therefore whether is it achieving its goals? This measure of success will differ depending on the R&D program, from any of the Framework Programmes to CERN, from EUREKA to the JRC. The number of European efforts complicates developing a single methodology for assessing whether and why pan-European R&D programs work. In the end, some efforts like CERN and the JRC appear to have widespread support and work well, as does EUREKA. On the other hand, efforts like ESPRIT and JESSI are coming under closer scrutiny and questioning by their sponsors. Americans who contend that the United States should develop transnational R&D efforts may need to take a more thorough and objective look at pan-European R&D objectives and "success" before advocating similar large-scale programs in this country.

COOPERATION OR COMPETITION

The future of Europe after 1992 includes a very important issue which will affect U.S. R&D priorities at the Government, industry and university levels. At what level can or should the Europeans cooperate with Americans and others, and at what point can or

---

[31] De Jonquieres, Guy. ESPRIT, JESSI Come Under Attack. *New Technology Week*, November 5, 1990. p. 2.

[32] Ibid., p. 2. In response to these anonymous sources, the Counselor for Science and Technology for the Delegation of the Commission of the European Communities in Washington, D.C., contended these were incorrect or untrue statements on the purpose and subsidization of these programs.

[33] European Community Court of Auditors. Special Report No 2/91 on the utilization of the results of community research work accompanied by the replies of the Commission, *Official Journal of the European Communities*. no. C133/1. May 23, 1991. 46 p.

[34] Ibid., p. 4–6, 7. It should be noted that the report did cite industry participation in ESPRIT II as a positive contribution, but also made several recommendations for improvement (p. 7). The Commission, in responding to this audit, contended that the complexity and specific nature of this R&D makes short-term evaluations difficult, and stressed the diversity of the EC R&D programs as a major factor (p. 34–36).

should they compete with the same parties? In basic research, such as that done at the JRC and CERN, non-European scientists, engineers and researchers are involved, although the participation of non-European individuals may be subject to restrictions. But in "pre-competitive" R&D—like JESSI or ESPRIT—there appears to be less consensus in the EC as to where cooperation in pan-European R&D ends and where industry, regional and global competition begins. But both the EC–92 process and the Framework Programmes send conflicting messages where proprietary information and technology and competitive goals contrast with a desire to share costs, risk and scientific exploration.

The regionalization process in general has the potential to exclude non-members.[35] But generally, the R&D process appears to thrive when few or no restrictions exist on the flow of people and resources across national boundaries, particularly if the flows are "pre-competitive" in nature. This issue was aptly addressed in a 1991 *World Monitor* article on the Pacific Basin region in which the author asked "Are globalization and regionalization compatible?"[36] If globalization can lead to a breakdown of barriers and less segmentation of R&D and industries, regionalization may create the opposite effect by fragmenting R&D along geographic boundaries. Europeans and non-Europeans have raised a fundamental question: should the EC Framework Programmes, EUREKA, JESSI and the 1992 process in general involve American, Japanese and other potential competitors?

While European and non-European firms have established a wide range of joint ventures, licensing agreements and other relationships, on the broader pan-European R&D program level, progress has been slower. In response to appeals from IBM Europe to join JESSI, officials initiated talks with the American semiconductor consortium SEMATECH in 1989. In late 1991 JESSI and SEMATECH officials signed an agreement outlining broad parameters for closer participation.[37] The EC has permitted some non-European participation in the Framework Programme, but this generally is limited to published research results and secondary and tertiary access to information disseminated through the Framework Programme. EUREKA, providing seed money for technological innovation, is open only to European participation.

The question of how to distinguish more clearly between cooperation and competition of R&D across regional boundaries is not an easy one to answer. The costs and benefits of participation versus restriction have to be weighed. By keeping non-Europeans out of R&D efforts, the Europeans may lose access to enormous resources in capital, innovative new ideas and expertise from abroad. Or the pan-European R&D programs may provide Europe with a fertile research environment, combined with intense transnational industry competition within the region, giving the world an archetype for

---

[35] Daniels, John D. and Lee H. Radebagh. *International Business; Environments and Operations.* Sixth Edition. Reading, MA, Addison Wesley, 1991.

[36] Three Blocs or One? Interview with Denis Fred Simon, Director of the Center for Technology and International Affairs at the Fletcher School of Law and Diplomacy, Tufts University. *World Monitor*, December 1991. p. 32.

[37] Zipper, Stuart. Sematech, JESSI to Cooperate. *New Technology Week*, September 23, 1991. p. 6.

closer cooperation in R&D. While either scenario may occur, current pan-European R&D efforts after 1992 may more likely combine some of both outcomes. This will require attention and skill by non-Europeans involved in European R&D in the coming decades.

DEVELOPMENTS IN ENVIRONMENTAL POLICY

by Mary E. Tiemann *

CONTENTS

SUMMARY

The Single European Act (SEA) of 1987 gave the European Community (EC) its first clear legal basis for issuing and enforcing environmental legislation. Consequently, EC integration is changing the way environmental issues are addressed throughout the Community. EC-92—and wider European integration—also has implications for a wide range of U.S. businesses and, perhaps, for U.S. environmental policy as well. A unified European voice on global environmental issues, for example, might influence U.S. positions on prominent international environmental matters, such as global climate change. Moreover, as other European nations join the EC, or simply harmonize with EC standards and regulations, U.S. policymakers may be prompted to review risk assessment and other standards-setting policies in domestic environmental legislation with a view toward greater harmonization with an increasingly powerful European market.

The achievement of a unified environmental policy, and whether it would result in the adoption of a strict set of Community-wide environmental standards and regulations, is expected to be constrained by differences among north-south EC members in terms of their relative economic strengths, environmental priorities, and

* Mary E. Tiemann is a Specialist in Environmental Policy, Environment and Natural Resources Division, Congressional Research Service.

current status of national environmental programs. Other factors that could affect the pace and direction of EC environmental policy include German unification and the associated cost of bringing eastern Germany up to west German environmental standards, and the vast needs of East European nations for environmental assistance.

The implications of EC–92 for U.S. businesses are multiple, and not all consistent. There is broad consensus that Community-wide harmonization of national environmental regulations and standards could improve the overall competitiveness of U.S. suppliers to that market. Concurrently, compliance with emerging EC environmental laws will increase the costs of doing business in the EC. A proposed environmental liability directive, for example, may force businesses to engage in environmentally safer but more costly waste management practices. If unification results in a comprehensive set of EC environmental requirements (and recent developments suggest it may), then U.S. manufacturers may realize increased competitiveness as environment-related business costs in the EC increase and approach those imposed in the United States. U.S. trade could also benefit from the European market for environmental goods and services which is expected to grow markedly with the number of EC environmental directives. However, if U.S. products fail to meet EC standards or associated technical requirements, the United States may lose market access, at least until products could be adapted.

Recent statements issuing from EC leaders suggest that the European Community intends to heighten the priority given to Community environmental matters and to challenge the United States for international leadership on global issues. This view is far from unified, however, and considerable disagreement exists among EC members and industry, as well as between the Commission and the Parliament, on the proper balance between economic growth and competitiveness, free trade, and environmental protection.

The SEA is unique among multilateral trade agreements and treaties in its attempt to balance trade openness with national and international environmental protection goals. However, a growing number of environmental measures taken by the EC members (and other countries) could be affected by the outcome of the Uruguay round of negotiations of the General Agreement on Tariffs and Trade (GATT). Thus, while EC–92 establishes authority, principles, and a policy framework for addressing environmental matters, many other factors will help shape the eventual form and practical effect of the Community's domestic and international environmental policies.

EC Environmental Policy: Background

Until the ratification of the Single European Act (SEA), the EC had no explicit authority to force member nations to implement its environmental protection directives. Despite the absence of express environmental powers in the Treaty of Rome, the European Community adopted an environmental policy in 1972 and passed more than 150 environmental measures between 1973 and 1987. [1] The legal basis for these actions was sometimes weak, however, and measures were generally described as efforts at harmonization in order to remove obstacles to trade. [2]

Initial actions addressed conformity among member countries' environmental laws, and adoption of broad authorizing directives to guide specific implementation by members. Later, national concern over the transboundary effects of pollution, particularly acid rain, heightened interest in multilateral cooperation among EC member nations. More recently, the EC has become an active participant in the development of international environmental agreements.

Three basic principles have guided EC environmental policies from its inception: (1) priority is given to pollution prevention over cleanup; (2) environmental degradation should be corrected at the source; (3) and the polluter pays. Also, individual nations generally may not adopt more stringent requirements, except where justified to protect the environment and human health.

As in other sectors, the primary mechanism for achieving Community-wide environmental protection has been the EC directive, a key purpose of which is to harmonize certain environmental standards and requirements throughout the Community to ensure that one country's environmental measures do not become another country's trade barrier. EC directives are not generally enforceable, but rather establish goals for member states to achieve through implementing legislation. The Treaty of Rome confers substantial flexibility upon member states in achieving the results that directives are intended to realize. [3] In contrast, EC regulations become law Community-wide without individual countries enacting implementing legislation and have precedence over national law. Given past noncompliance with EC directives, some EC officials have urged greater use of regulations in future Community environmental actions.

National environmental laws, like other activities, have been covered by the Treaty of Rome obligation that EC member states harmonize trading practices and avoid unfair competitive advantage through use of specific national policies. Individual countries can, nonetheless, be granted exemptions from the treaty's obligations on environmental grounds as follows:

> national legislation that results in obstacles to trade is nevertheless compatible with article 30 so long as the Community has not already regulated the same activity, and the national legislation is purely environmental in purpose, is applied evenly to imported and domestic products

---

[1] Zacher, Christian. Environmental Law of the European Economic Community: New Powers under the Single European Act. *Boston College International and Comparative Law Review*, v. XIV, no. 2, Summer 1991. p. 261.

[2] Heseltine, Michael. The Single European Market and the Environment. *European Business Journal*, v. 1, no. 3, 1989. p. 9.

[3] Smith, Turner T. and Roszell D. Hunter. The European Community Environmental Legal System. *Environmental Law Reporter—News and Analysis*, v. 22, no. 2, February, 1992. p. 10109.

> alike, and is necessary to satisfy imperative requirements such as environmental protection. [4]

In addition to EC directives and regulations, member states still have their own regulatory structures, and broad differences exist between individual countries' and Community environmental legislation. More than ever before, EC–92 will require member states to amend national environmental law to conform with an increasingly exacting Community structure.

New Environmental Powers Under the Sea

The key objective of EC–92 is to promote economic unity among member states. To achieve that goal, technical standards and regulations must be harmonized to reduce barriers to national markets. Many of the national regulations designated to be abolished in creating a single market involve environmental protection. [5] The framers of the SEA anticipated the potential for conflict between economic integration and environmental goals, and acknowledged that implementing unification measures could result in environmental deterioration. Accordingly, an environmental title, Title VII, was added to the Treaty of Rome that explicitly granted environmental authority to the Community. The SEA also subjected establishment of the internal market to a high standard of environmental protection.

The SEA contains specific references to EC environmental objectives (i.e., to preserve, protect, and improve the quality of the environment; to contribute toward protecting human health, and to ensure prudent and rational utilization of natural resources). The Act endorses current environmental policy (i.e., polluter-pays principle and pollution prevention), and mandates that "environmental protection shall be a component of the Community's other policies." [6]

SCOPE OF EC ENVIRONMENTAL AUTHORITY

Under Article 100 of the Treaty of Rome, the Community is empowered to establish regulations or directives as necessary to effect the functioning of the market. Thus, the EC may impose regulations (e.g., the content of products or product labelling) to remove technical barriers to trade resulting from differences in national environmental laws (or lack thereof). New Article 100a on harmonization includes a specific mandate to sustain a high level of environmental protection and authorizes the Council to act by a qualified majority to adopt measures to complete the internal market, including proposals "concerning health, safety, environmental protection and consumer protection." [7] This majority voting system enables most of the measures under the internal market program to be adopted much more quickly than would have been possible before. It also facilitates decision-making on environmental issues

---

[4] Zacher, Christian. Environmental Law of the European Economic Community: New Powers Under the Single European Act. *Boston College International and Comparative Law Review*, v. XIV, no. 2, Summer, 1991. p. 263.
[5] Ibid., p. 264.
[6] EC Treaty, Article 130r, par. 2.
[7] Smith and Hunter, p. 10116.

by limiting the ability of individual countries to block approval of environmental legislation which a majority of countries view as necessary.

The SEA further clarifies member states' authority to deviate from EC requirements for environmental purposes. Article 100a permits member states to take stricter action under the following circumstances:

> [i]f, after the adoption of a harmonization measure by the Council acting by a qualified majority, a Member State deems it necessary to apply national provisions on grounds of major needs referred to in Article 36, or relating to protection of the environment, . . . it shall notify the Commission of the provisions. The Commission shall confirm the provisions involved after having verified that they are not a means of arbitrary discrimination or a disguised restriction on trade between Member States. [8]

Title VII of the SEA, Article 130, delineates the environmental objectives of the EC Treaty, as amended, and articulates the Community's intent to balance trade openness and Community economic development with legitimate national efforts to protect the environment. It clarifies and strengthens the role for the Community in cooperating with international organizations and negotiating international agreements with third parties on behalf of member states. Among other things, Article 130 states that:

—Action by the Community relating to the environment shall have the following objectives:
- to preserve, protect and improve the quality of the environment,
- to contribute towards protecting human health, and
- to ensure a prudent and rational utilization of natural resources.

—Action by the Community relating to the environment shall be based on the principles that preventive action should be taken, that environmental damage should as a priority be rectified at source, and that the polluter should pay.

—Environmental protection requirements shall be a component of the Community's other policies.

—In preparing its action relating to the environment, the Community shall take account of:
- available scientific and technical data,
- environmental conditions in the various regions of the Community,
- the potential benefits and costs of action or lack of action, and
- the economic and social development of the Community as a whole and the balanced development of its regions.

Article 130s of the SEA explicitly grants the EC power to issue environmental legislation, but unlike Article 100a, it requires the Council to act through unanimous voting. This requirement responds to the concern of some member states that the EC's envi-

[8] Treaty of Rome, as amended by the Single European Act, Article 100a.

ronmental policy could affect national industries and create trade barriers among Community members. By contrast, legislative proposals relating to product standards or their impact on competitiveness would be subject to majority voting under Article 100a (e.g., pesticide residue standards and waste management), while broader environmental proposals would be subject to the unanimity requirement under Article 130s (e.g., habitat protection).

The new environmental principles incorporated into the Treaty of Rome could have far-reaching effects on various EC policies. Many doubt, however, that the ambitious goals will be realized. According to one EC observer, the principles have become more catchphrases than policies for action, since they are vague generalizations, and are not well suited to strict legal application. [9]

Others question the degree to which these principles should be pursued. Some EC officials argue that the Community should not attempt to manage all environmental responsibilities. In this view, the Community's abilities are best used in defining minimum standards in areas such as automobile and industrial emission limits, establishing a framework for common environmental action, negotiating international agreements, and introducing fiscal measures to encourage environmental protection. [10] The SEA generally adheres to the subsidiarity principle with regard to environmental matters; that is, the Community would determine whether or not an environmental proposal could be managed adequately at the national level. However, it also grants the Community broad law- and policy-making powers.

The SEA contains an additional provision that has implications for the Community's environmental course. Article 100a elevates the role of the European Parliament, granting it an advisory role and budgetary powers on environmental proposals. [11] Consequently, the Parliament could become more influential in determining EC environmental policy. This provision is potentially significant because the European Parliament has frequently advocated stricter environmental measures and has been outspoken regarding the balance of trade and environment—in favor of ensuring environmental protection. This position was most recently illustrated in the EC debate on international waste transport (both within and outside the EC), during which European Parliament members pressed for a ban on transboundary waste shipments, while the Commission favored continued shipments under tighter controls.

Environmental Impacts of EC–92

An EC task force report on the environmental impacts of EC–92 determined that expected increases in economic activity throughout the EC would result in higher pollution levels throughout the Community, unless additional environmental protection measures were taken. [12] The task force recommended that the Community

---

[9] Smith and Hunter, p. 10116.

[10] Bureau of National Affairs. EC Should not be Expected to Deal with all Environmental Issues. *International Environment Reporter*, January 15, 1992. p. 23.

[11] U.S. International Trade Commission. *The Effects of Greater Economic Integration Within the European Community on the United States: Second Follow-up Report*, Investigation No. 332-267. USITC Publication 2318, September, 1990. p. 4-30.

[12] French, Hilary F. The EC: Environmental Proving Ground. *World Watch*, November-December, 1991. p. 28-29.

rely on five principles to guide the development of an EC environmental policy, including:

- pollution prevention;
- polluter pays;
- subsidiarity;
- economic efficiency; and
- legal efficiency.

These principles incorporate preexisting EC policy and have been reflected in recent environmental measures taken by the EC Commission.

The task force also recommended much greater use of economic instruments to influence consumer behavior. Economic measures becoming popular at the national level in the EC include environmental taxes, investment subsidies, and pollution charges. Examples of national-level initiatives include subsidies for cars that use lead-free gasoline and have catalytic converters (Belgium, Denmark, Germany, Greece, and the Netherlands), and matched grants for investments in certain pollution prevention or control equipment (France). [13]

No EC-wide incentives (or disincentives) have yet been adopted, although EC environmental policy is already moving in this direction. EC Environment Ministers are considering proposals for (1) ecotaxes on carbon dioxide and CFC emissions, (2) a fossil-fuel tax at the point of production or importation, (3) deposits for recyclable packaging and containers, and (4) permits for toxic waste producers. [14] Given the economic implications of a carbon tax, it appears unlikely that the Community will act separately in the absence of similar action by the United States and Japan. Other measures, such as packaging and container deposit charges, are expected to proceed. EC adherence to the task force's recommendations would partially shape Community environmental policy under EC–92.

Environmental Policy Implications of EC–92

Conflicting views exist as to what EC–92 means for Community environmental policy, and ultimately for relative U.S. competitiveness. Much of the debate centers around harmonization of product standards in the member states, and opinions on the effects of harmonization vary among countries and industries. One view is that, given the growing awareness of the international environmental issues, and the emergence of consumer demand for environmentally safe products, creation of a single market could catalyze a strong environmental policy.

Another other view is that the general requirement of strict conformity with EC directives and regulations will lead to a lowest-common-denominator approach to environmental protection, with the more aggressive nations being prohibited from imposing, or being required to weaken, strict environmental regulations and standards. Subscribers to this view predict that poorer EC coun-

---

[13] U.S. International Trade Commission. *The Effects of Greater Economic Integration Within the European Community on the United States: Second Follow-up Report*, Investigation No. 332267. USITC Publication 2318, September, 1990. p. 4–35.

[14] USITC Publication 2318, p. 4–30.

tries would slow the general trend in the EC toward stricter pollution control requirements, especially when correcting this situation requires substantial financial or technological investment. Poorer, typically southern, EC countries could also inhibit individual country efforts to adopt more stringent environmental standards because EC law makes it difficult for member states to impose stricter-than-EC standards, especially where a product or process is exported.

If, as some predict, the EC will only be capable of consensus on lenient measures, then Community environmental standards and requirements could be less stringent that those imposed in the United States. Consequently, U.S. competitiveness would be diminished. The impact on U.S. industry could be substantial if, as some argue, EC standards should be considered a ceiling, not to be exceeded by individual countries, rather than a floor. [15] It is premature to discern a trend in EC environmental policy; however, there is no evidence to date of a downward trend in Community standards.

The ultimate shape and strength of EC environmental policy will depend on a variety of factors, including those EC measures taken to meet the social and economic goals of EC–92, and the persistence of the "green" mood that continues to be prominent throughout much of Europe. Community-wide policy may also be influenced by the EC Treaty provision which allows countries to maintain higher standards adopted for genuine environmental reasons, when verified by the Commission that the provisions do not constitute a disguised trade barrier. If stricter national standards meet this test, the EC may be prompted to harmonize toward the higher standard in order to achieve or maintain uniformity throughout the Community. This outcome has already occurred with several German measures, where the Commission has decided to conform to Germany's stricter standards. (See packaging and eco-labeling proposals discussed below.)

To date, the European Court has made several narrow rulings upholding member states' authority to impose stricter standards. In the first decision on European environmental policy under the SEA, the European Court ruled in favor of a Danish reusable container law, finding environmental protection to be a legitimate reason for subsuming the Community's free trade policy. [16] The Court further ruled that, in the absence of EC law, individual nations may enact their own laws, even if they contravene the Treaty of Rome free-trade policy. In other cases, the Court has held that environmental protection is an essential objective of the Community and justifies certain limitations of the principle of the free movement of goods. [17]

---

[15] O'Sullivan, Dermot A. Environmental Concerns Gain Prominence in Europe. *Chemical and Engineering News*, March 27, 1989. p. 11.

[16] Ibid., p. 10.

[17] Jerome, Robert. W. Trading With a Greener Europe. *The Journal of Commerce*, September 4, 1991. p. 12.

GERMAN UNIFICATION

The unification of Germany could influence both the substance of future EC standards and the rate at which environmental harmonization occurs. Long a leader in European environmental legislation, Germany now faces the costly challenge of cleaning up severe pollution in former East Germany, and bringing industries and municipalities in that region up to west German standards. Some analysts believe that Germany will be preoccupied with its own unification for some time, and thus, less interested in pressing for new EC environmental initiatives. At the same time, eastern Germany has presented Germans a compelling argument for pollution prevention and control.

In fact, Germany is proving to be a major force in the Community in pressing for strong environmental legislation. In several instances, the EC has already agreed to conform to higher German standards. The Commission, for example, is preparing a directive based on Germany's new packaging-recycling law. One German official anticipates that his country will continue to argue successfully for high Community environmental standards; however, poorer EC countries will be allowed more time to phase in those standards. [18]

PAN-EUROPEAN ENVIRONMENTAL COOPERATION

EC environmental policy under the SEA is influencing laws in other European countries as well. Several West and East European countries anticipate joining the European Community, and their chances of being accepted into the EC would likely be enhanced if their environmental standards are consistent with those in the EC. If EC and European Free Trade Association (EFTA) countries merge, the pressure to achieve higher environmental standards may result, as several EFTA countries have higher standards than the EC in many areas, and are strongly disinclined to weaken those standards. Additionally, the emergence of the European Economic Area (EEA) has also prompted several non-EC European countries to consider increased harmonization with EC laws.

The EC's proximity to Eastern Europe is also expected to sustain the Community's interest in improving the environment in those countries, in no small part in order to prevent deterioration of its own environment as a result of transboundary pollution. Poorer countries, such as Turkey and those of East Europe are also expected to be allowed to phase in EC standards over time, if they are accepted as members.

In sum, any effects of EC-wide environmental harmonization on U.S. trade and environmental policy could be magnified as EFTA and possibly East European nations join the trading block.

DEVELOPMENTS IN EC ENVIRONMENTAL HARMONIZATION

Community involvement in environmental matters is expected to be concentrated in the following areas: (1) pollution prevention and

---

[18] Personal communication with Roland Koch, German Member of Parliament, State of Hess. April, 1992.

control (air, water, waste, chemicals, and noise), (2) improving natural resource management, (3) international activities, and (4) developing means to promote environmental protection (research, standards and directives development, tax and grant measures, and information and education). [19] To date, the EC has adopted more than 280 environmental measures, and while many are narrow in substance, several have significant policy connotations. [20]

The EC Commission's effort to harmonize national environmental laws is likely to have mixed consequences for EC environmental policy and relative U.S. competitiveness. In many areas of environmental regulation, the United States already has stricter standards than EC countries, and upward harmonization of EC standards may make U.S. industry relatively more competitive. A proposed environmental liability directive, for example, would impose Superfund-type liability on waste generators. Among other things, this directive may force businesses to construct on-site treatment and disposal facilities, thus increasing costs of doing business in the EC. A new waste management and disposal directive (91/689/EEC) establishes strict, uniform procedures for handling, storage, transport, and disposal of hazardous wastes Community-wide. New EC bans on landfilling of certain wastes will require businesses to switch to more environmentally sound and costly disposal options, such as incinerating or recycling wastes. [21] (The United States has similar bans). The EC has also begun harmonizing certain vehicle emission standards up to U.S. levels, thus improving the outlook for U.S. auto manufacturers competitiveness in European markets.

In 1990, the EC Commission established the European Environment Agency. The Agency's primary function is to act as a center for coordinating and disseminating environmental information in the Community, thus assisting industry and other regulated parties to meet emerging environmental requirements. Many see the establishment of the European Environment Agency as an important step toward achieving a uniform environmental policy throughout the EC. Critics have faulted the Agency's lack of enforcement and policy powers, however, and the EC Commission has agreed to review and, perhaps expand, the Agency's authority in two years. [22]

Beyond EC–92, EC environmental policy is being influenced by growing support for Green candidates, recognition of the results of environmental neglect in Eastern Europe, wider European harmonization, and increased consumer demand for environmentally benign products. At this early date, it appears that these factors may result in more and stronger EC environmental regulations. As a result, U.S. industries may benefit from increased competitiveness as EC environmental costs come more in line with those now imposed on U.S. industries. Several significant EC environmental initiatives are reviewed below.

---

[19] USITC Publication 2318, p. 4–30.

[20] Haigh, Nigel. The European Community and International Environmental Policy. *International Environmental Affairs*, v. 3, no. 3, Summer, 1991. p. 169.

[21] USITC Publication 2318, p. 4–36.

[22] Curtin, Gerard V. Regulation 1210/90: Establishment of the European Environment Agency. *Boston College International and Comparative Law Review*, v. XIV, no. 2, Summer, 1991. p. 321.

CARBON TAX

In late 1991, European environment ministers suggested introducing a carbon tax in an effort to encourage energy conservation and, thus, reduce emissions of greenhouse gases and mitigate potential global warming effects resulting from fossil fuel combustion. The overall goal is to stabilize EC carbon dioxide emissions at 1990 levels by the year 2000. If adopted, the European Community's proposal to impose a tax on all carbon fuels (coal, gas, and oil) could diminish the Community's competitiveness in energy-dependent areas. The proposed tax would begin at a rate of $3 per barrel of oil, and increase by $1 per year until it reached $10 per barrel by the year 2000.

Such a tax could affect EC competitiveness in several ways; it would raise the cost of exports, and would increase the cost of entry for foreign companies interested in producing goods within the Community. Some analysts also predict that the tax would serve to decrease production of coal in the EC, and—in the short term—would provide an opportunity for more exports of cleaner U.S. coal to Europe. In the long term, coal use in the EC would likely decline as the Community shifts to reliance on other energy resources. Although many EC ministers for energy, economics, environment, and finance support the tax in principle, it is strongly opposed by industry, and its ultimate fate is uncertain. EC member states supporting the emission reduction targets have yet to issue specific strategies to achieve those targets. Moreover, poorer EC countries are particularly concerned that such a tax would hurt their economies.

The tax proposal was to have been ready for the United Nations Conference on Environment and Development (UNCED) in June, 1992, but appears to have lost considerable momentum since its emergence in late 1991. Outside the EC, few countries seem eager to follow suit. The United States has long opposed gasoline and other energy taxes, while Japan has expressed somewhat greater interest in using a tax to combat the threat of global warming. The EC is expected to eventually adopt some form of carbon tax, even without mutual action by other highly industrialized countries.

PRODUCT PACKAGING

By contrast to the carbon tax, pending changes in labeling and packaging requirements could make the EC more competitive in the world marketplace, as it moves to provide consumers with increasingly desired, environmentally benign, or "green" products. Conversely, outside industries interested in marketing their wares in the new EC may find barriers exist to market entry as a result of packaging and recycling requirements.

Prompted in part by Germany's new packaging law, the Community is moving toward adopting a similar measure. The 1991 German law provides that those who create packaging are responsible for taking it back. Already in effect is the requirement that producers and distributors collect and reclaim packaging used in transportation. Effective April 1991, secondary wastes (such as blister pack, exterior cartons and tamperproof packaging) must be accepted from consumers by retailers at the point of sale. Finally, beginning in January 1993, retailers must collect primary packaging. Primary packaging includes essentially all containers for liquids, and will be subject to a deposit charge of roughly $0.30. [23] Germany's law on packaging is likely to be adopted, all or in part, at the Community level. Given this development, U.S.-manufactured goods would be refused entry if manufacturers fail to meet new recycling requirements.

EC ECO-LABEL

In December 1991, the EC environment ministers adopted a Community-wide system for granting manufacturers "eco-labels" for products that meet certain environmental criteria. These criteria are to be set by a committee of industry, trade, environment, and consumer representatives. The purpose of the system is to encourage consumers to purchase those products that present fewer environmental problems either in production, use, or disposal. The decision as to whether a product qualifies for the label will be made by national officials. Industries have indicated support for a Community-wide eco-label system in lieu of disparate programs in each member state. Germany's "blue-angel" environmental labelling program is more than a decade old, and similar programs are under development in France, the Netherlands and Belgium. It is expected that the EC will encourage member states to phaseout national programs so as to have a single, uniform, environmental labelling system for all member countries. [24]

The eco-label program could prove detrimental to sales of U.S. products in the European market. As the EC-label program develops, U.S. companies may find it worthwhile to modify their products to earn the label in order to attract the rapidly growing "green" marketshare.

Similar proposals are under discussion in the U.S. Congress, Federal and State agencies, and the private sector. The EC experience in developing labelling criteria (which may involve participation by U.S. company representatives) and in implementing this program may benefit parallel efforts in the United States.

TRANSBOUNDARY WASTE TRADE

The extended EC effort to amend waste export regulations illustrates the challenge facing the Community in balancing free trade and environmental protection objectives. As of May 1992, the Commission and Parliament had failed to reach consensus on a proposal to implement the Basel Convention on international waste trade while meeting the goals of a single European market. Northern EC nations typically view waste as an environmental problem and support strict limits on international shipments. France opposes transboundary shipments even within the EC, and does not view waste as a commodity subject to EC free-trade rules. Conversely, several EC countries consider wastes commercial goods which should be al-

---

[23] U.S. Library of Congress. Congressional Research Service. *Recycling and Reducing Packaging Waste: How the United States Compares to Other Countries*. Report no. 91-802 ENR. Washington, 1991. p. 27-28.

[24] Bureau of National Affairs. Ministers Adopt System to Create Community-wide Environmental Labels. *International Environment Reporter*, December 18, 1991. p. 669.

Summary of Selected EC Environmental Initiatives

European Environment Agency (final 1990)	Established an EC-wide Agency to coordinate and disseminate environmental information.
Freedom of Information Directive (final, 1990)	Requires member states to establish measures to provide environmental information to the public.
Eco-label system (final 1991)	Authorizes establishing a system for granting manufacturers eco-labels for products that meet certain environmental standards.
Marketing and use of dangerous substances (amendment, 1991)	Adds toxic substances to list of chemicals restricted or banned from the EC market.
Transboundary waste shipment (proposed 1991)	Amends earlier directive to implement SEA, and to meet obligations under Basel and Lome Conventions.
Civil liability for damage caused by waste (proposed 1991)	Would impose Superfund-like liability on waste managers; allows public interest groups to sue for environmental damages.
Packaging waste recycling (proposed 1992)	Expected to follow German packaging law that requires producers and distributors to take back packaging from their products; may cover a wide range of wastes, impose deposit fees, and set recycling targets.

lowed to be traded internationally. Notwithstanding these differences, it appears that the measure finally adopted will permit the export of recyclable wastes only to OECD countries that have ratified the Basel Convention on international waste trade and allow exports for disposal only to EFTA countries that have ratified Basel.

The United States has not yet ratified this Convention which entered into force on May 5, 1992. Until and unless the U.S. Congress enacts legislation to implement the Basel Convention, U.S. industries may be prevented from shipping wastes for recycling to the European Community. Although most exported U.S. wastes go to Canada, industries involved in waste-metals recycling would be affected by the EC ban if adopted prior to U.S. ratification. Permissible trade could resume once the United States ratified the Convention, unless the Community ultimately agreed to more prohibitive waste trade legislation. The Basel Convention is pending in the U.S. Senate, awaiting advice and consent on ratification.

A Single Green Market?

Many European and American business analysts expect EC–92 to prompt higher environmental standards and, in turn, to stimulate pollution control research and "green" products development. If so, the European Community would be well situated to capture much of its emerging market for such goods and services.

In the products area, many Community manufacturers now voluntarily exceed required environmental standards in order to promote products and to capture the "green" consumer market. The EC Commission has encouraged industry to respond to the growing demand for less-polluting, "environmentally friendly," products (e.g., non-CFC containers, unleaded gas, and organically grown produce), and so-called "green capitalism" has grown along with consumer demand for such products. The single market notwithstanding, EC officials see the necessity for Europe to produce products that meet stringent U.S. and Japanese standards to enable European industry to improve international competitiveness.

If European industry responds broadly, Community members could increase competitiveness, while United States' businesses could lose market access for certain affected categories of goods. European companies would also have a competitive advantage in adjusting to emerging requirements, such as the proposed packaging and new eco-labelling directives. Many U.S. companies, however, are accustomed to high environmental standards, and adjusting to a greener EC market may not be difficult for them.

The growing pollution control services market also presents important business opportunities for U.S. companies. The U.S. International Trade Commission anticipates that the movement toward higher environmental standards could be beneficial for American firms involved in the design and sale of pollution control equipment. [25] Since many of these companies already manufacture products to meet strict U.S. standards, the firms are likely to be able to compete well in the European market.

In the waste management area alone, the 1991 EC market is estimated to have been $26 billion. [26] The Organization for Economic Cooperation and Development projects annual revenue in Europe from the environmental cleanup business (i.e., equipment and services for air and water pollution control, and waste management) will reach $78 billion by the year 2000, up from $54 million in 1990. [27]

As the countries of Eastern Europe and elsewhere begin to clean up their environments and adopt stricter pollution control requirements, the potential market for environmental goods and services in those countries is also significant. The EC could realize benefits from assisting its Eastern neighbors, both by transferring pollution control technologies and by offering new low-pollution products for their emerging markets. The United States faces similar opportunities in Eastern Europe, Mexico, and other developing countries.

Aided by the SEA, EC officials are able to address environmental problems more quickly than in the past. Timely and aggressive action could enhance EC ability to compete and possibly capture major portions of the pollution control/prevention market. Given the increasingly widespread perception in Europe that pollution control in unavoidable, and that pollution prevention is preferable, the EC appears to be moving rapidly to the subsequent question of how to create economic opportunities in doing so.

---

[25] USITC Publication 2318, p. 4–37.

[26] *The European Market for Hazardous Waste Management Services*, Report E1590. London, Sullivan House; as reported in *World Environment Report*, March 1, 1992. p. 52.

[27] Jerome, Robert W. Trading with a Greener Europe. *The Journal of Commerce*, September 4, 1991. p. 12.

Trade and Environment

The establishment of a single European market may influence the international debate how to accommodate environmental concerns within trade agreements. The trend toward establishing regional trading blocs (Europe, Asia, North America) has gained momentum in recent years; simultaneously, the major multilateral effort, the General Agreement on Tariffs and Trade (GATT) is seeking to expand its strength and scope. As these blocs solidify and trade agreements become more comprehensive, increased pressure is expected to be exerted on participating governments to harmonize environmental, and health and safety standards in order to realize greater efficiencies in commercial activities and to minimize interference with multilateral trade.

A unique characteristic of the SEA, in contrast to other multinational trade regimes, is that it includes significant environmental provisions in an effort to accommodate both trade and environmental protection objectives. Some believe the ratification of the SEA signalled the political recognition that environmental goals can be as important as, and sometimes more important than, free trade goals.

Consequently, EC efforts to harmonize environmental standards in the context of a trade partnership may inform other countries' attempts to form regional trading blocs. The EC model may also prove informative to the United States and other members of the GATT as they begin to grapple with the growing issue of the how to balance the sometimes conflicting goals of liberalized trade and environmental protection.

Conclusion

No clear consensus has emerged as to the effect EC–92 will have on European environmental policy and on U.S.-European trade. Under the new authority of the SEA, Community-wide uniformity will be promoted in many areas. Some environmental groups are concerned that harmonization will result in lower Community-wide standards. In contrast, many EC observers believe that, given the popularity of Green candidates, the growing demand for "environmentally friendly" products, and the EC policy shift toward pollution prevention, a unified market could result in stricter standards. Stricter standards could make U.S. industries more competitive as such standards would raise European pollution control requirements closer to those already incurred by many U.S. industries. The degree of this effect may be moderated by policy instruments supported by the EC (e.g., tax incentives, subsidies, grants, or EC-supported pollution-control research and development). The environmental equipment and services market is growing rapidly in the Community and presents significant opportunities to related U.S. businesses. In any event, an extended period of adjustment, and some confusion, can be expected as member states and their subdivisions adjust laws and regulations to meet EC directives. Moreover, although many environmental matters will be addressed and harmonized at the EC level, businesses likely will continue to encounter additional national and local environmental requirements.

Finally, EC unification may increase the force of the Community's voice in, and influence over, emerging international negotiations on global environmental issues. The experience the Community gains in attempting to balance trade and environment concerns may inform the international debate on this issue. Although the EC Treaty, as amended by the SEA, grants the Community broad legal and policy-making powers in environmental matters, it is expected that trade and environment measures may collide as unification proceeds. EC–92 marks a new era in European environmental policy; however, the ultimate shape and impact of that policy is currently uncertain and likely to be mixed.

VI. THE EUROPEAN COMMUNITY IN THE INTERNATIONAL COMMUNITY

MANAGING ECONOMIC INTERDEPENDENCE: THE EUROPEAN CHALLENGE

by C. Michael Aho and Bruce Stokes *

CONTENTS

The European Community (EC) is awakening from a long sleep to become a bold and dynamic force in the world economy. Widespread political and economic changes have unleashed pent-up energies and created a whole host of new political challenges for Europe and the world at large. The EC has embarked upon an ambitious program to achieve what was not accomplished 35 years ago: a unified, dynamic common market. But what began as an effort to create a Europe without borders (EC–92) has become an historic opportunity to form a much broader European Union with a common currency, a joint defense arm and a single foreign policy. If these efforts succeed, the EC will be richer and able to buy more from the rest of the world, to contribute more for common security and development assistance efforts and to take a leadership role in world affairs. [1]

At the same time Europe is arising from its slumber, the waning of the Cold War has put a symbolic coda to the end of the era of American global preeminence. U.S. military might is no longer needed to counterbalance the Soviet strategic threat. The U.S. economy no longer stands head and shoulders above its competitors. And America is grappling internally to define a new role for itself in a rapidly changing world.

It is little wonder that the transatlantic relationship is evolving and that the future shape of the alliance is unclear. The economy is replacing security as the primary focus of bilateral affairs. In the

---

* C. Michael Aho is Director of Economic Studies at the Council on Foreign Relations. Bruce Stokes is International Economics Correspondent for the *National Journal*.

[1] This article is adapted from a forthcoming book entitled *The European Challenge*. New York, Council on Foreign Relations, 1992.

past, economic disagreements took a backseat to security considerations in order not to disrupt the alliance's common front toward the Soviets. But without the constraints of the Cold War, Washington can be expected to aggressively pursue its economic self-interest. And in so doing, America will have less leverage with its allies. At the same time, Europe is more willing to assert its economic interests. In such a world, ongoing confrontation is inevitable.

Europe, and the European Community in particular, is the crucible of reform in the world today. Over the next decade and beyond, Europe will be the first among the major industrial powers to grapple with the challenges of the 21st century:

- how to redefine national sovereignty as individual nations surrender economic autonomy;
- how to mesh different cultures with different priorities and different decisionmaking processes;
- how to deregulate separate national economic regimes and to induce competition among national monopolies, and
- how to establish transnational incentives to promote innovation and technological advance without sacrificing the benefits from or being captive to laissez-faire economics.

As Joseph Nye of Harvard University has put it, the EC is the only entity that is capable of challenging the United States for center stage among the great powers in the next century. [2] But the EC lacks a common language and a common culture with generations of experience working closely together. And even though a common currency could be established by the turn of the century, Brussels lacks sufficient authority to tax and spend. For the immediate future, governmental responsibilities will reside in national capitals and the individual countries will have to negotiate among themselves on how to reduce regional inequities. Greater labor mobility would help, but the peoples of Europe, unlike in the United States, are well-rooted in the land of their birth. People don't even move north and south in Belgium, much less pick up and go to Portugal.

The European Community has an overloaded plate of political issues confronting it in the years ahead. It is likely that a common currency with a European central bank will only be achieved in a two-tier or two-speed process. Some countries will inevitably be on the outside of the new central bank looking in for the foreseeable future. The EC still needs to enact institutional reforms to correct its "democratic deficit" and to streamline its decisionmaking processes. New members will be admitted to the EC in the next few years, but which countries and on what basis? Political and security affairs will remain a source of contention as the Community wrestles over what should constitute a common defense posture and foreign policy.

With such wide-ranging issues at play and the possibility of significant dislocations perhaps exacerbated by a recession and/or a flood of immigrants fleeing the former Communist states of Eastern Europe and the republics of the late Soviet Union, the EC will

---

[2] Nye, Joseph. *Bound to Lead.* New York, Basic Books, 1990. See also Huntington, Samuel P. The U.S.—Decline or Renewal? *Foreign Affairs,* Winter 1988/89.

have its hands full. When push comes to shove, time and political will are scarce resources and the outside world could find that engaging the EC in multilateral initiatives is a challenge of the first order. Without sufficient prodding from the United States, the EC could become perennially preoccupied. The EC's stubborn refusal to make further concessions on reducing agricultural subsidies in the Uruguay round of multilateral trade talks could be a harbinger of things to come. If the EC refuses to act as a global power broker and chooses instead to remain a parochial regional power, it will constrain reform of the international economic system and hobble the management of global economic interdependence.

The European Community has attempted widescale reform efforts in the past, but has come up short. Could Euro-sclerosis once again settle over Western Europe? The pace of economic integration so ambitiously set out in the EC–92 program has unquestionably slowed. Contradictory visions of the future shape of Europe emerged at the EC's Maastricht Summit in December 1991, raising the specter of European political gridlock. And the Community's abject failure in mediating a peaceful solution to the Yugoslavian civil war has only rekindled earlier cynicism about Europe's ability to act in unison on the world stage.

While the Euro-optimism of the past few years has now been tempered, there is no need for a renewed round of Euro-pessimism. History suggests that each time the European Community has faced a major challenge, the struggle has driven the nations of Europe closer together, not further apart.

The train of European union is still on track. At Maastricht the 12 EC nations agreed to create a common monetary policy and single currency no later than 1999. "The momentum for progress is strong," said Keith Richardson, secretary general of the European Round Table of Industrialists. [3] Surely impediments to progress will arise, but the forces unleashed are irreversible. It remains for Europe's partners, most notably the United States, to deal with the consequences of Europe's emergence from its long slumber.

Macroeconomic Coordination

The unification of the European economy in the 1990s is the third great shock to the world economy since the Vietnam War, comparable to the oil embargoes of the 1970s and the Third World debt crisis of the 1980s. Europe is poised to be the global economy's next great growth engine, pulling along the stagnant North American economy, the collapsing economies of Eastern Europe and the moribund economies of Africa, South Asia and parts of Latin America. But a united Europe will also reorder the globe's economic priorities. Europe has suddenly become a focal point for investment and trade. And it poses a threat to U.S. preeminence in the global economy, a challenge that surpasses even that of Japan.

The original Cecchini report, done by Paolo Cecchini for the EC Commission, estimated that the integration of the European market could mean roughly 4.5 percent in additional economic

[3] Personal interview, December 16, 1991.

growth for Europe by 1998.[4] Richard Baldwin of Columbia University is even more optimistic, estimating that EC–92 could add up to 0.9 percentage points to Europe's long term growth rate, rather than only conferring a one-time rise.[5] Other economists are more pessimistic. But all analysts agree that Europe, which through the 1970s and 1980s was a drag on the world economy, has once again become a vibrant source of economic activity.

This revival of economic activity comes at a price. In the 1980s, the magnet for global capital was the United States. In the 1990s Europe has become an alternative pole for investment. DRI/McGraw-Hill estimates that fixed investment by business in Europe will grow an average of 8.3 percent per year from 1990 through 1995. By the end of that period European companies' annual capital demand will be more than triple what it was in 1986.

This investment will come from well-entrenched U.S. businesses expanding their European operations, American firms trying to gain a foothold in Europe, from Asian investors, and, most important, it will come from European companies keeping their money at home.

At the same time, public investment in Europe, especially by Germany in its five eastern *Länder*, has soared. Tens of billions of dollars have been poured into the former East German economy to rebuild infrastructure, to retool noncompetitive factories and to subsidize redundant workers. The German federal deficit, at a fifteen year low in 1989, has soared and Germany's current account surplus has disappeared.

Moreover, if the capital needs of the east German *Länder* are any indicator, the investment required to begin to improve the productivity of the economies of the other nations of Eastern Europe and the former Soviet Union will constitute a drain on the global capital market for years to come. Estimates by Harvard University's Jeffrey Sachs that the former Soviet Union may need $110 billion in Western capital over the next five years now look conservative.

This is of particular U.S. concern because investors from the European Community supply far more capital to the United States than does Japan. And Europe's future capital needs will make it much harder for the United States to attract the capital needed to finance its twin trade and budget deficits.

There is, of course, no scarcity of capital in the world, if the price is right. As a result, European demand for capital will keep interest rates higher than they might otherwise have been; witness the disparity in relatively high German and low U.S. interest rates in early 1992.

Such differentials are particularly damaging to the U.S. economy. Simulations by the London office of Robert Fleming Securities Ltd. suggest that a one percent rise in world interest rates will more adversely affect U.S. economic growth than European growth,

---

[4] Commission of the European Communities. *Research on the "Cost of Non-Europe"*. Brussels, 1988.

[5] Baldwin, Richard. The Growth Effects of 1992. *Economic Policy*, v. 4, no. 2, Fall 1989. p. 24781.

slowing U.S. growth by .4 percent in the first year and .6 percent in the second year, but slowing German growth by only .1 percent in the first year, and .3 percent in the second year. [6]

At the Maastricht Summit, the EC member states pledged to form a common monetary union and single currency by 1997, at the earliest, and by 1999 at the latest. To achieve sufficient convergence of national economies to permit a smooth transition to a monetary bloc, European governments have committed themselves to hold annual national government deficits to no more than three percent of gross domestic product (GDP) and overall government debt to no more than 60 percent of GDP. They have also promised not to allow national inflation rates to deviate from each other by more than 1.5 percent. While necessary preconditions for economic convergence, these commitments will impair future European governments' ability to use fiscal and monetary policy to lift their economies out of recession.

Of course, these criteria will be difficult to meet. With some member states' budget deficits approaching or exceeding 10 percent of gross domestic product and inflation differentials greater than 5 percent, not all member countries will initially be able to enter the European Central Bank. (The United Kingdom and Denmark reserve the right not to join at all.)

This two-speed monetary union will create political and economic management problems for participants and non-participants alike. At the same time, it will be impossible to have free flows of capital and fixed exchange rates on one hand and an independent monetary policy on the other. Even if European countries wait to join the new monetary arrangement, they will have little latitude to attack domestic problems using monetary or fiscal policies that significantly deviate from those of the core group.

Thus an inner circle of countries will then have the responsibility for making critical macroeconomic decisions affecting all of the EC. National politicians on the outside will resent being unable to deal independently with sensitive domestic issues, such as unemployment. They will find themselves highly constrained in using expansionary fiscal policy to generate jobs in lagging regions. And if their countries should get into the new European central bank, adoption of a single currency or irrevocably fixed exchange rates will entail sacrificing the possibility of exchange rate changes to stimulate aggregate demand.

Because of limited labor mobility in the EC and the lack of a strong federal role in Brussels, countries on the periphery have already begun to demand greater internal transfers and regional aids as the price for going along. The internal political debate in the EC will intensify but ultimately those countries will go along. The draw of a unified EC is too great to be left out.

The stringent criteria for joining the European Monetary Union (EMU), dictated at Maastricht by Germany's austerity-minded Bundesbank, and the political problems attendant with meeting those goals, also directly affect U.S. economic interests because the well-being of the U.S. economy is increasingly dependent on ex-

[6] Robert Fleming, private forecasts, 1990.

ports to Europe. Policies that hamper rapid European economic recovery will slow a U.S. rebound from the current and future American recessions. Moreover, U.S. domestic economic policy options will be limited in the future because use of debt- and inflation-producing fiscal policy to jump start the American economy will risk a run on the dollar.

Just as the crumbling of the Berlin Wall symbolized the end of the Cold War security regime, the decision at the recent Maastricht Summit to create a European Monetary Union (EMU) by the end of the decade signals the end of the dollar-dominated, Washington-led postwar international monetary regime. The days of a single reserve currency are waning. The ability of the United States to leverage European cooperation on interest rates, exchange rates and related monetary and fiscal policy is over.

The dollar's preeminent position as the world's key currency has been receding for years. The dollar's share of total official foreign exchange reserves held by the world's central banks fell from 71.4 percent in 1981 to 56.4 percent in 1990 and the percentage of trade invoiced in dollars by the major trading nations fell from 32.8 percent in 1980 to 25.7 percent in 1987.

The principal immediate threat to the dollar's preeminence is the German mark. The mark's share of European foreign exchange holdings nearly doubled over the last ten years and now accounts for nearly a quarter of all European reserves. [7] The ecu, which is already as widely used as the yen in many transactions, promises to be even more widely held than the mark. If all European currencies were folded into the ecu today, they would account for at least 34.4 percent of all foreign exchange reserves.

EMU, the planned creation of a European Central Bank, and the emergence of an ecu bloc will further alter the power relationship between the United States and Europe on monetary and fiscal issues. The depth and breadth of the market for the dollar has given the United States enormous leverage in the past. Washington could talk down the value of the dollar and force Bonn, which saw its U.S. export markets evaporating, to begin expansionary domestic economic policies. The emerging self-sufficient single European market will be increasingly immune to the arm-twisting effects of threatened dollar depreciation.

EMU is likely to transform the international economic coordination process that industrial nations have fitfully been pursuing over the last decade and a half. The emergence of an industrial world Big Three—Europe, Japan and the United States—places a higher premium on coordination. At the technical level, creation of a European Central Bank, with one currency and one bureaucracy, will presumably make that coordination easier—transaction costs will be reduced. But, in fact, coordination could at times become even more difficult. Greater symmetry could generate more instability if it creates more of an incentive to manipulate exchange rates for domestic purposes.

If the European Central Bank has in its charter a clearly stated mandate of price stability above all else, its ability to ease mone-

[7] IMF economist George S. Tavlas.

tary policy when conditions might require such relaxation for the purposes of international coordination could be hindered. Moreover, so much depends on the personal chemistry of the decision makers. U.S. officials have long found Bundesbank personnel much more difficult to get along with than the leaders of the Bank of Japan. An emboldened Bundesbank leadership, newly confident in its dominance of the European Central Bank may be even less likely to cooperate with Washington in the future.

And, if the new European Central Bank is truly independent of the political process, like the Bundesbank and the U.S. Federal Reserve, then it may be even harder for governments to insure that the international economic agreements they reach are put into practice. The Maastricht Agreement requires the unanimous consent of the European governments before the European Monetary Union can enter into irrevocably fixed exchange rate agreements. It remains unclear whether unanimity is also required for participation in informal target zone agreements, such as those struck between the major industrial powers in the Plaza Accord in 1985 and the Louvre Agreement in 1987. If Greece must sign on before Brussels can join with Washington and Tokyo in intervening in currency markets, European footdragging could sabotage future exchange rate management.

Because Brussels lacks substantial power to tax and spend, fiscal outcomes in the member states will condition the EMU monetary policy. But central monetary policy under EMU will put greater pressure nationally on fiscal policy to achieve domestic objectives. A situation like that in the United States in the early 1980's—tight monetary policy and loose fiscal policy—is possible if several of the large economies in the EC run large budget deficits simultaneously. The stringent criteria adopted at Maastricht are designed to avoid such a possibility. But if individual heads of state already in EMU are in a tough reelection fight the criteria could go out the window with adverse effects on interest and exchange rates and on the international economy in general.

International coordination of fiscal policy will also be more important and more difficult. The head of the European Central Bank might be able to agree with his or her counterparts in the United States and Japan, but who (among the twelve) will serve as the EC's finance minister to negotiate on fiscal policy? The United States and Japan could find negotiating macroeconomic policy with the EC as difficult as negotiating trade policy is today. Once the Community position has been negotiated it will be almost immutable.

Moreover, EMU will increase the market's oversight of U.S. economic policies. With the ecu representing an economy that is larger than that in the United States, currency traders will conduct a daily referendum on the efficacy of U.S. fiscal and monetary policies, driving down the dollar whenever they disagree with Washington's actions. This dollar volatility will complicate management of the U.S. economy.

Thus, EMU fundamentally changes the power relationship among Europe, Japan and the United States on monetary issues. Indeed, this may have been one of the primary driving forces behind EMU. The greater negotiating leverage the European Community gains through EMU will enable it to trade off macroeconomic changes for other objectives on trade or security issues.

Trade Cooperation

Politicians, trade policymakers, and business people in the United States have focused their attention almost exclusively on Japan in recent years. Their myopia could leave them unprepared for the policy challenges and business opportunities that will be greater in Europe than in Japan and the Far East in the 1990s.

Business people should not allow the competitive challenge from Japan to blind them to the enormous opportunities that lie across the Atlantic. The EC–92 unification effort has gotten its share of attention but most businesses have not yet recognized the size and richness of the emerging European market.

Europe, including the East European countries but not the former Soviet Union, houses more than 500 million people. Its gross national product of roughly $6 trillion is larger than that of the United States. And it has unleashed pent-up energies in its EC–92 unification effort.

What might the EC–92 effort mean? The economic effects will be substantial once all or most of the program is completed: European national income will increase by 9–30 percent over the medium term; up to 5 million more jobs will be created; consumer prices will be lower and a wider variety of products will be available; 12 different sets of regulations and standards will be harmonized; economies of scale might be achieved on a European-wide basis, enhancing competitiveness; and national cartels might be broken up, providing for greater flexibility.

Certainly this transformation of Europe will not be easy. The momentum generated by the EC–92 unification effort has undoubtedly slowed. The process will not be completed by December 31, 1992, but the shape of Europe will be altered forever. European businesses (and outside businesses) perceive that the process is irreversible and are beginning to act upon that perception. When businesses change behavior, perception becomes reality.

But many in the Community are apprehensive and have fears that United States and Japanese firms may be in a better position to take advantage of the EC–92 effort than EC firms; that labor standards will be eroded to the lowest level permitted among member states; that regional imbalances will be accentuated; that the dislocations will be significant; and that a two-tiered (or two-speed) Community will result, with the original six members moving further, faster than the United Kingdom and the newer member countries of the South.

How much will be accomplished? The road to unification is littered with a wide variety of obstacles. One of the most significant is surely fiscal harmonization, because establishment of a Europe without borders would see the removal of customs agents at internal frontiers. Those customs officials are responsible for charging national value added taxes on imports or rebating them on exports. And of course there is always the possibility of national objections to giving Brussels additional authority. Past unification efforts have foundered on national resistance to the sacrifice of autonomy.

National parliaments can be expected to react negatively to widespread dislocations or to the potential demise of national champions (e.g., Fiat and Peugeot). In addition, the member states will likely disagree over other issues including inconsistent immigration policies due to colonial preferences and preferential market access to the emerging democracies in Eastern Europe. Finally, of course, the EC will have to attend to the numerous petitions for membership. The richer countries of the European Free Trade Association (EFTA) have the inside track but how long can the EC say no to Turkey and eventually Poland, Hungary, and Czechoslovakia?

The odds against achieving economic—and ultimately political—union are formidable. Optimists in Europe are fond of looking at the United States as a model of integration. But unlike the United States, the European Community lacks a common culture based on 200 years of assimilation, a strong federal government with an interstate commerce clause and with the power to tax and spend, and a high degree of labor mobility among its regions.

The process will be difficult, but the potential for change in Europe should not be underestimated. A slumbering giant is waking up, and the United States had better pay attention. U.S. businesses stand to benefit from a united Europe, but European union also poses substantial trade problems for the United States. Vital American interests are at stake.

The EC is incrementally changing its rules of the game governing trade and domestic regulations. As the flap over beef hormones demonstrated, the U.S. trade policy process cannot ignore changes in laws and regulations abroad that discriminate against U.S. interests. The EC is experimenting with new programs to promote technical innovation and is revamping its competition policy, perhaps to the disadvantage of outside firms.

What should the U.S. policy responses be? The U.S. trade policy process fundamentally changed in the 1980s as the Reagan administration embarked upon a multifaceted approach mixing unilateral, bilateral and multilateral initiatives. Aggressive unilateralism under Section 301 of the 1988 U.S. Trade and Competitiveness Act has been wielded against several countries, but not against the EC out of a desire not to antagonize allies during the Cold War. But that may not continue if the EC discriminates against U.S. interests or is accused of "unfairly" supporting emerging industries.

In order to keep Europe open, or indeed, to open it further, some would prefer to use Section 301 as a crowbar and to pry open the European market. But such aggressive unilateral tactics will only weaken the transatlantic alliance. It would only be a matter of days before the EC responded in kind. Bilateral free trade agreements are also a new instrument in the U.S. trade tool kit but no one can agree which country to choose after Canada and Mexico, our neighbors. A bilateral free trade agreement such as the United States signed with Canada has been proposed by Representative Richard Gephardt, but why the EC and not a regional agreement in the Pacific? Senator Max Baucus proposed a free trade agreement with Japan. President Bush promised a regional agreement for all of the Western Hemisphere in his Enterprise for the Americas Initiative. Who will decide which bilaterals to pursue and on what basis? Regional agreements play favorites and create resentment on the part of outsiders. A misguided bilateral strategy could hasten the fragmentation of the world trading system into belligerent blocs and that would cause hardship for all countries.

There is, however, one policy instrument that is available to influence the Community in the implementation of its integration efforts—the Uruguay Round of trade negotiations. Emphasis on multilateral pressure confined to trade matters would help to minimize misunderstandings because more countries than the United States would be involved.

Many of the key issues in the EC–92 effort and the Uruguay Round of multilateral trade negotiations are the same—services, telecommunications, government procurement, and voluntary restraints. Can this coincidence be used advantageously by bringing international pressure to bear on EC internal decisions? Or, will the Uruguay Round be held hostage to the EC's restructuring—crowded out because of limited time and resources, pushed into the background with internal EC directives taken first? [8] With the internal rules of the game changing, creating uncertainty and new competition for EC firms, many EC firms would probably prefer to hold off liberalizing vis-a-vis the rest of the world. This is not to argue that the EC will raise new barriers, but it may not be eager to make new commitments or to lower barriers. After all, signing on to substantial agreements in the multilateral talks would limit its flexibility in reaching internal agreements.

If the past is prologue, countries outside the Community have reason for concern. One factor that has proved nettlesome in the past is the Community's cumbersome decision-making process on trade policy. Since negotiations over trade policy in the EC take place between the Commission and the separate nation states, the decisions are usually reached with difficulty, rendering the Community's position inflexible and, often, decisions are taken on the basis of the lowest common denominator. Gardner Patterson, a former Deputy Director-General of the GATT, states that "the Community's behavior creates serious problems and threatens [the] international trading system . . . It can be traced to the structure of the EC decision-making process, which is slow, hard to predict and has a protectionist bias." [9] The protracted disagreement over liberalization of agricultural trade in the Uruguay Round, largely because of French resistance, is a prime example.

Martin Wolf of the *Financial Times* has argued, "Another consequence of the [Community's] negotiating process is to externalize internal conflict. If, for example, the West German steel industry is hurt by subsidies from the Italian Government to Italian producers, the natural response is a combination of some limit on those subsidies with greater protection against outsiders. Furthermore, because of the nature of the European Community, it is only rarely that it can agree on any far-reaching initiatives in global arrange-

---

[8] Montagnon, Peter. EC 'Distracted' from Uruguay Round. *Financial Times*, March 24, 1990. p. 3.

[9] Patterson, Gardner. The European Community as a Threat to the System. In Cline, William, ed. *Trade Policy in the 1980s*. Washington, Institute for International Economics, 1983. p. 223–42.

ments, where the running has been left almost entirely to the United States." [10]

An additional problem is that business interests in the Community cannot be relied upon to promote trade liberalization. Unlike the situation in the United States, business interests in Europe do not lobby extensively on trade policy. Perhaps this is because at the Community level business interests are dealing with bureaucrats, not elected officials, who are more likely to side with particular sectoral interests. Business lobbying in the EC can be effective on internal issues such as the EC-92 effort where much of the impetus has come from an activist business sector. What is unknown is how business interests in the Community will react as the Uruguay Round approaches its critical, final stage. Businesses planning and operating on a global basis share a common interest in greater stability and reduced uncertainty, but you would not know that from the attitude of EC businesses toward the Uruguay Round. They appear to be too preoccupied with EC-92 and things closer to home.

Nonetheless, the battles over the external consequences of the EC-92 unification effort have not yet been joined. They will be fought out issue by issue, directive by directive, with alliances shifting from one issue to the next. The outside world should not let the Community lose sight of the implications for the multilateral trading system. Instead, it should be on the lookout to see: if Community directives are applied in a narrow reciprocal fashion and establish European preferences to discriminate against outsiders; if the directives' long phase-in times and safeguards for lagging sectors or for the poorer European countries are protectionism under a different guise; if regulatory standards effectively discriminate against outsiders; if local content provisions and rules of origin force new investment in the EC; how competition policy is revised and antidumping laws are used; and whether the implementation of directives is transparent or done behind closed doors with maximum uncertainty. All such efforts would have the same effect on outside firms as an increase in trade barriers. [11]

The external consequences will not be known for some time, but the outside world can not wait to see what the results will be because by then the Community's position will be set in concrete, with no room to maneuver. The Community's unification efforts should be made a focal point of multilateral discussions so that the Community feels constrained when reaching internal decisions. To the extent it is not constrained, the world risks willy nilly evolving into an economic order characterized by economic blocs. How benign these blocs might be would depend upon the strength of multilateral discipline. Greater multilateral discipline is on the table in the Uruguay Round, but if the round is to be completed soon, the Community may not be constrained and what little multilateral discipline that now exists in the world trading system may not be preserved.

---

[10] Wolf, Martin. *1992: Global Implications of the European Community's Programme for Completing the Internal Market.* Lehrman Institute Policy Paper, series on the United States in the global economy, no. 1, New York, 1989. p. 27-28.

[11] Aho, C. Michael, and Bruce Stokes. The Implications of European Integration for U.S. Trade Policy. In Baldwin, R. E., and J. D. Richardson. *The Uruguay Round and Beyond: Problems and Prospects.* National Bureau of Economic Research, 1991.

The Uruguay Round of multilateral trade negotiations is the first big test of economic cooperation in the post-Cold War era. Those talks were to have concluded in December 1990 at a Ministerial meeting in Brussels but they broke up because of the EC's refusal to make substantial offers to reduce its agricultural subsidies and to reform its Common Agricultural Policy (CAP, which the EC often refers to as the glue that holds it together). The Argentines and Brazilians (accompanied by the United States) walked out in Brussels vowing not to return until the EC was more forthcoming.

Agriculture is the linchpin for the talks. Some progress has been made since 1990 but the EC still insists on less of a cut than demanded by the United States and other agricultural exporters. At risk are substantial agreements covering the protection of intellectual property and the regulation of services.

If the Uruguay Round talks fail then there will be no ongoing multilateral process to scrutinize the EC's internal restructuring or to constrain the EC (and the United States) from reliance on discriminatory regional agreements and belligerent bilateral badgering. Both will look inward and trade tensions will heighten.

Even if the talks conclude with a modest result, the lack of an ongoing process could lead to heightened tensions. Meanwhile, the agenda of unresolved issues keeps growing as trade and environmental policy collide. American environmental legislation is increasingly using trade sanctions to enforce U.S. standards. On the other side of the Atlantic, environmental standards such as rules on the level of hormones in beef have been used to exclude U.S. products from Europe. But the environment is not yet on the multilateral trade agenda nor is it mentioned anywhere in the GATT Articles.

The Bush Administration is softening its agricultural position in the trade talks at the same time it pushes hard on the EC to budge. But even if an agreement can be struck it is bound to disappoint influential domestic constituents in services, agriculture, and industries looking for greater protection of intellectual property. What then? The Bush Administration has not developed a consistent multilateral plan. Without thinking through the consequences, the Bush Administration has only suggested that concluding a trade agreement with Mexico is next on the agenda, to be followed by negotiations for a regional agreement in the Americas.

How will the inevitable blanks be filled in the multilateral agreement? How can the EC be kept engaged in multilateral economic cooperation? How can the United States use its economic leverage to make progress on new issues like the environment without having to wait until the year 2000 to start another round of multilateral trade talks?

When an agreement is finally reached in the Uruguay Round, the U.S. Administration should grab it, but complain that it is inadequate. Agriculture, intellectual property protection and services will all come up short. In working with Congress, the Administration should draft the implementing legislation to make the agreement contingent upon further progress and call for the launch of a new set of talks to begin immediately. Although many business leaders and policymakers may be frustrated with the multilateral process, environmental groups could be instrumental in lobbying

Congress to approve further talks. They could get environmental issues on the trade agenda and the international trading system would get the added benefit of having established the means to constrain the commercial behavior of both the EC and the United States.

New Issues

The new transatlantic economic relationship will be further complicated by developments in Eastern Europe and the former Soviet Union, by the emerging EC-Japan relationship, by the changing nature of U.S.-European security arrangements and by political developments inside a united Europe.

Geography dictates that the former Soviet Union and Eastern Europe are within the EC's sphere of economic influence. But geography does not have to be destiny. If the countries of the former Soviet bloc craft viable Western-style economies, but do so with little or no U.S. help, their gratitude, their obligations and their new trade and investment relationships will only reinforce their centuries-old commercial ties with Western Europe. The United States will be dealt out of an important new production base and what could be one of the most rapidly growing markets in the world.

Currently, Eastern Europe and the former Soviet Union have little commerce with the world and account for only a small portion of U.S. trade: $3 billion in imports in 1990 and $4.8 billion in exports to the region. By comparison, in 1988, EC countries bought $49.1 billion worth of East European and Soviet products and sold the region $41.4 billion in goods.

Integration of the former Soviet Union and Eastern Europe into the world economy could increase world trade 2–3 percent in the medium run and by as much as 15 percent in the long run. [12] The EC is likely to monopolize those trade gains. For example, if the former Soviet Union is successful in opening its market to the world, the EC could end up providing it with over half of its imports, up from a third of the total today. [13] By comparison, without some initiative, the U.S. share of the potentially larger former Soviet import market could drop from one-fifth to one-fifteenth.

It will take a special U.S. effort to increase American commerce with the region. Currently, the United States is the only major Western government which does not provide substantial financing for its manufacturing exports to the former Soviet Union. Moreover, U.S. export controls impede the sale of high tech equipment to the region, ceding much of that market to European firms and creating new points of tension with Western Europe which favors fewer restrictions on previously controlled exports.

By allowing Western Europe free reign in the East, the United States will only reinforce the EC's inward looking trade and investment tendencies. The lonely burden of restructuring Eastern Europe will give the EC one more rationale for external trade discrimination and a go-slow attitude toward multilateral trade

---

[12] Collins. Susan M., and D. Rodrik. *Eastern Europe and the Soviet Union in the World Economy.* Washington, Institute for International Economics, 1991.

[13] Ibid.

reform and monetary policy coordination. Only a more aggressive U.S. economic engagement with the region, in effect changing U.S. stakes, can mute that potential discord.

Conversely, if the area's transition from a command to a market economy fails, the resultant inevitable social disintegration could lead to the reemergence of authoritarian regimes of both the left and the right, reigniting Cold War tensions. Hopes would be dashed for reducing the U.S. military burden and refocusing the U.S. economy to meet the competitive challenges posed by the European Community and Japan in the 21st century. And the region's nuclear arsenal could easily fall into terrorists' hands.

Moreover, the failure of job-producing Western capitalism to take root in eastern socialist soil threatens the advanced nations of Europe with a flood tide of economic refugees. These new "guest workers" could destabilize Western European society and undermine the role Europe will be able to play in sharing with the United States the financial burden of future world leadership. The United States economy could ill afford any weakening of its principal export market and the home of the vast majority of U.S. overseas investment.

Japan's rapidly evolving relationship with Europe poses a similar challenge to U.S.-EC relations. "Had there been no Japan, there might have been no 1992 project in Europe," wrote Daniel Burstein in *Euroquake*. [14] "A great many factors went into making EC–92 happen. But in the early days, Europe's fear and envy of Japan were particularly visceral catalysts."

EC-Japanese economic ties have come a long way since the 1960s, when French President Charles de Gaulle dismissed Japan as a nation of transistor salesmen. Since 1986, EC-Japanese trade has grown faster than either Japanese or European commerce with the United States. But this trade is precariously imbalanced, with Japan's trade surplus with France, Germany, Great Britain and Italy, expected to grow from $8 billion in 1990 to $30 billion by 1995. [15]

This imbalance directly affects U.S. interests. Japan's trade surplus with Europe is largely attributable to the undervaluation of the yen with respect to European currencies. This undervaluation places American exporters at a disadvantage when competing with Japanese manufacturers for a share of Europe's expanding unified market. Moreover, the one way nature of current EC-Japanese trade is bound to intensify anti-Japanese trade pressure in Europe. Such actions, while ostensibly aimed at Japan, could embroil Washington in Brussels' tussles with Tokyo and affect how the United States conducts its own commercial relations with Japan.

Moreover, the EC's attempt to confront the competitive challenge posed by Japan has forced Brussels and Tokyo into an unprecedented dialogue of ever widening scope. In the process, many Europeans and Japanese are finding that they share kindred philosophies about the structure of a modern economy.

---

[14] Burstein, Daniel. *Euroquake*. Simon and Schuster, 1991.

[15] Personal commentary, William R. Cline, senior fellow at the Institute for International Economics, April 1991.

The EC-Japan auto pact—which limits Japanese penetration of the EC market until the end of the decade—is a manifestation of this convergence of world views. The victim of such a deal could be the American auto industry. Japanese cars not shipped to Europe could end up in the United States, or more likely, in other markets where they will compete with U.S. exports. As the United States has ruefully learned from its own quota on Japanese cars, any European limits on the number of Japanese cars that can be sold will allow Japanese auto makers to charge higher prices. Increased profits will enable Toyota and Nissan to invest more to produce even better, less costly products to challenge Ford, GM and Chrysler.

Whether Europe and Japan draw closer together or merely find themselves involved in a more fractious relationship, their new rapport will forever change U.S.-EC relations.

Throughout the postwar period, U.S.-European defense ties have served as a lubricant in the transatlantic relationship, easing economic frictions. But the collapse of the Warsaw Pact means that alliance trade and investment problems will no longer be sublimated in the interest of maintaining a common front against an external threat.

The lack of a credible Soviet challenge to Western European security and the concomitant drawdown in U.S. forces stationed in Europe will inevitably undermine Washington's leverage with Brussels. European intransigence in the Uruguay Round in the face of obvious U.S. desire to move forward on a range of issues would have been unthinkable at the height of the Cold War. Similarly, Washington's blocking of European participation in the building of the Soviet gas pipeline in the early 1980s because of security concerns could not be repeated today. And European independence on monetary issues and its greater flexibility in fiscal policy is directly attributable to its lack of dependence on the U.S. defense umbrella and its ability to cut its own defense expenditures.

For now, European defense capacity is a hollow shell. The European nations lack the independent air and sea lift capacity to mount major operations without U.S. support. If the Western European Union (WEU) is charged with developing such capacity, funds for such an effort could draw down European commitments to NATO. And at a time when Western defense industries are desperate for business, the likelihood that much or all of those contracts will go to European firms will only heighten transatlantic tensions. Similarly, with allied armies reducing arms acquisitions, there is likely to be growing U.S.-EC competition in arms sales to the Third World.

Finally, domestic political developments in Europe are going to increasingly influence transatlantic economic relations.

In the past, a politically hamstrung European Community made U.S. dominance of the alliance all the easier. Moreover, the details of internal European political reform were considered a purely domestic European concern. But a European Community without the democratic authority and financial resources to act decisively on the world stage is a potential source of global instability that is not at all in U.S. interests. And continued sensitivities to national sovereignty no longer reflect the integrated nature of the transatlantic economy.

The Maastricht Summit signaled a growing discontinuity between Europe's emerging economic union and its lagging political union. For example, Britain's continued insistence that any EC member state has the right to disassociate itself from a common European currency or a joint set of rules governing workers' wages and hours potentially limits the benefits of a united Europe for U.S. companies. Moreover, a British precedent of opting out of a united Europe raises the specter that a nationalist-minded German government might also decide to go its own way before European union is completed, scuttling a half-century of American diplomatic efforts to preserve European peace by irrevocably tieing Germany into Western Europe.

The European Parliament's continuing inability to initiate legislation means internal European political debates over the EC Commission's accountability are likely to become increasingly divisive, threatening Brussels' political legitimacy. And the Parliament's inability to raise revenues means the Community is likely to have increasing difficulty funding its domestic and international commitments, such as Washington's demand that Brussels take a leading role in financing the rebuilding of the former Soviet economy.

On the other hand, to the extent that the European Parliament eventually gains greater powers, the social democratic tendency of many European parliamentarians could have a profound influence on the nature of doing business within a united Europe.

The next European intergovernmental conference will take place no later than the mid-1990s and will undoubtedly have to deal both with EC membership for Eastern European states and creation of a truly federal structure for Europe. If the enlargement question is mishandled, it could cripple the European economy, undermining many of the benefits American business hopes to gain from the EC–92 process. The reshuffling of decision making authority within Europe will centralize some powers in Brussels while decentralizing other responsibilities to the regional level. American companies and the U.S. government, which had to learn how to fight for influence on decisionmaking in Brussels, will face a far more complex challenge learning to deal directly with authorities in Scotland, Lombardy and Catalonia.

Conclusion

The next few years will test the metal of the new transatlantic relationship. The alliance was hardened in the heat of the Cold War. But it has now grown brittle with age. It must be fired again to stand the stresses of a new era, strains that can be expected from both sides of the Atlantic.

The United States is no longer the only giant on the world's economic stage. Now the United States must learn how to behave in the presence of the other economic giants—Japan and the European Community—but still exercise leadership as the first among equals. Leadership requires action, not just position. But foreign elites are beginning to question if the United States is shirking the mantle of leadership as it demands greater burdensharing on military affairs and aggressively asserts its position on commercial policy.

Great powers have great interests and great responsibilities that require great expenses. American demands for increased burden-sharing alienate allies and may make it even more difficult to find solutions to problems of common interest—increasing worldwide economic growth, ensuring peace and prosperity in middle Europe and improving the global environment.

International cooperation will be complicated by America's evolving relationship with other industrial countries. The European Community now has a combined national income comparable to that of the United States, and Japan is closing the gap. Although all have an abiding interest in promoting a stable global economy, none has taken the initiative to ensure it. All will have to bear more responsibility for the smooth functioning of the world economy. Joint leadership will be necessary. But joint leadership is less stable and more prone to delay than leadership exercised by a single dominant country. Nevertheless, each has a vital stake in the management of interdependence, because its welfare depends on other countries as never before.

Although America's dominance has waned, its initiatives still evoke a response. Ideas can inspire and influence others. As a great power, America should have great ambitions to lead the world into the next century. But the end of the Cold War and the growing realization that the American economy is no longer the world's preeminent competitor have engendered neo-isolationist sentiments in the United States. Traditional American disdain for foreign entanglements and the natural proclivity of a continental power to look inward are now reinforced by a growing desire to resolve long festering domestic social and economic problems.

This "America First" posture is far from benign. It manifests itself in the growing calls for a rapid drawdown of U.S. forces from NATO, threatening to loosen the glue that has enabled the transatlantic relationship to weather many a storm. It fuels Washington's increasingly aggressive trade posture—in the Airbus case and in the agricultural discussions in the Uruguay Round. And it heightens the possibility of new tensions over interest rates and exchange rates.

In Europe, the sheer size of the emerging unified European market will give Europe a larger and more powerful profile on the world stage. The Euro-optimism that has supplanted the Euro-pessimism of the past will add a swagger to the European character as it plays out its role. This new assertiveness, so much in contrast to the subordinate part Europe was forced to play for so many years in the transatlantic relationship, will increase alliance frictions as both Washington and Brussels psychologically adjust to the new realities of their partnership. And the extraordinary enormity of the endeavor Europe is now embarking upon—integrating its market, extending its borders and harmonizing disparate social and political systems—will only reinforce its traditional self-preoccupation.

But while the European Community is now a necessary partner for the United States, it is not yet a sufficient partner. It is not yet clear what interest Europe sees for itself outside of Europe.

The United States has long assumed that Europe shared American views on the importance of a global vision in shaping both international and domestic policies. But recent events suggest Europeans not only disagree with the United States on substance, they also do not share America's penchant for looking at the big picture.

Left to their own devices, the Germans and the French might likely have struck a deal with Iraq rather than confront Saddam Hussein over his invasion of Kuwait. Similarly, in the Uruguay Round Europe's domestic political concerns have consistently taken precedence over the tremendous benefits to Third World and East European farmers of reforming European agricultural policies.

Germany's interest rate increases in 1991 in the face of a declining global economy troubled both the United States and its European partners. But European Economic and Monetary Union will come to pass and then Europe will be able to call more of the shots.

The full ramifications for the United States of the macroeconomic developments in Europe have only begun to come into focus. But the need for eventual action already seems clear. It would be shortsighted if the United States did not realize that the growing global demand for investment will increase competition for savings. Now is the time for the United States to reduce its reliance on external savings. That means cutting the Federal budget deficit even further, while increasing incentives for private savings.

The United States should also contemplate taking some initiatives internationally about how the world economy should be organized, in the wake of German unification, Western European unification, and Eastern European liberation. Greater symmetry among the major countries means that the need for and benefits from closer economic coordination have swelled. The only question is will the coordination be led by the United States. Target zones for exchange rates may still be out of the question but the adoption of objective indicators to guide macroeconomic coordination could be the next step together with new procedures to ensure follow up and monitoring of Economic Summit agreements. Only such an initiative now can protect American interests while the United States still has some clout, before Europe feels its weight and the U.S. economic role has declined even further.

To cope with these inevitable future strains in U.S.-European relations and to recast the alliance in an economic mold more appropriate for the post-Cold War world, it is time for the United States to consider launching an overarching dialogue with Europe on the future of the transatlantic relationship—a discussion including trade, investment, monetary and fiscal policy, defense and global burdensharing.

This dialogue, effectively encompassing a series of multilateral and bilateral initiatives, would refashion U.S.-European relations for the 21st century.

- The first order of business is to rejuvenate the G–7 process of coordination among the major industrial economies. In the future, U.S.-European relations will not play themselves out in a vacuum, but will be only one leg of an emerging tripolar world, involving Europe, Japan, and the United States. The recent disparity among G–7 interest rates—especially the gap between German and U.S. interest rates—highlights fundamental differences over how to deal with the current global recession and the threat of renewed inflation. It is time for better coordination of economic fundamentals to avoid exchange rate instability and economic policies that work at cross purposes.

To ensure coordination and followup to decisions reached at the Economic Summits, the G–7 needs a permanent secretariat. Discussion should begin on how best to enforce joint economic commitments. And the expansion of G–7 cooperation into the political and other realms should be explored. The 1990s would seem to be a more propitious time than 1918 or 1945 for international institution building. Now is the time to define the objectives and functions of any new institutional architecture and determine who participates.

- The acrimony engendered by U.S.-European differences over the Uruguay Round underscores the growing stakes in world trade deliberations, the fundamental transatlantic philosophical dissonance on trade issues and the escalating costs of failure to resolve such disagreements. In the wake of whatever happens with the Uruguay Round, the United States and Europe should establish new transatlantic trade dispute resolution mechanisms, ideally as part of a new World Trade Organization (WTO) that grows out of a continued multilateral process or independently if WTO can not be created at this time.
- In the past, neither Europe nor the United States has been mindful of the external consequences of their actions. In a world of economic equals, such behavior will lead to unnecessary frictions. Moreover, with three economic giants on the world stage, relations between any two of them affects the interests of the third. Consultative mechanisms should be created to insure that the external consequences of special trade deals—such as the EC-Japan auto pact or the U.S.-Japan semiconductor agreement—are fully vetted with non-participants so that unanticipated negative consequences can be minimized. While not U.S. Commerce Secretary Robert Mosbacher's much-discussed seat at the table, it must be more than after-the-fact notification.
- It is evident that the EC will have more than 12 members by the end of the coming decade. The terms of accession of new members will affect U.S. trade and investment interests in Europe. The terms will also serve as a model for America's evolving relationship with Europe. U.S. interest in this process should be made clear to the Europeans and an informal process of ongoing consultation about the issues involved should be pursued. Similarly, the U.S.-Canada-Mexico regional agreement may be expanded by the end of the decade. Both developments suggest a compelling need to clarify GATT provisions on regional groupings (Article XXIV) and to strengthen multilateral discipline to minimize the distortions inherent in regional groupings.
- U.S.-EC economic friction is increasingly a product of differences over competition policy, taxes, environmental regulation

and other aspects of the business environment that contribute to rising U.S. concern over the evolution of a Europe Inc. comparable to a Japan Inc. and are not within the purview of the General Agreement on Tariffs and Trade. With the Structural Impediments Initiative talks between the United States and Japan as a model, Washington should begin laying the groundwork for a similar dialogue on these issues with Europe. This discussion could take place within the OECD framework or directly between Washington and Brussels. The goal would not be to harmonize policies in the two regions but to minimize distortions through competition among regulatory systems.

- A joint U.S.-EC effort should be initiated to promote the economic recovery of the former Soviet Union and Eastern Europe (with particular focus on Poland, Czechoslovakia, and Hungary, where there is the best chance for a successful economic transformation and where there is the potential for the greatest U.S. public support). This effort should include but not be limited to an activist U.S. role in the European Bank for Reconstruction and Development, and support for greater World Bank involvement in the region. The EC has the most to do for these former communist countries in terms of trade. Like the relationship between the United States and Mexico, either the EC takes their goods or it takes their people. But U.S. support for multilateral involvement in Eastern Europe and the former Soviet Union, not just passive acceptance of European involvement, will be crucial to a continuing U.S. influence in the region. If the United States is not more forthcoming and economic turmoil breaks out, America will have missed an opportunity and will not be forgiven. Japanese participation in these efforts should also be encouraged, but a reliance on Tokyo to be the banker for such initiatives would be shortsighted.
- Finally, if this overarching dialogue with Europe about the future of transatlantic relations is to succeed it must be a public dialogue, one that entails a vision of a better future that captures the imagination of the peoples of North America and Europe, much as the EC–92 effort has transformed Europeans' self-image of themselves. Americans in particular rally to large projects and inspiring challenges. With the end of the Cold War, lacking such purpose, the United States is turning inward. Building a new bridge across the Atlantic to better enable the United States to prosper in the 21st century can provide Americans with a rationale to turn outward rather than inward in the years ahead.

In short, the United States must remain engaged in and with Europe, not just for Europe's sake but for America's. Specifically, the United States should attempt to promote an outward looking, global role for the European Community to minimize the international distortions inherent in the formation and evolution of the expanding European Economic Area; to keep middle Europe peaceful by promoting economic growth and greater cohesion among the nations of Europe; and to establish international institutions and processes that minimize frictions and tensions and that include full participation by the major powers—the EC, Japan, and the United States.

THE U.S.-EC-JAPAN TRADE TRIANGLE

By Dick K. Nanto *

CONTENTS

The world has entered the age of the economic triad of Europe, North America, and East Asia. These geo-economic centers comprise the leading industrial regions of the world and increasingly set international trade policy, generate consumer and industrial trends, and provide much of the capital and expertise for the rest of the globe. Within these regions, the United States, the European Community (EC), and Japan take the leadership roles. As the triad goes, so goes the world.

During the Cold War, the security triad anchored on the United States, Europe, and the Soviet bloc dominated policy and debate. As the Big Power confrontation has dissipated, however, the focus now has shifted to the economic side of global relations. The questions center on who will gain the benefits of the globalization of economies, how to keep local industries competitive in world markets, how to devise trade and investment policies that will raise domestic standards of living, and in what directions to take the evolving economic order. International relations no longer turn on the fulcrum of collective military security. The new watchword is collective economic security and how to achieve it.

The overwhelming dominance of the market-driven economic system in the three industrial centers, compared with the collapse of centrally planned economies in the former communist bloc, provides the United States, the EC, and Japan with a unique opportunity to guide the course of world economic development. These leaders of the West now can look past the military Cold War and the ideological economic war at a golden opportunity to set new di-

* Dick K. Nanto is a Specialist in Industry and Trade, Economics Division, Congressional Research Service.

rections and trends for the world as mankind prepares to enter the twenty-first century. Unfortunately, this opportunity comes at a time of heightened tensions over trade, global and bilateral imbalances, new competitive challenges by Japanese companies, and difficulties by all three regions in coping with mature and declining industries.

Summary

For each corner of the triad, the economic questions are different. For Europe, the question is not only how to deal with increased competition from abroad in key industries, but how to address what is perceived by some as a U.S.-Japan axis in which Japanese and American companies, both alone and in concert, threaten weaker European producers. For the United States, the questions are how to resolve trade disputes with Japan, restore macroeconomic health to the economy, and how to continue to provide world leadership on economic matters despite economic problems at home, growing protectionist sentiment, and a Federal budget deficit that constrains international action. For Japan, the questions are how to cope with pressures from both the United States and Europe to open its markets further, how to internationalize its domestic economy, and how to deal with the backlash directed toward its aggressive export industries.

In a global sense, the important questions transcend the intra-triad relationships and settle on the ability of the triad to provide world leadership in the economic sphere. Given the collapse of the Soviet Union with its satellite states, the EC, the United States, and Japan have inherited global economic leadership. In virtually all international economic fora, the triad must supply most of the vision and expertise needed to forge policies not only for the industrialized nations but for the developing and newly industrializing nations as well.

The EC's Japan strategy has been influenced greatly by the record of U.S.-Japan economic relations. This strategy includes five elements: (1) to monitor imports from Japan to prevent market disturbances and to use antidumping or other measures when appropriate; (2) to negotiate voluntary export restraints or other curbs on sales of products in which Japanese exporters hold a significant competitive advantage; (3) to seek greater opening of Japanese markets; (4) to pursue a high technology policy designed to keep EC industries competitive in emerging technologies; and (5) to pursue cooperation, dialogue, and exchanges to deepen the EC-Japan relationship.

U.S. trade policy toward Japan has relied upon three basic tactics: (1) to use existing trade remedies to address problems such as dumping and unfair trade practices; (2) to ask the Japanese government to impose voluntary export restraints if the industry involved is large and has considerable political power and when protective legislation in Congress or sizable antidumping duties seem inevitable; and (3) to reduce the bilateral trade deficit by increasing U.S. exports to Japan rather than closing U.S. markets to Japanese exports.

Japan's strategies toward both the United States and the EC tend to be defensive. Constantly under pressure and being criticized for the aggressive actions of its exporters, Japan has been attempting to devise policies that will calm tensions, keep its industries competitive, smooth domestic economic adjustments, and attain a higher standing in the world community.

In building trading blocs with neighboring economies, Japan is far behind either Europe or North America. Japan belongs to no formal economic grouping, but it has been creating a *de facto* economic sphere through rising trade and investment relations with its neighbors in Asia. Japan's strategy has been to foster interdependencies and friendly links in Asia through trade, direct investments, and foreign aid, while at the same time containing trade friction with the United States and the EC. Its strategy for North America and Europe is to build production facilities inside the blocs and to become good corporate citizens. Once inside, Japanese firms today attempt to rely less on exports from Japan and more on local production.

Trilateral Interaction

The EC-U.S.-Japan trade triangle actually does not exist. What does exist is an interaction consisting of three separate bilateral relationships—each varying in intensity and balance. The EC-U.S. link is the strongest and deepest, and is based on cultural, political, economic, and military ties that have long historical roots. The U.S.-Japan link has deepened, despite trade friction, but still is subject to gaps in perceptions and relations, and appears to be in need of a major redefinition.

The Japan-EC nexus has been the weakest. Compared with the other sides of the triangle, the ties between Japan and Europe tend to be least developed. [1] For most Japanese, Europe has been a faraway land, a source of expensive luxury goods, first-class scientific research, some high technology, and the "largest open air museum in the world." For many Europeans, Japan has been an exotic country, crammed with people who seem to work too hard and who appear intent on destroying European industry.

While the EC-Japan connection will probably not develop to the extent of the EC-America link, relations are quickly taking on new dimensions. In a sense, Europe is rediscovering Japan, and Japan is turning its attention toward Europe. Both push- and pull-factors are operating. Japan is being pushed away from increasing exports to the United States and being pulled to the larger markets in Europe. Europe, meanwhile, is being pulled into linking more with Japan rather than risk being pushed aside in the new rough and tumble world of transoceanic competition.

THE CONTEXT OF INTERACTION

Modern technology has altered fundamentally the way in which the three economic regions interact. Improvements in communication, transportation, and human mobility over the past few decades

---

[1] See: Congressional Research Service. *European Community-Japan Trade Relations.* CRS Report No. 86-166 E, by Dick K. Nanto. Washington, 1986. 36 p.

have combined with liberalized trade and investment environments to link the economies of Europe, North America, and East Asia to an extent never before experienced. Young people in London, New York, or Tokyo may listen to the same music, eat hamburgers at the same fast food restaurants, dream of owning the same sports car, or wear identical faddish clothes. Life styles of their parents, although more different, also are converging. The emergence of this age of global tastes means that businesses now must cater to customers on three continents simultaneously. Companies must compete within each region, and regions also must compete with each other to capture business activity, savings, investment, top talent, and innovations.

The link between natural resources and manufacturing also has been largely severed. Except in primary products, no longer does a country specialize in producing certain products based predominantly on its natural resource endowment. In the modern world of manufacturing with brand-name products, any country can create a competitive advantage in any of several contemporary industries. There is no resource base that dictates that Japan should be competitive in mass producing automobiles, the United States in building airplanes, and Europe in producing chemicals and high fashion products. Since industries can develop almost anywhere, the questions of the 1990s revolve around how an economy can capture increments to world industrial production and what economic policies a nation should pursue to induce the economic development necessary for a rising standard of living.

International trade also is occurring within sectors as well as among them. While in the past, the United States might have traded generators for silk, it now trades microprocessors for semiconductor chips. While in the past, Europe might have traded fashion clothes for cotton, it now trades luxury cars for minivans or other luxury cars. In such trade, economies compete with, rather than complement, each other.

The trend among corporations is to cope with the new international competition by forming consortia and allying themselves with companies in different geographic markets. Competition is shifting away from national champion firms of one nation battling in the marketplace against champions of another. Instead, one international consortia of companies will compete with another that similarly crosses international boundaries. Competition in automobiles is not just GM-Ford-Chrysler against Toyota-Nissan-Honda-Mazda or Volkswagen-Mercedes-BMW. It also is the GM-Opel-Saab-Isuzu-Suzuki combination competing with Ford-Mazda-Jaguar-Aston Martin. [2] For example, Mazda of Japan makes Fords for sale in Japan, while the two companies share production from a facility in the United States. In Germany, Ford-Werke has agreed to begin making a car for Mazda to sell in Europe.

These changes in the nature of competition shift the economic strategies of nations. Nations no longer can be the exclusive beneficiaries of their own economic policies. Attempts to foster technology development in a domestic industry can also assist firms abroad.

[2] See: Ohmae, Kenichi. *Triad Power.* New York, The Free Press, 1985. 220 p.

The critical issues in international trade rely less on the principle of comparative advantage among and within nations as competitive advantage by firms within international industries. One policy objective of nations might be to make certain their industries are successfully integrated into such triadic consortia and networks. Production, furthermore, can shift from one economy to another as economic conditions change. Financial and capital flows are even more fluid. In such a changed global environment, competition among the triad economies and between the triad and the rest of the world becomes paramount. [3]

DIMENSIONS

The relative size of the three centers of economic power is like 1-2-3: 124 million people in Japan, 252 million in the United States, and 345 million in the European Community. Japan, however, has approximately twice as many inhabitants as either Italy, France, or the United Kingdom alone. In terms of total productive power, Japan's gross national product (GNP) at about $2.1 trillion is less than half that of the American $5.4 trillion or the EC's $4.8 trillion (based on purchasing power parity exchange rates). Converted to dollars at current exchange rates, however, Japan's GNP at about $3.3 trillion is more than half the American.

FIGURE 1. U.S.–EC–Japan Trade Triangle, 1990 (Billion dollars)

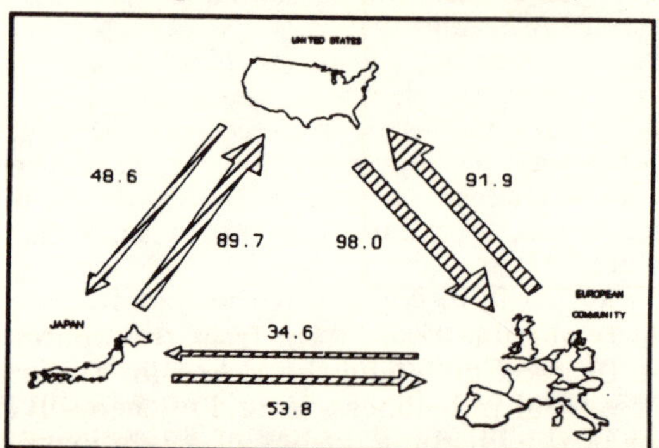

The triangular trading relationship is actually three bilateral relationships. As show in figure 1, in 1990, both the EC and Japan exported about $90 billion to the United States. The sales channels that support these transactions are deep and well developed. In U.S. exports, however, a significant difference is apparent. While the United States exported $98 billion to the EC to record a surplus of $6 billion in its balance of trade, it exported only half as much to Japan. The $49 billion in U.S. exports to Japan resulted in a deficit of $41 billion.

---

[3] For a comprehensive analysis of competition and policies, see: U.S. Congress. Office of Technology Assessment. *Competing Economies, America, Europe, and the Pacific Rim*. Washington, U.S. Government Printing Office, 1991. 375 p.

Over the 1980s, the trading relationship between the United States and the EC tended to be the most balanced. In 1980, it began with a $20 billion merchandise trade surplus in favor of the United States, dropped to a $23 billion deficit by 1986, and then recovered to a surplus of $6 billion by 1990. In contrast, the balance of trade between the United States and Japan began the decade with a deficit of $10 billion, grew by more than five times to $57 billion by 1987, and then diminished somewhat to $41 billion by 1990. The EC-Japan imbalance similarly stood at $10 billion in 1980, doubled to $23 billion in 1988, and then shrank to $19 billion by 1990. (See figure 2.)

FIGURE 2. U.S.–E.C.–Japan Trade Balances, 1980–90

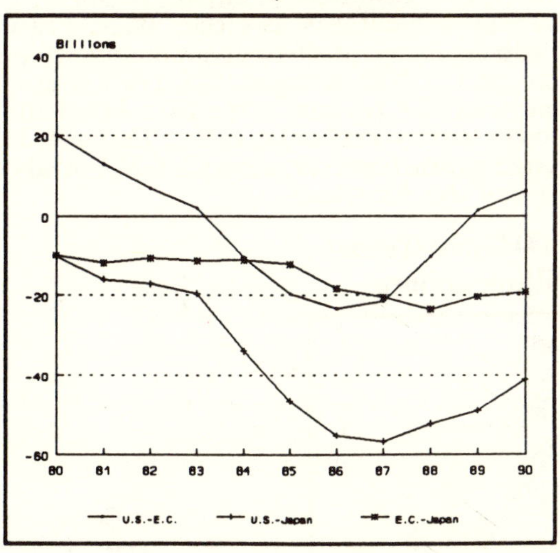

The imbalances in the triangular trade stem from the bilateral trade deficits of both the United States and the European Community with Japan. While bilateral imbalances, in and of themselves, are not the sole indicator of the economic health of a relationship, they do point to underlying problems and important issues. In an economic sense, if one bilateral imbalance is offset by a surplus elsewhere, there is no inherent reason one imbalance should be considered good or another bad.

In the political world, however, persistent bilateral imbalances do matter because import competition translates into a perception of lost jobs for the domestic economy, particularly in traditional industries. A trade deficit that is offset by an inflow of capital, moreover, is less than satisfactory for most nations, because citizens perceive that they are selling national, income-producing assets (such as real estate and corporations) for imports of consumer goods (such as video cassette recorders and clothing) that are perishable. Japanese industrialists are beginning to realize that unconditional and unlimited free trade does not exist and that economics and politics are inseparable in international relations. [4]

Investment relationships are similarly unbalanced. Japanese direct investment in both the United States and the EC far exceeds U.S. or EC investments in Japan. Over the FY1951-90 period, Japan's direct investments in France, for example, totalled $4,156 million, while France's investments in Japan came to $301 million. Likewise, over the same period for the United Kingdom, Japan invested $22,598 million while receiving $652 million; for West Germany, Japan invested $4,689 million while receiving $950 million; and for the United States, Japan invested $130,529 million while receiving $8,573 million. [5]

In terms of individual firms, the companies listed in *Fortune* magazine's Global 500 include 169 European, 164 American, and 110 Japanese. [6] Over the 1980s, however, the relative positions and market shares of the firms on this list changed significantly. The trend has been for American firms to lose their dominant position both in size and market share, while those headquartered in Japan and in some European countries are gaining. This has been noticeable even in high-technology and resource-based sectors, such as computers, office equipment, aerospace, pharmaceuticals, paper, and forest products. [7]

TRIAD LEADERSHIP

In a global sense, many important questions transcend the intra-triad relationships and settle on the ability of the triad to lead the world. Given the collapse of the Soviet Union with its satellite states, the EC, the United States, and Japan now share global economic leadership. In virtually all international economic fora, the triad must supply most of the vision and expertise needed to forge policies not only for the industrialized nations but for the developing and newly industrializing nations as well.

Some examples of this leadership can be seen in the Economic Summit meetings and in the Group of Seven (G–7—the United States, the United Kingdom, Germany, Japan, Canada, France, and Italy), which meet periodically to coordinate macroeconomic and exchange rate policies. [8] A proposal has been circulating to strengthen this organization by creating a permanent secretariat and possibly locating it in Japan. Other examples are the key roles the EC and the United States and, to a lesser extent Japan, play in the Uruguay Round of multilateral trade negotiations and on issues such as providing aid to the former Soviet Union.

A developing forum is the Quadrilateral Meeting between trade officials of the United States, the EC, Japan, and Canada. To date, the gatherings have been informal and without a rigid fixed agenda, but they could be the beginning of a coordinating mecha-

---

[4] Japan & Europe: New Relationship Needed, Our View. *Nikkei Weekly,* June 1, 1991. p. 6.

[5] Based on accumulated value of approvals and notifications. Japan Institute for Social and Economic Affairs. *Japan 1992, An International Comparison*. Tokyo, Keizai Koho Center, 1992. p. 55, 57.

[6] Knowlton, Christopher. Can Europe Compete? *Fortune,* December 2, 1991. p. 150.

[7] Franko, Lawrence. G. Global Corporate Competition II: Is the Large American Firm an Endangered Species? *Business Horizons,* v. 34, November-December 1991. p. 14-22.

[8] An excellent study of this process is: Henning, C. Randall. *Macroeconomic Diplomacy in the 1980s,* Atlantic Paper No. 65. London, Croom Helm, 1987. 74 p.

nism for trade. In a 1991 meeting, the trade ministers from each quadrilateral state discussed such topics as the Uruguay Round of trade negotiations and the impact of environmental regulations on the competitiveness of local industries in international trade. [9]

Future coordination within the triad will become increasingly important as formal border barriers to trade become less inhibiting, and attention turns to questions of how economies are organized or regulated and how businesses cooperate or compete with each other. Antitrust policy, in particular, has been breaking out of its primarily domestic orientation and being linked to international trade. On September 23, 1991, the United States and the EC signed an antitrust accord pledging to coordinate their antitrust enforcement efforts and to set boundaries on notification, information exchange, consultation, and confidentiality. The agreement calls for formal exchange of information on anti-competitive activities that may violate the other's antitrust laws and for meetings to discuss potential policy changes and to identify additional areas for cooperation. [10]

The U.S. Justice Department announced in February 1992 that it plans to issue new antitrust guidelines that would effectively extend the reach of U.S. law to foreign shores in a effort to address the problem of Japan's *keiretsu* or industrial groups. Ultimately, however, the U.S. court system would make the decisions on how to treat such attempts at extraterritorial reach. The U.S. courts have taken a fairly conservative stance relative to such attempts in the past. The interest in this issue, however, indicates that antitrust policy is likely to assume a higher profile among the advanced industrial nations. Japan has responded by strengthening its antitrust enforcement but has stated that it prefers questions on industrial competition to be addressed in the OECD (Organisation for Economic Cooperation and Development) rather than by attempts to make U.S. law extraterritorial. [11]

A point of cooperation in the triad has occurred in product standards. In 1991, the United States, the EC, and Japan agreed on guidelines for harmonizing pharmaceutical safety and quality standards. The negotiations took 18 months but resulted in measures that should speed up the time for licensing new drugs. [12]

The difficult challenge for triad leadership will be to shift perceptions within the member states away from the zero-sum mentality in which gains by one nation are necessarily perceived to be losses by another. [13] Instead, a system might be built in which economic cooperation and technology transfers bring rising living standards to all.

---

[9] Officials Said to Expect Little GATT Progress at Quadrilateral Meeting. *International Trade Reporter*, September 11, 1991. p. 1322.

[10] U.S., EC Commission Sign Antitrust Cooperation Accord. *International Trade Reporter*, September 25, 1991. p. 1407.

[11] Blustein, Paul. Japanese Spurn Plan to Break Up Cartels. *Washington Post*, February 25, 1992. p. D1.

[12] Abrahams, Paul. US, Japan and EC Agree Drug Testing Procedures. *Financial Times*, November 8, 1991. p. 1.

[13] Grewlich, Klaus W. Positive-sum Game USA-Japan-Europe. *Aussenpolitik*, v. 39, 1988. p. 229–33.

Battle of the Blocs?

Each economic pole of the industrial triad is linked to a surrounding region. The EC is itself a trading bloc, and in October 1991, announced that it was linking with the European Free Trade Association (EFTA) to form a wider European Economic Area [14] One by one, the EFTA nations are seeking membership in the EC. Combined with the EC's single European market and the greater role of Brussels, the Europeans have embarked on creating a European free-trade area rivaling North America in scope and exceeding North America in political, monetary, and standards unification.

Across the Atlantic, the United States and Canada are implementing their free-trade accord and negotiating with Mexico to possibly enlarge it into a North America Free Trade Agreement (NAFTA). President George Bush's Enterprise for the Americas proposal, which would create a free-trade area extending from Alaska to Argentina, indicates the direction in which the United States may proceed with future regional economic arrangements. Such economic unions are likely to be extended south before crossing the oceans to nations east or west.

Japan currently belongs to no regional trading bloc, although it is a member of APEC, the Asia Pacific Economic Cooperation council. Formed in 1990, APEC recently admitted China and Taiwan to bring its numbers to fourteen. Other members include the United States, Canada, New Zealand, Australia, and the nations of East Asia. APEC has been operating as a consultative body with working groups addressing specific issues. It has adopted trade liberalization as a goal, but as yet has taken no formal action.

The East Asian Economic Caucus (EAEC), also a consultative body, was proposed by Malaysia in 1990 as a formal economic grouping. It is intended to include only East Asian nations and is designed to serve as a counterweight to the EC and NAFTA. Japan was to take the lead in organizing it, but because of U.S. pressures and other reasons, Japan has not joined. Japan has supported the APEC process instead.

Anxiety is rising in Japan over what it perceives as its increasingly isolated position in world economic and political circles. On one side, it is being excluded from formal economic unions, while on the other side, it finds it is precluded from leading an East Asian grouping either because of U.S. pressures or historical enmity from its Asian neighbors. Japan can scarcely afford to alienate the United States by creating a trade bloc of its own, yet the probability is low that it will be able to link with North America or the EC in a free-trade agreement.

With no formal economic grouping in Asia, Japan has been creating a *de facto* economic sphere through rising trade and investment relations with its neighbors, in particular, but also with the United States and the EC. Japan's strategy has been to foster interdependencies and friendly links in Asia through trade, direct investments, and foreign aid, while at the same time attempting to

---

[14] Gardner, David. EC and Efta to Create 19-nation Trade Zone. *Financial Times*, October 23, 1991. p. 1.

contain trade friction with the United States and the EC. Its strategy for North America and Europe is apparently to build production facilities inside the blocs and to become good corporate citizens. Once inside, Japanese firms today attempt to rely less on exports from Japan and more on local production. This avoids some of the problems of protectionism, but Japanese firms still may not escape being considered foreign in public perceptions.

In many ways, the trading blocs of today differ completely from those in the 1930s. World trade now is relatively free. Average tariff rates for industrial nations are a scant two to four percent (although rates on individual products can be high). Regional economic blocs, therefore, are not exclusive. Still, such blocs can be quite significant because of the nature of manufacturing, the processing of commodities (particularly agricultural products), and performance requirements placed on foreign investments. Economic groupings that succeed in harmonizing standards, rules, and other nontariff trade barriers likely can become as significant a force for change as those that reduce formal border barriers to trade.

Triad Economic Policy

A triad economic policy is one taken by the EC, the United States, or Japan aimed at another member of the triad that arises because of a specific triad consideration. Most triad policies are not explicit. They appear primarily as bilateral policies or they may be couched as GATT negotiating policy, trade policy, high-technology policy, industrial policy, or microeconomic policy. In this section, only bilateral trade policies are examined.

Europe's Japan Policy [15]

The most obvious triad policy or strategy is that of the European Community toward Japan. The shape of this policy has been influenced greatly by the record of U.S.-Japan economic relations. Simply put, the EC seems to have decided during the mid-1980s that it would not allow certain of its major industries to be decimated by Japanese competition. Japanese companies are hindered in their efforts to gain market share by underpricing products and are encouraged to locate production facilities within the Community. Local production requires certain levels of European content. This strategy of Europeanizing Japanese production is combined with a policy of promoting European exports to Japan and developing a high-technology base to remain competitive with Japanese (and American) industries.

The policy to prevent European industries from being overwhelmed evolved as the EC watched traditional U.S. manufacturers in consumer electronics, automobiles, and machine tools steadily lose market share to imports from Japan and other Asian nations. In the EC, Japanese exports are the most competitive in particular sectors that require electronic miniaturization or lean production methods. These include office equipment (such as electronic typewriters, printers, photocopiers, facsimile machines, and personal and office computers), television receivers, video cassette record-

[15] Since E.C.-U.S. policies are discussed elsewhere in this volume, they will be omitted here.

ers, microwave ovens, compact disc players, semiconductors, motorcycles, and inexpensive automobiles. Europeans fear that a replay of the American experience could occur in these and other industries.

The perception among many in the Community is that Japanese firms take their most competitive products and attempt to slice through the European markets with a laser-beam type incision. Japanese exporters may focus on a product that has been a hit in other markets and compete intensely with each other to make a "beachhead" in Europe. The ensuing battle for sales based on slim profit margins and attempts to establish market shares by many Japanese producers can be devastating to local makers.

After watching the British motorcycle industry collapse under the onslaught of such competition, many European policymakers have concluded that they must do something to protect themselves against such sudden and radical changes in market shares. In 1970, the United Kingdom imported only $7 million worth of motorcycles and parts from Japan. By 1976, that figure had reached $113 million. It peaked at $244 million in 1980 as Japanese makers turned toward local assembly. By 1985, the traditional British motorcycle industry had all but disappeared. [16]

Many Europeans look at this example with horror. They feel that nations just cannot give up entire industries overnight, no matter what the consumer benefits. Unemployment in the Community is already too high, and labor markets in member countries can scarcely adjust quickly. Unemployment is so severe in many of the EC countries that layoffs and redundancies can become highly politicized. Even relatively small layoffs can trigger sizable labor disputes.

The first element of EC's Japan strategy is to ensure that Japanese exporters are unable to secure market share by underpricing products during initial incursions into markets. This has required that the EC Commission monitor closely Japanese exports to the Community in certain sensitive areas and respond rapidly in cases of market disturbance. [17]

The EC, for example, has vigorously pursued antidumping cases against Japanese exporters of office equipment. In some cases, such as photocopy machines, the dumping margins have been surprisingly large—as high as 69 percent. [18] The list of products which have been subject to antidumping levies has progressed from electronic typewriters, printers, and photocopiers to semiconductor-using electronic products, such as video cassette recorders, compact disc players, and microwave ovens.

The response by Japanese companies to EC antidumping actions has been to first shift exports from Japan to other production bases in the United States [19] or in South East Asia and then to build as-

---

[16] See: Nanto, *European Community-Japan Trade Relations*, p. 18.

[17] Commission of the European Communities. *Europe: World Partner*. Luxembourg, Office for Official Publications of the European Communities, 1991. p. 24.

[18] The average dumping margin was between 20 and 45 percent. A provisional duty of 15.8 percent was imposed on photocopiers from 9 of the 12 Japanese makers for 4 months. EC to Slap Duties on Japanese Copiers. *Journal of Commerce*, Aug. 28, 1986. p. 4A.

[19] There has been some dispute over whether products originating in Japanese assembly plants in the United States would be counted as Japanese or American in terms of EC quotas or antidumping duties.

sembly plants within the European Community. By 1990, Japan had accumulated $55 billion worth of direct investments in the European Community. Attracting such plants fits well into Europe's Japan strategy, because one of its elements has been to encourage local production as a substitute for imports. Direct Japanese investments also were encouraged by political pressures from the EC and attractive incentives from member states for Japanese companies to locate manufacturing plants in their districts. [20]

In order to insure that these Japanese plants would not be "screwdriver operations" and merely assemble kits imported from abroad, the EC also levied antidumping duties on imports of parts. It, furthermore, established rules of origin that required certain assembly processes or a certain proportion of the value-added to be performed in the EC. The rules of origin also applied to Japanese companies manufacturing in third countries, such as in nations of South East Asia or the United States, if they then exported to the EC. Japan, however, appealed the screwdriver law to the GATT and received a favorable ruling. [21]

The second element of the EC's Japan strategy has been to negotiate voluntary export restraints or other curbs on sales of products in which Japanese exporters hold a significant competitive advantage. In such cases, antidumping actions would not be effective because even at fair market prices, European producers still have difficulties competing. Until recently, all such trade restrictions were determined in country-to-country negotiations or in industry-to-industry discussions. Most of them resulted in gentlemen's agreements, informal import quotas, or voluntary export restraints.

Following the lead of the member states, in 1983, the EC negotiated a three-year accord in which Japan agreed to restrain the growth in exports to the Community of ten products. These included automobiles, motorcycles, television receivers, forklift trucks, quartz watches, and machine tools. Later, as the program to establish a single market in Europe by 1992 gained momentum, the EC Commission had to develop a common policy on imports and local production of Japanese cars.

Japanese car imports into EC member states had been restricted by France, Italy, Portugal, Spain, and the United Kingdom. The EC took eighteen months to generate a consensus among the EC nations on a new unified policy. As the single market in the EC was being debated, no other economic policy appeared to generate as much division among the member countries as did the automobile policy. On July 31, 1991 the EC and Japan announced that they had reached an understanding on automobiles. All details of the agreement have not been disclosed, but reportedly it does cap imports at the 1990 level of 1.23 million units and allows for production in Japanese-owned assembly plants in the Community to rise from 76,000 units in 1990 to 1.2 million units by 1999. Whether the 1.2 million units from local assembly plants is a forecast or a cap

[20] Japanese firms also invested in Europe to acquire advanced European technology, to establish distribution networks, or to obtain other expertise.

[21] Nishimura, Atsushi. *1992 and Euro-Japanese Economic Relations*. Tokyo, Long-Term Credit Bank of Japan, 1990. p. 24; and, Ishikawa, Kenjiro. *Japan and the Challenge of Europe 1992*. New York, Pinter Publishers, 1990. p. 82ff.

has not been made clear. After 1999, all restrictions on autos are to be dropped. [22]

This European agreement inspired similar attempts in the United States. In 1992, bills introduced in the 102nd Congress (H.R. 4100/S. 2145) would restrict sales of Japanese cars both imported and produced in American assembly plants if Japan did not reduce its trade surplus with the United States by 20 percent per year.

The extent of all European trade measures aimed at Japan is large. In 1989, approximately 40 percent of Japanese exports to Europe were subject to protective measures through 131 separate quotas. [23]

The third element of the EC's Japan strategy has been to seek greater opening of Japanese markets. Particularly high on the agenda have been markets for alcoholic beverages, cigarettes, cosmetics, chocolates, and automobiles, where European exporters are successful elsewhere in the world. EC tactics, however, have differed from those of the Americans. They seem satisfied to let the United States pursue the high-profile, pressure-filled trade negotiations that risk engendering a backlash in Japan but then quietly take advantage of any market opening that does occur. Germany now sells more cars in Japan than does the United States, and European cigarettes have done well as controls over distribution channels by Japan's Tobacco Monopoly were eased.

The EC, however, is gradually adopting more U.S.-style pressure tactics. It has agreed with Japan to start negotiations modeled after the Japan-U.S. Market-Oriented Sector-Selective (MOSS) negotiations and Structural Impediments Initiative (SII) talks. These would be aimed at market access in Japan for specific products, such as satellites and those of high technology, in which European exporters are competitive. The talks are to cover barriers on both sides, and the Japanese are expected to present their own list of what they consider to be examples of EC import restrictions on some 50 Japanese product categories such as television receivers, radios, and motorcycles. [24] Also, European automobile leaders have called on Japan to set a market share target for their exports to Japan of 10 percent by 1995 and 17.5 percent by 2000. [25]

Although both the EC and the United States share a broad interest in opening Japan's markets, they often differ in the specifics. While some Japanese concessions to American exporters do help Community businesses, others are of little help at all. When Japan expanded the list of approved ingredients for chocolates, for example, most of the items the Americans requested were approved, while an ingredient that a British company had submitted for approval long before was not. The success of the Americans in obtaining concessions in a certain area, moreover, often makes further

---

[22] Congressional Research Service. *The European Community-Japan Automobile Agreement.* CRS Report No. 92-94 E, by Glennon J. Harrison. Washington, 1992. p. 1–2.

[23] Korte, Karl-Rudolf. Japan and the Single European Market. *Aussenpolitik,* v. IV, 1989. p. 399.

[24] Andriessen Scores Japan on Uruguay Round, But Japan, EC Agree to Bilateral Talks. *BNA International Trade Reporter,* December 4, 1991. p. 1766; and, Cullison, A. E. EC, Japan Plan to Exchange Lists of Trade Barriers. *Journal of Commerce,* December 12, 1991. p. 5A.

[25] Oishi, Nobuyuki. Europeans Call on Japan to Increase Auto Imports. *Nikkei Weekly,* January 25, 1992. p. 1.

consideration of the problem in terms of European interests more difficult.

One fear among Japanese is that the EC and the United States might gang up and adopt coordinated policies against them. This has not materialized, however. Although some policies of the EC and the United States toward Japan are similar, neither seems to want to join in a united front.

In 1986, in a series of interviews conducted by the author with economic policymakers in the EC Commission and Parliament, West Germany, France, and the United Kingdom, a majority of those interviewed declared flatly that they opposed any coordination of policies, if such action gave the appearance that the European Community and the United States were ganging up on Japan. [26] Most policymakers felt that such a tactic would tend to isolate that nation and be counterproductive in the long run. A unified position blaming Japan for ills of the international trading system also would ease pressure on Community nations to make the difficult decisions necessary to induce their industries to become more competitive in world markets.

The need, according to one official, was not to coordinate an attack on Japanese import barriers and trade surplus but to design appropriate policies in each of the European countries in question. Some noted, however, that Japan realizes that it cannot exist in a vacuum and that being confronted with a united front could facilitate its consensus-building process. Some coordination among nations bidding for Japanese investment also might prevent it from playing disparate elements off against each other, which it seems to do so well.

EC attitudes toward Japan, however, now are in flux. In 1991, Sir Leon Brittan, the Vice-President of the EC Commission, began advocating that in certain cases, it would be a good idea for the EC to join forces with the United States and EFTA partners as part of a European strategy toward Japan, particularly in areas where there are common concerns and where the Community cannot make headway on its own. [27]

On the other hand, some in Europe have been pointing to the threat of a new Japan-U.S. challenge, a partnership in high-technology areas such as telecommunications, semiconductors, and computers. The fear is that European integration might have come too late and that EC firms might run a poor third in the technologies of the twenty-first century, behind those of Japan and the United States. Foreign investment in the EC might bring assembly jobs to the Community, but the research and development and other skilled jobs will be staying at home. [28]

---

[26] Conducted under the European Community Commission and Parliament's Visitors Programme. The German Foreign Ministry, Central Office of Information in the United Kingdom, and the French Ministry of Foreign Affairs also were helpful in arranging interviews and providing support.

[27] Brittan, Leon. *Getting the Best Out of European Industry: The International Dimension.* Speech to the Japan-EC Association, Brussels. EC Commission Press Release: IP/91/1009, November 14, 1991.

[28] Seitz, Konrad. *Die Japanisch-Amerikanische Herausforderung* (The Japanese-American Challenge). Munich, Bonn Aktuell, 1990; and, Harries, Meirion. Europe is the Wild Card in U.S.-Japan Relations. *Japan Economic Journal,* June 16, 1990. p. 9.

In some cases, Japanese and European interests coincide. On U.S. export controls relative to the Soviet pipeline and other issues, Japan and the EC have taken similar positions opposing the extraterritorial application of U.S. laws. They both also share apprehensions about a perceived tendency of the United States to act unilaterally. [29]

The fourth element of Europe's Japan strategy has been to pursue a high technology policy designed to keep EC industries competitive in newly emerging technologies. During the 1980s, a variety of programs designed to enhance European competitiveness in research and development sprouted in the Community. [30]

The fifth element is to pursue cooperation, dialogue, and exchanges to deepen the relationship. The dialogue is proceeding at several levels and is designed to bring both immediate and long-term results. Among the forums for dialogue are an annual ministerial conference, high-level government consultations, and technical meetings. Cooperation is occurring in key areas of scientific and technological exchange, including thermonuclear fusion, biotechnology, new materials, and the exchange of young research workers.

Although the elements of Europe's Japan strategy are not unique, they are pursued with a consistency that appears to bring results. Japanese comment that the Europeans seem to be more willing to protect their industries and less willing to yield on issues in order to maintain harmony in the relationship or because of political or security considerations. European consumers, of course, have to pay the price of the protection, and whether the EC's short-term protective measures will hinder or help their long-term efforts at developing competitive industries, particularly in high technology, remains to be seen.

AMERICA'S JAPAN STRATEGY

Trade disputes between the United States and Japan have been both more intense and longer lived than those between the EC and Japan. U.S. policymaking with respect to trade with Japan is driven by strong domestic interests, appeals to broad political principles, and numerous horror stories. The $43 billion U.S. trade deficit with Japan continues to be a focus of attention, but the deficit is an issue primarily because it is an obvious indicator of the imbalance in the relationship and because it reflects aggressive competition between Japanese companies and U.S. industries with powerful political muscle. Even if the bilateral trade deficit were to disappear, trade friction might likely continue.

U.S. trade policy toward Japan has relied upon three basic tactics that resemble those used by the EC. The first has been to use existing trade remedies to address problems such as dumping and unfair trade practices. In a period of a rising value of the yen, the antidumping law is a potent weapon, since the dollar cost of production in Japan rises with each appreciation of the yen, even

---

[29] Murata, Ryohei. Political Relations Between the United States and Western Europe: Their Implications for Japan. *International Affairs*, v. 64, Winter 1987/88. p. 5.

[30] See: Congressional Research Service. *The Europe 1992 Plan: Science and Technology Issues.* CRS Report No. 89-178 SPR, coordinated by Glenn J. McLoughlin. Washington, 1989. 23 p.

though nothing has changed when measured in yen. When the value of the yen rises, Japanese exporters have to either pass on the exchange rate change in the form of higher prices in export markets or they have to reduce both costs of production and prices at home. Since 1985, the value of the yen has risen by about 50 percent.

Although many antidumping cases have been brought by U.S. interests against Japanese exports, until recently, few have been used in conjunction with a broader U.S. policy to develop specific industries. Each case tended to be isolated and independent. The recent decision to impose antidumping duties of 62 percent on active matrix (flat panel) computer display screens, however, was taken specifically in tandem with a U.S. high-technology policy to foster this industry at home. Even though the result has been to push some American makers of laptop computers (which use the display screens) into producing overseas, the benefits apparently were considered to have outweighed the costs. [31]

The second tactic has been that when legislation in Congress or large antidumping duties seemed inevitable, the Japanese government has been asked to impose voluntary export restraints (VERs, also referred to as voluntary restraint agreements) if the industry involved is large and has considerable political power. Currently, VERs restrict imports of automobiles, machine tools, television receivers, and, until recently, steel from Japan. In the case of machine tools and steel, the restraints were, until April 1992, expanded to include exports from other nations. The appeal of VERs has been that they are temporary (although all have been extended), do not induce retaliation, and appear less protectionist.

The voluntary restraint agreements and antidumping actions are the two areas in which EC and American interests both coincide and clash with respect to Japan. Each intends to protect its local manufacturers against actions considered to be unfair, but as they protect their markets, each runs the risk of diverting Japanese exports into the other's market. The analog also holds true in U.S. agreements with Japan to provide for specific market shares for American exports in Japan. The commitment by Japan to raise U.S. exports of semiconductors, automobiles, or automobile parts to a certain level implies that the exports from the European Community will not receive such favorable treatment. U.S. sales might come at the expense of those from Europe. European policymakers have, therefore, openly criticized such American agreements with Japan.

The third American tactic has been to attempt to reduce the bilateral trade deficit by increasing U.S. exports to Japan rather than closing U.S. markets to Japanese exports. Americans expected that by forcing Japan to reduce barriers to exports of U.S. manufactures, both U.S. producers and Japanese consumers would gain. U.S. companies would increase production, would be compelled to learn to operate in the Japanese domestic market, might be able to replace jobs lost because of imports, and would become stronger

[31] Magnusson, Paul. Did Washington Lose Sight of the Big Picture? *Business Week*, December 2, 1991. p. 38.

international competitors. Equal access to Japan's markets also appealed to the American sense of fairness and reciprocity.

U.S. market-opening activities in Japan required special negotiations beyond those under the General Agreement on Tariffs and Trade (GATT). The United States undertook three major initiatives: the MOSS talks (led by the U.S. Commerce Department), the Super 301 (priority unfair trade practices) process, and the SII talks. The latter two were both led by the U.S. Trade Representative but, in the case of the SII, also included several other agencies. The MOSS and SII talks were strictly bilateral with Japan, while the Super 301 process also caught Brazil and India in its net.

There is considerable evidence that these U.S. tactics have brought results, even though many have been dissatisfied with the magnitude or outcome of the measures. [32] Between 1985 and 1990, U.S. exports to Japan in the sectors negotiated rose from $3.9 billion to $12.0 billion for an increase of 208 percent. This was considerably higher than the 119 percent increase in total U.S. exports to Japan or the 79 percent increase in total U.S. exports to the world. The problem, however, is that the process of identifying barriers, marshalling the evidence for a case, and applying the tools in the U.S. trade arsenal takes time, ends up addressing only a narrow range of products, has not increased U.S. exports enough to affect significantly the bilateral trade imbalance, and causes hostility in the relationship.

Some critics of U.S. trade policy toward Japan have proposed that the United States abandon its current strategy and adopt one of managed trade. Instead of changing the rules of competition and allowing market forces to determine outcomes, managed trade strategies focus on results and would put most of the burden on the Japanese government to guarantee those results.

Although managed trade is presented as a new approach to trade disputes, it essentially would be a system of government-administered trade targets and quotas. The quotas would be imposed by either side and would operate and have the same effects as any other protectionist measure. The import targets for Japan, however, would attempt to raise sales levels above those resulting from usual market forces. Such targets might be necessary in industries in which the Japanese government has an active industrial policy (high technology) or in mature markets which tend to be cartelized (chemicals).

The United States also pursues other policies affected directly by relations with Japan. Policies dealing with high-technology industries, education, antitrust and competition, business regulation, and the environment have been affected by competition from Japanese industries or represent mutual interests.

The rift that developed between the United States and Japan following President George Bush's visit to Tokyo in January 1992 has brought a new level of strain in the relationship. [33] The disputes

---

[32] See: Congressional Research Service. *Japan-U.S. Trade: U.S. Exports of Negotiated Products, 1985–90.* CRS Report No. 91-891 E, by Gold, Peter L. and Dick K. Nanto. Washington, 1991. 50 p.

[33] Oberdorfer, Don. U.S.-Japan Relations Seen Suffering Worst Downturn in Decades. *Washington Post,* March 1, 1992. p. A1, A28.

are primarily bilateral and are affected greatly by the U.S. recession and election year politics. European issues, however, hover in the background. In the dispute over automobiles, for example, American automakers know that European carmakers are making inroads into the Japanese market, while their exports are still stuck in first gear. In 1991, EC automakers sold over 150,000 cars in Japan, while the U.S. Big Three shipped only 14,000.

The United States is aware that despite the acrimony being tossed back and forth across the Pacific, Japan can ill afford to alienate America because it is unlikely to find a better friend in Europe (or in Asia). Japan is hoping that the security and business ties between the two nations will carry them through this period of U.S. recession and Presidential election without permanent damage being done to the relationship.

The challenge for the United States seems to be to restore industrial competitiveness to ailing industries, increase its rate of savings and investment, restore its macroeconomic health and economic growth, and strengthen its internal self confidence and international respect it needs for global economic leadership.

JAPAN'S TRIAD STRATEGIES

Japan's strategies toward both the United States and the EC tend to be defensive. Constantly under pressure and being criticized for the aggressive actions of its exporters, Japan has been attempting to devise policies that will calm tensions, keep its industries competitive, smooth domestic economic adjustments, and give it higher standing in the world community.

Japan's basic strategy has been to stretch out trade negotiations and to provide a series of concessions that would calm friction while attempting to minimize the political backlash from its industries hurt by those concessions. Recently, however, Japan has become more aggressive. It appealed to the GATT to rule on EC antidumping laws and in negotiations with the United States has pointed out problems and barriers on the American side.

The Japanese government no longer is able to control the competitive impulses of its industries. A debate is raging in Japan over whether Japanese business practices are dangerous to the world in general and to Japan in particular. The narrow focus of Japanese businesses on gaining market share, production efficiency, and product evolution has created such an adverse response from other nations that some Japanese business leaders are now questioning this managerial philosophy.

Akio Morita, the chairman of Sony, has proposed that Japanese businesses change their corporate strategy. He argues that the Japanese style of management is in danger. He proposes that instead of the intense focus on engineering, product quality, and manufacturing, Japanese companies need to broaden their economic goals to include shorter working hours, higher pay for workers, higher dividends for stockholders, fairer relationships with suppliers, more charitable contributions, and efforts toward greater environmental protection. [34] While these ideas are being debated in Japan, they

---

[34] Morita, Akio. Nihonkei Keiei ga Abunai (Japanese-style Management in Danger). *Bungei Shunju*, February 1992. p. 94-103.

are unlikely to affect the short-term relationship with the United States and the European Community.

In trade and investments, Japan is diversifying away from the United States and toward the EC and Asia. The Japanese investment boom in the American market has peaked for the time being, and firms are now focussing on building regional integrated networks of suppliers and factories in Europe and Asia. [35]

The Japanese government, however, tends to place the highest priority on policies toward the United States. During President Bush's visit to Japan in January 1992, the two nations issued a joint declaration initiated by Japan that lays down some of the objectives that the two nations have been pursuing in order to solidify the relationship. The declaration begins with the premise of interdependency which not only links Japan to the United States but to the EC and other nations of the world. The existence of this interdependency implies that each side has much to gain from cooperation rather than from confrontation. It lays out five areas for cooperation and includes a call to enhance openness and oppose protectionism in commercial, financial, and investment markets. [36] With Europe, Japan has made a similar declaration.

Japan is now at a crucial juncture in its postwar history. It is now an economic superpower, but it still tends to be treated like a second-tier nation—albeit a rich one. In international decisionmaking, it seems to have reached the point where it is less willing to be dominated by the United States and Europe. Many in Japan resent the fact that despite their $13 billion contribution to the Gulf War, for example, they were criticized openly and had no voice in the major decisions. The Gulf War scenario is being replayed in other multilateral fora (such as on the Cambodia question), and the issues go beyond securing a permanent seat for Japan on the U.N. Security Council. Japan is pressing for changes in its role in the triad and wants to change the perception that it is willing to sit back while the United States and Europe plan important initiatives and then expect it to write checks to help cover costs—even if it also benefits.

Japan would like to see a true tri-polar world economic order and a genuine sharing of power with the United States and Europe. Whether the economic strategists in Tokyo will be able to achieve this status without alienating the other poles of the triad, however, will remain an open question.

The immediate challenge for Japan seems clear. It is to internationalize its economy and put an end to the bad experiences of many American and European exporters trying to sell there. This may require aggressive reductions in barriers or customs that could cut deeply into the fabric of Japanese business culture. It also may require welcoming foreign investors and labor and restraining its aggressive exporters. Such policies would require strong political action by a government currently weakened by financial scandals, but the stakes are high and the potential consequences of inaction are great.

---

[35] Addison, Paul and Veldin Kattoula. Japan Placing Greater Focus on Europe, Asia, than on US. *Nikkei Weekly*, December 17, 1991. p. 1.

[36] *The Tokyo Declaration on the U.S.-Japan Global Partnership.* By the President of the United States of America and the Prime Minister of Japan. January 6, 1992.

THE CHALLENGE OF EASTERN EUROPE AND THE FORMER SOVIET REPUBLICS

By George D. Holliday *

CONTENTS

SUMMARY

The revolutions in Eastern Europe and the Soviet Union in 1989–1991 initiated a dramatic reorientation of the region's economic, political, and security relations with the rest of the world. Most policymakers in the region are opting for policies and institutions that will normalize diplomatic relations with Western countries and facilitate integration into the world economy. In the economic sphere, the new approach consists essentially of a transition from central planning to more market-oriented economies.

An integral part of such a transition is a repudiation of policies and institutions that discouraged trade with the West and limited the role of foreign capital in these economies. As a result, the reforming countries are developing more extensive trade ties with the rest of the world, especially with Western Europe, and making major demands on foreign capital markets to help rebuild and modernize their economies. The response of Western governments and the multilateral economic institutions will heavily influence the ability of the reformers to integrate their economies into the world economy.

Of utmost importance to the countries of the region is the response of the European Community. The countries of Eastern Europe and some of the former Soviet republics appear inexorably drawn to Western Europe, particularly the European Community. Common history and culture, geographical proximity, and econom-

* George D. Holliday is a Specialist in International Trade and Finance, Economics Division, Congressional Research Service.

ic complementarity lead many policymakers in the region to consider themselves natural candidates for integration into a united Europe. Many see membership in, or close association with, the EC as a means of solidifying and formalizing the break with their recent past. The governments of the smaller states see EC membership as an important safeguard against the kind of external domination that they have experienced since World War II. Reformers in the region believe that the prospect of eventual membership in the EC will buttress the democratic and market reforms that they have undertaken.

While full membership appears to be years away, the first steps of integrating the region into a European trade bloc are already underway. The association agreements and other agreements that the EC is concluding with countries in the region are providing a basis for expanded trade and economic cooperation. Moreover, capital flows, in the form of private investment and official aid, are likely to tie Western and Eastern Europe closer together.

Integration of the Former Soviet Republics and Eastern Europe into the World Economy

Most of the new governments in Eastern Europe and the former Soviet Union are intent on implementing rapid transitions to market economies. Successful transitions will require a fundamental reorientation of international trade and financial ties between the formerly centrally planned economies and the rest of the world. Such ties are important for several reasons. The commercial relationships that formerly promoted trade within the region, institutionalized primarily in the Council of Mutual Economic Assistance (CMEA), have collapsed. Even within the new Commonwealth of Independent States, commercial relations are strained. The reforming economies need new sources for imports and new markets for their exports. They also desperately need capital and technology from the West to modernize their industry, agriculture and infrastructure. Foreign trade and investment can also play an important role in the reforms by introducing competition and market discipline to economies that have been monopolized by state-controlled and subsidized producers.

The barriers to integrating the region's economies into the world economy are formidable. Most imposing are the systemic differences which are the legacy of Stalinist central planning. The new Eastern governments must bear the primary burden of implementing systemic reforms to overcome such barriers, though Western technical advice can be helpful. Western multilateral institutions and governments can also help the reforming governments overcome other kinds of barriers, including inadequate capital resources, lack of access to Western markets, and barriers to transfer of technology.

ECONOMIC REFORMS

Radical economic reform—sharp curtailment of the government's control over economic decisionmaking; privatization; price reform; new mechanisms for financing investment; and macroeconomic stabilization—is already creating the necessary framework in some of the East European countries. Poland, Hungary, and the Czech and Slovak Federal Republic are the pacesetters, while Bulgaria, Romania, and several of the former Soviet republics have either begun, or plan to initiate soon, fundamental economic reforms.

A prerequisite for reorienting their economies is a new institutional framework for conducting foreign economic operations. In the past, the governments of Eastern Europe and the Soviet Union controlled foreign trade, like other economic activities, to further the political leadership's economic goals. State foreign trade organizations, subordinate to the ministries of foreign trade, engaged in trade primarily to obtain essential imports needed to overcome critical bottlenecks in the domestic economy. They promoted exports, generally without regard to profitability or comparative advantage, primarily to finance needed imports. Central control over foreign currency earnings ensured that the foreign trade organizations imported goods in accordance with the central plan. Moreover, for political and ideological reasons, the governments severely restricted the role of foreign investment in the domestic economies. The net effect of central planning was to prevent the East European and Soviet economies from maximizing their potential gains from foreign trade and investment.

Centrally planned foreign trade led to the isolation of Soviet and East European industry from foreign competition and from the technological advances which have rapidly transformed products and production processes in Western industrial countries. It produced many manufacturing industries that were not competitive on world markets and lacked incentives to export. Government control of foreign exchange transactions and non-market exchange rates led to inconvertibility of Soviet and East European currencies. Inconvertibility, in turn, contributed to a propensity to conduct trade on the basis of bilateral trade and payments agreements with similar state-trading countries. Such bilateral agreements formed one of the underpinnings of the Council of Mutual Economic Assistance (CMEA), a grouping of the Soviet Union, six East European countries, Mongolia, Cuba, and Vietnam.

To integrate their economies into the world economy, the reformers must dismantle rigid government controls over foreign commercial relations and open their domestic economies to foreign trade and capital flows. In practice, an open economy means that all citizens and firms have a right to import and export with minimal interference from the government. In open economies, the government relies predominantly on tariffs and trade laws that are consistent with multilateral norms, rather than administrative fiat, to regulate trade. Currency convertibility, a termination of bilateralism, and an effective legal framework for foreign investment are important elements of an economy that is fully integrated into the global economic system.

REGIONAL TRADING ARRANGEMENTS

An immediate concern is to replace the CMEA system and the old domestic trade relationships among the former Soviet republics with new, market-oriented commercial relations. With the demise of CMEA in 1990 and the breakup of the Soviet Union in 1991, trade among the countries in the region has been based either on hard currency, which is in short supply, or on barter transactions, which are inefficient and difficult to arrange. Trade in the region has dropped precipitously, causing severe dislocations among suppliers and customers in the region.

One suggested solution is an East European payments union, patterned after the institution which helped to reestablish trade relations among the West European countries after World War II. Western credits would be used to establish a hard currency fund, which would provide multilateral financing for regional trade. Others have suggested that Western governments extend "triangular" aid—hard currency credits to one country in the region that would be used to finance imports from another. Within the former Soviet Union policymakers in the new commonwealth are considering several options. If a single, unified market proves politically impossible, they may consider a customs union with trade transactions among the republics settled in rubles.

Proposals for closer integration among the reforming countries in the East are a poor second best option for many in the region. Indeed, they are anathema to some East European reformers: such proposals remind many of the forced integration they experienced in the post World War II era. Even within the C.I.S., efforts to maintain or reestablish commercial relationships are meeting resistance. Most policymakers in Eastern Europe and many in the western portions of the former Soviet Union, look westward for help with economic reforms.

ROLE OF THE MULTILATERAL ECONOMIC INSTITUTIONS

Multilateral economic institutions, such as the International Monetary Fund (IMF), the World Bank, the European Bank for Reconstruction and Development (EBRD), and the General Agreement on Tariffs and Trade (GATT), could have a vital role to play in reforming the economies of the former Soviet Union and Eastern Europe and integrating them into the world economy. The IMF, for example, could support efforts to stabilize the economies and assist in building market institutions. The World Bank and the EBRD could provide financial assistance for new, economically viable industrial projects. By putting conditions on financial assistance, the international financial institutions can influence the shape of new economic policies and institutions in the region. Similarly, membership in the GATT brings both important benefits—nondiscriminatory treatment for exports from the region—and obligations—requirements that the reforming countries develop market-oriented trade practices and institutions.

Indeed, the multilateral institutions have already begun to influence the shape and direction of economic reforms. Poland, Hungary, the Czech and Slovak Federal Republic, Romania, and Bulgaria belong to the IMF and World Bank and have benefitted from both financial and technical assistance. Since the Soviet Union became an associate member, some of the former Soviet republics have received technical, but not financial, assistance from the IMF. The EBRD began making loans to countries in the region in April 1991. Poland, Hungary, the Czech and Slovak Federal Republic, and Romania are GATT members, and Bulgaria and the former Soviet Union have observer status. Thus, the countries in the region are becoming intricately tied to the multilateral economic system.

The Lure of the European Community

Although integration into the multilateral economic system and East European cooperation could help to further the economic goals of the reforming countries, many policymakers in the region believe that neither is sufficient to meet East European economic needs. The EC and its member countries are seen as the best hope for obtaining the financial assistance, private investment, and market access that are needed for a successful transition of the Eastern economies.

AID, FOREIGN INVESTMENT, AND TRADE

Aid from the EC, for example, can supplement the technical and financial assistance of the multilateral agencies. Indeed, the EC and member countries have taken a leadership role, coordinating and providing the lion's share of assistance to the reforming countries. The EC and its member countries, for example, have provided about 75 percent of the Western bilateral assistance to the C.I.S. and 73 percent of the aid to Eastern Europe. (See figure 1.) EC aid has included grants of food and medicine, balance of payments support, export credits, technical assistance, and assistance for withdrawal of Soviet troops and destruction of nuclear warheads. All forms of EC assistance for the C.I.S. totaled 47.5 billion ECU from September 1990 to the end of 1991 and for Eastern Europe, 18.8 billion ECU from the beginning of 1990 to mid-1991. [1] Of the member countries, Germany has been especially generous, providing 57 percent of the total bilateral assistance to the C.I.S. and 31 percent to Eastern Europe.

In the longer run, the economic reforms and recovery in the East are likely to require substantial inflows of private capital and technology from the West. EC-based corporations are likely to be primary sources. Since the reforming governments began to open their economies to foreign investment, companies from EC member countries have been among the most active investors in the region. German corporations, in particular, have been active, accounting for more joint ventures in Poland, Czechoslovakia, and Hungary than companies from any other country (though they trail U.S. firms in terms of the size of investments in Hungary). Companies based in Austria (a probable future member of the EC), France, the United Kingdom, and Italy have also made substantial investments in the three reforming countries. [2]

The EC has also become the largest trade partner of some of the reforming countries, as they have reoriented their trade toward the West. Figures 2 and 3 show the dramatic reorientation of trade for the three countries, Czechoslovakia, Hungary, and Poland, that have advanced most in economic reforms. Since the mid-1980s,

---

[1] One ECU = $1.25 (1991 average).

[2] PlanEcon, Inc. *PlanEcon Review and Outlook,* November 1991; and, Trying to Invest in East Europe. *Washington Post,* February 10, 1992. p. A1, A22.

FIGURE 1. Distribution of Western Assistance to Eastern Europe and the Commonwealth of Independent States

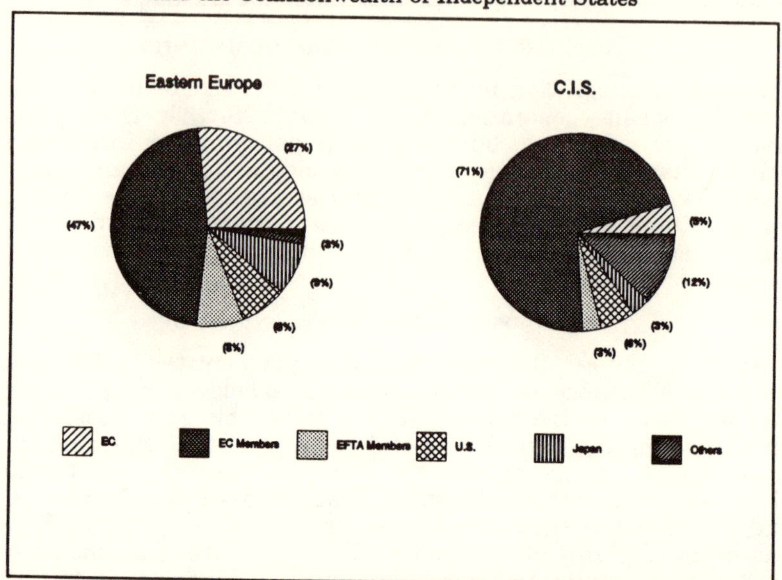

Source: *European Community News*, no. 2, January 21, 1992; and, Commission of the European Community cited in Congressional Research Service. *International Assistance to Eastern Europe*. Report 91–915 F, by Karen E. Donfried. December 23, 1991.

when their trade relations were dominated by intra-CMEA trading arrangements, trade with the formerly centrally planned economies has declined sharply, while trade with the EC and other Western countries has increased substantially. Western industrial countries now account for 67 percent of the combined exports and 64 percent of the combined imports of the three countries. The EC is by far the most important Western market. In 1991, it was the destination of about 29 percent of Czechoslovak exports, 45 percent of Hungarian exports, and 53 percent of Polish exports. [3]

BILATERAL AGREEMENTS

Because of the importance of EC aid, investment, and trade, the East European countries and the former Soviet republics have assigned high priority to negotiating agreements to formalize and deepen the emerging economic ties. Beginning in 1988, the EC negotiated agreements with most of the East European countries and the Soviet Union which provided for reciprocal reduction of trade barriers and encouraged economic and technical cooperation. Most

[3]All trade data are from PlanEcon, Inc., ibid.

FIGURE 2. Czechoslovakia, Hungary, and Poland: Destination of Combined Exports, 1985 and 1991

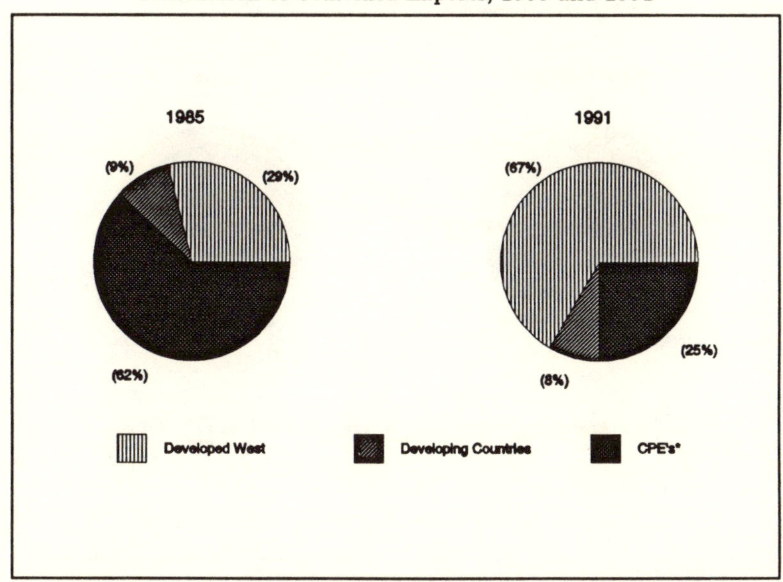

* Centrally–planned economies.

Source: PlanEcon, Inc. *PlanEcon Review and Outlook*, November 1991. Data for 1991 are estimated.

importantly for the Eastern countries, the EC agreed to reduce substantially import quotas and other nontariff barriers to imports from the East.

Responding to the radical economic and political reforms that began in late 1989, the EC extended financial assistance and more generous trade concessions to Poland, Hungary, and Czechoslovakia. By the beginning of 1991, the EC had reduced quantitative restrictions for all the East European countries and had extended preferential tariff treatment (that is, they became eligible for the Generalized System of Preferences, or GSP, accorded to many developing countries) to all except the Soviet Union. Thus part of East European exports to the EC were freed from all EC tariffs.

Important restrictions on imports from Eastern Europe remained, however. Antidumping actions, variable levies, and voluntary export restraints limit access to the EC market for some products. Most important, the EC maintained quotas on imports of such "sensitive" items as textiles, steel, and agricultural products. Such items constitute a major share of the exports of the Eastern countries: 25 percent of the EC's imports from Czechoslovakia, 45 per-

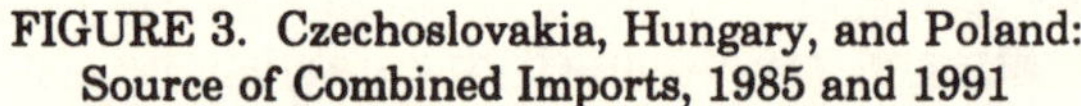

FIGURE 3. Czechoslovakia, Hungary, and Poland:
Source of Combined Imports, 1985 and 1991

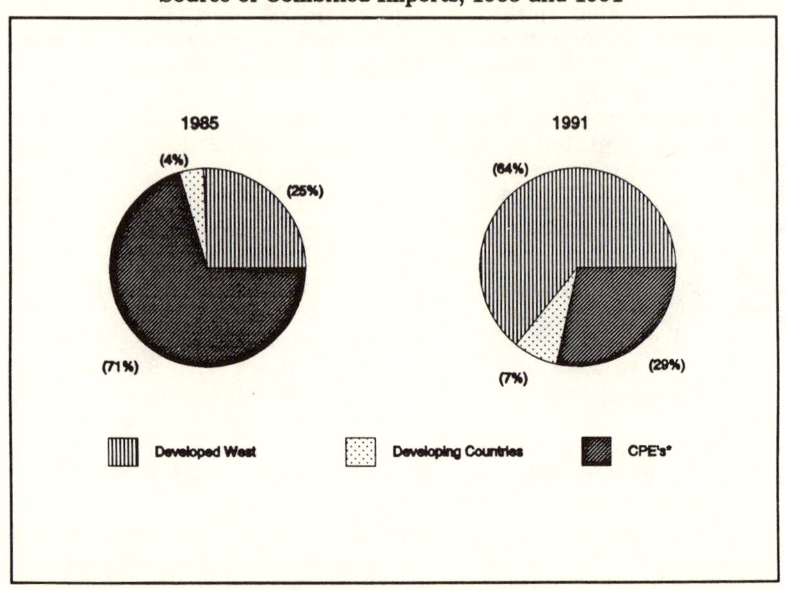

* Centrally–planned economies.

Source: PlanEcon, Inc. *PlanEcon Review and Outlook*, November 1991. Data for 1991 are estimated.

cent of imports from Hungary, and 55 percent of imports from Poland. [4]

Late in 1990, the three rapidly reforming East European countries and the EC began negotiating a new generation of agreements for association with the EC. While the two sides disagreed somewhat on the ultimate goal of the negotiations, all parties considered the agreements a significant step toward integrating the three East European countries into the West European system. Representatives of the EC, Poland, Hungary, and Czechoslovakia signed the so-called European Agreements on December 16, 1991. Each agreement includes provisions that reduce barriers to trade and investment, encourage political dialogue, and promote cooperation on economic, social, and cultural matters. [5]

---

[4] United Nations. Economic Commission for Europe. *Economic Bulletin for Europe*, v. 43, 1991. p. 46.

[5] The texts of the European Agreements have not been published. This discussion is based on a summary provided by the European Community Delegation in Washington, *European Agreements with Czechoslovakia, Hungary, and Poland.* IP/91/22, November 22, 1991; *European Community News*, no. 28/91, November 26, 1991; and various press reports, especially Mills, Jennie. The Shape of Agreements to Come. *Financial Times*, December 5, 1991. p. 38.

- Trade. The agreements remove many barriers to trade on a reciprocal basis and are designed to establish eventually a free trade area. They maintain, however, higher tariffs for Eastern European imports than for EC imports and continue some EC restrictions on imports of textiles, steel products, coal, and agricultural goods.
- Movement of labor. The agreements include measures to improve the situation of East European citizens who are already legally working in the EC.
- Movement of capital. The parties agreed to provide national treatment to foreign investors, allowing professionals and businesses the same rights as citizens of the host country. They also removed restrictions on repatriation of profits and movement of personal funds.
- Gradual application of EC law. The three associated countries undertook to harmonize many of their laws with EC laws. The EC's laws and regulations on competition, for example, will be adopted.
- Financial assistance. The East European countries will continue to be eligible for assistance under the program of aid for central and eastern Europe (PHARE), which is coordinated by the EC Commission, and for loans from the European Investment Bank. The EC agreed to consider giving macroeconomic assistance, such as balance of payments support.
- Economic, social, and cultural cooperation. The agreements encourage cooperation in standards, science and technology, education and training, statistics, regional development, social policy, transport, telecommunications, crime control, environment, and cultural affairs.
- Political dialogue. Through regular, high-level meetings, the two sides will try to coordinate foreign policy positions.

The association agreements will come into force only after ratification by the parliaments of the three associate countries, the parliaments of the 12 EC countries, and the European Parliament. Ratification by all of the member countries could take considerable time. The European Parliament, however, is expected to act promptly on aspects of the agreements for which the EC has competency. Thus, important elements such as trade liberalization are likely to be implemented quickly.

The EC has begun negotiating a similar association agreement with Bulgaria and envisages talks on a possible agreement with Romania once the Romanian political situation is clarified. The European agreements are not, however, prototypes for relations with all of the reforming countries in the East. The EC has negotiated more limited trade and cooperation agreements with Latvia, Lithuania, and Estonia and plans to negotiate various kinds of agreements with the other former Soviet republics. According to Frans Andriessen, vice-president of the EC's Directorate-General for External Relations (DG-I), future agreements with the successor states would depend on the economic and political progress of the republics. He warned, however, that not even the most European and economically advanced of the republics could expect quick integration into the EC. [6]

A PRELUDE TO MEMBERSHIP?

During the negotiations on the association agreements, representatives of Poland, Czechoslovakia, and Hungary strongly pressed for incorporating a clause that would give them automatic EC membership at a later date. Government officials in the three countries had made it clear that EC membership was their ultimate goal in the negotiations and a primary motivation for domestic economic reforms. Reformers such as Czech Economics Minister Karel Dyba and Professor Martin Kupka of Charles University, for example, emphasized that "close co-operation with the EC . . . is considered of prime importance for Czechoslovak external economic policy and foreign policy. The intention is to elaborate first a clear timetable for some form of association and for full membership in the not too distant future." With respect to domestic policy, the Czech reformers asserted that "all reform measures in Czechoslovakia will be realized with EC membership in mind." [7]

EC officials, however, were unwilling to make a firm commitment on membership for the three countries. While many in the EC think that eventual membership for the Eastern countries will serve EC interests—in particular, securing political and economic stability in the East—there are many objections to early membership. Many policymakers in the EC believe that they must further deepen integration before undertaking a major widening. Others are concerned about the incompatibility of Eastern legal, political, and economic institutions. Many in the EC are concerned about competition from low cost producers in the East. Another major concern is the difference in living standards between East and West: new Eastern members would compete with the poorer existing members for regional aid resources. Associate status offers EC policymakers a means of showing support for reforms in the three East European countries while putting off the problems of full membership. Thus, instead of a clear timetable for membership, the negotiators compromised by recognizing in the preambles to the agreements that the ultimate aim of the three countries is accession to the EC.

Compromise was an underlying theme to the agreements: while they represent an important step forward, they fall short of full integration in several key aspects. For example, they significantly advance the goal of establishing a free trade area by providing specific timetables for removing tariff and nontariff barriers for most industrial products. EC negotiators agreed to remove import quotas and eliminate tariffs over the next five years. East European exports of "sensitive" products, however, will continue to meet EC barriers. After long and sometimes acrimonious negotiations, the EC insisted on maintaining substantial restrictions. Quotas and

---

[6] EC Prepares Accords with Former Soviet Republics. *Daily Report, West Europe,* Foreign Broadcast Information Service, January 10, 1992. p. 3.

[7] Dyba, Karel and Martin Kupka. Economic Relations with Market Economies in Czechoslovakia. In United Nations. Economic Commission for Europe. *Reforms in Foreign Economic Relations of Eastern Europe and the Soviet Union.* Economic Studies No. 2. New York, 1991. p. 72.

tariffs on textiles, steel and coal will remain in place longer, though some gradual liberalization will take place in the meantime. The EC made relatively small concessions for agricultural imports, although some EC aid to the former Soviet republics will be allocated to the purchase of agricultural products from the associate countries. While many EC trade concessions will be implemented in five years, most East European trade liberalization will take place in the second five years of a 10-year "transitional period." In short, the agreements, while liberalizing trade, put the establishment of a genuine free trade area well into the future.

Another disappointment for East European negotiators is the lack of provision for free mobility of labor. Many believe that the East European countries could benefit greatly if workers were free to seek employment in the EC. Eastern workers could learn new skills and increase their earnings, and Eastern governments would be relieved of the political and economic burdens of high unemployment. The agreements, however, include only small concessions from the EC—measures to improve working conditions for Poles, Czechoslovakians, and Hungarians already legally working in the EC. Any future immigration is left to the discretion of member countries.

Despite the difficult negotiations and perceived shortcomings in the final agreements, most East European policymakers consider them a major accomplishment. The three associate countries achieved much of their short run goal of increasing access for their exporters to the EC market. They also consider their new associate status as a major step toward European unity and long-term security. [8]

In the long run, those measures that the East European countries agreed to undertake unilaterally may prove to be the most important aspects of the agreements. They agreed to apply EC models for their laws on competition, patents, standards, labor relations, environmental protection, and other matters. EC officials will provide technical assistance in implementing the agreements. By harmonizing their laws and institutions with those of the EC, the three associate countries are preparing a strong case for EC membership in the future.

The promise of participating in a free trade area and the possibility of future EC membership are likely to exert a strong influence on the domestic policies and foreign commercial relations of the associate countries. The agreements will probably provide a spur to domestic reforms. Reformers have begun to counter the arguments of conservatives who would delay reform by arguing that radical change is necessary for EC membership. The agreements are also likely to make it easier to attract foreign investment. Access to the huge EC market, either through a free trade agreement or membership, provides a strong incentive to foreign companies to locate production facilities in the associate countries.

---

[8] Interview with Polish Deputy Prime Minister Leszek Balcerowicz, *Rzeczpospolita*, December 19, 1991, cited in: de Weydenthal, Jan B. Czechoslovakia, Hungary and Poland Gain Associate Membership in the EC. *RFE/RL Research Report*, February 7, 1992. p. 26.

Implications for the United States

The United States and the European Community share broad foreign policy interests in Eastern Europe and the former Soviet republics. Both are working to ensure successful transitions to democratic governments and market-oriented economic systems. The U.S. Government supports closer economic cooperation between the reforming countries and the EC to the extent that such cooperation furthers common foreign policy goals. U.S. officials have encouraged the EC, for example, to play a leading role in coordinating assistance to the countries in the East.

In addition, the reduction of trade barriers between the EC and Eastern Europe could have some positive effects on U.S. commercial relations with the East. If the agreements contribute to faster economic growth in the East, they could stimulate demand in the region for imports from the United States and other countries. Improved access to the large European market may also make Eastern Europe and the former Soviet republics more attractive for U.S. investors. U.S.-based companies may, for example, take advantage of the low cost, well educated labor force to establish manufacturing operations, improving profitability in the European market and spurring exports of parts and components from the United States.

U.S. policymakers have expressed reservations, however, about preferential trade arrangements between the EC and the reforming countries. U.S. Trade Representative Carla Hills expressed concern to the House Ways and Means Committee, for example, that the association agreements would not be compatible with the parties' obligations under the GATT. [9] Article XXIV of the GATT allows countries to enter into free trade agreements, but forbids parties to such agreements from raising trade barriers to the exports of third countries. It also requires that a free trade agreement cover "substantially all trade" to minimize distortions of trade flows.

U.S. officials are concerned that the association agreements will violate both GATT provisions. First, the three East European associated countries are considering raising tariffs on imports from third countries as they lower tariffs on imports from the EC. If they do, U.S. and other exporters will be put at a competitive disadvantage, as higher tariffs divert trade away from third countries toward intra-bloc trading partners. Second, continued EC import barriers on "sensitive" products could violate the GATT requirement that substantially all trade be covered by free trade agreements. U.S. officials point out that the continued barriers would lead to further trade distortions that would prevent the East European countries from reaping maximum benefits from the free trade area. [10]

More generally, U.S. policymakers are concerned about the longer term consequences of integrating Eastern Europe and the former Soviet republics into a European trade bloc. If such integration is not compatible with multilateral rules for trade and invest-

---

[9] *Inside U.S. Trade,* Special Report. July 5, 1991. S–4.

[10] EC-Eastern Europe Association Agreements Targeted for Completion by Year-End. *Europe Now,* September 1991. p. 2.

ment, U.S. commercial relations with the region may suffer. U.S. ties to the reforming countries may increasingly be dominated by the sometimes contentious U.S.-EC relationship. Commercial disputes, such as disagreements over agricultural trade in the Uruguay Round or differences over the trade effects of directives for a unified market, could adversely affect U.S. commercial relations with countries in the region.

To ensure non-discriminatory treatment for U.S. exporters and investors, U.S. negotiators must persuade policymakers in Eastern Europe and the former Soviet republics to reconcile their aspirations for integration into Europe with their multilateral commitments. An important forum for pursuing U.S. commercial interests in the region is the Uruguay Round. Among the issues now being discussed is a reform of Article XXIV designed to provide stronger GATT discipline to free trade agreements and a more effective mechanism for resolving disputes arising from such agreements. If the Uruguay Round negotiations are successful, the threat posed to U.S. trade interests by a European trade bloc (or other trade blocs) could be diminished.

THE SINGLE MARKET AND THE URUGUAY ROUND: IMPLICATIONS FOR THE STRUCTURE OF WORLD TRADE

By Jeffrey J. Schott *

CONTENTS

About five years ago, the member nations of the European Community (EC) began the active pursuit of two important, and seemingly complementary, initiatives: internal market reforms pursuant to the Single European Act of 1987, and the Uruguay Round of multilateral trade negotiations in the GATT. Both initiatives sought to break down structural barriers to trade and investment in goods and services that have inhibited growth in developed and developing countries alike.

The juxtaposition of the two initiatives served to balance the implicit inward-orientation of the internal EC process, designed to remove obstacles to trade among the EC member states by 1992, and the outward-orientation of the GATT round, designed to open markets to competition from third country suppliers. To be sure, EC officials argued that there never was a conflict between the two, and that the initiatives were mutually reinforcing given the Community's predominant share of world trade. Others, however, saw both opportunity and risk: the Uruguay Round could open up substantial new trading opportunities for EC firms that would encourage the Community to lower its barriers to foreign suppliers, but the EC–92 process could also provide an excuse not to go forward in the GATT because of pending decisions in Brussels or the lack of consensus among the twelve member states.

Five years later, one can posit success for the EC–92 process, but the outcome of the GATT talks remains in doubt, in large measure because of a dispute between the European Community and most other GATT members on reform of farm support programs. The willingness to let the GATT talks fester, and risk collapse, over agriculture revives concerns that the Community places greater priority on its internal market reforms than on the GATT talks, and

* Jeffrey J. Schott is Research Fellow at the Institute for International Economics, Washington, D.C.

is willing to see a minimalist result in the Uruguay Round that effectively confirms the status quo ante. In addition, unfolding events in Europe, including most recently German reunification, the opening of the Eastern European economies, and the disintegration of the Soviet Union, seem to have distracted the attention of EC policymakers and lessened the urgency of multilateral trade reforms.

As I have extensively argued elsewhere (Schott 1990) [1], a minimalist result in the Uruguay Round would do nothing to deal with the problems that led GATT members to launch the Round in the first place. Indeed, the failure to resolve those problems after six years of multilateral negotiations would likely place the GATT process in disrepute and lead countries to seek solutions through alternative channels—either through unilateral actions under national trade laws or through the negotiation of bilateral and regional trade agreements.

By accident or design, both the EC internal market reforms and the Uruguay Round now seem to be heading for a 1992 climax. The outcome of the GATT talks may well determine whether EC–92 leads the Community to open up to foreign competition, or to curl up into an increasingly broadbased regional trading bloc. The implications of EC–92 for the structure of world trade can thus be examined in light of these alternative scenarios.

This paper will first examine the structure of EC trade, and the factors likely to guide EC trade policy toward its main trading partners in the 1990s as the process of European economic integration continues to broaden and deepen. The second section will examine how the EC–92 process has affected EC positions in the Uruguay Round, and how this could affect the prospective package of agreements. The final section concludes with some speculation on possible reactions to the expanding EC trading bloc.

The Structure of EC Trade

The European Community is the world's largest trading bloc, with EC member countries accounting for almost 40 percent of world merchandise trade, more than the United States and Japan combined. Reflecting the growing integration of the EC economies, trade among EC members represents around 60 percent of this total; Community exports to third countries account for the rest, or about 16 percent of world trade (see table 1).

Trade among EC member states has grown markedly in recent years, spurred by the accession of Spain and Portugal and the internal market reforms currently being adopted pursuant to the Single European Act of 1987. Since 1985, intra-EC trade has nearly doubled, and is now almost 60 percent greater than EC exports to the rest of the world. This trend is likely to hold in the near future as a result of both the income and efficiency effects of the internal market reforms, and increased integration with members of the European Free Trade Association (EFTA) and countries in Eastern Europe, and will likely affect EC policy toward third countries and its positions in the Uruguay Round. [2]

---

[1] All references are located at the end of this chapter.

[2] Indeed, if one took the EC and EFTA together, the combined markets would account for about 70 percent of the total trade of EC firms.

TABLE 1. EC Trade

(billions of $ and percentage)

	A. Total World Exports	B. Total EC Exports	Intra-EC Trade as % of A	Intra-EC Trade as % of B	EC Exports to ROW as % of A	EC Exports to ROW as % of B
1980	1,882.9	691.2	20.5	55.7	16.3	44.3
1981	1,855.0	636.9	18.1	52.7	16.2	47.3
1982	1,716.5	614.7	19.3	53.9	16.5	46.1
1983	1,666.7	598.7	19.5	54.4	16.4	45.6
1984	1,799.0	614.5	18.4	53.8	15.8	46.2
1985	1,820.1	647.5	19.4	54.5	16.2	45.5
1986	2,003.1	795.9	22.5	56.7	17.2	43.3
1987	2,359.2	958.4	23.7	58.5	16.9	41.5
1988	2,699.3	1,062.7	23.5	59.6	15.9	40.4
1989	2,913.8	1,135.0	23.3	59.8	15.7	40.2
1990	3,325.0	1,370.9	24.9	60.4	16.3	39.6

Source: *Direction of Trade Statistics*, 1986 and 1991.

The distribution of EC trade with third countries is detailed in tables 2 and 3. EFTA is the leading trading partner of the Community, followed closely by the United States; together the two areas account for almost half of EC trade with nonmember countries. The United States accounted for the bulk of the growth in EC exports to nonmember countries in the first half of the 1980s and the EFTA countries in the second half of the decade (see table 2). Dollar misalignment and differences in relative growth rates in Europe and North America during this period explain a good deal of these patterns. The following sections describe EC trade patterns with its major trading partners.

EFTA. EFTA countries account for 25 percent of total EC trade with third countries (see table 3). EFTA countries are even more dependent on the EC market: in 1988 EFTA exports to the EC were four times greater than intra-EFTA trade, and accounted for 56 percent of total EFTA exports. [3]

The EC-EFTA trade relationship should continue to expand in the 1990s for two main reasons. First, EFTA's strong dependence on the EC market virtually requires its members to adopt trade regulations and product standards consistent with EC norms, thus strengthening the integration of the EC and EFTA economies. Second, the new EC-EFTA treaty establishing a broader European Economic Area will promote even closer economic integration in the region, and extend existing institutional linkages between the two trading blocs. In some cases, EFTA members have opted to accelerate this process by applying directly for full membership in the Community.

While EC officials have stated publicly their desire to avoid action on new membership applications while the 1992 reform process proceeds, EC enlargement encompassing at least some EFTA members could proceed within a few years. Closer integration is

[3] Data are from IMF. *Direction of Trade Statistics Yearbook*.

TABLE 2a. Distribution of EC Exports to Rest of World: 1980–1990

(billion ECU and percentage)

Year	EC ROW Exports	U.S.		EFTA		Japan		4 Tigers		E. Europe [a]		Others	
		$	%	$	%	$	%	$	%	$	%	$	%
1980....	216.7	27.8	12.8	55.3	25.5	4.8	2.2	5.8	2.7	19.3	8.9	103.7	47.9
1981....	265.3	38.6	14.5	57.1	21.5	5.9	2.2	7.1	2.7	20.3	7.7	136.3	51.4
1982....	284.1	44.5	15.7	62.7	22.1	6.6	2.3	8.4	3.0	20.5	7.2	158.1	55.6
1983....	300.6	52.2	17.4	66.3	22.1	7.7	2.6	9.2	3.1	24.1	8.0	150.6	50.1
1984....	350.9	73.7	21.0	76.4	21.8	9.4	2.7	11.7	3.3	25.0	7.1	168.4	48.0
1985....	378.7	85.5	22.6	84.8	22.4	10.5	2.8	13.4	3.5	27.1	7.2	175.2	46.3
1986....	341.9	75.2	22.0	87.2	25.5	11.4	3.3	12.6	3.7	23.8	7.0	121.8	35.6
1987....	339.3	71.9	21.2	90.3	26.6	13.6	4.0	15.1	4.5	22.4	6.6	117.8	34.7
1988....	362.8	71.8	19.8	96.4	26.6	17.0	4.7	19.7	5.4	24.2	6.7	134.4	37.0
1989....	413.0	78.0	18.9	108.0	26.2	21.1	5.1	22.9	5.5	26.2	6.3	158.2	38.3
1990....	419.8	76.7	18.2	111.4	26.5	22.7	5.4	23.3	5.5	33.7	8.0	152.2	36.3

[a] includes inter-zone trade (FRG-DDR).
ROW = Rest of World.

TABLE 2b. Distribution of EC Imports from Rest of World: 1980–1990

(billion ECU and percentage)

Year	EC ROW Im-ports	U.S.		EFTA		Japan		4 Tigers		E. Europe [a]		Others	
		$	%	$	%	$	%	$	%	$	%	$	%
1980....	282.5	47.7	16.9	48.1	17.0	14.0	5.0	9.9	3.5	22.7	8.0	140.1	49.6
1981....	318.3	54.7	17.2	53.4	16.8	17.3	5.4	10.4	3.3	25.7	8.1	156.8	49.3
1982....	335.4	59.3	17.7	57.8	17.2	19.3	5.8	10.7	3.2	30.2	9.0	158.1	47.1
1983....	341.7	58.7	17.2	65.4	19.1	21.9	6.4	12.5	3.7	32.6	9.5	150.6	44.1
1984....	390.6	67.1	17.2	75.8	19.4	25.7	6.6	14.2	3.6	39.4	10.1	168.4	43.1
1985....	406.4	68.9	17.0	82.0	20.2	28.6	7.0	14.3	3.5	37.4	9.2	175.2	43.1
1986....	334.6	56.6	16.9	78.6	23.5	33.2	9.9	16.3	4.9	28.1	8.4	121.8	36.4
1987....	340.1	56.2	16.5	82.7	24.3	34.8	10.2	20.5	6.0	28.1	8.3	117.8	34.6
1988....	387.6	68.3	17.6	90.5	23.3	41.6	10.7	24.6	6.3	28.2	7.3	134.4	34.7
1989....	446.7	83.7	18.7	102.6	23.0	46.3	10.4	26.7	6.0	29.2	6.5	158.2	35.4
1990....	462.7	85.2	18.4	108.6	23.5	46.2	10.0	26.3	5.7	33.2	7.2	163.1	35.3

[a] includes inter-zone trade (FRG-DDR).
ROW = Rest of World.
Source: Eurostat. *General Summary of EC Trade*, and, *External Trade Eurostat*, (Monthly Statistics). December 1991.

likely to generate very little *additional* stimulus to growth in EC-EFTA merchandise trade since most industrial trade barriers have been removed pursuant to the free trade agreements signed in the 1970s between the EC and the individual members of EFTA—unless the agreements cover the agricultural sector.

Eastern Europe. The EC is the largest trading partner of the Eastern European countries, accounting for about one-third of Eastern Europe's total trade with the West, and is likely to benefit most from new trading opportunities created by the market-oriented movement of those economies. Trade finance and investment

TABLE 3. Distribution of EC Trade with Third Countries

(billion ECU and percentage)

Year	Total [a]	U.S.	EFTA	Japan	4 Tigers	E. Europe
1980..........	499.2	15.1	20.7	3.8	3.1	8.4
1981..........	583.6	16.0	18.9	4.0	3.0	7.9
1982..........	619.5	16.8	19.5	4.2	3.1	8.2
1983..........	642.3	17.3	20.5	4.6	3.4	8.8
1984..........	741.5	19.0	20.5	4.7	3.5	8.7
1985..........	785.1	19.7	21.2	5.0	3.5	8.2
1986..........	676.5	19.5	24.5	6.6	4.3	7.7
1987..........	679.4	18.9	25.5	7.1	5.2	7.4
1988..........	750.4	18.7	24.9	7.8	5.9	7.0
1989..........	859.7	18.8	24.5	7.8	5.7	6.4
1990..........	882.5	18.3	24.9	7.8	5.6	7.6

[a] Exports and imports.

Source: Eurostat. *General Summary of EC Trade*; and, *External Trade Eurostat*, (Monthly Statistics). December 1991.

guarantee authorities are already beefing up resources to facilitate increased EC trade in Eastern Europe. Nonetheless, a significant surge in trading volume in the near-term is unlikely due to foreign exchange constraints in most East European countries, and to instability in the newly emerging republics of the former Soviet Union.[4] Moreover, the value of trade is relatively small (about 8 percent of total EC trade), and is dominated by a few product sectors that are unlikely to expand for several reasons:

- The primary EC import from Eastern Europe is petroleum (mostly from the former Soviet Union), accounting for about 30 percent of imports in 1988–89. However, the volume of oil production from that region has declined due to inadequate oil-field maintenance and is unlikely to recover without substantial new investments.
- EC imports from Eastern Europe of iron and steel products, apparel, and other manufactured goods face strong competition from East Asian suppliers, and perhaps even stronger resistance from EC producers. Indeed, many of these products are already exempted from preferences granted in the bilateral trade agreements between the EC and Eastern European countries, and opposition to new preferences is already appearing. If new preferences for East European imports were to be granted for political reasons, then additional restrictions on competitive East Asian suppliers would likely be required to prevent a protectionist backlash by EC producers.
- Similarly, trade in agricultural products is often exempted or sharply constrained under the preferential trade arrangements negotiated between the EC and East European countries. Again, increased EC imports from Eastern Europe would

[4] For a fuller discussion of these issues, see Williamson (1991), Havrylyshyn and Williamson (1991), and Collins and Rodrik (1991).

heighten demands for even greater restrictions against other third-country suppliers.

In sum, adjustment concerns in sensitive sectors will continue to pose constraints on East European exports to the EC; substantial growth in EC imports from Eastern Europe will likely have to come in new product sectors developed with the help of significant foreign investment and technology in Eastern Europe. Trade is likely to lag such investment by several years.

United States. Despite the seeming continental focus of EC trade, the United States still accounts for 19 percent of total EC trade with third countries. Aided by a weaker dollar and strong European growth, U.S. exports to the EC have surged since 1987, generating increasingly large bilateral trade surpluses for the United States after years of substantial U.S. deficits. U.S. trade with the EC totalled $190 billion in 1990, equal to 21 percent of total U.S. trade, and is now greater than U.S.-Canadian trade. In 1991, the U.S. bilateral trade surplus with the EC reached $16.7 billion.

Bilateral trade flows in the 1980s have been—and will continue to be—strongly influenced by differences in relative growth rates and exchange rate movements between the dollar and European currencies. EC growth is projected to slow in the near-term but still outpace the performance of the U.S. economy. However, the short term outlook in 1992 seems unsettled: the dollar has strengthened against European currencies (and, indeed, has become overvalued against the yen) despite continuing large U.S. budget deficits; long term interest rates remain high, depressing investment; and inflationary pressures in Germany generated by the extraordinary costs of reunification have dampened EC growth prospects. These trends chart a much more ambiguous course for U.S. exports to Europe, and suggest that the recent U.S. export drive may wane to some degree.

Bilateral U.S.-EC trade is dominated by manufactured goods, which account for more than 80 percent of U.S. exports and almost 90 percent of EC exports. By contrast, agriculture accounts for only 10 percent and 5 percent of U.S. and EC exports respectively, although it generates the bulk of bilateral trade disputes (in which manufactured goods are often caught in the retaliatory cross-fire). This spillover effect explains why disputes over agriculture need to be resolved to avoid protectionist responses that result in broader disruptions of trade.

The evolving European trading bloc poses no inherent threat to the continued growth of transatlantic trade, although trade disputes are likely to continue to focus on the EC's common agricultural policy (the make-or-break issue in the Uruguay Round), and on EC subsidies that promote import substitution (especially in civil aircraft and steel). Both issues are likely to provoke bilateral trade frictions that lead to tit-for-tat trade retaliation, but most likely on a minor scale as in the pasta war and beef hormone disputes.

Indeed, closely following the prompting of major U.S. multinationals, U.S. officials have been generally supportive of the EC's internal market program, and only have complained about specific issues involving EC subsidies (agriculture; Airbus) and market access in particular sectors (e.g., financial services). [5] Note, however, that U.S. reactions to intra-EC developments are closely tied to U.S. efforts in the Uruguay Round; the failure of the GATT talks consequently would lead to a sharp increase in transatlantic trade disputes and significant new trade barriers.

Japan and the "Four Tigers". Although the value of two-way trade between the EC and the major trading nations of East Asia has almost doubled since 1985, and grown faster than with any other region, Japan still accounts for only about 8 percent, and Hong Kong/Korea/Singapore/Taiwan for about 6 percent, of total EC trade with third countries. These countries have run large trade surpluses with the EC in recent years, primarily due to exports of motor vehicles, machinery and equipment, and consumer electronics. These products have been the focus of growing protectionist pressures, which are likely to continue as competing EC industries restructure in response to the internal market reforms.

Following the U.S. model, EC trade policy toward the East Asian countries has resorted to a mixture of antidumping actions and voluntary export restraint arrangements to promote foreign direct investment (FDI) in the EC as a substitute for imports. Japanese FDI has grown substantially since 1985; in April 1987-March 1989, Japan invested $15.7 billion in Europe, of which about two-thirds was in the financial services sector and manufacturing. Japanese FDI in Europe totalled about $45 billion (on an approvals basis) by yearend 1989 (see Thomsen and Nicolaides 1991, p. 8).

While the U.S. experience with Japanese FDI indicates that at least at the outset foreign subsidiaries import a significant share of their components from their parent corporations (Graham and Krugman 1991), such import growth has been, and likely will continue to be, moderated by two factors:

- Resort to antidumping actions. Antidumping has been the most widely used approach to blunt the East Asian export drive, particularly in high technology products. From 1980–1988, the EC initiated 29 cases against Japan and 30 against East Asian suppliers (the Four Tigers plus Malaysia and Thailand). Of these, 22 cases involved high technology products during 1984–88 alone (see Messerlin 1989 and 1990).
- Pursuit of voluntary export restraints (VERs). Existing VERs already restrict EC imports of steel, some consumer electronics, and autos from East Asia. In autos, for example, Japanese VERs appear to cap EC import growth of assembled vehicles throughout the decade. [6] If the experience under U.S. VERs is a guide, the Japanese response will be to upgrade product lines, replacing subcompacts with new luxury models. [7] As

[5] U.S. interests have been narrowly focused on specific issues such as the reciprocity provisions in the second banking directive, the broadcasting directive, origin rules, antidumping, public procurement practices, and industrial standards. In addition, the United States has expressed concern about actions taken against East Asian trade because of their potential impact on US firms that are subsidiaries of foreign corporations affected by the EC measures (e.g., Ricoh; Honda).

[6] The EC has proposed a virtual freeze on the volume of Japanese car imports at 1.23 million units through 1999, as well as a cap on the growth of output from Japanese auto subsidiaries in Europe. See *Financial Times*, July 24, 1991. p. 4.

[7] However, Suzuki and Daihatsu have recently announced new ventures in Eastern Europe, holding open the prospect that lowend models could be shipped to the EC from subsidiaries in

Continued

such, the value of car imports may continue to rise even though the volume is restricted.

Taken together, these two practices tend to reinforce a policy of "investment protectionism," in which trade practices serve to encourage foreign competitors to invest in rather than export to the Community. This policy seems to serve two purposes: to increase production within the EC, and to promote trade diversion from East Asian firms to competing suppliers in Eastern Europe.

EC exports to East Asia should continue to grow from a very low base (about 11 percent of total EC exports), though perhaps not quite as fast as in the past few years. The recent weakness of the yen vis-a-vis European currencies will dampen EC export growth (except perhaps in luxury items like German cars), and there will continue to be strong competition from North American suppliers (aided by the political desire of Japanese leaders to see a sharp reduction in trans-Pacific trade tensions).

The EC and the Uruguay Round

Will the EC–92 reforms lead the Community to converge or diverge with the trade principles of the GATT? To answer this question requires the dexterity of a two-handed economist.

On the one hand, the EC–92 reforms are breaking down the implicit barriers to market access resulting from different *national* laws, regulations, public programs, and industrial practices. Many of these reforms benefit domestic EC firms and foreign participants in the EC market in a nondiscriminatory fashion. In addition, exporters to the EC also gain from EC reforms involving competition policy and state aids that establish a strong buffer against new protectionist measures.

The EC reforms seek to promote the convergence of national policies (which is also the implicit objective of GATT rulemaking), and in particular the harmonization of industrial standards (which holds the potential for substantial trade creation). The internal market reforms establish a model of deep integration that follows, but goes far beyond, the progress made to date in the GATT. By establishing the principle of mutual recognition of member state policies, based on a minimum level of harmonization, the EC policies have set an important precedent for future GATT talks.

In an important respect, GATT too has been moving in this direction as border measures have become less important than barriers created by domestic policies. The Tokyo Round was the first GATT negotiation to focus primarily on domestic practices, notably through the development of the subsidies and other nontariff barrier codes; the Uruguay Round has taken this trend several steps further by attempting to extend GATT disciplines to new areas such as services, investment, and intellectual property. EC reforms have already influenced the form and content of current GATT negotiations in those areas, and will likely help define the post-Uruguay Round agenda in areas such as competition policy and investment that go beyond the traditional GATT sphere of issues "in

Eastern Europe. How the EC decides the origin of goods will determine whether such production will fall under the VER limits.

order to adapt the free trade objective to the information-age economic, corporate and technological environment" (Bressand 1990, p. 65).

Nonetheless, any regional trading arrangement creates preferences that discriminate against nonmembers—that is the *raison d'etre* for the pact. The extension of European preferences to members of EFTA and perhaps newly emerging democracies in Central and Eastern Europe expands the scope of those preferences to such a large share of total EC trade that one can understand concerns that the marginal utility of additional multilateral trade liberalization is quite low for the Community.

This raises a political, not a legal, issue. The EC preferences have not been ruled inconsistent with the generally open-ended, and laxly enforced, exemptions to the most-favored-nation principle allowed under GATT Article XXIV. [8] One reason why the EC preferences have not provoked stronger reactions is that the value of those preferences has been continually eroded by progressive rounds of multilateral trade liberalization. [9] If progress on multilateral trade liberalization were to falter, causing the "bicycle" of trade policy to topple, the natural reaction of non-EC members would be to resort to their own regional preferences. This reaction would have the perverse effect of weakening the GATT system further.

The EC approach in the Uruguay Round so far has reinforced concerns that multilateral trade liberalization is not high on the EC's trade agenda. Only in services and government procurement have EC negotiators offered to enhance access to their market for foreign suppliers; in both cases the liberalization offer has been tempered by stringent demands for sector-specific reciprocity.

In services, EC reforms are creating a relatively homogeneous market from twelve formerly fragmented national regulatory systems. Foreigners already established in the Community should benefit accordingly; new foreign suppliers, however, may or may not gain access to the EC market, depending on the entrance fee established under the Community's reciprocity guidelines. For example, in financial services, the EC has adopted a mirror-image reciprocity standard in the banking directive to coerce other countries to open their markets to EC firms (thus emulating U.S. policy initiatives invoking section 301 cases); to date, however, the Community seems to be applying a more liberal reciprocal national treatment standard to determine whether foreign firms may participate in the EC market.

Similarly, the EC has offered to liberalize foreign access to its newly unifying public procurement market, if EC firms receive reciprocal commitments to additional access to procurement opportunities abroad. The EC proposal is comprehensive, but flawed, and will likely result in only a marginal increase in trading opportunities for two reasons: it qualifies its offer with the untenable

---

[8] For a more detailed discussion of the issue of the compatibility of FTAs and the GATT, see Schott (1989, p. 24–26).

[9] Indeed, the most recent and acrimonious attack on EC preferences arose in 1986 upon the accession of Spain and Portugal to the Community, which primarily involved agricultural products that had not been subject to liberalization in prior negotiations and which occurred at a time when the launching of a new GATT round was in doubt.

demand that procurement by private firms (notably in the telecommunications sector) be included under the coverage of the GATT code; and negotiating reciprocity for EC concessions in the four sectors (water, electricity, telecommunications, and transport) previously excluded from the GATT code will be difficult to achieve.

In most respects, EC interests in the Uruguay Round have centered on rulemaking in new areas such as services and trade-related intellectual property rights and institutional issues such as dispute settlement more than on liberalization of trade barriers. EC officials seem to be content with the status quo, so that they can proceed with their internal market reforms without the burden of also adjusting to external trade reforms.

EC concerns about compounding the adjustment burden (caused by internal market reforms) with increased competition from foreign suppliers (resulting from GATT trade liberalization) seem to be evident in several areas of the Uruguay Round agenda. These concerns are demonstrated most clearly, of course, in agriculture, which in most respects is not part of the EC–92 process; however, the trend is also evident in GATT talks on subsidies; safeguards and quota reform; and antidumping and trade-related investment issues (TRIMS).

In subsidies, EC–92 poses a direct conflict because of the extensive regional aids and adjustment subsidies that Brussels has offered as inducements to Mediterranean-tier countries. These policies have made the Community less willing to accept tighter disciplines on domestic subsidies (e.g., by placing some domestic subsidy practices in the prohibited or "red" category); indeed, the massive costs of German reunification—which have also involved substantial transfers from Brussels—seem to have weakened the resolve of the arch fiscal conservatives in Europe to commit to extensive new international subsidy disciplines. In addition, the rapid expansion of EC subsidies for research consortia in microelectronics and telecommunications, which are designed to promote European competitiveness in these sectors (and which emulate several U.S. programs such as SEMATECH), also seems to be running counter to efforts to curtail the use of state subsidies other than for "precompetitive" research and development.

The EC position in the safeguards negotiations suffers from a similar quandary of wanting to promote liberalization, but not too much. Such a conflict is inherent in the nature of safeguards, which are designed to facilitate liberalization by providing that the resulting trade could be restrained "temporarily" through the imposition of escape clause actions if import surges caused serious injury to a domestic industry. In the Uruguay Round, this dichotomy is reflected in an EC position that commits to bar the use of selective actions in most cases, but promotes selective actions as transitional measures in textiles and autos as well as the use of antidumping actions to achieve comparable results.

In that regard, the Community has been hesitant to liberalize existing quotas applied at the national level that will need to be consolidated at the EC-wide level after 1992; this problem is evidenced most clearly in the area of textiles and autos. In both areas, transitional safeguard measures under consideration raise concerns about whether the commitment to eventual quota elimination will be fulfilled.

Transitional safeguard arrangements often take on a life of their own; one need only recall the experience of the Multifiber Arrangement (MFA), the Davignon steel program in the EC, and U.S. auto VERs, to confirm this process. To avoid the risk that safeguards spawn chronic protectionism, transition periods need to be short enough to deter investment decisions that only augment the vested interests in maintaining the protection. Current EC policies in both textiles and autos seem to fail this test.

In autos, the Community appears to have effectively frozen the level of Japanese imports, and to have established subquotas for shipments to several national markets. EC policy seems to be following the U.S. model, which proved to be counterproductive. By demanding that the Japanese voluntarily restrain exports, the EC plan essentially creates a "coalition for protection" among both exporters and import-competing industries. Both gain from the scarcity rents generated by the continuation of the trade controls, and both thus lobby to maintain the quotas. Even worse, the Community proposes to monitor the production of Japanese subsidiaries established in the EC so that it does not exceed 1.2 million units annually, and thus sets an unhealthy precedent for other potential advocates of protectionism.

The experience in these sectors seems to belie the intention of the Community to develop more effective GATT safeguard procedures. Rather, EC policies on safeguards seem designed to control competition from third countries while internal barriers are removed under the 1992 process.

In antidumping, the Community has joined forces with the United States to augment GATT rules by incorporating new anticircumvention provisions as well as definitional changes in criteria for the determination of dumping, injury, etc. that would tend to facilitate the imposition of penalty duties. As Messerlin (1990) has argued, these types of provisions have been deployed to promote cartelization of several European industries—a trend that has been working at cross-purposes to EC–92 efforts to bolster Community-wide competition policy—and to implement a policy of export diversion, or investment protectionism, by which foreign suppliers are coerced to establish in the Community rather than export from foreign production bases. The EC position on antidumping may well explain the limited enthusiasm the Community also has had for the TRIMS negotiations, despite the fact that the EC reform process has been primarily investment-driven. [10]

Implications for the Structure of World Trade

The effects of the EC internal market reforms on the structure of world trade depend importantly on the pace of reforms within the

[10] Given the limited mandate of the TRIMS negotiators, the Uruguay Round will not achieve a very comprehensive set of obligations even under the most optimistic scenario; the lack of interest by the EC in this area makes even a limited result uncertain. However, the TRIMS negotiations should establish a foot in the door, but more will be needed in the future, particularly with regard to establishment issues, to extend GATT coverage to a broader range of investment issues.

Community, the pace of integration of the EC and its European neighbors, and the response of third countries to the evolving European trading bloc. This section will focus on three factors that are likely to influence trade flows: the growth effect, the adjustment effect, and the emulation effect.

The Growth Effect. The internal market reforms will both stimulate growth—increasing import demand—and increase the productivity of EC firms, making them more formidable competitors at home and abroad and thus spurring EC exports and generating some import substitution. I will not attempt to project how much trade will increase: projections by Emerson (1988), Baldwin (1989) and others provide a wide range of estimates of EC growth, which report either modest net trade creation or diversion.[11]

On balance, both Emerson (1988) and Dornbusch, Krugman, and Park (1989, p. 21) believe "that the trade diverting effects of the internal market reforms are likely to predominate." In contrast, Baldwin estimates that EC–92 will generate substantial trade creation as the dynamic effects of the supply side reforms stimulate robust growth. Note, however, that all these trade models have been rendered somewhat obsolete by the rush of events in Eastern Europe and particularly by the pace of German reunification. Quantitative projections of the trade effects of EC–92 are thus even more highly subjective than usual.

While the models generate mixed results regarding the net trade effects, the historical experience with European integration has been generally trade-creating. Instead of *trade* creation or diversion, however, it might be more appropriate to refer to the effect of the internal market reforms on foreign direct investment (FDI) in the region: in other words, do the EC–92 reforms yield trade-promoting or trade-substituting investment flows? The evidence to date is mostly anecdotal, since data on FDI are reported with a significant lag.[12] However, the experience so far in the auto and microelectronics sectors seems to indicate that Europe is following the U.S. model of trade-substitution rather than the trade-promoting model of Japanese FDI in East Asia.

The Adjustment Effect. The structure of world trade also will be influenced by an "adjustment effect," which is manifested in terms of political resistance to accommodating both internal market reforms and liberalization of trade barriers applied against third country suppliers. While the EC–92 process promises to yield large economic gains, there will be winners and losers as the reforms promote intra- and interindustry specialization within the EC market. Political considerations will undoubtedly enter the contest of dividing the gains and apportioning the adjustment costs.

The adjustment effect arises in part because of an imbalance in the degree of economic and political integration. The internal market reforms will create a more integrated European economy, but European politics will still be fragmented (and fractious!). This means that extreme positions can still dominate the trade policy debate (as we see now in agriculture), although the problem is

---

[11] For estimates of the impact on U.S.-EC trade, see Hufbauer (1990, p. 21–23).

[12] For the most recent report on FDI in Europe, which relies on data through 1988, see Thomsen and Nicolaides (1991).

somewhat mitigated in other areas as a result of the qualified majority voting procedures incorporated in the Single European Act of 1987.

The adjustment effect basically means that political considerations will increasingly come into play as each member state attempts to accommodate the redistribution of income and employment that will result from the reforms. This effect does not necessarily need to lead to increased protectionism, but it does create an inertial force against liberalization. Pressures could build either to retard the internal liberalization process (for example, by delaying enactment of EC directives into national laws or by lax enforcement or implementation of the new policies at the national level) or to restrict third country competition to ease the adjustment burden of EC industries.

There are already ominous signs that internal adjustment within the Community has generated strong political resistance to import liberalization. This problem is most evident in autos, where EC-wide quotas and monitoring of imports and the production of foreign subsidiaries established in the Community have been proposed to limit "foreign" penetration throughout the decade. [13] It is also manifested in the increasing use of antidumping actions (particularly against East Asian firms), and the unyielding opposition of European farm groups to basic reforms in the CAP.

The Emulation Effect. The third factor by which the internal market reforms could influence the structure of world trade is the emulation effect. Concern that the Community will place less focus on liberalized market access for third country suppliers, thus provoking a stalemate in the Uruguay Round which further undercuts confidence in the multilateral process, has prompted many countries to pursue alternative strategies, including the negotiation of free trade areas (FTAs), to enhance their access to important export markets. In essence, many countries have sought to emulate EC–92 either by seeking to join the Community, or by seeking closer ties with major export markets (especially the United States).

Interestingly, the emulation effect has had its greatest impact on the smaller countries that depend most heavily on the multilateral trading system; the reaction by the United States and Japan has been more restrained. Both have regarded bilateral and regional trading arrangements as imperfect substitutes for the GATT process, and have pursued such initiatives as complements to their multilateral obligations.

In the United States, for example, the negotiation of FTAs with Israel and Canada were designed to jump-start multilateral negotiations and to provide building blocs for broader multilateral accords. They also demonstrated that countries with large trade deficits have much to gain from trade liberalization, a lesson that many developing countries that have instituted unilateral trade reforms in the 1980s have taken to heart more readily than the major industrialized nations.

---

[13] See, for example, Buchan, David. Brussels Agrees on Japanese Car Imports Principles. *Financial Times*, May 1, 1991. p. 1.

The current negotiation of a North American FTA serves those and one other key objective: in response to the prospective resurgence of European competitiveness resulting from the internal market reforms, a NAFTA seeks to increase the efficiency and productivity of North American industries so that they can compete more effectively both in world markets and at home against foreign suppliers. The three countries of North America all run current account deficits; they all cannot solve their problems simply by exporting more to each other. Intraregional trade in North America accounts for only 40 percent of the total combined trade of the three countries, just the reverse of the EC.

For that reason the popular view that NAFTA and the new Enterprise for the Americas Initiative are attempts to create a comparable regional bloc are completely off the mark. All three countries need to maintain an outward orientation in their trade policies, and therefore seek to build their regional ties on the foundation of their GATT rights and obligations. By contributing to global trade liberalization and defending against resurgent protectionist pressures, the multilateral trading system provides a necessary complement for the regional trade goals of the North American nations.

Similarly, Japan recently has deflected overtures from Malaysia seeking to develop an East Asian Economic Group. Such a bloc would not account for the bulk of trade and investment flows from the main economies in the region, which tend to run across the Pacific rather than intraregionally. Indeed, the intraregional trade of the Asian members of the Asia Pacific Economic Cooperation (APEC), plus Taiwan and Hong Kong, accounts for only about 37 percent of total trade of these countries, about the same as the North American countries (see Schott, 1991).

The drive to emulate the Community has been most pronounced amongst the smaller developing countries dependent on the U.S. market for a substantial share of their export growth. In those countries, EC–92 has triggered a defensive reaction: to guard against the not unreasonable fear that the Uruguay Round will fail to strengthen GATT disciplines on the protectionist devices of the major trading nations, and thus trigger a protectionist backlash in the United States, they have sought to reinforce at least the existing level of access to the U.S. market through the negotiation of bilateral or regional pacts (see Schott, 1989).

In addition, the broadening European regional bloc has raised fears that the multilateral trading system could devolve into competing regional trading blocs, and that inter-bloc rivalry would then spawn a new wave of protectionism against outsiders. To date these concerns seem to be exaggerated, for three reasons. First, multinational corporations have a vested interest in the maintenance of the multilateral trading system; too much trade and investment flows between regions to lead to isolationism. Second, the evolution of the North American bloc is only a small increment to the existing bloc known as the United States, and, as noted above, that bloc needs to maintain an outward orientation. Third, there is little evidence of bloc formation in Asia; while intraregional trade has grown substantially over the past decade, so too has trade with third countries. All three points suggest that support for a strong multilateral trading system will continue to be maintained in North America and East Asia.

Even if the Uruguay Round falters, countries would still be bound to their GATT obligations. However, the failure to achieve results to longstanding trade problems after five years of negotiations would strike a tremendous blow to confidence in using the multilateral process to deal with trade problems in the future. Such a result would thus have a corrosive effect on GATT discipline and prompt the resort to alternative arrangements to handle trade relations.

In that event, regionalism would be promoted to complement the weakening multilateral system, and the rival bloc scenario could come to pass. Given the strong trade and investment linkages between North America and East Asia, it is unlikely that regional initiatives would generate three competing blocs; rather the fallout from a failure in the Uruguay Round could well lead to heightened interest in the elaboration of a Pacific Basin trading bloc, building on the nascent cooperative efforts under the APEC. This suggests that the alternative scenario could well be two competing blocs, pitting an expanding EC against the 15 main economies of North America and East Asia. [14]

If a bipolar world emerges, liberalization would continue to produce substantial trade gains *within* each bloc, but lead to a significant diversion of trade from nonmember countries—namely the bulk of the developing countries. Whether the negotiation of interbloc trade reforms could be engaged without a strong commitment to multilateralism is uncertain. Both the EC and the Pacific Basin blocs would likely be preoccupied with trade talks among their respective partners. As shown in table 4, in a Pacific Basin bloc, intraregional trade would account for 53 percent of the total trade of member countries, while trade with the EC would comprise only 17 percent. Similarly, about 59 percent of EC trade now takes place among the twelve member countries (and this ratio will rise as former EFTA members join), and only 16 percent with North American and East Asian countries.

Conclusion

An analysis of the net effects that the EC internal market reforms are likely to have on the structure of world trade can to date yield only speculative conclusions. It remains an open question whether the internal reforms will be matched by a complementary commitment to external liberalization. The answer may turn on two developments: whether the 1992 process succeeds in generating growth large enough to justify the political costs of accommodating the resulting economic restructuring in Europe; and whether the Uruguay Round results in substantial liberalization of longstanding trade barriers.

Despite the "Euro-optimism" that has been generated by the growth effects of the EC internal market reforms, this paper suggests that there remains a serious risk that internal adjustment

[14] For purposes of this analysis, the Pacific Basin bloc comprises the United States, Canada, Mexico, Japan, South Korea, Taiwan, Hong Kong, Australia, New Zealand, and the six members of ASEAN.

TABLE 4. Rival Blocs?: EC v. Pacific Basin, 1989

(billion dollars and percentage)

	1989	
	$	%
EC–12		
Total Imports	1,165.8	100
of which:		
intraregional trade	677.2	57
imports from ROW	498.6	43
from East Asia	104.5	9
from North Americaa	104.2	9
Total Exports	1,133.7	100
of which:		
intraregional trade	677.8	60
exports to ROW	455.9	40
to East Asia	66.2	6
to North America	100.8	9
Pacific Basin		
Total Imports	1,065.0	100
of which:		
intraregional trade	581.8	55
imports from ROW	483.2	45
from EC–12	165.0	15
Total Exports	988.8	100
of which:		
intraregional trade	513.4	52
exports to ROW	475.5	48
to EC–12	176.0	18

ROW = Rest of World.
[a] = United States, Canada, and Mexico.
Source: IMF. *Direction of Trade Statistics Yearbook*; and, GATT. *International Trade, 88–89.*

pressures within Europe will impede efforts to achieve external liberalization; current agreements regarding the auto sector already are demonstrating that threat. Furthermore, there is an additional risk that if external liberalization is implemented, the reforms could be applied in a discriminatory fashion, favoring one region (e.g., Eastern Europe) at the expense of another (e.g., East Asia). The fact that many countries have sought to emulate or otherwise guard against the potentially adverse trade effects of such developments confirms the problem while it compounds the risk for the GATT and the future of the multilateral trading system.

References

Baldwin, Richard. 1989. "The Growth Effects of 1992," *Economic Policy,* no. 9, 248–281.

Bressand, Albert. 1990. "Beyond interdependence: 1992 as a global challenge." *International Affairs* 66, no.1, 47–65.

Collins, Susan M., and Dani Rodrik. 1991. *Eastern Europe and the Soviet Union in the World Economy.* Policy Analyses in International Economics 32. Washington: Institute for International Economics, May.

Dornbusch, Rudiger, Paul R. Krugman, and Yung Chul Park. 1989. "Meeting World Challenges: U.S. Manufacturing in the 1990s." Monograph prepared for the Eastman Kodak Company, Rochester, New York.

Emerson, Michael et al. 1988. *The Economics of 1992.* London: Oxford University Press for the Commission of the European Communities.

Graham, Edward M., and Paul R. Krugman. 1991. *Foreign Direct Investment in the United States.* Second edition. Washington: Institute for International Economics.

Havrylyshyn, Oleh, and John Williamson. 1991. *From Soviet dis-Union to Eastern Economic Community?* Policy Analyses in International Economics 35. Washington: Institute for International Economics, October.

Hufbauer, Gary Clyde, ed. 1990. *Europe 1992: An American Perspective.* Washington: Brookings Institution.

Messerlin, Patrick. 1989. "The Uruguay Negotiations on Subsidies and Countervailing Measures: Past and Future Constraints." in Bela Balassa, ed., *Subsidies and Countervailing Measures: Critical Issues for the Uruguay Round.* World Bank Discussion Papers 55, Washington: World Bank.

Messerlin, Patrick. 1990. "Antidumping Regulations or Procartel Law?" *The World Economy,* vol. 13, no. 4 (December).

Schott, Jeffrey J., ed. 1989. *Free Trade Areas and U.S. Trade Policy.* Washington: Institute for International Economics.

Schott, Jeffrey J., ed. 1990. *Completing the Uruguay Round: A Results-Oriented Approach to the GATT Trade Negotiations.* Washington: Institute for International Economics.

Schott, Jeffrey J. 1991. "Trading Blocs and the World Trading System." *The World Economy,* vol. 14, no. 1 (March 1991).

Thomsen, Stephen, and Phedon Nicolaides. 1991. *The Evolution of Japanese Direct Investment in Europe.* London: Harvester Wheatsheaf.

Williamson, John. 1991. *The Economic Opening of Eastern Europe.* Policy Analyses in International Economics 31. Washington: Institute for International Economics, May.

INDEX